Heinrich Ewald

The Antiquities of Israel

Heinrich Ewald

The Antiquities of Israel

ISBN/EAN: 9783743347946

Manufactured in Europe, USA, Canada, Australia, Japa

Cover: Foto ©ninafisch / pixelio.de

Manufactured and distributed by brebook publishing software (www.brebook.com)

Heinrich Ewald

The Antiquities of Israel

THE
ANTIQUITIES OF ISRAEL.

THE

ANTIQUITIES OF ISRAEL.

BY

HEINRICH EWALD,

LATE PROFESSOR OF THE UNIVERSITY OF GÖTTINGEN.

TRANSLATED from the GERMAN

BY

HENRY SHAEN SOLLY, M.A.

BOSTON:
LOCKWOOD, BROOKS, AND CO.
381 WASHINGTON STREET.
1876.

TRANSLATOR'S PREFACE.

THE 'ANTIQUITIES OF ISRAEL' was primarily intended by its Author to be an Appendix to the Second Volume of the 'History of Israel.' Some of its assumptions will, therefore, hardly be understood by the reader who takes it up without previous acquaintance with the HISTORY. This applies especially to the titles of the Old Testament sources on which EWALD draws, and the dates which he assigns to their composition. Those, however, who do not care to study the entire History, will find, in Volume I. pp. 61–197, a section fully explaining what is meant by the Book of Origins, the Book of Covenants, and the several Narrators of the Primitive History.

But the present work is far more than a mere appendix. It is an independent treatise on the contents of the Pentateuch, having, as its main object, to reduce the heterogeneous and bewildering mass of laws to an orderly system,—a unity which can be grasped by the understanding and retained by the memory, and which shall exhibit the facts in their living connection with the history of the nation. The reputation which the book has long enjoyed on the Continent is chiefly due to its acknowledged success in attaining this object.

In presenting this work to an English public, the translator's first duty is gratefully to acknowledge the assistance which has been rendered him by Professor Dillmann, Rector of the University of Berlin, who has revised all the proof-sheets, and whose conscientious scrutiny, while it has served as a constant check on the translator's inclination to paraphrase instead of translating, will afford the real student no inconsiderable guarantee that EWALD'S meaning is correctly rendered on all important points. Still the difficulty of translating EWALD is so great, that the translator can hardly hope to have attained uniform success; he only asks that the work may be judged as a whole, and will be sincerely grateful to any critic who will enable him either to correct inaccuracies, or to improve the style without altering the meaning.

The translation has been made from the Third (and latest) Edition of the original, published in 1866; but all the additions and alterations which the author intended to appear in any subsequent edition have been incorporated here; on the other hand, one or two allusions to modern politics have been omitted, as they have from the HISTORY. The marginal paging gives the pages of the Second Edition, which is the one referred to in EWALD'S HISTORY and the English translation of the PROPHETS: pages 156–159 have been placed between pp. 360 and 361. At the end of the volume will be found a plan of the Tabernacle, added with the hope of making the verbal description more intelligible, but it must be used only to elucidate, not to supplement, the text. Anything that it makes determinate which the text leaves indeterminate cannot claim the support of EWALD'S authority. The Index also is an addition; but the Table of Contents is a careful reproduction of the author's own, and may materially assist the reader to understand the plan and unity of the work. All the Biblical references have been verified, and not a few corrected. They refer to the Hebrew text; where that differs from the notation of our Authorised Version ('A.V.') the latter is inserted in square brackets. These brackets are also used to distinguish three or four similar additions made by the translator. In references to German works the letter s. stands before the number of the page; when the work is not German, the letter p. occupies a similar place; the letters BK. before a Biblical reference correspond to the B. (Buch), which EWALD and others employ to intimate that the passage referred to is not the work of its reputed author.

The translator begs also to thank the various friends, especially the last Editor of the HISTORY, Professor J. E. Carpenter, M.A., for the assistance which has been so freely rendered him during the past two years.

PADIHAM: *February* 1876.

CONTENTS.

	PAGE
TRANSLATOR'S PREFACE	v

INTRODUCTION.

THE LAWS AND CUSTOMS OF THE THEOCRACY IN ITS TRANSITION
TO THE MONARCHY 1

FIRST SECTION.

THE ONE SIDE : HUMAN EFFORT AND ACTION TOWARDS GOD . . 12

I. SACRED UTTERANCES :

  1. The Sacred Utterances expressed by Words 14
    a. Prayer, and what is allied to it 14
    b. The Oath and Adjuration 16
    c. The Vow 21

  2. The Sacred Utterances expressed by Sacrifices . . . 23
    a. The Sacrifices of Property 25
      A. The Table-offering 27
      B. The Fire-offering 28
        i. The Materials of the Food-offering . . . 31
          The Blood and Entrails 35
        ii. The General Procedure with Sacrifice by Fire . . 42
        iii. The Individual Fire-offerings and their respective significance :
          The Whole- or Burnt-offering . . . 46
          The Thank-offering and its Varieties . . 50
          The Expiatory- and Guilt-offerings . . . 55
          Purification- and Consecration-offerings, Treaty-offerings 67
          The Effects and Issues of the Food-offerings . . 69

CONTENTS.

SECTION I. THE ONE SIDE: HUMAN EFFORT AND ACTION TOWARDS GOD—*continued.*

                       PAGE
- C. Simple Sacred Gifts 71
  - The Consecrated Gift 71
  - The Ban-gift (Ban-offering) . . . 75
  - Redemption of Consecrated Gifts . . 79
- *b.* Corporal Offerings and Sacrifices of Bodily Pleasures . . 81
  - *i.* Fasting and Similar Matters 81
  - *ii.* The Nazirites 84
  - *iii.* Circumcision 89
- *c.* The Offering of Rest : the Sabbath 97
- **3.** The Sacred Utterances expressed by Purifications and Consecrations . 107
  - The Sacraments of Jahveh 108

II. THE SACRED EXTERNALS 111
  - Sacred Men 112
  - Sacred Times. The Perpetual Light and Sacrifice . 113
  - The Sacred Appliances, Places, and Buildings . . 117

III. THE PROCEDURE OF DIVINE SERVICE IN THE COMMUNITY . . 130

SECOND SECTION.

THE OTHER SIDE: THE DIVINE DEMANDS FOR HOLINESS AND RIGHTEOUSNESS 134
  - The Power of Inflicting Punishment 136

I. THE SANCTITY INHERENT IN NATURE 142
  - **1.** What is Essentially Repulsive or Unclean . . . 144
    - *a.* What is Unclean for Food 146
    - *b.* What is too Unclean and Unholy, or else too Holy to be touched . 149
    - *c.* Material Impurities in Human Beings, and Elsewhere . . 155
  - **2.** Unnatural Combinations 160
    - Unnatural Mutilation and Disfigurement of the Body . . 163
  - **3.** Consideration for Nature 166

II. THE SANCTITY INHERENT IN HUMAN BEINGS 167
  - **1.** The Sanctity of Human Life 168
    - The Law of Corporal and Moral Integrity . . . 175
    - The Sanctity of Property 176
      - *a.* Fixed and Movable Property 177
      - *b.* The Law of Borrowing and Lending . . . 181
      - *c.* Protection of Property by Law 185
  - **2.** The Sanctity of the Home 187
    - *a.* The Relation between Parents and Children . . 188
    - *b.* The Relation between Man and Wife . . . 190
    - *c.* The Relation between Slaves, their Owners, and Free Men . 210
  - **3.** The Sanctity attaching to Foreigners 216

CONTENTS. xi

SECTION II. THE OTHER SIDE: THE DIVINE DEMANDS FOR
HOLINESS AND RIGHTEOUSNESS—*continued*.

                                           PAGE

III. THE SANCTITY INHERENT IN JAHVEH AND HIS KINGDOM . . . 220

 1. The Sanctity of Jahveh and Veneration for him . . . 220
  The Sanctity of Truth in the Kingdom 220
  The Opposition to every Form of Heathen Idolatry . . 222

 2. The Sanctity of the Nation 229
  The Vassals of the Nation. The Laws of War . . . 234
  Membership in the Community 237

 3. The Sanctity of the Kingdom 239

THIRD SECTION.

THE CONNECTION BETWEEN THE TWO SIDES BY MEANS OF THE
ORGANISATION OF THE KINGDOM 241

I. THE NATION AND ITS LEADERS 241

 1. The National Assembly 241
 2. The Overseers and Judges 253
 3. The Prince of the Nation 254

II. SPECIAL POWERS AND PROFESSIONS IN THE NATION . . 256

 Production and Trade 256
 Prophecy 258
 The Priesthood 260
  1. Its General Relation to the Nation 260
  2. Sphere and Nature of the Sacerdotal Functions . . 269
   a. The Regular Priests 273
   b. The Inferior Priests or the Levites . . . 281
   c. The High-Priest 288
  3. Maintenance of the Priests and the Sanctuary . . 298
   The First-Fruits and the Tithes 298

III. THE KINGDOM: ITS UNITY AND ITS AGENCIES . . . 307

 1. The Government 307
 2. The Administration of Justice 310
  The Legal Modes of Punishment 314
 3. The Sacred Tent 317

FOURTH SECTION.

HOW BOTH SIDES WERE SUPPLEMENTED IN THE COURSE OF TIME:
THE GREAT SABBATH-CYCLE 334

 The Division of Time among the Ancient Nation . . 339

 1. The Sabbatical Month and the Seven Annual Festivals . . 348
  a. The Traces of Pre-Mosaic Festivals 348

CONTENTS.

SECTION IV. HOW BOTH SIDES WERE SUPPLEMENTED IN THE COURSE OF TIME: THE GREAT SABBATH-CYCLE—*continued*.

	PAGE
b. The Festivals Established by Moses	354
c. The Three Annual Pilgrimages	366
2. The Sabbath-year	369
3. The Year of Jubilee	372
CONCLUSION	381
THE HUMAN KINGDOM	381
INDEX	383
PLAN OF TABERNACLE	387

Errata.

Page 14, line 8, *for* Indian, *read* Hindoo.
„   15, „ 4, „ Indians, „ Hindoos.
„   16, „ 9, „ Indians, „ Hindoos.
„   305, note 4, „ Mischna, „ Mishnah.

THE

ANTIQUITIES OF ISRAEL.

INTRODUCTION.

The Laws and Customs of the Theocracy in its Transition to the Monarchy.[1]

At the peaceful and elevated centre of the whole history, we purpose making a considerable pause, to learn more closely how the highest life of the ancient nation gradually found a way into all its lower springs of action, and how it sought to establish itself permanently in a variety of legal institutions. To understand this thoroughly and firmly is absolutely indispensable for a correct apprehension of the complete history; and the present opportunity is in every respect the most suitable for explaining it.

1. For it was not till the peaceful elevation of the last years of David, and of the succeeding rule of Solomon was attained, that the laws and institutions of the Theocracy could expand to their full extent. Not till then could they entwine themselves so closely with the whole national life as we find was the case in the next centuries, and which in essentials lasted unaltered during all their subsequent course. Only in those periods of a nation's life which are blessed with peace will its better customs and usages assume the most permanent forms, when the germs have had a long time, stormy and violent though it may have been, to strike deep into the soil. What would have resulted from all the institutions and customs of the Mosaic Theocracy if the storms of the period of the Judges had

[1] Comp. *History of Israel*, vol. iii. p. 202.

not been followed by the sunny days of David and Solomon? Ancient Israel was now for the first time firmly established in the country, and the finer manifestations of its life under the Theocracy, now also first assumed the forms which they ever after essentially retained.

This fact is confirmed by their literature. The important remains of the Book of Origins, dating from just this exalted period, supply us with the most complete and vivid descriptions of the laws of the Theocracy which we possess. The more strongly a greatly altered age tended to introduce modifications, the more scrupulously did the author of this Book[1] seek to preserve the remembrance of the laws of the Theocracy as they had existed and been developed from the august days of Moses. He was of course primarily not a legislator, but a writer of history; but his anxiety is evident to contribute all he can to save and establish the genuine old theocratic laws, so that his work is imbued with the true legislative spirit. For this purpose he strictly limited himself to the laws of the ancient Theocracy, without regarding those of the Monarchy, which was as yet too new to become the object of historical explanation and lengthy description. Moreover, to preserve by its side as much as possible of the old customs and principles of the Theocracy, and establish them for all future times, appeared a sufficiently important aim. It was still not too late to make a more complete collection of these ancient laws and legal germs, and to give an explanation of them; and no one has done this more satisfactorily than our author. Nor can there be anything at once more foolish and more unjust than to suppose that the laws and regulations of the Theocracy described in this book had no genuine historical basis, or did not in the main come down from Moses as their ultimate source. We have indeed no guarantee that each little section of the usages here described as legal came in that exact form direct from Moses. Many details may have been more fully worked out in the time of Joshua or later still, and would appear so sacred that the author would now never think of separating them from the rest. In what cases this has occurred will be explained more fully below. But to deny their historical basis, and their ultimate origin in Moses, is nothing less than completely to misunderstand, on the one side, the soul of ancient literature, and on the other, both the inmost essence and the grand connection of the most important laws.[2]

[1] *Hist.* i. p. 82.
[2] As, alas, was very common in Ger-many from twenty to forty, nay, even ten years ago. The best refutation of such

Accordingly we proceed everywhere on the broad and secure foundation furnished by the Book of Origins, composed at this very period. Nothing can give us such vivid representations of details, nothing can promise us so trustworthy a historical starting-point, as the precious relics of this book. But we shall always compare with them the remaining earlier and later sources; tracing back the origin and meaning of the usages to the earliest days of the community, or still further into the remotest primitive times; and also directing our glance forwards to the later, especially the Deuteronomic, development. If the usages prevalent in the brightest periods of the whole history are understood, as well as the way in which their ancient origin is to be regarded, it will be easy to survey the comparatively trifling changes which they underwent in the later days towards the end of this history; and this in most cases can be touched upon in no more suitable place than is afforded by the present work. On the other hand, the entirely new developments of later centuries, from the origin of the human monarchy in Israel and subsequently, can only be discussed when we come to those periods, and are explained in detail at the proper places in the third volume, from page 204 onwards, and in the succeeding volumes of the history.

2. If it were necessary to describe here the condition of the ancient nation in every respect, this discussion would have to be tolerably minute. But useful as it may be to know, amongst other things, how the ancient Israelites were dressed, or what sort of dwellings they had, yet we find that just in these matters of ordinary human life, the nation had few or no peculiarities, and still less set an example in them to other races. The ordinary clothing and manner of living of the men and women of Israel were, with trifling exceptions, of which some are mentioned below, the same as those of the nations then dwelling in that part of the world, and as still exist there very little altered. On this account in the Bible, too, very little comparatively is said on these matters, and the starting-point for all discussion in this province is a knowledge of the present condition of these lands and nations.

There is much besides of what was peculiar to the people of

misunderstandings is given in the whole discussion which follows.—I leave this remark from the first edition still standing (1866). Apart from the scholars of our days who do not go on historical principles, the earliest general doubt of De Wette, Gramberg, Bohlen, and others, has been now revived in a somewhat more serious fashion only by K. H. Graf in his treatise *Die geschichtlichen Bücher des Alten Testaments*, Leipsic, 1866. How little foundation there is for this is shown in the criticism of it in the *Göttingen. Gelehrten Anzeigen*, 1866.

Israel, and has far more importance for our object, which is explained at scattered but suitable places in the history, or is touched upon below only in passing.

What specially concern us are the institutions, considered as a whole, which existed in the ancient nation either by law or by public custom; or the life of the nation so far as it was determined and ruled by the truths and impulses of Jahveism which were stirring in it. Only what belongs to this has full significance for our purpose; but this significance is shared by even the smallest and apparently most insignificant thing, so far as the power of Jahveism contributed to make it exactly what it was, and thus confirms the principle that a powerful religion always completely penetrates the whole of the national life. And because a large portion of the history of Israel turns upon these institutions, it is this side of the antiquities of the nation respecting which we possess comparatively the richest sources of information, great as may be the carefulness required to understand many of the details aright.

When, however, we consider the particulars of even so limited a province as this, we meet with phenomena so excessively numerous and varied, that it appears difficult to describe them according to any arrangement which shall correspond to their essence and internal connection. In the ordinary text-books on antiquities, the most superficial, and therefore the most capricious and irregular, arrangements prevail; for they are content merely to handle certain principal subjects one after another. But as we are about specially to describe here such customs and institutions as were either created or put into more definite shape under the predominant influence of the higher religion, we cannot have much doubt as to the proper arrangement of our varied matter. All religion consists in a living relation between God and man, a striving of man to raise himself up to God and so draw Him down to himself, God yet ever remaining sublimely exalted, his Ruler and Governor. The conception of true religion expresses itself throughout the Old Testament [1] in the short phrase, 'Israel my people and I their God.' When the reciprocal relation between the nation and the true God, as it ought to exist according to this phrase, is perfect, then is all religion in that community perfect, for there can be no longer discord between man and God. But in the course of history we see only striving after this perfection; though this mere striving, when

---

[1] Comp. *Hist.* ii. 136 [first. ed. i. 559].

it is earnest and engrosses the whole energy, as was for the most part the case in Israel, secures a firm basis for progress in true religion. Man, then, on his side attempts everything to obtain the favour of his God. In every religion there arises in the course of its history a body of recognised and sanctified human efforts and institutions, which hope to secure without intermission the divine nearness and favour. It was, however, in Israel, where everything divinely-human, that is, religious, strove to reach the highest perfection, that the most perfect body of this kind was formed. But independent of all these human efforts, and of those which true religion recognises and protects by its own sanctity, there are the divine demands for perfect righteousness; demands which man ought to satisfy, and which he is very far from so doing merely by the above efforts; because these only lead him to the point at which he should begin satisfying them truly, and are therefore only the ways to heaven, and like other ways (methods) can be easily worn into holes. We have therefore a twofold subject to discuss in order and throughout its whole sphere : the human efforts and actions which Jahveism allowed in order to attain unto the true God, and the divine demands for true righteousness which it placed before man. In every case, of course, our treatment will have special reference to the actual customs and institutions which arose and were maintained among the people. —These two sides of the national life have indeed very different starting-points, and can even come easily into collision. But still there is a connection between them, and both have their seat in the kingdom and government, as the needful unity of national life, which links together all its various efforts, and must in its turn be maintained by special institutions.—And when a religion is really the highest and most perfect possible —as is Christianity—these two sides of the essence of all religion are in such perfect harmony within the firm ring of the unity of the kingdom, that the human efforts which it enjoins always lead again to the divine demands, and these to the right efforts; and it is thus that this religion ever shows its insurpassable perfection. But when a religion although true is yet defective, as was the case with Jahveism, this deficiency makes itself felt alike in the human efforts and in the divine demands, and gives rise to a feeling of ceaseless dissatisfaction with the Present and its arrangements, and hence to a continuous series of fresh institutions which shall supply, at any rate for the time being, the want which always exists, and therefore always grows. The discussion of these institutions aiming at the satisfaction of this felt want will form our concluding section; and it will lead up to the wider question whether the old Theocracy, as far as regards its customs and institutions, could have a perpetual existence in the special form in which it was founded under Moses. This will be followed, naturally, by the further discussion, whether the new institutions added by the human monarchy did or did not supply a stronger guarantee for its continuance unchanged.[1]

3. We have, then, chiefly to consider here, only that portion of the Antiquities of Israel which is stamped with its most characteristic life, and in which that spirit was revealed which operated in it as in no other nation of the old world. From this spirit there sprang not a few institutions of a truly creative character, which in their whole formation and style bear, so to speak, a peculiar stamp, so genuinely Mosaic and also so universally diffused, that they could have come into existence nowhere but within the community of 'the people of Jahveh,' and there even at no other time but the exalted days of Moses and Joshua. That among the various institutions and customs existing in ancient Israel there were some of genuine Mosaic origin, is a fact of high historical value; and to prove all this accurately in detail is not the least important aim of the following analysis.

The object of the great legislator was not to ordain a long series of new laws, and violently overthrow all that he found existing, but before everything to implant in the community the fear of the true God. The fundamental thought which he brought into the world and ineradicably fixed in the people of Israel in the first instance, was as a drop thrown into the wide ocean of the whole ancient world, although of infinite power, and destined gradually to penetrate all that was foreign to itself. Its consequences, so far as they belong here, are as follows:—

Many customs and practices which had previously existed in the nation were retained in Jahveism, and were modified sooner or later by its influence if they could be reconciled with its spirit; or were in the course of time more and more suppressed if they were essentially opposed to it. The proof

---

[1] The two sides which form the basis of the whole arrangement here are evidently in many respects the same as is given by a division into things '*sacra*' (*sacra*) and '*sicular*' (*civilia*), but it is equally clear that I do not draw this distinction so incorrectly and unfortunately as is done by the Papists and many Protestants. Moreover, the term '*civilia*' is altogether unsuitable for use, if the needful unity of the state is not to be destroyed. The distinction made here is given only because the Bible demands it, but I hold the thought lying at its foundation to be perfectly correct, as well as indispensable for our religion and politics.

of all this is due here, and inasmuch as many of these ancient customs carry us back to the larger circles of nations, under which Israel was comprised, either by descent or training, previous to the founding of Jahveism, these traces of the connection of Israel with other ancient nations, which are most instructive for the purposes of history, must be here carefully examined.

The legislation of Israel falls moreover in a period of very remote antiquity, all the peculiar features of which still existed among the nations which developed themselves the earliest. Antiquity as such has a most characteristic spirit—and this spirit ruled the world before the gradual advance of Jahveism, and of Christianity, which ensued as its goal and perfection, raised to power a completely different spirit, such as was alone capable of laying a sure foundation for a new era. As therefore there prevailed in the world when Jahveism was founded a spirit quite different from that which it vigorously manifested itself, the influence of the earlier spirit on Jahveism was from the first very considerable. Many customs and practices which had their origin in this spirit, still retained their place, some of them at first without even being called in question; but besides this the new views, institutions, and laws during that primitive creative period, were in many cases deeply imbued with that spirit which had hitherto ruled unchallenged. Accordingly we find amongst the institutions and practices of the community of Jahveh which sprang up and were legalised during the earliest times, very much that has an exact counterpart in those of all ancient nations, especially of such as stood on the same level of general culture; and great care is needed not to confuse the similarities which flowed only from the whole spirit of Antiquity, with those touched on above which sprang from the closer connection of Israel with a particular circle of nations. Countless similarities may be traced back to the life of the whole ancient world, but to trace these countless similarities is of far less importance than to understand somewhat better the essence of Antiquity as distinguished from our own times. The following are some of its main characteristics having special reference to our present subject.

Man, with all his sensitive endowments, stood much closer to creation (or Nature), felt more as a child towards what was living, and animated even what was dead with his ingenuous sympathy. He was the more exposed to the impressions of Nature, in proportion as he received less aid, on the one hand, from a religion standing far above her, and on the other, from a thorough investigation, and at the same time unsympathetic examination of her. But no less fresh and lively was the feeling of man for what was Divine; for this always lurks behind Nature and himself, and thus the feeling for it will always vary according to the kind of feeling entertained towards Nature and towards man.

The national customs, institutions, and laws were accordingly full of a keen though properly only passive sympathy for the animate and inanimate non-human world, of deep impressions of Nature, of grand attempts of men to draw her into a partnership of joy and sorrow with themselves.[1] All this repeats itself, moreover, with regard to the Divine.

But in spite of his standing so near to Nature, and as far as that went feeling himself gay and satisfied in her, yet, just because he knew so little of her, man cherished an almost blind terror of all her unusual phenomena, and so far felt towards her utterly strange and fearful. But he trembled yet more before all that was Divine, lying concealed behind her and behind himself. For he had also had experience of its strength and force, but attained respecting it little true and trustworthy knowledge.

To overcome this terror and the apparent hostility alike of Nature and of God, and to attain and uphold a special religion wherever the need of it was felt, was infinitely harder for Antiquity than it is for us. This accounts for the number of most elaborate regulations, of burdensome laws, and of harsh correctives, of which it is difficult for us to frame a correct representation.

An essential addition to these circumstances is the fact, that whatever Antiquity had once seized upon, it undertook with a youthful power and unjaded strength, with a magnificent consistency and simplicity, and with an openness and uprightness which are only too often found wanting in later times, and wherein it remains an eternal model for our own apparently or really more intricate relations. And as man stood altogether much nearer to Nature, his youthful open-hearted impulses drove him to express by outward signs, as strongly and appropriately as possible, his feelings and the deep meaning of his efforts and actions; particularly as the truths which thus sought for manifestation in the most forcible signs, were now for the first time looking for a lasting home on the earth.

---

[1] Compare also conceptions and expressions suggesting such thoughts; Hos. ii. 20 [22], iv. 3; Jer. xii. 4; Zeph. i. 3; Ps. xxxvi. 7 [6]; Jonah iii. 7, 8; iv. 11.—Hab. ii. 17; Jer. xxvii. 5, 6; xxviii. 14.

Hence we find so much that has symbolical meaning impressing itself through striking signs, and further leaving its mark in public customs and institutions.

4. As the explanation of these signs (*Symbols*) will form a main section of this work, it will be advantageous to consider more closely at this place their general nature and essential meaning. The sign has reference only to the thought existing in man, and therefore, strictly speaking, also to the words which he utters or might utter. It is nothing in itself, however elaborate it may be; but its meaning, its origin, and the need for it, exist only in the soul of man, which seeks to find expression in it. Now as human thought finds its most perfect expression in speech, the first question concerns the relation of the sign to speech, especially as it subsisted in the earliest days of humanity. We shall see that the sign can precede human speech, and in the earliest times for the most part actually did so. For thoughts which powerfully stir men and struggle to come forth out of their minds into the world, are already there before any words, and they may so take possession of the entire man, that all he does and is, may express them most completely and forcibly before the words come which shall make them plain. In prayer, e.g., it may be customary with one nation to stretch forth the hands towards heaven, with another to fold them; but this physical revelation, this sign of what moves the human soul, precedes and does not wait upon the words. Nor do words always satisfy. In this very case they seem too weak and too imperfect to express the whole soul of man that seeks to find an outlet. Its contents are of course infinite, and all words are but attempts to exhaust it. Or the words may be too thin, too inefficient, and too fleeting, to be able to give lasting satisfaction; and this would be especially felt as long as they could not be easily and permanently fixed in writing, comprehensible and accessible to all. Now, as all these causes coöperated most powerfully in just the earliest periods of humanity, such significant or symbolical actions of necessity arose then, in vast numbers, and took the most rigid forms, as an undesigned accompaniment and supplement of human speech, and served also for a long time as a needful witness, in the place of the art of writing, and the written documents which had not yet come into existence. The forms they assumed in each nation differed almost as much as their speech, with which their course ran parallel. But stil., like human speech, they have but one common source, and like languages assumed these varied forms in accordance with the o.igin and history of the nation. But from the very beginning they had an important significance and a place which nothing else could fill. They entwined themselves inseparably with the whole life of the nation, and won a permanency comparable only with that of human speech itself.

The most frequent occasion for them arose in all the intercourse and relations between man and God, where their significance is greatest and their employment even indispensable. Here all human words, however beautiful and perfect, remain for ever too weak and incomplete.

But they were also indispensable in human intercourse, especially as long as writing was little used. What, e.g. would be the good of one man binding another by an oath so long as this consisted of mere words? Words rustle past like the wind, and only when the one has indicated to the other by the most unmistakable signs the punishment which will fall on perjury, is there much hope that they will make a deeper impression and remain inviolate. But in truth both the impression and the emphasis of these symbolical actions rest ultimately on this—viz. that man considered, and acted on the belief, that they were executed not only before the witness of men where this was possible, but above all before the eyes of God himself.

Thus signs of this sort originated abundantly in primitive times, and kept their place even through the great changes of later days, though often they were for the most part retained only in current phrases. In this case it is often difficult to recognise their exact original significance: nevertheless it must be everywhere sought after as long as suitable means for the investigation exist. Even the sanctity and the frequent use of certain numbers, such as, amongst the Israelites, 5 or 10, or in a different way, 3, and more than all the rest, 7, are connected with the magic power of many such signs.

5. It is, moreover, a matter of course that the later documents, even when springing from the life of the ancient nation, are only to be used with the greatest caution, in dealing with these genuine Mosaic institutions and customs. There is nothing on which the Jewish schools employed themselves so zealously as the explanation and application of the laws of the Pentateuch; and this was the case both among the Hellenists, and in the new Jerusalem, and again with a fresh outburst of zeal after its destruction. In the numerous writings of Philo, we possess the most copious testimonies to the Hellenistic method of interpretation; in those of Josephus, tolerably frequent examples of the style at Jerusalem; and in the Mishnah and Talmud, the whole length and breadth of the exposition of the post-Christian schools. But how little do all these later sources help us to understand correctly the true sense of the old laws! How much that is totally foreign do they mix up with it! As has been shown elsewhere,[1] the life of the ancient nation experienced too severe a disturbance and break from the first destruction of Jerusalem, and it was gradually rebuilt on a new and too much altered foundation, for it to retain easily a trustworthy understanding of the old laws. Of the far severer consequences of the second destruction enough has also been said elsewhere.[2] Neither after the first, nor still less after the second destruction, did a science arise which is satisfactory for purposes of pure historical investigation. And the Talmud aids us least of all, for the historical sense in general, and in particular the true feeling for the essence and spirit of antiquity, are here already in the uttermost confusion and darkness. Long before the Christian era many of the more cultivated heathens had already been inquiring from curiosity about the customs and usages of this nation, and had sought to investigate more narrowly what seemed to them to be remarkable, and these endeavours continued to increase down to the second century after Christ.[3] But neither these, nor the Jews or Samaritans, who ought to have been their teachers, succeeded in attaining more correct views.

But many fragments of ancient customs and usages, of which we now, it may be, find no trace in the older works, may have been retained through all these later times, the frequency of their occurrence being proportionate to the antiquity of these times; and so far all the various later documents are useful for our purpose, whenever we can be sure of finding in them such scattered morsels. Still, for the whole picture and for all its main features, we must rely on the oldest sources alone, whether they are to be found in the Pentateuch or elsewhere.

[1] *Hist.* v. or iv. of the German ed.
[2] *Hist.* vii. of the German ed.
[3] This appears most clearly from such authors as Tacitus or Plutarch; especially the latter's *Conviv. disput.* iv. 4, 4-6, 2.

FIRST SECTION.

THE ONE SIDE; OR, HUMAN EFFORT AND ACTION TOWARDS GOD.

The above remarks—from page 7 onwards—on the earliest kind of dread (*religio*), find at once a special application in connection with the side of Antiquity which we must first consider. For undeniably correct as was the representation of the true God which Jahveism brought into the world, yet Israel at first, along with the whole ancient world, suffered the most painful dread of the wrath and of the chastisements of God. Indeed, this painful dread, common to all genuine Antiquity, was augmented in the community of Israel; partly because the general conception of God was there apprehended far more deeply and seriously, so that the anger and punishments of this true God naturally produced far truer and more lasting feelings there than among the heathen; but also because in the days succeeding those of Joshua the nation soon found itself again in such sore distress of all sorts, that its deep dread in the presence of the true God became more painful, and the fear grew keener of losing him and his guidance. Even in the Book of Origins, which was written during a period of great happiness and most joyous national life, this key-note of the life of the community in its early days is heard right through. 'This or that must be done that no great wrath, no punishment, come upon Israel,' is the frequent utterance, even when to us the occasion seems trifling, of its stern legislative voice,[1] and in the most instructive and vivid narratives it describes emphatically how often and how heavily such an all-annihilating punishment of Jahveh had come upon the community.[2] So difficult was it to enlighten this old gloomy fear of men, and make it yield to the glorified belief in pure love, of which the immortal germ was, of course, already supplied in the fundamental capacities and truths of the community of Israel.

This great dread, peculiar to Antiquity, of everything

---

[1] Lev. x. 6; Num. i. 53, xviii. 5; Ex. xii. 13, xxx. 12; Num. viii. 19. 46 seq.], xxv. 4 seq.; xxxi. 16. Comp. 2 Kings iii. 27, and many similar narra-
[2] Num. xvi. 4, 5; xvii. 11 seq. [xvi. tives not contained in the Book of Origins.

divine,[1] exercised an important influence on the formation of the Old Testament customs and institutions concerning human action towards God; and it explains why it is precisely on this side that the antiquities of Israel bear the greatest resemblance to those of heathen nations. But here again the early community did not disown the fundamental truths of Jahveism, so that in this way the points of these heathen customs and institutions were already blunted. And while the general spirit of the past still widely prevailed, there grew up imperceptibly here, a new spirit, opposed to all previously existing means of influencing God, and forming the commencement of an imperishable institution.

If now we pass in review all the sacred endeavours and acts of men which had the special aim of pressing in upon the Deity, and winning his favour, or drawing forth from him advice and revelation, we see that they are either complete with words alone, in some one or other of their infinitely various forms; or else that they pass over into something stronger, the surrender of one's own property, and so become a sacrifice, to use the word in its widest signification. There are further the purifications, bodily and otherwise, which are preparations for sacred words or deeds.

Moreover, they are readily connected with certain vessels, places, times, or persons, which seem specially adapted to excite, to strengthen, or to satisfy them.

These times, places, and persons can in themselves be very numerous, and similarly these endeavours may be infinitely various, whether it be as words, or as sacrifices, that they have found expression and become prevalent usages. But particular ones amongst them may acquire a peculiar sanctity, above that of many others, and become *Sacraments*. Whether there existed such in Jahveism, and how all the different usages in it were developed, must now be discussed in detail. As the whole province in consequence of its religious character is sacred, we can draw a short and clear distinction between the utterances by means of sacred words, and those by means of sacred gifts, or sacrifice. For all other significant gestures or actions which find a place here are seen, when closely considered, to be only an accompaniment of the words or the sacrifice, or else a preparation for them.

But it is only in human society and in a community which has a settled religion, that all these endeavours and actions

---

[1] This was retained longest among the Romans of all the nations of Antiquity known to us.

towards God are found united together with extreme vigour and durability. This combined action, accordingly, as the highest aim within our reach here, will in the last place finally engage our attention.

I. SACRED UTTERANCES.

1. *Those by means of words.*

a. Prayer and what is allied to it.

The ancient nation knew no fixed form of prayer, no Indian Gâyatri, no Lord's Prayer, no First Sûrah. The sacred words on which the new community of Israel was founded were, before everything, oracles which served as laws; no community has been founded so exclusively through the supremacy of the Oracle, as Israel. We find, indeed, in addition, many sacred words, phrases, and refrains of prayers, which were repeated both regularly by the priest in the assembled community, and often, too, less formally; and these undoubtedly come down from the creative times of the primitive community.[1] But of these some belonged to the priests alone, and others were repeated with so little formality, that we cannot recognise in them any fixed form of prayer for the whole community. We must therefore acknowledge that here, too, Jahveism, although laying an imperishable foundation of true religion, yet did not at once appear with its most perfect expressions and models, for it is pre-eminently in prayer that this perfection must show itself. With all the greater freedom and strength, did the practice and the wondrous might of true prayer gradually arise on this incomplete but sure foundation. Century after century did it produce ever richer and riper fruit, which finally, during the last period of the annals of Israel, appears in the Psalter in the clear light of history.

Still less did ancient Israel know of the perpetual repetition of certain sacred words, and of the evil art of accomplishing a sacred work by such repetition. Rather would this have been looked upon as heathenish in the earlier days of Israel's religion;[2] and not till the centuries under the Hagiocracy, is any inclination to it manifested.[3] — Nor do we observe much that is special or remarkable in the ordinary

---

[1] *Hist.* ii. 20, 21 [first ed. i. 443-4].
[2] Comp. Is. i. 15.
[3] Comp. *Hist.* v. 367 and [of the German ed.] vi. 152.

customs of that period connected with prayer. The posture of the suppliant varied much according to his tone of feeling;[1] but it was not the folding of the hands, the traditional custom among the ancient Indians and Germans, that was most common, but the eager stretching of them out towards heaven.[2] —Whether the countenance was then, as in later times, turned during prayer towards the place of the great sanctuary, we do not know.[3] It is, however, improbable, as the unity of the sanctuary was not yet so firmly established in the earliest times, and its locality was easily changed.

In the *blessing*, or prayer desiring the good of some being, which is so often mentioned, and is a clear token of the spiritual vitality of Jahveism, the laying of the hand on the head of the person to be blessed appears to have been, wherever possible, an invariable practice. On this point more will be found below in the description of the general procedure of the sacrifice.

The exact opposite of the blessing, the *curse*, appears indeed almost as frequently in the history of the nation, not only amongst the lower, but also amongst the upper classes, and not only in momentary excitement in songs,[4] but also closely connected with religion itself. It is as though the latter could only be rescued from the extraordinary hindrances which it encountered, by some such convulsive revolt of thought, word, or even deed. But yet we must notice a difference in this matter according to the date. In the earliest days of the community, that which appeared absolutely incompatible with the true religion, whether it was an inanimate object, an animal, or a human being, was not merely cursed, but was rather sacrificed to Jahveh himself, so that he might destroy it; on which point more will be said below under the ban-offering. The ban, and with it the ban-curse, had their direct origin in the very violent and warlike spirit which prevailed unchecked during the early days of the community. As in the course of centuries, the power of the ban became weakened, and its use less common, while yet Jahveism in the very heart of the nation fell into the most alarming distraction and dismemberment, the force of the mere verbal curse became so much the stronger; and Deuteronomy accordingly makes the people

---

[1] As some thing quite unusual, the posture of Elijah at prayer is described 1 Kings xviii. 42.
[2] Ex. ix. 29, 33: Is. i. 15: lxv. 2; 1 Kings viii. 22, 38; Ps. xxviii. 2: Lam. i. 17. ii. 19. iii. 41; and still later Ps. xliv. 21 [20], cxliii. 6; Ezra ix. 5; 1 Tim. ii. 8. Comp. on the other hand the प्राञ्जलि:
of the Indians.
[3] The *Qibla*, according to the Moslem expression. Comp. *Hist.* v. 23.
[4] Though it is found in the songs, it first appears more strongly during the tremendous internal religious warfare of the later times. See *Die Dichter des Alten Bundes*, vol. i. b. s. 238, third ed.

alternately pronounce on themselves the curse for non-observance and the blessing for observance of the Law, and thereby mutually bind themselves with respect to it, the Levites taking the lead.[1] Moreover we naturally find in the earlier period the belief that a curse spoken by a priest at the sacred place would be efficacious. But a legal application of this took place only in the most urgent and apparently unavoidable cases,[2] while no trace is to be found of the belief of the ancient Indians in the never-ceasing influence of a curse once spoken by priests (Brahmins).[3]

Still less did the ancient religion allow the use of words of imprecation and magic to avert some evil or procure some good; such as exist in the Avesta and even yet in the Koran.[4] Jahveism down to the later centuries was partly too young and vigorous, partly too healthy all through, and too sensible for this, so long as the power of the living oracle which had founded it maintained itself there. The oldest legal utterances already vigorously repudiated every kind of magic.[5]

b. *The Oath and Adjuration.*

We find no scruples about the employment of the *oath*; on the contrary seeing that in the earliest days humanity had for the first time to become accustomed to a mutual reverence for truth and fidelity, it was natural that its use should be the more frequent; and the means and signs by which it was expressed the more forcible. There are three kinds in particular to be distinguished here.

1. There is the simple kind, when a private individual believes that he must confirm something in a sacred manner by his own spontaneous action. That he should then call upon the God whom he believed to be the true one, and wish that he might be punished by him, if he consciously spoke falsely, was so much

---

[1] Deut. xxvii. 11-26; Josh. viii. 30-35.
[2] Numb. v. 11-31. Comp. below under the matters relating to marriage.
[3] On the contrary a very true judgment is passed on the empty curse, Prov. xxvi. 2. Balaam's history, too, related by the Fifth Narrator of the Primitive history, takes here quite the correct view, Numb. xxiii. 8.
[4] In this it is thrown quite to the end, in the last two Sûrahs.
[5] Lev. xix. 26; Ex. xxii. 17 [18]. Magic must have assumed early the most diverse forms, as can be seen from the unusually numerous names for it which occur in the Old Testament, many of which, but not all, are collected together in the passage Deut. xviii. 10, 11. But as all kinds were equally illegal in Israel, the frequent interchange of one Hebrew name for another became customary; and this is for us one of the main causes of the obscurity of the original meaning. A fuller explanation of the particular expressions, however, belongs rather to a work on the religion of the Bible. Comp. my *Die Theologie des Alten und Neuen Bundes*, Leips. 1871, vol. i. s. 234 seq.

a matter of course, that in the Hebrew, as it lies before us, the punishment imprecated is for the most part only briefly indicated,[1] not expressed and narrowly defined. Yet at least in ordinary conversation this indication was invariably given. To raise the right hand, as though in a challenge, to heaven,[2] was so universal a custom among the Semitic nations, that in some of their languages 'the right hand' is used as equivalent to oath,[3] in others a verb 'to swear' is derived from it;[4] whilst in Hebrew 'to raise one's hand' was quite a common phrase for 'to swear.' Along with the name of God, the person swearing would at the same time designate his other attributes, his power and greatness, or whatever else of the essence of this God appeared to him at the moment of swearing of special significance. One of the shortest and finest of asseverative phrases is that of the last king of Judah: 'As Jahveh lives, *who has created for us this soul!*'[5]—In the intercourse of common life it gradually became customary to weaken the force of this voluntary oath, by swearing merely by a valued friend, or by some honoured man, either alone or along with God.[6] But even during the time of the kings Israel allowed itself to go no further with this process of attenuation.

But even the former stronger style of oath was, according to traces from other quarters, far stronger still originally; so true is it that it cost the most gigantic efforts to get men at all accustomed, in the growth of the mutual relations of life, to respect truth and abhor perjury. A relic of the most distant times is to be found in Hebrew, and in this alone of Semitic languages,[7] in a word for the apparently simple idea of swearing, which yet originally meant clearly enough, 'to bind oneself by seven

---

[1] How definitely they can be named, and what fearful penalties were imprecated, is shown once in the great example, Job xxxi.; and such repeated and increasing self-imprecations best explain the meaning of the phrase 'so do God to me and so do he further,' which, according to *Hist.* i. 133 *note* 3, occurs so frequently in the Books of Kings, and from which the poetical application, Ps. cxx. 3, can be understood.

[2] Gen. xiv. 22; Ex. vi. 8; Deut. xxxii. 40, and elsewhere.

[3] In Arabic ى‍م‍ي‍ن.

[4] In Syriac and Deut. xxxii. 5, יָמָה. Comp. *Ausführliches Lehrbuch*, s. 160d.

[5] Jer. xxxviii. 16.

[6] The חֵי נַפְשְׁךָ of the Books of Kings. Generally, it stands after the name of God,

more rarely alone, 1 Sam. i. 26. During the early glory of the Monarchy the oath by the life of the king came into vogue, but this was assuredly never recognised by the law. The evil habit was much further developed by the time of the New Testament, though at the same time with a dread of the use of the name Jahveh. See my *Die drei ersten Evangelien*, s. 215. Here, too, the three great eras of this whole history can be most definitely separated.

[7] The way in which the chief Semitic languages separate from one another in regard to this conception of swearing is very remarkable. The Aramaic has ܐܳܡܶܐ, the Arabic has אלה, which is found also in Hebrew, though with a modified meaning, and also ح‍ل‍ف, which is the

(things),' and therefore presupposes an extraordinarily ceremonious kind of oath. In early days the person swearing deemed it necessary according to this, to call upon seven things as witnesses of his declaration, or as enduring monuments of the truth. It might be seven men whom he invoked, or seven gods, or else he might touch seven sacred objects, or take seven steps to a sacred stone.[1] If from special causes it were desired to make the oath yet more impressive (more solemn), e.g. in order to ratify a treaty, seven gifts also were taken, e.g. sacrificial animals, and the one most interested in the safe keeping of the treaty sought by the presentation of these to bind the other party more firmly to himself and to the oath, just as might be done by any acceptable gift. An instance of this out of the patriarchal times of Abraham is once actually related in the Book of Covenants.[2] This point will be more fully discussed below under Sacrifices. In the ordinary life of Israel indeed, this usage appears to have gone out of custom from the time of Moses; but the word which has remained the regular expression for swearing, still bears testimony not only to the primitive sanctity of the number seven, but also to the extraordinary degree of ceremony requisite in primitive times to secure on all sides a permanent recognition of a true declaration.

To this must be added that in the earliest times man already felt most keenly the necessity of making as conspicuous as possible, in the most varied but always telling ways, the penalties which would be incurred by breach of oath or promise. A somewhat strong physical encounter of the two parties pledging themselves, a *blow*, a *cutting*, even a *killing*, were employed.[3] The broken pieces or halves would remind each of the two parties of the common obligation, to fulfil which he

---

chief word, and probably too, gives the kernel of the idea, as well as بَيْع, with the above modified evil meaning. The Ethiopic has *maḥala*, which is the same as بَيْع, and *taḥalafa*, with the modified evil meaning related to حَلِبَ. With the Hebrew נשׁבע, the Sanskrit *çap* has perhaps an extremely ancient connection.

[1] This last was customary amongst the ancient Indians in concluding treaties. Comp. A. Weber's *Indische Studien*, v. 321 sq. 388.

[2] Gen. xxi. 27-31. The thought in verso 30 is especially noteworthy. It was an extremely early assumption, that a gift which one party concluding the cove- nant took from the other, made the contract more binding. Gen. xxxiii. 8-15.— Very similar is the old Arabic custom mentioned by Herod. iii. 8. At the present time in the Wadi-Muná (Miná) near Mecca, seven stones are now thrown where formerly seven idols stood. See Burckhardt's *Travels in Arabia*, ii. 57 sq. (61 of the 8vo. ed.). Comp. also Shahrastâni's *Kitâb Elmilal*, p. 442; 6 ed. Cureton.

[3] Hence the modes of speech which reach down from the most primitive times into those somewhat later, such as בְּרָת בְּרִית, ὅρκια τέμνειν, *fœdus icere*, *ferire*, phrases which differ much from our *ein bündniss schliessen*.

on his side had bound himself.[1] The blood would suggest the death deserved by him who broke his oath, a point on which more will be said below under Sacrifices at treaties.

The word *âlah* denoted this stronger form of swearing accompanied by a mention of the penalty, but because the act easily degenerated, especially in common life, and led to heedless or even false oaths,[2] the word not unfrequently bore a modified bad meaning. With this is connected the fact that in more cautious speech the express mention of the punishment was, as stated above, avoided by preference.

2. But to avoid uttering the *âlah* was impossible when the oath became adjuration, i.e. when it was used to compel another to confess a truth or observe a command. Then the punishments imprecated from heaven would undoubtedly be always expressed in the strongest language. It would, therefore, be in such instances that the *âlah* would find its most frequent legal application. Two principal cases of this were possible. A man might desire to bind or compel another by swearing in respect to his own private affairs, in which case, when the kingdom was in a settled state, the aid of the priestly authority would be invoked,[3] if such an oath was not to become a mere silent imprecation.[4] During the time of the patriarchs, when all these usages were still practised in much stronger forms, the person who desired to bind another to the strictest truth used to make the latter lay his hand under his own hip; on that part of the body, therefore, out of which, according to ancient ideas, posterity proceeded,[5] and which so far possessed in the homely notions of primitive days a certain sanctity. Thus he would refer the latter to the whole of posterity at once, and to its revenge should he break his promise.[6]—In the second place this formal adjuration found

[1] Comp. Al. Castrén's ethnologic lectures on the *Altaic races*, 116-7. Bastian's *Reise nach St. Salvador* in Congo (1859), 153-4, 236. Livingstone's *Travels in Africa*, ii., and more below under Sacrifices at treaties.

[2] Hence אָלָה can also denote heedless and false swearing, Hos. iv. 2; Zach. v. 3; comp. ver. 4, viii. 17. In Ecc. ix. 2, נִשְׁבָּע has quite this meaning, which already calls to mind the well-known expression, Matt. v. 37; James v. 12. But also among the most ancient Greeks, Horkos, son of Eris, already appears even as a dreaded evil God. Hesiod's *Theog.* ver. 231 sq. comp 783-806.

[3] A good example of this occurs Num. v. 21, 22, from which we can see that such an oath when complete would stand thus: שְׁבֻעַת הָאָלָה, 1 Kings viii. 31.

[4] As is described Job xxxi. 30.

[5] יָצְאֵי יְרֵכוֹ, 'which came out of his loins,' is a frequent description of posterity of which we cannot fail to be reminded, Gen. xlvi. 26; Exod. i. 5.

[6] Gen. xxiv. 2, 9; xlvii. 29, comp. xxiv. 41. The custom here depicted is certainly a very peculiar one, and only in modern times among the Egyptian Bedouins and the Kaffirs has anything parallel been discovered. See *Adventures of Colonel Somerset in Caffraria*, Lond. 1858. The usage is also found now among the lower classes in Turkestan. See Vambéry's *Reisen* there, s. 49 (1865).

an important application in public national life, when every effort was to be made for the discovery of a criminal, hitherto undetected. In such a case it is plain that the strongest oaths and imprecations would be uttered aloud by a priest or some other authority against all who might in any way whatever share the guilty secret. In a community like that of Israel, where in its best, and generally in the earlier times, a discipline of such unusual strictness prevailed, it is impossible to overestimate the potency and awfulness, and in most cases the efficacy, of such public oaths.[1] It is likely that on occasion of such oaths it was the traditional habit to repeat out of history instances of the fearful destruction of guilty persons in order to terrify and deter, and so bring into the words of the curse past 'names' of unhappy memory. Too frequent allusion to this custom is made in somewhat later times for us to doubt that it often found application in the cases lying before us.[2] But in the early nation, true to the simplicity of its religion, the ordinary phrase used in the public legal procedure was only this: The person supposed to be guilty was called upon to acknowledge the truth or to do this or that, *paying honour and giving praise to Jahveh, God of Israel*.[3]

The short word with which the person spoken to answered all such sacred addresses, including these adjurations, was the familiar *amén*, a little word which properly corresponds only to our yes! and which subsequently found the most diverse applications, but which in the use here explained goes back to the earliest times of the community.[4]

3. When finally the oath was employed in making contracts and alliances, each of the two contracting parties made the other

---

[1] Cases of this kind are presupposed, Lev. v. 1; Prov. xxix. 24; a similar one 1 Sam. xiv. 24. An ancient sacred phrase of this kind may in particular be traced in Mal. ii. 12, comp. Jer. xi. 3. This again enables us to explain such images as occur in Jer. xxiii. 10; Zach. v. 3; Mal. ii. 2. Josephus in his *Life*, c. 53, speaks of the recourse to φρικωδέστατοι ὅρκοι (which is so characteristic of his time, but only betrays its spiritual poverty); but among the Heathen we find the words of very long and strong oaths even on public monuments. *Corp. Jus. Grae*. ii. p. 410, 628 sq. Comp. further A. Danz, *Der sacrale Schutz im römischen Rechtsverkehr*, Jena, 1857. The important part played by the *dirae* among the Greeks and Romans is well known, and in regard to the Old Germans, comp. now Uhland's *Volkslieder* (1866), s. 269 sq. 365 sq.

[2] Comp. Jer. xxix. 18, 22; xlii. 18; xliv. 8, 12, 22; xlix. 13; BK. Is. lxv. 15, 16; Ps. cii. 9 [8]; Zach. viii. 13. Conversely in cases of somewhat longer and more precise blessings they liked to repeat the names of those who had been richly blessed in former generations, Gen. xii. 2, 3; xlviii. 20. But to what an extent later times learned to despise the ancient oaths is seen in Deut. xxix. 18 [19].

[3] Josh. vii. 19, where the ancient half poetical language is still retained. It is freely repeated Ezr. x. 11 (Ezr. Apocr. ix. 8), John ix. 24.

[4] According to the Book of Origins, Num. v. 22. Comp. *Die Dichter des Alten Bundes*, i.a. s. 247, 8.

utter aloud the words of the contract which concerned him,[1] these mutual promises being accompanied by similar oaths and imprecations. But if, as might easily be the case when the more important matters of state were concerned, one of the two parties was much more powerful than the other, the former considered himself above taking even the solemn oath, and 'brought' (according to the standing phrase) only the latter 'into the oath of imprecation,' i.e. the oath uttered with solemn imprecations.[2] Monuments of stone were erected as eternal witnesses, even in times when writing was already in use, and allusion is not unfrequently made to this fact in the oldest history of Israel.[3] Meals partaken of together both before and after the oath of alliance were also customary in the oldest times;[4] and it will be shown below how naturally sacrifices and alliances would be joined on to this.

c. The Vow.

The vow, in its original form, must not be regarded as the thought of a future performance conceived steadfastly but only in silence. It was spoken out loud before all the world, along with the most solemn invocation of God, as a sacred purpose, which a person swore by God he was determined to fulfil.[5] It could only refer to something sacred, i.e. to doing something directly for God in order to win his favour. In order to obtain from God some good thing, the want of which he felt with painful keenness, a man desired to give up on his part something dear to himself; but because his own weakness made him despair of being able to make this sacrifice, or at least because it could not be made immediately, he bound himself through an oath to God spoken out clearly and with the utmost seriousness, that he would fulfil it. This naturally inspired him with a strength which had previously failed him, and which, perhaps, without this spasmodic flight he would never have possessed.[6]

---

[1] The clearest description of this is found Deut. xxvi. 17-19, and here occurs the technical expression for it, הֶאֱמִיר, prop. to make some one say, i.e. promise, something. The actual oath then follows, xxvii.-xxx., comp. xi. 26 32. Comp. also Gen. xxvi. 28-31 ; xxxi. 44-54.

[2] Ezek. xvii. 13 ; comp. 16, 18; xvi. 59 ; Neh. x. 30.

[3] Comp. *Hist.* ii. 260 (first ed. p. 32); Gen. xxxi. 45 sq.

[4] Gen. xxxi. 54, which explains also the more exalted representation, Ex. xxiv. 11.

[5] It is plain too from the description that every one would at once clearly understand its meaning, Num. xxx. 5, 8, 9, 12-16.

[6] What is contained in the Bible on the subject of vows is further explained by the very numerous and varied votive inscriptions on Phœnician and Punic monuments which have been discovered in our days, and are being continually more and more perfectly decyphered. Comp. *Entzifferung der Neupunischen Inschriften*, Gött. 1852. and lately also the *Abhandlung über die grosse Karthagische und andere neuentdeckte Phönikische Inschriften* (Gött. 1864), s. 30 sq.

The vow was at first therefore the strongest possible utterance of sacred spontaneous impulses, by means of appropriate words. Accordingly during the first centuries of the community it was directed towards the entire mighty problem which then faced the people: viz. to live for the first time wholly within the religion which had been given it, and within its national development, and to supplement what was yet wanting by exerting the most deep-seated powers of body and of soul. Hence, as at that time the very hardest of demands was made on man, nothing less being required than a thorough inward change so that he should become capable of supplementing this great want, the subject of the vow was generally something extraordinarily hard to perform, or something that could not be calculated upon and was full of mystery. But it also stimulated the most deep-seated energies, and it appeared in the greatest strength, and with the most important historical consequences, among the whole nation just at the time when that want was felt most keenly.[1] After this deficiency had been removed as far as was then possible, and chiefly through the wondrous power of the vow, and when Israel in the second era of its whole history was to this extent enjoying greater peace, then, it is true, new and deeper wants began to show themselves, which gave rise on the part of some few of the nation to a new kind of vow, the performance of which was full of difficulty.[2] But in the community at large, it became the custom in time of need to vow only thanksgiving and rich offerings of the ordinary kind to be presented after deliverance,[3] on which occasions something laudable and acceptable would be vowed, especially if the thanksgiving was hearty and sincere, but nothing so very difficult or immeasurable.

In these first centuries, therefore, there was often a danger that many a one might make some tremendous vow, next to impossible to accomplish, by which he yet deemed himself bound, in consequence of the solemn way in which the vow had been audibly uttered, as described above. A true religion like Jahveism could disapprove neither of the utterance of sacred words nor of the ultimate object of all vows; but just as little could it demand vows at all, or cling tenaciously to the performance of what was impossible, thereby misunderstanding human conditions. On these principles the Book of Origins proceeds in the matter of laws on vows; and it has every token

---

[1] As is shown *Hist.* ii. 392 (first ed. 164).
[2] *Hist.* iv. 79.
[3] Vide *Die Dichter des A. Bs.* i.b. s. 162 of the third ed. Comp. also Prov. vii. 14.

of being the first work which treated this subject from a legal point of view. It assumes[1] that the man, i.e. the head of the family, may not violate his vow; it was expected from him that he should know what it was he was vowing. Still another law provides that in the case not contemplated here, and which religion could not sanction, of a vow uttered thoughtlessly, relief should be afforded by means of a guilt-offering.[2] But the father could annul every vow spoken by his unmarried daughter, the husband every one of his wife; though this could be done only if on hearing it he at once declared its invalidity (and that he should be able instantly to see through an inconsiderate one, must have been expected from the father and the husband or their representatives). But the mere loss of a husband, by death or separation, freed no woman from her vow.

So strict and yet so equitable are these laws, especially when considered from the point of view of the extensive ancient rights of the head of the family. In Deuteronomy as well as in still later writings similar prominence is always given to the general necessity of strictly keeping a vow, but at the same time it is said more plainly than in the Book of Origins that it is also no sin not to make vows, and that a heedless vow is before everything to be avoided.[3]

We are not yet in a position to speak more closely of the contents of the vow, or the things undertaken.

2. *The Sacred Utterances expressed by Sacrifices.*

Only a few kinds of sacred phrases, such as the ordinary oath or the blessing, constitute an end in themselves, and are complete with little or no accompaniment of motions and gestures. The majority, vows, or pure spontaneous prayers, should always lead to the corresponding action of man or of God. But in truth man must strain all his inmost powers of soul and body to their utmost, and when necessary, freely surrender his most cherished project, or the dearest of his external possessions, in order to attain what he is ever seeking, and which at every fresh step in his life is again impelled to seek.

A dim feeling of this has undoubtedly at all times been present to man. It drove him, when words addressed to the Deity were thought insufficient, to press in by stronger means,

---

[1] Num. xxx. 2-17 [1-16].
[2] Lev. v. 4. See below.
[3] Deut. xxiii. 22-24 [21-23], Ec v. 3-5 [4-6].

so as to draw forth from God what he lacked, and could obtain only from him. But what man sought, divine salvation and divine counsel, is still, and was then even more than now, the hardest and the darkest that he can seek after; something, moreover, which is inexhaustible, towards which he is ever conscious of fresh need. In regard to it, then, he soon felt himself ready for any undertaking and for the hardest service, or even the most painful and the strangest attempts. Something Vast and Awful stood over against him, and compelled him to give up or to dare all things in order to approach it, and draw it near to himself. But man can only offer what is human in order to get in exchange what is divine, and a dim impulse made him believe that he would the sooner win the divine boon, the more vigorously he sought the higher possession by the completest resignation of all his lower goods. Every such act, then, of practical surrender, by which man penetrates immediately to the Deity, and seeks not only to influence it, but more strongly, as it were, to touch it, in order to be touched again by it and blessed, we may designate by the general word sacrifice. The striving of men by means of an unusual act, as it were, to touch and draw to themselves Deity itself, and thus cause the sacred act to follow the sacred word of prayer, is assuredly the early commencement of all living individual religion. Without a renunciation, moreover, of what is valued and agreeable merely on account of its sensuous qualities, extraordinary efforts of the soul in striving exclusively after what is divine are impossible; and in so far as such renunciation is demanded of us, the idea of sacrifice has a meaning, eternally valid and imperishable, for us and for all futurity.

Nothing is more characteristic of remote Antiquity than the force, and at the same time the openness and integrity, with which the feelings of fear towards God passed over into corresponding actions; and this proves itself, before all else, in that chief constituent of every religion, the sacrifice. There seemed no more important task for a whole nation than not to neglect the sacrifices to its God; no greater misfortune could occur than for them to be violently broken off.[1] The individual knew no greater happiness than to draw near his God with offerings; no acuter pain and no deeper dishonour than for this to be impossible or forbidden to him.[2] And what the earth pre-

---

[1] This is seen best in Joel i., ii., but also in all Antiquity. 12. and the descriptions even in the Proter. Jac. i.

[2] Comp. the proverbial saying, Mal. ii.

sented to man seemed not to be blessed to him for his enjoyment until a portion of it had been offered to its Giver.[1]

Already, in quite the dawn of Antiquity, sacrifice had assumed a hundred different forms under these quick feelings of young humanity. In each of them the utmost efforts were made to reach the highest aim, viz. the right kind of the most fruitful influence of living religion. At the time of the founding of Jahveism the most varied forms of sacrifice had been long in operation, each with its special drift and corresponding belief; indeed, they were in the full bloom of their earliest development, and their evil side was but little known. Accordingly all the principal kinds of these ancient sacrifices were transferred to Jahveism. Some branches of them, indeed, it had from the very beginning to reject, as contradictory to its own spirit, and these included just the final points to which consistency had led them. But many others which it took, it developed the more thoroughly in consequence, pouring its new spirit into them, and seeking by means of them to awaken the power of higher religion. Being, however, a powerful new religion, it also founded a new form of sacrifice, which, though unpretending, was yet the only one which closely corresponded to its spirit. And while the attempt to develope perfectly the older forms of sacrifice only revealed more clearly their great deficiencies, completely new and purer kinds gradually became prevalent, and these are in a position to endure for ever. If the history of Israel is, before all things, the history of the growth of true religion, it shows also in particular, and with the utmost clearness, what is true sacrifice, and through how many imperfect kinds of it even the nation of Antiquity which was most advanced in religion had to pass, in order to learn at last what is this true and eternal sacrifice. Even the most imperfect and unsatisfactory sacrifice includes still undeveloped the whole tendency towards a true religion. When, therefore, this on any occasion reveals itself with greater vigour, it gradually kills off of itself the imperfect elements in the sacrifice, until there remains nothing but what is genuine and eternal.

a. Sacrifices of Property.

It follows immediately from all that has been said above, that sacrifices, in conformity with the feeling of Antiquity, and as they were customary also in Israel, especially during the first

[1] A striking expression of this feeling occurs Hos. ix. 4, comp. v. 6.

centuries of its history, were so manifold, and at the same time always so essentially dependent on man's free resolve at any given moment, that it seems scarcely possible to reckon them all up according to any strict arrangement.[1] When, e.g., three of his boldest warriors had, at the risk of their lives, brought fresh spring-water to David, when he was burning with thirst, and he, in sudden impulse, rather than drink it, poured it out on the ground in thanks to God, who had given him such companions in war,[2] he then performed no prescribed or even customary sacrifice, but one all the same which sprang from the deepest sacrificial feeling animating the ancient world.

However, if we desire to review the more usual ones among them, we must speak in the first instance of the sacrifices of *external possessions*, those being in themselves the most natural, as well as the most numerous. Such possessions, to which the name of property is usually confined, were, as the history of all sacrifice proves, what man first of all felt himself impelled to offer up, in order thereby to press in upon the Deity and obtain from it a greater good. We must remember that the external goods and treasures of men in the earliest times, before the arts of easily multiplying them were developed, were far from being as immeasurable as in later times. The oldest nations, like the first human beings, commenced their existence in poverty and need. The earliest efforts, prayers, and wishes of nations, turned almost exclusively on obtaining this sensuous ground of all higher development.[3] Thus we can understand what importance this sacrifice of external possessions had in primitive times, for in all ages the things sacrificed essentially resemble those which the person offering them is particularly anxious to obtain from God. But the conception of property and its surrender was capable of extraordinary extension in course of time. If no scruples held a man back from giving the dearest he had when a feeling in his heart drove him to sacrifice it to his God just as it was, then he would easily feel even the life of a beloved domestic animal not too dear to be given up at his heart's urgent demand. Nay, only in the offering up of life or soul, as the last that can be offered, did it seem to him that the highest was presented. But the logical consequence

---

[1] An attempt at a history of sacrifices was made at the end of the ancient world, by *Prophyrios* in his work *De Abstin.* ii. 6 sq. 59; but this most imperfect attempt stopped there, and rests on little else but guessing and conjecture. Nevertheless this philosopher refers to *Theophrastos*, ii. 20, 27 ; to *Empedocles*, ii. 21, even to old Phœnician writings, iv. 15 (probably the *Sanchuniathonic*).

[2] *Hist.* iii. 88.

[3] As can be seen most clearly and at greatest length in the oldest songs of the Vedas, comp. *Hist.* ii. 162 [first ed. i. 585], note 2.

of such feelings was that human life must ultimately be looked upon as incomparably the highest and most wondrous offering, whether the life offered be that of a stranger, or, as that which is dearest to one, that of one's own child, or even of oneself. Thus human sacrifice was everywhere the proper crown and completion of all these utterances of the fear of God. Whether Jahveism went so far as to justify this most consistent development of the sacrifice of property, can only be explained below at its proper place.

A. THE TABLE-OFFERING.

The simplest mode of offering a sacrifice of property was from the beginning connected with the liveliest wish to prepare therewith something pleasing, some enjoyment for the Deity. Accordingly the sacrifices which arose in the very earliest times were entirely furnished as food-offerings; they were presented as meals for gracious acceptance. Man parted with his own most delicious food in order to prepare enjoyment for a higher being, and to draw forth thereby a blessing over the earth;[1] and when he received this blessing from mother earth, thankfulness drove him to make ready a portion of the superabundance for a similar food-offering. Exactly in this way the custom arose among certain nations of western Asia and Europe, of setting out, at a sacred spot, a magnificent table, and replenishing it from time to time with choice provisions; libations of wine were always connected with this.[2]

A trace of this custom remained also in Israel down to later times. A table overlaid with gold stood constantly at the sanctuary of Israel; on it were twelve loaves turned towards the Holy of Holies, and accordingly named 'the bread of the countenance' (of God). After being there a week they were replaced (on each Sabbath) by fresh loaves, as is further described below.[3] Still this table-offering appears alongside of the other sacrifices, as they grew up in Jahveism, as something quite special, differing entirely from the numerous other kinds. For at the public sanctuary this simple offering stood by the side of the others like a sanctified relic of quite a different age; and at the domestic

---

[1] Here too the collation of Vedic hymns, so far as they are yet printed, is most instructive.

[2] Heathen *lectisternia*, as prepared also by many Israelites, are spoken of, Ezek. xvi. 18; xxiii. 41; Bk. Is. lxv. 11; Daniel xiv. 3–15. LXX. Even the religion of Zarathustra [Zoroaster], which in other respects rejects bloody sacrifices has something like in the *Draonas*, vide Spiegel's *Avesta*, ii. s. lxxii.

[3] See below, under the description of the national sacrifices and of the Sanctuary.

sanctuaries of the people it does not seem to have been in use from the time of Moses. Plainly, then it had only maintained itself in Israel out of an altogether remote primitive age. Similarly it will be made clear in many cases further on, that the characteristics of two earlier eras and cultures met in Jahveism after its foundation, and sought to maintain themselves in it; and this, after the fuller description of the primeval history of the nation already given,[1] cannot surprise us.

There can be no doubt, from general considerations, that originally the pouring out of wine (*libatio*) belonged to this table-offering;[2] and although it seems in Jahveism to have been completely separated therefrom (at least we must judge so according to our present sources), the sacred vessels for libations were nevertheless always preserved on this table.[3]

B. FIRE-OFFERINGS.

Great as was the readiness of remote Antiquity to sacrifice even its dearest possessions to the God, and present the most desperate offerings to the Mysterious One, whose favour it longed for, its desire was yet greater to receive conversely from heaven the signs of being heard, and of the gracious acceptance of its sacrifice. The listening for heavenly signs easily grew into the effort to attract them forth with all one's might, and wring them out from heaven. Many a nation value above all else the possession of at any rate one common easy sign of the visible mediation between heaven and earth. To the childlike feeling of remote Antiquity it appeared that such a one was met with in fire, with its wondrous nature. This, breaking forth, moving, and growing, like an unlooked for divine being, devouring, and bearing what was devoured aloft in its cloud, seemed to be the means for conveying the earthly gift to heaven.[4] And certainly in many nations, from very early times, this operated as a main cause why the sacrifice was most strongly developed in just this direction. It was only when the sacrifice had gone up to heaven in the fire that it was complete, a sweet enjoyment for the Gods,[5] and a token to the persons sacrificing

---

[1] *Hist.* vol. i.
[2] Comp. the two members of the ver. nx. Is. lxv. 11, and what is said below on libations of wine in general.
[3] See more below under the description of the Sanctuary.
[4] We see this nowhere so clearly as in the ancient sacrificial hymns of the Rig- and Sâma-Veda, especially in those addressed to Agni, the once so highly reverenced great God of Fire.
[5] Even in the Old Testament sacrifices are called 'a sweet savour for Jahveh,' according to a standing expression in the Book of Origins (רֵיחַ נִיחֹחַ לַיהוה). It sometimes appears in later writers (as Gen. viii. 21), but it is always borrowed first

that it had really gone to heaven and was accepted there. Another belief was easily and consistently added on to this. As fire can be kindled without human aid, e.g. by lightning or by catching the rays of the sun, the best sacrificial fire soon came to be considered that alone which was kindled even from heaven itself, as though God himself descended to meet and take the offering. The belief in the existence of such purer fire coming from heaven itself, had its root deep in many an ancient nation. It maintained itself also in Israel long after Moses, although with him it had no close connection with the higher religion itself;[1] and in many ancient religions the most active efforts were directed to the solution of the problem, how to obtain such heavenly fire.

It was, accordingly, through the fire- and food-offering that remote Antiquity felt the most palpable manifestations of that reciprocity between heaven and earth, between God and man, which ever constitutes the final ground of all religion. For here man saw his own prayers and wishes borne up to heaven, and God descending to meet them. It became, among every nation that introduced it, the highest and most brilliant sacred rite, it soon accompanied all the stronger utterances of religion, and assumed the most different forms just because of its endless application. It was therefore most closely connected with the strongest forms of all sacrifices of property, as well as with the profoundest views respecting them. The bloody sacrifice, with all its horror of flowing blood, became to the races that loved it, essentially only a fire-offering. The altar, i.e., in reality the hearth for the fire-offering, was regarded with quite other feelings than those which men attached to the sacred table

from this book. Similar expressions occur Amos v. 21; Deut. xxxiii. 10.

[1] Even sacrificial fire obtained by rubbing two sticks together is celebrated for its wonderful origin in one of the hymns of the Rig-Veda, iv. 1. 3. Amongst other ancient peoples the sacrificial fire was yearly renewed in spring by catching the sunbeams, and even according to the description 2 Macc. x. 3 (comp. with it the prolix legend, i. 18–36), when sacrifices were renewed in the temple after an intermission of three years, fire was obtained for the purpose from two heated stones (perhaps heated by the sun, i. 22?); comp. Ben-Gorion, iii. 13, the views of Philo in the *Life of Moses*, iii. 18; Clem. Rom. *Homil.* ix. 6; Plutarch's *Numa*, c. ix.; Prescott's *History of Peru*, i. ch. 3. But as Jahveism eagerly referred back direct to the true God all that it held sacred, and as it regarded him as the mysterious God of the heavens and the earth, the Book of Origins, Lev. ix. 24, makes the first sacred fire of the Sanctuary under Moses fall from Jahveh on to the altar, and in an instant consume the acceptable sacrifice. This a later narrator transfers to a case of similar extraordinary sublimity in the time of Elijah, 1 Kings xviii. 22-38. A like case is related 1 Chron. xxi. 26, and of Solomon's Temple, 2 Chron. vii. 1. Comp. also Sûrah iii. 179. The conception, or rather the representation, Jud. vi. 21, is peculiar, as also the similar one, xiii. 20. But these too come essentially to this, that a sacrificial fire kindled, as it were, without the aid of the person sacrificing, by a heavenly breath or staff, was deemed truly divine, i.e. miraculous.

mentioned above, and constituted far more the centre for numerous sacred rites. A warlike nation, longing for vivid impressions, will always give the fire-offering a preference to the simpler table-offering; so long at least as no new aversion of any sort to the destruction of all earthly life, including therefore that of animals, assumed predominance as the religion of the nation became enervated. For in this case an opposite tendency may cause continually more and more limitation of bloody sacrifices to the Deity, or completely forbid them, just as it may forbid the enjoyment of meat among men, and this we see in very different forms in the Egyptian worship of animals,[1] in Brahminism, and the religion of Zarathustra, but most strongly developed, in Buddhism.

The people of Israel maintained, especially after Moses, a straightforward, strong, manly religion, and never fell into the scruples of such over-refined and morbid principles. It was certainly acquainted with the fire-offering before Moses, for this had been long in use in those countries in Asia whence it sprang. Moreover if, on the one hand, the altar may be everywhere taken as valid testimony to the existence of sacrifices by fire, on the other hand it cannot be doubted that both long before and during the time of Moses altars were erected by Israel.[2] But it is just as clear that it had not yet acquired its perfect development by that time. Certain ancient historical testimonies show this,[3] and we saw that the table-offering must be the older of the two in Israel.[4] The fully developed sacrifice by fire is plainly connected closely with the development of the Levitical priesthood, which will be spoken of further on, and the two together probably assumed this fixed form only towards the end of the life of Moses, and the time of the conquest of Canaan. Thus at that time two essentially distinct kinds of sacrifices, the table- and the fire-offering, met together in Israel, and sought to harmonise; but in doing so, the sacrifice by fire, in itself the more developed and far more suited to those strong, warlike times, maintained much the superior position.

Thus these two principal kinds of sacrifice were compounded one with another in Jahveism, and as far as the idea of food-offering is concerned, stood upon the same footing. Accordingly, they were developed in other respects in as similar a manner as

---

[1] The silly things in this, which Josephus mocks at, *Contr. Apion.* ii. 11, 13, are only to be explained in this way.

[2] See below, under the description f the altars.

[3] See *Hist.* ii. 261 sq. [first ed. ii. 33]. This essentially agrees with what Ezek. says in a passage to be considered more closely below, xx. 25-6.

[4] P. 27.

the distinction between table- and fire-offering, as well as that between bloodless and bloody offerings would permit. This appears at once in considering :—

i. *The Materials of the Food-offering.*

Among the materials of the food-offering there is none which in itself would not serve also for human meals. Both the corn- and the slain-offerings, furnished the principal materials in Israel from early times, just as bread and meat did at human meals; and the 'bread of Jahveh' was, at the date of the Book of Origins, still a current name for all food-offerings.[1] In general a close connection runs through the ancient laws about eating and those about sacrifices, which is easily explained by the fact that the sacrifice of which we are now speaking was, in the oldest view, considered a meal for the gods. This, when possible, ought to be still purer and more choice than that of men; whatever was held to be the best meal for men should constitute the sacrifice. But what this is, will depend on the mode of life which is held to be the most noble and worthy among a people ; and it is an important fact for the whole history of Israel, that the Mosaic sacrifice was entirely suited to a nation which united agriculture and fixed settlements with the breeding of cattle. The pre-eminence of the slain-offering comes from the ancient preference for cattle-breeding; but with it is already inseparably connected the corn-offering, having relation only to an agricultural people.

1. Among animals, the wild ones, or those not accustomed to domestication among men, were not available for sacrifice. This was the case even when they were in themselves edible, and not forbidden as human food by religion, such as deer, gazelles,[2] and also fish and every kind of water-animal. For such animals as were living wild, could not be considered the actual property of men among a nation that had long passed out of the mere hunting stage, and they could therefore serve for no real sacrifice such as a man might offer up of his own possessions. There remained, accordingly, only the tame domestic animals, which from very early times were the real property of men, and in the times of the Patriarchs constituted their chief possessions, which stood in many respects so near

---

[1] Lev. iii. 11, 16 ; xxi. 8, 17 ; xxii. 25 ; Num. xxviii. 2.

[2] In accordance with the proverb, Deut. xii. 15, 22. The same principle was valid among the ancient Arabs, comp. the proverb in Ḥârith's *Mo'all.* ver. 69, and the *Hamâsa*. p. 442, line 6. with the narrative in the Scholia. It was different among the Phœnicians, who are treated of below.

to man, and almost seemed to share his very feelings. But as again from the tame animals there were excluded all that were held unclean for men (on which point more is said further on), the only ones that were available for sacrifice were cattle, sheep, and goats. Only in certain cases of an inferior kind, tame birds of the species of pigeons were permitted,[1] and these were also allowed when through poverty a prescribed sacrifice could not otherwise have been offered.[2] But at the time of the Book of Origins, cattle were the most natural and worthy sacrificial animals. Even sheep and goats were then considered in the eye of the law a poorer offering, which might be substituted for cattle only when a contribution was demanded of every individual, so that cases would arise when there would be a necessity for so doing.[3] That the animal must belong, as a condition of a proper sacrifice, to the person offering it, was so much a matter of course, that even kings could not take it in such a case as a present, but if they did not possess it, believed they must purchase it with their own money.[4]

The very conception of the sacrifice involved that the animal offered must be sound and free from blemish, and further that it must not have been impaired by work or other service for men, and as it were desecrated;[5] for the giving up of property already used and worn out, or faulty, would be no sacrifice. This feeling penetrated Antiquity so strongly, that it was not till the latest times—when the gifts, originally voluntary, had long been legally prescribed, when the childlike feeling of remote Antiquity was lost, and the people were become far poorer—that complaints are made of deception in the matter of blemishes in the animals brought for sacrifice.[6]

According to the Book of Origins the sacrificial animal must not be less than eight days, nor more than one year old; on this account those of one year old are generally spoken of as the best.[7] In considering the bodily defects of an animal a wide field of observation was opened for suspicion and superstition. The law, therefore, enumerated the particular blemishes which

---

[1] As in the cases Lev. xv. 14, 29; Num. vi. 10.
[2] As in the cases Lev. v. 6 sq., xii. 8; xiv. 21 sq. Comp. Luke ii. 24.
[3] This is clear from Lev. xiv. 10, 21, and from the whole mode of representation of this book.
[4] 2 Sam. xxiv. 23 sq.
[5] The usual expression for all this is מְמִים, 'without blemish,' still in its first fresh and full youthful vigour. But there are also more complete descriptions, such as Num. xix. 2.
[6] Mal. i. 7, 8, 13, 14. Comp. the bad figs. Jer. xxiv.
[7] This appears from Lev. xxii. 27, comp. xii. 6; xxiii. 12, 18; Num. vi. 14, and thence Mic. vi. 6. How animals for sacrifice three years old can be spoken of, Gen. xv. 9, is seen Hist. i. 325, note 1. The seven year old bull (Jud. vi. 25) appears even there as something unusual, which once in a way must, for want of another, serve for sacrifice.

FOOD-OFFERINGS.

rendered an animal unfit for the altar, and contented itself with demanding somewhat less strictness in this respect in the case of offerings which occupied a lower, and, as it were, a human grade.[1] Moreover, an animal that had not been reared among the Israelites themselves was considered quite unfit for sacrifice, as not coming direct out of the possessions of the nation itself, and out of its consecrated sphere.[2]

Distinction of sex in the animals for sacrifice was carefully observed in the case of quadrupeds, but not in that of birds. The male was held everywhere to be the most natural and most worthy. The Paschal lamb, as the oldest and by far the most widely extended sacrificial animal, was the standing type of this; and just as was the case with blemishes, it is only in a late age that attempts were made to evade the duty of offering male animals.[3] But still the female could not have been considered altogether valueless and unworthy. The ancient custom drew a remarkable distinction. The female animal was available for certain kinds of sacrifice, which were regarded as necessary under certain circumstances, it being eligible, as it were, for the whole dark side of sacrifice; and this gave rise to a distinct opposition between the sexes, as will be explained further on under the separate kinds of offerings. Moreover, the two sexes were not legally distinguished in sacrifices that occupied a lower, and, as it were, a human grade, such as thank-offerings.[4]—Further, the first-born was considered preferable, but the law did not demand it as a condition of correct animal sacrifice.[5]

2. Just as the sacrificial animals ought to be limited to the domestic ones among an agricultural people, so of vegetables, only *corn*, and what was prepared from it, should be offered up. This is enough to show how completely the law presupposed a nation which was already purely agricultural. Corn might be offered up in very many ways, but in ordinary cases it was only presented either as fine meal, or after being prepared as food; in the latter case, being baked in the oven in thick or thin cakes, fried in a pan, or else roasted.[6] To this was added, as at a meal, rich oil, which was either kneaded in, or spread on the thin flat cake, the quantity of each being accurately determined according to fixed proportions.[7] But because the oil pertained

[1] According to Lev. xxii. 18-24. See further on respecting some obscure expressions found here. This is more generally expressed Deut. xv. 21; xvii. 1.
[2] According to Lev. xxii. 25, which explains the expression Ex. x. 26.
[3] Mal. i. 14.
[4] Lev. iii. 1 [A. V. peace-offerings].
[5] According to Gen. iv. 4. Comp. what is said below about *firstlings*.
[6] Lev. ii. 1-10; comp. vii. 9.
[7] Num. xv. 2-12; xxviii. 5 sq.; Ex xxix. 40.

to the corn-offering just as the male sex to the animal offering, the want of it denoted the above-mentioned dark side of sacrifice, as will be made clear below. It was just the reverse with the leaven. Only bread which was quite pure, and would not yield readily to putrefaction, which was mixed therefore neither with leaven, yeast, nor honey, would do for the altar. But yet as leavened bread is more agreeable to men, it was not forbidden in thank-offerings, in so far as it was to be eaten by the person offering it.[1] But as unleavened bread alone was allowed for the altar, it was held the more necessary to season it with *salt*, which counteracts all corruption. It was, indeed, on this point that the special belief turned, that salt must accompany every sacrifice, as a new covenant which man concluded with his God; just as according to old custom it must never be absent from meals for ratifying human friendship and alliances, and only a 'salt-treaty' was held to be secure.[2]

3. Wine served as the drink-offering (nésekh) in conformity with the nature and fertility of the country, and was undoubtedly the red wine native there at that time, to which allusion is so often made in the Old Testament. It was employed, however, as at a genuine meal, only as an accompaniment of the proper 'bread of Jahveh,' and its proportion to the latter was estimated exactly as that of oil to corn.[3] But the same sadder kinds of sacrifice, at which oil was purposely not employed, did not admit of this joyous addition of a libation of wine.[4] Even on fast-days it was the national custom to offer up water alone at the holy place,[5] a usage which is fully ex-

---

[1] All this appears from the brief indications in Lev. ii. 4, 5, 11. 12; vi. 9, 10; vii. 12, 13; xxiii. 17. Comp. the still older and shorter utterance in Ex. xxiii. 18. More will be said on the subject further on under the Passover. I have already treated the whole subject in the article of 1835, *Zeitschr. f. K. des Morgenlandes*, iii. s. 423. We see from Amos iv. 5, Hos. iii. 1, that at sacrifices, more or less heathenish, as e. g. Philo, *Opp.* ii. p. 518, describes them, things leavened and sweet were esteemed. Still the Heathens themselves considered what was unleavened to be purer, see Gell. *N. A.* x. 15, Plut. *Quaest. Rom.* c. 109. — Theophrastus, according to Porphyr. *De Abstin.* ii. 26, makes the 'Syrian Jews' drop *honey* and oil upon the burnt-offering, but this view must have arisen from an error. In reality, at the time of Philo (*De Sacrific.* c. vi.), and Plutarch (according to his *Conviv. Disput.* iv. 6, 2), many were seeking an entirely incorrect reason why the ancient nation did not use honey at sacrifices.

[2] This follows from the short but clear expressions Lev. ii. 13; comp. the ancient proverbial phrases. Num. xviii. 19; 2 Chr. xiii. 5; Ezek. xliii. 24 says expressly that salt was also used at animal sacrifices: Lev. xxiv. 7 shows that it was not wanting from the bread of the sacred table, מֶלַח, from the LXX is to be inserted here after זָכָה.

[3] According to Num. xv. 3–13; xxviii. 4 sq., along with what has been said above.

[4] This follows from the limitation of the drink-offering to the thank- and whole-offerings, Num. xv. 3–12.

[5] 1 Sam. vii. 6. Among the Greeks, the Erinnyes, as being in everything the counterpart of the heavenly deities, received libations of water alone. Aesch. *Eum.* ver. 107, comp. ver. 327.

plained by that force of opposition frequently mentioned above, but of which the law takes no notice.—Widely different was the custom which appears here and there of pouring out, instead of wine, broth made of the flesh of the sacrifice.[1] It is, however, more simple, and is also only depicted as having formerly taken place in the time of the Judges.

The drink-offering was never poured on to the altar itself, but on to the ground, and probably at all times at the foot of the altar,[2] just as the blood. But all that was to come on the altar as 'bread' must finally be supplied with *sweet odours*, both because these belong to sumptuous banquets generally, and also to banish the unpleasant smell which the burning substances would otherwise have been likely to cause. Only when oil and wine were excluded was there also no place for incense.[3] But where it was allowed, as in the most usual and numerous sacrifices, its amount was not legally prescribed; it was therefore easy for it, as for the oil, to be consumed at times with the utmost profusion. At the same time its scent was deemed so pure and its substance so delicate, that the whole amount of it which was supplied with the 'bread' had to come on to the altar, and in certain cases it was even laid there as an offering in itself. Gradually it became in somewhat later times one of the most popular and elaborate constituents of the sacrifice. In particular many costly and rare substances were used as perfumes instead of the simple incense;[4] and in the period after the Book of Origins the most acceptable and valued offering generally is often that of incense.[5]

The Blood and Entrails.

1. But it was something quite different from this sweet savour on which remote Antiquity laid the chief stress in the food-offering, and this appears very clearly in the representations of the Book of Origins. In order to apprehend this rightly we must first investigate more closely the mutual relation of the two possible portions of the meal, these being the flesh- and the corn-offering.

[1] Judg. vi. 19, 20.
[2] Only in Num. xxviii. 7 is there a very brief indication of this spot. The language is more determinate in Sir. l. 15.
[3] According to Lev. v. 11; Num. v. 15.
[4] Porphyry, *De Abstin.* ii. 5, speaks of four substances. The sacred ointment, Ex. xxx. 23–25, was made up of this number of them mixed with an appropriate amount of pure oil. Accordingly the best incense for the altar probably consisted of four such substances; comp. DK. Is. xliii. 23, 24.
[5] As in Is. i. 13; comp. xliii. 4, 23, 24; Jer. vi. 20.—Ps. cxli. 2. Hence comes too the conjunction 'The sweet scent of rams,' Ps. lxvi. 15.

We find the corn-offering already driven quite into the background during the first centuries of Jahveism, and for the most part reduced to a mere accompaniment of the flesh-offering. To all the ordinary as well as the grandest animal sacrifices, a corn-offering always formed a necessary addition, the amount of it being determined by the species of the animal.[1] But from the opposite kind of sacrifice, more than once mentioned above, it was altogether absent;[2] and at compulsory sacrifices it was allowed only in case of extreme poverty on the part of those that offered them,[3] or in special cases where it seemed sufficient merely to accompany a peculiarly sacred action.[4] At certain sacrifices, which were early removed out of the ordinary course of the national life, the offering of corn always continued to hold a more independent position, and stood forth more on its own merits, as will be made clear in detail further on. But in the main line of the earliest history of a national development in Israel, the animal-offering so completely overshadowed the corn-offering as to represent the essential element of the whole sacrificial system.

Now, in the essence of sacrifice itself, there lay no ground for so decisive a preference for the animal-offering. Among many ancient highly civilised nations, as e.g. the Hindoos, the simple offerings of cakes, fruit and flowers, and also the still more simple presentation of fat (butter) and sacred water, remained always in high honour and common use. In the people of Israel too, or rather in an ancient nation from portions of which it was formed, the corn-offering must once have been far more respected and independent. The very name of it, *Mincha*, shows this; for the word originally denoted a free gift or an offering in general, and even in our present Hebrew text it is often used in a wider sense, not even confined to sacrifice at all. If then, it now of itself denotes the corn-offering, there must have been an earlier time in which this was regarded as the most natural and satisfactory offering, quite otherwise than in the present legislation. Accordingly it appears far more independent in reminiscences of the patriarchal times. The agricultural patriarch Cain brings nothing but a *mincha* of the fruits of the soil; Abel the shepherd offers, as suitable to his occupation, an animal sacrifice, but it also is there called *mincha*.[5]

---

[1] According to Num. xv. 2-13, cap. xxviii.-ix. Similarly among the Romans there was an old law never to offer sacrifice without meal. Plutarch's *Numa*, c. xiv.

[2] This appears from the limitation to the thank- and whole-offerings, of the injunctions given Num. xv., xxviii. sq.

[3] As Lev. v. 11-13; xiv. 21-32.

[4] As Num. v. 15 sq.

[5] Gen. iv. 3-5. We find the same word in the Hellenistic expression μαναά,

To account then for the animal sacrifice coming so prominently to the front among the people of Israel, two causes must have co-operated. In the first place the more powerful, warlike, and excited an ancient nation, or a tribe of it, became, the more it learnt to love the dread blood sacrifice, and the wider it extended its use. In Israel, too, everything goes to show that it was during the time of its first mighty wars and victories that the animal sacrifice became predominant in it.[1] It is a life, a warm young healthy life, which is here offered up and destroyed, in spite of the fact that every one readily feels the awfulness of this even in the case of animals, and in spite of the religion of such nations directing attention so early and so strongly to the sanctity of all life. If this feeling of awfulness was finally overcome, yet the less the sensibility for it was already blunted in early times, the deeper the impression it would leave; and it must have aroused many of the most profound and most incisive thoughts. Life for life, blood for blood, was already the rule in another case, where a human life had been destroyed by a living animal, because only like could balance like, and it seemed possible to compensate for one irreparable destruction only by another.[2] Here we have the converse case; man offers up a life to his God; but all the awfulness remained the same. When he was himself conscious of sin, must not the idea and the feeling have come across him, that this soul fell for his own, and that his own soul would only thus find reconciliation and peace? Or if at the moment when he prepared this sacrifice, he did not feel the inward pressure so severely, could he yet help having similar emotions of awe, and feeling himself in an unusually exalted mood?[3] It is as though this sacrifice alone were the proper means for putting men in such a mood, and the extremes of joy and sorrow meet.—But on this account the animal sacrifice could hardly come into regular use among nations already somewhat civilised, without, in the next place, the mood which ought to correspond to it, seeking to express itself completely by means of a special symbol, which should bring clearly before the senses the awfulness of the whole proceeding. This symbol was furnished by the *blood*, which to a great portion of remote Antiquity appeared to have about it something so utterly mysterious, so divinely sacred, that a belief became

which appears also in the still more corrupt form, μαννά, as Baruch i. 10.
[1] Comp. p. 29 sq. above, and *Hist.* ii. 38 sq., 58.
[2] See below, under the second main sec.

[3] It is the same mood, after all feeling has been blunted immeasurably, which to-day the King of Dahomey seeks to produce in this way at festivals, by the slaughter of thousands of human beings.

deeply rooted that true sacrifice could be carried out perfectly only by means of its intervention. A strong feeling of this had already completely transformed the whole department of sacrifice among the people of Israel, in times which we must consider as relatively very early; and the Book of Origins still depicts for us vividly enough the feeling in this matter which for many centuries penetrated the ancient nation.

2. Indeed, the warm blood of men, and of quadrupeds and birds, seemed to contain the very soul or life of the living earthly creature—to be almost identical with its soul. The Book of Origins hardly knows how to put this sufficiently strongly in the passages devoted to it.[1] Now when the life and the soul were held to be something sacred, and the more tender feelings of certain nations took this view very early, it would follow that the blood too must be considered a sacred thing, and be regarded quite differently from the rest of the body. The sight of that which was held to be the soul itself, carried the mind immediately to thoughts of God, placed directly before it something full of mystery, and filled it with that immeasurably profound awe which overpowers man whenever he sees any rent in the veil between him and the Divine. In accordance with such feelings, blood could be scarcely touched, still less eaten, by pious men; and ancient Jahveism impressed its immunity in every way as deeply as possible. Even the inviolability of human life received support from the sanctity of the blood.[2] To taste the minutest portion of animal blood was something horrible;[3] even the blood of such animals as were allowed for

---

[1] 'The soul of all flesh (i.e. of all things living on earth) is in the blood,' Lev. xvii. 11. This expression is exchanged for 'The soul of all flesh is its blood itself,' ver. 14, this latter being only somewhat stronger. It is certain that בְּנַפְשׁוֹ is nothing but our 'itself,' *Lehrbuch,* s. 314c. On the other hand, בְּנֶפֶשׁ ver. 11, can only mean that the blood makes atonement *for,* or *on behalf of,* the soul, i.e. reconciles or purifies it, according to Lev. vi. 23 [30]; xvi. 17, 23; and *Lehrbuch,* s. 282a. The LXX also rightly take it so. In this passage, Lev. xvii. 11-14, נֶפֶשׁ stands in such very different contexts, that great care is needed to understand it aright in each case.—The Book of Origins says the same with respect to men, Gen. ix. 5, and later the Deuteronomist repeats the principle in his own way, xii. 23.—It is further quite in accordance with this original significance of the blood that דָּם, just as *sanguis,* in direct oppo-

sition to the fine, thin, and apparently so fragile soul, is always strictly masculine. Sanskrit, Greek, and German, are the first to make the blood a mere thing (a neuter).

[2] Gen. ix. 4–6, after the Book of Origins. From this came further the horror among the heathens of blood shed apparently involuntarily, especially if it was in a temple, and the painful purification which would ensue, v. Jamblicus, *Vita Pyth.*

[3] The oldest expression of this is found in Lev. xix. 26; then in the Book of Origins, Lev. iii. 17; vii. 26; xvii. 10–14. From this it is repeated in Deut. xii. 16, 23 sq.; xv. 23. The Philistines, on the other hand, were not so particular in all this נְכ, Zach. ix. 17, and elsewhere complaint is made of the ὠμοφαγίαι connected with the Dionysos, Sanchuniathon, p. 44. ed. Or.; Clemens, *Protrept.* p. 9. ed. Sylb.; Eusebius, *Theoph.* ii. 58. But just as Hos. viii. 13, Jer. vii. 21,

eating, but not for sacrifice, was to be poured 'like water' upon the ground, and covered over with earth.[1]

It followed from this, as a matter of course, that the blood of sacrificial animals was not to be tasted by men. But the essential characteristics of sacrifice gave rise to a new and extraordinarily important idea. When he entirely surrendered the blood of the sacrificial animal without tasting the least portion of it, man gave it up to God; and having begged him graciously to accept it, the sacrificer could live in the glad belief that this had really taken place. But this belief in a gracious acceptance on the part of God is the very kernel and centre of the whole act of sacrifice, only when this is present does the act become spiritual and sacred, while altar and priest furnish the medium for the reciprocal intercourse between the man offering and the God accepting. Accordingly, as the blood was already looked upon as having a mysterious and divine nature, and was in addition offered up at the altar in this belief, and taken thence for the purpose of confirming and strengthening the same, it became the clearest expression of the highest aim of all sacrifice, as well as the special means appropriated to this aim. Sacrifice, in its fullest extent and widest development, is a sacred action done to arouse and impart as directly as possible the higher life of faith (it is a *sacramentum*) : the mysterious blood of the sacrificial animal became the strongest lever of this action, and by its means man most clearly saw with his own eyes, and at the same time felt with his own blood, what was supernatural and divine in it. It came therefore to be the most effective means of renewing confidence in the divine graciousness. God allowed it to be offered up on the altar, in order that man might thereby be continually reassured of his grace and reconciliation, and of the salvation of his own soul.[2]

Yet the internal activity, and the true might of the belief in the perpetual renewal of divine grace, is never in the least dependent on any special kind of external action. Rather does it spontaneously draw forth the external action, and then

comp. Ex. xii. 9, complain of the eating of raw sacrifices, so Enoch xcviii. 11. ed. Dillm., even complains of the eating of blood in Israel; and now there is still something similar in Ethiopia, see Sapeto's *Viaggio tra i Bogos*, p. 217, 232.

[1] Lev. xvii. 13 ; Deut. xii. 16 sq.—The question therefore never arose whether the eating blood is in general wholesome for men, or can be dangerous to them.

Certainly the example of the blood-eaters (*Kravjâd*) or blood-suckers in India is not inviting, but of such dangers the old laws of Jahveism assuredly never thought. See *Transactions of the Royal Asiatic Society of London*, vol. iii. p. 379 sq. ; Bunsen's *Outlines*, i. 345; comp. G. Müller's *Amerikanische Urreligionen*, s. 375.

[2] As is expressly said Lev. xvii. 11.

easily come to use it as its support and instrument. Every sacrament, as far as it is mere action, is merely human action. But what is internal, neither can nor ought for men to remain purely internal. For the sake of clearness and strength it presses out into action, and becomes itself visible; and the special form of representation and action assumed will be in accordance with the entire mode of internal belief, and the religion which gives rise to it. Thus the primitive feeling of the mysterious sanctity of blood only came to supply a want in the religion of the ancient people of Israel; nor can it surprise us that the blood of sacrificial animals seemed to other nations also to possess a certain sanctity. But no heathen nation had such ideas about human sin and divine grace, as had the people of Israel from the time of Jahveism; so that it was only in this nation that the blood assumed this unique, exalted significance, and only there that it became the one great centre of the whole sacrificial procedure.

All that sacred awe of the blood, and the use of it at sacrifice, as from the time of Jahveism this was more fully developed among the people of Israel, accordingly refers us back of itself to a yet more remote antiquity, whose existence the Book of Origins also indicates as a fact. This childlike awe at the first apprehension of the Infinite, deemed to lie in the soul and so in the blood, this equating of animal and human blood and life, and this horror of touching blood at all, leads straight enough to the view that man may destroy no life whatever, and may eat no animal. It leads therefore to the religion which prevailed in ancient India, whose yet untroubled existence is transferred by the Book of Origins to the first of the four ages of the world, as its divinely ordained law, with the express declaration that permission to shed the blood of animals was first given by God to the renewed race of men after the Flood.[1] Among many nations, then, at least a dread of blood remained as a relic of the entire tone of a still more remote antiquity, while others preferred not to offer animals at all, but let corn form their gifts to the gods. The people of Israel was composed in primitive times by the melting together of two elements, as shown by the numerous traces already explained;[2] and one of these two may have formerly given prominence to the corn-offering (the *mincha*), the other to the animal sacrifice

---

[1] Gen. i. 29, 30; ix. 3-6; comp. on this point, *Hist.* i. p. 85 sq., and what more is said further on with respect to the Sabbath. According to the Greeks the third and last of the commands of Triptolemus was τὰ ζῶα μὴ οἴνεσθαι, Porphyry, *De Abstin.* iv. 22.
[2] *Hist.* vol. i.

with its sacred dread of blood, until the form of sacrifice legally prescribed in the Book of Origins was arrived at by means of the complete union of the two. In this the animal sacrifice, as being not only stronger and more manly, but also more mysterious and available for far more varied and more developed sacred rites, took decisively the upper hand, but still without suppressing the other. The new name for both the slain-offering and the corn-offering was now *qorbán* i.e. offering.[1] All this certainly took place in pre-Mosaic times, but it was Jahveism which first gave the higher meaning to the blood of sacrifice.

3. Besides the blood, the entrails, as the mysterious seat of emotion, were a special object of the sacrificial art, and it is well known in how many heathen sacrifices they even became the instrument of soothsaying. They served for this purpose also among the neighbouring nations,[2] but never in Israel. Here, on the contrary, these parts were always to be consumed by the fire on the altar, even if the rest of the animal was not similarly treated; indeed, they were so indispensable an element in every act of sacrifice, that the eating of them was forbidden to men just as was that of blood.[3] Still they had no such directly sacred significance as the blood, which was to be poured out on the altar and not to be burned. The different parts were generally briefly called *the fat*, viz. the internal fat. The Book of Origins often gives them more in detail,[4] and the invariable omission of all mention of the heart and other blood-vessels is remarkable. Ancient custom plainly kept the strictest watch that these portions for the altar and proper supply for the fire should not be curtailed. All these practices, however, with unimportant modifications are to be found again in heathen sacrifices.—With birds these parts were never separated, but after the blood had been taken from them they were devoted whole to the fire on the altar.

---

[1] In accordance with such main passages as Lev. i. 2; ii. 1. Still the word would also contain the wider idea of a mere consecrated gift, Lev. xxvii.; Num. xxxi. 50-54; comp. Mark vii. 11; Matt. xxvii. 6, and more on the subject below.
[2] Ezek. xxi. 26 [21]. Even of human sacrifices, Porphyry, *De Abstin.* ii. 51.
[3] Lev. iii. 17; vii. 22-27.
[4] 'The fat above and about the intestines, the kidneys with their fat, and the large laps of the liver.' Lev. iii. 3, 4, 9, 10, 14, 15; iv. 8, 9; vii. 3, 4. This explains the abridged expressions in Lev. viii. 16, 25; ix. 10, 19; Ex. xxix. 13, 22; but it is possible that in Ex. xxix. 13 the words were abridged by a later hand, as just here no abbreviation was to be expected. When sheep are spoken of, such passages add the fatty tail; to so great an extent the mere conception of fat may have gradually worked its way in.

ii. *The General Procedure in Sacrifice by Fire.*

Such were the ideas and customs which of themselves determined a large part of the general procedure with respect to sacrificial animals and the other constituents of sacrifice. We shall now give a connected description of it so far as our sources permit this to be done.

It was so completely taken for granted that every one who wishes to approach his God with an offering has prepared himself for the sacred rite in a worthy manner, and knows well what it is he desires to do, that this is mentioned only in the historical accounts of the great days of sacrifice.[1] On such grand occasions the sacrificer had to purify himself for one or two days previously; that is, he had strictly to abstain both in thought and deed from everything that passed as impure or unholy; he had also to wash his clothes. If the sacrificial rite had to be performed with unusual haste, a purification in the shortest possible time was still necessary, but what were the usages then, we no longer know with certainty.[2]

The sacrificer was himself to bring his animal to the place where the sanctuary was, and before reaching its threshold he must in the fore-court, as it were, present it to his God with a petition for a gracious acceptance of it.[3] Hereupon took place, as something quite understood, the careful examination of the animal on the part of the priest, to see whether or not it were available for sacrifice and sound, and whether it just suited the special purpose of the sacrificer.

If the sacrificer and his gift passed this inspection, they drew near to the altar, and the sacred rite itself then began with his laying his hand for some time on the head of the animal. The Book of Origins, which evidently brings this part of the whole sacred rite into prominence as something specially important and indispensable, does not think it necessary further to explain its object and its meaning.[4] We must therefore look around in the circle of sacred usages generally. According to the Book of Origins, a man like Moses consecrated his follower Joshua to succeed him in his office by laying his hands on the latter's head, and thereby imparting his blessing,

---

[1] In the Book of Covenants, in reference to the sacrifice at Sinai, Ex. xix. 10, 11, with which the description in the same book of Jacob's sacrifice essentially agrees. Gen. xxxv. 2, 3; comp. such expressions as Zeph. i. 7; Jer. xii. 3.

[2] 1 Sam. xvi. 5. But see below.

[3] Lev. i. 3; iii. 1; iv. 4; and elsewhere. Hence, even in the latest times such beautiful images as Rom. xii. 1.

[4] Exod. xxix. 10, 15, 19; Lev. i. 4; iii. 2, 8, 13; iv. 4, &c.; from which it appears that it was to be found equally in all varieties of sacrifice, 2 Chron. xxix. 23.

along with his most sacred commissions.[1] It was as though the superior desired in so rare a moment to let his whole spirit stream over through the glowing nerves of his hands on to him whom he honoured with his blessing and highest commissions. Such a symbol of blessing and consecration, putting forth its utmost power and effort, was in use in Israel from primitive times,[2] and maintained its position down to the early days of Christianity,[3] when it, like many other things of the kind, came to life again with an entirely new vigour. This ancient custom even gave rise to the sacred practice that the priest in solemnly greeting and blessing the assembled multitude, since he could not lay his hands on them, at least raised them up, and stretched them out over the crowd.[4] Accordingly, when the sacrificer laid his hands on the head of the yet living animal, this can only indicate the sacred moment in which he, purposing at once to commence the rite itself, transferred to the head of the creature whose blood was about to be shed, and, as it were, appear for him before God, all the feelings which must now stream through him in full glow. Moreover, the ancient sympathy for the sufferings and conditions of loved domestic animals, and still more the above-mentioned idea of the sanctity of blood, contributed to the rise of this custom, and the public religion on its part could demand nothing less than this solemn commencement of the sacred rite, and the expression of such feelings and silent prayers on the part of the sacrificer. It immediately preceded the shedding of the blood; in this way the custom became as specially characteristic of the religion of Israel, as did the higher significance which they ascribed to blood in general poured out before the altar.—When, however, the same custom found further application in regard to criminals condemned to death in the community, inasmuch as the witnesses had all to lay their hands on the head of the criminal just about to be stoned,[5] the model on which this custom was based was clearly first given by the ancient sacrificial practice.

The slaughter which now followed was originally executed by the sacrificer himself, whether layman or priest, and this is still allowed in the Book of Origins. In later times it was,

[1] Num. xxvii. 18-20, where the expression, 'lay of thine honour upon him,' is particularly noteworthy; comp. vi. 27; Deut. xxxiv. 9.
[2] Gen. xlviii. 14-20. Somewhat different is the representation of the Fifth Narrator, chap. xxvii.
[3] In the first three Gospels and in Acts, the laying on of the hands is, as is well known, the symbol, the means, and the commencement of the communication of the spirit; hence, too, of the true salvation.
[4] Lev. ix. 22.
[5] This is also according to the Book of Origins, Lev. xxiv. 14. The criminal therefore was considered as חֹטֵא, see below.

according to certain indications, committed more often to the inferior priests.[1] The special place for the purpose, at any rate for the principal kinds of sacrifice, was, according to the Book of Origins, on the north side of the altar. Possibly we have here a relic of an old belief that the Deity dwells either in the East or in the North, and comes from thence. This much is certain, that all the nations of Asia to the south of the high mountains of Armenia, Persia, and India, have from primitive times placed the abode of their Deities in the lofty North. Now as it cannot be denied that the people of Israel also came ultimately out of this same North, as is proved in the *History*, vol. i., it is quite possible that such a belief in the greater nearness of the Deity in the North may have very long maintained its place in a particular sacrificial usage such as this, notwithstanding that Jahveism ascribed no further importance to it.

Under any circumstances the sacerdotal function commenced with the slaughter, in so far that the priest caught the fresh blood with sacrificial bowls, in order to employ it, while it was yet warm, in that usage which, as explained above, formed the essential kernel of the whole sacred rite. In later times, as we know for certain, the inferior priests caught the blood, and handed it over to a sacrificial priest to sprinkle it.[3]—The sprinkling of the blood was itself the most solemn moment: in ordinary cases the priest sprinkled it only on the corners and the sides, and on the foot of the altar,[4] but all round the latter; just as in general the ancient custom required on the most solemn occasions the party to go round the altar in a circle, praying, singing, and otherwise fervently soliciting the Divinity.[5] What the priest said while going round the altar to sprinkle it with the most sacred element of the sacrifice, how he supplicated thereby the divine grace for the sacrificer, and how he announced it, we no longer can tell in detail; but that it did take place in this way there can be no doubt.—A stalk of the shrub Hyssôp (*Ysop*) was, in accordance with ancient custom, used for the sprinkling, one end of it being dipped in the blood. This wood must once in early times have passed for pure and cleansing, just as among the Hindoos and Persians the *Sôma* (hôma) alone is used as a sacrificial drink; and only

---

[1] 2 Chron. xxix. 21-24; comp. xxx. 15-17; xxxv. 1, 11; Ezra vi. 20.
[2] Lev. i. 11; comp. vi. 18 [25]; vii. 2, and the position of the sacred table, Ex. xxvi. 35. Much the same is said, but on occasion of entirely different historical events, in the following passages. Ps. xlviii. 3 [2]; Ezek. i. 4; comp. bk. Is. xiv. 13; Enoch xxv. 5; comp. also *Bhâgavata Purâna*, t. iii. p. 79, Burn.
[3] 2 Chron. xxx. 16.
[4] Comp. bk. Zach ix. 15, with the descriptions in the Book of Origins.
[5] Ps. xxvi. 6, 7. Comp. *Meghadûta*, str. 56, with Wilson's remark.

by means of this instrument did it seem possible to complete properly the cleansing atonement.¹

Not until the conclusion of this principal ceremony, during which the feelings appropriate to the sacrificer would attain their maximum, did the cutting up of the slain animal commence, and at the same time the fire on the altar would be stirred up by other priests. But at this point the separate kinds of sacrifice begin entirely to differ one from another, inasmuch as each kind sanctified a different use of the parts of the bloodless animal, and it was only in certain sacrifices that the flesh, with the exception of what was invariably put on the altar, would be eaten either by the sacrificer or by the priests themselves. This is further explained below.—With birds, on account of their smallness, the latter part of the procedure, including the killing, was different. The priest himself took the small creature at once to the altar, wrung its neck without quite tearing off its head, sprinkled some of the blood on the sides of the altar, and let the rest of it run out at its foot. He then removed the throat and the offal, and tore open the body by the wings without completely dismembering it, and so prepared it for the fire on the altar, without, as it seems, the least portion of the flesh being eaten by men.²

All portions of the sacrificial animal which were destined for the fire on the altar were finally richly strewed with incense, as were also the corn-offerings, and laid upon the altar hearth, to be rapidly consumed by the long glowing fire. The Book of Origins invariably denotes this by the short expression, 'to burn upon the altar,'³ for which the LXX say with less significance, 'to put upon the altar.'

Far simpler was the procedure with the corn-offering. Each portion of it had its own incense, the whole of which the priest, after presenting and consecrating the portion at the altar, threw into the fire, along with a handful of meal and oil from the meal-offering, or a small piece of the cake. When the fire-

---

¹ According to Ps. li. 9, and what will be said further on in the second main section. The expression ὕσσωπος, comes from a Hebrew word אֵזוֹב, not from the Massoretic אֵזוֹב; on this point comp. Lehrbuch, s. 153b.

² The words, Lev. i. 15-17 contain some clerical errors which can to some extent be easily corrected from v. 8, 9. הִקְטִיר הַמִּזְבֵּחָה, in ver. 15 is quite out of place here; and yet there may be an original קִיר הַמִּזְבֵּחַ concealed in it. On the other hand there is at present no ground for changing, in ver. 16, נֹצָתָהּ, into צֹאָתָהּ, because it is a question whether the Aramaic ܟ̈ܦܶܐ ܘܶܢ, 'offal,' may not be brought into some sort of comparison with this. מֻרְאָה, as 'throat,' can at the same time include stomach. Compare Lehrbuch, s. 130 of the 8th ed.

³ Lev. i. 9, 13, 17, &c.

offering had come to predominate over the older table-offering, the twelve plain Sabbath-loaves also were strewn with incense, but when they were taken away only the incense was given over to the flames.¹ That portion of the corn-offering which actually came on the altar is called in the Book of Origins its *Azkâra*, i.e. its savoury portion; because originally at any rate it consisted either entirely or principally of the incense scattered on it.² At the time of the Book of Origins, the name was as specially appropriated to this portion for the altar, as was the name *Mincha* to the corn-offering itself.³

The libations of wine, on the other hand, were, as far as we know, simply poured out, this being done at the foot of the altar, but probably not at the places where the blood was sprinkled.⁴

Of the speeches, prayers, and singing, which went on during the sacrifice, mention is only once made in the law, in connection with sacrifice on account of the jealousy of a husband.⁵ Nevertheless, we still possess some of the most beautiful hymns, which must have been sung at the sacrifices in the sanctuary;⁶ and reference is still more frequently made to such singing.⁷ Undoubtedly it formed an important part of the whole sacred rite, although the ancient law prescribed nothing particular with respect to its kind and manner, and the individuals sacrificing were at liberty to enjoy the utmost freedom with respect to it.

*iii. The Significance of the different kinds of Sacrifice by Fire.*⁸

THE WHOLE- OR BURNT-OFFERING.

Sacrifice by fire or on the altar, the predominant kind and one most fully developed, took very different forms in accord-

---

¹ Lev. ii. 2, 8 sq.; vi. 8 [15]. Already Lev. xiv. 20, actually changes הָעֹלָה with הַקְטִיר, and it will be made clear below under the expiatory-offering that the word had some such meaning in the linguistic consciousness. How primitive is the entire mode of speech, is seen in the formation, found only there, הַמִּזְבֵּחָה. In general the sacrificial language preserves a good deal of the antique expression quite peculiar to it.

² According to the decisive passage, Lev. xxiv. 7, אַזְכָּרָה, although the LXX translate it μνημόσυνον, can mean nothing but scent; and it is indisputable that ذَكَّرَ, comp. ذَكِيٌّ, can also give the conception of a *pungent* smell. The verb, הִזְכִּיר, too, means, in sacrificial language,

to cause to give out scent, to make smoke (see *Die Dichter des A. Bs.*, ia. s. 284–5), and in Hos. xiv. 8 the meaning *scent* suits the connection of thought best for זִכְרוֹ, though it is to be pronounced somewhat differently. With regard to אַזְכָּרָה, Lev. v. 12 sq., see below, under the expiatory-offering.

³ P. 36.
⁴ P. 35.
⁵ Num. v. 18–26.
⁶ As Ps. xx., xxx., lxvi. 13–20, even apart from Ps. cxviii.
⁷ As in Ps. xxvii. 6; xxvi. 6, 7; xxii. 28 [27] sq.
⁸ The main section for the subject is Lev. i.–vii. It was copied in the Book of Origins, but there are many traces that it, along with a few kindred passages, is the

ance with the various occasions and significance which it might have. On this account we shall now pause to consider the separate kinds of sacrifice. We observe in the first place that they branch out into only two main divisions, which stand related to one another much as day and night, both in respect to the occasions which gave rise to them, and to the mode in which they were carried out. On the one side stands the thank-offering, joyous as the day; on the other the guilt-offering, shrouded in gloom.

But, in the midst between these two contrasted poles, Jahveism very early had already largely developed a third kind, which gave the most complete expression to an essential though one-sided idea pertaining to all sacrifice, and thereby lent such a glory to all sacrifice, that it seemed appropriate to every occasion, and to give additional value to every special kind of offering. This kind is known as the *Whole-offering*, or can also be named the *splendour-* or more exactly the *glow-offering*, and Luther not improperly called it the *Brand-opfer*.[1] In this, man's share in the consumption of the offering,

---

work of a different and somewhat older author; moreover, it is itself divided into two distinct works. *Hist.* i., 88, ii. 168.— The division of sacrifices into those: 1) διὰ τιμήν; 2) διὰ χάριν; 3) διὰ χρείαν τῶν ἀγαθῶν, which is given by Porphyry, *De Abstin.* ii. 24, is only imaginary.

[1] [A.V. burnt-offering.] The origin of the Hebrew word, עֹלָה, is obscure, and even the LXX translate it very differently in different places. As it is not unfrequently connected with הֶעֱלָה, and this appears capable of meaning *to put on* (the altar), we might think that the word was thence derived, in accordance with the translation of the LXX, Ps. li. 21, ἀναφορά. But in this nothing characteristic about this very special kind of sacrifice would be expressed. The assumption that עֹלָה, as the feminine form of עֹלֶה, means *that which goes up*, (in the fire), i.e., which is consumed, suffers from still greater difficulties, because everything which came on the altar was completely consumed. What is most probable is that עַל = עוּל, means properly a *glowing, burning*, like עוּר. The long burning is the distinctive mark of this offering, and the word itself seems to be thus explained in the passage Lev. vi. 2 [9], 'the burnt-offering,' that is, 'that which burns the whole night on its hearth (מוֹקְדָה according to the LXX), on the altar.' The translation, ὁλοκαύτωμα, of the LXX would thus be the most suitable, especially when we remember that the ὁλο- enters into composition in just the same way in the case of κάρπωμα and ὁλοκάρπωμα. Even the word occurs very early, comp. the ὁλοκαυτοῦν, among the Persians in Xen. *Cyrop.* viii. 3, 21. It is true that such a conjecture appears opposed to the fact that הֶעֱלָה, goes with עֹלָה, as its verb just as regularly and specially, as הִקְרִיב הִגִּישׁ, זָבַח go with the other kinds of sacrifice, so that the verb of itself even without the עֹלָה, can signify the offering of this particular sacrifice (Judges vi. 28, comp. v. 26; 2 Kings xvi. 12, where יַקְרִב is to be read). Even the intrausitive עָלָה is enough to denote the burnt-offering, Ps. li. 21. A departure from this linguistic usage is first found 1 Chron. xvi. 1; Esra viii. 35, where הִקְרִיב is used of עֹלוֹת. The Syrian ܐܣܩ ܩܘܪܒܢܐ may also be quoted here. But in everything which concerns the original significance of sacrifice, it is the oldest writings which must be consulted first, a Joel and a Hosea (ix. 3–5), however, as well as the Rig-Veda of the

being connected with sensuality, altogether vanished. The sacrificer consecrated to the Deity alone the enjoyment of the whole, and this not to punish himself, or because he was punished, on account of a special consciousness of guilt by deprivation of sensuous participation, but rather from free resolve and purest self-denial. The reciprocity, which as said above, originally existed at every offering of food, here totally disappears, inasmuch as man voluntarily withdraws his claim for sensuous participation, and consecrates to God alone that of which he might himself partake. Yet his entreaty for divine favour is now all the purer; his soul bent more exclusively on spiritual nourishment, and his hopes stronger of winning the divine favour. The whole-offering had no further aim than just to win the divine favour and reconciliation generally, apart from special circumstances; but this it sought all the more strongly and intensely,[1] with all the energy of which the once-existing sacrificial system of the Old Testament was capable.

Accordingly it became at the same time the true splendour-offering, at which the sacrificer thought from the first he might offer only the best that he had. The sacrificial animals, when offered by an individual, might indeed be the smaller quadrupeds and birds; but ordinarily they were cattle, or an equal number of cattle and rams,[2] and the law prescribed further that they must invariably be of the male sex. The number was quite undetermined, but often seven or some other round number. After the skin had been removed from the animal, and all the operations of cleaning properly performed, the separate pieces one after another came upon the altar with a quantity of incense, until all were entirely burnt to ashes.[3] A corresponding number of corn- and of wine-offerings belonged to every animal sacrifice of this kind; but the stringency of the

Hindoos. Moreover הָעֹלָה is also used of the *Mincha*, אך, Is. lvii. 6. even when this word has the ordinary meaning of *gift*, 2 Kings xvii. 4. Plainly then it denotes only *to offer*, with an allusion to an elevated or worthy place for it, but it does not mean, *to put on* the altar. Similarly עלה is first used in Ezra viii. 35, quite generally to embrace all kinds of sacrifice. Besides the word עלה itself is pure Hebrew in this sense (just as the above, וְהֶעֱלָה); but if ܥܠܬܐ, in the Inscr. Palm. 1, means the *altar*, we see from the Syrian plural ܥܠܘܬܐ that this genuine Syrian word ܥܠܬܐ, is yet of quite a different formation and derivation, and means originally, just like *altare* and בָּמָה, the *ascent* or *the elevation*.

[1] Lev. i. 3, 4, comp. with xvii. 11.
[2] This is seen very well from Num. xxiii. 1 sq., where פַּר וָאַיִל always serve for this sacrifice, while the בָּקָר יָצָא xxii. 40, are employed on the other hand merely for thank- and joy-offerings.
[3] Lev. i.; comp. vi. 1-6 [8-13]; ix. 13, 14, 16, 17; Ex. xxix. 17 [18].

whole-offering was so far modified (from causes to be explained under the expiatory-offering), that the priests could themselves consume the various sacrificial cakes,[1] and most of the meal, after giving over the indispensable portion of it to the altar. But the corn-offering, which the priest on duty had, daily, 55 to offer morning and evening on its own account along with the animal whole-offering, always retained too great a sanctity for this; all of it must be committed to the flames.[2]

In accordance with its all-comprehensive aim, this sacrifice admitted of the widest use, and easily connected itself with the most different offerings. On joyous occasions it was in keeping, and could accompany the thank-offering;[3] it could also serve as a general expiatory-offering,[4] and was added, as will be described below, to many a legally prescribed guilt-offering. It could not indeed suppress the more special kinds of sacrifice, which were too closely united, down from primitive times, with the whole national life. But it reduced them within far narrower limits, and was ever extending its own use. It was in the system of public offerings of the ancient kingdom of Jahveh that this sacrifice very early attained the highest rank. It became the foundation of all offerings presented on account of the kingdom, on behalf of which it was itself offered every evening and morning, and this alone prevented the fire on the altar from ever going out.[5] In the Book of Origins it accordingly occupies incomparably the highest place among sacrifices, and always takes the first place in the descriptions of all kinds of offerings. In later times, in consequence of its splendour and its comprehensive aim, it was the only one which the heathens were allowed to offer in the third fore-court of the Temple.[6]

The prominence thus assumed by this kind of sacrifice is 56

---

[1] This follows from Lev. ii. 4–10; comp. vi. 7–11 [14–18]; vii. 9–10, where the words have special reference to the whole-offering.

[2] The name for this was originally כָּלִיל, 'whole-offering.' Lev. vi. 12–16 [19–23], comp. Ps. li. 21 [19], although this word came gradually to be applied to animal sacrifices as well, 1 Sam. vii. 9; Deut. xxxiii. 10. It is impossible to doubt, on careful examination, that Lev. vi. 12–16 [19–23] does not properly mean the same as what is described in another connection in vi. 7–11 [14–18]; Ex. xxix. 40; Num. xxviii. 5.—The Koptic ϭλιλ is undoubtedly borrowed from the Hebrew, but hardly in consequence of the influence of the people of Israel. The question therefore arises, was the word in use among the Hyk-sôs or at least the Phœnicians? But with respect to the כליל of the Phœnician sacrificial language, compare the *Abhandlung* of 1849, s. 18 sqq. mentioned just below.

[3] As Ps. lxvi. 13–15.

[4] As Job i. 5; xlii. 8; Mic. vi. 6.

[5] This follows not only from the long description, Num. xxviii. 2 sq., but also from such remarks, in themselves obscurer, as Lev. iii. 5; vi. 2, 5, 6 [9, 12, 13]; viii. 28; ix. 17. Comp. more below on the whole subject.

[6] Comp. Josephus, *Bell. Jud.* ii. 17, 2; *Antiq.* xi. 4, 3.

E

undoubtedly characteristic of the life of the ancient religion of Jahveh. The resolute surrender and willing resignation which it taught, found vigorous expression there, whilst, conversely, among the Greeks and other nations such whole-offerings were rarities.[1]

But in the oldest times this kind also certainly passed through many forms before it arrived at the one described above. We still know, however, of an older and far simpler form which is ascribed to the time of the Judges.[2] According to it a kid was cooked at home as for an ordinary meal, the flesh then brought along with unleavened bread to some rocky altar, the broth poured out there as a drink-offering, and the rest dissipated by means of fire, it being customary to look for a Word of God (Oracle) in the way in which this fire blazed up. It is easy to see how much simpler this is on many sides, but yet it is essentially the same offering, excluding all human sensuous participation. Here, in fact, as well as in other passages recalling the earliest times,[3] we see very clearly what was its original aim.

The Thank-offering and its Varieties.

The Thank-offering[4] proceeded originally, at any rate, from the mere glad disposition of men, through whose longing for the continuance of benefits received from the Deity, thanks-giving passed of itself into an entreaty for a repetition of the divine favour. That the sacrificer did not celebrate a great sacrifice out of mere joy, without any view to the future, and without respect to the grand divine continuity of all human experiences, is a matter of course in the case of a superior religion like that of the Old Testament. The Deuteronomist

---

[1] This can now be seen more clearly since the sacrificial system of the Phœnicians and Karthaginians is somewhat better known. See the *Abhandlung über die neuentdeckte Phönikische Inschrift von Marseille*, Göttingen, 1849, also printed in the *Abhh. der Kön. Ges. der Wissensch.* iv. To this has now been added, partly modifying, partly enlarging and confirming, the *Abhandlung über die grosse Karthagische und andere neuentdeckte Phönikische Inschriften*, Gött. 1864.

[2] Judges vi. 17-21, is the principal passage, a later representation founded on it occurs xiii. 15-20.

[3] In particular, in the descriptions, Num. xxiii. 1 sqq., which are touched upon on p. 48.

[4] זֶבַח שְׁלָמִים in the Book of Origins, gradually expressed more shortly שְׁלָמִים, derived from שָׁלֵם, to pay, to reward, to *thank*, according to *Lehrbuch,* § 144 b; it is in the *plural*, like the Latin *gratiæ*; the *singular*, formed afresh from it, is found only in Amos v. 22. The translations of the LXX σωτήριον and εἰρηνικόν rest on erroneous views, although they are supported by the words in 1 Macc. iv. 56, θυσία σωτηρίου καὶ αἰνέσεως. We should then have to derive the word from שָׁלֹם, *well-being* or *joy*, but the very vacillation betrayed by this twofold interpretation tells against it.

is the first to think it seasonable to explain more distinctly what are the right words of gratitude with which man should consecrate his gift to the Sanctuary.¹ But just as that gay, childlike disposition—coming as the fair inheritance of humanity from a better time of youth—ever remained the foundation of the celebration of this thank-offering, so too the feasting together of God and of him who offered the sacrifice always maintained its position here as one of the oldest customs of all the sacrifices which men offered. This was because man desired not to keep his happiness or his gay enjoyment to himself, but wanted to share it with his God, and preferred to offer him everything in the first instance, and then become his guest, if he knew that God would be glad to have him, and see him by his side.

But in Jahveism the whole-offering early obtained such a preponderance that the far simpler, as it were, more human thank-offering, with the usages peculiar to it, retreated before it very considerably. The law indeed admitted the thank-offering with all its varieties, and invariably looked upon it as a sacred rite, but limited it almost entirely to the free-will of individuals, and only took care that its performance generally should be in due form. We do not know therefore so much about its particular usages as about the other kinds of sacrifice, which were more determined by law. Only from Nazarites does the Book of Origins demand that at the close of the period of their vow they should bring a ram as a thank-offering.²

A victim was always thought indispensable at it. Birds, especially as they did not seem to be shared between the altar and the man,³ were regarded as too poor to grace such a solemnity. The slaughter is so prominent here that the entire branch of sacrifice sometimes bears a name derived from it.⁴ The number of corn-offerings which should accompany every such sacrifice of a victim was determined by law, just as in the case of the whole-offering.⁵ Only those portions of the slain animal, which are mentioned above,⁶ were devoted to the flames. For these small portions, generally called the 'fat-portions' or the 'fat,' no special fire was kindled, but they

---

¹ Deut. xxvi. 3–10, 13–15.
² Num. vi. 14.
³ P. 45.
⁴ That זֶבַח is interchangeable with שְׁלָמִים, follows from 2 Kings xvi. 13, 15, and other passages. If a distinction is sometimes made between them, as in Num. xv. 8, comp. Josh. xxii. 26–7; 2 Chron. xxxiii. 16, this must be understood to refer to the different varieties, which are spoken of below.
⁵ Num. xv. 2–12.
⁶ P. 41, *note*.

were flung on to the top of the whole-offering, which was constantly burning in the Sanctuary.¹ The priest, by some special usages of consecration, which will be treated of further on, received the breast and the right hind-leg of every animal sacrificed. All the remaining portions were consumed by the sacrificer and those whom he had invited, for the law provided that none of this flesh which had once been consecrated and sanctified should be taken home, or put to any purposes without the precincts of the Sanctuary. On the same or following day it must all be consumed within the Sanctuary, and if any were left over, it must be burned to avoid human touch.² This very rule, therefore, tended all the more to induce the sacrificer, as the nature of a thank-offering would have already done, to invite others to join in his celebration, and share his joy and plenty at the sacred place. Allusion is not unfrequently made to a number of persons partaking of the celebration, or present for other reasons;³ and the Deuteronomist, regarding especially the needs of his own time, gives exhortations to remember the many poor, both of the laity and the Levites, and thus by means of human beneficence to render the best thanks to God.⁴

The thank-offering could assume different forms, either in accordance with special occasions, or with the less or greater degree of solemnity required. The Book of Origins distinguishes three varieties of the thank-offering.⁵ Of the last two it calls the one the slain-offering in accordance with an expressed *vow*; the other it speaks of as that which is offered without such vow, from free resolve, in brief, the *free* offering. This plainly indicates the two main occasions when thank-offerings were made. Distinct from these, and by all tokens exalted above them, was the Offering of thanksgiving or of praise.⁶ It would not, therefore, be the occasion, but the degree of solemnity, which would be its distinctive characteristic. It seems that then the sacrificer would perform magnificent songs of praise and thanksgiving with the aid of trained singers and musicians, and thereby impart a higher glory to the celebration.

¹ This follows from the passages mentioned on p. 49 *note*; Lev. iii. 5; vi. 5 [12].
² For further particulars on the subject in the Book of Origins, see Lev. vii. 15-18; xix. 5-8; xxii. 30.
³ Ps. xxii. 27 [26] with the other thoughts in this passage. Ps. xxx. 5; lxvi. 16; Amos iv. 5.
⁴ Deut. xii. 7, 12, 18, 19; xxvii. 7.

⁵ In the principal passage, Lev. vii. 11-21, comp. iii. The expression, Deut. xxiii. 24 [23], says nothing to the contrary.
⁶ Lev. vii. 11-15; xxii. 29, 30; comp. Ps. xxvi. 6-8; Amos iv. 5. In the first passage the LXX translate $αἰνεσις$, which is important on account of what is contained in the first Book of Maccabees. See p. 50 *note*.

THE THANK-OFFERING.

We have an instance of such a song of praise in the later Psalm c., according to its own title, and the numerous singers and musicians of the Temple will be spoken of further on in connection with the Levites. A choir of such singers of praise was itself called, like the offering, *Tóda*.[1] This also explains how the Book of Origins can elsewhere speak only of thank-offerings for vows or of free-will.[2] Each of them might be magnified into an offering of thanksgiving.

The higher sanctity of this latter variety found expression on the side of the sacerdotal regulations, in the rule that such a slain-offering must be consumed on the same day, whilst for the ordinary thank-offerings the following day as well was allowed for eating it.[3] No objection to the female animal was taken at any of the three kinds;[4] so much greater freedom must be admitted in these voluntary, and as it were more human sacrifices. But in the case of the variety which was altogether voluntary, when no vow was to be fulfilled, the law was less stringent even with regard to certain corporal blemishes, which elsewhere would have made an animal unfit for sacrifice.[5] Leavened bread, too, was permitted at every thank-offering,[6] that is, for the consumption of the sacrificer himself, and apart from the unleavened corn-offering which accompanied every slain animal. Not the least portion of it, however, might go into the fire; the priest on duty was to keep it for himself, if the sacrificer desired to make a gift of it to the Sanctuary.[7]

So far as all this goes, the thank-offering found its most natural application in the case of private individuals. But a further extension of its use clearly arose from the prominence of the whole-offering at all public assemblies of the people. On behalf of the kingdom the whole-offering only was then made, but if the assembled nation was on that occasion to partake of a sacrificial meal, slain-offerings were sacrificed along with the whole-offering, nor was this confined to joyous occasions. The law did not prescribe such a usage, but permitted it;[8] and the narratives, especially those concerning the earlier times, often tell of such a connection between the whole-offering and the slain-offering at public assemblies and on festivals.[9] A

---

[1] Neh. xii. 31-40.
[2] Lev. xxii. 18-21; Num. xv. 3, comp. 8.
[3] Lev. vii. 15-18. It is specially remarked of offerings of thanksgiving, xxii. 29, 30.
[4] According to Lev. iii. 1, 6. The expression, xxii. 19, is too brief to prove the contrary; but comp. p. 46 *note*.
[5] Lev. xxii. 23.
[6] Lev. vii. 12, 13 (comp. Amos iv. 5), where indeed this is said only of the offering of praise, but it would be more easily understood of the other kinds.
[7] This is the meaning of Lev. vii. 14.
[8] Lev. ix. 4, 18; Num. x. 10.
[9] Judges xx. 26 to be understood in accordance with xxi. 2-4.—1 Sam. xiii. 9;

great man, too, would generally sacrifice along with his whole-offering, thank-offerings, of which the people might partake.¹ In such cases, therefore, it was only a different application of what could be eaten, which this special kind of offering required. It is improbable that even on merely joyous occasions the public festivities would be complete without the whole-offering.²

But let us now look once more to the origin of the community and to the strict prohibition of eating blood, mentioned above.³ We shall then see that the ancient law consistently made every meal—which men prepared of animals available for sacrifice, i.e. of the best animals according to the old popular feeling—a sacrificial meal, and most naturally a free-will thank-offering of the lowest of the three kinds described above. For the precautions that the blood should not be applied to improper purposes could only be thoroughly observed by means of a regular sacrificial procedure; besides, the fat-portions were soon reckoned uneatable, like the blood:⁴ and it is likely that during the earlier and stricter days of the community a domestic quadruped, out of pure dread of what was Divine, was never slain and consumed, except as a free-will thank-offering. The Book of Origins still represents this as the law, but gives it not among the sacrificial laws themselves, but towards the end of its whole explanation of the laws, and only with express reference to the old camp-life of the nation.⁵ In Saul's time the people, in the heat of conflict, and exhausted with the struggle, tried to evade this requirement. But Saul arrested them, stopped the mere pouring out of the blood on the ground, and hurriedly erected an altar where it could be properly treated.⁶ The Deuteronomist, however, already allows every

---

² Sam. vi. 17; xxiv. 25. The 24 bulls, 60 rams, 60 he-goats, and 60 male lambs, spoken of Num. vii. would certainly have been made use of as a thank-offering at a festival for the whole people; but the narrative of the Book of Origins is suddenly broken off at vii. 88.
¹ 1 Kings ix. 25.
² According to 1 Sam. xi. 15, this would seem to be so, because there are great difficulties in the way of inserting ךְ from the LXX, and understanding זבחים of whole-offerings. But the doubt disappears after what will be remarked below under the treaty-offerings.
³ P. 37 sqq.
⁴ P. 41.
⁵ Lev. xvii. It is very remarkable

that the Pythagoreans were at most to eat beef. Jamb. *Vita Pyth.* ch. 18, 21 (85, 98).—Therefore, even in Islam the command is retained never to slay an animal for food without uttering a short prayer, and so consecrating it, Sûr. vi. 118–121; and the Ethiopian Christians even yet kill no animal without first speaking the *Basma âb*, &c.; comp. Sapeto's *Viaggio i Bogos et gli Habab*, p. 226, 232; comp. *Journ. As.* 1854, ii. p. 514. Among the Buddhists it is allowed in times of greatest need to slaughter flesh, but only as a sacrifice; vide Brockhaus' selections from the *Sômadêva* in the reports of the *K.S.G.W.* 1860, s. 109.
⁶ *Hist.* iii. 35.

animal, with the exception of the first-born without any blemish, to be slain without further ceremony so long only as the blood was not tasted. This was indeed necessary, for by his time the altar at Jerusalem was the only true one.[1]

The Expiatory- and Guilt-offerings.

The Expiatory- and Guilt-offerings form the exact opposite to the thank-offerings, and, as has already been more than once remarked, stand to them, in the ancient sacrificial system, in the relation of night to day. In speaking of them as the night-side of the ancient system, we have already implied that they first assumed their present form in opposition to another simpler and earlier side of the sacrificial system. But we have not denied that, in their ultimate origin and simplest form, they could be pre-Mosaic. On the contrary, we have indisputable evidence that they were; but it is just as certain, that it was within Jahveism that they were first developed more fully, became more important, and passed through a history quite different from that of the thank-offering.

We shall assuredly find the ultimate origin of this sort of sacrifice in the innate feelings of sin and guilt, which must arise in men in some shape or other from the very first, but which will be the more vigorous and potent the more the whole state of ideas and experiences in which it dwells, is developed. When once the extraordinary oppression and anguish of such feelings have become effective, what, if it will completely release men from them, will be thought too dear or too hard, so long as men believe (as all antiquity did, and every healthy man still does) in a God? How excited these feelings were in the better part of heathendom, is shown most graphically in the Old Testament itself in the case of the wicked patriarch Cain.[2] Indeed, the full vehemence and savageness of such feelings are to be easily seen only where they have not yet experienced the discipline, as well as the consolations, of the truths of a higher religion. We must remember, in addition to this, how powerful was the dread in early antiquity of an outbreak or further extension of the 'great wrath of God;' with what anxious care every evil, whether manifest or merely apprehended, was referred to the possible or actual guilt of man, and how hard it

---

[1] Deut. xii. 15-28; xv. 19-23.
[2] It is indisputable that Cain, as the Fifth Narrator, Gen. iv. represents him, is the type of one who has fallen away from the true religion, as well as from a higher grade of life that had been attained (that of regular agriculture), the type, therefore, of the heathen. Comp. for more about him now the *Jahrbb. der Bibl. Wiss.* vi. s. 5 sqq.

was for men to learn consistency in religion. We can then understand the wide extension of the expiatory-offering, with its array of atonements and purifications, which were already developed and in full bloom among many heathen nations before Jahveism came into existence. But in accordance with all that was said above,[1] it was just here that the *bloody* sacrifice found its most natural place.

Now within the circle of these existing usages, Jahveism aroused the feelings spoken of above all the more strongly, on the one hand, in proportion to the greater purity with which it placed before men the infinite holiness of the true God; and it is in the Old Testament generally that we see the deepest consciousness of guilt, which was possible previous to Christianity. But on the other hand, Jahveism saw in the same usages an ally in the struggle against all guilt, and thereby found the means for satisfying a crying want—a task which it undertook far more seriously than heathenism.

For the extraordinary striving after more perfect holiness and purity, which guided the ancient community in all its deepest feelings, met with no aid among the usages of an earlier state so important and efficacious as this expiatory-offering and the cleansing sacrifice allied to it. The ancient religion plainly seized with great power and consistency upon this long sanctified agency, in order to remove as far as possible whatever seemed to trouble and stain the sanctity of the whole. The community, as a standing whole, put itself into the same position as that occupied by a private individual. The one and the other must alike root out, by means of expiatory-offerings, every sad disturbance of the sanctity and purity before the eyes of Jahveh which had once been established; and as far as this was concerned, not the least distinction could be made between the great and the lowly. Accordingly, most of the expiatory- or guilt-offerings, even the very impulses to bring them, were no longer left to the free-will of private persons. The law endeavoured minutely to determine and arrange all of them without exception, the relatively voluntary along with the rest. On close consideration, a grand connection of ideas appears in the regulation of the details; and there are the most unmistakeable tokens that we have before us one of the creative institutions which must have sprung from the spirit of Moses himself.

1. The extreme solicitude which the law displayed in pro-

---

[1] See p. 35 sqq.

viding for the proper expiatory-offering, and the judicious strictness which characterised it here, appear at once in the distinction between an *expiatory-* and a *guilt-offering*.¹ Every sacrifice of the class here dealt with was properly in itself an expiatory-offering; for everywhere a distinct transgression of a Divine command or restriction is pre-supposed, and one so important, that it could only be effaced by means of a solemn atonement, by an expiatory-offering. A deliberate transgression could not indeed be effaced by means of a mere atoning sacrifice; grievous transgression of the kind was rather to be punished by the death of the sinner without any expiatory-offering. This was so thoroughly understood from the whole stern moral tone of the ancient religion, that in the Book of Origins the statement of the fact makes its first appearance towards the end of the sacrificial laws.² But where a committed transgression could be effaced by sacrifice, either an offering alone or one accompanied by something else, this sacrifice was always an expiatory-offering. If then a guilt-offering is deliberately distinguished from this,³ as a species is from a genus, the fact is enough to show an extreme solicitude in the arrangement of the whole expiatory system.

The distinction, which was not a superficial one, was of the following kind. On the one hand, provision was made for the case of a private member of the community who felt the pressure of conscious guilt, or an obscure religious distress which he might regard as similar (and which, as further explained below, was most closely allied to it), and who felt accordingly, or rather was obliged to feel, that he was shut out from the favour of his God as at present enjoyed by his co-religionists, and that he was therefore as good as excluded from the community. Such a man, if he would win once more this favour, and be received again into God's community, was to bring a *guilt*-offering, or as it can be also termed, an offering of *penitence*. Often, however, this was not enough without his making reparation for any damages which he had intentionally inflicted.⁴ A guilt-offering

---

¹ The first is briefly termed חַטָּאת, i.e. *expiation*, the second with similar abbreviation אָשָׁם, i.e. *guilt*; like שְׁלָמִים, for thank-offering, Num. iv. 16, and like ἱλασμός and ἁμαρτία in the New Testament.
² Num. xv. 30, 31, comp. with ver. 22-29.
³ As must be concluded from all indications, including such distinct utterances as Lev. vi. 18 [25]; vii. 2, 7, 37; xiv. 13;

2 Kings xii. 17 [16].
⁴ אָשָׁם, *guilt*, is used even when it is not applicable in its most usual, i.e. the legal sense; e.g. 1 Sam. vi. 3, it is used of the sacrifice which the Philistines offer, quite in accordance with their own usages, but yet as men who feel they have received corporal chastisement from Jahveh, and are imposing a sacred self-inflicted punishment on themselves. Another instance is אָשָׁם Is. liii. 10 of the

accordingly, like this, must specially abase the individual as an individual, and there were good reasons for making it a distinct kind, with special characteristics. Real guilt, however, can only exist, and can be ascribed as such to a man only when he has committed the deed consciously, and without just excuse. This condition therefore is always presupposed here.[1] If, however, an individual, whether an exalted prince or anyone else, had committed a transgression which was first remarked by others and pointed out to him, then a public offence and scandal had been committed, which must be at once atoned for, and since the scandal had become public, the atonement must be as conspicuous as possible; but still the simple expiatory-offering was sufficient penance for the transgression, and no special penance was to be superadded. Or if the transgression involved the whole community, so that no one felt himself more guilty than the rest, then consistency required that nothing but the simple expiatory-offering should be made. Still it might well happen on such occasions that certain persons would feel themselves specially compromised, just as when in Ezra's time certain heads of families, simultaneously feeling their guilt in the matter of unlawful marriages, brought the legal guilt-offering.[2] Finally, if the high-priest committed some error in the performance of his official duty, by which, according to the old belief, the whole community was involved in guilt, then, in this case also, the guilt-offering was not available, because the whole community, rather than he himself alone, was held to suffer along with him by the oversight. Accordingly, the simple expiatory-offering had more of a general and public character, while the guilt-offering was a more private affair, which was, however, morally compulsory on the individual, if he was again to take his place in the community and share its holiness with a glad feeling of freedom. To put the same thing in other words, the former sacrifice brings simple *expiation*; the latter adds to this *reparation*, in the form of a self-inflicted penalty, and makes this an indispensable condition of the atonement.[3]—This is the clear distinction between the two kinds of sacrifice;[4] but it is

---

sacrifice of one's own soul, which is offered up for the sake of others as an atonement demanded by God. Of course in these cases the word is only used *figuratively*.

[1] It is, therefore, important to understand the difference between the words אוֹ הוֹדַע אֵלָיו, Lev. iv. 23, 28 (on this אוֹ see *Lehrbuch*, § 352 a), and the words וְהֶעְלַם ... יָדַע, v. 3, 4. But in v. 17, וְהוּא is

to be read for וְלֹא, and לֹא is to be omitted from ver. 18.

[2] Ezra x. 19.

[3] The blood in the case of a guilt-offering was also considered as חַטָּאת, *expiation*, Lev. v. 9.

[4] According to Lev. iv. sq. and other more detached passages.

to be observed that the name 'expiatory-offering' may at any time occur in the language in its more general meaning, equivalent to an atoning sacrifice, and in particular cases is even frequent in that sense; while, on the other hand, a simple expiatory-offering can never be designated a guilt-offering.

The expiatory-offering could also be employed to make a consecration more solemn, a point on which more will be said hereafter. A guilt-offering would have been here quite out of place, so the former still preserves its more universal character. When, on the other hand, private persons were strongly suspected of transgression or sins, without the charge being proved, they were then permitted to bring the universal burnt-offering, but not an expiatory- nor yet a guilt-offering; the mere burnt-offering, if they were directed to present it, would have been here at any rate, of the nature of an indulgence.[1]—How it could become the sacrifice of the Nazarites and the Lepers will also be explained below. But here again the distinction of the two kinds appears at once, inasmuch as only that of the Lepers, not that of the Nazarites, could be treated as a guilt-offering.[2]

2. Every expiatory- or guilt-offering was essentially a mournful sacrifice, which had to be offered in order to re-establish the joy and the sanctity of the Whole after it had been actually violated, or was at least dimly felt to be no longer quite untroubled. It stood opposed, therefore, not only to the thank-, but also to the whole- offering; for though the latter was of the nature of a supplication for divine favour and reconciliation, it did not necessarily presuppose a definite violation of sanctity such as we have just spoken of, and could not in the least be considered to be of a sad character. A clear token of the wide distinction which always existed between the expiatory-offerings and the whole-offering may be at once found in the fact that the Book of Origins seizes every opportunity of lauding the whole-offering as 'a sweet and pleasant savour unto Jahveh,' but never [3] employs this, or any similar expression, of any form whatever of the atoning sacrifice.[4] However different were the purposes to which the atoning sacrifice was applied, and however much accordingly the varieties differed into which it was divided, this predominant spirit of sadness and of compulsion always cleaves to it.

[1] Comp. Job i. 4, 5, together with xlii. 8, 9.
[2] Comp. Lev. xiv. 12, 17, together with Numb. vi. 14.
[3] Except Lev. iv. 31.
[4] Just like other authors, e.g., Gen. viii. 20, 21. The Book of Origins, Lev. iii. 16, uses this expression of the portions for the altar of the thank-offering, but not of those of the guilt offering, which in other respects were quite similar, vii. 5.

A consequence of this was that only a single animal could be offered at an atoning sacrifice. The number of the animals cannot be increased, as at the thank- and whole-offerings according to the free-will of the sacrificer, as though he could thereby win a larger amount of God's favour. This single animal he must indeed bring, but it must stand in perfect isolation, as though in the midst of sad solitude and desolation, with nothing similar or comparable by its side.[1] On this account, however, it would be deemed a mitigation of this gloomy sternness when the law in certain cases allowed or ordered a whole-offering as well to be brought. This might be done only when the atoning sacrifices partook of the character of purification, where an individual had been rendered unclean by some obscure mysterious cause, e.g. on account of leprosy,[2] or where the sacrifice was made on behalf of the whole community, and the guilt of any individual did not come into prominence.[3] We can see how indispensable this isolation of the proper expiatory- or guilt-offering was deemed, from the fact that when a guilty person was allowed on account of poverty to bring two doves instead of a sheep, only one of them could be offered as the atoning sacrifice, the other must be sacrificed as a whole-offering.[4]

A female animal, in all likelihood, must have been originally chosen for these expiatory- and guilt-offerings. In the directions of the Book of Origins concerning the different varieties of this sacrifice, the cases in which the female appears still strikingly preponderate; and the *red cow*, whose ashes were to be used in preparing the water of atonement,[5] may be considered the type of all expiatory animals. The very nature of the whole institution involved this opposition between the sexes. If it had become law that the male sex was to be employed for all whole-

---

[1] The strictness of this isolation is seen very clearly in the enumerations, Num. vii. 12-88. comp. Ezra viii. 35.
[2] Lev. xiv. 10-20. comp. xii. 6-8.
[3] Numb. xv. 24-26. On the other hand, only an expiatory-offering is prescribed for the same case in Lev. iv. 14; on this deviation something has already been said on p. 46, *note* 8. Lev. ix. 2, 3, and often elsewhere. A whole-offering of this kind would consist of a bull, a ram, or a male lamb, according to the importance of the case.
[4] Lev. v. 7-10.
[5] Numb. xix. comp. more hereafter. Is. i. 18, shows us clearly that the red colour would signify guilt not yet expiated, still, therefore, to be atoned for, and though this colour is not distinctly insisted on in the case of all expiatory- and guilt-offerings, no conclusion can be drawn from the fact adverse to this being the type of an atoning animal. However, heathenism certainly went much further in the distinction of colours of sacrificial animals. See Aristophanes, *Ranæ*, 831. Virg. *Æn.* iii. 120. Gell. *N. A.* x. 15 *ad fin.* Plut. *De Iside et Osiri.* xxxi. But elsewhere black was often the colour which was considered to pertain to the infernal regions, as when, amongst the ancient Arabs, a hornless black buck was sacrificed as redemption-money for men. *Hamâsa*, p. 442 *ad fin.*—443. 7.

offerings without exception, and for thank-offerings in by far the most numerous cases, then the dark side of the ancient sacrificial system could not express itself more clearly in reference to the expiatory animals, than in the choice of the female sex.[1] Thus we may assume as certain that in pre-Mosaic times this sex alone was available for atoning sacrifices. When, however, Jahveism minutely distinguished and carefully arranged all possible varieties of this kind of sacrifice, then in particular pre-eminent cases the male animal came again to be deemed the most suitable and correct. And inasmuch as the different grades in the varieties of this kind of sacrifice sought to find expression in the difference between the animals required, the whole system assumed the following form, manifestly arranged with a certain amount of intentional art. The simple expiatory-offering for a transgression of which information had been given (the further subdivision being, therefore, of no importance) was, for an ordinary individual, always a young bearded she-goat or female lamb; for princes it was increased in such cases to a bearded he-goat; for the whole community, or for the officiating high-priest, it must rise to a bullock.[2] In these three grades a manifest advance is made, the starting-point being the expiatory-offering for the ordinary individual, since this was the most frequent.—On the other hand, the guilt-offering, which never concerned anyone save the single individual, but applied to him without distinction of rank, admitted of two or three grades, corresponding to the distinctions which could be drawn here between ordinary and more culpable transgressions. Ordinary transgressions were such as did not immediately involve any desecration of a sacred object; if e.g., when a solemn adjuration of the whole community took place in order to discover some truth, anyone had concealed it from fear of men, yet afterwards repented doing so; or if anyone needlessly and out of pure inadvertence had touched something unclean, yet perceived this himself or soon noticed it; or if he had uttered an oath inadvertently, and though inconsiderately, still without injury to his neighbour, yet afterwards noticed it himself. For all such transgressions,[3] which belonged to the lowest grade, the law prescribed a she-goat or female lamb, just as it did for the same grade of the expiatory-offering. If the person were too poor

---

[1] Verbal formations, to which the mere contrast gave rise, are to be found in the language (comp. *Lehrbuch*, § 267*c*) as well as others in the customs of ancient nations in considerable numbers. Some further ones are touched upon elsewhere in this work.

[2] Lev. iv. Such a bull was therefore similar to that required for the high-priest. Lev. xvi. 3.

[3] Lev. v. 1–13; Ps. xv. 4.

to give this animal for the sacrifice, he could defray its claims with two pigeons, or if too poor for that, with a corn-offering. On the other hand, for Nazarites in similar cases the requirement was augmented from the female to the male sheep.[1]—The transgression had immediate relation to a sacred object if anyone by mistake failed to discharge properly a tax due to the Sanctuary (e.g. the tithes), or in other respects had broken the laws of a sacred institution (e.g. the Sabbath or legal marriage). It was regarded as an equal transgression if on occasion of an oath being solemnly required of any person he had by mistake deprived a neighbour of a pledge or something confidentially intrusted to himself, or in some other way had done him injury, but afterwards became himself aware of his mistake. As in all these cases there was evidently a more serious transgression, the law required for the guilt-offering a ram, and in addition, if the rights of property had been infringed, required restoration, and also as compensation for the detriment which had been caused, an additional fifth part of the value.[2] This twofold reparation was so indispensable, that if neither the original possessor nor his heirs survived, the priest himself received it (as he did the sacrificial animal).[3] What was to be done in case the person was too poor to do this, we no longer know. Rams or female lambs were at any rate so usual for the guilt-offering, that the two pigeons or the corn-offering, which might be brought instead on account of poverty, received by preference the general title of expiatory-offering.[4]

Just as every animal to be available for any form of expiation must be a solitary victim, so in the next place it must approach the Sanctuary without any of the honourable and joyful accompaniments which pertained to the thank- and the whole-offering; it must be sacrificed without any corresponding corn- and wine-offering. In like manner the corn-offering which might replace the expiatory animal on account of poverty, might be accompanied neither by oil nor incense.[5]

3. But it was in the sprinkling of the blood, the proper sacrament of sacrifice, that the distinction between the guilt-

---

[1] Num. vi. 12; comp. also the case of the purification of the leper, Lev. xiv. 10–19.
[2] Lev. v. 14–26 [v. 14–vi. 7]; similar cases occur, Lev. xix. 20–22; Ezra x. 19. The ram is simply called an expiatory-ram in Num. v. 8.
[3] Num. v. 5–8.
[4] Lev. v. 7–9, 11, 12; compare with verr. 6, 7. It is a similar case when, along with the male guilt-offering of the leper, a female expiatory-offering also is brought, Lev. xiv. 19. The insignificant offering after child-birth is never called anything but expiatory, Lev. xii. 6–8.
[5] Lev. v. 11, 12; comp. vii. 10, the 'dry corn-offering.'

offering and the expiatory-offering in the narrow sense, came most clearly to the front; and it is easy to understand why it would reveal itself most plainly here.[1] As it was right that the blood of an expiatory-offering for public transgressions (as we may term it for the sake of brevity) should be made far more conspicuous to eyes and sense, so it was sprinkled on an elevated place or even on one which was extraordinarily sacred. The way too in which this was done was marked by three stages. If the atonement was made for an ordinary man or for a prince, the priest sprinkled the blood against the high-towering horns of the outer altar, and poured the remainder as usual out at its base;[2] if it was made for the community or for the high-priest, some of the blood was seven times sprinkled against the veil of the Holy of Holies, then some more against the horns of the inner altar, and only what was then left was poured out as usual at the base of the outer altar.[3] The third and highest stage of expiation was adopted on the yearly day of atonement, of which we shall speak hereafter. On the other hand, in the case of the guilt-offering, no reason existed for adopting any unusual mode of sprinkling the blood. It was sprinkled just as in other cases round the sides and foot of the outer altar.[4]

But as soon as this most sacred solemnity of the sprinkling of the blood was completed, then, according to the ancient belief, the impurity and guilt were already shaken off from the object to which they had clung. It seemed as though the drops of blood, sprinkled by the mighty hand of One who was pure, had called them up and irresistibly drawn them forth, for thus we must plainly interpret this procedure in accordance with the feeling of antiquity. Yet shaken off as they were, they only passed in the first instance according to the same view, into that body, whose blood had so irresistibly driven them forth (as well as into the officiating priest).[5] The rest of this body, therefore, was now deemed to have become in its turn unclean, and was regarded with all the dread with which anything that was unclean before God was looked upon, nay even with yet stronger dread; it was just here that the dark side of this whole order of sacrifices was felt most keenly. Consequently, all the remainder of the body just as it was, together therefore with the dung, was burned far away from the Sanctuary at

---

[1] P. 37 sqq.
[2] Lev. iv. 25, 30.
[3] Lev. iv. 6, 7, 17, 18.—At a mere sacrifice of purification, the outer altar was enough. Lev. ix. 9, 15.—The ancient Arabs even sprinkled blood on their idols. Shahrastâni's *Kitâb Elmilal*, p. 443, 2 sq. ed. Cureton.
[4] Lev. v. 9; vii. 2.
[5] See below.

some common but in other respects clean spot (outside of the camp or the city), as though it was an object of horror,¹ which could only be disposed of and annihilated in this way. Not till this was done could the Deity be implored that the impurity ⁷³ and guilt might now be really removed and destroyed. This burning, however, was eventually retained only at the most solemn kind of atoning sacrifices, at the great yearly atonement,² and at the expiatory-offering for the preparation of the water of expiation, about which we shall speak hereafter. The victim for the latter sacrifice was even slain outside the Sanctuary, as it was to be employed only in the preparations for another sacred rite.³ In ordinary cases the procedure was clearly so far abridged, that immediately after the sprinkling of the blood the divine grace was invoked to remove altogether the guilt which had now loosened its hold. The dead body of the ordinary victim was therefore regarded with extreme horror, as the mysterious instrument which the guilt seized upon, and at the same time destroyed; and any drop of blood which fell from it on to a man's clothes, had to be scrupulously washed out, in some part of the Sanctuary itself.⁴

The expiatory animal was to be slain within the Sanctuary on the same spot where the whole-offering fell,⁵ to the north of the altar; while probably the thank-offering was not slain on this more sacred spot, but just on the other side, to the south of the altar.⁶ Since the expiatory- and still more the guilt-offering, on account of their sad and gloomy character, might have been originally deemed unworthy of the sacred spot where the other offerings were made, the law expressly enjoins that the place where these victims are to be slaughtered shall be the same as the place for the whole-offering,⁷ thus overthrowing at the same time a piece of ancient superstition.

It was further a matter of course that the individual should have previously distinctly acknowledged his transgression, and

---

¹ As a חֵרֶם, see below. Similar is the practice of casting such an abomination into the *sea*: Homer, *Il.* i. 314; Herod. ii. 39. Allusion is made to this, Micah vii. 19, and frequently occur in the *Mishna*; comp. Porphyry, *De Abstin.* ii. 29, 30; iv. 10.
² Lev. xvi. 27; comp. vi. 23 [30]; viii. 17; Ezek. xliii. 21, determines it more closely in relation to the Temple. Allusion to this is made, Hebrews xiii. 10 sq. According to Porphyry, *De Abstin.*

ii. 54, such an offering must be sacrificed, ἔξω πυλῶν.
³ Num. xix. 3–9.
⁴ Lev. vi. 20 [27].
⁵ P. 43–44.
⁶ The recollection of this is in the *Seder 'Olam rabba*. vii. agrees very well with all else.
⁷ Lev. vi. 18 [25]; vii. 2; and with special reference to the guilt-offering, xiv. 13.

intreated divine forgiveness. In the case of the guilt-offering, where confession was especially important and necessary, the Book of Origins sometimes states this prerequisite with marked emphasis.[1]

4. We have already pointed out that the sombre feeling which necessitated the burning of the remainder of the carcase had already been to some extent overcome, and that, at any rate in ordinary cases, men had learned to pray for the divine removal of the guilt without this having been done, so that flesh doomed to destruction seemed as it were to be saved by higher grace. From this it was easy to venture a step further, and it became legal in Jahveism to cast into the fire on the altar a portion of every sacrifice even of this mournful kind. When an animal was sacrificed this portion consisted of the scanty parts which were always given to the fire even from the thank-offering,[2] and when corn was employed, it was a handful of meal; but all this would assuredly be offered with only just so much incense as the priests themselves found it desirable to add in the interest of the altar itself.[3] But neither did the original law permit the sacrificer himself to eat any part of the offering, nor was this ever allowed later.[4] It was a sad and' a compulsory sacrifice, the exact opposite of the thank-offering for men, as well as of the luxurious whole-offering for God. The flesh then of the ordinary offerings was preserved, but it was regarded as something marvellous, which had been saved from destruction purely by divine grace, as something 'most holy,' as it is often termed. Whoever touched it with common hand was looked upon as forfeited to the Sanctuary.[5] Only priests at the Sanctuary itself were competent to eat the dangerous food; but they were even expected to take and consume it, and the expiated guilt along with it. Nevertheless, it was a bold step for the law to allow the priests, or rather to make it their duty, to eat without scruple all the expiatory-offerings which did not belong to the two higher grades defined above.[6] How difficult it was to accomplish this at first is still

---

[1] Lev. v. 5; Num. v. 7.
[2] P. 41.
[3] This assumption explains rather more definitely how הקטיר, p. 46 nt. is also employed of these portions for the altar, Lev. iv. 10, 19, 31, 35; v. 12; vii. 5. It follows that the word had in this special case already taken the more general meaning ' to lay on the altar,' which is noticed on page 46, note. Similarly אַזְכָּרָה, Lev. v. 12, in accordance with what is said in pp. 62, 46, can no longer have retained its original meaning. The traditional technical term would of itself receive another signification in connection with this converse form of sacrifice.
[4] The ἀποτρόπαιοι θυσίαι are not to be eaten, says also Porphyry, De Abstin. ii. 44.
[5] See especially Lev. vi. 20 [27], and what will be said hereafter on the subject.
[6] Pp. 61, 63; Lev. vi. 19, 22 [26,

clearly depicted in the Book of Origins in a reminiscence about Aaron and his four sons. Aaron with his two elder sons burned the flesh and skin of a he-goat which had been used for an atonement at a festival. Afterwards Moses is angry with Aaron and his two younger sons for having burned instead of eating the expiatory-goat; for Jahveh had given it to them as the mediators of the atonement for the community, so that they were not only justified, but even bound to honour the sanctified flesh by consuming it themselves. So difficult was it in the earliest time to overcome the repugnance even of priests to such a meal; even Aaron excused himself and (as the narrative proceeds to state) with Jahveh's acquiescence, on the ground that he could not have eaten such flesh on a day when he had lost two sons.[1] Moreover, the vessels in which such flesh had been cooked must always be at once broken to pieces if they were of earthenware, or scrupulously scoured and rinsed with water if of metal, as though the traces of the impurity which had gone into the flesh were still an object of fear.[2]

Only under the guidance of this feeling of the most remote antiquity, shall we rightly understand the significance of the law which in like manner allowed, or rather commanded, the priest to cast into the fire only a part of certain sacrificial loaves, or even only the incense which was strewn on them, and themselves to eat them as bread which was indeed most holy, but was to be consumed by proper persons. These were (in addition to the twelve sacred weekly loaves already spoken of[3]) the corn-offerings which accompanied every whole-offering, and which on account of its splendour and frequency formed the most numerous contributions, and special prominence is always given to the injunction respecting them;[4] there were also those which would occasionally occur as expiatory-offerings. All this food, having once been received into the holy place and become itself 'most sacred,' must either be devoted at once to the fire on the altar, or else if only a portion of it was destined for this fire, the remainder having served its immediate purpose, was strictly speaking available only for destruction, and this could be best done by burning it.[5] Nevertheless, the ancient religion was soon sensible enough to introduce another use for it. In the case of the thank-offerings the participation of the priests in the consumption of them easily became a matter of

29]; vii. 6 sq.; x. 18. There is something similar in spite of all dissimilarities in the Brahminical usages; see Albr. Weber's *Indische Studien*, v. s. 274 sq.
[1] Lev. ix. 8-11, 15; x. 16-20.
[2] Lev. vi. 21 [28]; comp. xi. 33; xv. 12.
[3] P. 27.
[4] Pp. 48, 49.
[5] What speaks most clearly here is the expression 'Most sacred,' which the

course, but we may think how much there would be to overcome, before a priest would dare to eat even the bread of the whole-offering, or of those sacrifices which were regarded as having an equal sanctity! And even then the consumption of all such 'most sacred' food by the priests was always put under certain restrictions, to be spoken of further when we come to treat of the Priests.

Offerings for Purifications and Consecrations.
Offerings for Treaties.

It is easy to understand how the three principal kinds of sacrifice, when they had once come into existence, might be transferred to all sorts of corresponding occasions.

The various expiatory-offerings, either alone or in connection with other sacrifices, especially the whole-offering whose ultimate object was similar, might be transferred to the more solemn kinds of prescribed purifications, for the essential aim of atonement is purification. But this subject can be better treated of hereafter along with the very various purifications themselves, for the details assumed very different forms, and were mainly prescribed in the public interest.

These same expiatory- and whole-offerings were also appropriate for a solemn consecration of sacred objects, persons, or days, for in such a case the idea was always to establish something new and spotless, so far as human co-operation can effect this. According to the Book of Origins, at all the more important public festivals, where the high-priest himself officiated, an expiatory-calf must be offered, along with a ram as a whole-offering, for the consecration of the day on his own account, and an expiatory-he-goat, along with a calf and a lamb as whole-offerings, for the people, but the atoning sacrifices as most appropriate for the consecration invariably took precedence.[1] The blood of an atoning sacrifice like this, which served merely for a consecration, was sprinkled on the horns of the altar, but only on those of the outer one.[2] The procedure was similar when the altar, the inferior, or the superior priests were to be consecrated.[3] The latter priests were, in addition,

Book of Origins purposely reiterates, Lev. ii. 3, 10; vi. 9, 10 [16, 17]; vii. 6; xxiv. 8, 9: comp. the same expression applied to the expiatory-offering, vi. 18, 22 [25, 26]; vii. 1; xiv. 13. Num. xviii. 9, 10, classes both kinds together. See further, Lev. viii. 31, 32.—That the twelve weekly loaves were supposed to go finally into the fire, and that the table-offering was thus merged in the fire-offering (p. 30), appears also from their enumeration among the אִשִּׁים, Lev. xxiv. 9.

[1] Ex. xxix. 1-28; Lev. ix. 2 sq.
[2] Lev. ix. 9; comp. viii. 15; Ex. xxix. 12.
[3] Ex. xxix.; Lev. viii. 2, 15 sqq.; Num. viii. 6-12.

sprinkled in a peculiarly solemn manner with blood from the altar,[1] as though their consecration was to be made as overpowering as possible by the strongest contact with the most sacred element of sacrifice. When, however, at a consecration of superior priests only the one ram which was prepared as a thank-offering, was called the ram of consecration,[2] there was a special cause for this, to be explained hereafter.—Such an offering for consecration found also a suitable application on the occasion of the return from a foreign country to dwell again in the holy fatherland.[3]

78   Sacrifice was employed to sanctify treaties in a peculiar manner. Whole- and thank-offerings belonged to treaties by ancient custom; and thank-offerings were all the more important, since what was vowed on either side had, at the close of the ceremony, to be taken in, as it were, along with the meat and bread of the sacrifice by the parties swearing, as though it had to migrate into their flesh and blood, and since a common meal off the sacred instruments of the treaty was regarded as indispensable.[4] But before this concluding meal took place, the blood of the sacrificial animal was sprinkled, partly as usual on the altar, partly, however, in quite a peculiar fashion over those who took the oath, in order that the influence of this most sacred element might be the strongest and most binding possible. This is as the Book of Covenants describes it, plainly in accordance with a custom generally prevalent in earliest times.[5] The custom also took a yet more decided form, when the two contracting parties walked between the two halves of the sacrificial victim, in order to be reminded as strongly as possible of the fact that the victim had been slain for both of them. Nevertheless, the Book of Origins embraces neither this more sharply expressed kind of treaty-sacrifice, nor yet the simpler form of it, within the circle of laws, or even of typical actions, although frequent opportunities for so doing were not wanting.

[1] Ex. xxix. 22-34; Lev. viii. 30; comp. what is similar at treaty-sacrifices.

[2] Lev. viii. 22-33. A special question is, how the sacrifice of consecration can be spoken of, Lev. vii. 37, as having been described in chaps. i.-vii.; for the sacrifice described, vi. 12-16 [19-23], according to pp. 48, 49, cannot have been considered such a one. If, however, the sacrifice of consecration differed but slightly from the rest, especially from the expiatory-offering, this may perhaps explain its enumeration there.

[3] As is shown by the great example, Ezra viii. 35.

[4] Accordingly, even when the covenant between Israel and its God was concluded, the eating and drinking of the people at it is mentioned, as well as the fact that its God himself appeared then, and thus, as the one side, made himself somehow manifest to the other. Ex. xxiv. 11; comp. v. 5; BK. Zach. ix. 11. On this account again at the royal celebrations, when Israel concluded for the first time a treaty with a human king, it is only thank-offerings of which special mention is made, 1 Sam. xi. 15; similarly Gen. xxxi. 54.

[5] Ex. xxiv. 6-8; comp. p. 68, lin. i. sqq.

The simpler kind it could no longer sanction, because the blood had become too exclusively appropriated to the altar, and with the more sharply expressed custom, which we find had become very prevalent in the times succeeding David,[1] it was possibly quite unacquainted, or deemed it repugnant to the essence of the ancient religion.[2]

The Effects and Issues of the Food-offerings.

Such then were the forms assumed by the food-offerings (to include the table- and the fire-offerings under one name) during the earlier days of the community of Israel, and for a long time it seemed as though a most important element of the intrinsic life of true religion was to pass over into them. For Jahveism in its youth evidently embraced with the greatest fervour these sacred usages which were still blooming in their first innocence, and strove to let its own spirit operate also through them. But the apex of all these offerings, which we have already seen to be human sacrifice,[3] had nevertheless to be at once broken off in Jahveism. For there can be no doubt that the people of Israel were familiar with human sacrifice from primitive times. It is just among the nations of Western Asia and Greece, even among those most closely connected with Israel,[4] that we have abundant testimony to its having been in frequent use; and the nations in and round about Canaan early

---

[1] According to the testimonies of Gen. xv. 9-18 (where the birds which were not divided, certainly were to be used as a whole-offering); Jer. xxxiv. 18, 19; also Deut. xxix. 11 [12], may allude to it. Comp. Junghuhn's *Batta-länder* (1847), ii. s. 148. How among the heathen a contract and a promise was properly *struck* by sacrificial animals, is seen from Livy, i. 24; xxi. 45 *ad fin.*; Xenoph. *Anab.* ii. 2. 9.

[2] After all that has been said above, it is hardly worth while paying much attention to the manifold errors which are always seeking to rise to the surface in regard to Old Testament sacrifice; comp. the *Jahrbb. der Bibl. Wiss.* vi. s. 147 sq.; ix. s. 256 sq. It must be noticed, however, that in Western Asia the ancient sacrifices nowhere maintained themselves longer in full vigour than among the Ssabeans, comp. Chwolson's *Ssabier,* ii. s. 89 sq., 93 sq., 104 sq. They retained their position longer also in India under the Brahmins; but the ancient mysterious usages of a thousand forms are in our time

so near their final disappearance even there, that the description of them by M. Haug, in the *Göttinger Nachrichten,* 1862, s. 302 sqq., may be profitably studied.

[3] Pp. 26, 27.

[4] Even amongst the Arabs infanticide, partly, no doubt, as a precaution against poverty, but still more from superstition, was tolerably prevalent, as is clear from the account of the Dumatians in Eusebius, *Theoph.* ii. 62; *Præp. Ev.* iv. 16; and from Sûr. vi. 138, 141; comp. 152; lx. 12, and other passages. Comp. Origen, *Contra Cels.* v. 4. 3; and for what relates to India, Wilson's article *On Human Sacrifice among the Ancient Hindoos* in the *Journals of the Royal Asiatic Society,* xiii. (1851), pp. 60-95; Prof. Max Müller's *History of Sanskrit Literature,* p. 408 sqq., and Major-General John Campbell's *Thirteen Years' Service amongst the Wild Tribes of Khondistan for the Suppression of Human Sacrifice.* Lond. 1864. For human sacrifices amongst the Romans, comp. Alexandre on the *Libri Sibyll.* ii. 2, p. 218 sq.

became sufficiently polished and over-refined to take pleasure in this most refined of all bloody offerings. The narrative about Isaac when a child shows us how narrowly even such a hero of antiquity as Abraham, and with him the whole Israelitish nation, escaped the danger of child-sacrifice.[1] Jephthah actually did allow a delusion to bring him to sacrifice his only child.[2] Already does the Book of Origins sternly forbid sacrificing children to the Ammonitish God Moloch,[3] and much later Jeremiah has to make bitter complaints on the same point. An ordinary man too in Israel, even if he never thought of bringing such an offering himself, nevertheless experienced an insupportable horror when this most fearful sacrifice actually was offered.[4] So near to the nation did human sacrifice come. But the most characteristic instincts of Jahveism were utterly opposed to it, estimating man too highly to use him as an offering, as the very narrative of the child Isaac shows with such unsurpassable beauty. It is no doubt true that we find no legal ordinance against human sacrifice previous to this prohibition of sacrifice to Moloch in the Book of Origins; and it may well be that in the time of Moses no such absolute prohibition was as yet given, because the nation was not then in danger of being seduced into it by the Canaanites. For the offering of the dearest possession of one's own flesh and blood is everywhere relatively the latest, because the most refined, development of all these sacrificial usages. Even among the Ammonites the sacrifice of children may have been but little developed in the time of Moses. This would explain how Jephthah, who did not live far from the Ammonites, could be overtaken by the thought of such an offering. It is possible that in his days this sacrifice may for the first time have become more widely extended among the nations of Hebrew origin beyond the Jordan, and have exercised its first powerful magic over men of just the rank and culture of Jephthah. But in the same measure as we see it spreading among the heathen round about, do even the first commencements of it as an offering to Jahveh vanish from the midst of the ancient community, till at length the Deuteronomist, like the Prophets of the seventh century, deems it hardly worth while denouncing it as an abomination.[5] But how easily might all food-offerings have been deemed a per-

---

[1] See *Hist.* i. pp. 326, 332-3.
[2] For this instance, see more below, as well as *Hist.* ii. 395 [first ed., 167].
[3] Lev. xviii. 21; xx. 2; on the first passage comp. *Hist.* ii. 166 [first ed., i. 589], *note*.
[4] *Hist.* iv. 90.
[5] Deut. xii. 31. But on this question the section below, on the first-born, is also to be compared.

version, when true religion had utterly to reject just the most logical and refined of them!

Moreover, if we take the burnt-offering as the kind which was most esteemed in Israel and most characteristic of the nation,[1] we shall find that the very splendour which resulted from this costly sacrifice, the enjoyment of which was exclusively on the divine side, could soonest manifest the intrinsic emptiness of the whole sacrificial system.

On this account there arose tolerably early the view of the Prophets that all such sacrifices, and whatever was closely connected with them, stood in a false relation to the essence of religion, and one which might lead to grievous errors and perversions, and that the real sacrifice for man to bring is purely spiritual.[2] The Temple of Solomon was built while the old belief in the indispensableness of these offerings was yet unimpaired, and they attained their highest point of magnificence in it. But from that very time the germs of the very opposite views were maturing; and these, though they were to struggle on for a thousand years without external results, came at last to bloom in the New Testament. And even in the heathen religions the view that bloodless offerings were really superior, tried here and there to force its way gradually in direct opposition to the predominant bloody sacrifices.[3] With this indeed commences the dissolution of this whole development of Antiquity.

C. SIMPLE DEDICATION OF SACRED OBLATIONS. CONSECRATED PRESENTS.

If then all the gifts with which we have become acquainted as gifts of food, or as sacrifices in the primitive sense of the word, were unable to give satisfaction to the deepest needs of true religion, it is the more easy to understand how the feeling which strove to win the satisfaction of heaven attempted very early to reach the final goal by many other similar means. No sooner, in consequence of this activity and of these sacrifices of the very earliest religion, had there been established a congregation of worshippers of the same God, a local Sanctuary, and, as it were, an institution for the spontaneous propagation of

---

[1] P. 46 sqq.
[2] So Amos, Hosea, Isaiah, and all succeeding Prophets.
[3] E.g. among the Pythagoreans, who also tried to show historically that, in the most remote antiquity, it was everywhere wanting. Plutarch's *Numa*, viii., xvi.; Porphyry, *De Abstin.* ii. 15 sqq., 28; Jamb. *Vita Pyth.* cap. 5, 7, 24 (25, 35, 108). Comp. what is remarked, *Hist.* ii. 39 (first ed., i. 462), *note.*

this religion, than new wants arose, and opportunities increased for promoting higher, and therefore divine ends, by means of the simple surrender of property, and for sacrificing something of value without seeing it palpably accepted by heaven as food. This already gives us a more subtle and spiritual form of sacrifice, and in particular, in many situations of life, a pious man felt himself impelled to offer to his God possessions which were either from various causes not admissible as gifts of food or for the altar, or which, if they were admissible for this purpose, were yet voluntarily presented by him without any demand that they should be considered as food-offerings.

The most obvious kind of such simple gifts to God and his Sanctuary bore the closest resemblance to the above-described thank-offerings in respect of the ultimate motive which produced them. A spontaneous impulse of his heart induced a man to devote to some higher purpose more or less of his property without seeking the enjoyment and the honour of an ordinary sacrifice; and the dedication of property to God was at that time almost identical with its consecration to higher purposes. Even trifling possessions could be thus consecrated by a poor man. In the most important cases, however, where the transfer of a large amount of property must have been more difficult, there was always, or at least seemed to have been,[1] an antecedent vow binding the man to execute this most simple of all the forms of sacrifice.[2] Every description of property could be presented in this way. The Book of Origins does not yet make any exceptions; Deuteronomy, in consequence of the disordered state of its times, is the first to have to utter a warning against believing that it is possible to lessen the sin of encouraging unchaste religions (as e.g. when parents let their children earn money by prostitution at heathen festivals) by devoting a portion of the gain thence derived to the Sanctuary of Jahveh.[3]

When such gifts become more frequent and of wider scope, they presuppose not merely a deep religion, engrossing the whole heart, but also the existence of an organised priesthood. Only such a body can properly receive large gifts, and apply them in accordance with the wishes of the donor. From the frequency and amount of the donations indicated in the Book of Origins, we may therefore safely conclude that the power which Jahveism exercised during its first centuries over the whole life

---

[1] P. 21 sqq.
[2] Lev. xxvii. where a vow is throughout presupposed.
[3] Deut. xxiii. 19; comp. what is said, *Hist.* iv. 44, 50, *note.*

of the people, was very great. Many periods make of themselves greater demands than others on such self-sacrificing generosity; and thus the Book of Origins brings into prominence, as a model for all similar cases in the future, the willingness with which the whole nation, men and women, princes and people, brought their treasures together when the institutions of the great Sanctuary of Jahveh were first founded, and exhibits this as the result of an expression of the divine will and pleasure.[1] Similar mighty efforts for the revival and extension of the older sacred institutions were made by David and Solomon, as well as by some of their successors: a fact which the Books of Chronicles in particular everywhere take care to describe exhaustively in their own fashion.[2] What free-will offerings were given to the temple at Jerusalem after it had come into existence, whether as contributions to its treasury out of which the needful expenses for building and maintenance were met, or for the purpose of establishing a more independent institution of any kind which should adorn it, or enlarge the scope of its action and secure the attainment of its ends,—all these matters we can now survey better in general than in detail. We can, however, see clearly that the number and the magnitude of the consecrated gifts was at all times very considerable.[3]

Some kinds of such consecrated gifts, however, recurred so frequently and so regularly, that they began to lose their originally free character very early, and gradually became permanent taxes. This transition easily took place of itself, but it was of course favoured by the establishment of the Sanctuary and priesthood, so that gifts which had been originally completely voluntary, are already represented in the Book of Origins with all the exactitude and prolixity of law as imposts ordained by Jahveh for the Sanctuary. Such are 1), the share of the priests in every thank-offering;[4] 2), the firstlings of every kind; 3), the tithes. But we shall be in a better position to speak of these further on, in the section on the Priesthood.

But whether or not an originally free consecrated gift became a standing impost due to the Sanctuary, it must still on the occasion of its surrender be admitted into the sacred commonwealth by some sort of solemn rite, or at least through the instrumentality of some significant symbol. We do as a fact still find in many passages in the Book of Origins clear indications of such a symbol of consecration. It is the solemn action

---

[1] Ex. xxv. 1–7; xxxv. 5–9, 21–29.   17 [4–16]; xxii. 4–7.
[2] Hist. iii. 228 sqq.; iv. 50.   [4] P. 51.
[3] Comp. in particular, 2 Kings xii. 5–

74   SACRIFICE.

which has been too obscurely translated the wave and the heave,
and which we may name more correctly *the swing* and *the present-*
85 *ing*, or *the consecration* and *the dedication*.¹ There is no doubt
that the only essential part of the rite consisted in this, that the
priest held the gift aloft before the altar, and thus presented
it to the altar for acceptance, while he swung it to and fro,
uttering (as we may take for granted) certain sacred phrases
and prayers.² We must remember that the altar stood very
high,³ the object which was to be consecrated however was
held as close to it as possible, as though the altar were itself
that visible God to whom the heathens dedicated their gifts.
Such a consecration took place even at purifications and other
sacrifices before the rest of the ceremony was performed;⁴
indeed, this appears to have been the case in regard to everything that went into the fire on the altar.⁵ The most frequent
mention of it, however, is in connection with the two considerable portions of meat which were assigned to the priests from
every thank-offering, viz., the *breast* and the *right hind-leg*.
On both of these the priest first laid the smaller altar-portions
of fat and corn, solemnly raised up the whole before the altar,
then committed to the flames only what was indispensable,
and having once more presented the remainder to the altar
on its own account, took it away as consecrated.⁶ In the

---

¹ תְּנוּפָה and תְּרוּמָה, like the verbs הֵנִיף and הֵרִים, are essentially alike both in formation and meaning (Num. xviii. 11; comp. v. 8; Ex. xxix. 27, 28; xxxvi. 6; comp. xxxviii. 24). But the original distinction was this: הֵרִים means to *lift up*, or *take away something* from a greater heap of it (as I already translated it in 1840 in Ezek. xlviii. 8 sqq.); הֵנִיף, on the other hand, means to *swing*. Accordingly, only the תְּנוּפָה denotes the whole sacred rite which went on before the altar, and is a thoroughly sacred word, while תְּרוּמָה may sometimes be employed even with the bad meaning of extortion (Prov. xxix. 4), sometimes at any rate in a more general sense, and it gradually became the prevalent term. The former is in the Book of Origins, wherever it is speaking of sacrificial matters, the most usual, while the Deuteronomist even confines himself to the latter (Deut. xii. 11, 17), and in the same way later authors no longer use תְּנוּפָה and הֵנִיף in this signification. The word תְּרוּמָה is, however, in its wider signification of 'sacred contribution,' already familiar in the Book of Origins, as Ex. xxx. 13, 14. Probably the ancient usage lost much of its living character in later times, so that in reality only a תְּרוּמָה still continued to exist. To הֵנִיף corresponds in the old Roman sacrificial language the word *porricio*, substituted for *projicio*, as a dialectic form. The LXX in many passages very well express the subsidiary meaning of consecration, and at the same time the similarity of sound between the two words, by the translation ἀφόρισμα καὶ ἀφαίρεμα.

² This last is of course essential; and Isaiah, in a strong figure of speech, xxx. 28, alludes to this swinging to and fro; and in accordance with the same sacrificial language, he speaks in ver. 32 of מִלְחֲמוֹת תְּנוּפָה, *battles fought by swinging*.

³ Comp. the expression 'he descended (from the altar),' when the sacrifice was complete, Lev. ix. 22.

⁴ Lev. xiv. 12, 24; xxiii. 19, 20.

⁵ According to the description, Lev. viii. 25-28; comp. vii. 30, 31.

⁶ According to Lev. viii. 25-29. If in ver. 25 only the hind-leg is spoken of, and

same way the first sheaf was consecrated every year, and similarly no doubt every kind of valuable gift which piety caused to be offered.¹ Even the inferior priests were thus dedicated as it were by the whole people to the service of Jahveh and the Sanctuary, the high-priest probably conducting them on to a raised platform before the altar, in order to present them to the altar as sacred gifts, with a similar waving of the hand in prayer.² Every consecrated present bore after this the brief appellation of a 'Sacred Thing.'³

So long now as *human beings* themselves were reckoned available for acquisition or presentation (on which more will be said below), it was quite consistent for parents to dedicate their children to the special service of a God, or for a rich or mighty man to do the same with human beings who were his property, or for the whole national community to dedicate some of its own members to the various services of the established Sanctuary. The more needy the dedicator was, the more might the view be held that this was the highest and most sacred gift which it was possible to devote to the Holy One, and the forms which this assumed in Israel will be made clear in detail below. The instance of the inferior priests (Levites) has been already mentioned, and will be more fully explained further on.

Gifts placed under the Ban (Ban-offering).

But as in general the contradictions of the lower life came into sharper prominence in the utterances of religion, so in contrast to these peaceful and joyous consecrated gifts, there arose another kind of sacred offering which calls to mind, more strongly than anything of a similar nature, the dark side of ancient religious life. Some object or other might seem so dangerous to the existing piety, and its improvement so hopeless, or from some reason or other have appeared to its owner so mysterious and so horrible, that man knew of no way by which to be saved from it, except that of handing it over to the Divinity for destruction, or, if it were possible, for improvement. It was therefore presented to the Sanctuary, and thus

then in ver. 20 only the breast, another account, Lev. vii. 30–32, makes it plain that this is merely accidental; as a rule, however, the breast is mentioned first, just as תנופה is of the two words of consecration.
¹ Lev. xxiii. 11, 12; Ex. xxxv. 22;

xxxviii. 24; comp. xxv. 3; Num. xxxi. 41–54.
² Num. viii. 11–13.
³ לְקָדֶשׁ often means the same as ἀνάθημα, 2 Kings xii. 5 [4]; 1 Chr. xxvi. 20; Bк. Is. xxiii. 18; comp. Num. xviii. 19; Ex. xxviii. 38.

as it were withdrawn from the world, but at the same time the Sanctuary was required to undertake to destroy it or render it harmless, so that the owner might be saved from a plague; for which purpose the priest had no doubt to utter a ban-curse over it. This is the ban-gift or ban-offering, which in Hebrew derived its name likewise ultimately from consecration and hallowing,[1] but became the exact opposite of the ordinary consecrated gift. Corresponding to it, among the food-offerings we have the mournful expiatory-offerings; among the kinds of sacred phrases, the curse.[2] It is easy to understand that such a ban-curse when once solemnly pronounced was deemed irrevocable, the hated object on which it fell being regarded as completely banished from the world. And so long as the only way of escape from a dangerous object was by a most violent appeal for aid to the Sanctuary such as this, the *ban* always appeared to be invested with a sacred spell.

Such a usage is to be found accordingly among many an ancient people, and Israel was certainly acquainted with it long before Moses. But in early times it can scarcely have received among any other nation so forcible an application as it did in Israel, in virtue of the latter being the community of Jahveh; inasmuch as the stricter moral life, which soon completely separated this people from all others, specially adopted even this sacred usage to make a fearful weapon out of it. If the nation deemed the existence of its religion seriously imperilled by any of its enemies, it easily directed the whole power of the ban against the foe. Not only on the altars, images, and temples of enemies would the ban naturally fall,[3] even the greater part of the plunder of the enemy was put under it, i.e. destroyed as dangerous. So great was the dread of contact with what was heathenish, and so little longing prevailed after the riches and treasures of the earth! Especially did this horror apply to certain military insignia, which, in accordance with the primitive experience of the community of Jahveh, were considered un-Israelitish, such as horses and chariots, weapons, and even fortresses.[4] But though this horror

---

[1] חָרֶם is so called from the forbidding (separating), interdicting, shutting out from ordinary life; in contradistinction to חָלִיל, common (profane): הֶחֱרִים, 'to put under the ban,' is then derived from it. Similarly, the corresponding ἀνάθεμα was originally the same as ἀνάθημα. In Hebrew זִכָּרוֹן, μνῆμα, *remembrance*, or something to serve as a lasting memorial, corresponds to ἀνάθημα in Num. xxxi. 54; but also in a certain way to ἀνάθεμα, Num. v. 15; xvii. 5 [xvi. 40].

[2] Pp. 15, 16.

[3] In accordance with the ancient decree, Ex. xxiii. 23, 24; comp. Num. xxxiii. 52, 53.

[4] See *Hist.* ii. 130, 154, 155, 241, 242; iii. 145, 146. On the جـَـِـ spoken of there,

gradually became toned down, it was easily stimulated into a fresh glow in unhappy times by the power of the vow, as occurred in Samuel's case.¹ It had previously been usual to spare the lives of captives, and of much else that might be useful, e.g. cattle;² but through this relentless power of the vow, the demands of the ban increased till it was insisted that nothing, however insignificant, should be spared, as this same history of Samuel shows.³ The Book of Origins, therefore, endeavours in some vivid narratives to exemplify the law on the subject. According to it, the war against Midian, because that nation had seduced Israel into participation in an immoral worship, was a war of the ' revenge of Jahveh,' and Moses adds to the penalty of the slaughter of all the men, that of all the married women and male children, but nevertheless allows all else to be spared, and the whole punishment although resembling a ban of the highest grade, is not called here a ban-offering.⁴ Such a one, however, was laid upon Jericho; to spare or to hide as booty even the smallest portion of what came under the ban was deemed enough to completely overthrow the peaceable, blissful relation between Jahveh and his people. When Achor secretly retained some portion of it for himself, the tokens that Israel was in disgrace increased, until Joshua most solemnly adjured the culprit who still denied the deed, to give honour and glory to Jahveh by free confession. He then did confess, and with all his possessions and his whole house underwent the punishment of the ban.⁵ After the time of David this early harsh severity was indeed somewhat toned down,⁶ but still many great Prophets of the eighth century repeat the phrases which time had rendered sacred, just because they desire and anticipate a revival of stricter discipline in the Messianic times;⁷ and the Deuteronomist, in his own times, which were already greatly altered, endeavours to revive them at any rate against the ancient Canaanites, a point which will be further spoken of below.

comp. further, *Hamâsa*, s. 290, ver. 4 from below, s. 742, ver. 2. According to the *Cyropæd.* Cyrus in just the same way always caused the captured *weapons* of his enemies to be burned, for the strict religion of ancient Persia had many points of resemblance in such matters to Mosaism. Similar features occur among the earliest Romans, see Livy, i. 37.
¹ Comp. Num. xxi. 2. 3, 30, 35; Jos. ii. 10; Judges i. 17; 1 Sam. xv. 2 sqq.
² In the words which occur in Deut. ii. 34, 35, iii. 7, xx. 14, Jos. viii. 2, it is no doubt only the Deuteronomist who makes the remark, but the same is related, 1 Sam. xv. 9.
³ 1 Sam. xv.
⁴ Num. xxxi. 1–18. Also Jud. xxi. 11.
⁵ Jos. vi. 17–19; vii. 1–26.
⁶ Comp. *Hist.* iv. 74, 75. But it is the wish of the Prophets also that the ban should not exist for ever. *uk.* Zach. xiv. 11.
⁷ Is. ix. 14; Mic. iv. 13; comp. Ezek. xxxix. 9 sqq.

The ban either of the first or second grade was also turned inwards, with equal severity, against such members of the community as had violated the existing covenant, i.e. the existing sacred constitution, and this was done whether it were whole towns[1] or private individuals[2] that were concerned. In a song composed during the fresh moral indignation against such an execrable deed, we have an actual instance of the lively feeling which guided the people in such a matter. The very angel of Jahveh who, in peace and in war, moved on at the head of the nation, seemed to have pronounced his curse upon such an atrocity, and the destruction which the nation speedily awarded, appeared only to have been the consequence which resulted thence.[3] The extraordinary power exercised in early times by this custom, is plain even from the fact that the word for 'to ban' had come to convey the conception of the swiftest and most utter destruction.[4]—Now when the human monarchy arose and stood in its prime vigour in the Theocracy, this weapon of the ban also was consistently transferred to it. But the history of the first king shows immediately, in an illustrative example, how easily such a hand might employ it without due consideration, and what toil it cost the whole nation to ward off its pernicious effects.[5]

It was of course a somewhat different case, when an individual handed over to the priest some possession of his as a horrible plague, which he found himself unable to subdue. Scarcely any clear instances of this are mentioned in the Old Testament, but of the main fact there can be little doubt, as the Book of Origins lays down the law for such cases in the most unambiguous terms.[6] Even human beings, e.g. anyone sacrificing to idols, a seducer to idolatry, a child which appeared incorrigible, could be devoted to death in this way by the community or the head of the family.[7] Was a man troubled by some inanimate object in such a way that his soul was endangered, having, e.g. been led away into idolatry by it? He

---

[1] As in Jud. viii. 4–9, 14–17, xxi. 11; comp. Mal. iii. 24 [iv. 6].

[2] As even the Deuteronomist thinks legal and describes tolerably fully, Deut. xiii. 13–18 [12–17]. How this was altered in later times may be seen in Ezra x. 8; comp. what is said below.

[3] Jud. v. 23; comp. *Hist.* ii. 377.

[4] As Is. xi. 14, and ἀναθεματίζειν often in later languages. What an amount of superstition of all sorts may of course finally become connected with this ban, may be seen, e.g. from the Arabic usages forbidden by Mohammed, Sûr. vi. 139–141.

[5] Comp. *Hist.* iii. 35 sq.

[6] Lev. xxvii. 28, 29; comp. ver. 21. The Book of Origins certainly contained a section which is now lost on the ban-gift of the individual.

[7] This is distinctly presupposed in Lev. xxvii. 28, 29, nevertheless Deut. xiii. 7–12 [6–11], xxi. 18–21, already regards it as a purely civic matter without reference to the priesthood. The oldest and shortest utterance occurs Ex. xxii. 19 [20].

could get rid of it most thoroughly by the intervention of the priest's ban.¹ Even a whole field, which had inspired its owner with disgust and loathing, could be thus surrendered to the will of the Sanctuary.²

Finally, an object might evince its incompatibility with the holiness of Jahveh's community with such direct and palpable certainty, that it seemed sufficient to destroy it on the spot, even without having previously pronounced the ban over it. Such an object also was deemed to have been forfeited to the Sanctuary; but without anything further happening, its mere appearance was enough. It became accordingly sacred, i.e. received by the Sanctuary; only, however, to be instantaneously devoured and annihilated by the same Sanctuary, so that in its case the conception of making sacred coincides with that of annihilating.³ This final development of the idea of the ban found application chiefly in the case of contact with things that were too sacred and inviolable (a subject treated of below), but also in other cases when something horrible ventured to appear in the community in spite of legal prohibition, as in the instance just alluded to.⁴

The Redemption of Consecrated Gifts.

A ban-offering, which had once been accepted by the Holy One, was incapable, from its very nature, of ever reverting to its former possessor. It was for ever forfeited to the Sanctuary, and no abatement or change was possible; or, according to the technical expression, it was just as much 'most sacred,' as any portion of the food-offering which was destined for the altar-fire.⁵ Only the Sanctuary could now dispose of the object. When, however, it was such as could not be destroyed by fire, as e.g. a field, it was probably made to lie fallow until a time when a new state of things would commence for everything whether sacred or profane, until therefore the death of the high-priest or the Year of Jubilee; then, after atonement had been made for it, it could again come into the use of the Sanctuary.⁶ When booty which had fallen under the ban was

---

¹ Somewhat like this is indicated in Is. xxx. 22. a passage which, as noticed on p. 74, borrows many images from sacrifices.
² Lev. xxvii. 21, 28.
³ That this is the case with the verb קָדֵשׁ, follows clearly from Ex. xxix. 37, xxx. 29; Lev. vi. 20 [27]; Num. xvii. 2, 3 [xvi. 37, 38]; Deut. xxii. 9; as well as from the use of the Latin *sacer*, in the sense of *accursed*.
⁴ P. 78.
⁵ The name קֹדֶשׁ קָדָשִׁים, which was applied to such altar-portions, according to p. 66 *note* 6, is used also of the ban-offering, Lev. xxvii. 28.
⁶ According to the brief indication, Lev. xxvii. 21; comp. Num. xviii. 14.

being destroyed, only the noble metals were saved by the victors, in order that they might be presented to the Sanctuary as thank- and consecrated-offerings. The Book of Origins even gives a law to this effect for the ban of the first and second grade.[1]

Mere consecrated gifts, on the other hand, were treated less rigorously by the law, which admitted the possibility of redemption in case the man who had bound himself by a vow deemed this to his own advantage. Only the firstlings of all cattle, and those animals which were available for sacrifice, were not redeemable; the former manifestly because they were considered to be too singular in their kind and to belong indispensably to the Sanctuary (as we shall see below); the latter, because they were not more numerous than were needed for the public sacrifices of the temple. If the possessor from greed or other cause substituted a worse offering for a better, he was at once to be deprived of both.[2] Unclean cattle, i.e. those that were not available for sacrifice, houses and tithes, could be redeemed at an increase on their legal value of one-fifth;[3] but special regulations were necessary in the case of fields, on account of the privileges of the Year of Jubilee, a point on which more will be said below.

Most remarkable is the fact that human beings could be redeemed, the Book of Origins carefully determining the price for the redemption of every variety.[4] The law permitted[5] each head of a family to vow and present to the Sanctuary any human beings that were considered his property—slaves and children. It was, however, already sufficiently merciful to allow their redemption at an equitable rate (which was evidently reckoned by the priest according to the customary price of slaves), but more will be said on the subject below in connection with the temple-slaves. Only when a child had been consecrated for a Nazarite was no redemption possible; this will also be spoken of below.

We are now in a position to pass a proper judgment on the case of Jephthah's daughter.[6] Had it been Jephthah's will that the vow should involve a ban-offering, he would have seen that he was bound to carry it out even according to the Book of Origins;[7] but such an offering was not and could not have been intended. If, on the other hand, a mere con-

---

[1] Num. xxxi. 22, 23. 50–54; Jos. vi. 10. It is similar in regard to the brass in Num. xvii. 1–5 [xvi. 36–40].
[2] Lev. xxvii. 9, 10, 26.
[3] Lev. xxvii. 11–13; 30–32.
[4] Lev. xxvii. 2–8. In the Syrian church children are presented to a convent, but ransomed if they wished to marry. *Ausland*, 1850, s. 1047.
[5] P. 75.
[6] P. 70.
[7] P. 77 sq.

secrated gift had been meant, then Jephthah and those of his time might easily have thought of redemption, such as the Book of Origins permits. But what he vowed was to sacrifice as a whole-offering the first thing that met him out of his house. This is quite a different case, sanctioned neither by the Book of Origins nor any other legal authority in the Old Testament, because it springs from heedlessness, and may lead to monstrous perversions. The legal ordinance which is explained above,[1] and which proceeded out of the genuine spirit of Jahveism, would have left the individual who made the vow, after the sad consequences had manifested themselves, at liberty to make public confession of his heedlessness, and to obtain expiation from the priests by means of a guilt-offering. But such a man as Jephthah at that time, and occupying that princely position, was too proud to avail himself of such a way of escape; and in those devastated tracts beyond Jordan, no sensible man was to be found who would have had sufficient influence to free the triumphant warrior from his false notions of honour.[2]

In a different way the intention of the ancient law was overstepped in the late days of the Hagiocracy when it became a custom that anything to which anybody had applied the mere word *qorbân*,[3] should immediately be considered as necessarily forfeited to the temple, even though acts of injustice were thereby committed.[4]

B. CORPORAL OFFERINGS AND SACRIFICES OF BODILY PLEASURES.

i. Fasting and Similar Matters.

There are, however, kinds of sacrifice which lie deeper, and extend into quite another province, and which in their temporary effects are far more influential. The sacrifices which man imposes on his own body and its pleasures, in order thereby to obtain a blessing from God, touch him at a point where he is unmistakeably more sensitive, and they accordingly develope a power which has for religion a greater temporary force, and for the sacrificers themselves a more lasting influence, than all the above offerings of property. We saw, indeed, how the most

[1] P. 61.
[2] But compare more on this matter on p. 70.
[3] I.e. according to p. 41, *sacred gift*!
[4] See Mark vii. 10 sq.; comp. Ecc. v. 3–5, from which we can see how frequent were the discussions on this matter in later times. This also explains why, according to Theophrastus (Joseph. *Contra Ap.* i. 22), the Tyrians would not suffer this *qorbân*! to have the smallest legal value.

varied feelings or truths of religion might be connected even with the sacrifice of food or other possessions; but when man does not only offer external, though it may be most valuable property, when he lays hands on himself and offers to Deity the pleasures and pains of his own body, as well as its ornaments and embellishments, then such feelings or truths will from first to last affect him more strongly, and the reaction will easily excite them to greater intensity, and produce a more lasting impression. Everything here originates in the mightier impulses of the individual, although he does in the first instance hope as well to obtain from his God the coveted blessing through the instrumentality of his own body.

In thus connecting the feelings and needs of religion with one's own body and one's own pleasure, there clearly lies a danger of exaggeration and return to barbarism, into which self-mortification so easily falls. It is exactly such heathen religions as were seized with a more or less exalted impulse to discover and retain spiritual truths—among which we must especially reckon the Brahminical, and still more the Buddhist, but also the ancient Egyptian, the Canaanitish, and the Syrian—which easily fell into such exaggerations of the mighty strivings which had been aroused for the attainment of divine favour. The savage frenzy into which the prophets of Baal fell when they could not make their God do according to their wish, the way in which, after they had long called upon him to no purpose, they danced about the altar, and then, 'according to their custom,' cut into their flesh with swords and spears till the blood streamed down them,[1] may serve as an instance of such excesses as they were practised among the Canaanites and Syrians, and thereby became known also to the people of Israel from early days.

But the spirit of Jahveism was altogether too sensible, and in particular the human body as the dwelling-place of the 'image of God' was deemed by it too holy, for it ever to consent to such excesses. An express prohibition in its oldest written laws already forbids all mutilation of the human body, whatever be its purpose, as will be explained farther on. And this prohibition, moreover, was especially extended to the priests,[2] whilst in heathen religions the priests, prophets, and

---

[1] 1 Kings xviii. 26–28. Comp. Lucian, *De Dea Syra*, ch. l. sq., lix.; Layard's *Nineveh*. ii. p. 71. In India it is found specially among the worshippers of the Çiva and the Durga, *Journal of Sacred Lit.* 1849, ii. p. 55; *As. Res.* tom. xvi. p. 33.

[2] Not without cause does the Book of Origins, Lev. xxi. 5. apply specially to the priests what is said in the older source, xix. 27 sq., of the whole of Israel.

saints, believed in the meritoriousness of special self-denial and self-torture.

Under these circumstances the law could do nothing to hinder people from voluntarily undertaking to make such offerings, because they were capable of becoming a valuable instrument in calling forth true religion. The Book of Origins places them side by side with vows, which at that time were limited as far as verbal usage went, to offerings of property, and lays down the principles according to which vows of both kinds, those applying to property and those applying to self-torment, ought to be valid.[1] But this law, according to its clear meaning, certainly did not sanction any conceivable personal offering which at any moment a man had sworn somewhat inconsiderately to make; such cases of inconsiderate oaths were rather provided for in the opportunity given of bringing guilt-offerings.[2]

The law takes special cognizance of only a single case as the most usual one, that, viz. of fasting, which had been voluntarily undertaken by some one for a definite period, but this it gives with its usual detailed delineation.[3] What this fasting consisted in, is not definitely laid down. It occurs elsewhere not unfrequently as the involuntary manifestation of the deep grief and yearning prayer of an individual,[4] or as a public decree of the government on occasion of great national calamities, and those of the most different kind,[5] even when a town lay under an accusation of high treason.[6] If sacrifice also was to be offered at public fasts, pure water served for the purpose,[7] and such a fast lasted either from one evening to another, or for seven days without intermission. In the latter case it was certainly mitigated in the same manner as may now be seen in the annual month of fasting (the *Ramadhān*) of the Mahometans. The law claimed only a single annual day of fasting, viz., at the great festival of atonement in the seventh month, on which more will be said below. When, accordingly, anyone voluntarily made a vow to fast, it might last, as described above, for a single day, or for seven days, or

[1] Num. xxx. 2-16 [1-15].
[2] According to p. 61.
[3] Num. xxx. 14 [13], עַנֹּת נָפֶשׁ, to bow (*not satisfy*) the *soul*, i.e. the desire for eating, is the ordinary expression for to fast in the Book of Origins: the shorter expression for it, צוֹם, already in use in Joel, is unknown to the former. But the name for this vow, אִסָּר עַל־נֶפֶשׁ (i.o.

a pain to which a man binds himself to submit), is so general that it is by no means confined merely to fasting.
[4] 2 Sam. xii. 16; 1 Kings xxi. 27.
[5] Judg. xx. 26; 1 Sam. vii. 6 sq.; 1 Sam. xxxi. 13; 2 Sam. i. 12; Joel i. 14–ii. 12. Comp. the forty days, Ex. xxxiv. 28.
[6] 1 Kings xxi. 9, 12.
[7] Pp. 34, 35.

even for a longer time, no length of time being legally prescribed here. But the excess of fasting which characterised the times after the first destruction of Jerusalem,[1] was quite foreign to earlier days.

Other species of self-punishment were, it is true, possible. We meet later with the custom of offering the adornment of the hair;[2] or on being spared after a severe illness or from some other great danger, before bringing a thank-offering, a man might devote thirty days to frequent prayer, during which wine was abstained from, and the hair was shaven,[3] and it was usual to spend such a period of thirty days at the place of the Sanctuary itself offering sacrifices.[4] Even the power of the ban-curse, already spoken of,[5] might make its appearance here, so that, e.g. for the sake of attaining some end deemed sacred, a man might lay eating and drinking under its imprecations.[6] But all this received no further encouragement from the law.

However, the spirit of genuine Jahveism already placed an obstacle in the way of the voluntary assumption of all such self-punishment, in the fact that fasting was at least out of harmony with the Sabbath, as will be made clear below. It was not till the last days of the ancient nation that the spurious Pharisaic piety attempted to transcend this limit, and there appeared those who prided themselves on fasting once or twice even on the Sabbath, and who succeeded at certain times and places in securing the prevalence of so gloomy a tone;[7] but even in those times such an excess did not succeed in establishing itself permanently.

ii. The Nazirites.

If now a crisis in the nation's history was reached, in which the most deep-seated powers of the soul were called forth and put to the stretch, it was easier for the stronger forms of self-renunciation and punishment to develope themselves from such beginnings as has been described, into the employment of a life. They would be unreservedly devoted to effecting the more permanent rescue of man from his usual torpidity by

---

[1] Comp. *Hist.* v. 114, 200 sq., and other passages; see especially bk. Tobit, xii. 8.
[2] Acts xviii. 18.
[3] Josephus, *Bell. Jud.* ii. 15. 1. We shall see hereafter that, in exactly the same way, a day of repentance and atonement always preceded the great annual festivals.
[4] Comp. what is said below.
[5] See pp. 15 16.
[6] Acts xxiii. 12, 21.
[7] Luke xviii. 12; Sueton. *Aug.* ch. lxxvi.; Just. Mart. *Hist.* xxxvi. 2. 14. That these heathen accounts are not totally wrong in respect to so late a date, is proved by the first passage, and the 'Essaico-Pharisaic spirit itself.

means of extraordinary inward effort and its outward manifestations. The heavier and the more permanent the toil which such men took upon themselves, the smaller must be the circle to which such customs were limited. Smaller communities were therefore formed within the great one and connected with it more or less closely, which at times rapidly extended their boundaries, but gradually lost again either numbers or internal force, whenever the original mighty impulse which had called them into existence began to flag. That such smaller circles of a more intense religious life were formed from time to time within the great community, proves the existence of a strong vitality in the ancient religion; while the profound truth of the latter is shown by the fact, that those circles, after they had done what lay in their original impulse, always, without rending or overthrowing it, resolved themselves again into the great community. This, at least, remained the case until the last period of this history; then even this healthy impulse of the old community underwent a complete change.

Best known, and originating in remote antiquity, is the order of the *Nazirites*, i.e. the *Consecrated*,[1] those who had consecrated themselves by a vow exclusively to Jahveh,[2] and had given themselves up, along with the whole of their bodies, to be owned by him. In them an urgent desire was awakened to devote themselves more purely and more strongly than the ordinary people to Jahveh alone—to present him with their whole bodies and their greatest pleasures. Thus the vow to abstain from wine, which certainly existed here and there long before their time,[3] received under their efforts a new and more rigid application. To the priests it had been forbidden from the days of Moses to drink anything of an intoxicating nature before the commencement of their public functions.[4] Such

---

[1] The word is in itself only dialectically, and as it were sacerdotally, distinguished from the more common נדר, *to vow*, p. 21 sqq., which originally meant *to consecrate* (i.e. to set apart for a higher purpose); just as דֻּת, *votum*, is finally derived from וַר or וּ (*to preserve, separate, choose*). More on this word will be found below in connection with the *consecration* of the high-priest. In quite a different way εὔχομαι, and *geloben*, *verloben*, are terms derived from speaking and praying aloud.

[2] According to what was said on p. 21 sqq.

[3] See *Hist.* ii. 397; compare also Shahrastâni's *Elmilal*, p. 438, 9 sqq. It is quite true that the cultivation of the vine was also deemed the sign, and the commencement of a higher grade of human civilisation; see *Hist.* i. 270; but the possible evil effects of this civilisation—stimulated passions and spreading drunkenness—might be so deeply felt by some that they would long to return to a primitive simplicity.

[4] Comp. what is said below about the priests. That this command remained in force till the destruction of the second

ancient sacred prohibitions, however, are easily carried to excess by those who are anxious to acquire a special sanctity, and this was what happened in the case of the Nazirites. He who had once taken this vow of consecration to Jahveh might never again taste the least drop of wine or any part of the vine, neither pure nor mixed wine,[1] neither sweet nor sour drink of any kind prepared from the vine, no form whatever of the juice of the grape might he drink; neither fresh nor dried grapes, no dish which was made (as is still done in that region) of unripe grapes or of the pressed-out skins, might he eat.[2] So long as the Nazirite lived true to this vow, free from the infection and even from the touch of the intoxicating growths, he was deemed a consecrated, pure being; but since from the moment of his exit out of the world of ordinary enjoyments, he was deemed, along with the whole of his body, to be consecrated to God, no further alteration even of his body might be made. Accordingly, the hair of his head might not be reduced, still less shaved; and if this laid on him a new burden and hardship, on the other hand, the luxuriant growth and waving locks of this inviolable adornment of the head served, for himself and for the world, as the visible token and as the mighty spell of his own unbroken divine power and complete consecration.[3]

temple in Jerusalem, may be seen from Josephus. *Bell. Jud.* v. 5, 7; *Contr. Ap.* i. 22.

[1] The שֵׁכָר, σίκερά, Luke i. 15, mentioned here, and often elsewhere, *sweet-wine*, properly *intoxication*, seems to have been a wine mixed with honey, and other sweet substances, and accordingly only too well liked, just such an intoxicating drink as we find now, e.g. in Habesh, made by mere mixing. Fiery water (brandy, etc.) was then, according to all tokens, not yet known; and that שֵׁכָר was regarded as one of the more excusable drinks, follows from the real meaning of the words in Prov. xxxi. 4, where אַי, *K'tib*, according to the *Lehrb.* § 352a, means *even*, like the Latin *vel*. In later times the σίκερά, which was widely spread by means of the Phœnician commerce, appears to have been only a kind of beer, *M.* עבודה זרה, ii. 4. and Jul. Afric. κεστοί, v. 25 (in the *Veteres Mathematici.* Paris, 1693); but such a meaning is plainly in contradiction with Num. vi., where nothing but the vine and its products are spoken of.

[2] Both חַרְצָן and זָג, Num. vi. 4, are words hard to be understood. comp. the *Jahrbb. der Bibl. Wiss.* ii. s. 34 sq. In passages like *M.* נְזִיר, i. 2, they are merely repeated; and from places like vi. 2, we see how uncertain as to their meaning many of the later critics were. However, the LXX and a learned opinion in *M.* נְזִיר, vi. 2, give reason to think that חַרְצָן are the pressed-out grapes (in regard to which we must comp. the *Aram.* w. עֲצָר, which means the pressing out of the wine), and זָג the pips. Nevertheless the latter is found *M.* טהרות, x. 8; שבת, iv. 1, in a context which would make us think rather of the *skins*; the word would be then connected with חַי, *sediment*, comp. *recrementa.* חַצְרָן, then, reminds one forcibly of حِصْرِم, *unripe grapes (Hariri*, according to De Sacy, s. 427; *Fâkih. Chulaf.* s. 197. 2), a word which, from its formation, must rather have come to the Arabians from other nations, but which may mean originally what is *green*, i.e. unripe, just like حَضْرَان, خَضِر. On this account the words in the LXX seem only to have changed their places.

[3] The expression Num. vi. 7, 'the consecration of his God is on his head,'

The Book of Origins considers Naziritism sufficiently important and honourable to include it in the description of the legal religious orders.¹ But from the description we find there we should never guess what was its origin, nor its great historical importance; here, however, the accounts in the historical books come to our help.² These historical recollections leave no doubt that Naziritism displayed its greatest glory and power in the last of the three epochs into which we may divide the period of the Judges; towards the ninth century we see it already in a rapid decline, for the joke denounced by Amos of compelling Nazirites to drink wine,³ betrays an essential change in the popular estimation of this consecrated life. For a few centuries accordingly the spell of this extraordinary life maintained its position, and a phenomenon such as this cannot well retain its charm much longer. When we find, however, in much later times, this more rigid vow coming once again into respect and use,⁴ this is evidently already the result of the sacred estimation in which the present Pentateuch was held; the regulations of which in regard to the Naziritism which it had admitted into its sphere, were carefully observed in this very late period. But the Nazirites through whom this mode of life became so influential and famous in history—Samson, Samuel—were consecrated by their parents for their whole life; while the Book of Origins in its legal description presupposes rather that a man or a woman takes this onerous vow only for a definite period. Now is the stricter Naziritism of a Samson and a Samuel earlier or later than the easier practice? We must remember that Naziritism, as it is described in regard to those heroes, is only the final development of an already existing custom; that parents should come to such a determination in respect to their children cannot be the commencement of Naziritism in general. Examples of the simpler Naziritism

---

quite agrees with Judg. xvi. 17.—In just the same way the Brahmin, who was a hermit, might not, according to Manu, vi. 6 b, 12 sq., 16, cut his hair, nor eat honey, flesh, or oil; salt was allowed, but nothing grown on cultivated land.

¹ Num. vi. 1–21.
² Comp. *Hist.* ii. 396 sqq.
³ Amos ii. 11 sq.—If, further, a Nazirite devoted for life was esteemed to possess equal sanctity with a priest, and so might enter the inner temple, this will explain the narrative about James the Just, in Euseb. *Eccl. Hist.* ii. 23, and in Abdias, *Apost. Hist.* vi. 5 sq.
⁴ 1 Macc. iii. 49; Acts xxi. 23 sq.;

Luke i. 15. That he who offered the sacrifices necessary for Nazirites was himself regarded as consecrated (as the later teachers admitted to be legally allowed, Joseph. *Antiq.* xix. 6. 1; Acts xxi. 23 sq.; *Mishna*, נזיר ii. 5 sq.) is sufficiently proved from the fact that he must accompany them into the temple. But the Mishna *Nazir* shows here too what foolish ideas these later teachers of the law derived from the mere sacred letters. Since, at this late time, the vow was so largely revived, and extended in accordance with the words of the Pentateuch, its period was limited to thirty days: this became the most important of the innovations.

may therefore have existed long before the time of Samson and Samuel, and it might therefore be referred back by the Book of Origins to ancient times, and even to Moses himself, although, according to all the indications of stricter history, we can derive nothing with confidence from Moses but the higher prophetism which became the deepest foundation of the existence of the ancient community. Again, the Book of Origins [1] knows of children being presented to the Sanctuary, and thus admits the possibility of the stricter Naziritism.

When the period of Naziritism which had been only temporarily undertaken came to an end, this happy return into the full life of the people of one who had been consecrated and set apart was thus celebrated. A one-year-old female lamb was sacrificed as an expiatory-offering (for this we saw would either precede or accompany a very solemn thank-offering [2]), a male lamb as a whole-offering, and a ram as a thank-offering. As the consecrated person might now be released from his onerous vow, this thank-offering formed a fitting conclusion to the celebration; his load of hair was cut off in the forecourt of the Sanctuary, while preparation for this offering was made by the priest; the latter then took from the offering, in addition to the other portions of the flesh which were legally his share, also the right shoulder, and this having been roasted, was most solemnly offered at the altar by the sacrificer himself, together with a sacrificial cake and a wafer; [3] and in this respect such a thank-offering differed from an ordinary one. Not till this was over was he free from his original vow, and at liberty to drink wine.[4] A whole week was considered necessary for the completion of all these valedictory ceremonies.[5]

For all other purposes the Nazirites lived in the midst of society. When the respect for them was already on the wane, there was formed at the commencement of the ninth century the association of the *Rechabites*, who held to their fundamental principle of abstinence from wine, but gave up the vow to let the hair of the head grow, and vowed instead to perpetuate the ancient life in tents in the solitary parts of the country.[6] Abstinence in marriage,[7] and the total avoidance of it, which was the starting-point with the Essees,[8] appears wholly foreign

---

[1] P. 80.
[2] P. 67.
[3] According to p. 73 sq.
[4] Num. vi. 13–20.
[5] Acts xxi. 26–27.
[6] That they still maintain themselves in the East rests only on the doubtful reports of certain missionaries. See *Hist.* iv. 79, where more is said on the subject.
[7] About which Mahomet dares to proscribe laws, Sûr. ii. 226.
[8] *Hist.* v. 373.

to the early days of the nation, so healthy was its growth at the core under the influence of true religion.

iii. *Circumcision.*

Sometimes, however, a large community or a whole nation will pledge itself to a universal corporal offering of such a kind, that every member shall constantly bear about its mark on himself, and so make his personal appearance or condition a perpetual witness for the special religion whose vows he has undertaken. In such a case, the external form which this offering assumes becomes less and less burdensome, till every-one is able to adopt it without much trouble. It is reduced, therefore, to a mere token (symbol, sacrament), and becomes as little conspicuous as possible, being all the time capable of conveying a most important meaning, at any rate while it retains its original vitality, and of perpetuating itself from generation to generation.

Thus several Arabian tribes living not far from the Holy Land adopted the custom, as a sign of their special religion (or, as Herodotus says, after the example of their God), of shaving the hair of their heads in an extraordinary fashion, viz. either on the crown of the head or towards the temples, or else of disfiguring a portion of the beard.[1] This custom was extremely ancient; and in a very old legal passage similar mutilations of the hair of the head are already entirely forbidden;[2] later again, Jeremiah designates these races by the hereditary nickname of 'those who are shorn on the temples.'[3] Or it was deemed sufficient merely to brand or tattoo the symbol of a particular god on the skin, on the forehead, the arm, the hand.[4]—Israel, too, adopted from early times a

---

[1] More definite than Herod. iii. 8 is the description, Lev. xix. 27. The הִקִּיף here being allied with נגב has the force of 'hew down' used of the hair, as it would be of trees, a strong expression being purposely chosen.

[2] The prohibitions, Lev. xix. 27, may have been occasioned by heathen customs of a corresponding kind, because the usages, which refer only to mourning, are not spoken of till ver. 28 a. They are repeated in a somewhat different connection in the Book of Origins, Lev. xxi. 5, and differently again in Deut. xiv. 1.

[3] Jer. ix. 25 [26]; xxv. 23; xlix. 32, comp. the *Hamâsa*, p. 253. 10 sqq. What פֵּאָה may be in such a connection is shown in Lev. xiii. 41, comp. xix. 27. It was perhaps originally the same as ܦܶܐܬܳܐ, or even ܦܶܐܬܳܐ, or ܦܶܐܬܳܐ, although this now designates the mustaches, Knös, *Chrest.*, p. 50. 13, where ܦܶܐܬܳܐ is to be read, Barhebr. *Chron.* p. 355. 19.—See for similar practices, Lucian, *De Dea Syra*, ch. 60; and among such nations at the present day, Wellsted's *Reise zur Stadt der Chalifen*, s. 123, and the work of the missionary Halleur about the Ashantees. Also see Livingstone's *Second Journey*, i. s. 263 sq.

[4] See what is further said on this below.

custom which attained the highest sanctity in its midst, where no jest, however trifling, could be uttered on the subject, but which was essentially of a similar nature to those we have just mentioned. This was *Circumcision*, of which we are now to speak further.

Circumcision is far from being a usage lying so close at hand, and so easy either to be invented or to be brought into practice, that it would grow up of itself, like many other usages, among nations the most different and widely separated from one another. To the so-called Indo-germanic (more properly Mediterranean) races it was completely unknown in early days, and the same was the case with the Chinese and the nations of the North. In fact, it is something so unusually artificial and peculiar that we should expect it to be invented only in some one place on the earth, and it is besides something so strange that a nation would not easily adopt it of its own accord. But, on the other hand, just as little is it something originally confined to the people of Israel. The Book of Origins gives the legal description of it as it was practised and was to be deemed valid in Israel,[1] having, however, sufficient regard for history to refer it for its origin back to the age of Abraham. This already says as much as that all nations which derived their descent from Abraham may also have had the rite of circumcision, and the Book of Origins indicates this as a matter of fact as regards the Arabian tribes in the narrative of the circumcision of Ishmael.[2] Jeremiah, however, designates in addition, Edom, Ammon, and Moab, as circumcised;[3] but in the same passage he specially calls also the Egyptians circumcised. Herodotus, whilst confirming this, adds that the Ethiopians, the Phœnicians, as well as the Colchians, who were descended from the Egyptians, and certain Syrian tribes (amongst whom he undoubtedly reckons the Judæans, without mentioning them by name), likewise practised this strange usage, which outside their boundaries was nowhere to be found.[4] The Philistines, on the other hand, were always railed at by the people of Israel as the 'uncircumcised.'[5]

---

[1] Gen. xvii.
[2] Gen. xvii. 23–26. The circumcision of the ancient Arabs is spoken of by one who knows it, Bardâsân, in Cureton's *Spicil. Syr.* p. 18, 7 sq.
[3] Jer. ix. 24 [25] sq. Later Barnabas speaks more definitely, c. ix.
[4] Herod. ii. 104; comp. 36, 37, and Josephus, *Antiq.* viii. 9. 3; Aristoph. *Aves*, ver. 507. The Troglodytes in Ethiopia also had it, according to Diod. Sic. iii. 31; and among the Phœnicians, according to *Sanchuniathon*, p. 36, ed. Orel., Chronos was even deemed its originator. Philo, however, *Opp.* ii. s. 218 sqq. expressly speaks of the fourteenth year among the Egyptians, and others.
[5] 1 Sam. xiv. 6; xvii. 26; xviii. 25–27; xxxi. 4; 2 Sam. iii. 14.

Such, then, was the condition of this usage as it existed in the later days of Antiquity, both according to the Old Testament and to the information of Herodotus; and this shows unmistakeably that circumcision had its origin among an extremely ancient nation, as a practice and symbol of the civilisation peculiar to this nation. The civilisation of the Ethiopians stands in the closest connection with that of the Egyptians; and seeing that, at the present day, we still find circumcision in Africa, even in places where Mahometan influence is out of the question, among Ethiopic Christians and the Negroes of the Congo,[1] and among many other now savage tribes, extending far down towards the south, it cannot be doubted that we have here the remnant of a primitive African civilisation, which had its seat among the Egyptians and Ethiopians (which of the two was the earlier in attaining to it we need not consider here), and which was shared by many other nations reaching far into Africa. But the Asiatic nations mentioned above, who were acquainted with circumcision, were in part very closely connected with Egypt by relationship, as has been remarked of the Colchians,[2] and in part had, at some time or other, come into the closest contact with the Egyptians, either by war and conquest, or else by neighbourly intercourse and trade, as was the case with the peoples of Canaan and of Abraham.[3] From all quarters, therefore, we come back to the land of the Nile as that part of the earth where, in far-distant times, circumcision took its origin and received its significance. In particular we can see plainly that its transition from the Egyptians to certain Semitic races was effected through the Hyksôs. How complete was the intermingling at one time of the Hyksôs and the Egyptians is mainly proved by the long persistence of this usage among precisely these Asiatic nations, while they were living in the midst of others where it never found an entrance.[4]

We should therefore presuppose that the primitive signifi-

---

[1] See *Ausland*, 1845, s. 1353. Among the Tumálo it is performed in the nineteenth or twentieth year (Tutschek, in the *Münch. Gel. Anz.* 1848, s. 733; *Ausland*, 1848, s. 314 sq.), among the Kaffirs, Namaquas, and others, from the thirteenth to the fifteenth year; comp. Galton's *Bericht über das tropische Südafrika* (Leips. 1854), s. 109. Among other African races, such as the Wakuafi, it takes place in the third year, see Krapf in *Ausland*, 1857, s. 440; among the Betschuans, however, it is always the real transition to man's estate, comp. Anderson's *Reisen in Südafrika*, ii. s. 215. For the rest, the subject is best treated in Bastian's *Reise nach St. Salvador in Congo*, 1859, s. 85 sq., 152, and Livingstone's *Travels*, i. s. 180 sqq.; ii. s. 190; also his *Second Journey*, i. s. 263 sq.

[2] See *Hist.* i. 245 sq.

[3] *Hist.* i. 388 sqq.

[4] It is true that Origen, *Contr. Cels.* i. 5. 1 (comp. v. 6. 1, 7, 8), gives vent to his anger against those who thought that circumcision was more ancient among the Egyptians, but he is certainly not pursuing there any careful historical investigation.

cance and the origin of the strange usage would be best learned from Egyptian literature. But up to the present time the investigation of this literature has led to no disclosures of importance on the point.[1] When Herodotus, however, says that the Egyptians submitted to the rite from a conscientious feeling for purity and propriety,[2] he thereby tells us nothing but the view prevalent in Egypt at his time, when, however, the consciousness of its original significance among the Egyptians might long have become weakened and lost. That those who were the Circumcised deemed themselves purer than others, and explained the usage on grounds of propriety, is perfectly natural when it had once been in vogue from primitive days, but that it should have come into existence to promote such ends is just as unlikely as that it owed its introduction to a regard for health. These and other conjectures of later times have nothing to support them, and are right in the teeth of the spirit of Antiquity.

We shall be led nearer to a comprehension of the primitive meaning of circumcision by sundry indications in the Old Testament itself, because there we possess far earlier accounts. When Moses (as a very ancient source relates[3]) turned back to Egypt to effect Israel's deliverance, but was overtaken on his way by a dreadful sickness, and it seemed as though Jahveh required his life, Zipporah, his first wife, seized a sharp stone, with it cut her son's foreskin off, threw this before the feet of the father, her husband, and upbraided him as a bloody bridegroom (i.e. as a husband whom she now saw she had married under the grievous condition of shedding her child's blood unless she were to lose the husband himself). But just at that very juncture Jahveh released Moses, and the wife, full of joy for the restoration of her husband, broke out into the altered exclamation, 'a bloody bridegroom for circumcision' (i.e. I see now that the blood shall involve no one's death, but only circumcision). More clearly than is done in this brief typical narrative, the original essence of circumcision, according to its most ancient significance, cannot be described. It is a rite which cannot be performed without loss of blood, and there is, no doubt, a possibility that the patient may die of the wound;[4] it is therefore essentially a bloody sacrifice of one's

---

[1] See the picture of some Egyptian children about twelve years old, in the *Revue Archéologique*, 1861, 298 sqq.

[2] Herod. ii. 37. Perhaps, according to Joseph. *Cont. Ap.* ii. 13, only the Egyptian priests had to be circumcised, and to eat no pork.

[3] Ex. iv. 24–26.

[4] If the patient is too tender or weak in body, or if unexpected symptoms ap-

own body, difficult to render, such as man may regard with shuddering fear. But he who has offered up to his God this flesh of his own body and this blood, and bears circumcision on his person as a permanent token of this hardest sacrifice, becomes thereby for the first time a man well-pleasing to his God, and may even become the saviour of his father. Thus, the tender mother's horror at such an offering of her son's blood turns into peace and joy.

Circumcision was accordingly an offering of one's own flesh and blood sacrificed to a God. It may originally have served as the substitute for a sacrifice of flesh and blood at which far more was required. This very son of Moses, whom, during the deadly sickness of his father, the mother resolved to circumcise, might have been sacrificed for Moses himself by the mother, according to strictest custom, and it is already no small indulgence that a drop of the blood of his circumcision should suffice for the same end. It was, however, always more usual to regard it as an offering on behalf of the person himself who gave his blood and lost his foreskin, and therefore as a token that he had to devote himself—give himself up—to his God, inasmuch as he had perpetually to carry about with himself a constant reminder of this consecration to a higher being. It was properly a painful and violent expedient, such as could originate and become generally adopted only in a nation which was still very rude; and just as baptism now in the Russian Church has degenerated to so rude a condition that the endurance of it may almost serve as a test for the healthiness of the child, in the same way, and to a greater degree, the man who survived circumcision might, when the rite was first instituted, be deemed to have received strength and consecration from the Deity. At the same time, however, it is not too hard for it to become universal among the males of a nation.[1] But the fact that the offering was made to consist of just the foreskin, is due indisputably, not only to

---

pear. Comp. a book only suitable for medical use, Bergson, *Ueber die Beschneidung*. Berlin, 1847. The third day after the operation was anciently deemed the most dangerous, especially for adults, according to Gen. xxxiv. 25.

[1] Circumcision, or rather excision, for girls is mentioned as a custom of the Lydian, Arabian, and African tribes, first by Philo, *Opp*. ii. p. 218 sqq.. and by Strabo (*Terr. Hist.* xvi. 2. 37, 4. 9 ; xvii. 2. 5 ; comp. Athenaeus' *Deipnos*. xii. 11

(p. 515), and then by Arabian writers (Tabari, i. p. 154. Düb., and others), and further accounts of its present manner is given in particular by Rüppel (*Reise nach Nubien*, 1829); comp. on the point also Kölle's *Vei Grammar*, p. 147 sq., together with p. 209. But Strabo is altogether wrong when he calls this custom a Jewish one. Even Herodotus knows nothing of it, and whether it is as old as the circumcision of boys, or had originally the same purpose, is very doubtful.

an early discovery of the possibility of severing it, but also to the ancient sanctity of the organs of generation, of which we have already seen another proof.¹ We must also suppose that the operation was originally performed when the boys first passed out of childhood, and began gradually to enter on their youth. This was always the hereditary practice among the Arabs,² and on this account has remained precisely the same in Islam to the present day, and it may have been the case among the Egyptians and Phœnicians. If, then, it was first performed at this period of life, so that it may be compared with the Roman assumption of the *toga virilis*, it is the more easy to understand why just this corporal member should have seemed appropriate for the symbol. The initiation into the approaching period of youth became at the same time a special consecration to the service of the God of the fathers.

In this simple form, circumcision had undoubtedly been introduced among the people of Israel long before the time of Moses. But a narrative contained in an extremely ancient documentary source,³ tells us in a very remarkable manner how Joshua had the nation circumcised anew on the banks of the Jordan, because the operation had been neglected during the many years they spent in the wilderness. This, however, could not have been from lack of means; for the sharp stones which were made use of in early times for the purpose⁴ were certainly not difficult to procure in the desert. It was therefore negligence of some sort which had occasioned its total or partial discontinuance; in the same way as the Phœnicians, when living among the Greeks, had no scruples about neglecting it,⁵ and as the Arabians, previous to the rise of Islam, did

---

¹ P. 10.
² See the quotations from old Arabian narratives in the *Morgenländische Zeitschrift*, iii. s. 230; comp. Shahrastáni's *El-milal*, p. 444. 3. It is still just the same on the island of Socotra (see Wellsted's *Reise zur Stadt der Chalifen*, ss. 460, 466, and among the African heathens (see above). Most instructive, however, is the fact that the Kayan in Borneo have a custom for male children *like* that of circumcision (*Ausland*, 1850, s. 703), and certain tribes in Africa and Australia signalise the entrance of children from eight to nine years old into the world by knocking out three or four of their teeth. See Haygarth's *Buschleben in Australien*, s. 174; Kowalewski, in *Ausland*, 1849, s. 226, comp. s. 475. Essentially the same, too, was the so-called Nagualismus among the ancient Mexicans, Carabbeans, and others, see J. G. Müller's *Amerikanische Urreligionen*, s. 212 sq., 285, 398, 604, 640. Livingstone's *Second Travels*, i. s. 346.
³ IIK. Jos. v. 2–9.
⁴ Ex. iv. 25; IIK. Jos. v. 2, together with the important additions of the LXX at xxiv. 30. When, according to Jos. v. 3, there was a 'hill of the foreskins,' in that district by the Jordan anciently consecrated by Joshua's camp: this only shows that later also people liked to perform circumcision there, which quite agrees with what is said in the *History*, vol. ii. 225 sqq. The Rabbinical nonsense in Justin, *Contr. Tryphon*, c. 113, may be disregarded. A flint knife was discovered in 1864 during the travels of the Duc de Luynes in Palestine, *Ausland*, 1864. s. 455. See, too, Sauley's *Second Palestinian Journey* (French), i. p. 44; ii. p. 191 sq.
⁵ Herod. ii. 104.

not apply it universally.[1] In Egypt alone during remote antiquity does it seem to have been rigidly maintained, at any rate among the priests, while it was gradually neglected among the more distant nations. This accounts for the exclamation of Joshua, who, according to that ancient narrative, when he had reestablished it in all its strictness, cried out with unaccustomed joy, that 'now had Jahveh rolled off from them the scorn of the Egyptians' (who had reproached Israel with being no proper nation). We see, therefore, how in that early time, when among the most civilised nations of the earth, circumcision was deemed the surest token of civilisation, Israel would not allow itself to yield one jot in respect of this honour to any other people; and the time when it reintroduced circumcision with greater strictness than before, was just when, as the conqueror of Canaan, it established all its national institutions on a firmer footing. Certain it is, however, that already the God of Israel was entirely different from all the Egyptian and other heathen Gods, so that this symbol of circumcision was sure to assume in Israel a very different meaning, and ultimately receive, therefore, a very different application.

Circumcision was the symbol of consecration for the entrance into the community of Jahveh, and consequently for partaking of all the rights and duties of the latter. This community, with all its pure divine truths and its storehouse of spiritual powers, in which the new comer is about to share, is something infinitely higher than the corporal symbol, strong as this may be; but so far as the symbol of entrance does not remain powerless or without meaning, it becomes not only a reminder, but also, for believers, a motive force of the life passed amid the rights and the duties of the community, and in extending its meaning so far beyond its corporal significance, it becomes itself sanctified—a Sacrament. As such, circumcision further became obligatory on every male without exception; even including aliens who were desirous of entering the national community;[2] a matter which will be treated more fully when we come to speak of the Community. Such universality, such strictness, and such sanctity, as was to be found within the community of Jahveh, where, indeed, it experienced its proper regeneration, certainly never characterised its celebration anywhere subsequently to this period. And if among the Egyptians themselves, who still for the most part practised it, it yet

---

[1] This also is already explained, *loc. cit., Morgenländ. Zeitschrift.*

[2] As the Book of Origins shows typically in regard to the heathen house of Hamor. Gen. xxxiv. 15-25.

became preeminently only a symbol of the higher purity of the priests, so in Israel, at any rate after it had been revived under Moses and Joshua and made legally binding on every male, it could furnish an image of the higher purity which the whole people felt they possessed by the side of other nations.

But the benefits of the community of the true God, after it had once been called into existence, are not imparted for the first time to the human beings which live in it, at a definite period of their lives, at the fourteenth, or the twelfth, or the seventh year of their age. Everyone, on the contrary, that is born or brought up in it is received from the very beginning of his life by the spirit of love and kindness, of justice and truth, prevailing in the community; and who can say in how manifold and what early impressions this spirit would exercise its influence on the growing child! It is also well for the child, when it begins to be self-conscious, to be always met by an image of the good which had been thought, vowed, and done for it, before it had any consciousness. It is well, again, for adults to recognise the child as always partaking, as far as is possible for it, in every right and duty of the community. Thus it certainly became a custom from those days of Joshua just referred to, to circumcise the boy on the eighth day of his life, as the first day after the week of his birth.[1] The Book of Origins on this account relates how circumcision was introduced as a divine law and as a symbol of the covenant, at a time when Ishmael was just thirteen years old (the usual age for Arabian children), but when Isaac was not yet born, so that this typical child of the true community might at his birth be at once circumcised on the proper day.[2] Through this artificial transformation of circumcision to a consecration of the new-born child, the usage as practised in Israel made a further departure from that of heathen nations.

When circumcision in Israel had once attained this lofty significance, and served to mark the entrance of the man into the full rights and duties of the true community, it was only suitable, in the last place, to connect with it *the giving of the name*. The child received its name on this occasion; and to every adult who was admitted into the community by circumcision there was given at the same time a new name, which thenceforth seemed to correspond to his new worth as a member of the community. All this, too, is already shown in the Book of Origins[3]—a proof of how early these customs took definite shape.

[1] Lev. xii. 2 sq.
[2] Gen. xxi. 4, taken from the Book of Origins, according to xvii. 12.
[3] Gen. xvii. 4 sq., xxi. 3 sq. Well

There can be no doubt that it was in this special fashion that circumcision was always observed in Israel from the time of Joshua; many, too, in the nation might early have become the more easily proud of the sacred consecration, the more they remarked its complete absence or very different practice among foreign nations. Thus it is that the prophets of those days, taking an opposite line, speak of its being necessary, not so much to circumcise the flesh as the heart, i.e. to cleanse the heart of all that is superabundant and impure;[1] and the time would come when the rude old usage was no longer willingly regarded in its original aspect, viz. as a bodily sacrifice, but attempts were rather made to find in it an emblem of bodily, and therefore also of spiritual, purification, as though the foreskin taken away in the operation was in itself something impure that had to be removed. But this latter view does not accord with the feeling of remote antiquity, and no one would spontaneously arrive at the idea that the foreskin was less pure than any other part of the human body.[2]

C. THE OFFERING OF REST: THE SABBATH.

None of the offerings of the second series just described, accordingly, rise to the highest stage of life and activity in a true religion; just as all of them go back for their ultimate origin to a period anterior to Jahveism, and were only modified by its spirit.

But Jahveism, too, brought forward simultaneously with its appearance a sacrifice absolutely peculiar to itself, the first which corresponds truly and directly to its significance, and

---

worthy of consideration, apart from circumcision, in the primitive widely extended custom of giving the child a name on the seventh, or eighth, or (fifth) tenth day. The tenth day is to be found among the Indians (A. Weber, *Ueber die Naxatra*, s. 316, and *DMGZ.*, 1853, s. 532), and the Greeks (Arist. *Aves*, ver. 493, 923 sq.); the eighth among the Romans; the seventh among the Khands in India (*Ausland*, 1856, s. 703), and the Negroes in Borneo (Kölle's *African Native Literature*, p. 131 sqq.), but also among the Greeks (Apollod. *Bibl.* i. 8. 2). This is connected with the old reckoning and sanctity of the week, of which we shall soon speak.

[1] Lev. xxvi. 41; Deut. x. 16; Jer. iv. 4; vi. 10; ix. 24 [25] sq.: comp. Ezek. xliv.

9. Still earlier the ideas of 'uncircumcised' and 'unclean' began to be convertible.

[2] As for the controversy so vehemently carried on in modern times (since 1841) about the necessity of circumcision for the present confessors of the religion of the Old Testament, it is undeniable that the later prophets down from the eight century already held very free opinions about this necessity; that, moreover, circumcision does not stand so high as the sabbath in the Law itself; and finally, that it is essentially a barbarous usage, and that if it costs but one life among thousands, yet that even this life must be valued more highly than the custom. Christians, at any rate, ought to take good heed how they oppose its abolition.

which is of a totally distinct kind from all the innumerable offerings of both the preceding series. This is the Sabbath, an institution in its essence purely Mosaic, and as such the greatest and most prolific thought of Jahveism.

1. Yet it would be an error to imagine that this institution of the sabbath, or of the sacred rest on the seventh day, found nothing of an earlier date which could furnish an occasion for it, when it was introduced for the first time on the earth in Israel, and that it was in this respect an entirely new discovery of the great founder of the true community. Many very ancient nations were acquainted with a weekly circle of seven days,[1] which is quite in accord with the fact that such a week is spoken of in the primitive history of Jacob.[2] These traces leave no doubt that the division into weeks of seven days, and all consequent distributions of time, were widely extended over the earth long before the time of Moses. But that it was originally adopted by all nations can by no means be inferred thence. On the contrary, there are certain regions in Eastern Asia where, at the present time, a shorter week of five days is still in use,[3] and this, according to many other traces, is just as ancient. Indeed, there are some indications even in Israel itself in the earliest times of the use of a corresponding great week of ten days.[4] Accordingly, almost the same as was said

[1] Philo, *Vita Mos.* ii. 4, and Joseph. *Contr. Ap.* ii. 39, are only too partial in explaining this as an imitation of the Jewish week; a still wider view is taken by Theophilus, *Autolycus*, ii. 17. It is a fact, however, that in particular the seventh day, but the eight as well, after the new moon, was held sacred, and dedicated to some special god (Apollo, Herakles) by many heathens, including the Greeks. See Philo on the *Decalogue*, xx; Aristobulus, in Euseb. *Præp. Ev.* xiii. 12 (p. 667 sq.); Jamb. *Vita Pyth.* xxviii. (152); comp. Müller's *Orchomenos*, ss. 221, 327, and Valekenär, *De Aristobulo*, xxxvii. p. 89 sqq.; also *Hitopadeça*, i. 3, and for what specially relates to the Buddhists, Spence-Hardy's *Eastern Monachism*, p. 236 sqq. That the ancient Arabs were acquainted with the week follows from *Hamâsa*, p. 268. 7, according to the correct interpretation and reading والبدر ليلة. The celebration of the sixth day by some of the ancient Hindoos (see Max Müller's *Hist. of Sansk. Liter.* p. 424) does not, on the other hand, affect these considerations.—Comp. also what is said below under the Festivals.

[2] Gen. xxix. 20, 27.

[3] See Selberg's *Reise nach Java* (Amsterdam, 1846), s. 264 sq., and Léon Rodet, in the *Journ. As.* 1858, ii. p. 408. The Japanese and Chinese have, it is true, lunar months, and accordingly esteem more highly the first, fifteenth, and twenty-eighth day of each month, but distinguish no week of seven days with a celebration, but rather refer the great week of sixty days (see Siebold's *Nippon*, iii. s. 107) to an original one of five days. Very remarkable, compared with that, is the fact that the seven days were unknown to pre-Christian Americans; whilst, on the other hand, a week of five days was customary among the Mexicans. This affords striking evidence that the former came from Eastern Asia.

[4] In the expression 'some days, or a week of ten (days),' Gen. xxiv. 55. The word שׁבוּעַ, of the same rare formation as שָׁבֻעַ a week of seven (days), signifies, according to Ex. xii. 3, Lev. xxiii. 27, the tenth day of the month, as one which was distinguished from those which immediately surrounded it; the fifteenth corresponds to it; comp. ثُلْث, for a third of the month, in

above¹ in regard to circumcision may be repeated here, viz. that we have here a custom very widely extended in primitive times, but still definitely limited to a large circle of nations, and which in particular was unknown in Eastern Asia. Still, the use of the week of seven days seems to have been more limited in Africa, and to refer us rather to Asia.²

The very fact, however, of there being these two systems may assist us in recognising the origin of the divisions into weeks. As the moon certainly affords the most natural term for all such reckoning of days, the month may have been early divided into four parts; and the fractions over and above the four times seven days may originally at least, as long as the real month was strictly maintained, have been intercalated somewhere or other when they amounted to a complete day.³ Only in this way can we explain how the sanctity of the number seven became so universal, for there must have been a foundation for this fact somewhere. And just as easily could the month be divided into three greater weeks of ten, or into six smaller of five days each, in which case one of the weeks would lose a day when necessary to keep in with the lunar month;⁴ though here the solar year, with its 365 days, comes very near to thirty-six greater, plus one of the smaller, weeks. It cannot, then, be denied that the reckoning by five and ten days is relatively the more original, partly because it can be more easily harmonised with the course of the moon, partly because these numbers primitively suggested themselves with such unique readiness, and formed the basis of all counting,⁵ whilst the sanctity of the number seven manifestly finds its first support in the more artificial reckoning of weeks of seven days, and the great importance which this subsequently attained.

In the people of Israel traces are still to be found, as has been already remarked, of this most primitive division of time into periods of ten (five) days, as well as of thirty, but reckon-

---

the *Chron. Samarit.* p. 35, and in other Arabian writings.
¹ P. 90 sqq.
² For the question whether it was known to the Egyptians, see Lepsius, *Chronologie der Aegypter*, s. 131 sq. But other Africans certainly had it from earlier times, as the Ashantees and the Gallas, see Tutschek, *Grammar of the Galla Language*, p. 59.
³ As in the ancient Persian division of weeks (which seems also to have kept its place among some Buddhist nations); see the treatise in the *Morgenländische Zeitschr.* iii. s. 417.
⁴ That a period of thirty days was very common among the people of Israel from the earliest times will be made clear below in many ways. When, however, according to *M.* ברכ, iii. 2, fifty-nine instead of sixty were reckoned sufficient when the thirty days were doubled, the meaning of this can only refer to the course of the moon. But the *Mishna* no longer knows the reason, and introduces one which is quite perverse.
⁵ According to *Hist.* ii. 159 sqq.

ing by exactly equal weeks of seven days, without further reference to the course of the moon, must very soon have been established among them;[1] even as this week was already in existence among many of the neighbouring nations. Standing, as it did then, entirely on its own merits, this circle of time, with its eternally-constant periods, easily came to be regarded as having something sacred in it; and among heathen nations it was but a short step from this to consecrate each of the days to a god or a corresponding star (planet), and then it was only natural to dedicate the last day of the circle to Saturn as the god of a remoter antiquity, or as the last tardy-pacing planet.[2] Now as Saturn is also the god of dull quiet time and of repose itself, the conjecture was already made by some of the scholars of the fast-disappearing Old World,[3] that Moses had made the last day of the week the sabbath solely because he regarded it as the day of Saturn. But there is nothing to confirm this conjecture. Unfortunately, we do not now know when and how the week of seven days was introduced. But if (as was certainly the case) it was long prior to Moses, and, moreover, among a nation where an accurate knowledge and even a veneration of the solar year was prevalent, so that we may say that the aim of this week was to establish a single self-recurrent period of time, without regard for the moon and the lunar year, then it is altogether probable that the week was established with reference to the number of the seven planets,[4] the individual days of it being severally named

---

[1] This is plain from the Book of Origins, Lev. xxiii. 15 sq., in a passage where (as will be shown below) it describes the genuine Mosaic arrangement of the fifty days after the Passover.

[2] This we find to be the case, not only with the Nabatians (see *Morgenl. Zeitschr.* iii. s. 416), but also with the Hindoos, who call Saturday *çanirâra*; their planet Saturn takes its name *çani* from its slowness, and is also represented as a God slowly driving in a carriage with piebald mares, comp. Wilson's *Vishnu-Purâna*, p. 210. It is also by no means necessary that Saturday should be the sacred day among such nations as possess the weeks of seven days from primitive times; the Ashantees, e.g. have this week, but do not hold the Saturday or the Sunday as sacred, see *Ausland*, 1849, s. 511. Again, we find that in Islám it is Friday, with the Druses Thursday, and with the Jezidi, even Wednesday, which is become the sacred day (Layard's *Nineveh*, i. p. 302).

[3] Tacitus, *Hist.* v. 4, collects a multitude of such conjectures; Dion Cassius, *Hist.* xxxvii. 17–19, speaks most definitely on the point, giving instructive information. On the further conjectures of modern scholars in this topic, which for the most part erroneously appeal to Amos v. 26, it is already needless to say anything.

[4] Even the series of the days of the week, as far as we can follow it back among the earliest nations, is everywhere the same, and rests on a primitive heathen belief: 1) that the series of the seven planets, commencing with the moon, and ending with Saturn, is something sacred; 2) that the twenty-four hours of the day were also in like manner of a sacred character; and 3) that the planets in this series had an influence on the particular hours and days, as though the planet which ruled the first hour of each day possessed that day. The twenty-four gave three times seven and three over, when divided by the series of planets, and the fourth planet which came next with the

after them. But this makes it all the more necessary to assume that in Israel, at any rate from the time of Moses and preeminently through his instrumentality, the violent transformation which then took place caused this original nomenclature to be totally rejected, just because it referred to the celestial deities. For when the days of the week are once named in a nation after deities or planets, these names easily keep their place unchanged, even when heathenism is relinquished; but of such names there is no trace among the Hebrews, nor again among the Syrians, so far as we can now trace back their history, or among most of the Arabian tribes. The last day of the circle is called by all these nations simply the day of rest; the first is, in the Old Testament, 'the one which follows next to the sabbath' (or the first after it). The remaining days do not happen to be mentioned in the Old Testament,[1] but were undoubtedly then, as later (e.g. in the New Testament), distinguished merely by their numerical order, as the *second, third*, &c., *of the sabbath*, i.e. of the week as regulated by the sabbath. In the same way the months in the Old Testament were, at a tolerably early date, named according to their number only, although it is possible to show that prior to Moses, and even after him, they were also named differently.[2] The difference is due merely to the fact, that the names of the months were not originally derived from such artificialities, and accordingly appeared less irreconcileable with the true religion than those of the days of the week.

Accordingly, when Moses fixed on the last day of the week for the day of rest, this was only done inasmuch as rest of

twenty-fifth hour, became the consecrator of the new day, and thus the name of each of the seven days was determined. Here, the perpetual repetition of this sequence seemed finally to be its most sacred attribute. The only doubtful point is whether the most ancient Egyptians were acquainted with this entire system (comp. J. Brandes: *Die sieben Thore Thebens*, in *Hermes*, 1867, s. 259 sqq.); if this is not the case, the origin of the whole must be referred with all the more certainty to Babel. But how little the sabbath had intrinsically to do with Saturn, is once more shown by the above facts.

[1] That ancient Israel during the time of Moses, even held in high esteem the influence of the seven planets, or other astrological systems, is extremely improbable, comp. the treatise in the *Morgenl. Zeitsch.*

iii. s. 418, and *Hist*. iv. 169.—Whence indeed finally come all astrological systems, and how and when they spread abroad, has not yet been accurately investigated. But though the Rabbis in the time of the Romans called Saturn, שַׁבְּתַי, it by no means follows that the ancient nation cherished the same ideas, and expressed them in the same manner.

[2] See below, in the last section. No doubt the names *Quintilis, Sextilis*, etc., show that the Romans also at first only counted most of the months, and the mere numbering of them was still more prevalent among certain races in Greece and Asia Minor, *C. Inscript*. iii. p. 22 sq. But we shall show below that with regard to the months, at any rate, totally different relations prevailed from the very commencement.

itself comes best not at the beginning, but at the end of the circle of ordinary daily toil, as is depicted with unsurpassable truth by the Book of Origins, in its typical narrative of the week of the Creation. And when heathen nations called the same day after Saturn, they may have therein arrived half-way at the expression of the same idea, without its following thence that Moses had previously honoured it as the day of Saturn, or that the meaning which Jahveism put into it was first of all borrowed from the conception of a God Saturn.

2. The most important point is the last mentioned. What Moses made of the last day of the week was something quite new, something which had previously existed among no nation and in no religion. The last day was to be devoted to rest; all ordinary human toil was to cease, an unwonted quiet to reign. Man must therefore renounce the gain and enjoyment which he sought in his ordinary occupation and labours. This is the self-denying sacrifice which he must here offer, something quite different from all the sacrifices which the world had ever known before, but one which is often far from easy for man to make, seeing how covetous he is, or otherwise plunged in the world's unrest and turmoil.[1] But yet man shall not rest on this day for his own sake alone, so as to sink into a vacant condition characterised only by the absence of activity, or yield himself up to dissolute, savage pleasures for the sake of passing the time; the rest, says the law from the very first, shall be unto the Lord Jahveh, shall belong to him and be sanctified to him. Man, then, shall release his soul and body from all their burdens, with all the professions and pursuits of ordinary life, only in order to gather himself together again in God with greater purity and fewer disturbing elements, and renew in him the might of his own better powers. If, then, the interchange of activity and rest is already founded in the nature of all creation, and is the more beneficial and healthbringing the more regular its recurrence, so should it be found here too; yet not as when in the night and in sleep the body is cared for, but as when in a joyous day of unfettered meditation, the spiritual man always finds his true rest, and thereby is indeed renewed and strengthened.

To do this, however, is the peculiar object of Jahveism, as of all true religions. The sabbath is therefore the first sacrifice which is appropriate to it, such a one as the spirit alone produces

---

[1] This is shown not only in the figurative narratives about the introduction of the sabbath, Ex. xvi., Num. xv. 32-36; but also in such prophetical descriptions from life as Amos viii. 5.

and brings to perfection. External property man does not offer, to his body he does not the slightest harm; all the purer does he present his soul to the Creator. Nevertheless, the realisation and celebration of this lofty repose of human life must show itself also externally, in the cessation of all labour; and there was already something solemn in this universal cessation during a whole day, from the evening of the one to that of the other. On this account the sabbath possesses some external and visible attributes, so that it can be deemed a symbol, but at the same time a sacrament of Jahveh, which all the members of his community must observe together. In this sense the sabbath 117 was deemed of sufficient importance to be assigned a place among the Ten Commandments,[1] although not a single other sacrifice or sacred usage is there required. The same conception of it prevails in the other laws of the oldest times, and it is there exalted to a position of the highest importance.[2] Indeed, its final and eternal prototype seems to the Book of Origins to have been given by God himself at the Creation,[3] for the alternation of motion and rest goes like a divine rhythm throughout the whole world, and equally certain is it that the existing condition of the world, which, considered on a grand scale, preserves a constant method, must have been preceded by conformations of a totally different order.

The grave importance of the sabbath to the history of humanity is exhibited by the Book of Origins, with its profound legislative insight, in a grand review of all the epochs of the world. According to this conception each of the four epochs into which the whole of man's past history is divided,[4] has its special divine commandment and decree, by which men were bound to God, its covenant therefore with him, and an external token as the visible confirmation of the latter.[5] Every law is at the same time always a limitation for man, which he ought not to overstep, and above which he is nevertheless always trying to rise, and the whole development of humanity properly consists in 118

---

[1] *Hist.* ii. 161 sq.
[2] Lev. xxvi. 2; xix. 30: comp. what is said below on this; Ex. xxiii. 12, already speaks with more circumlocution and explanation.
[3] Gen. i. 1–ii. 4; Ex. xx. 11; xxxi. 17.
[4] *Hist.* i. 79, 256 sqq.
[5] Only in the case of the first epoch of the world, where this description is altogether of the briefest character, Gen. i. 29 sq. there is no token added, because neither is there any distinct mention of a covenant which God then concluded. For when a contract is concluded, the mutual understanding may already be deemed disturbed, and accordingly a new arrangement needful which shall bind both parties; and this had not yet taken place at the commencement of all creation. So far as this goes, all must here be onesided, simply the command and law of God; but the existence of a law binding two parties is always just what is essential for every covenant.

such a ceaseless struggle against a limitation lying right before it, until this is perhaps once broken through, and a new law can at once come into being to suit the relations which then exist. The prohibition of the first epoch contained accordingly the straitest limitation to human life and action, viz.: to slay no living thing, to eat only of vegetables and fruits.[1] When man transgressed this first law more and more, and the first world was therefore destroyed, the peaceful commencement of the second epoch, brought him permission to shed the blood of brutes, but human life was made all the more sacred, and the bow of peace in heaven was the token of this epoch. When in its course human blood was continually shed more and more, and for the sake of upholding human society, a sharp distinction between ruler and subject had been established by the force of circumstances,[2] there appeared with the commencement of the third epoch, Abraham the pattern of the true ruler and father of many people; along with a new covenant and circumcision as its token.[3] After this covenant also had been transgressed worse and worse, and good rulers had given place to evil Pharaohs, there commenced with Moses, in the fourth epoch, a new covenant, viz., the rule of Jahveh over his people, so that the true God appeared, and at the same time in closest relation to him—the true community, the mutual token being the sabbath.[4] Accordingly the sabbath stands yet higher than circumcision, and the Book of Origins loses no opportunity of enforcing its supreme importance.[5] The book, however, always seeks to illustrate its legal instructions by appropriate narratives, and in one of these it shows how God himself by the difference in the fall of manna, taught the people in the wilderness the distinction between the sabbath and other days;[6] and in another how the punishment of death was incurred by him who infringed this sacrament.[7]

3. This extreme penalty was not so heavy, considering the

---

[1] P. 40.
[2] The part of the Book of Origins where this feature of the second epoch was described is, it is true, now lost, but that it once existed may safely be concluded from the arrangement of the whole as indicated by the portions which still remain. How great are the losses which a keen observation of the surviving portion will still detect with certainty!—We can here only briefly touch upon other important consequences of this circumstance, e.g. that the murder of Abel belongs properly to the commencement of the second epoch, and that his very name is probably borrowed from הֶבֶל, Gen. iv. 10.
[3] P. 95.
[4] Ex. xxxi. 12–17; but the description of concluding the treaty which should stand before ch. xxv. is no longer contained in the Book of Origins.
[5] Ex. xxxi. 12–17; xxxv. 1–3. To a later time belongs Ex. xxxiv. 21.
[6] Ex. xvi.; comp. *Hist.* ii. 221 sq.
[7] Num. xv. 32–36; comp. Ex. xxxi. 14; xxxv. 2.

whole position of the ancient kingdom of the people of Jahveh, as will be shown below in its proper place. The early recollections, too, collected in the Book of Origins, still let us recognise clearly enough that it was deemed no easy task to enforce at first the strict keeping of the sabbath throughout the whole community and permanently accustom men to it.

That it was strictly kept from quite the first, and that the law was urgent on this point, is not to be doubted. None of the business of ordinary life, such as the crafts and agriculture, buying and selling, might be carried on, as many passages in the Old Testament clearly show. And for a long time it seemed all the harder to observe this prohibition, and all the more justifiable to evade it,[1] inasmuch as all nations were accustomed to hold a market on exactly these exceptional days, the new-moons and festivals, and to make use of the concourse of many men at leisure, for the purposes of trade. Even fire might not be kindled in their dwellings, a point on which the Book of Origins lays special stress,[2] plainly meaning only that during the sacred day nothing might be eaten which had not been on the previous day procured and prepared.[3] Of its haughty violation, or conversely of an over-anxious erroneous conception of the sabbath, we hear no complaints till we come to the latest prophets.[4] However, the notion that people were to sit quite still all the day, and might hardly walk the necessary number of paces to and from the sanctuary which in later times was called a sabbath day's journey,[5] is a view far too scrupulous, which was derived in later days from a misunderstood passage in the Book of Origins.[6] Considerable strictness in observing the sacred rest was of course involved already in the general nature of the very strict discipline prevailing in the early community, which reached its maximum in regard to the sabbath, that being the loftiest and most peculiar sacrament, as well as the one instituted latest, a fact which would have alone secured special stringency. The community had first to learn to feel that it was altogether the community of the one true God,

---

[1] Comp. Amos viii. 5.
[2] Ex. xxxv. 3; probably only the commencement of a further amplification of the duties of the sabbath, which is now lost. It is remarkable that Philo, *Vita Mos.* iii. 28, says it was *frequently* forbidden.
[3] As may be seen also from the typical narrative about the use of manna as food, Ex. xvi. 22-31.
[4] Jer. xvii. 19-27; comp. ux. Is. lvi. 1-8; lviii. 13.

[5] Acts i. 12: comp. Matt. xxiv. 20. It was reckoned at 2,000 ells, which was the distance from the west side of the Mosaic camp (see below), to the east where the Tabernacle stood, as the people were at any rate obliged to go to the sanctuary on the sabbath.
[6] Viz. in the passage, Ex. xvi. 27-31, which the context and true meaning of the speech show to relate to going forth for purposes of gain, not to other going forth.

and to look up to him alone; on his account too, peremptorily to interrupt and suspend all the trades and occupations of the lower life, in order that they might wait in perfect quiet and retirement on their Lord and his voice alone. Here the strictest custom and discipline were not too stringent, and for every member of the nation without exception the sabbath was surrounded by the circle of this strict discipline. But that in the earlier days, when the national life was stronger and healthier, this strictness did not degenerate into the subsequent scrupulosity, is certain from general considerations. On the contrary, the sabbath was looked upon, like every other festival, as a time of glad recreation and elevated joyous life.[1] What were the particulars of its celebration among each local community in early times, we no longer know; but it was certainly not celebrated by a torpid sitting still, but with prayer and exhortation; and we do still know that on it the people were wont to seek the instruction of the prophets.[2]

The more strictly the sabbath was kept, and the more preparation was required in order to avoid all work while it lasted, the more customary did it become to regard the last hours before it as a mere preparation for it, and even to designate the whole of the day immediately preceding as the *pre-sabbath*,[3] or as the *preparation*,[4] or as *high-evening*.[5] All this, however, was not fully developed until the last days of the ancient nation, when all that concerned the sabbath was observed with the most painful scrupulosity, and a thousand new laws were passed about it.[6] The same was the case with regard to the other festivals.

Of what superlative importance the sabbath was, moreover, to the community during its earliest days, and how this perpetual sacred circle was regarded in the mind of the great

---

[1] Hos. ii. 13. It is expressly declared in Judith viii. 6, that even all *pre-sabbaths* and festivals of every kind are incompatible with fasting. Down to the latest times care was taken not to appoint a sabbath as a day of fasting or lamentation; and the dread of so doing was still lively enough even among the Christians of the first century; comp. what was still the right feeling in *Protev. Jac.* ii.; *Ev. Nicod.* xvi.; *Can. Apost.* 45, 46. Confusion of these ideas is first found only among heathens, see Just. *Hist.* xxxvi. 2; comp. above, p. 84. And how little inclination there was in earlier times to the later scrupulous dread of war and the use of weapons on the sabbath, how, rather, a brilliant victory was expected on the seventh day, may be seen in the exalted narrative, Josh. vi. 3 sqq.; *Hist.* v. 307, 400, 416.

[2] 2 Kings iv. 23.

[3] προσάββατον, Judith viii. 6.

[4] παρασκευή of the Gospels.

[5] The word, appearing chiefly in the Aramaic form עֲרוּבְתָּא, which signifies *Friday* also among the Syrian and Arab Christians, but which yet occurs nowhere in the Old Testament, would properly denote *the day made (turned) into the evening*, i.e. the high (sacred) evening.

[6] See on the point *M.* שַׁבָּת, and the intimately connected *M.* עֵירוּבִין; further light is thrown on it in *Hist.* v. [German ed.].

founder of the community as the pattern for every period of time, may be further seen from many periods of time which appear in other laws modelled on this pattern, as will be further explained in the course of this work[1]. Here again is something genuinely peculiar to the time of Moses and his immediate followers.

But the application on the largest scale of this sanctified circle of time, and of the number seven, was with regard to the determination of all the remaining festivals of the community and their dates. We shall, however, be better able to speak on this point towards the end of our whole description.

3. *The Sacred Utterances expressed by Purifications and Consecrations.*

Purifications were sometimes legally ordered on account of such transgressions or impurities as the supreme law in the community of Jahveh did not tolerate. So far they hardly concern us here, and will be fully spoken of below.

They were, however, also undertaken by men as a fit preparation for sacrifice and other imposing solemnities, as has been already noticed.[2] On such occasions they no doubt varied very much so as to suit the importance of the solemnity which was to follow; in their main features, however, they were very strict, true to the spirit of Jahveism. The lowest grade of purification demanded a washing of the body and changing of the clothes,[3] as well as the removal of any objects of heathen superstition which might be about;[4] on occasions of very great solemnity sexual abstinence for three days was further required.[5]—For the priests on duty purifications wholly special to themselves were necessary; they must, e.g. bathe with hands and feet, i.e. with the whole body, in the fore-court of the Sanctuary when they desired to enter the sanctuary or approach the altar.[6]

Related to these are the consecrations for sacred or dangerous undertakings, e.g. for a general fast,[7] a war,[8] the meeting of the national assembly,[9] or for a new building, not only of an

---

[1] Comp. what has been already said under Circumcision, p. 96 sq.; for other cases, see below.
[2] P. 12.
[3] According to Ex. xix. 10, 14; Gen. xxxv. 2, and the purifications described below.
[4] Gen. xxxv. 2, 4; Ex. xxxii. 5 sq.
[5] Ex. xix. 15. At ordinary celebrations, e.g. when the national assembly met, a single day's preparation sufficed, Josh. vii. 13.
[6] Ex. xxx. 17–21; xl. 30–32.
[7] Joel i. 14; ii. 15.
[8] Ps. cx. 3; Joel iv. 9 [iii. 9]; Mic. iii. 5; Jer. xxii. 7, and elsewhere. An historical instance occurs 1 Sam. vii. 9 sq.; a song, Ps. xx. Josephus, *Antiq.* xv. 5, 4, speaks of sacrifices before a combat being still offered under Herod.—Philo, *Vit. Mos.* i. 57 *ad fin.* speaks of a purification of warriors on their return from the combat.
[9] Joel ii. 16; comp. i. 14.

altar,[1] and a temple,[2] but also, e.g. of a town-gate.[3] They are all called 'sanctifications'; but we do not now know much about the particular phrases and rites which were employed on these occasions.

Sacrifice was connected with all the more important purifications and consecrations[4]; the songs and phrases being for the most part freely composed and selected.[5] For the consecration of the sacred vessels, as well as for that of the high-priest, oil, mixed up with various costly perfumes, was employed,[6] a matter which will be spoken of again. This oil was what grew in Canaan, and of itself furnishes an image of happy luxuriant growth, and therefore of a blessing. The various perfumes also which were mixed with it in certain technical proportions grew in that neighbourhood, or in Arabia and Syria, countries not too far from Canaan.

THE SACRAMENTS OF JAHVEH.

Every religion, however, has finally some few usages in which she seeks to comprehend her entire significance and spirit, as well as her external validity and her sanctity. These are her sacred rites, by us usually termed *sacraments*,[7] and their existence is quite inevitable. For while every religion, particularly if it be an elevated one, starts from some few fundamental truths, but finds her fulfilment and goal only in life and action, she has also a craving finally to put forth again her whole contents in some few usages, and to cling to these as eternally valid in the world and for the world. Religion, so powerful and at the same time so simple, especially in her strictest and purest forms, must finally collect her truly inexhaustible power in certain equally clear and expressive symbols of her life. These symbolic actions

---

[1] Ex. xxix. 36 sq.; Ezek. xliii. 18–27.
[2] Comp. 1 Kings viii.; *Hist.* iii. 126 sq., 245 sqq.
[3] Neh. iii. 1.
[4] In the heathen purifications they were of the same terrible kind as the sacrifices of covenants (p. 68), so that those who were to be purified had to *pass between* the halves of the sacrificial victim, Livy, xl. 6, 13. What Israel retained of similar more rigorous usages will be explained below, under the Passover.
[5] As is shown by the examples, 1 Kings viii.; Ps. lxviii.
[6] Ex. xxx. 22-33.

[7] The proper Hebrew word for them is מְקֻדָּשִׁים; for, on a close inspection, it is impossible to doubt that this word must be so understood in the very ancient passages, Lev. xxvi. 2; xix. 30. The sacraments are here given in a series as things 'to be feared' along with the sabbath. On this account the plural מְקֻדָּשִׁים is to be read, as is actually found in Lev. xxi. 23. In the last passage, as likewise in Lev. xx. 3; Num. xviii. 29, the word refers to the sacrifice. The words הֲקֹדֶשׁ or מִקְדָּשׁ, in Ezek. xxii. 8, 26; xxiii. 38, are to be understood and read in accordance with this.

have their origin in the life, and the whole power and activity of this particular religion itself, and so when repeated in their original vitality, propagate and renew this whole significance and spirit of the religion. But as soon as they come into being they serve perpetually to remind alike adherents and opponents of the existence of this religion, with its many various commandments and laws; the believers however having these things recalled to mind very differently from the unbelievers. This at least is their original essence.

These few usages of more than ordinary rank, are accordingly very properly described in the Old Testament as symbols of the covenant of Israel with Jahveh. A symbol in itself is dead, the spirit which created or took possession of it first gives it all its significance, as well as its powers of persistence. It is then very possible that such a symbol may have existed earlier, before it is seized upon by the higher religion, and receives from her quite a new meaning, which shall correspond to her nature. This we have already shown to have been the case with regard to circumcision[1] and sacrifice, especially the bloody sacrifice.[2] Nevertheless, a vigourous true religion will always create as well out of its most intrinsic spirit a completely new symbol. Such an one Jahveism possessed in the sabbath.[3]

Never, however, can such a symbol exhaust, in its mere phenomenal manifestation, the significance of that which it tries to reveal to the senses, least of all where it is employed to express the deepest thoughts and the highest aspirations of true religion. If the life and the power of every religion, and most of all that of the true religion, includes an incalculable element, something secret and miraculous, then for every common mind which does not like to penetrate into their full vital meaning, these symbols of it become still more full of secrecy, so that these sacraments become identical with *secrets* (*mysteries*).[4]

That such sacraments are to be deemed more sacred than aught else that is visible, is a matter of course; they are the seat of the public conscience and consciousness of religion. So long as the religion is surrounded by many powers bitterly hostile towards her, and is limited to a narrow circle, or even single close nationality, the latter will seek to protect her, and therefore her most intrinsic and sacred symbols, with the greatest anxiety. As in the case of blaspheming the name of Jahveh, so also designed and conscious violation of these symbols of the

[1] P. 89 sqq.
[2] P. 40 sq.
[3] P. 97 sqq.

[4] As even this word מְקֻדָּשִׁים may signify *secrets*, Ps. lxxiii. 17.

covenant was to be punished according to the Book of Origins, by death; as though he who despised or disturbed these symbols of their life, robbed himself of all life in the sacred community.

The individual sacraments, moreover, so far as they were vehicles of this lofty significance, assumed the form of a coherent Whole. *Circumcision* was the sacrament and symbol of reception into the community.[1] It is thus a very strong symbol, derived from a ruder primitive time; it always remained visible on the person of him who had received it, and would always serve as a most vivid memorial for himself and a witness for others. *Sacrifice*, especially the bloody sacrifice with its inseparable deep dread of all blood, was derived from still earlier days; it could not, in the form in which it was taken and employed, be so readily connected with any of the new truths of Jahveism, and it is accordingly termed a sacrament, but not, as a rule, one of the symbols of the covenant. Only the Passover and its blood is depicted as a sacred symbol,[2] and therefore strictly insisted on every year for at least every male member of the community.[3] On the other hand, such a symbol of the covenant appears from the very foundation of the community in the *Sabbath*, and it presents itself not only as something quite new, but also as the most worthy symbol of this religion and community, being altogether incorporeal, and one which, without the complete participation and free act of the spirit, could not become manifest in the community, but which does become a glorious revelation of the existence and efficiency of religion, as soon as the nation celebrated it with one accord and from their hearts.[4] At the same time it is a sacred symbol in which all members of the community without exception may have an equal share. As then circumcision, a single act incapable of repetition, marked and sealed the entrance into the community, and still more into a state of obligation towards Jahveh, so the proper celebration of the sacrifice, which could be repeated after longer or shorter intervals, and still more that of the sabbath, gives the symbol of this obligation, and at the same time when properly celebrated, the continual fresh power for its maintenance. And as this alone is the final aim of all true religion, her whole intrinsic unity and might is brought to a focus in her having,

[1] P. 95 sqq.
[2] Ex. xii. 13, 21-28. The symbol given by God to Cain to bear on his body (Gen. iv. 15), is, on the other hand, more of a heathen character; comp. above pp. 55, 94 *nt, Apocal.* vii. 1-8.
[3] See below.
[4] As has been all further explained on p. 97 sqq.

taken strictly, only one such rite of the highest sanctity (*sacrament*), the true sacrifice. To this the former kind now only stands in the relation of a suitable prerequisite and preparation. How far these sacraments were really held sacred in the life of the ancient nation has been already explained.

II. THE SACRED EXTERNALS.

When a religion passes out of her purely spiritual province, and enters a particular community or nation, there to abide and bear her fruit, she needs more than the above-described sacraments, which do bring out her deepest truths, but only so far as they are capable of external representation and communication. She needs, in addition, a number of outward means and instruments, which are not meant to produce and represent her truths themselves, but only to enable the latter to be maintained, imparted, and advanced. There must be persons whose lives may be spent in their promulgation—priests, and these possibly of different grades. There must, further, be implements, places, and houses, which may be used as the instruments of this promulgation; and lastly, there must be definite times, when they may be promulgated again and again as efficaciously and vigorously as possible.

All these we call the sacred externals; and that they are indispensable as conditions of the existence and maintenance of every religion which has attained historical importance, is undeniable. But their special conformation and development is most intimately connected with the whole individuality of each special, i.e. historical religion; and Jahveism shows also here the duality which characterises its temporal origin.

On the one hand, Jahveism, in its inmost nature and impulse, as far as it was something new in the world, was so simple, and at the same time so true and so deep, that in its necessary assumption of human, moral, and temporal externals, it was nevertheless obliged to strive to uphold, securely and clearly, its own pure truths, which stood far above these things, and were quite independent of them. It cannot take the view that the truth and power of religion depends on priests, or even on prophets, or sacred vessels and houses, or festivals and seasons. This dependence it nowhere teaches, for all that is Sacred it refers back ultimately to Jahveh, to his volition and action, his election and rejection. How completely, on the contrary, it exalted the eternal and unchangeable Sanctity alone, and only thence derived all else which was called sacred by men, we see most clearly in the fair commencement of its course, when its divorce from all earlier religions, and new arrangement of all conditions after its own impulse, proved most favourable to a noble simplicity in all sacred externals.

On the other hand, the founding of Jahveism fell in a time when all living religion was still more than at present bound up with persons and places, and when especially the genuine religion with its truths could only make its way with great toil. This was reason enough why Jahveism had to become accustomed to relying much on external supports, even if these were not to become to it what they were to Heathenism. And when we remember what terrible risks this commencement of true religion ran at the time from the most opposite quarters, and with what difficulty for a long time it maintained itself in the struggle against the world, we cannot be surprised at the excessive anxiety with which it sought to attach itself to certain persons and races, to vessels, and places, and seasons. True religion seemed always ready enough to vanish again out of the world; all the more anxiously did the conception of it gradually connect itself with certain externals, without which it appeared unable to exist.

In this way, then, these two impulses interpenetrated one another from either side till their co-operation resulted in the remarkable historical conformation of sacred externals about which the Book of Origins gives us our most perfect knowledge.

SACRED MEN,

be they priests or prophets, preachers or monks (the sanctity of the last mentioned being that on which Buddhism was specially reared), or any other human beings, could find no place in Jahveism, for this had too profound a knowledge of the relation of human weakness to Divine strength; and accordingly represented sanctity for men only as a requirement of God, but on this very account as something which applied equally to all the members of the community. Of the worship of relics, into which Buddhism fell so early, there is in Jahveism not the most distant trace. Even the exalted figures of the patriarchs of the nation, with all that was closely connected with them, were allowed to be neither deified nor canonised by the strict true religion which became law in Israel.[1] Nor were Moses or the other ancient heroes of the first founding of the

---

[1] *Hist.* i. 295 sq.

community, ever made the subjects of such an application of the idea of sanctity.[1] How much less could this religion ascribe sanctity to a living man and member of the community as something which cleaved to him and was to be reverenced in him!

When, nevertheless, a certain sanctity is often ascribed to the priests and to the high-priest in particular, this is to be explained from the narrowness of those times, in which religion did not seem able to maintain herself without the closest alliance with particular classes and persons; and, moreover, in such cases the expression 'sacred' must be understood in conformity with the ruling principle of Jahveism.

We shall, however, be better prepared to speak on the point further on in treating of the position of the priests.

SACRED TIMES. THE PERPETUAL LIGHT AND SACRIFICE.

Of all sacred externals none is more necessary and unavoidable than the appointment of sacred times, when not only the individual, but still more the whole community, shall have leisure, as well as a summons, to recognise the higher truths which it is so easy to leave unheeded amid the bustle of ordinary life, and to strengthen themselves afresh by partaking of their vitality. It is desirable that such seasons should recur regularly at intervals not too distant from one another, and for this Jahveism made the best provision in the already described institution of the Sabbath[2]—that greatest and most enduring of the creations of the arch-legislator. The more important festivals, which ought to stand out prominently even in the series of ordinary sabbaths, will, however, be treated of below at a more suitable place.

But again, the mere observance of holy days like these was not enough, inasmuch as religion must exist and operate without break or intermission, and there should not be an instant in which the individual may doubt whether he is in the presence of God, or whether he sighs after his light in vain. Especially were the cravings of Antiquity utterly unsatisfied by this constant renewal of the public religion as the sacred days recurred. For every nation then believed that its gods, and in particular its head- and guardian-god, might be easily lost again, and wished therefore to put forth all its might to secure his actual and continuous presence in their midst. Every

[1] *Hist.* ii. 225 sqq.   [2] P. 97 sq.

nation, accordingly, which felt a craving for such *sacra diurna*,[1] took measures in its sanctuary for giving assurance by means of appropriate symbols of the eternal presence in its own midst of a God ever ready to succour; and other symbols of the never-ceasing worship of this God were easily connected therewith. Now the craving for such symbols was felt also by the people of Israel, and after the founding of Jahveism more strongly than ever, inasmuch as its God could be represented by no image made with hands, and the setting up of any such image in the sanctuary was strictly forbidden. It was as though it desired to make it perfectly clear to the Heathenism which surrounded it, that its God too, though purely spiritual, was none the less actually in its midst, and was honoured there with no less magnificence. Many things of this kind, then, passed over from the earlier condition of affairs to Jahveism, in order to indicate the abode where Jahveh dwelt, who, though invisible, was certainly and eternally there. And yet it is almost more important to notice how at that time the true religion only partially submitted to such temporal limitations, still clinging to the more eternal view, at any rate in anticipation and contemplation, and letting the light of pure truth stream through.[2]

All the particular symbols of this perpetual sacred service recur in their essential features in heathen religions. It is, as has been already said, as though Israel was ever desirous of showing by a similar institution, that its totally distinct, invisible God, was not less continually present, than all the gods of the nations in whose midst it lived. And when we turn to the essential elements, it appears that we always meet with two distinct symbols: a light (or fire) kept perpetually burning as the symbol of the mysterious presence and activity of the Divinity in this abode, and some kind or other of perpetual sacrifice as its never-failing human worship.[3] In other respects a close investigation shows that the separate parts of which this daily

---

[1] The תָּמִיד in the Book of Origins, the ἐνδελεχισμός, in Joseph. *Bell. Jud.* vi. 2. 1. How much importance was ascribed to it even in later times, is seen from such expressions as Acts xxvi. 7, which are frequently to be met with at that time. Something similar appears in the Temple of the Tyrian Herakles, see Sil. Ital. *Pun.* iii. 29.

[2] This is proved in a great variety of ways; in the long passage, e.g. which concerns us most here, Ex. xxxii–xxxiv., we see that the original Decalogue 'written by the finger of God' was shattered, and a new one put in its place, and the sacred tent was not looked upon as necessary till after the great backsliding of the people.

[3] Before a Chinese idol there stand at the present time two great candles and dishes containing dainties of every sort; among the Cossacks and similar races a light, never permitted to go out, burns by the side of an image of the Virgin, see Wagner's *Reise im Kaukasus*, i. s. 65 sqq.; Bodenstedt's *1001 Tage*, s. 32. But in the Acropolis of Athens, too, Athénè sat by the side of a sacred lamp never extinguished (*Berl. akad. Monatsber.* 1849, s. 212).

sacred worship was composed in the final arrangement of it were of very different origins.

1. As we have already seen,[1] the primitive table-offering always maintained its position here, and consisted of twelve loaves, carrying us back by means of this number to the primitive time when the number of the tribes determined everything. This offering is termed in the Book of Origins the 'eternal bread'[2] and elsewhere the 'bread of the countenance'[3] because it was placed *in front of* the innermost sanctuary, in two rows, on the similarly named sacred table. But in true Mosaic fashion these twelve loaves were unleavened and served up only with incense and salt, and had to fall in with the Mosaic arrangement of time in being renewed every sabbath-day, the old ones becoming the property of the priests.

2. A perpetually burning light must assuredly have been an invariable accompaniment of this table-offering; but its arrangements, as they are known to us, have a thoroughly Mosaic stamp. Seven lights were to burn on the lamp of the sanctuary, manifestly in accordance with the number which the sabbath had made sacred. Every evening they were prepared, i.e. filled with the finest oil, every morning they were examined and cleaned; by day it appears that not so many, three or still fewer out of seven, were kept burning.[4] The description of it in the Book of Origins is at present somewhat imperfect, but it is not in itself probable that there was no sacred light at all burning during the daytime. We should rather remember how calamitous it was deemed when the 'eternal light' was by any accident completely extinguished; and this is enough to make it likely that by day more than a single flame was kept alight.

When in the evening the priest filled the seven lamps and in the morning put all in order for the requirements of the day, it was his duty at the same time always to offer incense at the smaller altar in the inner sanctuary. In this way perfect expression is found for the correspondence between light and sacrifice.[5]

3. After the brilliant fire-offering described above[6] had

---

[1] P. 27 sq.
[2] Lev. xxiv. 5–9; Num. iv. 7.
[3] 1 Sam. xxi. 6 [5] sq., rendered by Luther *Schaubrode* [A. V. shew-bread]. In a more artificial manner the name 'the bread set out in order,' 1 Chron. xxiii. 29, is formed out the words in Ex. xl. 23.
[4] According to the passages, Ex. xxvii. 20 sq.; xxx. 7 sq.; Lev. xxiv. 1–3; 2 Chron. xiii. 11; and 1 Sam. iii. 3, it seems as if the light burnt only at night; but the passage, Ex. xxx. 7, speaks of a trimming of the lamps every morning; and Joseph. *Antiq.* iii. 8. 3. may be right in informing us that by day three out of the seven were burning. Comp. Mal. i. 10, where no intermittent illumination would suit.
[5] Ex. xxx. 7 sq.
[6] P. 46 sq.

established itself in Israel, a new and final, but more costly, form of the daily sacrifice was its logical consequence. Every morning and every evening a male sheep was consumed as a burnt-offering, together with the fruit- and drink-offering which went along with it, and on every sabbath a second offering of the same kind was added.[1] The fire for it on the large altar was made up every morning and evening till it was sufficient to reduce the offering then consigned to it to ashes in the course of half a day; it was therefore never too low for all other offerings which were brought to the sanctuary to be at once placed upon it.[2] A similar perpetual fire, which, however, probably did not yet consume the same expensive sacrifice, must have marked out the sacred central spot while Moses was alive;[3] and we have already shown the use of this constant great sacred fire, according to the remembrance of those who lived later, during the many and long wanderings of the people under Moses.[4] As soon as the great sanctuary obtained a fixed abode in the Holy Land, this sacred fire, too, must have assumed a different shape. It was no longer possible or desirable that it should mark the high central spot of the encamping nation, visible afar in a wild desert. But something similar at any rate was once more instituted. Thus it was transferred to the Temple of Solomon,[5] and the prophets of the eighth century can still declare that Jahveh has at Jerusalem a hearth which was ceaselessly burning, and a sacred fire.[6]

The particular time in the morning or the evening when this sacrifice never failed to rise aloft, was according to all indications, the same as that when, as has been just said, the incense was daily kindled on the more refined altar of the inner sanctuary. The time was so universally known, and the sacrifice with the prayers which undoubtedly accompanied it, was deemed so sacred, that use was made of it in common life to distinguish two of the hours of the day,[7] and it gradually became customary for the pious all over the country to pray daily at the same hours.[8]

[1] Num. xxviii. 1-10; comp. Ex. xxix. 39-42; Lev. vi. 1-6 [8-13]; ix. 17.
[2] P. 51.
[3] See *Hist.* ii. 218 sqq.
[4] *Hist.* ii. 218 sqq.; with which we may compare the gleaming jewel, bright at night and dull by day, in the temple of the Syrian Hierapolis, Lucian, *De Dea Syra*, c. xxxii.
[5] Comp. *Hist.* iii. 246 sq.
[6] Is. xxxi. 9. The Samaritan Chronicle, xli., also gives an account of the dying out of the sacred sacrificial fire.
[7] According to 1 Kings xviii. 29, 36; 2 Kings iii. 20.
[8] This daily prayer at certain hours of the day was not, it is true, fully developed and in general use among the people, before those later times when, as we have shown (p. 14) prayer generally became a real popular power. Allusions are, however, already made to a similar, more informal, custom among pious individuals in Ps. cxli. 2; v. 4 [3]. Mid-day is

There was, however, in the earliest times still another sacrifice which the high-priest, as suited his peculiarly lofty position and importance (of which we shall speak later), offered up every morning and evening as his own. This was very simple—a corn-offering, which was reckoned as a full burnt-offering,[1] and was half the size of the one which was daily offered on behalf of the kingdom along with the flesh-offering. It is plainly something extremely ancient, and very different in kind from the other fire-offerings.[2] It is, nevertheless, possible that this more simple sacrifice gradually ceased after the animal-offering became prevalent.

THE SACRED APPLIANCES, PLACES, AND BUILDINGS.

An altar can be dispensed with by no religion which attaches importance to sacrifice by fire, and the extraordinary importance which was attached to it in the pre-Mosaic times has already been explained. The altar is in the first instance nothing but a hearth for fire; but this very fact caused it to become the centre of all divine worship, and the sacred spot where earth and heaven have their meeting-place, where religion seeks to impart her whole strength to man, to reveal to him what is most full of mystery, and to exhaust before him what is most inexhaustible. All religion, especially all true religion, is a reciprocal relation between God and Man; all real religion, is an intercourse between them. The altar, and the man standing opposite to it, only declare that this reciprocal relation and intercourse, as certainly as it had once existed, and as certainly as the altar stands there, shall continue to be renewed and to operate for ever. If it is the case that all other symbols of religion which are displayed to men serve to indicate this mutual intercourse, and their very existence is an exhortation unto its accomplishment,[3] still the altar,

---

added to morning and evening by the poet in Ps. lv. 18, but he is only speaking freely.

[1] Luther translates it here and elsewhere in similar cases by *Speisopfer* [A.V. 'meat-offering'].

[2] We are, it is true, acquainted with this offering only from Lev. vi. 12-16 [19-23] (where it is an utter mistake to think of a single offering of dedication made once for all by the high-priest), but the words מִנְחָה תָּמִיד in ver. 13 [20], comp. Num. xxviii. 3, allow no other meaning; and possibly the same sacrifice is intended in Num. iv. 16, as the name מִנְחָה is convertible in other authors (Judg.

vi. 18, and p. 36 above) with עֹלָה, but never in the Book of Origins. For the rest, compare p. 48 sq.

[3] E.g. it may be, at a still more simple stage of religion, a sacred stone, about which more is said below. Every object, however, simple and rude it may be, which is employed just for reminding men of what is Divine, may be termed a *fetish*, if people like the name; it is better, however, in Antiquity to avoid the modern word. It is, however, true that it was almost as natural then to hallow certain trees or staffs. *Sanchuniathon.* p. 8. ed. Orelli; *Evang. Luth. Missionsblatt*, 1849, s. 36 sqq. How arbitrarily a *Qibla* could

as the hearth of the fire which mounts to heaven, has the advantage of representing the perpetual realisation of this intercourse, while at the same time, in the absence of other symbols which have been given historically, and are therefore more definite, it is the one nearest to hand and the most indispensable. The numerous ways in which it received further special honours from sacrifices, and how it came to be regarded as the unique and lofty centre of the whole sacred rite, have already been described.[1]

1. An altar, therefore, was all that was originally wanted, and we know that it was enough even for the people of Israel in the very earliest pre-Mosaic times; wherever a patriarch settles down for a while, there he builds an altar.[2] On the other hand, it was a most ancient custom in Canaan to erect a monument of stone, either quite simple or more elaborate, as the memorial of a place which man gratefully remembered as the spot where he had drawn near to the Divine presence;[3] and such a one would also be naturally erected where a single individual, or a family, or a tribe, or nation felt themselves surprised by an exhibition of the Divine nearness and favour for which they had not looked, and which took place before an altar had been built there.[4] Sacred monuments of stone of just this character formed from early times one of the main peculiarities of Canaan and of the other regions lying round about the country where the Hebrews and the races allied to them dwelt, and the preference for the purpose of stones remarkable for their strange origin, colour, or form, can only be ascribed to the same cause.[5] Indeed, we can almost follow the whole history of the Palestinian-Syrian religions in the wide difference in the views regarding, and in the application of, such sacred stones. In the primeval days—more than two thousand years before the birth of Christ—when the Patriarchs lived, many of the Canaanites may have used a sacred stone as a mere monumental symbol of a god, and consecrated and anointed it, as is related of Jacob.[6] At that time there must in particular have been one sacred stone of the kind in the middle of the country at Bethel, which was deemed of great sanctity, so that the

---

he issued only to get a fixed point for direction of prayer is seen from *Sûr.* x. 87.

[1] Pp. 44-46.

[2] This is the account of the oldest sources about Jacob, Gen. xxxv. 1, 3, 7, also of the Fourth Narrator, in regard to all the ancients, Gen. viii. 20; xii. 7; xiii. 4, 18; xxii. 9; comp. xxvi. 25.

[3] According to Gen. xxxi. 35, where

this custom is presupposed, Lev. xxvi. 1, and other passages cited below.

[4] Of which Gen. xxviii. 10-22, gives the ever valid type.

[5] Like the black stone of the Ka'ba at Mecca.

[6] Gen. xxviii. 18 sq.; xxxv. 14 sq.: comp. Tacitus, *Hist.* ii. 2 sq.; Dion Cassius, *Hist.* xvi. 33.

Hebrews and the Canaanites struggled for centuries for its possession (as the Arabs did for the Ka'ba).[1] It is always the name of the one patriarch, Jacob (Israel), about which the strongest recollections cling from primitive times of his having attached so great an importance to a stone, and, before all, to this stone at Bethel; and down from those earliest days when the people was still a race of wandering shepherds, there was retained the designation of its God as the *shepherd of the stone of Israel*.[2] But even down to the time of David, the numerous local names compounded with the word -*stone*, prove, when taken along with these ancient legends, what a sanctity these stones possessed in the popular estimation.[3] While, however, 'Jacob's stone' at Bethel was deemed so sacred in the eyes of that people, and the ancient feeling was so hard to eradicate, the Phœnicians even gave the name of *Bätylos*[4] to an ancient god who had certainly at one time been highly reverenced by them at the place of this very stone, and sacred magic stones generally they termed *bätylien*; and while in Israel even this stone continually lost more and more of its sanctity, as the true religion was more and more developed from the days of Moses, stones received among the Phœnicians and other heathens an increasing superstitious reverence, their character varied more and more (pillars and portable stones being the most common), and the smaller round portable ones were deemed to be living things with which men versed in magic liked to practise their art.[5]

When man came to possess an image of the Deity, some kind or other of shelter or case was allotted to it, or even a house, this being at first certainly a very small one.[6] But it is plain that in the earliest times, each separate household began

---

[1] *Hist.* i. 302 sq., 343 sqq.; ii. 277 sqq.
[2] *Hist.* i. 409 sqq.
[3] Comp. the narrative given in *Hist.* ii. 427. The Eben-ha'ézer, 1 Sam. vii. 12, something like our *Helfenstein* [helping-stone] is already mentioned, iv. 1. v. 1. only for the sake of more clearly describing the mere locality, for it was undoubtedly not another place.
[4] Comp. the Deus Carmelus of Karmel. Tac. *Hist.* ii. 78.
[5] *Sanchuniathon*, p. 26, 30, 18, ed. Orel., with the essay on the Phœnician views of the creation of the world, pp. 24, 62. Comp. further the reminiscences in Livy, xxix. 11; Pliny, *Nat. Hist.* xxxvii. 51; Pausanias, *Perieg.*, ix, 27, 48; x. 24; Porphyr. *Vita Pyth.* c. xvii., and especially Damaskius in Photius's *Bib-*

lioth. i. p. 342, 348, ed. Bekker, as well as the remarks of Theophylact, according to Cyril, on Acts vii. 43. Similar, if not so highly developed, superstitions existed among the Greeks (see Æsch. *Eum.* ver. 41; O. Müller's *Orchomenos*, s. 179, 211; Gerhard, in the *Berlin. akad. Abhandl.* 1818, s. 277 sq.), and the Hindoos (see O. Frank, in the *Münch. akad. Abhandl.* 1834, s. 613 sq., 837). See also Theoph. *Ad Autolykum*, i. 15; Irby and Maugles, *Travels in Arabia Petr.* p. 461. الزب
Sûr. v. 4: *Ausland*, 1849, s. 510 sq., 514. Ehrenberg in the *Berl. akad. Monatsberichten*, 1849, s. 345 sqq.; *DMGZ*. 1853, ss. 498, 500, and 1864, ss. 452, 456 sq.—For the rest comp. more below, and the *Jahrb. d. Bibl. Wiss.* v. s. 287 sq.
[6] This is seen from Jud. xvii. 5.

by coveting an image of this kind for itself alone, in order that it might be able to enjoy quite privately the perpetual aspect and immediate proximity of its divine protector. It was placed by the hearth as the innermost sanctuary of the house, and kept locked up in a case only in troubled times.[1] It was already a higher stage when a whole nation desired to assemble round an image of its god in the same way as the family had done. Not till this was the case would the images as well as the corresponding receptacles or *houses* probably be much larger and more handsome.

The highest summits of the earth have always been deemed places essentially sacred; but in these countries a certain sanctity was also attached, from a most remote period, to some kinds of long-lived wide-spreading trees, so that men, especially when they wished for some sort of sacred worship in valleys and plains, liked to celebrate their rites, erect their altars, and keep their other sacred possessions, under the shade of one of these trees.[2] Such was the condition of local sanctuaries in the earliest times, according to all the traces which we can still discover.

Jahveism, which, at any rate in its stricter conceptions rejected all idols from the very first, could at no time tolerate a 'house of God' of the kind that had hitherto been customary; and the truth that every house of God, however great and however magnificent human hands may make it, will yet always possess features which have little correspondence with the full majesty of Jahveh, is one to which it bore clear witness, especially on all decisive occasions, although here too in the course of centuries, art tried what it could do in the matter.[3]—Nor could sacred trees or groves agree with the spirit of Jahveism, so that all the remnants of the old Canaanitish superstition

---

[1] This also may be seen equally clear from Jud. xvii. 5 sqq., and other traces of the early religion which will be explained below.

[2] As is even still clear from the reminiscences of the patriarchs, *Hist.* i. 302 sq. The same belief is familiar in just those northern districts whence the patriarchs came, see Mose von Chorene, i. 15, 19; Tschamtschean, *Armen. Alterth.* i. 13; Assemani's *Bibl. Or.* iii. 1, p. 492 sq. For the rest comp. *DMGZ.* 1853, ss. 481, 483; Spence-Hardy's *Eastern Monachism*, p. 25, 212 sqq., 325 sq., and Lajard's *Recherches sur la Culte du Cyprès pyramidal*, p. 65 sqq. For palms, as oracle-trees, see Orpheus, *Fragm.* 40, p. 496, Herm. See how vividly the belief is still described in Ibn-'Arabshah's *Fak.* in the omen furnished by the viridity or non-viridity of a grand old palm-tree.

[3] 2 Sam. vii. 6 sqq.; BK. Is. lxvi. 1 sqq. No doubt this same simplicity in this matter might be found also among certain nations, partly inherited from primeval times, partly due to the reaction described on p. 71. So Origen, *Contr. Cels.* vii. 8. 1, maintains that neither the Scythians, the Lybian Nomads, the Seres, nor the Persians, had either temples, pillars, or images. Still more to the purpose is the instance of the simple altar of the Phœnicians on Mount Carmel, Tac. *Hist.* ii. 78.

which still lingered on in subsequent times, or which crept
back again among the people, were continually more and more
decidedly regarded as heathenish.¹ The high places of the earth,
on the other hand, had something of a sacred character even for
the earliest Jahveism. Just because this religion was utterly
unable any longer to find and to hold fast its God in any single
earthly object which was visible and could be handled, it was
all the more eager and anxious to find the tokens of his existence and activity, at any rate, in heaven and in all heavenly
phenomena, and therefore in the clouds which touch the highest
and holiest spots of earth. This was a primitive belief, which
maintained itself in Israel down to later days, and was not
severely shaken until the highest and most illustrious sanctuary
of the nation was permanently established on the but slightly-
elevated Mount Zion, before which the incomparably higher
peaks of the earth now seemed to bow their heads for ever.²
But even when the old belief was beginning gradually to waver,
a piece of rocky ground, at any rate, was selected by preference as the best locality for an altar.³

While to early Jahveism the places of the earth which were
high and difficult of access were long regarded as spots which
had ever been sacred, nevertheless in its legislation it always
held fast to a lofty truth, which was far more special to itself,
viz. that wherever the true God reveals himself to men, even if
it be in the valley or the desert, the ground is sacred to him ;⁴
and in the earliest tones of the law the happy promise is heard,
' Everywhere where I let my name be praised, will I come to
thee,'⁵ an utterance closely resembling that of the Gospels,
' Where two or three are gathered together in my name,' &c.
Many an ancient reminiscence of the former roving life of the
people, and the revival of it under Moses, might here unite
with some of the less restricted sympathies of the new religion
which was working its way up under his influence, so as to
clothe such a view with even a legal sanctity. An altar of this
kind, according to the same earliest law, ought to be built in
the simplest manner possible of nothing but turf. If, however,
it were desired to build one of stone, the stones must not be

---

¹ See below under the review of
heathenism.
² Ps. lxviii. 16 sq. [15 sq.]
³ According to Jud. vi. 20; xiii. 19.
But just lately there has been discovered,
on the same place where formerly Solomon's Temple stood, the *rock* which was
covered over by the *Ssachrâ Moschee*,
الصخرة whose name is derived thence.

How Isaiah deals with this *rock* or *stone*
from his own point of view may be seen
from Is. viii. 14 sq.; xxviii. 16; xxxi. 9.
⁴ The Fourth Narrator represents this
most magnificently, Gen. xxviii. 10–22;
comp. xvi. 13; xxi. 14–19.
⁵ Book of Covenants, Ex. xx. 24;
comp. xxiv. 4.

artificially hewn, so as to have been much touched by human hands and tools [1]—a prohibition which is similar to the command to offer no sacrificial animals which had in any way been desecrated, but which is a remarkable expression of the spirit of this earliest Jahveism. Stone monuments of the heathen sort were, it is true, forbidden distinctly enough,[2] but the old custom lingered on of erecting twelve monumental stones—one for each of the tribes—at a celebrated place where the whole people desired to offer thanksgiving and sacrifice to their God.[3] The same purpose was served by a single stone of larger size under a tree,[4] irrespective of any special sanctity in the latter. And it was but a slight modification of the primitive custom to use twelve stones to build an altar large enough for the solemnity of the occasion when it was to serve for the whole of Israel.[5]

2. But this extreme simplicity which prevailed under Moses, and for some time after him, did not remain very long, and there are several causes to account for the fact. In the *first* place, many an object within the sphere of a new religion will quite imperceptibly become invested with an extraordinary sanctity, though it arose at first very simply out of the needs of the time, and claimed originally, on its own behalf, no special holiness.

This is the case with the *Ark of the Covenant*, whose original position was the following. A chest is used for keeping documents, jewels, and sacred articles, therefore for signs or images of a god, when these, as was customary in the earliest days, were of small size;[6] the Ark of the Covenant had essentially no other purpose. But for Israel the most precious and sacred things of inestimable value, to be kept in such a chest, were—so far as they were preserved in writing—just the great truths and divine commands on which its whole earthly existence rested, as well as its faith and its hopes. And we know that in that chest the two stone slabs of the earliest law, and consequently of the earliest contract between Jahveh and the people, were preserved; and with equal right the documents of other laws and contracts of supreme importance might have been deposited there. Nothing is more characteristic of the earliest Jahveism, nor yet of greater historical truth and certainty, than that in

---

[1] Also Ex. xx. 24 sq.
[2] Lev. xxvi. 1, according to *Hist.* ii. 165, from a very early fragment. Ex. xxiii. 24.
[3] Ex. xxiv. 4; BK. Josh. iv. 2 sqq.
[4] BK. Josh. xxiv. 26.
[5] 1 Kings xviii. 30-32.
[6] This has been rediscovered even among the ancient Mexicans, comp. J. G. Müller's *Amerik. Urreligionen*, s. 594. Something similar has lately been discovered in the Phœnician Amrit; comp. Renan's *Mission de Phénicie*, p. 67.

place of the idols in which common heathenism took delight and of certain artificial symbols which served the same purpose for a heathenism which was aiming at something higher, it was only the documents of these purest truths and of these contracts, concluded as it were for all eternity, which acquired the most precious value and the highest sanctity.

It was in accordance with this fact that all the special arrangements connected with this chest were made. It was certainly constructed in the desert, a fact shown by every indication, and as we should suppose from the description of its component parts in the Book of Origins.[1] The very durable wood of the acacia-tree, which grows in certain places in the desert, was taken for the purpose. Its length was two and a half ells, its breadth and height one and a half. Inside and out it was covered with thin plates of gold, and further adorned with a sort of ripple of gold running round it,—a form of construction which, as regards materials and decoration, exactly reappears in the sacred table and great altar, to be described further on. But as this chest was to have contents so precious, two Cherubim were fixed over it, to symbolise the fact that Jahveh had, as it were, descended upon it, and eternally protected what was contained in the chest. For the Cherub signified in the first instance the descent of the Deity, and consequently the spot whither it had descended and would again descend perpetually, and there manifest itself.[2] In this symbolical application the Cherub was also much utilised elsewhere,—in the sacred tent and in the temple, as will be shown below. But its primary and most significant position was over the Ark of the Covenant, where, for artistic reasons, two were placed lying face to face;[3] and in this application they indicate, in the first instance, how strict is Jahveh's watch and guard over the sacred words contained therein. The two Cherubim were fixed to a plate of pure gold, which was suspended as a footstool over the ark, and was like a second cover of corresponding length and breadth, but separable from it. Its proper name was 'the footstool,'[4] and

[1] Ex. xxv. 10-22; xxxvii. 1-9; xl. 20 sq.
[2] I have said sufficient on this point in the *Propheten des A. B.* vol. ii. s. 220.
[3] So far, no doubt, the Sphynxes lying facing one another over a sacred shrine or sepulchre, etc., are very similar, see *Description de l'Egypte antiq.* pl. i. 11, 12; Wilkinson's *Manners and Customs*, second series, ii. p. 276, and Lepsius's *Denkmäler*, iii. bl. 14; Fellows's *Second Excursion in Lycia*, p. 185, along with the picture accompanying it. Comp. also the *K. S. G. Berichte*, 1854, ss. 54-62. There is a remarkable representation of a Garuda (i.e. a cherub), as the altar for the ancient Indian horse-sacrifice, *Râmâyana*, i. 13. 30 (28 Gorr.). But the greatest resemblance of all is found in some lately discovered Assyrian pictures, which are given in Layard's *Monuments of Nineveh*.
[4] כַּפֹּרֶת can by no means signify simply the cover, as though the chest had no other; for it would have one of its own,

it indicated the spot where Jahveh had, as it were, his footstool and abode. The two Cherubim, constructed of similar gold, lay over it, with their faces turned one to the other, and spread wide their mighty wings, as though protecting the ark. How deep was the space which separated this second covering from the first we do not precisely know, but we may very well suppose that there must have been room enough underneath the 'footstool' for the lid of the ark to have been opened and shut. No other sacred article was similarly distinguished; for none included in itself such an infinite depth of meaning, or called to mind anything so superlatively glorious and sacred as did this ark with the equipment we have described.

Now if this ark had of itself, from the very beginning, a significance so lofty that it could not but be deemed the most sacred of all the sacred externals, then in the days after Moses the reverence felt towards it must ever have been on the increase. It held the documents of the law in its greatest purity and of the covenant in its fullest divinity, as they were guarded by Jahveh himself. Thus it became the representative of the presence of Jahveh himself among the community,[1] the symbol and pledge of all the revelations and promises of this God, and accordingly a place was allotted to it in the Holy of Holies of the sacred tent or house. This would make it seem more sacred than the altar itself, and on occasion of the most solemn sacrifices, e.g. at the annual Festival of Atonement the blood was sprinkled on the footstool which hung over it,[2] as the most sacred of all visible

whilst the *Cappóret* is described from the first, Ex. xxv. 17-21; xxvi. 34, as something of different dimensions, and elsewhere in other respects as separable, and as an object of special importance in itself more important even than the ark. The word is manifestly very ancient, and only to be found now in this meaning, but it clearly denotes a stool, being formed from כפר, i.e. to rub off, scrape off (to obliterate, and therefore to *forgive* guilt), just as *seamnum* or *seabellum* from *seahere*, and just as גָּבִי, 2 Chron. ix. 18, a word of similar derivation and meaning, takes its name from *treading*. There is also a correspondence even in the Ethiopic word ደጐላፊ, which is plainly a passive formation from a word of similar signification. The word is formed like בָּרְכַת, according to *Lehrbuch*, § 166 a. In the legendary history, according to the Book of Covenants, the corresponding feature is 'the work of art of gleaming sapphire,' which was to be seen under the feet of Jahveh when he had descended on to Mount Sinai, Ex. xxiv. 10. – Moreover, it is the Ark of the Covenant which first gives the name to Jahveh of 'him who is enthroned upon the cherubim.'

[1] Just as the expression 'before Jahveh' is convertible with 'before the revelation,' i.e. the ark in the Holy of Holies, Ex. xvi. 33 sq.

[2] The LXX already think that the name כַּפֹּרֶת owes its origin to this circumstance, as though it denoted atonement, lid of atonement. This conjecture was not far wrong, for, as has been said above, כפר can also signify the effacing of guilt. But in this case, the ornament could, from the very beginning, have served for no other purpose than for expiation, which is quite impossible. The LXX also begin by translating the word very freely by ἱλαστήριον ἐπίθεμα, and it was only gradually ἱλαστήριον alone came to take its place, although the latter

places, and the step nearest to heaven. For it will be easily understood that this footstool assumed far greater prominence than did the mere ark, from which it might be distinguished as absolutely the most sacred of all places. It seems as though the people had had still so imperative a craving to represent materially and locally the presence of the Divine Being in its midst, that this ark became gradually more and more of a centre, both for the whole nation and for the priesthood and the invisible sanctuary, and this in peaceful sojourn as well as in roaming and in war.

But soon the consecrated receptacle passed into a new stage of its existence. As it contained the highest ancient revela- 142 tions, so, too, it was but natural that new ones should proceed from its mysterious interior,—that, at any rate, the high-priest should receive the oracle which he sought for most easily and correctly in its immediate neighbourhood. This is the aspect in which the Book of Origins especially treats of the sacred ark. What Moses had placed inside, it calls absolutely the 'revelation,' or more properly the sacred convention (parley), to which a peculiar name is given here;[1] the ark it invariably terms 'the ark of revelation,'[2] and even the place in the Holy of Holies where this stood it also calls simply the 143

---

is already so used in Philo's *Vita Mos.* iii. 8. Saadia, on the other hand, held fast to the idea of ἐπίθεμα, and translated it, *covering, lid*. The same conclusion has been reached by J. D. Michaelis and the moderns generally, without their thinking that כפר cannot possibly allow this meaning, and that כפרת must merely from its formation be an architectural expression similar to פרכת.

[1] Ex. xxv. 16, 21; xl. 20. The expression עדות will only become clear when we remember that, 1) in the Book of Origins, מועד is not only convertible with עדה in the sense of 'congregation,' Num. i. 16; xvi. 2; xxvi. 9, but in the connection אהל מ, sometimes also with עדת, Num. xviii. 2-6; xvii. 22 [7] sq.; ix. 15; comp. מִשְׁכַּן הָעֵדֻת, which always stands thus; 2) when either the ark or the sacred tent is spoken of, these nouns are sometimes explained by a corresponding verb, Ex. xxix. 22; xxix. 42 sq.; xxx. 6, 36; Num. xvii. 19 [4]. We cannot doubt that עדת signifies the revelation (or a legal code thence derived) so far as God and man meet together in it, and speak to and understand one another; whilst מועד rather indicates the place of it, and is therefore coupled with the word *tent*. The meaning, 'tent of the assembly,' in favour of which the words Num. x. 3 sq., may be cited, destroys the manifest connection of מועד with עדת, and is contrary to the spirit of Antiquity. The roots ועד and עוד are therefore convertible here, according to *Lehrbuch*, § 117 sq.; but the LXX have derived the words incorrectly from עד, *witness*, and translate by μαρτύριον, which could, however, give a meaning in so far as every convention is an attestation. In perfect correspondence both as regards origin and signification are the Arabic ࢩ‎, and, with the ancient termination in -*ân* (which is essentially the same as the -*ût*), the Ethiopic ነቋሬ:, where *k* interchanges with ע. The allied meaning of *witness* is also to be met with, but this is more frequently expressed by ࢩ‎, ࢩ‎.

[2] Also 'the ark for the revelation,' Ex. xxxi. 7.

'revelation.'[1] It thinks that on to that stool with the Cherubim the glory of Jahveh himself descended, as it were, in a cloud,[2] and, according to it, Jahveh even promised to speak to Moses on that very spot, and reveal himself for Israel.[3] With this persistent view of the Book of Origins is connected, as we cannot fail to recognise, that excessively high reverence felt for the ark in the centuries between Moses and Solomon, about which the historical books tell us. And in war-time this greatest sacred possession of the people was, in the first instance, carried about with them not merely in order that they might be protected by it, as by a miraculous image which could be handled and kissed (for so deep into heathenism Israel could never really sink), but in order that, with the aid of the high-priest, it might be everywhere used as the seat of the oracle,[4] and, of course, also in order that they might rejoice over it as over the presence of Jahveh himself during the greatest crises of their lives. Accordingly its capture by the Philistines gave the first powerful blow to this oldest religion.[5]

By the 'revelation' to be placed by Moses in the ark, the Book of Origins undoubtedly intended the two stone tables of the law;[6] and we can still understand enough to see plainly that they were deemed by it to have been given to Moses by God himself, but the passage where this book speaks explicitly on the point is now lost. The old Book of Covenants simply makes Moses write down the Ten Commandments, and they belong to it as part of the Covenant Book.[7] But from the time of Moses to the building of Solomon's temple there is not likely to have been any one who dared to open the ark. Important legal documents, which came into existence after Moses, were not deposited in, but by it.[8] When it was opened and newly decorated on the occasion of the building of Solomon's temple,[9] the writing on the slabs may already have become antiquated, and so the more easily have been supposed to have been written by the finger of God.[10] It was certainly less and

---

[1] Ex. xvi. 34; xxvii. 21; xxx. 6, 36; Lev. xvi. 13; xxiv. 3; Num. xvii. 19, 25. [4, 10].
[2] Lev. xvi. 2.
[3] Ex. xxv. 22, and the similar passages quoted on the preceding page.
[4] We might, therefore, consider the reading of the Masoretic text in 1 Sam. xiv. 18 (comp. *Hist.* iii. 34), to be correct—as against the LXX ἐφούδ in particular, no one would say the 'Ephod of God'—if only the passage were quite trustworthy in other respects.
[5] See *Hist.* ii. 412 sq.
[6] This follows from Ex. xl. 20: comp. xxv. 16, 21, although there is no mention here of slabs. After Ex. xxxi. 17, the Book of Origins must have further represented how Jahveh gave this agreement to Moses in writing, but what now stands in ver. 18 is but a poor remnant of it.
[7] Ex. xxiv. 4, 7.
[8] 1 Sam. x. 25 (so to be understood) Deut. xxxi. 26.
[9] See *Hist.* iii. 242.
[10] This is first said in the passage,

less used, as time went on, for the purpose of seeking oracles, just as was the case with the grand attire of the high-priest, which is spoken about further on. It, therefore, completely lost the name which it bears in the Book of Origins,[1] and all later writers call it the 'Ark of the Covenant of God,' or, more briefly, the ark of the covenant, or the ark of God.

These facts further show us how peculiar to the people of Israel was this greatest of their sacred possessions, and what slight grounds there are for regarding it as a mere imitation of the sacred things of other nations. For it can be easily understood that heathen religions, too, might possess a sacred chest which contained their most sacred objects, which were to be exhibited to the people only on certain festivals, and which the priests might carry round in solemn procession.[2] As far as this goes, Moses introduced nothing new; but just as the contents of the ark were quite exceptional, so, too, was its position as the centre of all that is holy.

The existence of the ark of the covenant and its sanctity—which went on increasing for centuries—was the first and most powerful cause which put an end to the primitive extreme simplicity of the sacred appliances. A *second* cause may be found in the necessity which was soon recognised for founding, in the midst of the whole great community, a single sanctuary of corresponding greatness and worthy of its position. When, after the first founding of the community all its arrangements acquired some stability, it became necessary that it should have, somewhere or other, a more permanent sacred place, or else, in some way or other, a more permanent symbol of such, round which the community could always assemble in a manner worthy of its entirety. If it did not suffer this place to remain a mere simple altar, but adorned it with its finest decorations, it thereby only paid honour to itself, and did what was demanded not, it is true, by the stricter side of its religion, but by human feelings and human thankfulness. Every ancient nation honoured its gods with costly sanctuaries, and gladly erected for them the most superb house at the place which it made its own centre of rejoicing. Israel neither could nor would be left behind in this display of zeal.[3] Its task was only this, to

---

Ex. xxxi. 18, then with a notable increase of strength by the Fourth Narrator of the primitive history, Ex. xxxii. 15 sq.; xxxiv. 1, and on this Deut. x. 4, is based.

[1] There is just one exception to this in BK. Josh. iv. 16, owing to imitation of the name in the Book of Origins.

[2] It is to be found even among the Greeks (Gerhard, in the *Berl. akad. 'Abh.* 1847, s. 492). For similar circumstances among the Phœnicians see the *Abh. über die Phönik. Ansichten von der Weltschöpfung* (Gött. 1851), s. 19.

[3] Comp. the way in which the Book of Origins represents this, Ex. xxv. 1 sqq.; xxxv. 20 sq.

make the great sanctuary which it erected in its midst correspond as closely as possible to Jahveism.

A *third* cause, moreover, lay finally in the institution at this sacred central point of never-ceasing sacrificial rites. This, we have already seen, existed even in Israel, which had, moreover, to unite the two essentially different kinds of the table- and of the fire-offering, so that to the sacred hearth there was necessarily added at the same time a *sacred table*.[1] This perpetual sacrificial service (to be further discussed below) is most intimately associated with a hereditary priesthood, which, as will be further described hereafter, developed itself sufficiently early in the community, and separated itself from the latter tolerably sharply. As then this ceaseless sacrifice at the sacred place demanded special arrangements, so, too, the separation from the rest of the community of hereditary priests who were specially charged with this duty, led the way to a similar separation also in the Sanctuary and its appliances.

The cooperation of all these causes led before long to the establishment of a special sacred house or tent, more briefly termed *the Sanctuary*,[2] with numerous appliances and fixed institutions, as will be described below in its place. And even these appliances, belonging to this great sanctuary in the centre of the people along with the building itself, gradually acquired a certain sanctity, even if none of them could rival that of the ark of the covenant. More will be said on the matter below under the Priesthood.

3. Along with this great central Sanctuary, there existed, in the earlier days of the community, a multitude of smaller ones, for the most part consisting of nothing but an altar with a stone monument. We can have as little doubt of the original plurality of sanctuaries as of the fact that, during the period of the healthier and stronger national life, a stricter unity of the national religious life was sought through the establishment, in the midst of this plurality, of a single great sanctuary. Just because, in the oldest times, there were a multitude of sacred places, the individual altars were distinguished by special names. These, however, were not, as in Christendom, borrowed from early saints (*St. John*, &c.), but were derived

---

[1] See pp. 113 sqq., 27. In this way we still find in heathen temples many τράπεζαι of the kind dedicated to a god merely in accordance with a vow. *Revue Archéol.* 1866, i. p. 105 sq., 224.

[2] הַמָּקוֹם in the Book of Origins, Ex. xxv. 8; nк. Jesh. xxiv. 26, and elsewhere. This, as the name of a place, is easily distinguished from the sacraments (p. 108) designated by the same word. It is expressed in passages specially concerned with it more briefly, קֹדֶשׁ. Ex. xxvi. 33; xxviii. 43; xxix. 30; xxxv. 19; xxxix. 1.

more immediately from great historical events which the people had themselves experienced. Thus it is related how, after the victory over Amalek, Moses erected an altar and called it 'Jahveh my banner.'[1] This monument of the old warlike days of the community certainly existed not far from Sinai down into later times, and the Israelites may have long laid claim to it, if (as is related of Elijah) they made pilgrimages to Sinai. When, after the conquest of Canaan, every tribe possessed its own province, and in each of these provinces certain Levitical cities were to be found, each of these forty-eight towns would contain its own altar.[2] What relation existed between these smaller sanctuaries and the great one we do not exactly know; probably the perpetual sacrificial service[3] was maintained in its majestic splendour only at the centre of the community. —But at any other place, down to the reign of Solomon, it was a natural thing to erect an altar,[4] at any place, e.g. where a man had received a special favour from heaven, and desired to return solemn thanks for it by means of sacrifice;[5] sufficient reason for one was even to be found in the old strict law to slay no domestic animal without solemnly sprinkling its blood on an altar,[6] and the extremely simple construction of all that was needful,[7] rendered it possible to erect one with very little delay.

But in this plurality of altars there was always a danger, attaching, in particular, to such as were remote from the central sanctuary, of their being gradually misapplied for purposes of strange religions, or of the Jahveism in connection with them not retaining its strict purity. This, at certain periods, may have been of frequent occurrence, and in times when the unity of the nation became impaired, a further danger soon appeared, that, viz., of several larger sanctuaries being formed in the outlying districts. To this must be added, that a sacrificial service, if it is to be carried on in a worthy manner, always seems to be increasing its demands for costly and difficult preparations, as will be further shown below in treating of the priesthood. Reasons such as these induced men to think during the better days of David of establishing a stricter unity, and when an immense step in that direction had been ventured on in the

---

[1] Ex. xvii. 15: comp. xxiv. 4; the short account of the latter passage is certainly very ancient, like the verse xxxiv. 16. For similar cases see *Hist.* i. 303, and Judg. vi. 24. So far what is said in *Hist.* ii. 100, must be somewhat qualified.

[2] *Hist.* ii. 308 sqq.

[3] P. 113.

[4] As Judg. vi. 24–28; xxi. 4; 1 Sam. vii. 17; xvi. 2–5.

[5] As 2 Sam. xxiv. 18 sqq.

[6] As Saul erected more than one of the kind, 1 Sam. xiv. 35.

[7] P. 121 sq.

building of Solomon's Temple, the Book of Origins seized every favourable opportunity to forbid sacrifice outside of the one proper place for it.[1] This, however, was far more rigidly insisted on by the Deuteronomist, after the kingdom of the Ten Tribes had made its attempt to procure a total repudiation of this seasonable claim.[2]

148 III. THE PROCEDURE OF DIVINE SERVICE IN THE COMMUNITY.

With the way in which divine service was celebrated by the priests when the great community was assembled, we are still tolerably well acquainted, at any rate in regard to certain main features.[3] The celebration was one of magnificent splendour, but on this very account of somewhat rare occurrence, and it was only at the annual festivals that it was on so large and complete a scale, as will be here described.

In the more ancient times the community was assembled in the early morning by the priests with the sound of trumpets and loud shouting, almost in the same way as if the summons were for battle.[4] In this not only the inferior, but also the higher priests, with trumpets peculiar to themselves, took an active part, a matter which will be spoken of below in connection with the priests.

One of the necessary consequences of the feelings of all Antiquity as they have been described above, was that sacrifice should form the commencement and most important part of the whole celebration. The sacrificial animals were solemnly brought in, the celebrants marched round the altar singing, perhaps going round it several times, and this would furnish an occasion

---

[1] Lev. xvii. 1-9; גַּם Josh. xxii. 10 sqq. On the other hand, this agrees with the fact that in 1 Kings xix. 10, the existence of many altars in the kingdom of the Ten Tribes is presupposed by Elijah himself, whose sphere of activity was there. In the same way he readily builds one himself, xviii. 30-32.

[2] Deut. xii. 5-14, 18-26; xiv. 22 sqq.; xvi. 2, 5 sqq.; xvii. 8 sqq. Comp. *Hist.* iv. 225.

[3] The chief passage from the older times is Lev. ix. 22-24. The description here is certainly very brief, giving little more than indications; and, moreover, in accordance with the habit of the Book of Origins, it is highly figurative.—But we may remember that a historical reality must correspond even to what is figurative, especially with this author. From the time of the Hagiocracy we have a more detailed description, though it suffers from rhetorical exaggeration, Sir. l. 5-21: comp. *Hist.* v. 273. But the two do not appear to contradict one another in main points, and it is of itself unlikely that the chief constituents and fundamental arrangements of the divine service should have been completely altered in later times. We must rather wonder at the casual similarity of the two which is something which may easily be overlooked.

[4] According to Joel i. 14; ii. 1: comp. Num. x. 2; Lev. xxiii. 2.

when most beautiful choruses might be sung in turns by the people and the priests.¹
The sacrificial priest would now come forward out of the sacred house invested with his official decorations. He would in like manner march round the altar singing, and ascend its steps, surrounded by other priests of the higher rank, probably at least twelve in number.² The fire on the sacred hearth had been made up long before, and all was now ready for the actual offering. The sacrificial priest then received from the hands of his subordinates the portions for the altar in order to place them on the hearth, whilst the congregation, beholding the proceedings with feelings full of awe, were engaged in prayer.³ If the celebration was a full one, the sacrifice consisted of a combination of its three main kinds, the expiatory-, the burnt-, and the thank-offering; the expiatory-offering coming first as a consecration, but being itself preceded by an expiatory- and a burnt-offering, which the sacrificial priest offered on his own account.⁴

The conclusion of the proper sacrificial proceedings was reached when the priest had poured out the drink-offering on the steps of the altar,⁵ and immediately the priests joined in exultantly with a loud trumpet-blast, but the whole community swiftly flung themselves to the ground, praying aloud.⁶ Not till this was over did the singing of the whole congregation, led by the sacerdotal singers (the Levites), commence. This was always of a highly elaborate character, especially after the time of David and Solomon.⁷ The intervals in it were in part filled up with alternate choruses,⁸ in part, also, when it seemed

---

¹ According to Lev. ix. 1–21; Sir. l. 5: comp. Ps. xxvi. 6; hence comes too the sacred name جَأَر or جَأْر; Iuurial-qais M. ver. 63. A song of this sort is certainly to be found in Ps. cxviii.: for the correct divisions of the periods, and entire meaning of which, see Die Dichter des Alten Bundes, I. b. s. 394 sqq. 3rd ed. Comp. also Ps. lxvi. 13 sqq.
² This number may be inferred from what is said, Hist. v. 189; comp. Sir. l. 12 sq.
³ All this according to Sir. l. 5–14: comp. Joseph. Antiq. xiii. 13. 5.
⁴ Lev. ix. 1–21; comp. xvi. 3 sqq.
⁵ P. 35.
⁶ According to Sir. l. 14–17.
⁷ Hist. iii. 248 sq., 282 sqq.
⁸ Of which we can see clear examples

and models in Ps. xx, xxi., lxxxv., cxv. A close investigation of the poems of the Old Testament undoubtedly reveals a most beautiful system of choruses at the solemn services of even the earliest times, as is more fully shown in the Dichter des A. B. I. a. s. 46 sqq., 172 sqq.—It is true that, according to Sir. l. 18, it seems as if in the days of the fully-developed Hagiocracy, only the Levites sang, while the people prayed in silence. But in those better times when songs like Ps. xx. were heard in the Temple, we have every reason to assume a closer participation of the whole congregation also in the singing. Only in the still earlier times antecedent to David does it seem to have been assumed that there would not be much singing or participation of the community in it, Lev. ix. 21 sq. But such brief description must be supplemented out of

needful, by shorter or longer addresses to God, succeeded—the face being turned in the opposite direction—by addresses to the assembled congregation;[1] and it was, of course, also the case that during the happy days when kingdom and theocracy were at one, the king as priest might deliver such addresses to the congregation either from his own place or from the altar.[2] Still the sacrificial priest remained standing on his elevated post all the time that the congregation were singing, and when that was over, before he descended, he pronounced with outstretched hands the blessing on the people.[3]—But after doing this he only went into the sacred house in order again to return thence to the neighbourhood of the altar, and after the gracious acceptance of the sacrifice by heaven, to speak to the congregation a few comprehensive words full of the highest sublimity, after which, with repeated blessing, he dismissed them.[4] It was here that the solemn rite attained its highest point, and it was then, at least according to reminiscences of the Mosaic days, that the glory and power of God often seemed to stream forth over the whole people, while at the same time the offering had risen joyously to heaven, and the people with loud exultant cries repeatedly sank down in prayer.

On one of these two occasions, probably with inconsiderable alterations on both of them, the priest accordingly uttered the benediction to the assembled congregation, which the Book of Origins has handed down to us,[5] and which without doubt always remained in use from the time of Moses. Simpler, and yet at the same time more pregnant and satisfying, nothing can be. It consists properly of three short half-poetical sentences, which gradually extend their length, each one (as in a verse) has a break in the middle, and all three, while constantly varying the words, only contrive to exhaust more and more

---

fuller ones, as Ex. xv. 1, and others; and at any rate the indisputable meaning of all parts of the poems is here decisive.

[1] We have some important examples in the speeches at the temple, 1 Kings viii. 12-61.

[2] See *Hist.* iii. 251.

[3] P. 42.

[4] That this second coming forth out of the sacred house was the more solemn, and that the whole divine service only then reached its highest point, is plainly involved in the description, Lev. ix. 22-24, where we must note that only then did Moses appear along with Aaron. We can understand now somewhat better the connection with the whole service in which we should regard the lofty answers in Ps. xx. 7 sq.; xxi. 9-13 [8-12]; lxxxv. 9-14 [8-13]; they were proclaimed as prophetic utterances on the return of the sacrificial priest, and before lxxxv. 9 [8], we can easily supply in idea the words 'I thought,' for the proper answer is first taken up in ver. 10 [9]. Comp. also the explanation, *Hist.* iii. 297 *note*. That this conclusion is altogether wanting in Sirach's description is a matter for great surprise; however ver. 21 is certainly to be read with the Compl. ἐδευτέρωσαν and ἐπιδέξασθαι, which alone gives it any meaning at all.

[5] Num. vi. 22-27; comp. *Hist.* ii. 21.

completely the one pure thought. The threefold repetition, therefore, only expresses thorough confidence; there are also other traces to show that in primitive times it was only a three times repeated Yes! which was accepted as regular and binding.[1] —A similar and probably shorter form of blessing was undoubtedly also pronounced at the commencement.[2]

Nevertheless, the grand feature of the divine service was always the sacrifice and its proper preparation and presentation. Here, as elsewhere throughout the whole of the ancient world, it was deemed an achievement of the highest but also of the most difficult nature, to draw down the Deity, as it were, with all its living power and aid quite close to man, this being regarded as only possible at such solemn moments as these. Here too the fear existed lest this Deity should be lightly lost, and what had been undertaken at so much cost should have been undertaken in vain. This will account for the anxious scrupulosity and timorous caution which characterised the whole procedure, for the rigid fencing-off of the consecrated space, and the deep dread of any disturbance,[3] and for the universal trembling and quaking at the most sacred moment of the rite.[4] This was but the strongest manifestation of what expressed itself in other respects when the Sanctuary became a visible object of the outer world, as will be further shown below in connection with the priests. Nevertheless, the best conclusion of the whole celebration was always deemed to be an exalted joy and cheerfulness irresistibly spreading forth below from the heavens above.[5]

These and similar facts we can learn clearly enough from the fragments of the ancient literature, and we may thence conclude how rich and stirring even in early days was the divine service of that nation whose religion was the most perfect in Antiquity.—In later times instruction in the law by the priests was added, perhaps during the middle of the day or at some other time when no sacrifice was offered.[6] But no doubt there was also much that was similar in earlier times.

---

[1] This is seen most clearly from Ex. xix. 8; xxiv. 3, 7, according to which the people have to answer 'yes' three times to a proposed law. What is essentially the same to be found in the members of the utterance about Canaan, Gen. ix. 25–27, and even in the words John xxi. 15–17, where the same is repeated thrice both as question and answer.

[2] According to 1 Kings viii. 14: comp. ver. 55.

[3] What is related in Ex. xix. 12 sq., 21–24, is only the highest of its kind, which, however, is just on this very account to be applied elsewhere. The same was the force of the *Procul profani* of the heathen mysteries: comp. *Hist.* iv. 100.

[4] What is related of it also in Ex. xix. 16, 18; xx. 18, can only be deemed here the highest of its kind.

[5] Lev. ix. 24.

[6] See *Hist.* v. 146.

SECOND SECTION.

THE OTHER SIDE : THE DIVINE DEMANDS FOR HOLINESS AND RIGHTEOUSNESS.

THE POWER OF INFLICTING PUNISHMENT.

1. Such then were the endeavours and exertions of man to press in upon the Deity in order to obtain from it that in which he felt himself to be deficient; and it was the aim of the laws of Jahveism either to mould and guide as much as possible in accordance with its own spirit all such forms of human activity, the force and employment of which were in existence long before itself, or else completely to transform and remodel them.

But all these divinely-human exertions and strivings, let them do what they will, were always met from the beginning by the divine demands for holiness and righteousness of life, demands which are universally valid and not to be rejected, which are so far from being dependent on these human exertions, that the first question is always whether the latter satisfy them in particular cases or in general, and which can even remain essentially unaltered when the insufficiency of many kinds of these human exertions has made itself manifest. These are just the eternal divine truths in their application to human life, so far as they can be plainly recognised in a religion, and at the same time be proclaimed as universally valid in their application to the infinitely various emergencies of human life. They form, therefore, a very important part of the privileges and of the laws without which ancient religion could not see how to exist, and which she drew into close partnership with herself.

In each religion, as well as in the laws of a community based upon that religion, all depends on the extent to which these paramount truths are known. Here, accordingly, ancient Jahveism first displayed its most intrinsic essence and its lofty speciality. And the exalted stage in this knowledge, which it had already attained at its very dawn, is revealed at once by the fact that it comprehends with the utmost clearness all the infinite variety of details which might give rise to questions, under a single fundamental principle, viz.

the divine command: 'Holy shall ye be, for holy am I.'[1] In these words the member of the community was referred to the absolutely perfect eternal authority which was totally free from moral deficiency. It was this of which it was even his duty to partake, which was therefore the measure of his obligation and for which he would not be too weak or poor. In all that he did or thought the member of this community was only to have before his eyes the unimpeachable pure sacred Being, something which he could indeed misconstrue, but could neither remove nor render inoperative, which would rather turn round upon and destroy him, so soon as he ceased to give it a lively recognition and appropriate it to himself. This utterance, therefore, involves the inexhaustible claim of a task that is infinite both as regards the individual and the community, and it already properly contains in itself all particular claims.

And just as Jahveism compressed with the utmost exactitude and truth into one main principle all the infinite variety which may here arise, so too it embraced all that it deemed sacred with an earnestness and decision of which there is no trace in lower religious and national constitutions. It raised itself far above much that the latter considered holy and salutary, but its grasp was all the firmer of whatever it did hold sacred. The moral strictness which characterised the community as a whole, as well as each particular tribe or household, was almost the only great force which the ancient nation possessed from the time of the establishment of Jahveism; and it was all the more indispensable, as during the pure Theocracy the highest authority could not be rendered visible and its presence shown to men. But how strict was the protection of whatever the community held sacred, and how long this state of things endured, has already been to some extent indicated in the particulars of its history, and will besides be touched upon below in many ways.

This extraordinarily strict discipline, which lasted with little diminution or change down to the time of Solomon, and which it is difficult for us fully to realise, by no means depended merely on the existing authority and the heads of the nation. On the contrary, Israel, subsequent to the leading of Moses, was so inured to it that the consciousness of its necessity and the actual practice of it extended to all the

---

[1] This is found at the head of the ancient fragment, Lev. xix, 2 sqq., but it is elsewhere repeated in the Book of Origins, xi. 44 sq.; xx. (7) 26; comp. xxi, 8; Num. xv. 40.

members of the nation, and its influence was not less exerted from below upwards, than in the contrary direction. In this respect the whole people felt at all times almost as a single closely united household, in which there dwelt something absolutely inviolable, holding all members together, and affording them protection and happiness, something whose violation and destruction would therefore be an affront to all, which all must indignantly repulse. A certain sphere of what was holy and pure for men, as well as conversely of what was vicious and to be avoided, had been distinctly defined by the foundation and primitive history of the community. Every violation of what was pure and holy, even though it were unintentional, was immediately punished and expiated with zealous severity, so that 'the majesty and the name of the guardian God of Israel might not be desecrated,' and no stain attach itself to his people, so that to Jahveh alone should honour and praise be rendered.[1] And should it be for the moment impossible to punish a desecration in this community, it was so little lost sight of, that long after, and under totally changed circumstances, the vengeance was inflicted, often with all the greater severity on account of the delay; and so vigilant was now the universal heed paid to every such violation, so powerful the dread of the 'wrath of Jahveh,' that people were ready to detect signs of it everywhere, and in every other misfortune which the community suffered they could see only the warning of an injured God. Indeed, it would often happen that such a misfortune would induce them to restore some insignificant, and, in other respects, despised member of the community to its rights even when the legal claim to them had been lost by prescription, e.g., a tribe under their protection which had been unfairly treated.[2] A discipline as strict, as watchful, even as painfully anxious, may indeed be found in other ancient kingdoms so long as they were contained within narrow limits, and had become neither too powerful through brilliant success in warfare, nor yet demoralised by misfortunes of another kind. But nowhere else in the ancient world do we find this spirit so strongly infusing a whole nation, nowhere is it equally persistent amid so many and such momentous changes, or does it serve to protect such important truths.

2. But should the Sanctity which alone ought to prevail in this community, and there carry on its work, be desecrated,

---

[1] Frequent expressions, as in the Book of Origins, BK. Josh. vii. 19; Amos ii. 7: comp. iii. 2; Jer. xxxiv. 16.

[2] Comp. the instances, *Hist.* ii. 351-353; iii. 135 sq., 214-215; iv. 98-99, and elsewhere.

whether by its members or by aliens, then the discipline which must oppose the offence, the penalty which may be attached to it, and the superintendence and precautions which have to keep a ceaseless watch over the observance, and anticipate any outrageous desecration, must in any case be under human management so far as human ability is available for the purpose, and the men who undertake the task must themselves belong to the community. Thus there arises an apparent contradiction. On the one hand, true religion, which ought always to be the deepest life and the purest motive power of the national community, ought to put all the members of the latter on an equal footing, alike as regards their rights and their duties. All equally ought to hearken without ceasing and exclusively to the voice of the true God, their sole king and lord. On the other hand, certain members ought to exercise a superintendence, hold the reins of discipline, and inflict penalties on the rest. Thus the equality of all should be subject to such exceptions as will permit human authority and even human lordship to arise in their midst, and for these a perpetual maintenance should be secured! What power there is, and yet what apparent arbitrariness in the right to inflict punishment, and this ought to be placed in the human hands of individual members of the community! An additional consideration is that those in the community who raised themselves to be human rulers would be compelled to extend their supervision and power of punishment over everything that was permitted or forbidden there, even over the affairs of the established true religion when they came under the law as described in the preceding main section. For it was the healthy feeling of those times that there should be one supreme universal law, whose penalties should apply, with the utmost impartiality possible, to all the movements and strivings which attained power in the nation; and this, in spite of the many confused notions which at the present hour are continually making more and more desolating inroads, will continue to remain for all times the unspoiled feeling and the self-preserving instinct of every nation.

But at the same time we must not suppose that Jahveism, from its commencement, and also later during the long centuries of its more vigorous existence, did not perceive the possibility of this contradiction, and had no clear ideas how to obviate it. When once it had clearly recognised in the light of the true religion what must be the true Divine rule among men, and in the first instance in a nation, it could comprehend all the more clearly how far men might cooperate with this Divine rule in maintaining and protecting its institutions. Human rule and right of punishment have but a limited meaning and aim. They only become possible under certain conditions; but as long as these conditions last, so must they. It is accordingly historical circumstances which best determine their essence and the sphere of their competency as well as their limitation. The people of Israel, however, had experienced from the time of Moses enough real history to prevent them for all eternity from ever taking wrong views in this matter. And thus the author of the Book of Origins, in his equally lofty and marvellously happy review of all the periods of the world's history,[1] anticipates and teaches the true view. We must, however, now give special prominence to what necessarily concerns us here.

In the first of the four epochs there is as yet no mention of human sovereignty. When, however, it came to an end, and apparently for want of this, and when a new order of things, more complicated but also higher, is established at the beginning of the second period, there is heard for the first time the sentence, 'Who sheds the blood of men, *by men* shall his blood be shed.'[2] These words can only be fully realised when we remember that previously all shedding of human blood had been most strictly forbidden, and that God had reserved to himself the punishment of the transgressor of this prohibition. Thus man is now charged with the execution of punishment on other men, and even of the extreme penalty which God had reserved to himself, and which in the strictest sense does pertain to him alone; and this right to inflict the extreme penalty which can be exacted of a human being, is committed by God himself to men, because otherwise (as God foresaw, so to speak, from what had happened), it would not have been exacted with the same care and certainty. During the second epoch in the progress of the struggle of human freedom against its immediate limitations, a divinely guaranteed liberty is indeed won for all human action; but where the sphere of freedom for all kinds of human activity is enlarged, especially if its growth be rapid, so much the more serious may be its excesses; and thus in order to suppress the license of individuals, it becomes necessary to have a human sovereign, who takes the place of God in inflicting punishment. And as with each new progressive epoch human effort assumes greater variety of form and hue, and all human relations grow more complicated, the simple equality of all men

[1] P. 103.
[2] Gen. ix. 6: comp. ver. 4, and especially ver. 5.

one with another must cease. The sharp distinction between authorities and their subjects makes its appearance, and what would have been deemed impossible becomes a possibility—a single member of the community exercises the Divine power of inflicting punishment on the rest. But it should be understood as a matter of course that the human ruler who owes his position to this state of things ought to consider this power only as something intrusted to him for a time by God and for which he is responsible, and he ought to exercise it only in accordance with the meaning and intentions of the Divine law as it has been revealed to all and is universally accepted. Should the human rulers forget these their limitations, and degenerate in the same way as, according to the old tradition, the fathers and founders of the earliest great nations did in becoming malicious Titans and Giants, then such a period meets once more with the only fate it deserves—universal destruction. Accordingly the true fathers of nations, as they ought to be, and as the people of Israel on a retrospect of their first days could pride themselves on having had, do not appear before the commencement of the third epoch. With the three Patriarchs the real nation, or the community of the true religion, now endeavours to form itself as the goal whither all temporal history is tending. When, however, this was about to be crushed at its very birth by the Pharaohs, the most hopelessly degenerate of the human rulers, then, at the commencement of the fourth epoch, and engaged in the severest conflict with these rulers, there appears in Moses the true Prophet and national leader, and simultaneously with him, the true community, along with all its eternal possessions, its permanent institutions and its laws, including those relating to punishment.

This position the Theocracy never abandons. The image of the true prophet becomes to this community, i.e. to this nation, the imperishable type also of all ruling and punishing power as it ought to be exercised by men. Much as those who rule may differ from one another in respect to the greater or less importance of their office, and much as the highest rulers, so far as outward appearances go, may vary to suit the exigencies of their times, and actually did vary during the centuries between Moses and the permanent establishment of the human monarchy, it was still indispensable for them to retain some most essential features of Moses, or rather of his time and his spirit. The immediate Word of God (or Oracle) as it might lead Moses, and thereby first introduce the nation to its new constitution, does not appertain to every human ruler; it could not easily return with any later one as it was with Moses; nor was there, after the community had been founded by its means, such imperative need for it. But if the true prophet cannot but give the supremacy in himself to the Divine demands for holiness and righteousness, and ought to derive his surest strength and a God-sent confidence in commanding other men, only from feeling these powers reigning in himself, so every ruler in this community ought only to exercise his functions as far as he is warranted by these objects and this belief. He must totally renounce his own personal desires and inclinations, pay heed only to the Divine will and law, and thus exercise in the place of God—as far as it is possible for a man to do so—this power of inflicting punishment on men. He must reign, command, and punish, as though it were not he that reigned, commanded, and punished, but the One to whom he never ceases to be responsible, and as though he might himself be in the position of any other member of the community, and the latter in his own. This is the genuine Mosaic element which ought to be retained by every human ruler of this nation, whether he be High-priest, Duke (like Joshua), Judge, or King, and which should extend downwards in due manner to all the officials of inferior rank.

The forms which human sovereignty actually assumed in Israel, so far as they endeavoured to establish themselves as permanent institutions, and the extent to which the power to punish was carried into practice, will only be described in the third main section.

3. We may, however, consider more closely here, what were the particular things which were either forbidden or commanded; apart from all questions respecting the person by whom, and the way in which, the legal punishments for sacrilege were enforced. A little reflection will then show us that each one of these things, at least in its strictest and most original essence, must contain in itself the ground of its own sanctity or opposite character. The original constitution of individual things, and of individual truths as well, as it is given to men in creation, is at once their most original and most inalienable right, their goodness, and (so far as man ought to realise this goodness and respect this right) their sanctity. And though this sanctity, goodness, and righteousness, may attach themselves to individuals in an infinite degree, they are nevertheless, included and protected, from the first and for all time, in the sanctity, goodness, and righteousness of the Creator

himself, as the eternal sustainer and lord of his creation. There exists no Divine sanctity which we can think of as ever being arbitrary, and by which we can determine in a manner no less arbitrary the sacredness of individual things and truths. The sanctity of the latter must show itself in the possession of an unimpeachable holiness which extends to the highest sanctity of the true God, and is again sustained and protected by him.—But just because the sacredness of things and of truths depends on their essential qualities, and therefore in the eyes of particular men and times on the degree of their knowledge of these, we cannot expect that in those early days it would appear to Jahveism in all its details just as it appears to us now after the whole development has reached its completion in Christianity. We shall be able to approach the subject somewhat more closely if we consider the distinctive marks of the main divisions under which all the details that belong here will come.

There are three great departments into which all these rights and laws will fall. There is a sanctity, i.e., in a lower or higher sense, an inviolability for men, inherent 1) in *creation* (*nature*), or the *world*, as that which the human mind knows to be the work of a wise God, the order of which man can despise or disturb only to his own hurt.—Contained in this there is 2) the sanctity of the *human being*, as something formed in the image of God, standing in the midst of and yet over the world, occupying an independent position as well as being a member of the greater Whole into which humanity always organises itself, viz., that of the community and the kingdom. Again, the existence and activity of what is spiritual in man sanctifies *property* also as that which is always won originally by human exertion. —Finally, this sacredness attaches 3) to the true *God*, to his revelations when once they have been recognised as real and accepted as decisive, as well as—when it has been recognised as binding the community—to the whole constitution of his *kingdom*, from its greatest and most indispensable constituent elements down to what was of less importance and apparently less needful. All this pertains here, even though particular details in its wide sphere may appear to us to have very different degrees of sacredness,[1] and the arrangement just given of the three great departments into which all the infinite varieties of detail separate themselves, is the proper one, in

---

[1] If we compare Lev. xi-xii. as the passage where, according to *Hist.* i. 88, the phrase 'holy shall ye be' has its special home, we shall not find everything which we comprehend here expressly touched upon there. But the greatest and most important part of it is treated of there as fully as the character of the Book of Origins allows; and this is a sufficient justification for us.

order to ascend from the lower and so far apparently more comprehensible stages, to those that are higher and so far really harder to understand.

But of these three all-embracing departments, that of nature was the one least known to remote Antiquity. For as regards main features, it must needs be that first of all man learns to know himself perfectly, and God, who though invisible stands nearest to him, so that, having become secure in matters that lie closest to him, he then becomes familiar, gradually but continually more and more completely, with nature, which stands with its hidden depths and infinite diversities between himself and God. Lofty, then, as is the general level of those laws of Jahveism which concern man and God, and full as they are of eternal truth, those laws which decide about physical matters are equally full of transitory elements, especially when it is not the physical nature of man which is in question.

I. Sanctity in Nature.

We understand here by nature not the original true essence of all possible things or relations, but the whole of the animate and inanimate creation, so far as it stands over against the human mind, and therefore human activity or passivity,—what in fact may be termed *matter* or the *world*. In this sense it was just in the earliest times that nature made the strongest impressions on men. This was the case so long as his mind had not sufficiently learned clearly to recognise and realise the higher mind which is over him even as it is over nature; and so long accordingly as he knows not how to give any clear account of these impressions, and indeed has hardly begun even to get the first grasp of their real character, nature appeared to man to be endowed with extraordinary life, spontaneity, and even understanding.[1] But to him she was not merely a friendly being, but also, so far as his knowledge of her was little trustworthy, far more a hostile living being, dark and terrible, which he must take heed not to disturb and insult, and whose evil actions were hard to avert. The more direct and therefore the more powerful were these obscure impressions which man received from nature, the more troubled became his dread of doing anything which seemed antagonistic to her,

---

[1] Comp. the *Hebr. S.L.* § 171 sqq., and further the treatise *Ueber die haupt- eigenthümlichkeit des Kafir-sprachstammes*, in the *Gel. Nachrichten*, 1866, s. 175– 190.

and the more diligent were his efforts to remove to a distance from himself any repulsive object which he might anywhere happen to meet with. However, the whole of nature in all its infinite details could not be always making such impressions on man; where therefore he thought he had no need to fear, he soon acted with all the greater recklessness and cruelty, as, e.g. towards the human body itself.

A treatment of nature so heathenish was far beneath the level to which Jahveism was raised by its deeper principles. In teaching a knowledge of the true God and Creator, it frees the human mind from the dark bonds of nature, and impels it to seek after the hidden causes of all that is alarming as well as of all that is repulsive. And inasmuch as it regards the whole creation with all its infinitudes as having been well constituted, it condemns all blind horror of any one of her manifestations, unless it has been polluted by sin; still more does it condemn any rough treatment of her. Thus the legislation is characterised by a remarkably tender anxiety for the rights of animate nature, and for the eternal laws of what is inanimate. Indeed, this ancient legislation shows a far more delicate feeling for nature than the modern often does, where, alas! the true connection between religion and law is as good as forgotten. The former legislation is still penetrated by the strong, healthy feeling that even nature, as the work of God and cognisable by man, has her inviolable laws and rights, and therefore her special sacredness for men.

Since, however, it was developed in a time when the essential features of nature and the causes of her phenomena were very little known or closely studied, this legislation nevertheless bears many a trace of the primitive troubled dread of natural objects. Here, too, we can recognise an instance of Jahveism not being at once able to attain in actual life to the pure elevation which was shown to be its destiny by the vigorous deeper principles which it already contained in itself. Numerous prohibitions have their only ground in the prevalence of this primitive dread, though the special occasions on which it displayed itself may have varied much. It is accordingly just on this side that Jahveism has retained many features of those primitive times when it was still more closely allied with other religions of the nations which were earliest developed. Nowhere does it bear so much resemblance to other earliest religions as here, and in the above-described department of sacrifice, which, so far as the ancient sacrifice was not purely spiritual, likewise falls into the same category.[1] Where, however, Jahveism of its own impulse desired to go a step farther, in order to exalt the sanctity of the nature which often received such scurvy treatment at the hands of heathenism, then, following its general plan,[2] it found no difficulty even here in lighting on some of the most widely prevalent uniformities without having regard to possible or even advantageous exceptions of less consequence, which a wider experience and acquaintance with nature would have brought under its notice.

1. What is Repulsive in Nature or Unclean *per se*.

164 The important consequence of this ancient troubled dread is that Jahveism deemed a tolerably large number of the objects and conditions of nature to be *unclean*, i.e., such as were not to be tolerated either under any circumstances or in certain respects in the community of Jahveh, which, therefore, would make a man unclean and unworthy of communion with Jahveh and his worshippers if he did not keep himself away from them, or if after having been defiled by them, he did not hasten to free himself from them. The ultimate grounds of this dread seem to have been very different in the various instances. In part, they were purely natural, here there would be a repulsive and often sound experience of what was prejudicial to health and life, there the only too easily aroused repulsion which the living feel towards the dead, or again, perhaps, a repulsive look, or some other such obscure feeling. In part, however, and probably to a greater extent they were due to historical events, and determined by the formation of national peculiarities. It would thus be necessary to know far more about the earliest conditions of Israel and of other nations long anterior to the time of Moses, before we could give an accurate explanation of each detail. But since the dread of these things always remained an obscure feeling, Jahveism did not concern itself with its ultimate grounds, nor were many questions asked on the subject as the laws were developed. Rather was there but one single effective feeling about them, viz. that they were things not to be tolerated in Jahveh's community, and as it were before the eyes of the exalted Pure Being,—that Jahveh repudiated and abominated them. This view being once adopted, the ancient religion applied her whole strength to

---

[1] Comp. *Hist.* ii. 151 sq.   [2] See p. 8 sq.

the task of warding them off from that community which was to be the purest and holiest among all nations; and the extraordinary earnestness which found a home there, and the might of its influence on the entire life of the nation may again be recognised here with the utmost clearness. No doubt similar efforts, originating in a similar dread, are also to be found characterising other ancient religions, which were specially exacting in their demands on men.[1] None, however, embrace so firmly and consistently a whole nation, and stamp their prohibitions on it so deeply.

But the ways to avoid or destroy the unclean things which might be met with must differ much according to the very various kinds and grades of the latter. Now in the determination of these kinds, whether of the unclean things themselves, or of the modes of dealing with them, and ways and means of getting rid of them, there appears a Unity in the prescriptions and laws so well studied and so consistent, that we cannot help recognising here the most unmistakeable traces of the spirit of a single great legislator. The laws of the Book of Origins, moreover, are here very complete, and this also shows us how rigidly these ancient regulations had been upheld till the time of the composition of this historical work. As regards general characteristics, there are three main classes of unclean things; and these are arranged in the following order, beginning with those of least, and ending with those of most consequence.

---

[1] Especially those of Zarathustra and of the Hindoos. The laws of the ancient Hindoos about eating (Manu, v. 5–16) are very like the Hebrew ones in certain fundamental points, and in particular we see very clearly from them how close was their original connection (according to p. 54 sq.) with the laws of sacrifice. That, on the other hand, the Egyptians had, on the whole, totally distinct laws of eating is plain from many indications, and is explained in Gen. xliii. 32, xlvi. 34; but it leads to quite a false conception to suppose that Moses gave his people their special laws on the subject *in order* thereby to procure for them greater isolation. This is to substitute for the origin and first unprejudiced meaning of the laws, the consequences to which, no doubt, they gave rise more and more, and which are on this account conspicuous in the representations of the Book of Origins, Lev. xx. 22–26, comp. xi. 44–47. Rather was there much that was similar among the Egyptians and Phœnicians, e.g. the prohibition of pork, even if, especially in later times, the particular application of it was developed in very different degrees, just as was the case with circumcision. See Porphyry, *De Abstin.* i. 14, iv. 7, comp. ch. 14; Herodian's *Hist.* i. 6. 22. Sextus Empir. *Hypotyp.* iii. 24. 223.—But we cannot take any fuller notice here of the innumerable attempts of later writers to explain, by allegory and other artificial methods, the meaning and purpose of the primitive laws about eating contained in the Pentateuch, although they begin before the Church Fathers.—Mahomet speaks sensibly about such laws, Sûr. iii. 87, but to what an extent superstition in the matter prevailed earlier in Arabia, is seen in Sûr. vi. 139 sq., and as a fact he himself sank back into its tone.

L

a. *What was Unclean for Food.*

Of vegetables the law takes no account, leaving the few that are not eatable to be distinguished by experience. But in respect to animals it draws the sharpest distinctions, counting in round numbers, however, far more species as unclean than as clean.[1] We see indeed that the only animals which ancient custom and religion permitted in Israel were cattle, sheep, and goats, and this is manifestly connected with the whole of the primitive formation of Israel as a pastoral people. We should try and think ourselves back in the times when Israel placed alike its strength and its honour in separation from the tribes of the desert, and so refrained from the flesh of the camel or similar animals of the desert, as well as in elevation above the morally degenerate town-life of the Canaanites and Egyptians, and therefore held aloof from the rearing of swine, or of other smaller or more dirty animals which are often eaten of necessity in thickly populated towns.[2] In those early days the strict and proud limitation of the use of meat, to beef, mutton, and goats' flesh, was undoubtedly very closely connected with the entire condition of the civilisation and of the aims of Israel. The scale of preference and the particular estimation of these animals, which is seen so clearly in the old sacrificial laws,[3] was unaltered in common life. Nevertheless the list of animals allowed for food exceeds that of the sacrificial animals in certain respects, and the law, seeking to determine everything as far as possible by inseparable attributes, decreed as follows:—1. Of the larger quadrupeds all were clean which both possessed completely cloven hoofs and also chewed the cud. This would include, besides the above-mentioned sacrificial animals, the many species of deer and gazelles inhabiting the forests and deserts.[4] Specially excluded by name were the

---

[1] Lev. xi. 1–38. We easily recognise in the enumeration of the species of animals the same order as is found in the history of the Creation in the Book of Origins. Gen. i., only that here the large quadrupeds, as the most important, are taken first, and that finally a particular kind of small animal (שֶׁרֶץ) is distinguished as the most uneatable and especially repulsive. But for this very reason we must suppose verr. 24–28 to be out of their proper places, and transfer them back to after ver. 8.—A short selection of the most important cases, along with a few additions, is given in Deut. xiv. 1–20, but already with the addition of permission to give or to sell such animals to the heathens, ver. 21.

[2] As the Carthaginians are bitterly reproached with eating dogs' flesh, Justin. *Hist.* xix. 1, and as pork in many heathen countries was even used for sacrifice, see comment on Is. lxvi. 3.

[3] P. 31 sq.

[4] Their partly obscure names occur Deut. xiv. 5, with the surprising omission of the רְאֵם so often mentioned by the poets, supposing this really to belong to the family of gazelles; perhaps because it was so difficult to catch that it was hardly

camel, the coney, the hare,[1] and swine,[2] manifestly because these were largely used as food among the surrounding nations, and further, all carnivorous animals which walk upon paws.— 2. Of fish and all allied animals only those were admitted which have fins and scales, as though from an ancient obscure dread of snakes and animals like them, such as eels.—3. In the case of birds we have only an enumeration of those that were forbidden, the list being of some length. Many of the names in it are now of very doubtful meaning, but it is clear that all birds of prey as well as most waterfowl were reckoned unclean. However, not only the different kinds of pigeons which were used for sacrifice,[3] but many others were considered clean, as the narrative about the birds of the desert[4] suffices to show.— 4. For all the smaller land animals, whether winged or not, an ancient disgust continued to prevail in great strength.[5] The various kinds of locusts are the only exception, and they may have been too indispensable as food for the people during their marches through the desert for the law to pronounce them unclean, but it is a noteworthy fact that this exception is made only in the Book of Origins, no longer in Deuteronomy.

But even with clean beasts the flesh was deemed unclean if the animal were torn to pieces in the fields, suffocated, or in other respects not put to death in the proper manner. This, however, was not only on account of a natural repugnance for every dead body, or because of experience of injury to health, but principally on account of the blood not having been taken from it in the proper way. The prohibition of the use of such flesh belongs therefore to another class,[6] and marks the tran-

---

ever eaten, see the note on Job, s. 301 of the 2nd ed. On the other hand, the Phœnician law permitted even wild animals for sacrifice, as is clear from the treatises mentioned above, p. 50 *note*.

[1] Here we must disregard the question whether the hare really does chew the cud, as stated in Lev. xi. 6; and also whether this is the case with the *Hyrax Syriacus* (שָׁפָן), the same animal as is still to be found in great numbers in Palestine, living in holes in the ground, but now called וֶבֶּר, for neither does this chew the cud, according to John Wilson's *Lands of the Bible*. ii. p. 28 sqq. Whether the LXX understood by אַרְנֶבֶת, the χοιρογρύλλιος or the δασύπους, is so far doubtful, as, without the substitution of שָׁפָן for the latter, which occurs in Deut. xiv. 7, comp. Lev. xi. 5 sq., they preserve the same

arrangement in both passages. But it is in any case remarkable that they avoid the use of the word λαγώς. *hare* (see *Hist.* v. 249, *note*), and probably in both cases they had the arrangement of Deuteronomy.

[2] That Mahomet was not the first to disallow the eating of swine among the Arabs is clear from the remarks in Solini, *Polyhistor*, xxxiii. 4, and Jerome, *Adv. Jovin.* lib. ii. (iv. 2, p. 200 sq. ed. Mart.).

[3] P. 32.

[4] *Hist.* ii. 221 sqq.

[5] We may notice how expressly the denunciation of them is repeated at the end, Lev. xi. 41-44.

[6] Not without reason is it wanting in Lev. xi., although the Deuteronomist, no doubt, at once supplies it, xiv. 21. On the other hand, it is found in the old legislation, Ex. xxii. 30 [31], though this

sition to the prohibition, of very different origin, against eating blood and the altar-pieces of the animals which were sacrificed.[1] But while the Book of Origins[2] insists that all meat which might not be eaten in Israel, was also not to be eaten by the heathen in their midst, we recognise in Deuteronomy[3] the token of a later and degenerate age, when permission is given to dispose of it to the heathen as presents or by sale.

How much these two prohibitions differed from one another both in origin and importance, is further sufficiently manifest from the penalties which are legally attached to the transgression of them. In what way eating an unclean animal was to be punished, the law does not tell us, the surest sign that the observance of this prohibition was largely left to the care of conscience alone, and in stress of hunger it was not difficult for it to be gradually set aside.[4] The most extreme penalties, on the other hand, are denounced against the eating of blood![5] Even towards the close of this whole history, when the prohibition of these unclean meats fell altogether in abeyance, this was still quite properly distinguished from that relating to blood and the flesh of suffocated animals, as well as from that referring to heathen sacrifices.[6]

Of a somewhat different character was the custom not to eat, but carefully to search out and remove, one of the sinews of the hip-bones which is necessary for walking well, and especially for movements in wrestling. This custom was certainly very ancient in Israel, and its explanation is therefore given in the primitive history,[7] but probably it rested on some old belief which the law could not allow. There may have been an ancient belief that the sinew which was indispensable for walking well was too sacred to be eaten with the rest of the meat, just as in the case of the blood. This might have become interwoven with the history of Jacob 'the limper,' so that the narrative represented him as limping because God had touched this sinew, and his posterity must accordingly reverence it to guard themselves against a similar injury. But while Jahveism

does not think it worth while saying any more about clean and unclean meat.

[1] Special prominence is given to the last, Lev. vii. 23–27; comp. above p. 37 sq.
[2] Lev. xvii. 15.
[3] Deut. xiv. 21.
[4] As 2 Kings vi. 25.
[5] P. 110.
[6] Acts xv. 29, xxi. 25; 1 Cor. viii. 1 sqq., comp. Ex. xxxiv. 15. Nevertheless, complaints against eating what is bloody

are already made in Ezek. xxxiii. 25 (comp. p. 38), and proper conduct is required only of the priests, xliv. 31.
[7] Gen. xxxii. 25–33. With נָשֶׁה, comp. ﻟﺴﻲ, Tabari, Ann. vol. i. p. 194, 17 sq., where the sinew is somewhat more closely described; Hârit's Moall. ver. 53; Chalef el-Ahmar's Qasside, ver. 45 (s. 216 sq. ed. Ahlw.).

retained the sanctity of the blood, it would have had much greater difficulty in connecting the old belief about this sinew with any higher truth, and it only followed its better impulses when legally it ignored the matter, and only spoke of it historically.

b. What was too Unclean or too Unholy, or else too Sacred, to be touched.

By merely touching an unclean animal even the holiest man in Israel did not contaminate himself. There were, however, natural objects whose touch was so contaminating for every member of the community that a special purification was needed before he could be again received into full membership. This is particularly the case with all dead animal matter. An ancient horror of stiffened life and blood, along with fatal experience of the exhalations from corpses, may have contributed to give occasion to this belief in the strong contaminating influence of every dead thing.[1] This is the unmistakeable source of the euphemism by which, instead of a 'dead man,' they said merely a 'soul,' i.e. a 'person,' a mode of speaking which was still quite prevalent at the time of the Book of Origins.[2]—If a horror of stiffened life and blood as such was a cooperating cause here, it is easy to understand why the law drew so sharp a line between human corpses and others, and required a far more thorough purification after contact with the former than with the latter. We see here only another consequence of the deep dread of human blood which was so characteristic of Jahveism.[3]

Now whenever from this or some other cause, a man, and it was the same with any other object, was deemed unclean, i.e. polluted, he was thereby excluded from the community, and

---

[1] Later refinements on the subject may be found in Joseph. *Contr. Ap.* ii. 24–26; Porphyr. *De Abstin.* iv. 19 sq. p. 366–370. The same custom also occurs among the Egyptians and others, see Origen, *Contr. Cels.* iii. 6, 3, and we see how many legal similarities there were among the Hindoos in Manu, v. 57–146.

[2] The existence of this euphemism is seen plainly in Lev. xix. 28, comp. Deut. xiv. 1, Lev. xxii. 4, Num. v. 2, comp. vi. 6, Lev. xxi. 11; and, without assuming a euphemism, the phrase cannot be explained. A perfectly similar euphemism occurs in the Book of Origins in בָּשָׂר, flesh, for the sexual organs, Lev. xv. 2 sqq.—It was probably this impurity which once kept Jeremiah at home, Jer. xxxvi. 5; comp. a similar case, Neh. vi. 10; and as those who were 'prevented' from coming to public business or processions from this or any other of the causes which will be explained here, would be at once known, and the whole people, therefore, be separated into two divisions, we can understand from this fact the meaning of the proverbial phrase עָצוּר וְעָזוּב, *Hist.* i. 124, *note* 3, 133, *note* 3.

[3] P. 37 sqq.

could not re-enter it till his purification was completed. The simplest way of effecting this was by washing, and when human beings were concerned, washing the clothes was always included.¹

1. Accordingly, whoever touched, even though only accidentally, the corpse of an animal, clean or unclean, whoever came into closer contact with it, e.g., in order to carry it away, or whoever ate of the corpse of a clean beast, was to be unclean till evening, i.e. for a whole day. This meant being shut out from society, and having first to wash oneself and one's clothes before one could re-enter it.² This shows, however, of itself that the slaying and preparation of a clean animal had no contaminating effect. But what was competent to defile a man had the same effect on everything that pertained to him —clothes, skins, bags, tools, must be washed and be unclean until evening; earthenware must be broken and its contents, ordinarily cooked food or drink, be regarded as unclean, i.e., as uneatable, a cooking-oven or a seething-pot (things very simply constructed in the earliest times) must be destroyed. Springs and reservoirs were nevertheless not polluted by the corpse of an animal which had fallen into them, nor were seed or corn, except when they had already been moistened with water and destined for food.³ Even in war no exception could be made to these rules.⁴ While the smallest animals, e.g. flies, have no notice taken of them, it was different with somewhat larger species like mice and lizards, which lived here and there in houses in considerable numbers, and are on this account carefully enumerated.⁵

2. The above-mentioned first grade of necessary purification is succeeded, when there had been contact with a human

---

¹ This last is also clear from Gen. xxxv. 2, Ex. xix. 10-14.

² Lev. xi. 8, 11, 24-28, 31, 39 sq., comp. Num. xix. 7 sq., 16, 21 sq., Lev. xvi. 26, 28. From such passages as Lev. xi. 24-28, we might suppose that there were cases when a person was unclean till the evening, without being compelled to wash his clothes, but only to take a bath himself (for that uncleanness in every case could only be removed by washing is obvious). But that the phrase 'to be unclean till the evening' is merely an abbreviation follows from passages like Lev. xv. 16-24, to say nothing of other reasons. Washing clothes in the earliest times was done without much difficulty. Conversely, we often find washing clothes as an abridged phrase.

³ Lev. xi. 32-38. The Deuteronomist omits all these distinctions, perhaps because in his time they seemed no longer applicable.

⁴ Num. xxxi. 19.

⁵ Lev. xi. 29 sq. Altogether there are eight of these 'creeping things' enumerated here, and it is remarkable that no mention is made of that small animal spoken of in Prov. xxx. 28, to be found in abundance creeping about the finest houses, but it may yet be reckoned as belonging to some one or other of the *species* of those that are mentioned.—The unclean birds, Lev. xi. 13-19, must probably have been, according to a fuller catalogue, Deut. xiv. 12-18. originally twenty-one in number; and round numbers show that by the time of the Book of Origins such regulations had been long in force.

corpse, by a second grade of sevenfold stringency, and extreme solemnity.[1] For the purpose of this purification, a water was specially prepared with peculiar materials and appropriate sacrificial rites, as though pure water was far from being adequate here. But whilst the rite, which elsewhere retained its simplicity, appears here in fully developed and pronounced forms, these only bring into the clearer daylight the most intrinsic thoughts and impulses which are the source of all such purifications. And accordingly in the case of other purifications of equal efficacy, which will be described below, very similar phenomena make their appearance. We have then now to speak more closely of the general meaning of sacrificial purification.

When any pollution had arisen in the sacred community, some one of its fundamental laws had been transgressed, something repulsive and unholy introduced into it, and the serene countenance of Jahveh become clouded. This necessitated an expiation, and an expiatory-offering if the pollution were of sufficient importance. In the second place, the special impurity attaching to a member of the community must be removed. This must be done where the impurity was very great by the aid of certain special materials which were endowed according to ancient belief with potent cleansing powers. Such materials,[2] according to old custom in Israel, were to be found primarily in the wood of the cedar-tree, to which a special medicinal virtue was also ascribed in those regions; further there were the threads of scarlet cloth, to which was ascribed a special healing virtue, just as in Italy at the present day the same is believed of the red viper's-grass, as it is called, and to which the impurity which was to be expelled was expected to cleave; finally, there were the leaves and stalk of the hyssop, a small plant which Antiquity supposed to possess a like purifying power, whose leaves were mixed up with bread to purify it, and whose stalk was on this account employed by preference whenever blood or water was sprinkled for cleaning purposes.[3]

In the next place an expiatory-offering was made, but this was brought into the closest connection with the specially pre-

---

[1] Num. xix.
[2] Lev. xiv. 4, 6, 49-52; Num. xix. 6.
[3] See p. 44. This last circumstance follows from Ex. xii. 22, Num. xix. 18, also Ps. li. 9 [7]. In respect to this virtue of cedar-wood, reference has already been made by earlier writers to Dioscorid.

Mat. Med. i. 105. For the use of hyssop among the Greeks, who coupled it with cedar-oil for purposes of sanctification, see the same passage, and also iii. 29, ed. Spreng.; comp. my *Erklärung des Schriften des Apostels Johannes*, i. s. 412 sq.

pared water of purification, or rather, as it is more exactly termed, the water of pollution, i.e. to purify from pollution.[1] At the same time, in view of the great frequency with which contact with human corpses is unavoidable, every death rendering this necessary, it became desirable to find a suitable substitute for bringing an expiatory-offering for every separate case. A red heifer was therefore chosen as the most perfect type of an animal for expiatory sacrifice,[2] and this was slain before the eyes of a superior priest as the representative of the whole community, and outside of the camp (or town). Its blood was sprinkled by the priest seven times in the direction of the Sanctuary, and then the whole of its body along with the rest of the blood was at once burned in the way already described,[3] while the priest threw into the flames the three purifying materials just spoken of, and all was reduced together to ashes. These ashes were next brought to a clean spot, still without the Sanctuary, and there carefully preserved. When a pollution was to be effaced, they were mixed with fresh water into a kind of lye, and sprinkled with a stalk of hyssop on the polluted man, as well as on all implements or places that were considered to be tainted. Everything which had to be sprinkled was excluded as unclean for seven days from the community, and sprinkled on the third and on the seventh day, if they were to be purified in the course of the sacred period of a week.[4] Moreover, not only the priest who received and sprinkled the blood of this expiatory-offering and rendered active assistance at its burning, but also the man who carried the ashes to the clean spot, and he who sprinkled the water mixed with them, and even everyone who touched this compound only accidentally, at once incurred the above-mentioned first grade of uncleanness.[5]

3. A still more stringent law applied to the priests, which will be described when we come to them. Most severe was it, however, in the case of the Nazirites.[6] If one of these had unawares been made unclean through a corpse, in addition to the above purifications, he must on the seventh day shave the hair of his head, i.e. recommence his whole vow from the very beginning, then on the eighth day he was to offer two pigeons, one as an expiatory- and the other as a whole-offering, in order that he might therewith be freed from the impurity, and

---

[1] מֵי־נִדָּה.
[2] P. 60 sq.
[3] P. 64.
[4] Num. xix. 12 (where, according to the LXX, instead of the first יִטְהָר we should read 'יִ, as explained in *Lehrbuch*, § 347a), 19, comp. xxxi. 23 sq.
[5] This is sufficiently manifest fro the explanations given on p. 63 sq.
[6] P. 84 sqq.

finally he had to pay for the suspension of his consecration by a lamb as a guilt-offering. At the same time, if his consecration had been vowed only for a definite period, the time which had already elapsed was not counted.[1]

The transgressors of any of these stringent laws were punished with extirpation, because they had 'defiled the sacred dwelling of Jahveh,'[2] and in the actual life of the ancient nation there are many other traces which clearly show the penetrating effects produced by the laws. Since the man in whose house any one died found himself with his whole household rendered unclean, and as even the food which might be standing there in open vessels at the time shared the same fate,[3] good manners required that his friends should come to him to share his solitude, to eat with him the funeral meal at the risk of making themselves unclean thereby, and even of bringing their own bread and drink with them, that there might be no want either of the necessaries of life or of consolation, a practice to which allusion is not unfrequently made.[4] Again, the custom of deeply lamenting a departed one for seven days finds a natural place for itself here,[5] although this period was easily extended to thirty days in the case of deceased persons of high distinction.[6] Again, the speedy burial of the dead, now so general, appears to have gradually originated in consequence of the burdensome character of the corpse; this custom, however, is probably not particularly ancient.[7] On the other hand, the undefinable shrinking from a corpse was not carried to such an extent in Israel as it was among other ancient and in part highly civilised nations, where it was a custom either to expose corpses on high places to be consumed by the birds, so that no trace of them might remain (as was done among the Zarathustrians, and is still by many tribes of Central Asia), or else to burn them and collect only their ashes, as was done among the Greeks and the Romans. It is true that the interment of a king,

---

[1] Num. vi. 9–12.
[2] Num. xix. 13, 20.
[3] Deut. xxvi. 14; comp. with Num. xix. 15.
[4] 2 Sam. iii. 35; Hos. ix. 4; Deut. xxvi. 14; Jer. xvi. 5, 7; Ezek. xxiv. 17, 22. The degeneration of this custom, at any rate in later times, when the house of mourning was compelled to go to most inordinate expense, is touched upon by Joseph. *Bell. Jud.* ii. 1. 1. It is the same now in Central Africa, see Tutschek, in *Ausland*, 1853, s. 16 sq., 1855, s. 1222. Hanoteau's *Grammaire de la Langue Tamachek*, p. 104 sq.—Ghevond, *Hist. de l'Arménie*, p. 147.
[5] 1 Sam. xxxi. 13; comp. similar instances, Job ii. 13; Ezek. iii. 15 sq.; Sir. xxii. 11, 12; Joseph. *Bell. Jud.* ii. 1. 1. It is still the same among the Lesghians, *Nouv. Ann. des Voyages*, 1852, i. p. 75.
[6] Num. xx. 29; Deut. xxxiv. 8.
[7] Undoubted allusions to it are not to be found before the New Testament, e.g. Acts v. 6. Totally different customs are, however, everywhere presupposed in the primitive history, Gen. xxv. 9, comp. xxi. 20 sq.; xxiii. 2, comp. xxiv. 62.

or possibly of any rich man, was accompanied by the burning of much costly incense, as its traditional mark of honour,[1] so that to *burn anyone* came to be the standing phrase for *honouring him* in this way.[2] But the burning of the corpse itself was deemed (as will be shown below in connection with the modes of punishment) an aggravation of the penalty of death. Embalming, however, and preserving the bodies of the dead, which can be explained only out of the Egyptian religious belief about death, was indeed introduced during the temporary sojourn of the people in Egypt,[3] but from the time of Moses it was completely abandoned as a custom essentially connected with a false religion.

As the law further decreed that anyone who touched a human bone or a grave must submit to this onerous purification,[4] it became customary to make arrangements for burial in places as far removed as possible from human habitations or from temples, and by preference on high ground and in deep caverns in the rock, and in addition even to strew them over with lime, and thereby make the ground safe again to tread upon.[5] What a complete contrast this presents to the custom of building Christian churches exactly over graves and round about the scenes of martyrdom! When, later on, certain kings began to erect tombs for themselves within the temple of Solomon the act is expressly censured.[6]

The possessions of an enemy when taken as booty had the same contaminating effect as dead bodies. All which were not fireproof were merely to be washed, but whatever could be purified by fire, such as metals and the like, had to be cleansed in the fire, and then purified with the water of pollution.[7] This stringent treatment is explained by the profound horror which Israel felt towards all heathen goods, which expressed itself most strongly in the ban described already,[8] and about which there will be more to say below.

---

[1] According to Jer. xxxiv. 5; 2 Chron. xvi. 14, xxi. 19, comp. what is said *Hist.* iii. 273 sq.

[2] 1 Sam. xxxi. 12.

[3] According to the reminiscences in Gen. l. 2 sqq., 26, comp. Ex. xiii. 19. It evidently connects this with the rejection of the whole of the Egyptian ideas about death and immortality, which is spoken of *Hist.* ii. 133 sqq.

[4] Num. xix. 16.

[5] The latter is alluded to Matt. xxiii. 27, Luke xi. 44, comp. Beulé's *Fouilles à Carthage*, in the *Journ. des Sav.*, 1860, p. 569.—The magnificence and scrupulously protected purity of the tombs of rich men was in striking contrast to the 'graves of the common people,' or the places where the corpses of all the poor, of criminals, and other despised beings, were all thrown together, and this made the latter graves seem all the more horrible. bk. Is. liii. 8 [9], Jer. xxvi. 23. Such a place was *the valley of corpses and ashes* to the south of Jerusalem, Jer. xxxi. 40.

[6] Ezek. xliii. 7-9. This may not have been done till the time of some of the latest kings, comp. *Hist.* iii. 273 sq.

[7] Num. xxxi. 20, 21-24.

[8] P. 76.

—But just as, according to this ancient feeling, there existed things too unclean or too unholy for man to be allowed to touch, so also were there things which, from the same cause, were *too holy* to be touched without the contact being immediately penal. The two feelings are in mutual correspondence; and the more imminent seemed the possibility of the Holy Presence vanishing again from the world, the more anxiously, nay, the more recklessly, did the endeavour to keep guard over it assume its different forms. Jahveism, too, thought it possessed objects so sacred that their mere contact with improper hands must necessarily be punished by nothing less than the ban.[1] As accordingly, the highest sacrifice was deemed *most holy* [2] (i.e. a sacrament) anyone who touched its flesh when it was already consecrated, was forfeited to the Sanctuary itself, i.e. came under the ban; whilst any of its blood which might have been accidentally spattered on the dress must be scrupulously washed out at a sacred place.[3] Similar rites will have to be explained below under the Priesthood. But all this gave rise to further scruples of the strangest kind,[4] and it was one of the Messianic hopes that all such painful fetters would finally disappear.[5]

c. Material Impurities in Human Beings, and elsewhere.

In the last place it was the ancient belief that certain substances in living human beings rendered them unclean. This arose in part from a natural dread of mysterious, enervating, or shameful issues from the body, which sometimes of themselves remind humanity strongly and suddenly enough of its helplessness, and chain the sufferers to their homes. In part it was at the same time due to the bitterest experience of infection, and the propagation of appearances on the human body, which, being incomprehensible, were the object of special dread to remote Antiquity. The law here only regulated more carefully

---

[1] P. 75 sqq.
[2] P. 108.
[3] Lev. vi. 20 [27]; comp. Lucian, *De Dea Syra*, liii. sq. When, later, the Rabbis, according to the Mischna Jadâjim iii. 5, passed a law that the holy Scriptures made the hands unclean (so that anyone who touched them, or anything in contact with them, must wash their hands), its source is to be found in the same feeling. Among the Peruvians even every article of clothing or vessel which had belonged to the king had to be burned, as too sacred for another, as soon as he ceased to use it. Prescott, i. s. 347.

Comp. also the *Can. Apostol.* lxv.
[4] Li e Haggai ii. 12 sq.
[5] BK. Zach. xiv. 20 sq., comp. xiii. 1. —If anyone would see how many utterly trivial laws of purification were ultimately derived from the few that occur in the Old Testament by the schools of the Pharisees, and with what strictness they were to be observed, he should read the long articles *M.* דמאי, כלים, אהלות, טהרות, and others, but also compare with them such passages as Mark vii. 3 sq., which clearly show that these laws were not even confined to the Talmud.

a force which had long been operative in vague feelings and impulses, but it gives us a vivid illustration of the extraordinary striving to keep the sacred community perfectly clean and pure, which was peculiar to Jahveism, and of its unparalleled scrupulousness in avoiding everything which would destroy this, or in stamping out again whatever had actually made its appearance. The details are as follows:—

1. Seminal issue, whether in the usual case of the copulation of the two sexes, or in the unusual case during the sleep of the man, caused the above-mentioned uncleanness of the first grade; at the same time, any clothes or skin that was stained with it had to be washed.[1]

2. The monthly period of the woman brought with it the second grade of uncleanness, which lasted the space of seven days, but without rendering necessary the use of specially prepared water. Everything on which the woman sat or lay during this time, and every one who touched such things or her, incurred the uncleanness of the first grade, but the man who slept with her during this period had to suffer the same more onerous uncleanness for seven days.[2]

The similarity to the latter case[3] was of itself enough to cause every mother to be unclean for seven days after the birth of her child; on the eighth day a son would be circumcised, in which solemnity she would participate quietly at home; but after this week she had still to remain for thirty-three days longer in the house, without touching anything sacred or going to the Sanctuary. If it was a female child the seven days were extended to fourteen, and the thirty-three to sixty-six, manifestly in accordance with the ancient belief that a female child causes the mother more labour and a longer illness. This belief (even though it may have little ground in fact) was itself caused by the well-known primitive disfavour with which the birth of a girl was regarded; and like every ancient custom in this par-

---

[1] P. 150.—Lev. xv. 16-18, comp. Deut. xxiii. 11 [10] sq.; and as historical examples, 1 Sam. xx. 26, xxi. 5 [4] sq., 2 Sam. xi. 4. Comp. Jamblichus' *Vita Pyth.* xi. (lv.), and similar instances among the Babylonians, Arabs and others. Herod. i. 198 ; Shahrastâni's *Elmilal*, p. 443. 11.— Josephus quotes an example of it, remarkable on account of its consequences, *Antiq.* xvii. 6. 4.

[2] See Lev. xv. 19-24, and the corresponding historical incident, Gen. xxxi. 35, with the allusions to it, Is. xxx. 22, lxiv. 5 [6]. This is how the Book of Origins legally determines it; but according to the words in Lev. xviii. 19, xx. 18, the oldest law assigns the penalty of death to this breach of purity, probably meaning in cases where it was becoming a regular practice. Nevertheless, we find complaints of contempt of these as well as of other similar enactments in Ezek. xviii. 6, xxii. 9-11.

[3] It was even similar with the λοχεῖα of the Greeks, Thucyd. *Hist.* iii. 104. Eurip. *Iphigen. in Tauris*, ver. 384; still more so among the Zarathustrians, see *Vendîdâd*, xvi.

ticular sphere, it was able to persist for a very considerable time, although under Jahveism the disfavour gradually declined.[1] —When the one or the other period had elapsed, and when therefore the bodily purity could be restored, the mother had to bring an offering of purification which was of a similar kind to those that belonged to the other still more stringent purifications which will be next described. After deliverance from so trying a bodily evil, it seemed too little to bring a single expiatory-offering, at least a whole-offering seemed due to Jahveh from one who was again to be received into partnership in all the good things of life. So what was required was a one-year-old lamb as a whole-offering and a pigeon as an expiatory-offering, or if poverty interfered with this arrangement, at any rate the latter was to be supplemented by a second pigeon as a whole-offering. Not till all this was over did the priest officially pronounce the mother's restoration to purity.

3. What the nation found most intolerable were the extraordinary tedious appearances on the human body which told of dire internal disorder. Two such kinds have prominence given to them, undoubtedly only because they were then the most frequent.

In the first place there was the issue from the sexual organs, to which both men and women were liable, which might also cease without being healed, and then only grow worse again. Everyone who touched such a patient, or whom he touched with unwashed hands, as well as all utensils of which he made any use, became unclean in the milder sense, even his spittle defiled anyone who was clean. If he was cured, he might, when seven days had elapsed, be purified in body, and on the eighth day had to offer a couple of pigeons.[2] That this was, at that time, a formidable disorder is plain, and we can have equally little doubt that it bore the greatest resemblance to gonorrhœa prevalent in Europe among males, and the fluor albus among females. The whole description would make it seem that it was not infectious.[3]

The other, and still far more fearful disease, was *leprosy*, 'the stroke of God,' as it was universally termed, an evil which suddenly produces small white spots, especially on the counte-

---

[1] That the law in Lev. xii. really presupposes a longer weakness of the mother in the case of the birth of a girl, follows from the word בְּנֶקְדָּתָהּ, ver. 5, comp. the corresponding, only more definite, words in ver. 2. With this was long ago compared what Hippocrates says just at the beginning of the fifth chapter of the *De Nat. Pueri.*

[2] Lev. xv. 1–15, 25–30.

[3] Perhaps we have an historical example of the illness with women in Mark v. 25–34, where it is true no allusion is made to uncleanness.

180 nance, but which is so wearisome and so hideous, that the ancient belief held that it always came as a curse ordained by God on him who felt its sudden stroke,[1] as though God had so marked him, as an enraged father might spit in the face of his child.[2] The cure of it, too, was regarded as requiring extraordinary skill. This evil was very common in Israel during the latter years of its stay in Egypt,[3] and appears to have grown rarer during the new elevation under Moses, so that it was related of the great national leader that he had removed it by his intercession, and that he could draw his hand out of his bosom either in a leprous state or not, just as he, or rather as his God, willed.[4] It lasted, however, among the people, long after his days down into the latest times. The law, therefore, strictly commanded the priest to examine most carefully and repeatedly every one who was even suspected of leprosy, and to pronounce him unclean if the evil really did show itself on him.[5] On account of the danger of infection, such a person, with clothes rent for mourning, and bare head, concealing his chin with his hand, and proclaiming aloud his own uncleanness, must withdraw from all society and only settle down in some utterly lonely spot, where at most he would have the company of those who were suffering the same affliction.[6] Should his cure be effected, a most solemn, and, at the same time, most cautious reception back into society was prescribed. When the priest was satisfied that the cure was thorough, the simple cessation of the evil was first celebrated. The convalescent appeared with two clean birds, one of which was slain in an earthen vessel over fresh water; the other, still living, along with cedar-wood, threads of scarlet cloth, and hyssop, was then baptised in its blood,[7] and after the blood had been seven times 181 sprinkled towards the person who was to be purified, the bird was allowed to fly away free, as though it were itself to bear away into the wide world all the impurity which was now unattached.[8]

---

[1] Comp. 2 Chron. xxvi. 19.
[2] According to Num. xii. 14.
[3] *Hist.* ii. 80 sq. *Berlin Akad.* MB. 1859, s. 341 sqq.
[4] Num. xii. 11–13, Ex. iv. 6 sq., undoubtedly with ancient legends as their foundation.
[5] The remarkable, from a medical point of view, and exhaustive description, Lev. xiii. 1–44, is clear enough of itself; the whole law is briefly referred to Deut. xxiv. 8. Comp. also Seetzen's *Reisen*, ii. s. 315 sq.
[6] Lev. xiii. 45 sq., comp. the historical case, 2 Kings vii. 3.
[7] P. 151.
[8] Comp. what is said of this imagery under the day of atonement. Similar and stronger symbolical language is not rare either among ancient or modern nations; e.g. in Bali at the present time, when the *Satî* spring into the fire, a dove is let loose from their heads as an image of their pure soul soaring to heaven (see *Ausland*, 1852. s. 40); just as formerly, according to Herodian, *Hist.* bk. iv., 2. 22, an eagle (the spirit, the soul) was allowed to fly to heaven from burning funeral piles. For the rest comp. Knudsen's *Gross-Namaqualand* (Barmen, 1848),

The convalescent washed, shaved, and bathed, and was now pronounced clean for civic purposes, but had to keep away from his house for seven days more, and this interval was deemed so indispensable for repentance and for preparation for the great joy of his life that was coming, that, according to the ancient narrative, even Miriam the sister of Moses could not escape it, when, on account of an offence towards Moses, she was punished with a brief attack of leprosy.¹ On the seventh day the shaving, washing, and bathing were repeated with still greater carefulness,² and on the eighth day a most solemn sacrifice of purification was offered. A male lamb was slain as a guilt-offering, the priest put a streak of its blood on the tip of the man's right ear, on the thumb of the right hand, and the great toe of the right foot (i.e. he cleansed the whole man); then, holding in his left hand the sacrificial oil (to which a healing virtue was ascribed), he sprinkled it seven times towards the Sanctuary, anointed with it these same terminal members of the man, and poured the rest of it upon his head. Thus the man was once more sanctified, and now a female lamb as an expiatory-offering, and lastly a male lamb as a whole-offering together with the corn belonging to it, were offered on his behalf. The last two animals might, in case of poverty, be replaced by pigeons.³

All who were unclean on account of any of the above-explained causes, were not only to avoid the Sanctuary, but were excluded from all assemblies of the community, and in particular from the army and the military camp, a point which in the early times was no doubt very strictly insisted on.⁴ Deuteronomy is still very strict as regards the military camp, and has the additional requirement that every warrior shall go to a certain place outside the camp to ease nature; and a mattock, which in other respects would be very useful in war, was to be carried in his girdle in order that the excrements might be at once covered up.⁵

—The law further assumed the existence of a similar leprosy in clothes and houses, and laid down similar enactments for the priests to observe in respect to it. It required that an

---

s. 27; and for the Hindoo Badaga, see the *Ev. Heidenboten*, 1849, s. 103 sqq.
¹ Num. xii. 14 sq. The Book of Origins gives at the same time, according to its custom, an example of the law it describes; if even Miriam had to submit to it, how much more must everyone else!
² Comp. p. 152.

³ Lev. xiv. 1-32.
⁴ Lev. xv. 31, Num. v. 1-4. For the rest comp. *Dichter des A. B.s*, iii. s. 22 sq., 80, 2nd ed.
⁵ Deut. xxiii. 10-15 [9-14]. For אָזֵן we must read with the LXX אָזְנְךָ, and וְיָשַׁבְתָּ must be understood as derived from יָשַׁב, according to *Lehrbuch*, § 234c.

article of clothing on which the signs of leprosy had appeared should be burned, and that a house in which the disease was gaining ground, should, if an attempt to cure it proved futile, be utterly destroyed, and all the materials be transported to some solitary unclean place. But a house which was, as it were, restored to health at the first attempt to heal it, must be reconsecrated by the same solemn procedure of purification which was necessary for the human leper[1] (though as a matter of course without the seven days of penitence or the guilt-offering). What was the nature of this leprosy which attached to clothes and houses, it is very difficult to determine with our present knowledge of the facts. It may be that human leprosy then, as a new disease, possessed such far greater powers of devastation that under certain conditions its matter might even communicate itself to clothes and houses (in a similar way as infectious disorders are believed to propagate themselves amongst us). Or it may be that the ancient nation, on account of its extreme horror of human leprosy, thought they detected it in appearances where the resemblance was only superficial, and have acted accordingly.[2] The whole matter must await future investigations for its closer determination.—With regard to contagious diseases in cattle, the law is silent, at least so far as it is preserved.

2. Unnatural Combinations.

Two things, though neither of them of a nature to cause impurity of themselves, might nevertheless by being united and intermingled produce something quite repulsive, shocking to a pure taste, and at the same time injurious. That things which are of two different kinds, i.e., which cannot be united, should not be mingled contrary to the order of nature, and therefore also against the will of the Creator, is indeed a universal and quite justifiable prohibition, to which Jahveism, with its indwelling delicate feeling for whatever is fitting, and its stringent horror of all that is unnatural, gave emphatic prominence, and endeavoured with no less consistency to carry out in common life. It is the lofty simplicity and purity of all its sentiments and aims so peculiar to Jahveism, which here, too, finds expression, and maintains its position against so many unnatural

---

[1] Lev. xiii. 47–59, xiv. 33–57.
[2] Thus J. D. Michaelis thinks that the leprosy in houses is corrosion due to saltpetre, and that that in clothes is mort-lings, as it is called. But the description of the latter in Seetzen's *Reisen*, i. s. 204, does not harmonise, and neither are just the thing.

or even pernicious excrescences of Egyptian or other heathen advanced civilisations. No doubt the horror of this mixing of different things may easily be carried too far, and in the dawn of Antiquity when the special applications of this principle passed into law, man had not nearly enough knowledge and experience in order to settle the unalterable boundaries in all particular cases. But we need not on this account fail to recognise the truth of the principle.

The individual applications of it which the oldest law[1] already gives as examples are the following:—1. Animals of two different species were not to be allowed to copulate. This was right enough; only the question arises here, how far the animal species are related one to another, or whether they are totally unrelated? However, the law could not have forbidden the crossing of the horse and the ass, so far, at least as the oft-mentioned mule proves this. Deuteronomy forbids in like manner yoking cattle and asses to the same plough.[2]—2. The field (as well as the vineyard, according to the later addition of the Deuteronomist[3]) was not to be sown with different kinds of seed. What primitive custom may have given occasion for this prohibition, we are now unfortunately unable to determine; but the law assuredly meant more than that bad seed should not be mixed with good, or that weeds should not be tolerated on cultivated land.—3. No clothing was to be worn which was made of two different materials, e.g., of wool and of linen. There are clear traces[4] that this was common in Egypt, and probably the material was adulterated for purposes of deception. All the more stress, therefore, would the law place on absolute purity and simplicity in articles of clothing. The full meaning and the final occasion of this enactment may, however, be recognised somewhat more closely when we remember the ancient estimation in which wool was held as a material for dress, a point which is spoken of below in connection with the dress of the priests.—Nor must we suppose that the law lightly

---

[1] Lev. xix. 19, the oldest law concerning כִּלְאַיִם, *different things*, which must not be brought into union. The way in which the Deuteronomist translates such primitive phrases into the language of his own day may be seen very clearly in xxii. 9–11.
[2] Deut. xxii. 10.
[3] Deut. xxii. 9.
[4] In the primitive law, Lev. xix. 19, שַׁעַטְנֵז, the Egyptian name for such mixed material, is added, clearly for the purpose of explanation. It must, therefore, at that time have been a name still generally understood. But as by the time of the Deuteronomist the word may have become obscure, he explains it, xxii. 11, by the addition 'of wool and linen.' In fact, it may easily be the same form with dialectic changes as the two words still retained in Coptic, ⲥ̄ⲡⲧ ⲛ̄ⲥⲉⲛⲧ, i.e. wool-linen, as a compound. The transition of an *r* into a *y* can be explained, and the last word may have ended in the earliest times with a *z* (*r*), passing finally into a *u*.

regarded the transgression of these enactments. There is one passage[1] which shows us that a field improperly sown, together with its fresh seed or with its crop, was in danger of being confiscated without further ado.

A similar prohibition forbids men to boil a kid in its mother's milk. It seemed as though it was most harsh and shocking to all humane feeling to cook the young creature in the very milk which should properly nourish it, and as though even in death it, as well as its mother, could feel the pain occasioned thereby. We no longer know what more or less shocking spectacle may have given occasion to this prohibition, at the very least it may have been the growth of a custom of slaying and cooking both the old and the young animal at the same time. The words, however, evidently became a kind of proverbial saying by which Jahveism was reminded of the gentle kindness and considerate forbearance which ought always to distinguish it from ruder religions. As a short pithy maxim of this sort, this sentence concludes the whole series of laws in the Book of Covenants, and in later legal compilations it recurs in a position which of itself shows its importance.[2] In like manner the Book of Origins requires that a full-grown animal and its young shall never be slain for eating on the same day.[3] But when the Jews much later thence derived the theory and established the practice that meat should never be cooked with butter[4] (because it is impossible to tell whether the butter does not come from the mother of the calf or bullock), they then in part exceed the meaning of the saying, in part fall short of it.

In the next place forbidden marriages would in great measure belong to this section, but they will be better spoken of below. This, however, is quite the place to notice the stringent prohibition of all the unnatural lusts mentioned by the law,[5] as well as of intercourse between men and beasts.[6]

---

[1] Deut. xxii. 9. For the verb קָדַשׁ see p. 79. הַמְלֵאָה הַזֶּרַע means, according to *Lehrbuch*, § 281 *b*, 290 *c*, 'that is filled with the seed,' i.e. the vineyard in which the seed is about to spring up.

[2] Ex. xxiii. 19.—xxxiv. 26; Deut. xiv. 21. If it said here only 'thou shalt not slay (sacrifice),' we might perhaps take the intermediate words in the sense '*on* its mother's milk,' so that the prohibition would only apply to the slaying of a very young animal. But then it could not be to 'cook' or 'seethe;' and the special significance which it is manifest the saying has would not be explained.—Even the conjecture to read, as in ver. 18, בְּחֵלֶב, '*in

the *fat* of its mother,' would not suit the case; the sense would be the same, but the connection between the milk and the still sucking kid would be lost.

[3] Lev. xxii. 28. A similar prohibition, Deut. xxii. 6 sq., is further touched on below.

[4] Or בִּישֵׁר בְּחָלָב, as it is found *M.* שׁ״ע, v. 9, and which they would deem absolutely forbidden.

[5] Lev. xviii. 22, repeated in the Book of Origins xx. 13; comp. also what is said below in connection with marriage.

[6] Lev. xviii. 23; xx. 15 sq.; Deut. xxvii. 21.

All such abominations were to be punished with death, and the animal was to be killed along with the human brute.

Even the prohibition against interchange of dress between the sexes[1] finds its place here, so far as it is capable of bearing a general significance. For as an actual fact, such interchange, when made on purpose and of itself worthy of censure, occurred for the most part in certain heathen mysteries, where men put on the dress of women or women that of men.[2] Nor need we doubt that some such abominable spectacles were present in the mind of the legislator, for they were in existence early enough in Egypt and among the Canaanites. But the law, in the universal form in which it was conceived, undoubtedly admits a more general application.[3]

Unnatural Mutilation and Disfigurement of the Body.

Nearly allied to the prohibitions of unnatural combinations, are those which relate to the mutilation and disfigurement of the body. It is really very surprising to see the warmth and decision with which at so early a date Jahveism set its face against every kind of savage disfigurement of the body, and especially of the human frame. Only a religion which saw in the whole of creation the self-constant power of a single, infinitely exalted, wise and good Creator, and in the human body the possible abode of the holy spirit of this all-perfect God, could have successfully demanded in its legislation so deep a horror of arbitrarily injuring and defacing the lovely work of God. No doubt circumcision presents a manifest exception in this legislation;[4] but apart from this case, which came down unaltered from a very early time, the law shows here as elsewhere, the grand self-consistency with which it endeavoured to carry out what it deemed needful. The details of the following cases specially concern us here.

In the first place, the law forbade every sort of human

[1] Deut. xxii. 5.
[2] It was just the same habitual conception and desire which expressed itself, e.g. in the representation of Hermaphrodites; comp. Gerhard on *Eros*, in the *Berl. Akad. Abh.* 1848, s. 290 and 109. Raoul-Rochette in the *Mémoires de l'Institut*, xvii. 2, p. 92 sqq., 287. The best known case is the clothing of the priests of Kybele as women, comp. *Hist.* iv. 100 sq., and Meliton in Cureton's *Spicil. Syr.* p. 28, 2. It was done, e.g. in this way. The men brought their richest attire as an offering to a goddess, and received in its place for the period that the mysteries lasted women's clothing which the priests kept in readiness, and which they received back again when all was over. —There is a ludicrous reference to change of clothing in a battle in Joseph. *Antiq.* bk. iv. 8. 43.
[3] As Tiberius, in the *Annals* of Tacitus iii. 53, severely condemns in sweeping terms the *promiscuæ viris et fœminis vestes*.
[4] P. 89 sqq.

castration, so much so that any man thus mutilated was shut out from the community and its rights.¹ The life at the Egyptian and Assyrian courts had undoubtedly introduced this immoral practice at a very early date.² All the more strongly, therefore, did Jahveism oppose it; and it is plainly due only to a renewal of the Egyptian and Assyrian influence when in later days eunuchs are to be found at the courts of the kings of the Ten Tribes and of Judah.³ David certainly did not introduce this court-practice, nor yet in all probability did Solomon. Nevertheless, when later on, an undeserved contempt for those who had once been castrated had not unnaturally become prevalent, we find one of the later prophets speaking strongly enough against the universal belief in the inferior moral worth of a eunuch.⁴—The consistency so often mentioned of the primitive legislation procured the extension of this command even to all domestic animals.⁵ This must have caused the rearing of cattle to have assumed a remarkable form in many respects, but we cannot doubt that at one time the law was carried out with extreme stringency.

In the second place, there prevailed in those countries from very early times, the varied expressions of a wildly-excited mourning for the dead, which had no scruples in exercising its raging violence on the body, and thought that propriety demanded its disfigurement or mutilation. The hair of the head and beard, man's adornment according to the oldest representation of the Hebrews, was shaved, wholly or partially, and the body beaten or scratched to wound it.⁶ The law did not indeed forbid those signs of excited grief and wailing which can soon be effaced, such as tearing of the clothes in front downwards from the breast (which was but a sign that mourning garments must now be put on), or beating of the breast; but it did prohibit the above-mentioned manifestations which would permanently disfigure the body.⁷ However, the Book of Origins is moved to increase the stringency of this prohibition, especially in regard to the priests, as though elsewhere it was not always adhered to so strictly;⁸ and this latter fact,

¹ The law on the matter is now to be found only in Deut. xxiii. 2 [1]; but according to all tokens it dates from the origin of the community, and its omission from the earlier sections of the Pentateuch which are preserved to us is only accidental.

² As may be seen so vividly, as regards the ancient court of Nineveh, on the Assyrian antiquities dug out by Botta and Layard.

³ See *Hist.* iii. 271.
⁴ ex. Is. lvi. 3–5.
⁵ This is implied in the words Lev. xxii. 24, although this law is spoken of here only in connection with sacrifice.
⁶ The הִתְגָּדֵד, Deut. xiv. 1: comp. 1 Kings xviii. 28.
⁷ Lev. xix. 28, and with a fine reason for it, Deut. xiv. 1 sq.
⁸ Lev. xxi. 5.

especially in relation to cutting the hair, is plain also from other tokens.[1]

In the third place, just the same disfigurements of the beauty of the body were customary as an imagined mark of reverence for a Deity, as has already been more fully described.[2] These superstitious practices were forbidden by the oldest law with the utmost decision,[3] and here there can be no doubt that the practice in ordinary life in Israel was no less strict. Even the branding or tattooing on the skin of the name or symbol of the Deity, as well as of sundry sacred guardian words, which was a custom very extensively prevalent among many ancient nations of those regions,[4] is forbidden by the earliest law;[5] and as a matter of fact the practice does not seem to have prevailed extensively in the nation, although the Bible not unfrequently alludes to such symbols on the body by which the confessors of a God deemed themselves protected.[6]

Finally, it was undoubtedly another consequence of Jahveism's peculiar horror of all mutilation and laceration of the human body, that it did not legalise any intentionally horrible capital or corporal punishments, so that wherever such are to be found in the Bible, they appear to have been first introduced from the royal courts among the heathens.[7] The matter cannot be further discussed till we come to the judicial penalties.

Equally decided, however, is the injunction of the law not to despise nor yet deride or persecute anyone on account of a bodily infirmity or of an obscure terrible disease and

---

[1] Amos viii. 10; Is. iii. 24, Mic. i. 10, Jer. xvi. 6. xli. 5 (comp. xlvii. 5).
[2] P. 89 sqq.
[3] Lev. xix. 27 sq. That in these two verses, only the first member of the second verse refers to mourning for the dead, is also clear from the addition לָנֶפֶשׁ, which is found only here, and on which comp. p. 149, at. 2.
[4] It is the وَسْم which the women used to do in the early days of the Arabs, Lebîd's Moall. ver. 9; and even now the pilgrim to Mecca receives three cuts on his face (Maltzahn's Wallfahrt nach Mecca, ii. s. 132, 244). Comp. also the Britonum stigmata, in Tertull. De Vel. Virg. x.
[5] Lev. xix. 28 b.
[6] See note on the Apocal. vii. 3, comp. Ezek. ix. 6, but not nx. Is. xliv. 5. For the Maccabean period see Psalm. Sol. xv. 10; 3 Macc. ii. 29, and on the तोलक of the Hindoos see Gött. Gel. Anz. 1852, s. 187 sq.
[7] Like the death inflicted in a thousand cruel forms by slowly tearing apart or cutting off the limbs, e.g. a right hand and a left foot, the διχοτομεῖν or قطع من خلاف which Mahomet so often speaks of in connection with crucifixion, Sur. v. 37, vii. 121, xx. 74, xxvi. 49, and which is still practised e.g. in Ethiopia (Sapeto's Viaggio tra i Bogos, p. 119), as it also was in Persia, Dan. ii. 5, Matt. xxiv. 51; or by sawing in pieces (comp. Cureton's Ancient Syriac Documents, p. 59 sqq., and ܐܪܒ in Lagarde's Anal. p. 57. 22; Suet. Calig. s. 27; also mentioned in Shâhnâmeh as practised among the Persians), and smashing in pieces, Heb. xi. 35-37; by crucifixion, comp. Hist. v. s. 482 sqq. [German ed.]; by slowly roasting e.g. in glowing ashes, Jer. xxix. 22, 2 Macc. xiii. 5; lastly, by blinding. In war vengeance was often very severe, see below.

distress.¹ On this matter the Book of Job has something more to say.

3. THE CONSIDERATION SHOWN FOR NATURE.

All these prohibitions lead up to the one great command, to honour and be considerate towards Nature as the work of God, nay, even to sympathise with her and live in her life. Thus, not only will the Creator's will be done, but the benefits which man is instructed and permitted to draw from her will increase. Even the legislation of Jahveism is penetrated with a kindly feeling of this sort. The young fruit tree was to be three years before it was pruned on man's behalf, and even if it bore fruit, no use was as yet to be made of it. In the fourth year its fruit was to be offered to Jahveh, and only in the fifth year did it belong regularly to man. This is what the Book of Origins prescribes,² and promises thereby with justice that he who does not prematurely usurp or use greedily the fertility of Nature, shall reap all the richer blessing. Deuteronomy even enacts that in war no fruit tree in an enemy's country shall be cut down for the purpose of using its wood for the operations of a siege,³ and thereby puts to shame those of our time who would forget 'that it is not with trees that war is carried on, but with men.'

In particular the law enjoined consideration for animals, as the objects which in all nature stand nearest to man, and whose sufferings he himself is most able to share. No doubt Deuteronomy, true to its whole spirit, is the first to find a definite place for these feelings in the various details of legislation, the ox treading out the grain was not to be muzzled, eggs or young ones were not to be taken out of the nest along with the mother, but the latter was to be allowed to fly away.⁴ But the genuine Mosaic comments on the Ten Commandments already show that even as the benefits of the Sabbath were especially to be shared by all the hard-toiling dependent human beings, so too they were to come to the relief of the similarly toiling domestic animals,⁵ and an equally kindly tone sought to prevail permanently among the people.⁶

¹ Lev. xix. 14; brought very strongly into prominence, Deut. xxvii. 18.
² Lev. xix. 23-25.
³ Deut. xx. 19 sq.
⁴ Deut. xxv. 4, xxii. 6 sq.; comp.
p. 162.
⁵ Ex. xx. 10, Deut. v. 14, comp. *Hist.* ii. 163 sq.
⁶ Comp. Prov. xii. 10, Hos. xi. 4.

II. Sanctity in Human Beings, or Personal Holiness.

For man as distinguished from other beings, Jahveism set up a highest truth, which was capable of serving in all laws as a guiding principle in respect to man's various legal relations. This is the conception that man from the time of the creation, bears the image of God, that is, possesses a worth which raises him above the rest of creation, which, just because it had been given to him at the creation, never again could be wholly lost, of which all men without distinction essentially partake, and which, as a germ implanted in each individual, must freely develope itself there, so as to fulfil its divine destiny and bring forth the flower of its hidden nature. This is already the position taken by the Book of Origins;[1] and the same fundamental view of the worth and destiny of mankind, even apart from this fine idea of man being formed in the image of God, penetrates the whole of the Old Testament in the most manifold representations and phrases. Thus a sure foundation was laid for all particular legal enactments in regard to man in all the conditions of his life, if only this fundamental truth were carried, with unfaltering consistency and determination, right through all the ancient obscurities and complications which had become traditional in the common and lower life.

But nowhere have so many difficulties been at all times accumulated against the carrying out of a lofty truth, as in that province in which a man feels himself primarily a member of a particular household, or tribe, or nation; and these relations are mostly to be found where the distinctive characteristics of man are concerned. Long before the truths of an elevated religion tried to penetrate the world, the sanctuaries of the house, of the tribe, and of the nation, were the firm seats of customs which offered the most stubborn resistance whenever it seemed as if the only things that were concerned were man himself and the lower primary conditions of the existence of a human household. If this fact still proves true everywhere, how much more would it be the case in those early days when, for the first time, such higher truths were revealed, and the establishment of their authority was attempted! In conformity

---

[1] In order to understand the complete idea of the Book of Origins we must compare Gen. i. 26 sq. with v. 1–3, ix. 6, and remember that the fundamental truth (ix. 6) is repeated in a primary law on the worth of man; it may also have been repeated along with other similar primary laws. How other writers, though without this special conception, proclaim the same fundamental truth, may be seen in the example Job xxxi. 15.

with this fact, we can distinctly observe that this loftier principle was allowed freer play, and soon secured greater successes in all those distinctions where it was least hampered by primitive domestic customs. At the same time so much genuine motive power dwelt in it, that in the course of time it did imperceptibly modify and finally completely transform the life of the ancient community in spite of all the mighty force of opposing customs.

We shall now consider this personal sanctity of man in its separate aspects, and commence with the one which is nearest to hand and is at the same time the most momentous of all.

1. THE SANCTITY OF HUMAN LIFE.

That the life, or, to express the idea in another more Hebrew word, the 'soul' of a man, possesses of itself an inviolable sanctity, is one of the first principles which was firmly established among the nobler races from the very earliest times, and in which all those presentiments of something Infinite being implanted in man sought to find the clearest expression possible. All more particular historical reminiscence begins with the fact of the sanctity of human life being already terribly violated in every variety of way; and the sinful impulses had also become sufficiently pernicious and excitable in this direction before the human race set about repressing them energetically. Then, in order to uphold the true principle, there arose among the nobler and more spirited races what is known as the *vengeance of blood*. This was already an established custom in the primitive days when the household was still everything, and when a kingdom embracing all individuals was either extremely weak or altogether wanting, and at that time it alone furnished this most indispensable reciprocal protection for life. The avenger of blood is the *redeemer*,[1] he is the next heir; he inherits not merely the goods but the corresponding debts and duties of the dying man. If, then, it is one of the first duties of a living man not to endure any wrong that has been put upon him and to avenge all insult, if, moreover, having been wrongfully murdered, he is himself unable to discharge this duty, then the nearest of kin or his representative inherits, along with his other new duties, the vengeance of

---

[1] It is originally גֹּאֵל, the redeemer, ransomer, he who desires to redeem a person or a thing which belongs to himself from another who now possesses or retains it contrary to justice.

blood as the most sacred of them all, and the full burden of infamy rests on him should he not discharge this most burning obligation. Accordingly, it was a further and natural consequence that the whole family of the murdered man took this duty upon themselves,[1] and however long, or with whatever craft, the murderer might seek to baffle the avenger, this only called for more craft and persistence on the part of the latter. The investigation whether a murder were intentional or not undoubtedly led very early to simple *expiation* for what was done without purpose; but among many nations, even in the case of intentional murder, it became a custom to compound with *blood-money* for the life which was forfeited to this right of retaliation.

Among the people of Israel this ancient vengeance of blood lasted a very long time with little essential alteration. Even in David's time his first general Joab suffers himself to be carried away in executing it with the aid of his brother, without being at once seriously punished by the king;[2] and images and phrases originating in its practice, and in the most vivid ideas about it, abound in the Old Testament.[3] It is true that the Book of Origins requires that the community should first institute an investigation into the guilt of every murder, and that at least two witnesses should come forward against the accused, a regulation which assuredly comes from Moses himself.[4] But this law may have been often infringed, especially by men of high station full of vain notions of their social honour; and in all cases there at any rate remained this significant relic of former days, that the murderer when condemned to death was simply handed over to the avenger of blood and his family for the vengeance to be inflicted. Thus it was still the avenger of blood alone who insisted on the accusation and the passing of the judgment.[5]

---

[1] Like 2 Sam. xiv. 7, from which the plural אֱלֹהִים may be explained, Ruth ii. 20. Among the Bedouins at the present day, the ڎو extends even to the fifth degree of kinship: Burckhardt's *Notes on the Bed.*, p. 85. Layard's *Discoveries*, p. 305 sq. If we reckon this number five according to a series of consecutive generations, and remember that so many, according to Gen. l. 23, were the utmost that could be thought of as living together with the father of the race or his sons, we shall be able to explain from it the incient way of speaking of the Divine vengeance extending unto the fifth generation, Ex. xx. 5, comp. xxxiv. 7. For that the שִׁלֵּשִׁים, are great-grandchildren (and therefore בְּנֵי שִׁלֵּשִׁים, great-great-grandchildren), reckoned as the third generation from the father of the race, is proved by the derivation of the Mongolian word *ghotschi*, great-grandchildren, from *ghe*, three. Comp. also *Lehrbuch*, § 155 c.

[2] 2 Sam. iii. 26-30, comp. ii. 23.

[3] Gen. iv. 10, Job xvi. 18 sq., comp. xx. 27, Is. xxvi. 21; the expression 2 Sam. i. 21, has less connection here.

[4] It follows from Num. xxxv. 12, 24 sqq., 30.

[5] Num. xxxv. 19, 24 sqq.; repeated Deut. xix. 12. Very similar was the

194   But what is really peculiar to Jahveism in this matter is the universal extreme dread of in any way polluting the holy land by human blood, and the mighty efforts corresponding to so unusual a dread which it made to wash out any stain of this kind which had been contracted. Here, again, we have a fine manifestation of the earnest moral tone of Jahveism, which, partly by means of the persistence of these most vivid ideas about the vengeance of blood, partly by means of the loftier conceptions which now for the first time began to prevail respecting the worth of mankind, stimulated the feelings till they appeared in the form of this most profound dread. With the prohibition of murder the second half of the Ten Commandments begins;[1] the legislation in the Book of Covenants in like manner assigns with terse emphasis the penalty of death for every murder,[2] and wherever the nature of its theme gives occasion for it, the Book of Origins repeats the same lesson with a fine copious flow of the most serious discourse;[3] and again, Deuteronomy commands that no outburst of pity shall stand in the way of removing the stain of innocent blood from Israel.[4] It is besides distinctly stated that this law shall come into operation in the case of every murder without exception, so that even the sanctuary of the house, should a murder take place there, will not protect the criminal.[5] Even if a human life is destroyed, e.g., by a bull, this must not pass without punishment. The bull himself, as bearing an immeasurable weight of guilt, must be stoned, and as an unclean beast might not be eaten; even the life of its master, if he were acquainted with the animal's tendency to gore, must also at the same time be forfeited. Such were the requirements of the earliest law, which came 195 into existence while this profound dread was still fresh.[6] But if the murderer of a corpse, e.g., found lying out in the fields, could not be discovered, then the Elders of the nearest town were to slaughter a young clean heifer over the waters of a brook which was never dried up, and then while the water was carrying away the blood of this heifer—which was shed instead

procedure of the Arabs under the first Chalifs; comp. the conclusion of the narrative, a most instructive one for this whole legal system, Hamâsa, p. 235 sq. Comp. also the ancient phrase, Gen. xvii. 14, which will be explained under the judicial punishments.

[1] In the Cod. Vat. of the LXX in Ex. xx. 13, the prohibition of murder comes after that of stealing; not so in Deut. v. 17. The transposition seems to have been arbitrary.
[2] Ex. xxi. 12.
[3] Gen. ix. 5 sq., Lev. xxiv. 17, Num. xxxv. 33 sq.
[4] Deut. xix. 11-13.
[5] Ex. xxi. 20, Gen. ix. 5, Lev. xxiv. 17, 21.
[6] In the legislation of the Book of Covenants, Ex. xxi. 28-32; comp. above p. 8 sq.

of that of the criminal, and for this reason could wash away the innocent blood of the murdered man—they were to protest their own innocence and make entreaties for Divine compassion. Deuteronomy is the first to give this command,[1] but here, as in certain instances elsewhere, it is plainly only supplementing, according to its own style of composition, a primitive sacred custom which had not till then been committed to writing. For the essential element in this practice is wholly derived from this profound dread belonging to the original Jahveism.

It was an important consequence of this stringency that the acceptance of blood-money was not permitted in any form whatever, and so deep were the roots of this feeling that no special Hebrew word was found to express this mode of compensation.[2] The guilty owner of a bull with a propensity for goring was the only one who could redeem himself by such a payment, the amount of which was to be determined according to the will of the avenger of blood.[3] All other blood-money is expressly forbidden by the law,[4] although there are many tokens[5] to show that in later times it was nevertheless sometimes accepted.

Still more remarkable is it that even for unintentional manslaughter[6] no money might be paid as an expiation, notwithstanding that this had always been allowed by the ancient Arabic legislation. The holy land seemed to be too much desecrated by human blood shed even in this manner, for it to be possible to efface the stain by so inadequate a means as money. The law provided for such a case in this way: a man who, through no fault of his own, against whom no evil purpose (i.e. hatred) could be established, and who without any lying in wait for his victim, but purely through misfortune, had slain another, might flee to a sacred spot, and there shelter himself under its superior sanctity from the human vengeance of the victim's relatives. No place, however, but one specially sacred, was competent to protect one whose hand had been dyed with human blood, and accordingly when the holy land was taken

---

[1] Deut. xxi. 1-9. This would be accordingly the θύειν τὰ κωλυτήρια, Ἀνιρρuncatoria Sacra, Jamblich. Vit. Pyth. ch. xxviii. (141).

[2] כֹּפֶר, properly *expiation*, according to p. 123, *nt. 4*, stands for blood-money. Comp. Sûr. vi. 69.

[3] Ex. xxi. 30.

[4] Num. xxxv. 31.

[5] Not such phrases as את, Is. xliii. 3, 1 Sam. xii. 3, which, on account of the more extended use of money as compensation, do not apply here; the only ones that are decisive are such as Prov. xiii. 8 (if we are not to think here merely of the case in Ex. xxi. 30) and Ps. xlix. 8 [7] sq., בך. Job xxxvi. 18 (here, however, heathen practices may have given occasion to use the phrase).

[6] Of course heathen legislation, too, punished this, see the later subtleties on the point in Porphyr. *De Abstin.* i. 9.

possession of and divided, three specially sacred places on either side of the Jordan had this right of refuge assigned to them, receiving however along with it the duty of executing the blood-ban.[1] Each one of these places was at such a distance from the rest that six cities of refuge were enough for the whole of the twelve tribes. Nevertheless, as during the period of the Judges, the possessions of the nation passed altogether into a state of great insecurity, it may be that only the one place where the ark of the covenant stood was deemed a consecrated secure refuge.[2] On the other hand, in the later times of the kings, the growing population seems to have necessitated an increase in the number of those on the nearer side of the Jordan, as is proved by the expression in Deuteronomy.[3] The fugitive had to state the grounds of his petition for security at the gate of such a city; and only when these reasons were approved was he admitted and taken under the protection of the community of the sacred place. The avenger of blood could, however, still demand a legal investigation before the great national assembly.[4] If this investigation proved the real guilt of the manslayer, he was bound and handed over to the avenger of blood and his allies, and these executed the death-penalty upon him in what way they pleased.[5] But if the result was to show that the man had caused the death of the other without intention, he was then permitted to dwell quietly within the precincts of a secure place of refuge of this kind; being sufficiently punished in never being able to leave its narrow boundaries, for should the avenger of blood meet with him outside, he might kill him without punishment. Only when the death of the High-priest took place, did a new era of judicial decisions commence, and the innocent manslayer, if in the mean time no new grounds for suspicion had been discovered against him, regained his full freedom.[6] The reason of this will be explained hereafter. The law, however, forbade as utterly inadmissible, and defiling the sanctity of the place, any convention between

---

[1] Book of Origins, Num. xxxv. 9-24, Josh. xx. Of the three on the nearer side, the most northern city, Kedesh, was already, by its name, a sanctuary in the north from primitive times; Shechem and Hebron were so also by other well-known adequate tokens. We know less of those beyond Jordan: Bezer in the south, Ramoth in the middle, and Golan in the north.

[2] This appears from Ex. xxi. 13 sq.

[3] Deut. xix. 8 sq. That the three cities which the Deuteronomist wishes to see added are to be placed on the nearer side of the Jordan, is clear from the expressions in ver. 1-7, comp. iv. 41-43. for there is no reason for making the Deuteronomist contradict himself here.

[4] Num. xxxv. 12, 24 sq., according to which the words in Josh. xx. 6 are to be understood.

[5] It follows from the words 2 Sam. iii. 34, as well as from the nature of the case itself.

[6] Num. xxxv. 25-28, Josh. xx. 6.

CITIES OF REFUGE. 173

the manslayer and the avenger of blood. The former, if he were really guilty, might pay no blood-money to the latter in order to obtain the privilege of sheltering himself within the sacred place of refuge.[1] Nor could any altar to which he might have fled protect the guilty criminal.[2]

The Book of Origins seeks further to define the cases of intentional murder more closely,[3] but the law allows no intermediate cases between intentional murder and unintentional manslaughter. So long, therefore, as the stringency of Jahveism prevailed, we may be sure that unintentional manslaughter was restricted within extremely narrow boundaries, so that a man of a more noble disposition even expresses his pity for the unhappy one, who 'laden with blood' has to make his way, perhaps through a thousand perils to a distant place of refuge,[4] and it was censured as an infamous transgression to slay such fugitives on the way ere they reached the sacred spot, and a regular judicial procedure could be instituted.[5] And while Jahveism gave great prominence to the inconsolable state of the guilty man tortured by an evil conscience, even though he had committed a murder only in unpremeditated haste and passion;[6] so also did it depict in the example of the wicked patriarch, Cain, the possibility of the control of a higher Divine grace being exercised in the case of a murder, and the fearful consequences of a wild vengeance for blood.[7] Indeed, we cannot fail to recognise that it clings to the possibility of sparing the life of the murderer, and maintains, at any rate in this example out of primitive times, that even he may become a member of the human race, and one not without its utility. This was as though to prove that what seemed impossible in the actual state of the human race, might yet be restored in the days of Messianic perfection, even as it had been in the remotest primeval times."—When the institution of the human

---

[1] Num. xxxv. 32.
[2] Comp. 1 Kings ii. 28-34.
[3] Num xxxv. 16-24; comp. the much briefer distinctions of the earlier legislation, Ex. xxi. 13. Unintentional manslaughter is distinguished most clearly of all in the example Deut xix. 5.
[4] Accordingly Deut. xix. 3 gives an exhortation to smooth the way to the sacred places; and this, along with the addition similar in spirit explained above, is all that is new in Deut xix. 1-13.
[5] Hos. vi. 9.
[6] Prov. xxviii. 17. Gen. iv. 10-12.
[7] Gen. iv. 13-15.
[8] As regards the question so much agitated in our times about the possible abolition of capital punishment, we must primarily commence in the Bible with a correct explanation of this legend, Gen. iv. 1-17, as it is given in the *Jahrbb. der Bibl. Wiss.* vi. s. 1-16, and is supplemented here. If the issue of all history may correspond to its origin, and the Messianic perfection restore the simplicity and purity of primitive days, then the Divine power to inflict punishment entrusted to mankind (p. 138) for these extreme cases, as it was given in the course of history, may in like manner be recalled in the course of history. After the Divine permission to inflict capital punishment,

monarchy made it possible to make the rigid, stringent law more humane and mild in certain suitable cases, without its becoming too pliable and yielding, we see the kings using their highest and fairest prerogative—that of remitting a deserved penalty—for the benefit even of a murderer. History, however, teaches us how extraordinarily difficult it was to take the first step towards bending the rigidness of the old law.[1]

As a precaution against causing accidental death, Deuteronomy requires that the (almost flat) roof of any new house should be surrounded with a parapet, so that the owner might not bring upon his house the guilt of blood in case of a fatal fall.[2] Probably a house where this did happen would need some sort of expiation.

Suicide in the earlier and healthier days of the nationality was of very rare occurrence among ordinary people, and the ancient law determined nothing special in regard to it. Nor does it seem, if we may draw this conclusion from an ancient narrative, to have involved any civic disgrace as its penalty.[3] It was not till later times when all ideas of soul and life were in greater and more desperate confusion, that it occurred more frequently; then, however, it was always abhorred at least in the popular estimation as a transgression of the deepest hue. The corpse was not buried before sunset, the soul was supposed to wend its solitary way to the deepest hell, while the murderer himself was deemed for ever cursed in his posterity.[4]

Equally little is said of infanticide, because to the ancient nation it was as good as unknown. On one side it is true this abomination penetrated deep into the heart of the highly civilised nations of antiquity, as well as of those that were uncivilised. The ancient prejudice that the birth of a daughter was an undesirable event, nay was even a misfortune, as well as the poverty of many parents, and the perverse notions of social position (as was the case among Hindoo hereditary royal families) were causes which early led to a very wide extension of the practice of putting daughters to death,[5] and it still

which had been given for a considerable period of time, had displayed itself as the most extreme madness in the execution of Christ, the question of its abolition has become only a question of time. The question is whether Christ may not have done enough for this.

[1] *Hist.* iii.117 sq., 173 sqq.
[2] Deut. xxii. 8, comp. the important historical example, 2 Kings i. 2.
[3] Comp. 2 Sam. xvii. 23.

[4] Fl. Josephus, *Bell. Jud.* bk. iii. 8. 4-7. There is an allusion to the conception in regard to hell in John viii. 22.
[5] Exposure, and therefore the murder, of daughters occurs already in the Veda (A. Weber, *Über die Naxatra*, ii. s. 314). The ancient Arabs had even a special word, ا‍ٔد, for burying daughters alive, see *Hamâsa*, p. 117, last line, sqq., with the further remarks there.

prevails extensively in the Chinese Empire. So long, moreover, as the rights of parents over their children were upheld in their earliest one-sided stringency, it was not easy to make child-murder of any sort punishable. But the spirit of the higher religion of the Old Testament was evidently opposing such violence from the first with all its might. If Mahomet, along with all his perversities, has at any rate this great merit of having rigidly put a stop to all infanticide, especially with regard to daughters,[1] Moses deserves the credit of having done the same much earlier and in a more enduring form.

Legal Rights in regard to Corporal or Moral Integrity.

If human life as a whole is sacred, it must also be inviolable in all its several corporal or mental constituents, and damage done to these by neighbours must be punishable.[2]

With regard to corporal injuries, the law which is so stringent in the case of murder, proceeds consistently to demand that as life must be exacted for life, so must eye for eye, tooth for tooth, wound for wound, and so on. The ancient legislation of the Book of Covenants enacts this with the utmost distinctness,[3] and the Book of Origins deems it sufficient to repeat this incidentally in a shorter form.[4] That unintentional injuries would not be intended here, is a matter of course. Even in the case of those that were intentional, the law interfered only at the express suit of the injured person, and undoubtedly in later times compensation for injuries were mostly made in money.[5] Such compensation, to be estimated by the judges, was already allowed by the ancient law, where a woman with child was so injured as to be brought to premature confinement;[6] and only 200 indemnity for time and expense was required when anyone was seriously hurt in an angry quarrel.[7]

But freedom from moral injury is as needful as from cor-

---

[1] Sûr. lxxxi. 8 sq., comp. xvi. 59 sq. They had even a ڪَبَاتٌ‌‌ ‌‌‌‌اَلْوَءَادِ of the old narrator el-Kelbí, *Journ. As.* 1861, p. 142.

[2] Here the question arises, whether the law, if it had no more adequate civic penalties for those who injured themselves corporally or morally, could punish the above-mentioned suicide with civic penalties? The presumption, according to the connection given above, must be in the negative; at any rate, in times when suicide was still very rare, tho law (as we saw above) will be able to pass over it.

[3] Ex. xxi. 23-25. How such a law is still put in force at the present day may be seen in Munzinger's *Ostafrikanischen Studien*, s. 502.

[4] Lev. xxiv. 19 sq.

[5] Although passages such as Prov. xix. 19 are too general for them to prove this, the fact itself admits of no doubt, see p. 171.

[6] Ex. xxi. 22, which has no close connection with ver. 23-25.

[7] Ex. xxi. 18.

poral. It is a duty of equal importance not to slander, not to hate, not to bear false witness, not to be partial towards either rich or poor, and the law is equally bound not to tolerate anything of this kind. Already the Decalogue forbids bearing false witness, and the earliest laws treat all that pertains to this as of great importance.[1] Nevertheless, they do not assign any penalties for particular cases, manifestly because they deemed it sufficient to leave this to the estimation of the judge. Deuteronomy is the first to demand with great earnestness the application of the old law of retaliation against deceitful witnesses, who out of malice seek to destroy the innocent.[2] In earlier times so much wickedness within the meshes of the external legal institutions may have been unheard of.

The Sacredness of Property.

Property is one of the fruits of personal activity, and this is especially true in the sense in which it is ordinarily taken, viz., the possession of earthly goods and utilities of every possible kind. For whatever be the extent to which property may also be merely inherited by a son from a father, or conveyed in various other ways from one possessor to another, and however obscure the origin of much of it may have become in the long course of centuries, still there can be no doubt that all property was due in the first instance to the suitable exertion and capacity of some particular human mind in appropriating the utilities of Nature, mastering and guiding her forces as well as her matter, and founding a new and more salutary order of things which becomes a power in the world. Property is accordingly the fruit of the activity of particular individuals, whether one man works by himself on his own account, or several co-operate at the same task, and when once the intelligence of any individual has been at work in a special way and for special reasonable ends, whatever portion of the goods of the world he has conquered and won, (of course) by fair means, belongs to him as his private property. However, it is equally correct that true religion teaches man not to estimate all that is called property in this sense, viz., the external possessions of life, higher than the spirit which first brought them into existence, and again, not to place them higher than the maintenance and well-being of the spiritual commonwealth on the earth, where he is placed as an individual moral being. All this

---

[1] Lev. xix. 15-18, Ex. xxiii. 1-3. [2] Deut. xix. 19-21.

finds full justice done to it in the various laws and the advice which Jahveism utters in respect to property. Only we must here connect properly together all that belongs to the subject, and in reality, according to the strict meaning of the truths, cannot be entirely torn asunder. We shall then readily see that the ancient law was no doubt still imperfect in this respect, but nevertheless already contained the soundest principles.

a. Fixed and Movable Property.

1. The existence of property is assumed by every system of legislation, even the earliest, because such a system can only follow on a long period of social development and exertion. But Jahveism assumes more than this. For according to it each of the twelve tribes of Israel is to have its landed possessions, and each individual household in the tribe is to have its definite portion of the land belonging to the tribe, which is for ever to remain the inalienable *heritage* of this house, and form the sure basis of all property. This is the enactment of the Book of Origins,[1] manifestly in accordance with a primitive settlement in the community after it had obtained a permanent residence.

Of a truth nothing is more desirable among a people for the most part engaged in agriculture than that each household should possess a landed inheritance of this nature, the cultivation of which shall afford its members the most indispensable necessaries of life, assure to them a trustworthy foundation for further toil and acquisitions, and bind them firmly to their fatherland and all their fellow-countrymen. And where a state, like that of Israel under Moses and Joshua, is founded by conquest, it is only fair that the conquered fields should be divided as equally as possible among those who shared the burden of the war and conquest, and thus form such hereditary estates. Accordingly, we find a similar institution among many an ancient nation which desired to cultivate its conquered land in peace, and to defend itself against fresh attacks.[2]

The Book of Origins was to this extent justified in referring

---

[1] It is true that just that passage in it, where this is properly dealt with and established, is no longer extant; but in many places this legal institution is presupposed, such as Lev. xxv. 13, 23; Num. xxvii. 1–11; xxxii. 18; xxxiv. 13; xxxvi.; comp. in particular xxxiii. 54. Allusion to the circumstance is made in such images as Ps. xvi. 5 sq.

[2] The constitution of Lycurgus in Sparta is especially to be compared, but also in Peru the legislation took similar precautions, see Prescott's *History of the Conquest of Peru*, i. s. 37.

this institution, which in his time had been long in force to a settlement made by Jahveh himself; just as in general it treats as divine the entire occupation of the holy land, and the division of it among the twelve tribes.[1] It was not the people of Israel by their merely human desire and ability that had won this fair domain. In a higher and a better sense God had conquered the country for them. Their God was therefore the real lord also of it, only from his hand did they receive possession of it, to enjoy it so long as they were-worthy of it; and along with the whole nation, each individual member received accordingly an hereditary estate, which nevertheless permanently belonged not to him as something contingent on his personality, but to his God.[2] This is the light in which the whole relation is conceived, and in its higher aspects nothing could be more true. How happy a valiant Israelite could be in the possession of his share of landed property, and how tenaciously he would cling to his ancestral estate, is seen in the story of Naboth, who refused to give up his even in exchange for a better one, and at the demand of the king.[3] If any external institution could serve to secure the attachment of the entire nation to the possession of the land which they had won, and to stimulate a peaceful diligent life in it, it was this agricultural settlement which was carried through with a firm hand immediately after the conquest. But it was equally the case that the settler might always have the consciousness that this possession which he rejoiced in as his own property, even as it had been given him by a higher power, could be taken away again from him in the same manner. And thus in this conception we find the impress of what alone is the true way of finally regarding all human property.

It will of course be understood that this hereditary estate was only the minimum of landed property which the head of a family might possess. Further possessions, especially in the case of the chiefs, were of course not excluded; they would consist partly of larger sections allotted to a deserving chief after the conquest or on some similar occasion, partly of private acquisitions. Instances of these larger sections are given in the Book of Origins, in the case of the estates of Caleb, of

---

[1] *Hist.* ii. 255 sqq.

[2] Lev. xxv. 23.—What would now be called state-loan land, or royal loan estates, was at that time regarded as being more directly Jahveh's estates, as hereditary lands which the individual had on loan from Jahveh. But assuredly this by no means meant that the priesthood, or some other ruling house, could take Jahveh's place as ultimate owner or feudal lord.

[3] 1 Kings xxi. 3 sq.; 2 Kings ix. 10, 25 sq.

Joshua, and of the high-priest Eleazar.[1] To manage these larger properties a grandee would keep a steward as 'servant,' i.e. as a bondsman or a vassal, a relation of which we have a clear example in the case of Ziba the 'servant' (i.e. client) of the royal house of Saul, who also appears to have been well off on his own account.[2] But there are other distinct allusions to it in the Old Testament.[3]

2. How this ancestral estate was to be inherited in the family of which it was the inalienable possession, we cannot now definitely tell. It is not likely, however, that the law forbade its being divided among all the sons of the father, or in general being cut up. Probably, however, the double portion which the first-born legally received,[4] consisted not only in the share in the ancestral estate, but also in a corresponding portion of the movable wealth, and of whatever other fixed property there might be. As far as this goes, all the domestic arrangements always remained during the formation of the laws of Jahveism as they had been established in the primitive times. The first-born was the principal heir and the proper representative of the family, but undoubtedly under the condition of taking on himself more of the duties of the head of the family than the other brothers, of maintaining the widows, and of providing for the unmarried daughters. Exceptions to these rights of the first-born were always occurring, as the legendary history reveals in its own way in the leading examples of Reuben and of other early heads of tribes; and in consequence of the great power and responsibilities of the heads of families in early days, such exceptions may often have been salutary. But it is quite in harmony with the progress of social development, that for the later times of civic peace and order the Deuteronomist forbids any exception of this kind, if it rests merely on the arbitrary will of the father.[5]—Sons of a concubine had only gifts to hope for;[6] those of meaner origin could expect nothing.[7]

Daughters inherited fixed property only under exceptional circumstances, with the consent of their father or their brothers, so that when a case of this kind occurs the reason for it is always expressly mentioned, sometimes as a rare instance of the utmost mutual affection of all the members of a family.[8] If

---

[1] Josh. xiv. 6-14; xxiv. 30, 33: comp. Num. xxxiii. 54.
[2] *Hist.* iii. 135, 181, 191.
[3] The whole imagery of the 'servant of Jahveh,' BK. Is. xlii.-liii. is only to be explained in this way; comp. *Die Propheten des A. Bs.* ii. s. 404 sqq.
[4] We learn this only from the incidental mention of it, Deut. xxi. 17.
[5] Deut. xxi. 15-17.
[6] According to Gen. xxv. 6 comp. xxiv. 36.
[7] Judg. xi. 1-7.
[8] See the narrative of Caleb's

there were no sons, the daughters shared all the property alike; but this was a new right acquired by the female sex, the origin of which only goes back to Moses.[1] The inheritance of a daughter then accompanied that of her husband, and if he belonged to another tribe, it must have passed over into the bounds of the latter. But from the time that the boundaries and the constitutions of the separate tribes in the holy land were properly determined, such a dismemberment of the boundaries of a tribe became more and more prejudicial; so that the Book of Origins enacts that heiresses may marry only within the limits of their own tribe.[2]—If there was not even a daughter, the inheritance came in due course to the father's brothers, next to the father's uncles, and finally, if these too were wanting, to the nearest of kin.[3] But it was not rare for the law to be evaded by treating a faithful slave as a son, marrying him to the heiress, adopting him altogether if there was no child, or even putting him on an equal footing with the sons of the house.[4]

3. This last fact is also an indication that to a certain extent an owner was at liberty to make his own will, and so dispose of his heritable wealth at pleasure.[5] An oral declaration of his wishes seems to have been adequate to this purpose; but we have now no further information on the subject.

Buying and selling, or exchange and cession, according to the above conditions, could apply without limitation to fixed property only when it formed no part of the ancestral estate. The latter, if it ever went out of the possession of the original owner, reverted to him in the year of Jubilee (which will be spoken of below), so that only the usufruct for the intervening time could be disposed of to another, and it must be then redeemed if this had not been done previously.—In the earliest times all business of this kind was done by public transactions in the market, so that the witness of the whole community, or at least of ten of its elders, served to confirm it.[6] As, however, at such times the strongest visible tokens would be needed to assist the memory, the custom of drawing off the shoe at a

---

daughter, *Hist.* ii. 285; further see Job xlii. 15; comp. i. 4; Langlois' *Harivansa*, i. p. xi. sq.

[1] Num. xxvii. 1-8.

[2] Num. xxvi. 1-11; Josh. xvii. 3 sq.; 1 Chron. vii. 15 sq. The five daughters of Zelophehad, however, originally indicated, according to Josh. xvii. 5 sq., the five bastard races of Manasseh (*Hist.* i. 378 *note* 1) as contrasted with the five ruling on this side of Jordan. Instances from a more historical time are found in 1 Chron. xxiii. 22; Ruth iv. 1 sqq.

[3] Num. xxvii. 8-11.

[4] 1 Chron. ii. 34 sq.; Gen. xv. 2 sq.; Prov. xvii. 2. Comp. also Prov. xxx. 23.

[5] Other instances are 2 Sam. xvii. 23; Is. xxxviii. 1 sq.

[6] Gen. xxiii.; Ruth iv. 1 sq.

redemption or an exchange long held its place; the man who gave up a possession drawing off his shoe so as plainly to strip himself of something before the witnesses, and thus indicate that he withdrew from and handed over the property.[1] From the time, however, when it became more and more customary in Israel to use writing for all the incidents of ordinary life, written documents became usual in such cases, so that the old practice fell out of usage. The documents signed by the witnesses were then prepared in duplicate; one copy remained public for everyone's use, the other was sealed, to be opened only officially and compared with the public copy, if anyone doubted the genuineness of the contents of the latter.[2]

b. The Law of Borrowing and Lending.

Whoever possesses external property, and makes a diligent use of it, finds it increase under his hands. It is therefore no more than fair that such a possession, if borrowed for a time by another, whether merely in consequence of indigence or in order to extend his business therewith, shall be returned by him to its owner along with a corresponding increase. Thus even property, money or anything else, which is lent to another bears fruit for its owner, grows, sometimes most luxuriantly, and increases for his benefit with greater or less rapidity.[3]

1. But the evil of this among the ancients was that the percentage of the interest was entirely left to the freewill of individuals. The rate varied much, but was for the most part

---

[1] Ruth iv. 7: comp. Deut. xxv. 9 sq. Such antique images, as in Ps. lx. 10b [8b], are quite a natural product of the living feeling embodied in this usage. In the *Râmâyana*, ii. 2142 sq. a similar custom is described; comp. also *Qirq Vezír*, p. 70, 12. According to the ancient Saxon custom (in Adalb. Kuhn's *Sagen in Westphalen*), the bride, on becoming the wife, forfeited her shoe to her husband.

[2] Jer. xxxii. 9-14: comp. Is. xliv. 5: comp. the closely corresponding γραφή and ἀντίγραφον, 1 Macc. xiv. 48 sq.; Leemann's *Description raisonnée des Antq. Egypt.* p. 118 (Ms. dem. 374); and the *Charta indentata*, θεσμὸς δίπλαξ; also the examples in the *Gött. Nachrichten*, 1864, s. 138, which have lately been discovered on inscriptions. Comp. the *Propheten des A. B.* ii. s. 272, and *Ausland*, 1867, s. 610.

[3] Hence the name מַרְבִּית, prop. increase, and נֶשֶׁךְ, comp. נָשַׁךְ and נָכַר prop. birth, for *interest*. So with τόκος; and in Egyptian ⲘⲎⲤⲈ from ⲘⲒⲤⲈ, *progeny*, in Javanese *hanak dhuwit*, i.e. child of money, in Dajaken *matak*, have the same original signification, see Hardelands, *SL.* s. 128. comp. also the good explanation in the *Clouds* of Aristophanes ver. 1260 sq. Nevertheless, we see from Lev. xxv. 37, that the former word was more frequently used of the increase of the fruits, the latter for increase of money; but later, Deut. xxiii. 20, [19] מַרְבִּית is also put for the increase of fruits. An expression exactly corresponding to our *zins*, i.e. *centesima*, is first to be found in Neh. v. 11.—In other cases words meaning dividing, gaining, like בֶּצַע, قرض have been readily applied to this idea.

extravagant, and this often led to a cruel oppression of the
poorer classes, and consequently to dangerous disturbances of
the public peace. A debtor was regarded as completely at the
mercy of the creditor, almost as his bondsman and subject, as
the ancient languages are of themselves enough to show in the
208 strong expressions they employ to express this relation.[1] In
addition, among nations which took as little part in foreign
trade, as was the case with Israel in its earliest days, loans
were demanded not so much in order to carry on the business
of production and commerce with greater energy, as in consequence of sheer poverty. We must remember that every
family in Israel ought properly to have possessed its hereditary estate, and in it the means to support life decently, and
further that such a nation at first formed a compact unity
and a close brotherhood, especially towards other races subjugated by it. We cannot then be surprised that the law, rather
than suffer the pernicious usages which existed elsewhere, preferred trying to abolish all taking of interest whatever. The
same prohibition is to be found under similar circumstances
outside of Israel among many nations which led a life of upward striving, including some of the early Greek races. But
it was incumbent on Israel to show itself a nation more ready
than others to follow wherever possible the laws or rather the
counsels of the higher life, a nation whose members willingly
sacrificed the advantages of the lower life to the higher good
of the whole. And as a fact, it is worthy of wonder, how long
and, comparatively speaking, with what unusual stringency the
legal exhortations not to take interest kept their place in the ancient kingdom of Israel, and what prominence was given to the
importance of this higher duty of life for one who truly honoured
Jahveh. The legislation of the Book of Covenants exhorts
men to exact no interest,[2] and the Book of Origins repeats this
209 with greater distinctness;[3] but both legislative codes expressly

---

[1] To owe interest (to borrow) is to *bind oneself*, to become bound to the creditor, לָוָה, comp. the Talmudic הִקִּיף, *borrow*; to be a debtor is as much as *to be knocked, to be crushed, to toil* (suffer), נָשָׁא or נָשָׁה, taken from the active meaning of this word to *knock* (elsewhere push away, seduce, deceive): and hence is formed נֹשֶׁא בוֹ, the *creditor*, like עֶבֶד בּוֹ the *liege lord*; hence also the combination מַשָּׁה יָד, a *debt*, i.e. a pressing of the hand (violence). Deut. xv. 2; Neh. x. 32 [31]. In the Book of Covenants, Ex. xxii. 24 [25], the LXX. translate נֹשֶׁה very happily by κατεπείγων (exigens). Again תֹּךְ, pl. תְּכָכִים, Prov. xxix. 13, *interest*, is properly *pressure* or *compulsion*, which the debtor could be forced in any way to give. Also in Arabic غلّ is to be *pledged*, or to *owe, Hamâsa*, p. 148. 15.

[2] Ex. xxii. 24 [25].

[3] Lev. xxv. 35-38, comp. the rhe-torical exaltation of the law, 4 Macc. ii. 8. The same is even to be found in the Korân, Sûr. ii. 278 sqq.; xxx. 38: comp., lxviii. 24; lxix. 34.

limit this exhortation to the poor brethren of the national community, without saying whether it should hold good of any ne else who sought a loan. When, however, the Deuteronomist repeats the ancient prohibition, he found it already needful to speak more clearly in regard to this exception, declaring that to those who were not Israelites, e.g. the neighbouring Phœnician merchants, it was lawful to lend money on interest.[1] For by his time foreign trade and commercial intercourse had long become so widely extended and so complex among the people of Israel, that it seemed all the more necessary frankly to abandon in regard to strangers what was still to be maintained in its integrity among their own countrymen.

From these facts we cannot doubt that the ancient prohibition in the kingdom of Jahveh remained intact throughout the whole of the thousand years of its existence down to the first destruction of Jerusalem, at any rate in regard to their own countrymen. It is equally clear that for the national and commercial relations of the times from Solomon onwards, it was no longer equally applicable, and in these later days did little to secure the maintenance of the kingdom, if it did not actually contribute gradually to weaken it. It may also be readily understood that such a law (as the above passage in the Book of Origins especially shows) had only a moral position, and interfered only to teach and exhort, not officially to inflict penalties, and thus all the passages referred to denounce no legal punishments for those who will not conform to the law. Accordingly, all didactic poets and prophets from the time of David do no more than exalt the not taking of interest as the higher duty of a true worshipper of Jahveh,[2] and thereby give us clearly to understand that there was already in the nation a vigorous endeavour to act contrary to this brotherly duty taught by the ancient religion.

2. Lending to needy brethren, however, without interest, was strongly encouraged by the law. As the creditor is always anxious for some outward security for the replacing of his loan when it falls due, it was the more important that the ancient legislation should regulate this.

We have, then, first to consider the system of *pledging*.[3]

---

[1] Deut. xxiii. 20 [19] sq., comp. the words, very characteristic, but still in prophetic diction, Deut. xv. 6; xxviii. 12, and the similar cases explained above, pp. 146, 148.—But from Joseph. *Antiq.* iv. 8. 25 sq., it is clear that by that time the scribes had hunted out all sorts of further restrictions.

[2] Ps. xv. 5; Ezek. xviii. 8, 13 sqq.; xxii. 12.

[3] A pledge is called חֲבֹל or עֲבֹט, prop. a *band*, it is therefore essentially the same idea as that which gives its name to lending, p. 182 nt. 1. In Phœnician,

The creditor naturally wished to appropriate as pledges whatever was best or most prized of the debtor's goods and contained in his house, nor could the law forbid such keeping in pawn, because it would only ensure a reasonable security, especially when no interest was to be paid, for repayment. Nevertheless, the legislation in the Book of Covenants tries to put limits to the hard-heartedness which might be displayed here, forbidding that a poor man should be deprived for a night of anything so indispensable as the broad upper garment which served him during the night as a covering,[1] and the Deuteronomist makes a further exception of the implements of the handmill which was at that time indispensable to every household,[2] and in addition demands that the creditor shall not himself enter the house of the debtor to seize as pledges whatever things were most attractive to himself.[3] But here too the law could inflict no civic penalty, and in somewhat later times complaints are not rare against creditors who took away the most indispensable articles, such as clothes, the ploughing ox or ass, from those who were in distress.[4]

In the second place, the *personal security* of a friend on behalf of the debtor became of all the more importance if the latter had nothing which he could or might pawn. The law is silent on the matter; frequent allusions to it, and warnings, especially to young folk, not to stand surety without due consideration, are first to be found in the Books of Proverbs and of Job.[5] According to these indications it was a very formal proceeding. The surety gave his hand both to the debtor and to the creditor before an assembly legally convened, he deposited a pledge, and in accordance with this two-fold promise was regarded by the creditor in just the same light as the debtor himself, and treated accordingly.

3. If the debtor, or in his place, the surety, was unable to pay the debt when it fell due, he was entirely at the mercy of the creditor. The authorities troubled themselves but little about these relations, and the law, so far as it is preserved to

---

on the other hand, a pledge was called עֲרָבוֹן, a word which came into circulation through the Phœnician and Carthaginian commerce in the form ἀρραβών and *arrhabo*, and abbreviated, *arrha*, with the meaning of earnest money. It is, however, also found in Hebrew in the primitive history, Gen. xxxviii. 17–20; comp. the verb עָרַב, *to give as a pledge*, Neh. v. 3, but also *to stand for a man*, i.e. to make oneself a surety for him, Job xvii. 3.

[1] Ex. xxii. 25 [26] sq.; Deut. xxiv. 12 sq.: comp. Matt. v. 40.
[2] Deut. xxiv. 6: comp. xv. 6. Comp. similar cases in the early Greek legislators, Diod. Sic. i. 79.
[3] Deut. xxiv. 10 sq.
[4] Amos ii. 8; Job xxii. 6; xxiv. 3, 7–10; Ezek. xviii. 7, 12 sqq.; xxxiii. 15.
[5] Prov. xi. 15; xvii. 18; xx. 16: comp. xxvii. 13; xxii. 26 sq.; vi. 1–5; Job xvii. 3.

us, gave no directions in the matter. We see, however, from many allusions and narratives what harsh forms these relations actually took, especially in later times, when the ancient national brotherly love which the law presupposed was more and more dying out. The creditor could not only forcibly appropriate all the ᴵmovable, but also the fixed property including the hereditary estate (this at least till its redemption in the year of Jubilee), nay he could even (if he could find nothing else of value) carry off as a prisoner the body of his debtor, or of his wife or child, to employ them in his service, though this could only be done for a definite period (as will be explained below under the subject of Slavery). The violent abstraction of such valuables may in like manner be called pledging;[1] and already in the time of David one who could pay with nothing but his own body and service, found refuge from his creditor only in flight.[2] Indeed, in the eighth century there were already bitter complaints made in Judah over the accumulation of too many acres in a few hands.[3]

Hiring of either human or animal power was not forbidden by law. If an animal hired for agricultural purposes died during the work, nothing but the hire was to be paid; if it had been merely lent, and if the owner was not present when the misfortune happened, its full value was to be replaced.[4]

c. *Protection of Property by Law.*

So far as property possessed a sacred character, according to all the explanations already given, it was taken very strictly under the protection of the law. The universal prohibition of theft seemed weighty enough to occupy the eighth place in the ten fundamental Commandments of Jahveism; and as the true religion felt that there was more to be required than the avoidance of the open transgression, it also prohibited in the tenth and last fundamental law every sinful desire for whatever was the property of another, and thus condemned the first step to countless secret or open offences which no law can enumerate and punish.[5]—The details in respect to this law are as follow:—

[1] Such cases as Job xxii. 6; xxiv. 9, for the rest, comp. 2 Kings iv. 1; Mic. ii. 9; mk. Is. l. 1; Neh. v. 5.
[2] 1 Sam. xxii. 2.
[3] Is. v. 8; Mic. ii. 2: comp. the phrase, very significant for the primitive system of dividing the land, in ver. 5.—Prov. xxxi. 16. Of special significance here is also what Ezekiel says, xlv. 8 sq.; xlvi. 16–19.
[4] Ex. xxii. 13 [14] sq.
[5] Comp. a similar, very ancient, expression, Lev. xix. 11.

1. The thief was to replace the stolen property, if it was found with him still uninjured, along with its equivalent in value. Should he be struck dead whilst effecting his burglary, this involved no blood-guiltiness if it took place during the night. If, however, the stolen property had already been appropriated to some purpose or other, then he was to replace one ox with five oxen, as the most useful and valued domestic animals, and one sheep or goat with four; but if poverty prevented him from furnishing the requisite compensation, then, even if hunger had induced him to commit the theft, his own body was at any rate legally forfeited to the person who had been robbed and he became his slave, though only for a definite period,[1] (as will be further explained below). These are the regulations of the Book of Covenants for these relations as they existed in the earliest, simplest times, when domestic animals (which alone are separately specified by the law) still formed the great bulk of the nation's wealth. This penal code will not be found too stringent. In the case of theft induced by hunger it was properly only house-breaking which the law punished, for the poor and helpless were allowed to glean freely among the fields and vineyards; indeed anyone without distinction might pick so much of the grapes or the ears of corn as should suffice for his needs for the time being.[2] Far more stringent, as is fitting, was the penalty for the theft of human beings. The thief was punished with death, whether the stolen persons had been sold by him or were still found on his premises. This stringent law was deemed worth repeating in Deuteronomy in relation to the slave-trade, which in later times was continually expanding.[3] Another serious transgression, which it is remarkable to find mentioned for the first time by the Deuteronomist,[4] was the removal of boundaries, whose sanctity ancient nations often sought to protect by the erection of special Divine images (*Termini*).

2. Property intrusted to another was to be protected in just the same manner.[5] If it was inanimate and was stolen from its keeper, it was to be replaced by the thief in a similar

---

[1] This is the meaning of Ex. xxi. 37; xxii. 3 [4]. A seven-fold restitution is spoken of, Prov. vi. 30 sq., only poetically and colloquially.
[2] Lev. xix. 9 sq., and the latter explanation of it, Deut. xxiv. 19-22; Ruth ii. 2 sqq.—Deut. xxiii. 25 [24] sq.; Matt. xii. 1.
[3] Ex. xxi. 16; Deut. xxiv. 7.
[4] Deut. xix. 14; xxvii. 17: comp. the proverbial phrase, Hos. v. 10. The utterances of the earlier legislation must have been lost; however the Tenth Commandment may be brought forward here. Comp. Alexandre on the *Libri Sibyll.* ii. 2, p. 169.
[5] To intrust anything to anyone is הִפְקִיד, prop. to make him its over-seer, comp. Ps. xxxi. 6 [5].

manner. If, however, it was not to be found, and the person intrusting it would not be satisfied, then the highest court was to decide whether the person in charge of it was to blame for the loss, and if he was, he had then to pay double its value. If the intrusted property consisted of cattle, and was therefore particularly exposed to various mishaps, then its keeper had to replace what was stolen, but not what was torn in pieces if he produced evidence that he had vainly called for help; nor was he reponsible for other misfortunes if he could swear to his innocence before the court.[1]

All property that had gone astray, that was in distress, or was lost, was to be brought back, assisted, and kept in safety by the finder as though it were his own. This is already the exhortation of the oldest law.[2]

3. When property was damaged in such a way that another than the owner was more or less responsible, e.g., by a man's ox, the latter person was to make good the damage, either in full or as much as was equitable, of which the earliest law gives several instances.[3]

2. THE SANCTITY OF THE HOME.

From first to last, however, the law regards the individual only as a member of a household,—the primary, and the closest, and also the most permanently enduring human community, whose benefits he shares, and where on this account he inherits such benefits as are capable of being bequeathed. This community is, therefore, the ultimate foundation of all human culture and activity, and acquires from all these causes a peculiarly important sanctity which exists long before there is any attempt to establish a similar but infinitely wider and freer community in the state. Accordingly, the national customs, good as well as bad, nowhere maintain their position with greater persistency than when sheltered by this almost impregnable sanctity of the home. Much which was more or less opposed to the purer

---

[1] Ex. xxii. 6-12 [7-13].
[2] Ex. xxiii. 4 sq.; repeated, Deut. xxii. 1-4.
[3] Ex. xxi. 33-36; xxii. 4 sq.; more briefly in the Book of Origins, Lev. xxiv. 18. The case in Ex. xxii. 4 [5] is, however, obscure, according to the Massoretic interpretation; we must here insert after אחר the words contained in the LXX, and which still stand in the Samaritan recension. The meaning is this: if the cattle merely eat some of the crops on another man's land, their owner shall make a proper compensation from the crops of his own land; if they eat up the whole of the crop, then the compensation shall be taken from the best land of the owner (because it could no longer be told whether the fields that had been injured, would have borne good or bad crops). Only in this way again is the series of ten made complete, comp. *Hist.* ii. 166 sq.

215 laws of Jahveism was still retained for many centuries in the 'houses of the fathers' (i.e. families) of Israel, and yielded only very gradually to higher claims. This point is to be carefully attended to in regard to details, to avoid confounding things which have very different origins and only external points of resemblance. But the indispensable basis afforded by the home and its eternal sanctity, no superior religion and legislation should seek to destroy or even to disturb, and if the token by which to recognise a true religion is its promoting a strong, healthy, domestic life, and powerfully protecting its indwelling sanctity, then, in this respect too, Jahveism has triumphantly vindicated its lofty station. On a comprehensive survey we cannot fail to recognise that there is no other ancient nation in which, during the days of external power, domestic life remained for a long period so vigorous; and secondly, during the gradual decline of the external power, became so little weakened and corrupted, as was the case in Israel. We shall equally see that whilst the higher religion and more stringent tone was at first hard to be reconciled with the ancient customs of the home, so conversely it finally transformed the home most thoroughly, and in the sanctity of the latter established its deepest and most indestructible seat. Let us look at this more closely in respect to the three principal relations which are possible in every home.

a. The Relations of Parents and Children.

The closest union between child and parent, and the strictest dependence of the former on the latter until marriage, is a consequence of the ancient domestic life, so long as it is able to develope its own tendencies undisturbed. How important were the duties of the child to the parent, is shown in the primitive typical relation of Isaac to Abraham,[1] and may be at once learned from the placing of the law on the subject among the Ten Commandments, and from its position here in immediate proximity to the commands relating to the duties of man towards God.[2] Tender affection for parents and childlike reve-
216 rential awe we see pervading the whole history of Israel from its very commencement. This is the clear utterance of the old legends and histories; and the evil nature of the Canaanitish, i.e, non-Israelitish, character, is nowhere delineated more strongly than by pictures of its undisciplined relations, dis-

---

[1] *Hist.* i. 339 sq.   [2] *Hist.* ii. 160 sqq.

honouring alike father and child.[1] So again, in later times, the same profound horror of improper domestic relations is displayed in the strongest expressions, just as the delight felt in a true home is revealed in the most touching phrases.[2] In particular the contempt existing among many nations for old people who have grown weak and helpless, is so far from being characteristic of Israel, that the law never alludes to such an impropriety, but in its earliest portion it does expressly command every one 'to stand up before grey hairs, and to honour the hoary head.'[3] Just as little do we find the remotest trace of exposing or even putting to death new-born infants, particularly girls; although numerous traces of such a custom are to be found among the ancient Arabs.[4]

But the one-sided development of the strict dependence of the child easily leads to evil consequences; and the next question is how the law dealt with such cases.

Disobedience and other improper conduct was left by the custom of many ancient races to be punished by the father just as he thought best, even with death. The ancient law of Jahveism requires with equal strictness that death shall be the penalty for the child who strikes his parents or even curses them,[5] the latter clause being repeated with great emphasis by the Book of Origins.[6] But that parents themselves without further responsibility could inflict this penalty is so far from being herein implied, that the ancient proverbs of Solomon, which in other respects desire to draw the reins of discipline as tight as possible, utter an express warning against doing so;[7] and afterwards Deuteronomy distinctly lays it down that in such cases parents were to have recourse to the whole community, and that only the latter could inflict the penalty of death.[8]—A perplexing antagonism between the filial duties owed to parents and those owed to the priests as protectors of what is sacred, is a thing not heard of till the time when the hagiocracy was fully developed.[9]

When, again, child and parents form so close a unity that

---

[1] Gen. ix. 20–27; xix. 31–36.
[2] Prov. xxx. 15–17, a fuller expansion of xx. 20; Ps. cxxvii. 3–5; cxxviii. 2 sq.
[3] Lev. xix. 32.
[4] Comp. above p. 174. Such a girl, if she survived the exposure, was termed ﻣﻮﺀﻭﺩﺓ, originally ﻣﻨﺒﻮﺫﺓ (comp. Hemâsa, s. 4, 6 sq.) *one who is picked up* on the ground. The words, Job iii. 12 a, on the other hand, refer only to the father's right either to recognise a new-born child as legitimate, and to place it on his knees to bless it, or else to repudiate it.
[5] Ex. xxi. 15, 17.
[6] Lev. xx. 9; also Deut. xxvii. 16.
[7] Prov. xix. 18, in another application xxiii. 13, 14.
[8] Deut. xxi. 18–21.
[9] Mark vii. 11; comp. the treatise on *die drei ersten Evv.* s. 264, and more particularly Philo in Euseb. *Præp. Ev.* viii. 7. 3, 4, for one of his lost works on the Mosaic legislation.

no superior power of the state separates them, then they cannot be legally distinguished, and the former, as far as externals are concerned, may have to atone and suffer for the latter. Thus, while the old law did not lend its sanction to the practice, neither did it forbid a child (most likely a daughter) being sold by its parents to relieve their distress,[1] or being accepted by a creditor as a pledge.[2] In fact, so long as the strict conception of the ancient household was upheld in its integrity, the fact that the house stood or fell with the father readily affected not only the children, but also all its other members; and in extreme cases of high treason it was long customary to make the children as well as the guilty party expiate the offence.[3] But by the seventh century the principle was already felt in full force, that every human being, as he was estimated before God according to his individual worth alone, must be treated in the same way by human law, so that the son ought not to suffer for the father, nor the father for the son.[4] And from that time it was only a question of temporal legislation or interpretation of the laws whether the asperities of the kind we have mentioned, which the ancient legislation permitted without enjoining, were any longer to remain in force or not.

b. *The Relations of Man and Wife.*

The relations between the sexes took a very similar form, as we see in the following respects.

1. There is no ancient religion which of itself is so sternly opposed to misconduct in these relations and yet so free from unnatural limitations of their due rights as Jahveism. What importance it attached to their purity, and how it sought to protect real marriage as the primary basis for all true life in common among human beings, is at once shown by its stringent laws on the subject. The universal prohibition of adultery was deemed of sufficient moment to be received among the Ten Commandments, and to be placed here in immediate conjunction with the one protecting life, as though chastity were a good equal to life itself.[5] This same law is repeated in the oldest legal compilations with similar, but still more definite

---

[1] Ex. xxi. 7.
[2] P. 185.
[3] Josh. vii. 24; 2 Kings ix. 26 (*Hist.* iv. 74 sq.); comp. similar cases among the Romans even in the times of the emperors, Tacitus, *Ann.* v. 9. This severity is explained, if such cases were regarded, as חֶרֶם, see p. 75 sqq.
[4] Deut. xxiv. 16; Jer. xxxi. 30; Ezek. xviii. 20; comp. 2 Kings xiv. 6; but even the sons of Korah were not exterminated, according to Num. xxvi. 11: comp. xvi.
[5] Comp. above p. 168 sqq.

expressions, and the legal penalty here was death, not only for the adulteress, but also for the adulterer.[1] The mode of execution, as was almost understood of itself from what will be explained below, was stoning in the assembled community. Simple prostitution, which did not involve adultery on either side, was not punished with loss of life; but just as little was it regarded with indifference,[2] and neither the man nor the woman escaped with impunity. If, however, the guilty one were the daughter of a priest, then the bodily punishment must be the severest possible,[3] just as was the case among the Romans with regard to the vestal virgins—only with this great difference, that Jahveism forbade marriage neither for the daughter of a priest, nor to anyone else connected with the sacerdotal orders. Public prostitution, as it was practised undisturbed and even required in the temples of certain heathen divinities, was in no way to be tolerated; and parents were to be severely punished who brought up or disposed of young children, especially girls, for such practices.[4] Nor might money or gifts which come from such a source be accepted by any sanctuary in Israel,[5] although there were Israelites by birth who would often seek to quiet their consciences by devoting a portion of the 'reward of harlotry' to their country's sanctuary. It was not indeed till the days of Solomon that Israel had sunk so low that it became necessary to include such a prohibition among the laws, and the history shows clearly enough with what vigour all unchastity, if it only tried to find entrance into their midst, was put down in the earlier days.[6]

[1] Lev. xviii. 20; more definitely with a statement of the penalty, xx. 10; similarly Deut. xxii. 22. The almost literal repetition of the sentence, Lev. xx. 10, is due entirely to the emphatic diction. Comp. Ezek. xvi. 40; Joseph. *Contr. Ap.* ii. 24.—Later writers have imagined from Deut. xxii. 24, that only in the case of the betrothed bride the penalty was death by stoning, and that in other cases the execution was simpler; but all this is without foundation, according to ver. 25, comp. ver. 22. On the contrary, there can be no doubt that originally every adulterer incurred death by stoning, although it is only in the former passage that it is expressly mentioned as not too severe even for that case, and as not to be neglected. Accordingly, in John viii. 4 sq. we need not think of such a betrothed bride.

[2] Comp. the judgment in the cases, which it is true were strengthened by special causes, in Gen. xxxiv. 7-11; 2 Sam. xiii. 12 sqq.

[3] Lev. xxi. 9.

[4] Nevertheless the prohibition in the Book of Origins, Lev. xix. 29 is still made quite general, just as according to the narrative of this book, Num. xxv. 1-15, Israel only becomes seduced to unchastity by foreign women. The prohibition in Deut. xxiii. 18 [17] sq.; Apoc. xxii. 15, runs quite differently; but all surviving historical tokens indicate that the names קְדֵשָׁה, for a consecrated professional or temple-harlot, and קָדֵשׁ or כֶּלֶב (*dog*), for a male similarly consecrated, did not enter the country till after David's time, along with the corresponding heathen religions. Comp. *Hist.* iv. 44.

[5] This too is first enacted, Deut. xxiii. 19 [18].

[6] *Hist.* ii. 351 sqq.

Another mark of the strict discipline which Jahveism introduced into the relation between the sexes, may be found in the laws relating to prohibited marriages. What unions were not allowed can only be explained in detail further on; but in general terms we may notice that Jahveism was far stricter in this respect than even the more serious of the ancient heathen religions. Now if we enquire into the source of such prohibitions in general, we must guard ourselves against seeking for only a single cause for all of them without exception. Of course there does prevail here one chief and fundamental cause rooted in the very nature of marriage. Only in the riper years of life should marriage unite those who have been separated, but have been ultimately created for one another, so that they may come together in the firmest bond, and form the commencement of a new house. It seems as though the partnership thus founded is to be quite other than that given from the commencement by common blood, or birth, or by living together in one house. It gives something new as an addition to what has already existed, a love distinct from what is always bestowed among blood-relations, which is indeed great enough of itself and can satisfy its own demands. The more distinct and remote therefore the graft which is inserted into the stock, the freer and the fresher may be the inter-action and the new unfolding of the good on both sides, and the less propagation is there of what is one-sided and therefore weak. It is as though that which is isolated were itself seeking with all the greater force to supplement its nature from foreign sources, and in like manner it becomes a thing of national importance, inasmuch as marriage is one of the most powerful and happy means of preventing a pernicious isolation and estrangement of the households and tribes, and of nations and communities of every kind. An obscure recognition of this leaning towards what is foreign, and therefore a dislike to marriage within too close a degree of relationship, may have been excited very early in Antiquity among the upward-striving, healthy races, and this is undoubtedly the primary cause of the prohibitions which we are considering. To this was soon added, however, regard for good discipline, and a salutary mutual reserve among the members of a household which such prohibitions endeavour to provide. But still both causes have not of themselves sufficient power to prevent many a nation allowing itself considerable freedom in this matter, and the heathen races with which Israel came into close contact, whose life was never of a really high order and gradually became less and less restrained, set aside matrimonial relations with great freedom.[1] Even among the early ancestors of Israel these limitations were far laxer, for unless there had been distinct reminiscences to this effect, the legend of Abraham's marriage with his half-sister Sarah, or of Jacob's with two sisters at the same time, could never have originated. When, accordingly we find Jahveism from the very first[2] laying down in the matter the strictest limitations—such as had the widest sphere of operation—and when history teaches us with what thorough consistency it maintained their sanctity inviolate,[3] then we see how decisively it took a chaste domestic life under its protection, and with what success it promoted the formation of valid marriages.

Totally different in kind is the prohibition against alliances with heathen families. As far as the mere nature of marriage is concerned, we should not expect to find this restriction by the side of the ones already mentioned. And we also see as a matter of external fact that the two laws were by no means originally placed together in one series, for this latter is completely wanting just where the ancient legislation gives an exhaustive enumeration of forbidden marriages. An obscure dread of close connection with alien races is naturally found in every nation; and it is certain that he who enters on such a contract, even if he does it with his eyes open, may thereby expose himself to new embarrassments and undertakes heavier responsibilities. Especially a proud victorious race will never be much inclined to mingle its blood with that of a nation which it has conquered or which it regards with contempt. Such a pride had Israel during the early days of its power and dominion; and at that time it would have been a most unlikely thing for any of the noble stock of Israel to have mingled their blood with aliens. But no kind of prohibition against such marriages was at that time uttered, and exceptions to the prevailing custom found entrance here and there,[4]

---

[1] The expression, Lev. xviii. 24, is quite confirmed by our other sources of information. It is true that we know little of Israel's nearest neighbours beyond what may be learned from Gen. xix. 32-38; but the Egyptians and the Greeks may furnish us with a picture of heathendom in general.

[2] The oldest legislation treats this and kindred matter exhaustively and systematically, Lev. xviii. 6-23; the Book of Origins repeats the principal points in its own way, Lev. xx. 11-21; still briefer is Deut. xxiii. 1 [xxii. 30], xxvii. 20-23.

[3] Of course in extreme cases these prohibitions were sometimes set aside, as by Herod Antipas, who is, however, severely reproved on this account, Mark vi. 17 sq. But that Moses himself was born from a marriage of his father with his (Amram's) aunt on the father's side, does not necessarily follow from Ex. vi. 20; for דּדָה, as the LXX take it, may also denote a cousin, comp. Jer. xxxii. 7, at any rate just as well as a brother's son may more briefly be termed a brother, Gen. xiv. 16; xxix. 12.

[4] As Josh. vi. 25 (Hist. ii. 247 sq.); Judg. xiv. 1-3; nk. Ruth. Often an excuse for this was deemed needful, and even

especially many a foreign wife captured in war became grafted on to the stock of Israel.[1] Not till the days of the gradual decline of the national might of Israel from the time of Solomon onwards, when heathenism in continually more and more seductive forms was pressing in by a thousand ways, and experience had shown often enough how easily a heathen wife might lead her husband astray to heathen practices, does the Fourth Narrator of the primitive history utter his warning definitely against such alliances, and the Deuteronomist follows still more strongly.[2] These alliances were then doubtless becoming more and more frequent, in proportion to the increased influence and wealth which the heathen were threatening to acquire here and there in the midst of Israel.[3] In the times after Solomon it would not be so much the proud and the high-born who shrunk from such marriages, as the pious; nor was this without consequence, since on its account quite a new truth could be found in the lofty words [4] which spoke of Israel as 'a people dwelling apart, not mingling with the heathen, neither reckoning itself with them.' Nevertheless, this boast was the boast of a race that was already on the way to meet its outward doom,[5] and what unhappy complications developed themselves out of it in course of time will be learned in the later volumes in the history of the new Jerusalem.

The fair type of true matrimony which the old legend presents in Isaac and his Ribeqa (Rebecca),[6] accordingly does no more than represent with little alteration marriage as it really existed in the majority of families during the best days of the nation. Simple fidelity, pious love and attachment, and hence a certain amount of foresight in the choice of a wife from a worthy race, were not less in reality than they are in that type, the foundation on which a new family in Israel was erected.[7]

Moses had to listen to harsh reproof from his relatives on this account, Num. xii. 1 sqq.; but the very narrative shows how groundless and how worthy of divine punishment such reproof may be.

[1] As is even admitted in Deut. xxi. 10–14.

[2] Ex. xxxiv. 15 sq.; Deut. vii. 1–4: comp. Josh. xxiii. 12. In these passages, according to the context, the prohibition refers in the first instance to the tribes of the Canaanites, and undoubtedly in those times it was those who were most dangerous to the people of Israel, as is further indicated by many earlier descriptions, Gen. xxiv. 3; xxvi. 34 sq.; xxvii. 46–xxviii. 9. But as a fact, no reason presented itself why the prohibition should not be extended further, and that this did not absolutely contradict even the spirit of the Deuteronomic legislation is shown by the final editor of the Books of the Kings, 1 Kings xi. 1 sq.

[3] P. 183.

[4] See *Hist.* ii. 303 sq.

[5] Just as the more modern prohibition of mixed marriages within the pale of the Romish Church have only been a sign of internal weakness, and of the commencement of disruption.

[6] *Hist.* i. 339 sq.

[7] We may accordingly compare in many respects the example of the Caucasian nobles of the present day, who marry

All else that we know from history is in harmony with this; and here, too, we may clearly recognise the mighty working of an elevated religion.

2. But another powerful influence was exercised on these relations by customs which had become firmly established long before the origin of Jahveism during the undisturbed dominion of the primitive household system. So long as no higher power, superior to all the various families, is securely founded, and the head of the family possesses a legal and unlimited power, the consequences of the fact will appear in an unduly inferior station for woman, in polygamy, and in great facility for divorce : three phenomena which are most intimately associated one with another, and of which the one invariably leads to the others. It was the more difficult for Jahveism to break with these consequences of primitive family life, inasmuch as its origin in opposition to an Egyptian civilisation tended to drive it back into the freedom, marked with so little external restraint, of the ancient Israelitish mode of life. It is instructive in the highest degree to see what a struggle took place between the loftier truths and the noble impulses of Jahveism and family customs consecrated by immemorial usage, and how the former here too gradually achieved the victory.

The truth—which survives all else—of monogamy is already represented as alone worthy of imitation in the two narratives of the creation, all the more so as the second narrative makes use of the occasion to throw the true light on the essence and the higher necessity of every marriage.[1] To this may be added the genuine national type given, as has been already mentioned, in Isaac and Rebecca. And whenever a prophet alludes to matrimony he invariably presupposes monogamy, faithfully and sacredly observed for life, to be alone right. Again, the true prophets, so far as their real life is depicted, never have more than one wife at one time (for any doubt as to the lawfulness of a second marriage entered the head of no one). Moses, it is true, when he was advanced in years, took a Cushite woman to wife ;[2] but undoubtedly at that time the Midianitish Zipporah, who was the wife of his youth, was already dead. Hosea, Isaiah, and also Ezekiel, are shown by clear

in their own rank, but not among their own relatives, see Bodenstedt's 1001 *tag*, ii. s. 134, 136.
[1] Gen. ii. 18-24 : comp. *Jahrbb. der B. W.* ii. s. 154 sq.

[2] Num. xii. 1 : the death of Zipporah is not, it is true, alluded to in our present Pentateuch, but this is indisputably due only to the abridgment of the original narrative.

indications about their domestic affairs to have had each but one wife. But the law did not insist on monogamy, and there were many chiefs or other rich men in Israel who preferred to follow the example of Jacob with his two wives, in spite of the accumulated warnings afforded by his example,[1] instead of the purer type given in Isaac's case. Just this number of two wives was very frequent in such circles in accordance with ancient custom;[2] a larger number served only to give splendour and distinction to a powerful national leader,[3] and to the kings. Rulers, moreover, in polygamous countries, even at the present day, often take wives out of powerful houses or tribes for no other reason than to secure the greater fidelity of the latter. Nevertheless, as the kings had gone to excesses in the matter, the Deuteronomist enjoins a wise moderation.[4] The legislation does not approach the question in general at all closely till we come to Deuteronomy, even to obviate the injustice which might easily arise from a man's preference for one of two wives.[5] But although polygamy was never abolished by law, it evidently gradually disappeared as the improvement which the higher religion was in the course of time imperceptibly bringing about in morals became more and more decided; so that the history of Israel concludes, at any rate in Christianity,[6] with the unforced but decisive victory of monogamy.

The possibility of this polygamy is taken into account by the ancient law in regard to prohibited degrees of marriage, thereby adding to their number. This number was further increased owing to the fact that the prohibition presupposes all through the strict domestic life of primitive days to be intact, where a very large number of relatives were firmly linked to a single father, and the immense respect for this father could be easily transferred to any member of the family holding a similar position. If now we also take into consideration the principles already spoken of,[7] it will become clear why all the particulars assumed the following forms. Marriage was

---

[1] For in Gen. xxix. sqq., this double marriage of the patriarch is represented as not having been desired by himself, and as being moreover the source of countless ills to himself.

[2] 1 Chron. ii. 18; viii. 8-12; 1 Sam. i. 2: comp. Gen. xxxi. 50; also iv. 19, and Deut. xxi. 15; 2 Chron. xxiv. 3. It is something peculiar to find in 1 Chron. vii. 4, the richness of the tribe Issachar in wives and sons praised.

[3] As already in the case of Gideon, Judg. viii. 30 sq.

[4] Deut. xvii. 17.

[5] Deut. xxi. 15-17.

[6] For apart from Herod's many wives, some of the men spoken of in Ezra x. 44, still had a plurality; and even Joseph. *Antiq.* bk. xvii. 1. 2, calls polygamy a πάτριον in Israel (as opposed to the Roman practice), but manifestly only lays any weight on the fact because his own inclination went in that direction.

[7] P. 191 sq.

forbidden 1) With the mother; 2) With the step-mother, or with any of the father's wives, even if they were not step-mothers in our sense of the word[1]; 3) With the mother-in-law[2]; 4) With the daughter or grand-daughter of any kind[3]; 5.–7) With the aunt on either the father's or the mother's side, as well as with the wife of the father's brother (on the other hand —what is quite opposed to the ancient Roman practice,[4]— connections between the uncle and the niece were allowed, manifestly because here the respect due to the father appeared to be less infringed); 8) With the daughter-in-law, should she be widowed or put away; 9) With the daughter or grand-daughter by marriage; 10) With the sister (including the half- or step-sister); 11) With the sister by marriage on the father's side; and 12) Probably also on the mother's side[5]; 13) With the sister-in-law, i.e. the brother's wife (who accordingly was on the same footing as a sister, and often dwelt along with the brother-in-law in the house of his parents) if she were widowed and had children by the brother (the opposite case of her being without children will be spoken of below); 14) With the sister of a wife who was still living.[6] It is easy

---

[1] The step-mother in Semitic languages is ordinarily coldly designated the *father's wife*, the step-father, the *mother's husband*, and, in like manner, *sons of the mother* are step-brothers, see a remark on Sol. Song, i. 6. This can be understood, if polygamy was very ancient among the Semites.

[2] That this prohibition is wanting in the text of Lev. xviii. is very surprising, but assuredly it was there originally. It is found even now where the author of the Book of Origins is speaking more independently, Lev. xx. 14.

[3] Evidently in Lev. xviii. 10, the daughter is omitted from the present text through oversight, for she cannot possibly be included in ver. 7.

[4] Comp. Suet. *Claud.* xxvi., xxxix.

[5] In the present text of Lev. xviii. the traces of an originally well-considered arrangement are so clear and numerous, that we certainly do no wrong in assuming that verses 9, 11, and 16, originally stood before ver. 18. And as there is no reason why a sister by marriage should come within the prohibition only on the father's side, it is probable that either before or after ver. 11, there is a verse fallen out commencing with the words: עֶרְוַת בַּת אִישׁ אָפוּךְ. If we restore the primitive text in this way, a further remarkable arrangement appears. The prohibitions commence with an introductory verse (ver. 6), or rather the prohibition of marriage with a daughter is regarded as independent of the rest, and then follow three series of five verses each, the whole being arranged with equal precision and appropriateness. This was probably succeeded by five verses of more general but cognate import (comp. verr. 19–23); comp. *Hist.* ii .166. For the case in respect to the wife of the mother's brother was still more remote, and can hardly have been regarded as parallel.—All these laws are summed up, certainly very briefly, in three very general ones, Deut. xxvii. 20, 22, 23.—Indications that even the ancient Arabs possessed similar laws, derived from an earlier, purer religion, will be found in Shahrastâni's *Elmilal*, p. 440. 10 sqq.

[6] That the first wife is still living is so expressly presupposed in the words, Lev. xviii. 18, that any one might have seen long ago how groundless is the repudiation by the English law of marriage with the deceased wife's sister. The words can mean nothing but that the sister shall not be taken in marriage along with the still living wife לִצְרֹר, *in order to stir up jealousy*, like ڍﺎﺭ. The verb is, according *Lehrbuch*, § 238 *b*, an infinitive of a strong, because new and purely active, formation. Comp. on the

to explain, however, why marriage between brothers and sisters in the widest sense was forbidden, while that between cousins was permitted.[1] The latter did not form one united household, and the more each house stood strictly by itself in the ancient fashion, the wider seemed the separation between cousins. If now we take into consideration the true grounds of these prohibitions, we cannot fail to recognise in these regulations not only an arrangement externally most suitable, but also a well-conceived and internally compact system. Nor will this fact surprise us if in this, as in similar cases, we think of the regulative spirit of Moses as determining the exact form which they assumed. The penalty for breaking these laws is always death, viz. by stoning as it will be subsequently described, or in the worst cases,[2] by burning; and the punishment with which prohibited marriages of this description were visited, applied also (as something which was self-evident) to all fornication between such persons.

These laws preserved Israel not only from the grosser offences against healthy morals, examples of which were furnished by many a nation kindred to itself though profoundly degenerated from former better days,[3] but also from the subtler errors of marriage between children of the same parents which was permitted even by such peoples as the Hindoos and Persians, the Greeks and the Egyptians. And with all its brevity the old law in Leviticus xviii. indicated, by its mode of speech in expressing all the prohibitions, the profoundly abominable character of such actions. In graphic brevity and comeliness this ancient section far surpasses all later passages of similar import; more delicately and at the same time more seriously such matters cannot be spoken about. 'The shame of a woman who may not be thine thou shalt not uncover'; what hateful shamelessness would be involved in this first step of the outrage! And in this connection the feelings of abhorrence which ought to exist in every human being are very briefly enumerated as follows: 1) The feeling of filial dread towards relatives who stood above him: who might lay bare his parent's shame! 2) The paternal feeling of shame in regard to those who come below him: he who dishonours his daughter, dishonours himself![4] 3) Among those who were

---

subject the *Gött. Gel. Anz.* 1862, s. 1193 sq.

[1] Although this had already come under the Christian prohibition, according to the narrative in Abdias' *Apost. Hist.* iii. 11.

[2] As Lev. xx. 14; Gen. xxxviii. 24; for the rest, comp. Ezek. xvi. 40; xxiii. 47.

[3] Gen. xix. 30-38.

[4] In ver. 17 we have accordingly to read with the LXX שְׁאֵרָהּ for שַׁאֲרָה.

sisters in the widest sense,[1] the feeling of shame on behalf of one's own flesh, i.e. on behalf of those who are most nearly related to, and consequently on behalf of oneself; and in the case of the second sister, there was added the abhorrence of exciting a hateful jealousy between two sisters. This will enable us to recognise what were the feelings on such matters which were most active at the time of Moses, or rather under the influence of his spirit.

3. When once polygamy is recognised as lawful, the possibility of different estimations and positions of wives is naturally admitted at the same time. And thus Israel from the earliest times allowed the half-wife or wife of the second rank (the concubine); she would be taken either from the prisoners of war, which would be the most frequent case in the better warlike days, and in regard to which Deuteronomy utters some humane precepts,[2] or else from a man's other possessions. Nevertheless the special name for a concubine[3] suffices to show that the custom of taking them in those countries spread further and further outwards from an ancient luxurious court, and that their whole relation is artificial rather than natural. All that related to forbidden connections was of course equally valid for wives by every form of marriage.[4] A concubine and her children, however, had not an equal legal title to authority, she was evidently neither taken nor put away with the same degree of formality as the real wife by marriage. The earlier legislation did not trouble itself about this relation except in so far as the question of slavery was mixed up with it.[5] How frequent it was, at any rate in the earlier days, is shown in the old

---

[1] 'The daughter of the wife of thy father, who is (as good as) one of the family of thy father, thy sister,' ver. 11. This is how the words should be understood.

[2] Deut. xxi. 10-14.

[3] Pilégesh lengthened from pillégesh. It is equally remarkable that the Hebrew is here similar to the Greek and the Latin, as it is noteworthy that every other Semitic language, even the Syriac (ܦܠܩܬܐ) and Samaritan (כבלנת) always has a different but genuine Semitic term for the same idea, and that the Chaldaic לחינא only bears a slight resemblance in sound. So little does this conception belong to the original conceptions of humanity and of the earliest nations, although this agreement of the Hebrew with certain languages of a different stock undoubtedly goes back a couple of thousand years, more or less, before Christ! It would be instructive for primitive history to learn from what spot this word pellex originally came; we can, however, see with sufficient certainty that it was derived from an ancient Aryan language of more northern Asia, comp. the Gött. Nachrichten, 1862, s. 371 sq. And the remarkable fact remains that only the Hebrew language used this northern word, foreign to Semitic speech, for a concubine.

[4] Comp. Gen. xxxv. 22; xlix. 4. The kings certainly form an exception, in the case of their numerous wives taken to increase the splendour of the palace, 2 Sam. xii. 8; xvi. 22. In the History, iii. 170 sq. notice is taken of other exceptions to the stringent law, due to the urgency of special causes, as, e.g. when each wife of a king formed a distinct household for herself.

[5] See below.

legends respecting the two concubines of Abraham as well as of Jacob, while conversely in the model marriage of Isaac with Rebecca no inferior wife finds place. Where many wives were taken merely for the sake of splendour, e.g. at the courts of the early kings, there the same splendour would require more concubines and female slaves.

The concubine was regarded as little more than one of the external possessions of her master, so that the terms maid-servant (female slave) and concubine are frequently convertible;[1] although elsewhere they are also carefully distinguished,[2] and the concubine was looked upon as living in real marriage, and therefore as only to be put away on competent grounds. Many a one, too, in the earlier days undoubtedly took a concubine only because it was less expensive.[3] But the complete wife as well was for a long time in many respects regarded more as an external possession than as a being of independent worth; so difficult was it to cause the lower view, which had firmly established itself in actual life from primitive days in consequence of the one-sided development of family life, to give place to the higher view, although this made its appearance early enough, and was exhibited with equal beauty and clearness.[4]

230   The wife, accordingly, did not yet enter into full marriage with her husband as an equal in consequence of her own pure inclination and deliberation. The old custom maintained itself very tenaciously of buying a wife from her relatives, or of winning her by giving them presents, or by performing some service which would be acceptable to them and was appointed by them. The special and most natural protectors of a free maiden were, besides her parents, her brothers, especially the eldest of them, who often showed themselves far more jealous and active in the matter than the father while he was yet alive.[5] This caused the betrothal and marriage of daughters only too often to be a pecuniary transaction between these protectors and their future husbands.[6] The legislation did not concern

---

[1] אָמָה, *female slave*, occurs as identical with *pellex*, Judg. ix. 18 : comp. viii. 31 ; also Gen. xvi. and xxi.

[2] Sol. Song vi. 8.

[3] Like the priest, Judg. xix.

[4] As in the earlier proverbs, see the *Dichter des A. Bs.* vol. iv. s. 19 sq. : comp. Hos. ii. 18.

[5] Comp. *Hist.* iii. 171 sq.

[6] Gen. xxxiv. 4–12; Sol. Song i. 6, 8: comp. Gen. xxiv. 53; xxxi. 15; xxix. 18 sqq.; 1 Sam. xviii. 23 sqq. The word מֹהַר (מָהַר is identical with מָכַר, *to buy*) denotes the bride-money, which was to be paid to the bride, or to her father's family; its amount might vary, but without it marriage was not valid. On account, therefore, of its legal character, it was natural to distinguish it from the more voluntary *gifts*, מִגְדָּנוֹת or מַתָּנוֹת, Gen. xxiv. 53; xxxiv. 12. The latter, however, are more modern terms than the former primitive one, which recurs in all Semitic languages

itself with the matter. However, there would necessarily be a minimum price for ordinary cases, and the law took this into account so far as to compel the seducer of a maiden to make her his wife in the ordinary way, consequently by purchase, or if the father refused to give her to him, to pay the latter the ordinary and therefore the average price.[1] The Deuteronomist, in case the seducer had employed the smallest violence, increases the penalty by enacting that he must not only take her at the ordinary market price, but that he might never subsequently dismiss her, so that he would be compelled to support her all her life.[2] A maiden, who had sinned without being seduced either by words or by violence, may have been deemed sufficiently punished by the loss of the tokens of virginity (which are spoken of below); at any rate the present Pentateuch does not inform us whether there was any additional legal penalty. One who was betrothed was regarded in almost the same light as one who was married; the stern penalty of death was enacted in the case of sexual transgression here. It applied invariably to the seducer, and to the betrothed as well, in case she had neglected to call for aid when the place was one where she might have done so.[3]—Parents in good circumstances would give the young wife maid-servants or some similar dowry of small amount towards the new establishment,[4] but for the rest only rarely and exceptionally a share in the actual fortune.[5]

From this we see that even full marriage was little more than a particular kind of contract, legally valid only to the same extent as any other similar contract. But assuredly Jahveism regarded it in respect to its real essence and its higher function, as a sacred covenant concluded before God,[6] and it may be taken for granted that a consecration appropriate to this conception took place on the day of betrothal or wedding. But the particulars have not been preserved in any

(except the Ethiopic), but which met with a somewhat different historical fate among the individual races.

[1] Ex. xxii. 15 [16] sq. That the average price for a half-wife was from 20 to 30 shekels of silver, and for a whole-wife about 50 shekels, follows from Hos. iii. 2; comp. Ex. xxi. 32; Deut. xxii. 29.

[2] Deut. xxii. 28 sq. That violence is supposed here follows from the selection of the words in ver. 28: comp. 25-27: and it is the only passage which treats of the rape of a virgin.

[3] Deut. xxii. 23-27.

[4] Something of the kind is presupposed in Ex. xxi. 9.

[5] As in the case mentioned, *Hist.* ii. 264 sq. At what date writing became part of the procedure in determining matrimonial settlements, as spoken of in Tobit vii. 14, is not precisely known. Deuteronomy, however, already mentions written procedure in regard to marriage generally.

[6] According to Prov. ii. 17; Mal. ii. 14. This idea of the bond was brought into prominence in other respects by the Prophets; Hos. ii. 20 [18] sqq.; Ezek. xvi. 8.

ancient description,[1] and it cannot be proved that the ceremony by means of the assistance of a priest crossed the boundaries of mere private life. As a matter of fact, the Levitical priesthood, as one particular national tribe, still stood at too great a distance from the life of the individual households of the nation, while on the other hand, each individual household was too much shut up within its own limits.

232 The national wedding customs in Israel, however, with their public parades and processions at night by torchlight which usually accompanied at any rate a full marriage, were much the same as they have ever been among all the nations of those regions, and as they still exist at the present day.[2] It is more important to notice that according to the primitive custom of those countries the characteristic token of a woman's being married or betrothed was wearing the veil, by which she became easily and purposely recognisable everywhere in public;[3] but even when she met, or suspected the presence of, the man to whom she was betrothed, etiquette required that she should veil herself. The veil over the concealed head might thus pass as an undesigned proof that the woman no longer belonged to herself, but had something on her head which would always remind her of him to whom she belonged, and who was so far her lord, and was, as it were, the visible head of her own head. This is a true thought, and it moved the Apostle to call the indispensable veil itself, in an appropriate context and in the heat of discourse, briefly and sharply a *power* or a *compulsion* which the woman must have on her head.[4] And inasmuch as the woman's veil had been a subject of conversation, playful as well as serious, for thousands of years previous to this, it has even found its way as a thing of significance into the typical narrative of the model marriage of Isaac with Rebecca.[5]

---

[1] The most complete description of this is still, Ruth iv. 11–13.

[2] See a brief notice in the *Erklärung der drei ersten Evv.* s. 339.

[3] That widows did not wear it during their days of mourning because they might not appear in public, is clear from Gen. xxxviii. 14, 19.—At the present day the maidens of Tuârik still wear no veil, see Hanoteau's *Gr. de la langue Tamachek*, p. xix. The same is the case in North-east Africa (Munzinger's *Ostafr. Studien*, p. 146), but also by the Tigris (Loftus, *Trav. in Chaldæa and Susiana*, p. 383 sqq.).

[4] 1 Cor. xi. 10. All that is obscure in this passage which, in other respects, is perfectly plain, verr. 3–15, is whether Paul includes here the maidens, as Tertullian supposes in his well-known treatise *De Velandis Virginibus*. But both the words themselves, as well as the ancient practice, show that maidens are not spoken of here at all, and that Tertullian arbitrarily extended the meaning of the passage to them.—But the same conclusion may be inferred from the words which are so easy to misunderstand, which describe Abraham as the *eye-coverer*, i.e. the veil of Sarah; only the fact that he was her husband enabled him to protect her adequately from every lustful eye, Gen. xx. 16; comp. *Lehrbuch*, § 327, eighth ed.

[5] Gen. xxiv. 62–67. The meaning of this whole passage will be sufficiently

Rebecca is betrothed to Isaac of her own free determination, [233] and without having seen him first, and makes the long journey over the Euphrates and the Jordan to him accompanied by Eliezer alone. She is seated aloft on her camel and throughout the long wearisome journey has no thought about a veil, as she expects to meet her betrothed first in his own house. But he one day, having just returned to his dwelling in the south after attending his mother's funeral, and full of anguish for her loss, is gone out alone into the fields towards evening, in order the more freely to indulge his grief. He, too, on his side, is as far as possible from expecting the compensation and comfort which is so near him. But at the first quite unexpected view of the solitary wanderer in the distance, whom she has never seen before, she is as suddenly as irresistibly filled with the conviction that he is her betrothed. Down she comes from her camel in all haste, afraid of having to meet him in an unseemly fashion, and not till then does she ask Eliezer who it is, veiling herself almost without waiting for his answer. So truly did her feeling guide her here, as it did in all that she thought or did in the matter both previously and subsequently. This is the type of true love from beginning to end ! And this appropriate and beautiful trait concludes this whole typical narrative section, which was not above depicting even the mysterious omens and bounding presentiments of genuine love.

4. Finally, we must not blame the husband severely, if when the preliminaries to his marriage were such as have been described, he considered that he still kept in his own hands a certain right of dissolving it. The earlier legislation contains [234] nothing definite in regard to this marital authority; and in the earlier days when all domestic life was marked by a stricter morality, it would only be in exceptional cases that a husband would make an evil use of his rights in this respect. Just as the great prophets of the eighth and seventh centuries depict Jahveh as repelling the community of Israel which had become unfaithful, and driving it from its visible home back into

clear after what has been said above. It is true that the whole of chap. xxiv. has been borrowed somewhat abruptly from the Fourth Narrator, so that we do not at once see the relation of the first words of ver. 62, 'Isaac was come from coming,' i.e. 'was just come to Beër L. R.,' for nothing is said previously of his having been present at the death and burial of his mother in Hebron, and of Abraham having then sent him to Beër L. R. to take possession of the inheritance, including the ancestral estate of his mother, which now came to him. The Fourth Narrator must have made mention of this earlier in an account which has not been preserved to us. Nevertheless, it is easy to supply the deficiency from ver. 67: comp. xxiii. 2, xxv. 11. Something very similar is related in Munzinger's *Ostafr. Studien*, s. 147.

the desert, but nevertheless cherishing in the very bottom of his heart no malignant wrath, and ever ready to receive the penitent once again into his glory: so, undoubtedly, every honourable man felt in regard to his own little household. But the morals of the whole people were gradually becoming more and more licentious from Solomon's time, and when the ancient conscientiousness and feeling of honour had become impaired to an intolerable degree, the Deuteronomist attempted by some stringent enactments at any rate to limit the excessive arbitrary power of the husband. One of these laws, which really supplemented the ancient legislation, shows us that by the time of the Deuteronomist these matters had long been so far reduced to system, that the husband was obliged to give a bill of divorce to the wife whom he put aside.[1] This would serve her as a token that the marriage had been legally dissolved, so that she might marry again; and undoubtedly such a bill did not contain further charges against the wife, as though it had been a bill of accusation, but served as a proof that nothing stood in the way of her second marriage. But by that time experience had already shown that couples who had been thus separated, often wished to be again united in marriage, after the wife had found a second husband. Not only was all the permanency, but also all the worth and sanctity of marriage destroyed by the dissolution of relations which might go on being formed and broken off again indefinitely, even in respect to the same two men. It was, therefore, very properly enacted that a wife who had been put aside might never again be married to the same husband; he had accordingly to consider well from the first what he was doing if he demanded a separation.—The other law related to an allegation of the lack of the tokens of virginity made by a young husband. The old custom was that a maiden who lacked these tokens should be punished as a prostitute, and consequently, in this case, as an adulteress,[2] and this the law could not alter, because it was manifestly the most powerful means of deterring daughters from prostitution. But on this account it required with all the more justice that he who made such an allegation

---

[1] This, in the law, Deut. xxiv. 1-4 (comp. Jer. iii. 1, 8) is not commanded for the first time, but assumed as well understood; comp. BK. Is. l. 1. The controversy mentioned by the commentators on Matt. v. 31 sq., between Hillel and Shammai about the meaning of the words עֶרְוַת דָּבָר, Deut. xxiv. 1, could only have arisen in a time when the arbitrary power, which was still left to the husband by Deuteronomy, was beginning to be looked upon as too great. The phrase there (comp. xxiii. 15) is equivalent to 'a hateful thing of any kind,' i.e. according to Lehrb. § 286 d, anything hateful, displeasing.

[2] P. 201.

out of mere malice, should have to pay a pecuniary penalty to the aggrieved parents of the young wife, amounting to twice as much as the price paid for the marriage,[1] and should lose his right to a legal separation from the wife whom he had maliciously calumniated, the last clause having the same ground as the similar case already mentioned.[2]

Still, in the earlier and better days, if a husband was stung with matrimonial jealousy but did not purpose immediate separation on mere suspicion, the Book of Origins interested itself in the case of the defenceless wife, at any rate as far as the spirit of that age rendered possible.[3] If the husband was troubled about the fidelity of his pregnant wife on grounds of suspicion which he could not prove, the law bade him neither keep silence nor yet take vengeance into his own hands. Rather did it recognise his obligation to act in the matter, and his guilt if he neglected to do so,[4] just as might have been expected from the extreme dread shown everywhere by the ancient community of even any possible defilement of their corporate sanctity. But the belief still prevailed that in such a case the possibly defiled external sanctuary must and could itself render assistance, and that accordingly an ordeal, procured through the instrumentality of a priest, was to be sought for at the most holy place. The husband was to bring the wife to the priest, who would conduct her right in front of the inner Sanctuary, in order that the ordeal might be obtained by means of a sacrifice and a peculiar drink which the priest himself prepared. The sacrifice, since the guilt of the wife was assumed in the first instance, was a kind of guilt-offering, being without oil and incense.[5] Nevertheless it could not be deemed a complete guilt-offering; its purpose was rather to warn the wife of what was so strongly denoted by the husband's jealousy, viz. the possibility of her guilt and its fearful consequences. Accordingly it was not as much as a complete guilt-offering, it consisted simply of meal and even of the poor barley-meal, and was called a warning-offering or a jealousy-offering. When all was made ready for this sacrifice, the priest was to take an ordinary earthen vessel and mix in it sacred water (i.e. water drawn from a fountain in the temple) with dust taken from the floor of the inner Sanctuary. In this way he prepared a most peculiar drink, holy in a twofold degree, and very hard to swallow. Next, as the woman

[1] P. 200 sq.
[2] P. 201. Deut. xxii. 13–21.
[3] Num. v. 11–31.
[4] This is clear from the arrangement of the words in ver. 31.
[5] P. 62.

was standing with bare head and holding the sacrifice right in front of and facing the inner Sanctuary, he told her beforehand what would be the fearful curse which would befall her, in case she were guilty, when she had swallowed this drink; then he took her oath, next dipped in the water a document on which was written the words of the curse, and when all this had been gone through made her drink some of it; after this he took the sacrifice from her hand and solemnly offered it up, and lastly made her swallow all that was left of the drink. The effect of this long and awful rite was believed to be that the woman who knew herself not to be innocent, could not fail to be instantly destroyed by the water and earth of the Sanctuary drunk under such impressive circumstances, her pregnant body to be burst,[1] her hips to rot into dust. And as a fact, in the early simpler days, as long as the belief remained operative, a consequence like this may have been of no such rare occurrence; while, on the other hand, the drink was without serious danger to the woman who was conscious of her own innocence, and did not impede the progress of her pregnancy. The author of the Book of Origins undoubtedly found this usage already existing, and it is quite in accordance both with the old sacrificial ideas of Jahveism, and with certain other traces of the early belief in ordeals to be found there.[2] But we know also that it passed out of use tolerably early.[3]

What was the fate of a divorced wife who found no other husband,[4] we do not exactly know. A priest might not marry her.[5] It cannot be proved that the husband had to endow her at the separation with even the smallest portion beyond the fortune which she might herself have brought him,[6] (as Mohammedanism prescribes, assuming a much greater frequency of such cases); they are often placed side by side with the

---

[1] צָבָה, ver. 21 sq., 27, can by no means signify merely to swell, but must also indicate the consequence of this, viz. bursting. In like manner מָרִים, verr. 18–27, certainly means according to *Lehrb.* § 179a, as much as מָרָה, 2 Sam. ii. 26, and is used as a circumlocution for *misfortune, death*. The LXX. already went far astray in their interpretation of this description of a matter which had become obscure to them.

[2] The following are such: The oracle of the high-priest, the oracle through the rods described Num. xvii. 16–28 [1–13]; see below on the point.—For similar usages to those described here, see e.g, *Not. et Extr.* tom. xii. p. 649; *Recueil des Voyages*, tom. ii. (Paris, 1825), p. 9. II. Hallenr, *Das Leben der Neger West-africa's* (Berlin, 1850) s. 34; *Ausland*, 1852, s. 1075 sq.; Livingstone's *Travels*, ii. s. 82 sq., 281 sq.; Bastian's *Reise nach S. Salvador* (1859), s. 90.

[3] The instance given in the *Protev. Jac.* xvi. is nothing but a learned repetition.

[4] They bore the special name גְּרוּשָׁה.

[5] Lev. xxi. 7, 14; Ezek. xliv. 22.

[6] P.,173.

widows,[1] and shared, if they inherited no fortune from their paternal home, the fate of the latter so often bewailed in the Old Testament.

If, in conclusion, we once more look away from these details to the whole condition of woman as it is revealed in its larger and more general features in the history of the ancient nation, we then for the first time see clearly what an influence ancient Jahveism exercised in determining her worth and position in the realm, in spite of the surviving restrictions of an earlier stage of civilisation. There is no trace of the contemptible and preposterous life to which Mohammedanism has gradually degraded women. A woman, should she be possessed of extraordinary gifts, might even be recognised as a prophetess and a poetess, as a national leader and a ruler, and retain such dignities till she met with a renowned death;[2] although this stepping out of the sphere into which she was born never became frequent or connected with superstition. With what success even a defenceless country damsel could defy the mightiest king, is seen in the Song of Solomon. Again, the fact that the wife of Isaiah is called simply 'the prophetess,' not on account of her own office, but of that of her husband, is a sufficient proof that the true estimation of the better nature and influence of woman and of her position towards her husband early made powerful efforts to establish itself.

5. During almost the whole period of the nation's existence it retained undiminished its eager delight alike in the cultivation of the soil and other arts of industry, and in matrimony and the continuance of the family in the tribe and the great community. Nothing is more alien to those days than prudish and melancholy views in regard to marriage and children. In the earlier times, however, this fresh delight in life and this zeal for the honour of the house not only found far more open utterance, but assumed very peculiar forms in relation to those blessings which at that time were regarded as almost the highest of ordinary life. This shows itself most in the custom of marriage by the brother-in-law (the *leviratus*, termed also a marriage of duty). We know[3] that to every free-born Israelitish family there belonged a plot of land which could not be alienated, that the continuance of this institution had the closest connection with the whole national constitution, according to which such a hereditary portion was almost inseparable

[1] Lev. xxii. 13; Num. xxx. 10 [0]. [3] P. 177 sq.
[2] *Hist.* ii. 374 sqq.

from the family that should possess it, and was deemed its dearest and most sacred possession. We know also,[1] how self-contained every family was in the earliest days, and how firmly all its members grouped themselves around their common father. If the owner of such an estate died without leaving a son behind him, so that a whole family in Israel was threatened with extinction, which, just as among the ancient Hindoos and indeed among every healthy primitive race, was reckoned a great and dismal misfortune, inasmuch as none remained to uphold the fame of his house and his forefathers in the community,[2] then the widow, as though she were no true widow,[3] was strictly bound to continue in the same house, and to marry again no one except the nearest relative of the deceased, who could best represent his flesh and blood, his brother, therefore, or if such did not exist, a kinsman of the same standing. This relative, whether already married or not, and whether or not he wished to take another wife, was on his side bound to beget by her a son, who should inherit the name and house of the deceased. In return, however, he enjoyed together with the widow, the usufruct of the outstanding estate, till the son whom he had to bring up came of age. Thus the house which was threatened with extinction was given a new lease of life with as far as possible the same blood. The law, moreover, only applied to brothers living at the same spot; and a service of love like this performed from a feeling of necessity or of duty, thus made an exception to the laws already explained concerning forbidden connections.[4] If the nearest brother-in-law refused to accept the obligation, perhaps because he did not feel himself competent to undertake a second household, he could then legally transfer his claim on the widow and the property to the nearest relative whom he found willing to take it.[5] Even a widow who was no longer marriageable and who was without a son, and who desired to give up her hereditary estate and rest in peace, might legally summon all who laid claim to it in virtue of relationship, in order that they might establish their respective claims in turn, under the condition that he who was willing to acquire it should complete this marriage-at-law with an equally childless daughter-in-

---

[1] P. 187 sq.
[2] Comp. Jer. xxix. 32; xxxv. 19; Mal. ii. 12. This was of course the case with the houses of the grandees of the nation, 1 Sam. ii. 35; 2 Sam. vii. 11; 1 Kings ii. 24: comp. the opposite case, Is. xxii. 16.
[3] This important particular appears clearly from the order to burn the harlot as an adulteress, Gen. xxxviii. 24.
[4] P. 197.
[5] All this is according to Deut. xxv. 5-10, and Ruth iv. 1-10, the two representations mutually supplementing one another.

law. The jokes and surprises to which this might well give occasion, are described pleasantly enough in the Book of Ruth.[1] Moreover, the ancient custom was liberal enough in these matters to excuse the wife for many a step which would otherwise have been intolerable, just as when Tamar finally succeeded with impunity in obtaining a son from her recalcitrant father-in-law,[2] or when Ruth gave Boaz to understand by means of a strong hint, though with every propriety, what was the matrimonial protection which she desired him to afford her.[3]

It is, however, most improbable that Moses was the first to introduce this custom of marriage-at-law, since the circumstances and views of such primitive nations are alone sufficient to account for it, and it is actually to be found in a very similar form among other, and completely alien races.[4] Nor is it mentioned in any earlier legislation than Deuteronomy. And deeply rooted as the custom undoubtedly was during Israel's earliest days,[5] it was not difficult to see that this exception to the other matrimonial laws ordained by Jahveism, might easily lead to most unfortunate complications, if in somewhat less primitive times no willing relative could be found, and the widow nevertheless believed herself bound to insist on her right. This, indeed, is represented with the utmost ingenuousness in the narrative of Tamar and the patriarch Judah.[6] This caused the custom to die out tolerably early, so that it is already explained as an antiquity in the Book of Ruth. But the Deuteronomist, who was always seeking to restore the ancient customs which had become obsolete in his own days, revived this too; not, however, without allowing the responsible person to free himself from his obligation by a public declaration before court. At the same time he obviously revived it out of pity for the widow, whose marriage with anyone else never seems to have been regarded with favour. But we find an indication of the extent to which the custom had then fallen into disuse in what this legislator permitted the

241

---

[1] For this correct interpretation of Ruth iv. 3–5, see the *Jahrbb. der Bibl. Wiss.* viii. s. 156. For אמוני, ver. 5, אַתְּ דָּא is to be read, comp. verr. 8–10.
[2] Gen. xxxvii. 24–26.
[3] Ruth iii. 1–14.
[4] As is the case among the Caucasians and many other widely separated nations, see Bodenstedt's *Völker des Kaukasus* (Frankfurt. a. M. 1848), s. 82. For Africa, see Livingstone's *Travels*, i. s. 222; for ancient America, in Guatemala, see Franc. Ximenes' *Las Historias del Origin*

de los Indios, edited by Scherzer, Vienna, 1857. The same, however, is to be found among the ancient Hindoos and Persians, see *Manu*, ix. 57–70, 97; Spiegel's *Avesta*, ii. s. xxviii.
[5] This is also shown by the fact that a special verb was formed to express the idea: יִבֵּם, to *marry-at-law*, i.e. to take a wife in this marriage-at-law. An historical instance of this occurs, Jud. x. 1, according to the rendering of the LXX.
[6] Gen. xxxviii.

woman to do in court to the man who refused to accept his responsibility. She might take his shoe off, call him a barefooted one, and spit in his face. For it will be easily understood from what has been already said,[1] that the drawing off of the shoe in court was originally what a man did himself when he gave up a right, and was consequently intended to signify nothing but the renunciation of a right and of a possession; so that in this respect the description given by the Book of Ruth is more ancient than that of the Deuteronomist, who desired only to retain so much of the custom as was valid and could be valid at his own time.

The *adoption of children* was permitted, but not very favourably regarded, as the typical case of the patriarchs shows.[2] The custom seems to have been for the adopter to throw his mantle over the child which was to be adopted as one of his own, and a similar custom prevailed among other ancient nations.[3]

c. *The Relation between Slaves, Masters, and Free Men.*

A respected and powerful house will always be a centre to which a greater or smaller number of people of less power and consequence will attach themselves, as long as either birth (nature) or fortune give rise to different grades of human capacity or power. These weaker strangers will be the more closely attached to the house, and the more a part of its possessions, the more independently each house exists for itself alone, and the more exclusive its dependence on the paternal authority. Thus the earliest form which this attachment took was that of slavery, i.e. of household property, its origin extending back into pre-historic times. In the Old Testament it makes its appearance abruptly in the history of Abraham as a fully-developed institution, without any earlier mention of it, except its prediction by Noah at the commencement of the history of the present human race.[4]

However, we are able to recognise very accurately in the Old Testament what were the sources from which slavery grew up. The great majority of slaves may have originally

---

[1] P. 180 sq.
[2] Gen. xvi. 2.
[3] Comp. the German *Mantelkind*. This affords the easiest explanation of the application of this custom to a similar case, 1 Kings xix. 19-21; similar, again, is the instance mentioned, Ruth iii. 4-14. Comp. further, Shahrastâni's *Elmilal*, p. 440, ad fin., ed. Cur.; *Qirq Vezîr*, p. 91, 5 par.; also the Arabic passage given by Quatremère in the *Mémoires de l'Acad. des Inscr.* xv. 2, pp. 319 sq., 326 sqq., and the descriptions in Sapeto's *Viaggio tra i Bogos*, p. 119 sq., 173.
[4] Gen. ix. 25-27.

become such by their lives having been spared when taken captive in war, although the ancient practice of Jahveism, as will be shown below, put very narrow limitations to this sparing of human booty, and consequently the number of male slaves in Israel could not have increased in this way to any important extent. The extensive trade in slaves carried on at an extremely early period,[1] may have arisen in consequence of a surplus of such prisoners of war. But human robbery on a great scale was soon added to this by means of military inroads, against which the prophets of the Old Testament declaim indignantly.[2] Stealing human beings was punished by the laws of Jahveism as one of the very worst offences.[3]—But, on the other hand, many from poverty, laziness, or moral degeneracy, fell into a condition of dependence, or even chose to offer themselves as slaves merely to escape the cares of providing for their own maintenance. Thus, too, the patriarch Noah, in the passage referred to above,[4] proclaims slavery as particularly the curse and consequence of moral turpitude. When, again, the individual houses were united in the higher organisation of an administrative realm, the debtor whom other means failed would be then compelled to pay with the person of his children, his wife, or even himself.[5] Many parents, however, would also sell their children merely on account of poverty or from slothfulness.[6]—Finally, slavery spread by means of the home-born children of slaves, who shared every variety in the fortune of the house, and even in Israel were from the first deemed the most faithful and best.[7] Thus the mightier houses early became the centres of very large assemblages of slaves of every variety of character, who according to their several capabilities and trades discharged the most diverse, but often most important household duties,[8] and whose overseer, termed the

243

[1] Presupposed already in regard to Abraham, Gen. xvii. 23, 27.
[2] Amos i. 6, 8.
[3] P. 186.
[4] Viz. in that prophetic passage at the commencement of the whole history of the present human race according to the true meaning of the entire narrative, Gen. ix. 18–27.
[5] P. 184.
[6] Ex. xxi. 7; BK. Is. l. 1; comp. Munzinger's *Ostafrikanische Studien*, s. 245, 483.
[7] Ex. xxi. 4; xxiii. 12; Gen. xiv. 14; xvii. 23, 27. When Eliezer (*Hist.* i. 294) Gen. xv. 3, is called a home-born slave of Abraham's, and yet in ver. 2 Damascus is called his native city, this need not signify anything more than that this city was the one to which his family belonged, and he would himself go by preference should he receive his freedom. But we must also remember that ver. 3 is only an explanation of the obsolete mode of speech in ver. 2. Moreover, the terms 'home-born' or 'son of a female slave,' as indicating the best kind of slave, are often put for slave in general, Ex. xii. 12.
[8] We may also notice that in the ancient view the slave had properly no personal name, enjoying no such honour, but as a mere thing, used to be distinguished, just like an animal, only by a number. Hence the witty enumeration in *Hariri*, s. 376 sqq. *de Sac.*

eldest of the household, although taken from their midst, was often a most exalted personage.[1]

In ways like these, slavery in the old world had long struck its roots very deeply into all domestic institutions when Jahveism made its appearance. To abolish it at once was not to be thought of; but no other ancient religion, either in respect to its actual origin[2] or its unextinguishable impulses, was ever so emphatically opposed to it, or at least to all inhumanity connected with it, or made such sure preparations for its abolition. The fundamental principle here finds clear utterance. If Israel had once been the slave of Egypt, and knew therefore how to value genuine liberty, what excuse could it have for treating its own slaves harshly? How could it help (this further consequence at any rate follows easily in thought) trying to extirpate all slavery? And even the earliest law took for the first time a decisive position above the traditional household usage, inasmuch as it ordained universal commandments for the benefit of all slaves without distinction of nationality, for Hebrews and for aliens. Its requirements were as follow:—

1) Slaves were at any rate to be placed on an equal footing with free men in regard to life's spiritual privileges; before God the former were not more insignificant than the latter, but on the contrary enjoyed with equal rights all the blessings of the higher religion. They were to rejoice in the sabbath,[3] to be circumcised,[4] and therefore to enter the community of Jahveh as thoroughly as those who were free; how much was already implied in that! That their masters should also let them partake of the joys of sacrifice is especially enjoined by the Deuteronomist.[5] Among heathen nations the customs in respect to all these things were for the most part totally different.

2) The law gave them certain civil rights in regard to their masters, without, it is true, putting them quite on a par with free men. The slaughter of a slave shall not remain unpunished, says the oldest law, but it does not determine here the amount of the penalty, and it leaves the master quite unpunished if the slave does not die till some days after a chastisement; severely maiming him was to be expiated with his manumission.[6] All these regulations applied equally for the benefit of female slaves.

Nevertheless the presence of national feeling even here cannot be wholly denied, as the law was more merciful to the

---

[1] *Hist.* i. 294.
[2] *Hist.* ii. 138 sq.
[3] Ex. xx. ii., and the passages corresponding to this one.
[4] Gen. xvii. 10-14, 23-27; xxxiv. 22; Ex. xx. 44.
[5] Deut. xii. 12, 17 sq.; xvi. 11, 14; still more simply Ex. xii. 44.
[6] Ex. xxi. 20 sq., 26 sq.: comp. ver. 32. Very finely expressed, Job xxxi. 13-15.

Hebrew slave than to others. It decreed[1] that such a slave after serving for six full years should be set at liberty, leaving behind, however, the wife who might have been given to him by his master during this period, and any children whom she had born him. If he already had a wife when he lost his freedom, e.g. on account of debt, then they both went free. A period of seven years in such a case was fixed by ancient custom, if not for slaves, still for hired servants.[2] But the limitation of the period of servitude to six years, and the express proclamation of the seventh year as the year of freedom, is undoubtedly a subsequent result of the conception of the sabbath; but it is equally certain that it was established at the time when the community itself was founded, a time when all these conceptions were in such full vigour as will be shown further on. An appropriate addition to this, accordingly, was that anyone who did not desire to avail himself of this consecrated year of freedom, should receive from his master at the Sanctuary, under the sanction of the highest judicial court,[3] a token which should serve as a memorial of his solemn determination to remain a slave for ever. This was done by the priest holding the slave's ear against the door or door-post of the Sanctuary, while the master bored it through with an awl, much in the same way as the nose is pierced of an animal which is about to be tamed.[4] This might always take place at one of the yearly festivals when they were in the habit of making a pilgrimage up to the Sanctuary. The fact, however, that it was always necessary in the first place to take such a bondsman up to the Sanctuary, proves that the Deity was deemed the supreme guardian of the freedom and the freeing of the members of his community. Still the priests had to investigate the case more closely, were able to hear what the bondsman had to say, and only permitted the ignominy to be inflicted on him when they were convinced that he really did not desire his liberty.

---

[1] Ex. xxi. 2-11.
[2] Gen. xxix. 18 sqq. An apparent interchange of a similar kind between the numbers six and seven is found Gen. ii. 2, as well as Jer. xxxiv. 14.— Relics of this primitive custom are even yet to be found in these regions, having been revived by means of the Bible, see several passages in Lynch's *Narrative of the United States Expedition to the River Jordan* (London, 1849). Among the Lesghians the period of service is ten years, see *Nouvelles Ann. des Voyages*, 1852, i. p. 90.
[3] According to the context the second הגישׁי, Ex. xxi. 6, is to be referred to האלהים, on this, however, see below.
[4] Comp. Is. xxxvii. 29; Ezek. xxxviii. 4. It was an ancient custom with certain Arab tribes to bore through or shorten (جدع) the ear of a captive who was to become a slave, and whose life was therefore to be spared, *Hamâsa*, p. 114, 7. Similar facts in Munzinger's *Ostafrik. Studien*, ss. 312, 383; Petermann's *Reisen im Orient*, ii. s. 108.

The servitude of a Hebrew female slave, a daughter e.g., sold by her father (as often happened) on account of domestic poverty, was of course limited in the same way to the period of six years;[1] moreover, her master might not sell her again as an ordinary slave.[2] If he had chosen her for a concubine for himself (as in the earlier days was undoubtedly often his purpose from the first), and after she had become marriageable had publicly recognised her as such and thereby raised her to a higher stage; (for a concubine always stood higher than a mere female slave,[3] and was more like a *liberta*), then, in case he afterwards got tired of and repudiated her, he might not sell, but at the most might marry, her again to a stranger. If, on the other hand, he selected her as a concubine for his son, he had to give her a bridal portion as though she had been a daughter. If he kept her but took another half-wife along with her, then he was bound either to withdraw from her none of the prerogatives of a half-wife, or else at once to set her free,[4] possibly before the expiration of the six years.—Such a girl would undoubtedly often not know what was her real position, in case her master had neither set her free nor betrothed her to his son, nor yet practically emancipated her in order to marry her to someone else like one of his own daughters. Accordingly, if under such indefinite circumstances, anyone were to lie with her, it would have been too harsh to have punished him as an adulterer, as her owner would be often ready enough to demand. The law was content with requiring from him a guilt-offering,[5] in addition to the legal penalty inflicted on both parties for simple fornication, as we may conclude from what has been said above.[6]

---

[1] As is said still more distinctly in Deut. xv. 12, 17.
[2] This is the meaning of the words, Ex. xxi. 7: comp. Lev. xxv. 39, 42.
[3] P. 199 sqq.
[4] This is the meaning of Ex. xxi. 7–11; ver. 10 sq. certainly refers to the master himself, with whom the whole passage is dealing, not to the son. Ver. 8, already misunderstood in many ways by the earlier translators, only becomes intelligible if we consider לֹא the same as לוֹ, and give to the Hifil of פדה, which occurs only here and in Lev. xix. 20, the meaning of 'to free, i.e. to make a concubine.' For the concubine must have held a far higher position, she had, e.g. nourishing animal food assigned to her, as indicated in ver. 10. Comp. اَنْذَلَ, to emancipate, *Hamâsa*, p. 442, last line, and more on the meaning of the whole passage in the *Jahrbb. der Bibl. Wiss.* x. s. 275 sq.—This also makes the passage Lev. xix. 20, clear; only the words בִּקֹּרֶת תִּהְיֶה (which the LXX already obscured by supplying αὑτοῖς) must be taken thus: 'So let there be distinction! i.e. thus is this case to be kept distinct from another case with which it is not identical,' viz. actual adultery. נֶחֱרֶפֶת is much the same as 'given up' in the sense just explained. But that בִּקֹּרֶת signifies *punishment* cannot be proved from the Ethiopic በቀለ :.
[5] Lev. xix. 20–22.
[6] P. 58.

But this emancipation of a Hebrew slave after six full years of servitude must have gone out of usage at a tolerably early date. This we see plainly from the Book of Origins, which gives great prominence to the distinction between Hebrew and non-Hebrew slaves, and requires the former to be treated with the utmost consideration, but nevertheless limits their emancipation to the year of Jubilee (which is spoken of below), a period which not nearly all of them could live to see.[1] The Deuteronomist, it is true, re-instates here too the ancient law, and even enjoins that a small portion should be given out of kindness to the emancipated slave, to help him at the commencement of his new independence.[2] But even after the national reformation effected under Josiah, the proper feeling to procure the observance of this particular law was wanting. The law had become obsolete for many centuries; it touched the civil rights of rich individuals; and therefore no king at that time, even if he desired to do so, could introduce it on his own personal authority, after a totally different usage had been long established. As a matter of fact, too, the execution of this law would by this time have become far more difficult, because the pecuniary circumstances of the citizens had now become for a long time far more unequal and more complicated than they were in the simplicity of the earliest days when the community was founded. If an effort was now to be made to carry out the spirit of the ancient law, it would seem comparatively more easy to abolish slavery altogether in regard to their own countrymen, and to substitute for it labour for hire, just as the Book of Origins had previously recommended that these slaves should be treated exactly like hired servants.[3] And it is really remarkable that an attempt to abolish by law all slavery of this kind actually was made under the last king of Judah, even though it achieved no permanent success.[4] The opinion was still maintained that a slave did double the daily work of a hired labourer,[5] and on this or other pretexts the attempt was soon brought to nothing. The total overthrow of the ancient kingdom was necessary before an end could be put to a slavery which no one was able to take any further steps to banish. In the days of the New Jerusalem, however, slavery although not legally abolished, nevertheless seems to have been more limited to the household institutions of the most powerful and wealthy of the nation.

---

[1] Lev. xxv. 39-46.
[2] Deut. xv. 12-18. In speaking of boring the ear, ver. 17, all mention of the Sanctuary and the co-operation of the priest is entirely omitted.
[3] Lev. xxv. 40.
[4] *Hist.* iv. 271.
[5] Deut. xv. 18.

—During the course of these centuries, however, a new relation had been growing up, which occupied an intermediate position between slavery and free service for hire, a sort of feudal dependence or allegiance (*clientel*). The client is no longer the absolute property of his patron—his position is far more independent; but he attaches himself to his patron's household, and receives his paternal protection in return for discharging certain services. Thus both have a new object in life, one of permanent significance so that the relation becomes hereditary, and one which neither patron nor client feels he can easily achieve independently of the other. Such a client in Israel might often be called the same as a slave (serf), but for all that the difference is most essential. That a relation of this kind was formed among the Hebrews, especially whilst the simplest modes of life were gradually disappearing, even as it existed among many of the ancient Arabian tribes,[1] has been shown beyond doubt by what has been already said,[2] and the advance which this implies can be learned in the Old Testament itself from two exceptional delineations of a similar nature. One of the earlier narrators of the Primitive History depicts the extraordinary grandeur of the function discharged by Moses as the servant of Jahveh towards the community, under the image of an overseer of slaves.[3] The great Unknown designates the true nature of the future Messianic servant of Jahveh under the image of a client of Jahveh, who executes his work independently.[4] How much easier it is to give an appropriate representation of the function of the higher religion under the latter, than under the former, of these images!

3. Sanctity pertaining to Strangers.

By strangers we mean here all those who, in the widest sense of the word, are aliens to a particular household, clan, or tribe, or, finally, to the whole nation, but who nevertheless come into close contact with one of these communities. Just as the household in its most ancient form shuts out roughly

---

[1] A client was called جَارٌ a plebeian زَرْبِيَّة. But just as the old Hebrew גֵּר, i.e. *guest* or *cottager* (tenant), easily passed, as will be shown below, into the meaning of client or vassal, in the same way among many Arabs the client was called جَار, as *Hamâsa*, p. 148, 7 sqq. 149, 3.—Similar relations still exist in these countries : comp. Munzinger's *Ostafr. Stud.* s. 155, 311 sq.
[2] P. 179.
[3] Num. xii. 6-8 : comp. p. 179.
[4] P. 211 sq.

whatever is external to itself, so does every newly-arisen, more comprehensive community act, so long as it has still to attain to its full perfection. But the law, as has been already explained, strives to break down this narrow exclusiveness of the primitive household wherever its effects may be prejudicial; and thus in respect to strangers Jahveism further reveals its higher impulses. The circle of love and esteem, of righteousness and equity, shall extend to those who are strangers to the private individual, and who therefore so readily meet with want of consideration and harshness at his hands. Even the law demands this extension, and gives by way of example some plain injunctions, the execution of which it must, it is true, so far as they set forth equitable and handsome treatment, leave over to the individual conscience. Certain portions of the rich blessings of the fields and the gardens were already ordered by the earliest law to be left ungrudgingly for the needy, just as opportunity occurred in each case.[1] Whatever the hungry man picked with his hands for himself of the harvest was not, according to the Deuteronomist, to be made a matter of accusation against him.[2] Even the foreign slave, whom ill-treatment had caused to run away from his master— the case quoted as the most frequent—is taken under the protection of this legislation.[3] In particular no unfairness of any sort was permitted towards those who worked for hire, in order to wring something to one's own advantage out of their

---

[1] Lev. xix. 9 sq.; Deut. xxiv. 19–22: comp. from the history, Ruth ii. 2 sqq. The former and earlier of these two passages requires that both at the corn-harvest and the vintage, the gleanings shall be left for the poor, and adds that in reaping the harvest a corner of the ripe field shall be left untouched for them; while in picking the grapes, only those that were first left from pure oversight were not to be gathered later for the owner; for as grapes do not all ripen at the same time, those that are unripe are naturally left, so that the gleaning of the vintage came to be distinguished by quite a special name, viz. עוֹלֵלָה, i.e. *second picking*. Thus a distinction is made between the ordinary gleaning of the grapes that ripened later, and that of grapes which had been overlooked. The Deuteronomist, on the other hand, only speaks of the gleaning in either case, but adds to both, the olive-harvest, betraying in each respect his later date. The word פָּרַט, Lev. xix. 10, should signify what has been over-

looked in haste, for, corresponding to لَجَّ, it signifies to precipitate, to overlook through excessive haste, or (where the arts are referred to) to attempt to do what a man has not been willing to learn to do properly, or to bungle, Amos vi. 5. In Hebrew this rare word פֶּרֶט evidently became obscure, and in accordance with later, more Aramaic linguistic usage, it was interchanged with פֶּרֶד and פְּרִישׁ, so that it was thought to mean, what was *scattered*, as though the vintagers were forbidden to pick the scattered grapes. Thus is it explained in *M.* פֵּאָה vii. 3: comp. iv. 10, but manifestly incorrectly. We may see generally from *M.* פֵּאָה with what scrupulosity, pettiness, and want of success these teachers of the Law expounded all these words in the Pentateuch, and forgot over the letter all the spirit and higher significance.

[2] Deut. xxiii. 25 [24] sq.: comp. Matt. xii. 1, and the description of the harshness of the opposite treatment, Job xxiv. 10 sq.

[3] Deut. xxiii. 16 [17] sq.

scanty earnings.[1] And that every stranger possessed a sacred right to protection and assistance, that between one's own countrymen and dependent foreign tribes no difference in this respect should properly be made; nay, that under the forms of even the least known and most foreign-looking suppliants, nothing less than the Divinity may draw near to mortals with an entreaty not to be badly treated, this the twofold narrative of the opposite conduct of Abraham and of the Sodomites shows in a clear light and with insurpassable beauty.[2]

But if it was a hard matter for Jahveism to break down the exclusiveness of the ancient household, it was still harder for it to remove the boundaries of nationality. For the nation was then only beginning to come into existence, and while therefore it was vigorous enough, it was in the highest degree narrow and rough; and this was all the more the case in Israel since Jahveism itself had to endeavour to enlist the national feeling as one of its supports. Sharp opposition to other races was therefore essential to this nation. National antipathy to the Egyptians was formed in the cradle of the community, and was succeeded by the same feeling towards the Canaanites and the Philistines; this again, after the days of David and Solomon, by aversion towards the smaller kindred tribes which surrounded them; and, finally, towards the great heathen dominions in the three continents of the old world. All this time the opposition was continually growing deeper and stronger with the growth of Israel, in proportion as nationality and Jahveism gradually became more and more intertwined one with another. Thus even the earliest law is unable wholly to conceal a warmer inclination towards its own people. It enjoins love, and readiness to give help, to make peace and atonement in regard to one's own countrymen.[3] It takes the slaves of Hebrew blood in quite a special manner under its own protection,[4] although its tone towards strangers is invariably far gentler than that of other ancient religions. But the step from this position to a command to hate foreign nations and their inhabitants, is a tolerable wide one, and the ancient law guards itself carefully from uttering any such thing, demanding, on the contrary, that a man shall love even the stranger as himself.[5] Not till

---

[1] Lev. xix. 13 b; comp. Deut. xxiv. 14 sq.; Tobit iv. 14.
[2] Gen. xviii. sq.: comp. *Hist.* i. 330 sq., and Heb. xiii. 2.
[3] Lev. xix. 18: comp. Deut. xxii. 1–4. When in Matt. v. 43, the second member of the first passage 'thou shalt love thy neighbour as thyself' appears to be extended by the addition 'but hate thine enemy,' this is due entirely to later interpretations. Comp. *Die drei ersten Evang.* s. 217.
[4] P. 212 sq.
[5] In this way the expression of the

towards the period of the destruction of the ancient kingdom did the growing needs and privations of the time secure a place in the legislation itself for the expression and impulse of so strong an aversion towards certain nations and inhabitants. In this respect, too, it is a new feature to which Deuteronomy introduces us. We have already seen this in regard to intermarriage with heathen women;[1] and it is very characteristic of Deuteronomy to find it concluding a long series of commands respecting relations towards human beings with the stringent order to extirpate Amalek.[2]

When the class denoted by the word stranger, as would often be the case, coincided with the poor and helpless, then neither the later nor the earlier legislation made the smallest distinction between countrymen and strangers. On the contrary, it is Deuteronomy which repeats with the greatest emphasis and frequency the principle which had already found utterance in the earliest times, that the helpless of every kind and every race, widows, orphans, strangers—i.e. those who were not Hebrews—should meet with kind and gracious treatment.[3] The most intrinsic impulse of Jahveism had a most powerful influence in arousing such kindness towards the poor and a readiness to assist them. This impulse exerted itself everywhere, and operated vigorously at every period; but it manifested itself most on the surface in the requirement that the poor in particular should partake in the joys of the sacrifice;[4] for no joys could rival the elevation and comfort of these.

The particular relations of strangers and their customs and institutions in regard to the civil and religious community of Israel and the extent to which they were allowed the right of citizens in it, can only be explained below in another connection.

---

second member, Lev. xix. 18 (comp. verr. 16–18) is to be supplemented from ver. 34.
[1] P. 194.
[2] Deut. xxv. 17, 19; but here we also see very plainly how what had occurred earlier merely in history, and is narrated as such in Ex. xvii. 14, may at last pass into the legislation in almost identical words.
[3] Deut. x. 18 sq.: comp. xiv. 29; xvi. 11; xxiv. 19, 21; xxvi. 12 sq.; xxvii. 19; all these are after Ex. xxii. 20 sq.; Lev. xix, 33 sq.
[4] P. 212, 52.

III. THE SANCTITY OF JAHVEH AND OF HIS KINGDOM.

1. THE SANCTITY OF JAHVEH AND VENERATION FOR HIM.

The Sanctity of Truth in the Kingdom.

Over the sanctity alike of nature and of humanity stands that of the true God, as human beings in Israel learned to know him. It is he alone in the last instance who is absolutely holy, who is the sole ruler and the only one to be feared, who is perpetually giving his community fresh means to recognise him and reasons to fear him. He also it is through whom all that is sacred in man and nature first receives its sanctity.

He is accordingly the sole person who shall be deemed absolutely holy even in speaking and words, the sole name which is not to be defamed even to the most trifling extent, for otherwise in him the existence also of all law and order would be called in question, and at the same time that which was dearest to every pious heart would be polluted. That the glory of the true God really stands too high to suffer defamation at the lips of a man, even in an exalted community, was an idea too hard to be grasped at that time. The knowledge of this God and the founding of his community were then too recent, the worship of him too much restricted to this one people, and the reverence towards him easily became over-anxious. He alone, according to the ancient constitution, was king of Israel, so that the crime of high-treason could only be committed in respect to him, and as the Ten Commandments would lead us to expect, the penalty for blaspheming his name was death.[1] The Book of Origins accordingly relates how on one occasion a semi-Israelite, son of an Israelitish woman and an Egyptian father, in a brawl with the rest of the people, reviled and cursed[2] the *Name* (that above all names, therefore the glory, majesty), how the community, shocked at the unlooked-for event, sought counsel of the oracle, and how this commanded the man to be stoned. A reminiscence of such a case had doubtless been preserved out of Moses's time, although the Book of Origins, according to its wont, only avails itself of this narrative in order to explain, from its own point of view, the most fundamental principles of the criminal code valid in the community.

That a nation might not publicly defame, at any rate, its

---

[1] *Hist.* ii. 161.

[2] The word נקב in the narrative Lev. xxiv. 10-23 is distinguished from קלל, ver. 11, 14-16, only as 'verwün-schen' (revile) is from 'fluchen' (curse). The latter is a more independent conception, and also a worse one.

chief god, by whom public and binding oaths were sworn, was, it is true, established as a custom also among the heathen.[1] But the far greater truth and depth of Jahveism caused the sanctity of the name of Jahveh to be regarded with much greater seriousness, and expressed itself in far more decided consequences, than did similar phenomena among the heathen. It is true that in ancient Israel we have no sign of the excessive servile scrupulosity in regard to the use of the name of Jahveh, which attained full development towards the end of its whole history.[2] But we have clear indications in the history that the healthy tone prevalent during the fairest period of the nation's life counselled an avoidance of the most sacred name in certain forms of speech,[3] and that the pious felt a delicate dread of even using the name of God openly at all in connection with captious thoughts.[4] Here, then, we see the first beginnings of the latter scrupulousness in regard to the use of the 'name,' the exaggerations of which, however, gave rise to new manifestations which are altogether repugnant to the ancient usages.

Next after the majesty of Jahveh himself, comes that of the sacraments already described.[5] So high did they stand as the symbols mediating between Jahveh and his community that the conduct of those who maliciously injured them seemed as intolerable to their co-religionists as that of warriors who railed at or abandoned their colours would to an army. He who injured these seemed in most cases truly to wish to injure and drive away that which lay concealed behind them—the sway of the true religion and its laws. Capital punishment in these cases was undoubtedly always inflicted with the utmost promptness.

If, finally, even improper handling of the ark, or of any of the other articles deemed most holy, was punished with death, this is only to be explained historically from the whole position occupied by the external Sanctuary among the people, a topic which is dealt with further on.

—But again, of what avail is the sanctity of the true God and his worship in the realm, however watchfully it is protected by all its members, however sternly it is revenged when injured, unless truth itself as the bond of the very existence of all solidity and all real progress in this realm, is similarly protected as something equally inviolable? As with the individual man, so with the kingdom : it can only exist and hold its own

---

[1] To which the Book of Origins itself refers in the narrative ver. 15 sq. This is how ver. 15 is to be understood.
[2] Comp. *Hist.* v. 198.
[3] This was already explained in my pamphlet on *Genesis*, 1823.
[4] Such as Job iii. 20.
[5] P. 108 sqq.

where truth, trustworthiness, and fidelity are everywhere required, everywhere protected, and everywhere honoured, along with all the means and institutions (such as the oath and adjuration)[1] whereby this aim is advanced. But where, as in this case, the religion of a nation desires to be reared on what is the sole foundation of all truth, then nothing more is wanting to vindicate the authority of truth. Mere laws cannot achieve much in this matter; Jahveism gives no one single law against lying and to protect truth, although its whole spirit is far more born of truth and dependent on its might than Zarathustra's law of life. But in procuring admission to the stone tables of the primitive Ten Commandments for the duty not to bear false witness against a neighbour, thus placing it on a level with the few fundamental commands, it gave sufficient proof how it took truth under its protection, as the basis of the very existence of the realm and of the common well-being of all its members.[2] That the infringement of this law was punished with death, requires no further proof;[3] and if Jahveh was invariably thought of as being close to his people, and if his holy eyes grew angry at matters of far more trifling import, how was it possible to think of him in any way but as moved to the profoundest wrath in the presence of the false witness?[4]

Opposition to every form of Heathen Idolatry.

The rigid exclusion of all worship of images and of heathenism was from the first most intimately associated with the requirements of Jahveism, i.e. of true religion, and we must remember that in this case it is ultimately the public regard for truth itself that is concerned. But the extraordinary difficulties which this religion began more and more to experience in maintaining its position intact in the midst of an utterly different world, naturally gave rise as time went on to greater and greater strictness. The Book of Covenants already commands the violent destruction of all the manifold tokens of heathenism, while still earlier legislation was content with uttering warnings against the imitation of heathen religious practices, and even (as they were used to swear by) against speaking the names of heathen gods.[5] The Book of Origins,

---

[1] P. 16 sq.
[2] See *Hist.* ii. 161 sqq.
[3] The words in Deut. xix. 15–21 only express more distinctly what may have been said in Ex. xxiii. 1. Comp. for the rest p. 176.
[4] Deut. xxiii. 15. [14].

[5] Ex. xxii. 19 [20] (where אחרים is to be inserted, as in the Sam. Pent.); xxiii. 13, 24; comp. the Ten Commandments and Lev. xix. 4; xxvi. 1. Then, again, the tone is similar in the Book of Origins, Num. xxxiii. 51–53.

written during the fairest period of Israel's nationality, contains special cautions against worshipping the spirits of the desert (Demons) given in connection with its description of Israel's sojourn in the desert,[1] and this connection is the reason why the ghost-like, mocking spirits of the desert are mentioned in the place of all other false gods. The Deuteronomist is the first to legislate more minutely in this field, and he is the first to give distinct directions that all apostasy from Jahveism, even if counselled by a prophet or anyone else, even if committed by a nearest relative or friend, whether it appeared in an individual or a whole community, should without pity be punished with death.[2]—An important difference, however, was made here between a strange worship which endeavoured to accommodate itself to Jahveism, and one which stood in hostile opposition.

1. Forms of worship which were in force and honour in Israel before the founding of Jahveism, sought for many centuries after that event to hold their position alongside of it and accommodate themselves to it, and this they did all the more in proportion to the difficulty which pure Jahveism, with all its simple grandeur and freedom from images, had in becoming a permanent possession of the community. Strictly speaking, the law forbade even this accommodation, by which Jahveh was revered through an image and man sank again into heathenism; but in reality it was not till during the times of the kings that a stop could be put to this popular mingling of old and new. There are three different sides on which this tendency is specially manifested.

First and foremost it appears very strongly in connection with the images of the primitive Teraphim, or family divinities,[3] of Israel. About these we know, comparatively speaking, a good deal, and yet far too little for us to frame a perfectly distinct representation of them. What, however, we can gather from the scattered notices concerning them may be represented as follows:[4] An image of this sort did not consist of a single object, but of several distinct parts, at any rate when the owner cared to have one of the more fully adorned

---

[1] Lev. xvii. 7. If the same are meant by the word שְׂעִירִים Deut. xxxii. 17, the word is nevertheless employed in this song in a far less restricted meaning, just as שְׂעִירִים, Satyrs, 2 Chron. xi. 15.

[2] Deut. xii. 29–xiii. 19 [18]; xvii. 2–7.

[3] The Svîjakuladêvatâs in the Veda.

[4] The clearest description of them is found only in the narrative, Jud. xvii. 4 sq.; xviii. 14, 17, 18, 20, 30; the words in xviii. 18 are to be restored according to the LXX. When the words are carefully considered, it will be seen that all four names signify only one image.

and perfect specimens. The essential kernel of it, made either out of stone or else out of wood,[1] always attempted to exhibit the image of a god in human form, even life-size ; but already in the earliest times this by itself was readily regarded as too plain. It generally received therefore a coating of gold or silver, either over the whole body or only particular portions; and hence the caustic speech of the stricter worshipper of Jahveh, who detested all worship of images, and delighted in mocking at the product of the chisel and the ladle which formed the two constituent elements of such idols. It may, moreover, be understood of itself, that where the noble metals were plentiful enough the idols might be cast entire of them.[2]—
Up to this point, then, a family god, without regard to its special form, was prepared just like the image of any other god ; it was something added to this which formed the specific distinction of the primitive family god of the Israelites. In order to understand what this was, it is of the utmost consequence that we should remember that these domestic deities were employed from the earliest times to furnish oracles, so that the word *Teraphim* is absolutely identical with oracular divinity.[3] For this purpose the first addition to the image was an *Ephod*, i.e. a magnificent robe put over the shoulders, having on its breast a casket containing the lots employed in determining the oracle, just as will be described further on in connection with the adornment of the high-priest. In the second place a kind of mask was placed over the head of the image, in which the priest who was seeking the oracle probably had to perceive by sundry tokens whether the god was willing or not to give an oracle at all at that particular time. These masks alone made the image properly complete, and from them the divinities received their name of Teraphim.[4]

---

[1] פֶּסֶל is originally only an image of stone according to *Hist.* ii. 160*nt*. but it gradually came to signify any idolatrous image, Ex. xx. 4: comp. Jud. xviii. 30, and assumed a meaning as general as that of ξόανον.

[2] As in the cases mentioned, Ex. xxxii. 2-4; nk. Is. xl. 19; comp. Jer. x. 3-9; nk. Is. xl. 20; xli. 7: xliv. 12-17: xlvi. 6.

[3] Jud. xvii. sq. ; Hos. iii. 4 ; BK. Zach. x. 2 ; Ezek. xxi. 26. [21].

[4] תְּרָפִים may, after طرف, اشرف be equivalent to a nodding countenance or living mask, and may even be such a plural as פָּנִים, face, properly features. The LXX already usually abstain from translating the word; in 1 Sam. xix. 13, 16, however, they translate it by κενοτάφια, a seemingly strange word, of which, however, so much is clear, that it may mean the same as *larvæ*. On the other hand, in Hos. iii. 4, it is rendered by δῆλοι, on the supposition, revived also by modern critics, that it was identical with אוּרִים (see below under the dress of high-priest). But the latter opinion rests only on the frequent conjunction of the *Ephod* with the Teraphim, which is to be understood in quite a different way. Aquila's translation μορφώματα is accordingly still the clearest. Then there is a perfect parallel in the *lares* as the *dii larvarum* ; and the extent to which *nodding* was

At the same time we can understand from this how the Teraphim can be sometimes described as of a similar size to that of a man,[1] sometimes as smaller, and therefore capable of easy concealment under the saddle of a camel,[2] for the principal element consisted of the two proper oracular constituents, especially in the case of a household divinity which had been preserved for a long period, and was regarded with great affection.—Somewhat like this were the forms of the family gods, dating, as we cannot doubt,[3] from the most ancient days of the nation; and if we consider the extraordinary tenacity with which everything of a domestic character held its ground with little alteration in spite of the opposition of the fundamental principles of Jahveism, it will not surprise us to find many continuing for centuries to seek for protection and counsel from these family gods, only finding in them now an image of Jahveh himself. From individual houses this materialisation of Jahveism may have extended itself over a somewhat wider circle, as when at the extreme northern border of the land, in the territory of Dan, a grandson of Moses undertook with his posterity the priesthood of such a Jahveism.[4] But that this abuse crept into the heart of the kingdom is contrary to all probability; and so soon as a vigorous revival of the genuine religion sprang up under Samuel, such an abuse could no longer maintain itself, at any rate publicly, as is distinctly stated in this narrative about Dan.[5] In private houses, however, the Teraphim were held in reverence till much later.[6]

Of a different kind was the reverence paid to the image of a *horned bull*, for which a prejudice existed from the days of the Hyksôs among certain sections of the nation, and which though suppressed by triumphant Jahveism, yet at certain periods regained the ascendancy with unexpected obstinacy. This image never denoted domestic protecting deities, but the guardian divinity of the whole realm and people, and was

expected from such images is shown in the passages in Chwolson's *Ssabiern* ii. s. 152 sqq. The rest of the conjectures of modern writers on the original significance of the word (including Bonomi's *Nineveh and its Palaces*, p. 179 sqq.) are wide of the mark.— Moreover, it will easily be understood from what has been said, that the *Ephod* by itself may denote the same idolatrous image elsewhere called Teraphim, Jud. viii. 27: comp. Is. xxx. 22.

[1] 1 Sam. xix. 13–16
[2] Gen. xxxi. 34.
[3] Particularly after what is said, Gen. xxxi. 19, 30.
[4] Jud. xviii.
[5] The ancient words, Jud. xviii. 31, clearly indicate that after the removal of the ark from Shiloh, i.e. after the fall of Eli and the rise of Samuel, a religious reformation took place extending even to the extreme north of the Holy Land, manifestly through the agency of Samuel himself; in ver. 30, perhaps אֲרָן is to be read for אָרָן.
[6] They occur for the last time, 2 Kings xxiii. 24.

undoubtedly like all other images borrowed from animals, originally nothing but a symbol for weapons and standards. In history, it appears in the earliest annals of Israel as the token of the former supremacy of Joseph in Egypt, and therefore also of his tribe,[1] and would of itself have been innocent had not the people imagined they had found in it an image of Jahveh himself. Strictly suppressed, therefore, by Moses, it nevertheless rose easily to the surface again, in the first instance in the tribe of Joseph, at times when the remembrance of the former alliance with the mighty and fair Egypt was revived, and it finally became dominant in the kingdom of the Ten Tribes with all the greater facility as the origin of this kingdom caused it to incline more closely to Egypt.[2] All remembrance of Egypt, if it contained nothing unfavourable, could call to mind only the great state institutions existing there. Even the honouring of Jahveh under the image of a bull was manifestly related to such great state institutions, while the former earliest veneration of the Teraphim always possessed a more purely domestic, or at most family, importance.

In Canaan itself, finally, a peculiar worship had found a home from the earliest times, which continued to exercise a powerful influence on Jahveism long after this had been founded. It is the above-mentioned[3] worship of sacred stones of peculiar origin, colour, or form, as monuments or even as images of a God,—a worship generally connected with the veneration of sacred trees. It early extended itself from Canaan far into foreign lands, and undoubtedly assumed in the course of time the most manifold variety of forms; but its essential character can everywhere be recognised, even in the descriptions of the latest authors.[4] That among the ancestors of the people comprehended under the name Jacob who settled in the primitive days for the first time in Canaan, there were those who followed the custom of the country and

[1] Also comp. *Hist.* ii. 181 sq., 183 note 1.
[2] See further, *Hist.* iv. 26 sqq.; comp. ii, 181 sqq.
[3] P. 118.
[4] Nothing was more astonishing to Roman notions; comp. the way in which the temple of the Paphian goddess and other temples are spoken of in Tacitus, *Hist.* ii. 3; Sil. Ital. *Pun.* iii. 30 sq.; Herodian's *Hist.* v. 3; Curt. *Hist.* iv. 7; Arnob. *Adv. Nat.* i. 39; vi. 11: comp. still similar features in Rüppel's *Reise nach Abyssinien*, i. s. 353. That the smaller magic stones which were moved about in the hand, and at last made to produce sounds by striking, only came into fashion in consequence of a much later art, will be easily understood from what has been said on p. 119. In the same way the largest and heaviest sacred objects became, and still become, among the heathen, diminished to the smallest and most delicate copies.—The last allusion to it is in the seventh century, see Bk. Is. lvii. 6.

imitated this worship, is proved by the highly significant reminiscences concerning the stone of Jacob at Bethel, as well as by the ancient sanctity of this genuine Israelitish Sanctuary. Again, the beautiful description by the Fourth Narrator of how Jacob in the midst of the desert plain found for his night-quarters a hard stone, which became for him and his whole house an instrument and a monument of the highest blessings of his God,[1] still contains a clear recollection of this kind of Divine worship as it existed in Israel down from its earliest days. It is not then surprising that these images of the Holy One once more became influential in Israel, when after the founding of Jahveism it conquered Canaan, found again its ancient sanctuary at Bethel, and came into friendly relations with Canaanitish civilisation. At the time of the Judges many worshipped Jahveh in a sanctuary built after this as a model, and gradually the word *bâmah* established itself as the name for a sanctuary built after the Canaanitish fashion.[2]

2. It was a totally different case when foreign sacred rites were introduced with a purely hostile purpose into the midst of the existing Jahveism in order to suppress it. In the earlier days this took place but very rarely and without any results whatever. It did not become frequent and dangerous till after the days of Solomon. This is not the place to give a full description of all such foreign religions as from time to time endeavoured to penetrate into Israel. Besides, the details of many of them can now hardly be discerned by us. This much, however, is clear, that in every century the struggle in Israel against all such religions was far more bitter and desperate

---

[1] Gen. xxviii. 10–22: comp. the primitive designation in the blessing of Jacob, 'the shepherd (protector, God) of the stone of Israel,' Gen. xlix. 24.

[2] See further, *Hist.* iii. 305; iv. 238. In Ezek. xviii. 6, 11, the names of *mountains* are interchanged with those of *bâmoth*, yet it is possible that only the artificial mountains, viz. the conical stones, are to be understood thereby. So far the conical monuments and sacred trees of the Druids are also to be compared (comp. Renan's *Essais de Morale et de Critique*, p. 404 sq.). Such sacred groves existed also in ancient Ethiopia; the demons had their abodes in them, and fled when they were cut down, as the Snskâr relates in Dillmann's *Chrest.* p. 38, 14.—It is only another name for the same thing, indicating a somewhat different form of these artificial cones, which we find in תַּמָּנִים, 2 Chron. xxxiv. 4. They are therefore connected with בָּמוֹת, 2 Chron. xiv. 4 [5]; Lev. xxvi. 30; Ezek. vi. 4, 6, and with the אֲשֵׁרִים, Is. xvii. 8; xxvii. 9. This latter term is explained, *Hist.* iii. 306 (see also *M.* עוּז, iii. 5, 7–10 which still gives the right interpretation). The word itself is certainly compounded from חַרְמוֹן, comp. حُرْم and حَرَم, as though they were little Hermons.—This, too, shows the word not to be pure Canaanitish; and a last trace of it is shown by the בַּעַל חֲמָן on Punic inscriptions, although in the latest of them it is already abbreviated into בַּעַל מָאן. Copies of such sacred symbols are continually found on Cyprian and Phœnician coins; see *Revue numismatique*, 1860, p. 8 sqq.

than that against the mere mingling of old and new, of home and foreign elements. Examples of this may be seen in the most important cases.

The sanctuaries of Canaanitish origin which are comprehended under the name *bâmah*, were also erected shortly after the time of Solomon for the reception of the worship of Astarte, and were therefore more thoroughly adapted to the Phœnician mode,[1] while at the same time the earlier types of these sanctuaries continued to exist. But we still know that the most strenuous declamations of the prophets were directed against this new type of Canaanitish sanctuaries.[2]

The practice of sacrificing children to the God Moloch, as well as the name of the God himself, are mentioned for the first time in the Book of Origins.[3] The rite may therefore have been first introduced about the commencement of the reign of Solomon, when the conquered surrounding races could revenge themselves on their conquerors through the extension of their pernicious sacred rites. That this sacrifice came across a tendency which had already manifested itself here and there in Israel at an earlier date, cannot be denied;[4] but it is equally certain that this God Moloch was a total stranger to the people of Israel before the period just alluded to. We cannot at present say clearly from what nation this sacrifice extended itself to Israel; it is not quite certain that it was from the Ammonites.[5] In any case we know that a similar sacrifice was widely extended at an early period throughout the region

---

[1] See *Hist.* iv. 44, 49 sqq. The proper symbol of Astarte was undoubtedly a star (as though one fallen from heaven), *Sanchuniathon*, p. 36, 1 Or.; the same, therefore, as Amos v. 26, speaks of: comp. Ugdulone *Sulle Monete Punico-Sicule*, p. 44 sq.—If, however, the Hellenists were accustomed to say ἡ Βααλ (comp. Rom. xi. 4), we must remember that they preferred this contemptuous *feminine* in the case of all idols with which they were not acquainted: comp. the LXX. 2 Kings xvii. 30 sq. In the same way, at a later time, instead of Teraphim the word תְּרָפוֹת was used with a general meaning of *idols*, *M.* עי, ii. 3.—A disgraceful practice of their lascivious female worshippers is described in the Epist. Jer. v. 43. The custom, scanty remnants of which have lasted into our own time, of consecrating all sorts of ornaments to the gods in consequence of a vow, or, at any rate, of hanging them up on sacred trees, is referred to *Hist.* iii. 306, note 1; iv. 208: comp. Aristoph. *Aves*, 825, *Equites*, 568; Virg. *Cir.* 21 sqq.; Ovid, *Metam.* viii. 727 sqq.; Fletcher's *Narrative of Nineveh*, ii. p. 276; Badger's *Nestorians*, i. p. 99; *Ausland*, 1851, s. 280; *Revue Archéol.* 1853, p. 528; Lajard in the *Mém. de l'Acad. des Inscr.* xx. 2. p. 146 sq. 150; *Journ. of the Royal Geographical Soc.* 1858, p. 240; Furrer's *Wanderungen in Paläst.* s. 229; John Mill's *Nablus*, p. 54.

[2] When the prophets speak against the *bâmah*, it is for the most part these which are meant, as may be seen from the particulars of the descriptions. This word *bâmah* gradually acquired the wider signification of an idolatrous temple, just as the name *Baal* stands for any idol, Jer. xxxii. 35.

[3] Lev. xviii. 21, xx. 2–5.

[4] P. 69, sq.

[5] According to *Hist.* iii. 297, note 3: comp. 2 Kings xxiii. 13, along with ver. 10.

of the Canaanitish or Phœnician civilization,[1] while in the kingdom of Judah it made its first appearance in the higher walks of life after the mournful days of King Ahaz, as the prophets of this later date bitterly complain.[2]

The worship of Baal as the highest Phœnician god (the Herakles of the Greeks), along with his numerous subordinate deities, in large and brilliant temples, and celebrated with mysterious rites, was first introduced by the kings of the house of Omri. It extended during their dynasty as far as Jerusalem. The violent convulsions, however, which it excited in both kingdoms are well known, and also how it scarcely maintained itself in either realm for half a century.[3]

The worship of the constellations, of the signs of the zodiac, and of the planets, was according to all tokens first introduced into Jerusalem in the eighth century.[4]

2. The Sanctity of the Nation.

1. This all-surpassing sanctity attaches to Jahveh in the eyes of Israel, only so far as the latter recognises his entire inviolable grandeur and truth, and out of the spontaneous impulse of its heart, takes him eternally as its sole lord and king, just as any king in whom his people have confidence may be elected by them their lord. In this province, as everywhere, the first impulse, according to the right feeling of the true religion, proceeds straight from God. But Israel was once mightily stimulated and moulded by the spirit of the true God, and was too deeply imbued with all the infinite truth of the real redeemer and helper for it to be able to depart from this at any subsequent time. In this way there arose that inextinguishable eternally progressing and eternally fruitful reciprocal action and reaction between the Truth which has already been previously recognised and experienced, and that which in every epoch is newly recognised and experienced,—a reciprocity which

[1] When Diodorus Sic. *Hist.* xx. 14, calls the corresponding Carthaginian god *Kronos*, he does so only in the well-known Greek fashion, and we may not immediately infer that Moloch and Saturn are the same.—But that הַעֲבִיר does not merely signify (a supposition lately revived by G. Müller's *Amerik. Urrelig.* s. 653) a dragging of children through the fire, is certain from every indication, and is proved merely by the language. Comp. *Parthenon*, 1862, no. 21 sq.

[2] *Hist.* iv. 169 sq. 207 sq. Not till the monarchy itself had sanctioned a new religion by its own example could it be adopted even into the temple of Solomon. It is true that we are informed of this in relation to the sacrifice to Moloch only by Ezek. xxiii. 37-39, but it is clear how he might do so, from what is mentioned *Hist.* iv. 169 sq.

[3] See *Hist.* iv. 40, 44, 78, 92, 94 sq., 136.

[4] See *Hist.* iv. 169 sq., 217 sq.: comp., as belonging just here, Job xxxi. 26-28; Deut. iv. 19, xvii. 3. In regard to Tammuz and the Zarathustrian sacred rites comp. my remarks on Ezek. viii. and xvi.

is the ground and motive of the 'covenant' between Jahveh as king and Israel as his people. Accordingly, as the nation is ruled and swayed by the commandments and revelations of the true God, and an active relation exists between this God and the people, the latter also no longer consists of itself alone, but has a share in the glory and sanctity of this its God himself. The lower national life and aims, such as any nation may possess, are not, so far as they contain nothing false, thereby abolished, but a door is opened for the free operation of all higher spiritual truths in the midst of the nation. Wherever the genuine worth and majesty, the unimpeachableness and inviolability, or even the higher destiny and duty of Israel, are to be brought into prominence in contrast either with its foes, or with human potentates, or with perversities in itself, there the earliest times already use the phrase—full of endless significance—the 'people of Jahveh,'[1] or (what occurs more rarely) the 'people of God;'[2] and with the most profound significance the words 'my people' are heard on similar occasions in the mouth of the prophets as the immediate interpreters of the true God.[3] The Deuteronomist in a few passages where something of the greatest moment is to be explained, speaks of the 'holy people of Jahveh;'[4] and in lofty speech the short expression 'the Saints' was gradually formed to designate Israel in suitable passages.[5]

But correct as was the truth denoted by these lofty ideas and names, it was at any rate never made too much of by the law, which was careful to guard against false deductions from it. Penal transgression against the glory and sanctity of the community, such as blaspheming the people, is unknown to the law. It places the sanctity of the nation in this respect on a far lower level than that of Jahveh.

In the spiritual elevation attained by the nation through this regeneration, and in the fact of its becoming the 'people of God,' the foundation is laid for a permanent condition of higher worth, or even of higher duties, with a standard of measurement the same for all its members. The whole of Israel with all its members, without exception, is legally become 'a kingdom of priests, a holy nation.'[6] No one in this com-

---

[1] In Deborah's songs, Jud. v. 11, comp. Ex. xv. 13, 16; also Num. xvii. 6 [xvi. 41]; 1 Sam. ii. 24; 2 Sam. i. 12, vi. 21; 2 Kings ix. 6; Num. xi. 29. This is exchanged, in suitable passages, for the expression 'community of Jahveh,' Num. xvi. 3, xx. 4, xxxi.16; Josh. xxii. 16 sq.; Deut. xxiii. 2-4 [1-3], 9 [8]; 1 Chron. xxviii. 8.

[2] Jud. xx. 2; 2 Sam. xiv. 13 The more general name 'God' appears here as a weaker form which gradually took the plan of the more definite term.

[3] As Is. iii. 12, x. 2, 24, and often elsewhere; Mic. ii. 8 sq., iii. 3.

[4] Deut. vii. 6 and xiv. 2, 21, xxvi. 19.

[5] Ps. xvi. 3, xxxiv. 10 [9]; Deut. xxxiii. 3; Dan. viii. 24, xii. 7.

[6] See *Hist.* ii. 135 sqq.; comp. also Hos. iv. 6.

munity stands so high and no one so low that all are not alike before their God. Every member without exception has free access to the same highest spiritual truth and spiritual freedom, but is also bound along with all the rest by the same duties. Earlier human distinctions which interfere with this equality are abolished, and even slaves are free in this respect and on an equal footing with their masters.[1]

The corresponding tokens and pledges of the sanctity of which in this sense every member of the community ought to partake, were the three great sacraments of Jahveh already mentioned.[2] He who was competent to partake of them, had also his share of the whole worth and sanctity of this community, but was bound to manifest a corresponding holiness in his actions. Jahveism, however, unmistakeably sought after some token to be constantly borne by every one of its adherents, which should represent this truth still more easily and uninterruptedly than could be done by circumcision. For the latter being for the most part concealed beneath the dress served rather as a private reminder to the individual of his obligations, and moreover it was related to the peculiar civilisation of a far earlier epoch.[3] In heathen religions a man would wear the symbol of the God whom he wished to worship scratched (tattooed) on the skin of his forehead or hand. All such symbolical disfigurement of the body was forbidden by Jahveism.[4] In its place every male Israelite is ordered by the Book of Origins to wear, hanging from the tip of his robe, a tassel hanging by a dark blue cord [5] (of the colour of the sky); and it is evident that the custom of wearing a simple token of honour like this was prevalent for a long time in the early community. No further sanctity attached to this symbol, so that also from this we can see that a sacrament must be much more than a mere symbol.

2. But notwithstanding this sanctity and worth of every member of the community, it must still always have its human governors and leaders. A hundred different cravings and efforts of the people want the cleverest men in its ranks to inspect, satisfy, and conduct them. Thus the most diverse organizations always spontaneously arise or are retained in the

---

[1] P. 212.
[2] P. 108 sqq.
[3] P. 89 sqq.
[4] In the primitive law Lev. xix. 28*b*: comp. the comment on Apocal. vii. i. sqq. See p. 165.
[5] Num. xv. 37–41; the κόκκινον βάμμα of which Justin speaks in his own manner, *Contra Tryp.* ch. 46. How ostentatiously, after the symbol had manifestly been for a long time out of use, this simple law was re-introduced by many in the latest times is clear from Matth. xxiii. 5.

ordinary course of history, and in a hundred different ways numerous weaker or less capable members of the nation range themselves under a single member, or a few who are stronger and more capable. If, accordingly, the nation is to become an organized community, the indispensable human governors and leaders must also have the privileges and powers without which they cannot discharge their function. They must, although themselves but men and members of the same community, be entrusted with power to rule over men and the members of this community.[1]

Jahveism was not unaware of this fact. But a human king, such as the kings of the earth had hitherto been, was incompatible with its original strictness, especially in regard to the name, while human leaders and authorities generally it could tolerate. It is true, that when the principle of the sanctity of the community and of the equality of all before God was established in this nation for the first time upon earth, it was extremely liable to be misunderstood. That this soon actually occurred and gave rise to the most serious disturbances, and even to positive rebellions of all kinds, is proved by the ancient legends of the envy of Aaron and Miriam towards Moses, and of the revolt of the sect of Korah against Moses and Aaron.[2] But these very narratives also show clearly how sensibly and how decisively Jahveism opposed from the first any caricature of the ample freedom of which it had laid the foundations in this world. The equality of all before Jahveh only lays on all the same duties without which the community of Jahveh cannot exist, and guarantees them also an equal share in the justice which ought to prevail everywhere in it, so that no member of it may be illegally oppressed or straitened either as regards body or soul. This equality, however, abolishes neither the varied nature and grades of mental powers, so far as these serve a higher purpose and thus operate under the influence of the spirit of Jahveh, nor the infinite divisibility of the employments and enterprises of human life, nor yet the possibility or even the demand for human privileges and powers of rule which spring from the two previous real diversities.

The conception of human authority and rule receives accordingly in this community no more than its true significance and application. Where the spirit of Jahveh—that spirit of genuine religion, wisdom, and power,[3] which has formed the

[1] P. 136, sqq.
[2] Num. xii., xvi.: comp. *Hist.* ii. 176,
[3] According to the brief but exhaustive designation, Is. xi. 2,
sqq.

community and now continues to work in it, and ought to penetrate and guide it more and more—becomes more powerfully active in an individual, a human authority and rule is ripening, such as may be hoped for in this community, and will in every way be salutary. In this way it is possible for even the most insignificant and temporarily oppressed man to achieve power and rule in small or great matters under the protection of this community. Joseph was favoured with the spirit of Jahveh while he was in prison, so that there as everywhere, he became a wise governor and leader of others; and during the ripest development of the community of Israel it became a proverbial saying that a wise slave becomes the master of a bad son, and a joint heir with the brothers.[1] In addition, this capability ennobles every useful employment and dignifies every vocation in the community. Even the sculptors and artists of every kind were filled with the spirit of Jahveh, and received high honour and distinction for the work which they completed in this spirit just as much as any national leader or prince.[2] Finally, not only the more indispensable or traditionary powers and authority are thus justified, but also new kinds of capacities and powers were always tolerated in the true community, so far as they satisfied a genuine need, and were instigated in doing so purely by this genuine spirit of Jahveh. Thus the so-called Judges, in the days after Joshua, were originally invested with no power provided for them by law, and yet they gradually became almost a settled power in the realm. When, however, an extraordinary or a newly-ripening power and capacity finds entrance and foothold entirely through a stronger stirring of the spirit, then the established and more indispensable authorities of the realm ought never to forget their source and their destiny in this community; but rather the only principle by which they ought to rule should be this, that each one in his own sphere follows the higher will which is made truly known unto him, and suffers himself, in leading his subjects, to be himself led by this. Every standing power is in this respect alike responsible in an upward direction to God and the laws of the community, and downwards to its subjects; and every human ruler sees the twofold nature of his obligation, and attains happiness so far as, and no further than, he satisfies this.

Such supreme principles of government in the kingdom of

[1] Prov. xvii. 2.
[2] Ex. xxviii. 3, xxxi. 2-6, xxxv. 30-35: comp. 1 Kings vii. 14.

Jahveh follow from the above narratives which depict the evil result of a misunderstanding of liberty and equality, as well as from the whole of the Old Testament.

3. But to what purpose is the principle of the sanctity even of the nation, and to what purpose arise out of its midst leaders, who, if they are worthy of their vocation, must possess a double portion of this same sanctity, unless the sanctity proves its existence by people and princes always acting heartily together in accordance with that holiness of the true God and of his will through which they first receive their own? The co-operation of all is needful to protect the sanctity of the laws and of the kingdom, and the morals of the household. Whatever violates this must be immediately repelled and punished, and the luminous glory of the Divine holiness which has streamed down upon the community, must ever be kept bright and pure. And, as a fact, this was the feeling and spirit which the nation realised during its most glorious days. The success, however, especially in regard to punishing every transgression and every infidelity, with which this spirit can operate in the heart of the community, and give rise to a power to which even the criminal has involuntarily to submit, so that his necessary punishment becomes a wholesome discipline for himself and for the whole community—is depicted in the Book of Origins according to its custom in a luminous example.[1]

THE VASSALS OF THE NATION. THE LAWS OF WAR.

1. If, however, the conception of the sanctity of the nation in its true meaning refers only to an internal relation between it and the true God, then this can give occasion to no contempt for other races or pretended right to act unjustly towards them. A profound aversion towards Egypt, Amalek, and other nations did, it is true, characterise the commencement of the community of Jahveh; and before long fair Canaan became so homelike to them that every foreign country with its food and its treasures appeared to them unholy and unclean.[2] But this aversion and this horror ought not in all strictness to lead further than to a more intense love for their own higher religion and its abode, and a more scrupulous avoidance of everything heathenish. The proud consciousness of being distinguished from all the other races of the earth, no doubt penetrated the people of Israel sufficiently vividly during its

---

[1] In the history of Achan, Josh. vii.
[2] Amos vii. 17; Hos. ix. 3; Ezek. iv. 13 sq.; and above, p. 155.

best days; but alas for that nation which does not feel similar proud aspirations, and does not at any rate recognise and claim as its own a lofty work in life which shall leave its mark on the world's history; and Israel in claiming as its own at once the noblest and the hardest of these tasks, never fell during the fair period of its earlier history, in consequence of this pride, into danger of becoming insolent and unjust towards other nations.[1] It is the peculiar mark of every true religion that she gives profundity within themselves to the individuals, as well as the whole nation, who give themselves up to her, and protects them from a vain contempt or hostility towards what is foreign. Jahveism never demanded, as Islâm did, that the sword should be used against everything foreign.

2. If now certain legal decrees required Israel to conclude no covenant, i.e. no treaty or friendship with the Canaanites, it is evident that these were not issued until it had already been proved how dangerous any connection with them was to the religion and morality of Israel. In the earliest legislation we find no such decree. The law in the Book of Covenants, which, although relatively very ancient, was still not written till about a century after Moses, is the first to command Israel not to dwell with them, but to drive them out and overturn their altars.[2] When, again, the Deuteronomist repeats and emphasizes these commands at a later date, his very words are enough to show clearly that he is only inspired by the fear of being crushed by the heathenism which was everywhere powerful, by no delight in destruction, no blind hostility. We must, indeed, admit that even this earliest law had been preceded by actual facts and experience. From the last years of Moses and the time of Joshua, it had been proved that Jahveism could not obtain a firm abode on the earth without the violent dispossession of at any rate one ancient nation. But we also see that from the first commencement of the formation of the community, it was only maintained by the most stringent treatment of all that lay outside it.[4] We must, then, pay attention to the above-mentioned historical origin of these laws. It is only then that we understand how they have but a temporary significance.

Accordingly, the law itself admitted further exceptions. What the Book of Origins relates of the crafty inhabitants of Gibeon, to whom Joshua, though almost against his will, had

---

[1] Even such expressions as Ex. xxxiii. 16, xxxiv. 10, are accordingly not too lofty.
[2] Ex. xxiii. 32 sq.; comp. 20 sq. It is repeated and amplified by the Fourth Narrator, Ex. xxxiv. 12-16. Another earlier utterance occurs Num. xxxiii. 51-53.
[3] Deut. vii. 1-5, 16, 25 sq., xii. 2 sq. xx. 16-18.
[4] See p. 75 sqq.

to promise protection for life and property,¹ is clearly, according to the custom of this work, nothing but a model for similar cases. The relation of such persons to the kingdom became, as a matter of law and custom, the same as that of vassals to a single powerful family.² They were even named in like manner the *guests* or *settlers* of the realm, who had a right to live and dwell there. But as they would not readily forget their former full freedom, and conflicts would often arise, these dependent communities for the most part sank gradually into greater and greater servitude. They became 'public hewers of wood and drawers of water,'³ i.e. they were bound to perform villein-service for the community of Israel. They nevertheless always retained certain rights which might not be violated.⁴ The Deuteronomist desires, however, that milder proceedings should be adopted only with the non-Canaanitish cities, and that the Canaanites should fall under the ban of the second grade.⁵

Even individual heathens might be admitted as vassals into the community of Israel. Here and there this took place from the time of the conquest;⁶ but it was chiefly after the time of Solomon that foreigners, through commercial intercourse, became numerous in the cities of Judah. They formed a class of half-citizens, possessing many rights the same as the Israelites. They appeared at the gate, i.e. publicly on the market, and before the tribunals of justice; they could always count on protection at least for their life and moveable property. Real property, however, they were not permitted to acquire.⁷ In return, they were obliged to observe the most universal laws of Israel, e.g., not to eat blood.⁸ Distinguished from these were the absolute foreigners,⁹ whose presence was tolerated, but who possessed no rights. The Deuteronomist is most solicitous on

---

¹ Josh. ix. 3 sqq.
² P. 216.
³ Josh. ix. 27. (The last four words may be by the Deuteronomist.) Comp. the same idea in other words, Deut. xx. 10 sq.; 1 Chron. xxii. 2; 2 Chron. ii. 16 [17] sq.
⁴ See *Hist.* iii. p. 135 sq., and p. 136, sq. above.
⁵ P. 77; Deut. xx. 10-18.
⁶ Josh. vi. 25 (*Hist.* ii. 247 sq.) evidently only mentions an important example of what often occurred.
⁷ Comp. below under the Year of Jubilee.
⁸ Lev. xvi. 29, xvii. 8-11, xviii. 26, xxiv. 16, 22; Num. ix. 14, xv. 14-16,

xxxv. 15; Ex. xii. 48 sq., all from the Book of Origins. That the Philistines, e.g. regarded blood in a totally different light follows from בך, Zach. ix. 7. Such foreigners had to give up their customs.
⁹ נָכְרִי, *Foreigner*, opposed to the גֵּר, *guest* 'within the gate of Israel,' Deut. xiv. 21; comp. i. 16, x. 18 sq. That in later times some of them were very wealthy follows from Deut. xxviii. 43. Very plain language is also found in Ezek. xlvii. 22 sq.; comp. xxii. 7, Mal. iii. 5. The most accurate name for a half-citizen is גֵּר וְתוֹשָׁב, *guest and settler* or more briefly ג' ח' without ו, Lev. xxv. 35, 47; comp. 45.

behalf of both classes, but lets the distinction between them be clearly recognised.

3. The way in which the ancient nation carried on war was no doubt unusually stern, on account of its frequent exercise of the ban in its two grades, particularly as this ban was not only turned outwards, but also inwards, against members of the general army who were lukewarm and dilatory.[1] This makes it the more noteworthy that Deuteronomy, even in dealing with these stern old customs, without whose protection Jahveism could not have maintained itself in the world many centuries after its foundation, seeks to introduce the same spirit of gentleness and forbearance, which in other directions had long become a part of the law. Towards the members of the general army, in which, according to the ancient custom, every man capable of bearing arms without exception was compelled to serve, it enjoins forbearance and consideration, when urgent grounds for such really exist.[2] Towards enemies it sanctions a procedure of three gradations. Those who submit peacefully are to be taken under protection. Of those who are forcibly conquered only the men are to be put to death (ban of the first grade). The ban of the severest kind was to be confined to the Canaanites.[3] In carrying on war the utmost consideration was to be shown to a hostile country, e.g. no fruit trees were to be cut down.[4]

The Membership of the Community. 272

The complete membership of the community was, on the other hand, under so strict an administration in its details, that the title of a 'holy nation' remained anything but a mere conception. In regard to recognised members the ancient law knew of no deprivation of civic rights or expulsion from the country,[5] but it was all the stricter in its requirement of a

[1] Pp. 75-80.
[2] Deut. xx. 4-9.
[3] Deut. xx. 10-18. How readily the usage had extended itself to other nations may be gathered from *Hist.* iii. 149 sq., 157, iv. 88 sq.
[4] Deut. xx. 19 sq.: comp., however, 2 Kings iii. 25 for the sort of events which certainly furnished the first grounds for the law. The reason given here for it is as follows: 'Is the tree of the field a man that it should be distressed on thy account?' This is uttered quite in accordance with what is said on p. 7;— why should the tree suffer when only men

have done amiss? The reverse of this may now be seen in the numerous magnificently executed frescoes of the cruel wars of the Assyrians, Layard's *Nineveh*, ii. p. 29 sq.

[5] When, on the other hand, the community of the new Jerusalem lost under the Persians the right of inflicting capital punishment, they consistently claimed the right of exclusion from the community, and exercised this in its stead. This is now the שָׁרֵשׁ, *extirpate*, Ezra vii. 26: comp. x. 8; Neh. xiii. 28. The utmost that was connected with this was the ban

sacerdotal expiation of such offences as could be expiated, and secondly, where this was not admissible, of capital punishment. as will be further explained below. The reception of new members, on the other hand, was not indeed limited by the narrowness of privileged families in Israel itself, for such earlier limitations had been wholly abolished by the spirit of Jahveism. It was, however, in the first place, limited by the cautious spirit of the old world and the stern discipline which we have already described. Deuteronomy still retains two of the results, the exclusion of eunuchs of every kind,[1] and that of bastards with all their posterity without exception. By a bastard,[2] however, it is certain that we must understand only a child of fornication between persons of two distinct nationalities between which sexual connections were not allowed, particularly if an Israelitish woman prostituted herself to a born alien. Nothing seemed more disgraceful and intolerable than this.[3]

The fact last mentioned leads us to the second main limitation. The national descent from the blood of Israel still seemed indispensable for full participation in all the rights of the community. This shows how impossible it was for Jahveism in the earliest times to maintain itself apart from the nationality of Israel, and for the latter to do the same without being sharply separated from other nations and rigidly secluded in itself. It is true that this limitation is no original feature of Jahveism, and therefore eternally essential. On the contrary, a far greater freedom prevailed in this matter under Moses just during the lofty period when the community was founded.[4] But from the time that Israel had conquered and partitioned the land of Canaan, which was continually becoming a less and less secure possession on account of the foreign nations which threatened Israel on every side, it separated itself as the ruling people continually more and more sharply from the rest. All foreigners by birth who lived under its rule were only tolerated

of moveable property (a kind of proscription), Ezra x. 8. Of course the hagiocracy during the last centuries again laid claim at favourable opportunities to the right of inflicting capital punishment.
[1] P. 164.
[2] מַמְזֵר, Deut. xxiii. 3 [2], although מַמְזֵר in Arabic is ممْز, and in Syriac ܡܡܙܪ, may correspond to the Arabic ممزج, bastard, according to Lehrb. § 51 c-e; the intermediary term being the Aramaic ܒܐܕ bad (Knös, Chrest. p. 65, 6).

But the formation which is altogether similar and only somewhat weakened in sound is the Ethiopic ᎣᎾᎻᏨ, Enoch x. 9 (Dillm.). That, however, it possesses the above defined narrower signification follows from Zach. ix. 6: comp. what is said Hist. iv. 142; for here what is clearly meant is a family in the Philistine Ashdod which sprang from a connection of the women of this subjugated city with the conquerors.
[3] Comp. the narrative, at the same time a typical one, Gen. xxxiv.
[4] Hist. ii. 118 sq.

ADMISSION OF STRANGERS. 239

as vassals. Yet a distinction was made here, as soon as the nation permanently obtained a strong and peaceful supremacy. If a complete foreign community or tribe was under the protection of Israel, it always remained in this dependent condition, and those who happened to be its princes became vassal princes.[1] If, however, a single foreigner lived in one of Israel's communities, then his descendants could after three generations enter into full participation in all the common rights, in case he did not spring from one of the races between which and Israel the hostility was too great. When the latter was the case, they could not even in the tenth generation (i.e. never) become full citizens. The last distinction is given by Deuteronomy plainly in accordance with ancient practice. When, however, it reckons the Moabites and the Ammonites among the strangers who were to be perpetually excluded, and the Egyptians and the Idumæans, who are often elsewhere closely united together,[2] among those who were to be gradually adopted, its classification is due entirely to the special circumstances of the time when it originated.[3] Many foreigners had also been adopted from time to time at an earlier date.[4]

3. The Sanctity of the Kingdom.

The kingdom is the unity and the active co-operation of all its constituents and powers to the single end of its existence and its well-being. If it derives its name from its lord, and if what we are speaking of here is always named in the highest sense the kingdom of Jahveh, this by no means implies, that even this absolutely invisible lord administers or desires to administer it without laws, for even between this eternal lord Jahveh and his community there stands a covenant obligatory on both sides. All the individual members of the community, in spite of their external and temporal inequalities, whether human subjects or human rulers, priests or laymen, prophets or not prophets, ought always to hearken to the voice of Jahveh alone, and therefore to the eternal truths, whether these were given at an earlier time or newly revealed, in order that he who alone can succour may impart the true help and the protection

---

[1] P. 236. מַלְכֵי הָעֶרֶב; see comment on Jer. xxv. 20, 24.
[2] Comp. *Hist.* iii. 217, iv. 44 sq.
[3] Deut. xxiii. 4-9 [3-8]; comp. *Hist.* iv. 221 sq.
[4] If the foreigners by birth mentioned Ex. xii. 38; Num. xi. 4, had been merely vassals, and even if this son of an Israelitish woman and an Egyptian father, Lev. xxiv. 10, had belonged to them (though this is nowhere indicated) still the fact would be abundantly proved by the cases cited, *Hist.* iii. 144.

that never fails. A kingdom built on this foundation is essentially necessary, eternal, and holy. But he who touches this foundation when it has once been laid, trespasses against the sanctity of the kingdom, and thereby incurs the penalty—to be more fully explained below—of violating what is absolutely holy.

But the unity, as the essence and strength, of the kingdom always depends in reality on the mutual relations of the various forces which either exist in it from the first or gradually develope themselves there. All the more is this the case when the highest bond which is to hold together all the human constituents is as purely spiritual as it was in the ancient strict theocracy. We must accordingly examine more closely these human forces which encountered one another in the kingdom of Jahveh, in order to comprehend how far their unity was developed there, and what form the kingdom consequently assumed in history.

If, however, the kingdom is the living unity of all the individual members, and of all the special powers and aspirations of the nation under its God, it must also form the true union and the necessary connection between the two sides of the institutions, laws, and customs which we have described more fully above.[1] Here both these sides are united, here both must be equally protected. The question now is how they may both be brought together, and made to act on each other in a salutary manner, how each may develope itself freely and advance as far as is healthful, and also how each may limit, discipline, and restore the other to the right path when and where it has lost itself in error and corruption. This is the *organization of the kingdom*, which needs a special description all to itself.

There also exist great and permanent institutions in the kingdom which are specially destined to uphold this organization and its firm unity. These now call for particularly careful delineation.

[1] P. 4 sq.

THIRD SECTION.

THE CONNECTION BETWEEN THE TWO SIDES BY MEANS OF THE ORGANISATION OF THE KINGDOM.

I. THE NATION AND ITS LEADERS.

1. *The National Assembly.*

The essential constituents of everything which was of a purely national character already existed in Israel previous to the foundation of the Theocracy. This is the case with the national assembly, and therefore with one of the most important and indispensable constituents of a healthy and vigorous nationality.

1. It has already been thoroughly explained[1] how Israel as a nation possessed from primitive times a permanent organisation, which was extremely hard to subvert, and which embraced the whole of the internal national life. Regarding it all from below upwards, we see three well-marked stages,[2] in which the whole broad and firm edifice rises aloft. First in the great social union comes the individual *household* (the family). This we have already seen[3] maintained itself very strongly in its original wide independence and power, and therefore as a rule embraced numerous human beings, and these of a very diverse character, and still gave to its head (the father) very extensive rights.—Several single households together form, in the second place, a *clan*, or as the Romans would have said, a *gens*.[4] This firmly embraces all its households together, like a single greater household. It may therefore have a father at its head, whether he be regarded as its historical founder, or as time went on as the prince of the clan, and so far it may also be termed a *father's house*.[5]—Several

---

[1] *Hist.* i. 362 sqq.
[2] The clearest descriptions of them are found בK. Josh. vii. 14-18, 1 Sam. x. 19-21. The former passage is more definite than the latter. Comp. also 1 Sam. xxiii. 23, Jud. vi. 15.
[3] P. 187 sqq.
[4] Or a δῆμος; this is how the LXX most correctly translate the כְּמִשְׁפָּחָה in Num. i. 20 sqq.
[5] That 'father's house' may be another term for 'clan' clearly follows from

Ex. vi. 14; Num. iii. 24, 30, 35. We cannot therefore understand the word differently even when it is placed alongside of the other term in the Book of Origins, in accordance with the prolixity characteristic of this work, Num. i. 2, 18 sqq.; ii. 34; comp. i. 4. It then generally stands for the ordinary expression, but before it in Num. iii. 15. What, on the other hand, the father's house is when a single man is being spoken about, needs no further explanation.

clans in the third place are united together into a *tribe*. This, too, embraces all its members like a compact household; has accordingly its 'father,' and is in like manner termed a 'father's house.'[1] But again, all the tribes together form the people, which may be termed not only Israel, but more solemnly 'the house of Israel.' Thus the conception and organisation of the household (the family) penetrated everything in the actual life of the nation from ancient times. The carefully executed genealogies[2] were only the result, not the cause, of these national relations.

The nation was therefore divided from primitive times into greater and smaller exclusive communities. These were no associations formed to carry on in common particular operations or arts more successfully. Certain distinctions in this respect did, it is true, display themselves very early, and might readily develope themselves while the individual communities readily separated from one another. Thus the tribes of Reuben and Gad, perhaps also Simeon, always had a greater inclination than the others for a peaceful life, with the breeding of cattle for its main occupation.[3] On the other hand, the tribe of Benjamin was devoted to war, and was famous for its special warlike arts and dexterity,[4] so that we are justified in regarding this smaller tribe as having been the vanguard in primitive times of its larger brother-tribe Joseph. But in general the only associations which were formed within the nation were political and military. When it became customary to give the name of a *thousand*[5] (a Chiliad) to a larger association, tribe, or clan, aspirations for military companionship and considerations about capability for bearing arms were manifestly prevalent. It might be that from such an association only 1,000 warriors in all were required, or that it embraced 1,000 households, each one of which had to furnish a warrior. We are therefore taken back to the primitive times when domestic life first overstepped its narrowest limitations, when one household, if only for the sake of external security, endeavoured to bind itself as closely as possible on to another, and thus formed clannish unions, which were in part founded on blood-relationship, and in part,

---

[1] In the Book of Origins; Num. xvii. 17, 21 [2, 6]; Josh. xxii. 14. Even in Num. ii. 2, the word is probably to be understood in this way, since it is enough for each tribe to have its own ensign.
[2] *Hist.* i. 23 sq.
[3] See *Hist.* ii. 296 sq.
[4] *Hist.* ii. 281 sq., 573.
[5] The name אֶלֶף, about which there will be more to say immediately, can originally only mean 'thousand,' and only from thence a fraction of the people or tribe. This needs no proof, and therefore is poetically interchanged with *Myriads*, Num. x. 36; Deut. xxxiii. 17. (Elsewhere the two words occur together, Gen. xxiv. 60.)

and to a greater extent, on common aims and for the sake of external security, and which formed a firm graduated unity, endeavouring to build a higher household, without its being possible to break down the internal partition-walls between the individual families. They therefore readily broke apart again from one another at this stage of civilisation, and this we see happened during the period of the Judges, when even the clans in one tribe, that of Manasseh, split apart.[1] Only the long affliction in common in Egypt, then still more the lofty religion and civilisation from the time of Moses, finally, as the consequence of this, the great victory over the Egyptians and other nations and the subsequent development of a firm kingdom, gradually established a more intimate union of the long allied communities, and made the 'house of Jacob' into the 'people of God.' Still, however, the Book of Origins is acquainted with the earlier stage, and describes its essence very accurately; and the primitive phrase, which will be further explained below, 'the soul shall be rooted out of its nations,'[2] is a standing witness to the ancient feeling that Israel had properly grown up out of many nations, i.e. clans and tribes.[3]

A nation growing up out of such materials may easily at the time when it is in process of formation double itself by the adoption of new materials, and in conformity therewith may even change the name of its communities. We can still prove from many indications that something of this kind actually took place in ancient Israel. For we see in its ordinary language two names for 'clan,' of identical signification, but of which the one must earlier have denoted the 'tribe.'[4] Only a new formation of the whole people at an early date, of which other traces are apparent, can have brought it to pass that what was previously a tribe, and therefore the highest division of the nation, should be degraded to a mere clan; whether this

---

[1] *Hist.* ii. 321 sq.
[2] Gen. xvii. 14, and elsewhere
[3] Just as the Athenian δῆμος grew out of the individual δῆμοι.
[4] The אֶלֶף we have just spoken of interchanges in most books (not, however, in the Book of Origins) quite commonly with מִשְׁפָּחָה. That it must, however, have denoted a tribe at an earlier date follows in the first place from the use of it in the Idumean language, where it always signified the highest division of the people (Gen. xxxvi. 40-43); and in the second place from some extremely ancient phrases in Israel itself, which even the Book of Origins repeats in some passages with great emphasis, as though they were genuinely Mosaic, Num. i. 16, x. 4; Josh. xxii. 14, 21, 30; comp. the Mosaic pæan, Num. x. 36.—Even the usual word for tribe is beginning to mean the third part of a great tribe, Num. iv. 18. We must understand in quite a different way the conjunction מִשְׁפַּחַת מֹטֶה, 'the race, i.e. the relationship of the tribe,' Num. xxxvi. 6, 8, comp. ver. 12. Moreover, in lofty speech, מִשְׁפָּחָה always readily occurs in a wider sense.

took place in pre-Mosaic times,[1] or what is more probable, not till after the days of Joshua, when the whole community was more fully developed.[2]

But even this lowest grade, the 'household,' by no means remained so simple that every adult or married man would form a valid 'household' in the national assembly. We rather see clearly from sundry tokens[3] that, at any rate from the time of Moses and Joshua, every household which was counted in a clan was divided into many individual 'men,' and therefore into many simple families or households in the strictest sense of the word. The organisation, therefore, was carried to such an extent that it can only be fully described in the five grades, man, household, clan, tribe, nation.[4]

But the organisation would have been very imperfect if each of the middle three grades had not been further organised upon fixed principles. We have already shown it to be probable, for many reasons,[5] that as the nation had always been divided into twelve tribes, so each tribe was divided into twelve clans. How many households a single clan embraced we cannot determine from our present historical sources. That their number, however, was limited, is certain from what we have just explained, and we may conjecture from the other proportions that every twelve households formed a clan, while the number of the men who formed one household might be extended at will. The fundamental lines of such an all-embracing organisation were plainly given from the earliest times, and maintained their position very tenaciously, however various were the forms adopted in the course of time in this connection. When the tribes from the time of Joshua had taken firm possession of the Holy Land, there were formed, out of the landed properties of the clans of each tribe, an equal number of districts with a town as 'mother,'[6] and we still know that Bethlehem, with its territory, was too small a town to form a district by itself, although after David's time it perhaps laid

---

[1] *Hist.* i. 371.
[2] *Hist.* ii. 259 sqq.
[3] According to HK. Josh. vii. 14–18 every 'household' is again divided into 'men,' and the individual man and warrior who occurs there, Achan, belongs to the house of Zabdi, as whose grandson he appears in the genealogical tables. This of itself is clear enough, but the mention of the 'patriarchs of the clan of Gilead,' Num. xxxvi. 1, speaks with still greater clearness; for neither according to the title nor the meaning of this narrative are these all heads of families in the proper sense of the word, and for both reasons can only have been few in number.
[4] Comp. for the lower developments and the essential necessity for them the example of the present Arabs of the desert. Layard's *Discoveries,* p. 239.
[5] *Hist.* i. 362 sqq.
[6] Like Abel Bêthma'akha, 2 Sam. xx. 19. The smaller towns belonging to a larger one such as this, are often called in ordinary language her 'daughters;' see *Hist.* ii. 257, nt.

claim to such an honour, and then may have had a district-count living in its midst.¹

Each of these greater or smaller unions had from the first a head around whom they assembled, and whose power was more or less extensive. The Book of Origins calls the ruler of a household the head of the fathers or the patriarch, that of a clan the patriarch of the households, or *prince*, and also more generally the 'head' or head of the fathers, that of a tribe the prince of the princes, or simply the prince.² In the first instance, at any rate originally, the head of the first house was always the head of the clan, that of the first clan also that of the tribe. All these three grades of the heads of the people, who would thus reach the total of 1,728, might certainly be also designated by one common name, and in all probability this was furnished by the names 'head' or 'father,'³ also more definitely the 'head of the fathers,' but most frequently by the name we so often meet with of *Elders*. It would be, on the one hand, a complete mistake to assume that every father of an actual family would have been deemed an Elder. The name clearly had a far weightier significance. But, on the other hand, we know that the number of the Elders of Israel far exceeded so low a number as seventy.⁴ And if this name had so wide a significance, it will explain why the Book of Origins for the most part avoids the use of it, preferring to express its own meaning in particular cases with more precision. When an entire community actually assembled under its head, e.g. in war or when the nation assembled under arms, this head stood forth in front like a firm corner-stone in a large house, and this explains how in such cases the Elders could be termed the *corners* (corner-stones) of the whole nation;⁵ for in other respects no distinction is to be found between these two names. Where, on the other hand, the giving of counsel and

---

¹ Mic. v. 1 [2]; comp. אך, Zach. ix. 7. Also Amos v. 3 assists in the comprehension of this.

² According to Num. xxxvi. 1; Num. iii. 24, 30, 35; xiii. 3; xxv. 14; Ex. vi. 14 sqq.; Josh. xxi. 1; xxii. 14; 1 Chron. v. 6; Num. iii. 32; i. 4–16: comp. ii. 3 sqq.; vii. 11 sqq.; xxxiv. 18 sqq.; and the entire series with Num. xiii. 2 sqq.; Josh. xxii. 14. It was similar among kindred nations. Gen. xvii. 20; xxv. 16.

³ Hence may occur such epithets as 'father of Tekoa,' 1 Chron. ii. 24, 42, 45, 50 sqq.; iv. 5; or the name 'head,' Num. xxv. 4.

⁴ According to Ex. xxiv. 1; Num. xi. 16.

⁵ Judg. xx. 2: comp. the other names, xxi. 16; 1 Sam. xiv. 38; Zach. x. 4. According to the first two passages such a *corner man* never appeared or moved without his troop of armed men.—The Book of Covenants, Ex. xxiv. 11, uses for this a name of probably similar meaning, אציל, from אצל, 'the side, corner;' for the Arabic أصل, *noble*, comes from quite a different and purely Arabic word, and means properly *one of a tribe* or *clan*, *noble* in this sense.

incidents of general interest to the national life are spoken about, they are always called the 'Elders.'

2. When the nation was gathered together, arranged somehow according to this organisation and with these leaders at their head, the *assembly* was present. These heads were of course originally also always the leaders of the nation in war and its protectors against every enemy. But one of their principal functions was also to meet in the collected assembly in order to give advice and pass decrees in respect to the common interests of the people. Indeed, the precise organisation of the nation manifestly had particularly in view a careful system of voting at the national assembly.

The people of Israel, therefore, constituted from its earliest days a well-organised assembly which took counsel and came to decisions about their own affairs. This was arranged with so much consistency and thoroughness that every smaller community within it, every tribe and every clan in the Holy Land, as well as every district and town, was organised, met for counsel, and managed their affairs in like manner. Nothing could become a law binding the community which had not previously been discussed and approved of in the assembly. No important measure could be framed in matters belonging to the whole people without the previous sanction of the 'Elders.' Even a recognised and popular Prophet could introduce no important change in the national life without a discussion in and the agreement of the assembly. This fact is confirmed on a closer examination of all that we know of the primitive and earlier history of the nation down to the times of the kings; indeed, without it it is impossible to understand the details of the whole of that portion of history. If even the Mosaic fundamental constitution, and with it the foundation of all the better national life of that long period, was adopted, according to the earliest view, after a voluntary acceptance on the part of the assembly, and by a covenant concluded betwixt it and its lord,[1] then we are able to see from this most important example how deeply the idea of a free discussion and acceptance of all laws in the assembly, and of contracts which were to be concluded by it, had taken root in the nation from primitive times.

Representative institutions were essential to every well-organised nation, and no ancient upward-striving nation divested itself of the right to deliberate and issue decrees by means of them. Ancient Israel, during just the purest period of its

---

[1] *Hist.* ii. 143 sqq.

existence, never suffered itself to be deprived of this fundamental right of a healthy national life. Nothing is more erroneous than to suppose that representative institutions are peculiar either to the Teutonic races or, in the ancient world, to those of Europe. But their composition, organisation, and prerogatives, were important questions, just as is the case at present, and to understand these details accurately in the case of the ancient nations of which no very abundant literature has been preserved, is a task of great difficulty. What may be recognised in the case of ancient Israel is as follows.

The heads above described had the right of meeting in assembly when and where they chose. They therefore constituted the national assembly, which never allowed itself to be deprived of its right of deliberating and deciding upon the most important general affairs of the nation. When the heads met together, each one, after the ancient military custom, was always attended by his following of men capable of bearing arms. More than 400,000 men completely equipped were at times counted at such gatherings.[1] The actual deliberation, however, undoubtedly took place in the midst of only the 'Elders.' The share which the common people had in the matter lay in the fact that each Elder had previously to come to an understanding with his men. This would readily take place, since these heads were not arbitrarily set over the nation, but undoubtedly originally proceeded from the communities themselves. That they were elected is, as far as we know, not probable.[2]

But it is not needful to show how difficult it would be for a deliberation of any length, or even a co-operation in carrying on the supreme direction of the people, to take place in the presence of the whole of this great original assembly. It is not surprising that very early a sort of committee of Elders was formed, which was specially empowered to carry on together the supreme direction of the people, and to represent the perpetual living unity of the deliberative and executive assembly. These are the Seventy Elders.[3] If we assume that the number

---

[1] Judg. xx. 2: comp. xxi. 16. In the same way in 1 Chron. xii. 23–28, there appear at Hebron to do homage 304,822 men out of all the tribes, in which number in the case of some of the tribes—it is clearly said of Naphtali in ver. 34—only the leaders appear to be reckoned.—That round numbers were often chosen is seen also in Num. xi. 21 : comp. i.

[2] Nevertheless, the description, Num. xi. 16, includes also the possibility of the election of a few out of many who stand on an equal footing. And in general the choice of national representatives and that of kings stand mutually related, so that in proportion as the latter falls into disuse the former becomes more indispensable. The many causes of this are easily understood.

[3] The Book of Origins, strange to say,

of these Elders was properly seventy-two, but that perhaps the two presidents (in the Book of Origins Moses and Aaron) were not counted, or that from some other cause the number seventy-two was reduced to seventy, then we evidently have on an average (i.e. apart from the special changes which might take place historically) six heads for each of the twelve tribes as representatives of the whole, the twelve clans of each tribe only sending half the number of their heads to this smaller assembly. This committee of Elders (or, as we may say, *Council of Old Men*, Senate) had, according to all tokens, been long in existence in early times, and had contributed in determining a large portion of the fate of the nation. From the narrative, which will soon be spoken of more fully, contained in Numbers xi., we might suppose that it was not instituted by Moses till some period subsequent to the Sinaitic legislation. But the fact of its earlier existence, especially during the time of this very legislation, is conclusively shown in the far more ancient accounts of the Book of Covenants.[1] That this committee never ceased to exist during the days of Moses is obvious. It lasted undisturbed under Joshua,[2] and thus aided in the establishment of the extraordinarily important national and territorial settlements which were then made,[3] and which brought to a conclusion the whole labours of the new legislation and constitution. Even after Joshua this seat of authority (as it may be termed) continued to exist, and it seems only to have developed its whole force then, in the absence of any great and universally recognised national leader.[4] It is undoubtedly the same as 'the honourable men who managed all things in Israel' who used to be appealed to centuries later.[5] The last relics of the

does not afford any mention of this Seventy. This may be accidental, since we only possess fragments of it. Or we may conjecture that the 'princes' who are always represented in this book as accompanying Moses and Aaron are only another name for the Seventy, as in Num. xxvii. 2; xxxvi. 1: in the first quotation the 'whole community' are named at the same time; but not in the second, where, however, the same relations are to be found. This title 'princes' is interchanged in a similar connection with that of 'heads of the tribes,' Num. xxx. 2 [1]; comp. the more definite title, 'patriarchs of the tribes,' xxxii. 28; very rarely the name 'elder' occurs, Num. xvi. 25. But that these 'princes' were not merely the twelve princes of the tribes, but that others as well were 'summoned to the Council' (i.e. the smaller Council), is clear from Num. xvi. 2; xxvi. 9; comp. i. 5-16; and thus it is undoubtedly probable that the Book of Origins was thinking of seventy 'princes,' and that the number seventy is only accidentally omitted.

[1] Ex. xxiv. 1, 9, comp. 14. They are also designated with the rare expression of ver. 11, the 'fore-men,' the nobles.
[2] According to the Book of Origins, Josh. xiv. 1; xix. 51; xxi. 1.
[3] *Hist*. ii. 259 sqq.
[4] Josh. xxiv. 31; Judg. ii. 7. It is needless to explain that the elders mentioned here formed a united body; comp. *Hist*. ii. 311 sqq.
[5] 2 Sam. xx. 19. According to the reading supplemented in *Hist*. iii. 195.

respect for and of the operations of this Seventy, which certainly possessed great power through long periods of time, may very probably be found in some strangely brief narratives concerning the seventy children of celebrated judges.[1] It is needless to explain that every judge after Moses and Joshua, if his rule lasted any length of time, was desirous of having by his side a similar assembly of seventy great men. If at the time the original senate had already been destroyed from any cause, so that it could no longer be composed of the heads of the ancient races, then such a judge might be glad to form out of his own sons and near relatives an assembly which should bear the closest possible resemblance to it, and which after his death inherited his dominion in common. On this account they might together be briefly termed his 'sons,' even if they were not all so in the proper sense of the word. Thus we are told that the 70 legitimate sons of Gideon, while they were ruling after his death, were murdered by his bastard, since he desired to become despotic; that Abdon had 40 sons and 30 grandsons, and that the whole 70 even during his lifetime have also been national leaders; that Ibzar had 30 sons and 30 sons-in-law, but that Jair had only 30 such sons. We cannot well fail to recognise here brief recollections of important state arrangements, and it would be ungrateful to remove these out of their living historical connection, and to assume that the numbers 70, 40, 30, were chosen at hazard. Even in every large town a similar institution appears to have been formed during the period of the Judges, as the 77 Elders of Succoth show.[2]

But apart from these later phenomena, we have every reason, on the grounds quoted above, for placing the origin of this Council of Elders in the most ancient times long prior to Moses. A fuller proof of this is contained in the primitive tradition that Israel consisted of seventy souls when it journeyed into Egypt.[3] That this means, according to the original sense, the

---

[1] Judg. viii. 30 sq.; ix. 1 sq.; x. iv.; xii. 9 sq., 14. What else is remarked, *Hist.* ii. 388 sq., on the point also retains its validity. Even the fact that the numerous sons of Ahaz, 2 Kings x. 1, are briefly given at seventy, may have a distant connection with this, so far as this number came to stand for a large body of 'princes.' See also Ezek. viii. 11 sq. In the same way the Iliad and the Sháhnámeh (the latter, e.g. in the case of Guderz with his eighty sons) speak of many such sons of princes, but in the Old Testament we can even trace this particular number to its real origin.

[2] Judg. viii. 14. This may mean the seventy along with seven others as 'princes,' i.e. magistrates, a permanent body of supreme officials according to ver. 6, 14; comp. ver. 16.

[3] Gen. xlvi. 8–27; Ex. i. 1–5. The deviations of the LXX in both passages, according to which seventy-five souls went into Egypt (which reappears also in Acts vii. 14), rest on an ancient gloss following Gen. xlvi. 20, whose contents recur 1 Chron. vii. 14–20, but which appears not to be original there. Even the LXX have no variation on the number seventy in Deut. x. 22.

seventy heads of seventy small Israelitish communities, is sufficiently manifest from the fact that among the seventy souls only such names appear as are elsewhere quoted in genealogical tables of the primitive times as fathers or mothers of these very communities, so that at any rate the original purpose was not to give here the number of the individuals who journeyed with 'Israel' to Egypt. Nevertheless, the latter view is partially adopted by the last editor of the table, and we can distinguish very clearly in it an earlier and a later redaction. In the first instance it brings all the heads of Israel under the four wives of the patriarch, and, therefore, under the four main divisions of the nation in the following proportions: 33 (Leah), 16 (Zilpah), 14 (Rachel), 7 (Bilhah). This exactly amounts to seventy, and we cannot doubt that at one period the proportion of the main divisions and heads of the nations was correctly represented thus. If, again, we observe that these numerical relations only differ very slightly from the perfect proportion, $32 : 16 :: 16 : 8$, we are, in this way, led to the above-mentioned fundamental number seventy-two. In the second instance, however, the last editor endeavours to arrive at the individual persons who might have been living in Canaan at the time when Jacob moved into Egypt. Thus he enumerates from the genealogical tables sixty-six sons, grandsons, and great-grandsons of Jacob, and adds to these Jacob himself as well as Joseph and his two sons who were already living in Egypt. This again gives the number seventy, though in a different way.[1] So clear is it that the number seventy or seventy-two rests in this connection on a primitive reminiscence which reaches far beyond all the present narratives.

3. The rise of Jahveism produced very little alteration in these ancient political arrangements. It may only have re-established the primitive institutions which had been dissolved during the last period of the Egyptian oppression. But at the same time it animated the ancient institutions with its own peculiar spirit, and in that way it remodelled them more than would have been possible by sudden and outward changes.

When the community came together for solemn counsel and decision, it constituted the assembly of the people of God.[2] It usually took place as near the great sanctuary of the nation

---

[1] Viz. he allows the number 33 to stand in Gen xlvi. 15, but only reckons up 32 names. Even the LXX have no variation here; and we see at present no reason for treating the number 33 as an incorrect reading.

[2] Judg. xx. 2.

as possible,[1] and the lofty destiny, unto which in general the nation was summoned in Jahveism,[2] ought to be realised in so solemn a moment as it would be realised at no other time. Nor was this always an empty hope. Even when a war had already broken out, the assembled community—especially if a man of God like Moses or Samuel fired its genuine valour—felt itself suddenly seized by a mighty stirring of its God, and rushed upon its foe with resistless victory.[3]

Especially was this inspiration realised when the Elders met in assembly. Those whose position and office brought them, in the exercise of their functions, nearer than others to the pure divine truths and forces, must approach the latter more closely even in recognising and discharging their duties, and thereby receive an insight and a power which had previously been unknown to them, unless they were to be destroyed sooner and more hopelessly than others by these very truths and forces just because they had approached them more closely. Yet the former alternative is possible. Jahveism assumes that it is what is to be expected, and its history justifies this in striking examples. Thus the very ancient Book of Covenants relates how the seventy went up the holy mountain with Moses and Aaron, when the legislation was being given, and how they there gazed upon the purest, highest glory; nay, how they even celebrated the common meal of the covenant with the highest One, on terms of the closest intimacy, and yet were not destroyed by the most perilous nearness of the Unapproachable. They saw and tasted what was without parallel in mortal experience, and like new men they returned enlightened and reinvigorated to the rest of the nation.[4] Like unto them might all the Elders of the same community be!—This truth is apprehended with still greater profundity by the Third Narrator of the primitive history.[5] To him it appeared as though the whole institution of the Seventy had been first founded by Moses, and at a somewhat late period; for he understood them purely in their higher vocation and worth as men of that same spirit which rested most powerfully and uninterruptedly on Moses himself; and it is true that such perfection and glory can have attached to this smaller assembly for counsel only subsequently to Moses and his legislation. Thus he

---

[1] According to Num. xxvii. 2; Jer. xxxiv. 15.
[2] P. 229 sqq.
[3] As 1 Sam. vii. 7-11; comp. Ps. xx.
[4] Ex. xxiv. 1 sq., 9-11. The whole narrative about the covenant-sacrifice is to be compared with Gen. xxxi. 44-54. Comp. the *Jahrbb. der Bibl. Wiss.* xii. s. 198 sqq.
[5] Num. xi. 10-30.

relates how in a moment when Moses had felt the burden of his sole rule to be too grievous, and had on this account cried to Jahveh for help, he was commanded by the latter to choose out seventy Elders and place them round about the Sanctuary. These who now stand nearer to the most holy place than the rest of the nation hear the miraculous conversation between the true Prophet and the true God. Their head and mouth too are suddenly taken possession of by the same power; they too share the spirit of Moses and speak with the matchless prophetic tongue,[1] and accordingly become from that time thoroughly competent to advise with Moses and to assist him. Nevertheless, it seems as if in this delineation of what is so hard to describe, there had been a feeling of how easily it might be misunderstood, and the mere propinquity of the external sanctuary be supposed capable of producing the inner stirring of thought and speech. Accordingly the higher truth of Jahveism here contained is immediately represented afresh in a beautiful appendix. Two of the chosen men, Eldad and Medad,[2] happen to have remained at a distance from the Sanctuary among the rest of the people in the camp, but they too suddenly revealed themselves as Prophets, and when Moses was called upon to quench their spirit, he uttered rather a desire that all men without distinction of rank might be immediately and powerfully stirred by the spirit of Jahveh! So let no one feel envy towards the higher gifts of the spirit wherever they may be found, but let none in whom they do arise fancy that he cannot fail to possess them on account of his privileged position alone!

That even much later, under the monarchy, a kind of popular representation always maintained its place, we can tell from sufficiently sure and numerous traces.[3] Its position and activity varied, no doubt, much according to the fortune and estimation of the kings and the changes of the times. It

---

[1] This idea of the *ut non plus ultra* is contained in the verbal addition ולא יספו after a preceding verb. Precisely similar is Deut. v. 19 [22]; comp. also अनुत्तम :

[2] The descent of these two men is not mentioned here, but we know that they were elders; and a tribal prince of Benjamin, Num. xxxiv. 21, in the Book of Origins bears the name of Elidád, corresponding to Eldâd.

[3] Comp. *Hist.* iii. 11. 310 sq., 312 sqq., iv. 234. Allusion is briefly made during these times to a national representation in the expression in Prov. xi. 14; xv. 22 (xxiv. 6). For when the king is warned not to lend an ear to private prejudiced counsellors who would desert him at the hour of need, but to hearken to as many as possible, this can only refer to such as regularly assembled about the king to give him their advice. That indeed under the mantle of the public character of such discussions the meanest disposition may all the more cry aloud, is said later in the Proverb xxvi. 26.

became most powerful only in periods when the regal position itself became degraded, or the complications and requirements of the realm increased. But the kingdom never became prominently degraded to the rule of mere force.

2. *The Overseers and Judges of the Nation.*

Superintending and judging the nation (for these two functions were then rarely separated) would undoubtedly be adequately provided for in the earliest times by the existence of these Elders,[1] and even later they always retained a certain share in the judging.[2] To uphold the rights of the weaker members against every form of injustice was of course the special duty of every born 'prince' within the limits of his clan or tribe. But the whole national life soon became too intricate for this, so that the weaker member sought for his protector (patron) wherever he could find him,[3] and the relation already described[4] was continually extending.

After the earliest national constitution had been shattered in Egypt, we find overseers or bailiffs set over the people, who superintended their forced service, but at the same time no doubt also acted as inferior judges. They were of Hebrew descent, but were under Egyptian head-bailiffs—the so-called Taskmasters.[5] Their name *Shôter*, meaning much the same as rulers,[6] was retained even during the later centuries, with a similar meaning, at any rate in certain authors (who seem to belong chiefly to the kingdom of the Ten Tribes). This explains how quite at the commencement of the departure from Egypt, Moses, as prophet, was at the same time the sole judge of the entire nation. The *Shôter* as Egyptian officials were then without office, the Elders had long ceased to exercise any regular judicial authority, and the new great prophet possessed the full confidence of the people.

We still possess in a very ancient document the narrative —characterised by so much ingenuousness—where it is related how this duty had become an insupportable burden on Moses, and how he by Jethro's advice appointed judges over tens,

---

[1] Comp. how in the Book of Origins, Num. xxv. 4 sq. the name 'chieftain' interchanges with the name 'judge.' That judges caused this interchange of the two names is a matter of course.
[2] Comp. 1 Kings xxi. 8 sqq.; Jer. xxvi. 16-19.
[3] Comp. Jer. xxvi. 24; xl. 10; and

Hist. iii. 70.
[4] P. 216 sq.
[5] The description of the Third Narrator, Ex. v. 6-23, is very plain.
[6] שׁטֵר allied with סדר is properly to *set in a row,* hence to *rule,* comp. سطرون, Sûr. li. 37.

fifties, hundreds, and thousands, who should settle disputes in gradation, so that only the cases which were too difficult for them should come to him for decision.[1] Genuine as is the historical ring about this, we shall easily fail to comprehend it if we think of judges like our own. So many judges, and in so many grades, appear scarcely needful. But judging, in the wide sense of those times, included the overlooking of the entire management; and not rarely these *Shôter*, i.e. overseers, are treated as almost identical with Shôfet, i.e. judges, the only difference perhaps being that the overseer is then the same as the inferior judge.[2] And in the second place we must remember that the nation was at that time always in the position of an army in the field, and therefore organised in true military fashion; even during the fairest period of its dominion it always retained this military organisation; so that those who were the overseers in ordinary times undoubtedly in campaigns and battles became the leaders of their subordinates. Then the overseers would not be too numerous. The Elders, on the other hand, if the preceding assumption is correct,[3] were far too few in number for the overseers to be taken from their ranks alone.

It was specially in this application to the army that these ancient authorities over tens, fifties, hundreds, and thousands, were retained under the monarchy, as we clearly recognise from many sources.[4]

3. *The Prince of the Nation.*

Nevertheless this military organisation certainly did not at the time of its origin overthrow the former primitive constitution according to tribes and elders. It did not even intersect this, but completed its arrangement within each particular

---

[1] Ex. xviii. 13–26.

[2] As Deut. xvi. 18–20; whilst from Deut. xx. 5–9 we can see that a *Shôter* in the first instance only exercised his personal supervision over all the affairs of his subjects. When the *Shôter* are coupled with the Elders (as Num. xi. 16 and often in Deut.) they are manifestly of inferior dignity to the latter. In the higher sense of prince or judge, so far as this conception coincides with that of prince, the name *Shôter* never occurs.

[3] P. 245.

[4] A *decurio* by himself does not happen to occur again (Deut. i. 15 is mere repetition); a captain (שׂר) of fifty occurs Is. iii. 3, 1 Sam. viii. 12, 2 Kings i. 9–14. Captain of hundreds (*centuriones*) and thousands are frequently mentioned. Comp. also Jud. xx. 10.—Similar divisions were not uncommon elsewhere; for the ancient Persians see Xenoph. *Cyrop.* ii. 2. 1, 9; while in 1. 12 he speaks of twelve tribes. In China all have been divided from primitive times into groups of 10, 100, and 1000 households. In Peru the organisation of the people into groups of 10, 50, 100, 1000, and 10,000, was strictly carried out (Prescott's *History of Peru*, s. 33). Even the ancient Germans—and the usage still exists among the Anglo-Saxons—were divided into tens and hundreds. See *Gött. Gel. Anz.* 1860, s. 887 sqq.

household, clan, and tribe. The tenacious mutual adherence of the subjects of each household, clan, and tribe, the ready separation of the great divisions of the people, and the antagonism between the tribes or clans which had in any way increased their power, remained after its establishment what they had been before. When the assembly met in its full strength, no doubt the august image of Israel, or even Isaac or Abraham, might be present to their minds as their common ancestor, and as an exhortation to unity and harmony. Yet the fact that these three ancestors were usually thought of together was enough to prevent the idea of unity being sufficiently distinct. The Seventy, too, even when they sat, could ensure no strict unity, at any rate in the execution of their resolutions. And the rigid external unity of the rule of a single despotic prince or king was an object of dread.

It is undeniable that this national constitution did much to promote the new formation of the Theocracy during the all-important days of Moses. Of course the Theocracy proceeded from totally different and far more powerful causes; but it is equally clear that the establishment of the sole supremacy of Jahveh would have been a far harder task if a single house or clan, with hereditary claims to regal power, and an externally strict national unity, had already been in existence.

The marvellous vitality of a true, previously unknown, religion, brought the nation for the first time under the rule of one great eternal truth. Once it felt all the lower aims and all the wrangling of its former life here annihilated; once it felt itself here marvellously renewed, invigorated, and filled with eternal hope. This is the ineradicable germ of a new life, and so also of a new unity, of a new community, and of a new kingdom, which, however varied might be its fate in more distant times, can only cease with its own perfection. At the time of Moses all the sections of the nation for the first time bowed beneath one realm, i.e. beneath the strict unity of national life as this is upheld by one higher will standing over all, against which no private person and no individuality may assert a personal will destructive of the unity. It received through its covenant but one head, one king; there was only one whom all were willing to hearken to. This one was the eternal invisible true God, whose very incorporeality, however, made it hard for men always to realise him, and easy for them again to forget him.

On this account, in the period characterised by inspired fresh recognition of the true God, and by the charm of being subject to him alone, the ancient national constitution remained essentially unchanged. The tribes recovered their complete independence, and much may have been restored which had been long suppressed in Egypt. Each tribe forms a separate unity in all its purely national relations, has its special army and ensign,[1] its prince springing from its midst as its military leader[2] and external representative. The whole twelve tribal princes represent the entire nation when the interests of all are involved, or on solemn occasions.[3] If an embassy is to be despatched on behalf of the realm to deal with matters concerning all, then out of the wider circle of princes we have spoken of, twelve, according to the tribes, are selected for the purpose.[4] For specially urgent cases—e.g. for conducting an unavoidable war—a national leader may be raised up from the midst of the nobles, as Joshua was by Moses, with the approval of the community, and as Jephthah, after making certain conditions, was appointed their leader [5] by the Elders of Gilead. However, the powers of such an officer properly come to an end with the completion of his work, although there was no special law on the point.

Jahveism, then, had no intrinsic objection to the rule of a national leader, whether he were a private tribal prince or a prince universally recognised. On the contrary, an ancient law forbade the cursing of such a prince as much as of the spiritual authorities.[6] But what is of supreme importance is that, in its ancient strictness, it gave him no regal power, i.e. none that extended over all, unchecked and compulsory, and in general feared to intrust such powers to a human individual.

II. SPECIAL POWERS AND PROFESSIONS IN THE NATION.
PRODUCTIONS AND TRADE.

In a nation whose life is regulated by ancient customs, there always arise a variety of particular crafts and professions demanding special knowledge and instruments, which form smaller private circles, and so become distinct powers. Or

---

[1] Num. ii. 2.
[2] Num. i. 4-16, ii. 1 sqq.
[3] Num. i. 4, 44, vii. 2 sqq.
[4] P. 245. Num. xiii. 2 sqq. xxxiv. 16-29. Similarly the national monument consisted of twelve pillars. *Hist.* ii. 246.
[5] Jud. xi. 5-11.
[6] Ex. xxii. 27 [28]. Here, as in the Book of Origins, a prince is always called נָשִׂיא; even the name נָגִיד would have been more distinction. The word אֱלֹהִים, however, on account of the corresponding national princes, must signify the spiritual authority; and just this is involved in the peculiar language used in the Book of Covenants. Comp. more on the point below.

new occasions may give rise to special powers and cause them to become great, as a progressive favourable development causes the important capacities and crafts in the nation to be continually more and more exclusively and vigorously devoted to the satisfaction of the special needs of both the lower and the higher life. So long as a nation is absorbed in satisfying the most immediate and universal of the wants of life, or thinks of nothing but wars of conquest or defence, other crafts, professions or sciences, are hardly able even in the most favourable countries to make any head, and so ripen into special powers in its midst. But as soon as a favourable opportunity is granted to these, each one of them collects together its own community (they may be called guilds, societies, corporations, &c.) within the great national association, draws its wider or smaller circles through the whole nation, and operates from its own centre with greater or less force upon the whole. Many a corporation, indeed, exercises the most powerful influence on the body of the nation at large, moulds it according to its own life, upholds and protects it when danger threatens, or pours into it the destructive poison which may be gradually formed within itself.

Production and trade among the Canaanites (Phœnicians) must very early have become highly-developed individual powers of this kind in the national life, and have stimulated the formation of a great variety of close corporations.[1] Even in Israel many guilds and companies drew more closely together, the better to carry on the various higher or lower professions and crafts of life; they grew accustomed to the hereditary practice of living closely together in towns and villages, and, especially during the regal times, often received powerful aid from the government. We possess on the point at any rate some scattered and only too brief items of intelligence.[2] But Israel was little adapted to develope such modes of life perfectly during the times when its national force stirred it most powerfully and

---

[1] Comp. the treatise *Ueber die Phönik. Ansichten von der Weltschöpfung*, s. 16; the remarks on Job, s. 317 of the 2nd edition; and the treatise *Ueber die grosse Karthagische und andere Phönik. Inschriften*, s. 49–58.

[2] Specially noteworthy, but difficult to understand on account of the abridgment in the representations of Chronicles, are (1) 'the families of *literati* resident at Jabez,' 1 Chron. ii. 55 (comp. on the point *Hist.* iv. 94 *nt* 4, 192); (2) 'the smiths' in the 'valley of the smiths,'

'whose father,' i.e. master and type, 'is Joab,' 1 Chron. iv. 14; (3) 'the families of the byssus-makers of Bath-Ashbea;' and (4) 'the potters dwelling at Netaim and Gedera, who dwelt at the royal works (factory) on these domains,' 1 Chron. iv. 21–23; where in ver. 23 the ־י before יְשֵׁבוּ is to be struck out, or rather is to be understood from its position in accordance with what is said in *Die Dichter des A. Bs.*, I b. s. 15 of the 3rd edition.

gave it its most permanent form—in the days of Moses, Joshua, and David—no more than the Romans were when they persevered in their ancient simplicity, and then raised themselves to world-wide dominion. But in all times when peace at all permitted it, we see the nation, from its earliest centuries, devoting itself to every peaceful occupation in life, and contesting the palm in such matters with all the most civilised nations that adjoined it.[1] The peculiar turn of its spirit, however, never permitted it, through all the fate-fraught changes in its history down to the latest times, to surpass the Phœnicians in such arts, but was continually drawing it away from them with inceasing force. So strongly was it stirred from the days of Moses with impulses and powers of a totally different kind.

Prophecy.

On the other hand, Israel, from the time that it appears in the clear light of history, found such a lofty power in Prophecy, which arose in the midst of the great national corporation, had the strongest and most salutary influence on it, and indeed first gave the nation that unique worth with which it appears in the world's history. A prophet, especially if he had already vindicated his position, had the right, according to the very fundamental constitution of the nation, i.e. the Theocracy itself, of speaking in the national assembly or elsewhere in public. This right was maintained uninterruptedly even to a late period, however much the public authority of the prophets might gradually decline after the ninth and eighth centuries B.C.[2] The ancient law assumes this as a matter of course. The Deuteronomist is the first who finds it needful both to guard this prophetic right, as well as to decree the punishment of death for the crime, which had already appeared in his time, of misusing this most invaluable but possibly most pernicious prerogative.[3]

But the very fact that prophecy in Israel, from the all-decisive commencement, worked through long eras with the purest grandeur and perfection which Antiquity allowed previous to the consummation of all religion, was a reason why it hardly ever attempted to secure external propagation in the nation as a mere profession, or to become hereditary, or yet to

---

[1] See more of the details in *Hist.* ii. 292 sq. 342 sq. 354; iii. 226 sq. 260 sqq.; iv. 191 sqq.

[2] Comp. Amos v. 10 and similar passages. The ground of the inviolability of the true prophet is shown very briefly in Amos iii. and Jer. xv. 16, comp. xxvi. 12–15.

[3] *Hist.* iv. 224.

create out of itself a corporation or even to have a fixed external place of operation. And if at times during the long course of this history it inclined that way, so as to threaten to become a kind of heathen prophetism, it was always soon enough led back again to the true way as it had been pointed out to it, and only developed in consequence the more purely its most peculiar and true essence. For this would not tolerate any such external propagation and inheritance.

A consequence of this is that there is not much to say concerning the outward appearance or dress of the prophets. Everything about them of an external nature remained very simple. Samuel wore an outer garment something like that which the priests wore;[1] he was, however, himself a Levite by birth. The large mantle which it became customary for the later prophets to wear, along with other articles of the simplest kind, appears to have first attained this honour through the person of Elijah.[2]

In the same way the prophetism of Israel was prevented, by its most deeply-seated instinct, from accepting the aid of any external instrument, the adoption of which is the genuine token of the heathen oracles. But it is true that the longing to obtain signs of the future and higher assurances of success was as great among all early nations as was the effort to draw forth such divine premonitions and indications; and the more mysteriously spiritual was Israel's God, the harder it appeared to win from him an oracle. Now if this longing of the whole of remote Antiquity for oracles, and the extraordinary difficulty of obtaining a true one, did produce even in Israel certain traces of an appeal to external aids, such as the whole ancient world was filled with, these could not permanently keep their position; at length even the last shadows of the ancient system of oracles in Israel disappear, and nothing remains on this hearth of God but the glow of the purest fire. Strictly speaking, the only thing of the kind which the earliest Jahveism did not repudiate was the casting of sacred lots in the oracle of the High-priest, to be described below. Nevertheless, in representations of sacred truths we find such clear indications of oracles being expected in dreams while sleeping on a sacred spot,[3] as well as of asking

---

[1] 1 Sam. xv. 27, xxviii. 14.
[2] See *Hist.* iv. 68, and Zach. xiii. 4.
[3] The *incubatio*, see *Hist.* i. 330, iii. 50 sq., even Sir. xxxi. 1–7 says much about it; but Strabo is in error in quoting it as a general Judaic custom, *Geogr.* xvi. 2, 35. In the ancient Egyptian kingdom and its history, dreams and their interpretation play an important part, as well as the belief that it is possible to see and hear the gods in them (comp. *Hist.* i. 419, ii. 76); but allusions are often made to the subject also on Phœnician and Greek thanksgiving inscriptions. Apart from

the will of the Deity by means of rods deposited at the sacred place,[1] that we cannot fail to recognise a close connection, at any rate in the earlier times, between these ways of seeking an oracle and the prevalent religion. It appears that just these three ways of obtaining oracles were the commonest in Israel before Moses; a reason why they, like the ancient household divinities,[2] were held in esteem long after his time. Even of the ancient belief in the mysterious rustling among the tops of certain trees being significant of the coming of the Deity, a trace is still to be found in David's time,[3] and as the belief in sacred trees was itself extremely ancient in Israel,[4] we cannot wonder at this special belief which is thence derived. Conjuration of the dead,[5] on the other hand, as well as all other materialistic arts of extracting answers from the Deity, were strictly forbidden, and only forced their way into the community at times from foreign religions.[6]

The Priesthood.

1. Its General Relation to the Nation.

It is, however, possible for a craft and profession in which proficiency is hard to attain, and which in the first instance is reached only by individual members of a people, to be of such a kind as to seem indispensable for upholding the existence of the nation and its kingdom. As it is only the universal spiritual truths which constitute the light and the animating spirit, and therefore also the firmest unity of a nation, it is needless to explain that it is only crafts and professions related to these which are spoken of here. In the ancient Egyptian

---

the Spartan temple of Pasiphaë it was much in vogue at Athens even in the time of Hypereides, see *Gött. Gel. Anz.* 1853, s. 794, and Marcus Aurelius in his *Meditationes*, i. 17, does not scruple still to express his high regard for it. Comp. also Müller's *Orchomenus*, s. 158-160; Xen. *Anab.* vi. 1, 14 sq.; Pomp. Mela, i. 8, 50; Tabari's *Arab. Annalen*, i. p. 169 sqq.; Muh. Shahrastâni's *Elmilal*, p. 437, 4 sq. *Revue Archéol.* 1860, p. 116 sqq.

[1] A kind of ῥαβδομαντεία (comp. Deinôn's *Schol. ad Nic. Ther.* ver. 613, ed. Otto Schneider). No proof of this is to be found in Hos. iv. 12, but there certainly is in the entire representation, Num. xvii. 17 [2] sqq. For the purpose green rods of different sorts were put down before the sacred spot, and the next day were examined to see which had bloomed best in the night; the individual thus designated was deemed to be favoured by God.

[2] P. 223 sq.

[3] 2 Sam. v. 23 sq. (1 Chron. xiv. 14 sq.); this has already been explained, *Hist.* iii. 147.

[4] P. 120.

[5] Which even at the present day is practised in a cave in Mount Moriah; see Bartlett's *Walks about Jerusalem*, p. 167 sq. The same is the case on the soil of Nineveh; Layard's *Nin.* ii. p. 71.—The explication of the kinds of heathen divination mentioned here and there in the Old Testament belongs to biblical theology. See my *die Lehre der Bibel von Gott, oder theologie des alten und neuen bundes*. Band, i. s. 231 sqq. 1871.

[6] Comp. above, p. 16, nt. 5.

kingdom the prophets and the priests were thus regarded as the two branches of the order which was competent to maintain the spiritual, and therefore the best, bond of the unity of the nation. They took the position accordingly of great permanent guilds, of which all the higher knowledge of the kingdom, both theoretical and practical, became the hereditary possession. In Israel prophecy, since it was deemed an impulse of the freest spiritual activity, could never be regarded as it was in Egypt. The priesthood, on the other hand, was rightly deemed to be a profession devoted to the constant protection and maintenance of the religion whose foundation had been already laid, and which had been recognised by the nation as true and eternal.

. 1. And, as a fact, the priesthood, as it is mainly concerned with sacrifice and prayer, with action therefore and administration, is everywhere essentially employed less in creating than in upholding and administering what has been created. True, the priesthood in that most remote period, when for the first time in the history of mankind it learned to develope its own peculiar powers, must not only have been in its own way creative, but must have been armed with the most extensive authority. When for the first time the priest, by means of his sacrificial art and the might of his petitions, learned to draw, as it were, the gods down from heaven to earth, and to become for thousands the mediator between heaven and earth, then the enchantment which proceeded from him was of the most powerful kind, and many thousands would hang on the sacrifice and prayer of one priest as on the lips of a great prophet. The rank of the priest was then equal to that of the prince;[1] nothing could be happier than when a king, who was at the same time a priest, possessed the confidence of all.[2] It is a reflection and a relic of this earliest exalted authority of the priest when Aaron, and every one of his followers,[3] is designated as *the priest*, as though even the name *high-priest* were unnecessary. But a different state of things arises as soon as the priesthood, as was already the case under Moses, no longer exists in its pure spontaneity and original vitality, but is already dependent on a prophetic religion given outside its own borders.

So soon as the priesthood in this nation under Moses acquired the courage and made the determination to devote all its activity and skill to the protection of the true religion,

---

[1] As in Job xii. 19, where the hue of patriarchal times is so admirably represented.
[2] Gen. xiv. 18, comp. *Die Dichter des* *Alten Bundes*, I *b*. s. 40 sqq. of the 3rd edition.
[3] Still the case even on the Asmonæan coins.

which had come into existence and had been faithfully adopted there, a single priest of this earliest kind was no longer sufficient, however great the reverence felt for him. Still less could mere domestic priests of private households or clans be tolerated. For it is easy to understand that when once a great priest of the earliest kind had arisen and become an exalted type of sacerdotal activity and benefits, every household or every clan would be glad to possess a similar living sacred treasure, and the head of the household, or he to whom the latter intrusted his prerogative, would then be the genuine priest; and this in a good sense has no doubt its truth. But although this convenient dismembering of the priesthood of the true religion tried at times to creep back into Israel, even after Moses, it always met with a sufficiently stubborn resistance from the latter's deeper spirit. The function, and one of the first duties of the priesthood, could now only be to uphold the true religion *for* the whole nation, and also thereby to protect the right feeling, the power, and the unity of the nation. To discharge this new function the priesthood must now branch into numerous ramifications in the midst of the people, and be represented by numerous agents. Every power which thus spreads itself from one individual to thousands readily loses its strict unity more and more, and only in the earliest days Aaron and his immediate followers had much in common with the most ancient priests, until quite other causes in the last days of the nation restored something similar. But while the priesthood of the true religion became more and more divided in its personality, its individual members acquired increased power permanently to fill the whole nation with the spirit and force of the religion to which alone they owed allegiance.

Thus the great truths and powers which prophecy had at the commencement, and with greater vigour then than at any other time, established in Israel, merely required the priesthood to be an instrument capable of maintaining them in their integrity and perpetually renewing them from one generation to another. This instinct during the youth of the community of Jahveh at any rate produced the priesthood of the tribe of Levi. Thus a new corporation arose in the heart of the nation; and because the holiest and the highest impulses awakened in the nation were committed to its care, it ramified continually deeper and deeper into the ancient national life with the most wonderful force, and more than once appeared completely to dominate the nation and absorb it in itself. Nor did it, amidst all the changes and overthrows which time brought about, ever entirely cease to exist, but rather, along with the kernel of the nation, always renewed its youth and persisted until the close of this history, as though it were Israel in little, and as though the nation could no longer exist and live without it. In this way the attempt was made to give stability to that which in its original essence is too fine and spiritual, too much the spontaneous stirring of one great spirit; and if there was as yet no other way of securing its permanence, it was well that for a time, even if this lasted for many centuries, it was at any rate kept secure with greater vitality and purity in this stiff form and narrow sphere.

Of course a priesthood had been long familar to the people of Israel before it became the inheritance of the tribe Levi. For it is implied in the existence of every, even imperfect, religion, which requires sacrifice and the permanent sacred rites connected therewith. Duly to discharge these is what every one does not feel himself at once competent to do, nor is every one at once worthy. We have already seen [1] at what an early date, undoubtedly long before Moses, sacrifices became customary among the people of Israel. This alone is enough to prove that Israel had priests before the Levites. This proof is confirmed by the fact that besides many other sacrifical terms, the word for priests themselves (*Kôhen*) is extremely ancient, and must have been in use long before Moses, since it stands quite by itself in Hebrew, and its original significance can scarcely be explained.[2] But as in those days before Moses the exclusive life of each individual household was at its greatest height, each liked to have its own priest, and the father would choose for the purpose one of his sons who seemed best adapted for it. Young innocent lads, by preference (as will be explained below) the first-born of every household, seem to have been deemed the most

---

[1] P. 23 sqq.

[2] We should be entirely without firm ground within Hebrew itself for determining the original meaning of כֹּהֵן, if the verb had not survived in a single poetical instance, ex. Is. lxi. 10, with the meaning of *to equip*, hence e.g. to *put on* an ornament; comp. the Syrian ܟܗܢ (*cahin*) *glorious*, properly *adorned*, Is. Carm. ver. 32 in Knös. The priest according to this would be named from the management (הֲכָנַת) of the sacrifice, as ῥέζειν is employed of sacrificing, and this agrees with the meaning of a manager, an administrator of business, which the word, according to the Kâmûs, may have had among some Arabian tribes. The word in Arabic certainly first derives the meaning of *soothsayer* or *magician* (Sûr. li. 29) from an ancient kind of priests, who in virtue of the inspection of victims were deemed also soothsayers; for we know from other sources that the word was once in use in a great variety of Arabian races (see Tuch's *Sinaitische Inschriften*, s. 78). That the word in Hebrew describes in its stricter meaning only the service of the altar, also follows in particular from Num. xviii. 1–7.

suitable.[1] This was still the condition of affairs during the first period of the activity of Moses;[2] here and there it may have existed for half a century after him.[3] Many of the ancient sacred usages of this earliest priesthood were retained even later, and in particular the sacerdotal administration and action, aims and endeavours, passed over from this earliest time to that of Moses. Yet in respect to its deeper spirit this ancient priesthood had now to give place to its superior.

In the first place the new, more elevated religion introduced a whole circle of new extraordinarily lofty truths, views, aims, and commandments, which gradually found expression in a variety of corresponding rites and customs. The very simplicity of the fundamental principles of Jahveism gave them force to seize hold of and transform the details of the national life. Equally stubborn were their powers of resisting destruction. Where they could not at once penetrate and shine forth from the materials which they had mastered, they could grow rigid, at any rate temporarily, and retire into a shell. For it is everywhere the essential nature of simple truths, when once they come into existence, to be thus powerful in aggression and thus firm in defence. We have seen above in detail what profound truths, and what a multitude of new institutions and customs corresponding to them, were founded in the community, and we can now understand that to keep them faithfully and always apply them properly would require a totally new priesthood. The same Ephraimite who at first, according to the old custom, had consecrated one of his sons to be head-priest, preferred to take a Levite to be his 'father and priest' so soon as he had the opportunity.[4]

In the second place it is involved in the force and instinct of every true religion, that it endeavours to extend its dominion with the utmost equality possible over all the individuals, clans, or even tribes and nations, which have embraced it; so that its existence and operation bring about a higher spiritual unity and concord where previously the most mutually repug-

---

[1] Comp. נַעֲרִי Ex. xxiv. 5 with נַעַר Jud. xvii. 7-13, xviii. 3. A similar custom, though tinted with a heathen hue, is described in Pausanias *Periïg.* vii. 24. 2, comp. Porphyry *De Abstin.* iv. 5 p. 307; Jamblich. *Vita. Pyth.* x. (li.). Even in the heathenism of the present day, when it descends from those primitive times, similar customs are found, as among the *Khonds* of India and in the most interior parts of Asia, comp. *Ausland* 1847. s. 656; 1849, s. 47. It seems, however, from Acts v. 6, 10, as though there was an attempt to restore this simplest state of things at the commencement of young Christianity.

[2] According to the ancient passage Ex. xxiv. 5, where the reference is only casual, but perfectly definite.

[3] According to Jud. xvii. 5.

[4] Jud. xvii. 7-13.

nant errors and perverse endeavours had ruled triumphant. Jahveism directed the efforts of Israel for the first time towards a high aim, and united it by eternally saving and imperishable truths. When, then, the whole people had undertaken to find salvation in it—had once concluded the covenant with Jahveh—Jahveism could not fail to feel the strongest impulse to bind to itself all the members of this nation in a permanent manner, and never again to tolerate anything opposed to itself; but to annihilate everywhere the remnants or the new encroachments of Heathenism, as has already been more fully explained.[1] But for Jahveism to be able permanently to exercise this salutary rule it must be secure of very different priests for its instruments from those ancient ones who varied with every individual household, and were quite incapable of leading a large nation everywhere alike towards higher truths.

In the third place, every elevated religion, if she desires constantly to afford protection to her rule, her truths, and her institutions, over a wide field, has to contend with an infinite variety of errors, claims, and foes, of which scarce a trace appears on the stage occupied by the lower religions. Even in Israel, soon after the time of the first pure inspiration there ripened germs enough of such unexpected conflicts over the continuance and development of the true religion which had been founded.[2] This was another reason why it needed a stronger, more consolidated, and more vigorous priesthood.

2. In this way a priesthood of entirely novel character in regard to enlightenment, knowledge of how to govern, and decision, arose in Israel after Moses.[3] It undoubtedly excelled its predecessor as much as Jahveism did the earlier religion, and in spite of the many dangerous idle habits and errors into which it fell in the course of centuries, it nevertheless leaves far behind it every other form which Antiquity produced.

It is therefore no matter of surprise that this priesthood, when it arose, should obtain in quite a new class of men a pliant material out of which to form itself, and that the remnants of the earlier sacerdotal system were soon totally lost in the public life of the nation during the decades immediately succeeding Moses and Joshua, while the traces of it, which we have already mentioned,[4] remained somewhat longer in the private life of particular households. New men were needed at the time of Moses to become his immediate assistants in upholding

---

[1] P. 222 sqq.
[2] Comp. *Hist.* ii. 177 sqq.
[3] The finest description of the original preference of Levi as the sacerdotal tribe occurs in Mal. ii. 4–7.
[4] P. 263 sq.

the better things, of which he had laid the foundations, and which the entire nation had accepted. There could be no doubt of this. But the fact that these new men came solely from the tribe of Levi, and that the entire priesthood was soon most intimately associated with it, is an ultimate consequence of the ancient tribal-life,[1] according to which an individual tribe under the guidance of a leader of its own, with its clans and households firmly clinging to one another, was in the best position to direct all its compact forces so as to satisfy a single but specially important national want.[2] The fact of the priesthood soon settling hereditarily in the tribe of Moses and appearing inseparable from it, was also a result of the coincidence of the favourable settlement of all national interests in Israel under Joshua, with the mighty efforts made by this tribe at that time and the high estimation in which it was held. The occupations of life easily glide into a hereditary state wherever the ancient life of tribe and clan is still dominant, and the special sciences, arts, and crafts, are therefore still confined to narrow circles. Antiquity began with it, and could not dispense with it till the arts and sciences had worked their way to such a height that the merits of the individual in them passed for more than descent and guild. It was not a little that Jahveism at so early a period liberated Prophecy from all such limitations.[3] The priesthood—which must exist in the realm without a break, and has always the same work among the people, nay, whose whole essential aim is to maintain the established religion—could only be dealt with by making it hereditary.

Nevertheless, we must here remark that the priesthood was by no means so exclusively confined to the tribe of Levi during the early centuries that this could not be to some extent broken through in extreme cases. The sons of David were priests, as we are told in an ancient historical work[4] quite briefly, so that this was intelligible enough for its time. This would only refer to their rank, and at the solemn meeting of the assembly to their dress.[5] It was certainly not the case with Saul's sons, and is accordingly mentioned as something new in regard to

---

[1] Described on p. 241 sqq.
[2] See more on the subject *Hist.* ii. 141 sqq. Among the Greeks the priesthood was actually offered for sale, comp. *C. I. Gr.* ii. p. 453 sq. and the inscription of Andania.
[3] P. 258 sq.
[4] 2 Sam. viii. 18. When the Chronicler, 1 Chron. xviii. 17, puts instead of priests 'the nearest (in rank) to David,' he gives indeed no unsatisfactory explanation, for the priests may have come next to the king in honour, but he plainly avoids on purpose using the name of priests of those who were not such by birth.
[5] Like David, 2 Sam. vi. 41.

those of David. This agrees with the fact that the kings David and Solomon on the most solemn occasions officiated as priests, and received the honours due to the office,[1] while it was the somewhat later kings of Judah—when the kingdom generally was in a state of decadence, and, as a consequence, internal petty jealousies, misunderstandings, and rivalries were constantly becoming more and more dangerous—who were the first to see their right to exercise sacerdotal functions challenged by the priesthood.[2] Moreover, it is probable that in earlier days the most skilful persons in the art were occasionally taken even out of other tribes in preference to the more remote branches of the Levites.[3] For a long time the nation could not entirely forget that the sacerdotal prerogative of this tribe was not original, so that particular infringements of it, especially during the earlier centuries, may have seemed not wholly without a warrant.

But, apart from such trifling fluctuations, the priesthood had long been the hereditary unchallenged possession of the tribe of Levi by the time of the Book of Origins. Thus this book refers the special inheritance of the priesthood by the Levites to a divine institution and confirmation, and explains in accordance with this their whole legal position. It is the first book, according to our present sources, which inculcated the view of a divine prerogative held by this tribe, but at the same time it sets forth this view with such decision as to show that it must have been firmly established, at any rate as a historical fact, for a considerable period. And, in truth, if every honest human calling in the community has for itself a divine justification, so of all the individual professions the priesthood would naturally be the one which would be most certain to be regarded as consecrated by divine installation and appointment, since the higher religion had to be maintained in the realm in its perfect purity as well as in its full activity, and since this was not possible without agents properly qualified and with full authority. And though in the course of history the priesthood came

---

[1] See *Hist.* iii. 127, 246 sq.
[2] What is said 2 Chron. xxvi. 15–21 (comp. *Hist.* iv. 145 sq.) about the attempt which King Uzziah made to offer sacrifice in the temple with his own hand, and which was frustrated by the priests, may contain a trace of historical tradition, inasmuch as Uzziah was the last of the more powerful and vigorous kings of Judah, just such an one as might propose to act towards the temple after the manner of David and Solomon. The kings of Judah after Jehoshaphat appear to have lost all influence over the priests of Jahveh till Uzziah attempted to restore it; nor can it even be denied that from the later years of Solomon's rule a jealousy grew up among the priests of Jahveh towards a monarchy which also favoured heathen religion, and that this led finally to greater and greater estrangement.
[3] See *Hist.* iii. 278 nt. 2.

to be confined to the tribe of Levi, and to be regarded as its divine inheritance, yet there must have existed within the ancient true religion and the limits of the kingdom of Jahveh so clear a perception of the true nature of every priesthood corresponding to such a religion, that the very limitation of it to the tribe of Levi appeared only as a matter of minor importance. Filled with this feeling, the Book of Origins describes with its fine copiousness all the duties as well as the rights of the priesthood; and even the other writings of the Old Testament, wherever they have to speak of it, suffer the light of its lofty vocation to manifest itself.

3. Yet, indispensable as it was for the Levitical priesthood to develope itself in those early days, and gloriously as it did develope itself on many occasions in the community of the ancient true religion, this religion could not have been what it is if, in spite of its becoming continually more and more intertwined with this form of the priesthood, it had not had the feeling —here more clearly, there more obscurely—that the form had only a temporal nature and value, and did not supply the unchangeable deepest basis of the Theocracy. There may be individual passages in the Old Testament where the Levitical priesthood is with right treated as of divine installation. There are others which sufficiently indicate that it assumed this definite shape only in consequence of the needs and narrowness of the times.[1] These temporal needs may change. And if on one occasion, in the long course of those times, the perpetual existence of the Levitical priesthood is demanded even by a great prophet,[2] in the times in which he thus spoke, it really was indispensable for a period whose termination none could see; and, moreover, Levitical priests came gradually in common usage to mean the same as the true priests generally, of whom the prophecy is in every sense correct. Accordingly, the best representation and account from a historical point of view, is that of the Book of Origins, according to which the Levites were only placed in office with the consent and approbation of the representatives of the whole community.[3] If they were thus put in office, they stand ultimately as so many men of Levi under the community as the entire living household which was the abode of the Divine spirit; and the community may, under other temporal conditions, intrust the sacerdotal authority to others than these hereditary priests.

[1] See *Hist.* ii. 142 sq.
[2] Jer. xxxiii. 21.
[2] Num. iii. 1 sqq.; comp. more on the point below.

2. *The Sphere and Nature of the Duties of the Priesthood.*

1. The priesthood has accordingly one single permanent function, viz. to protect the true religion which had been founded in the community, so that it may perpetually flourish throughout the entire nation. Or, to say the same thing more in the words of Antiquity: the true Holy Presence was dwelling in Israel; the priesthood had to serve it without ceasing, as the servants standing closest to a lord who, besides them, has many other servants at a greater distance in his wide domain. The priesthood of Israel only became possible by means of and within the community; while the community of Israel rather became possible in contradistinction to the expanse of Heathenism. The former, therefore, can have no duties which, originally and in strictness of speech, were not also duties of the whole community, and even of every individual member of it. The true priest ought before all to be holy,[1] pure, and blameless; but this ought also to be the case with regard to the whole community of Jahveh,[2] which would not otherwise be distinguishable from the heathen. He should stand in the closest proximity to Jahveh,[3] should personally approach his most holy place with confidence and intrepidity, have a full and accurate acquaintance with his laws, and care for his affairs like a confidential body-servant. But the whole of Israel too should be close to the true God, should belong to Jahveh more than the other nations, should be his heir,[4] his first-born son.[5] The priest ought to be entirely devoted to Jahveh, dedicated to him alone, and should possess no inheritance, i.e. external property besides;[6] on his account the priest should leave father and mother, disown brother and sister;[7] and to fight unto death on his behalf should be unto him a joy:[8] but all this is equally true of the whole of Israel. The priesthood is therefore only an Israel in Israel, a higher grade in the same community. As Israel was separated from the heathen, so again within Israel was there a narrower circle which immediately surrounded the Sacred Presence. In many ways like this all healthy vigorous life falls into gradations; and it is a fact that those who desire to vivify and protect for others what is sacred,

---

[1] Lev. xxi. 6–15, comp. more below.
[2] P. 229 sqq.
[3] Ex. xix. 22, Num. xvi. 9, xviii. 2.
[4] Ps. lxv. 5 [4], Ex. xix. 5, Ps. xxviii. and elsewhere.
[5] Ex. iv. 22.
[6] Num. xvi. 5; especially Deut. x. 6–9, xii. 12, xviii. 2. On these passages of the Deuteronomist see more below.
[7] Ex. xxxii. 27–29, Deut. xxxiii. 9.
[8] Ex. xxxii. 28.

must themselves first possess it in its greatest purity and exercise it in highest power.

These facts, however, render it necessary that such internal prerogatives, capacities, and merits should already be in existence before they receive their full recognition and divine justification. All who are Jahveh's own are then also marked by him with an external indication of the fact. He who is holy and loved of God is then declared before the world to be worthy to approach him. This universal truth is directly taught by the Book of Origins in regard to the true priest.[1] Not till Aaron and his son and grandson, not till the whole tribe of Levi had most gloriously proved their pure devotion and self-sacrifice under the severest trials, did they receive from heaven full credentials for their sacerdotal office.[2] On the other hand the higher grade and dignity, when once attained, brings with it greater dangers and fearful penalties. Those who bear the dignity of the priesthood and approach the Sanctuary must also be the first to undergo the punishments which are brought about by official error and the slightest violation of the holy place. An extremely ancient divine oracle runs as follows:

*On him who nearest to me stands show I my sanctity,
And before the whole nation is my glory manifest.*[3]

This was to explain how it was possible for the two eldest sons of Aaron to be at once pitilessly annihilated by the altar-fire when they drew near to it with strange fire.[4] Only when the priesthood works entirely as it ought to do, from its own good foundation, can its actions be rich in blessings for the rest of the community. In the same way it is taught later that Israel can only turn successfully against the heathen when its internal state is perfect.[5]

This is the general meaning of the priesthood of the tribe of Levi. It was accordingly regarded as a privileged holy tribe, occupying an intermediate position between the remain-

---

[1] Num. xvi. 4 sqq.
[2] Num. xvi. 20-xvii.; xxv. 7-12, out of the Book of Origins; Ex. xxxii. 29.
[3] Lev. x. 3. Jahveh manifests his greatest glory (majesty) publicly before the whole nation in the fact that he exhibits his sanctity most on those who stand nearest to him, and therefore punishes their transgressions most severely and instantaneously; comp. *Hist.* ii. 138 sq.—It is noteworthy in this connection that, according to the Chronicler, the priests and Levites alway purify themselves first, and only then do the same for the people.
[4] Lev. x. 1 sqq. What strange fire may be at any rate in its original sense is explained below under the Sacred Tent; here, however, the expression manifestly already occurs in a more general, i.e. in a higher sense.—That it may be dangerous to linger in the inner temple, and that the priest frequently issued thence disfigured by God, is a belief which finds expression even in the representation, Luke i. 12 sq.
[5] See *Die Propheten des A. Bs.* vol. ii. s. 404 sqq.

ing tribes and Jahveh. Nor was this high regard confined to the recognition of its prerogative and rule, or this praise given only to the courage wherewith it frequently defended Sanctuary and sacred rite with the utmost decision. A still higher estimate was made of the bold sudden determination with which it opposed with the confidence of faith the progress of the worst national misfortunes, throwing itself in between the other tribes amid the wildest raging of internal national discord and infatuation, and like a divine mediator repressing the fury.[1] Did strife burst out concerning the pure truth, and was there a call to rescue the highest conceptions of Jahveism? Then 'Moses and Aaron' may perhaps be found standing alone against the entire nation; the true priest, even if the whole people take the side of error and he is left alone, must remain standing on the other side, where he is upheld in spite of everything, and wins the final victory. But if it might thence appear as if he alone deserved the reward of fidelity, and if there were indications that God himself meant to save him alone and destroy the whole unfaithful nation, then most of all he feels that he is nothing without the community, and in the midst of his victory makes supplication for the deluded crowd.[2]

2. It is at this point that we first meet with the highest function of the priesthood, according to the feeling of the earliest times. In the sacred community of Jahveh the original purity, which, strictly speaking, ought always to be maintained there, is constantly receiving various stains, noticed or unnoticed, expiated or unatoned for; and the whole community, while it felt the necessity for strictest purity, felt also that Jahveh's Sanctuary dwelt in the midst of the countless impurities of his people, and was never free from their defilement.[3] Between the sanctity of Jahveh and the perpetually sin-stained condition of the community there is therefore a chasm which seems infinite. All the offerings and gifts which the members of the community bring are only like a partial expiation and payment of a debt[4] which is never entirely wiped out. To wipe out all these stains, to bear the guilt of the nation,[5] and constantly to restore the divine grace, is the final office of the priest. How hard a one duly to fulfil! A hundred precautions in every direction were framed by Antiquity for the sacerdotal office in sacrifice and

---

[1] Num. xvii. 11–13 [xvi. 46–48].
[2] Num. xvi. 20 sqq., xvii. 9 sq. [xvi. 44], comp. Ex. xxxii. 9 sqq.
[3] The principal passage is Lev. xvi. 16; comp. Num. xv. 31, xix. 13, 20.
[4] According to the remarkable phrases which at first sight are so obscure, Ex. xxviii. 38, Num. xxxi. 50.
[5] This is the explanation of the strange phrases, Num. xviii. 1. comp. 3, 22 sq.; Ex. xxviii. 38, Lev. x. 17, Num. viii. 19.

elsewhere. A prolix science was developed in order to ensure without fail the real reconciliation of God by means of sacrifices of every kind. Yet all sacerdotal activity was frequently of no avail, and if misfortune broke upon the people (a 'wrath of Jahveh') it was only too often imputed to some error of the priests.

It was the duty and it was the desire of the developed Levitical priesthood to step into the breach and to take the full responsibility of this on its own shoulders. It undertook always to bear the entire guilt of the nation. This was the way in which it was its duty and its desire during its best days to administer and to protect the Sanctuary. This, however, was a reason— and the anxious dread of what was too holy already mentioned [1] cooperated in the same direction—why the demand early arose that no stranger, i.e. no one save a priest, should approach unauthorised the Ark of the Covenant, the interior of the Sanctuary, and the other sacred appliances, that no one should touch them and interfere with their office. The penalty which the law in the Book of Origins attaches to the infringement of this requirement is death,[2] and reminiscences contained in the historical books show that it was not unfrequently inflicted in the days of early zeal.[3] Thus the Levitical priesthood became a most important member in the body of the whole realm, and one which must soon have appeared absolutely indispensable to the people themselves. But of course all this tended to widen the yawning gulf and sharp distinction between the Sanctuary with those attached to it, and everything else which existed and lived in the land, between priesthood and people. And though Jahveism would never suffer this separation to take so one-sided and rugged a form as it did in heathenism in corresponding cases,[4] it still would never again (as the history at last irrefragibly showed) entirely erase it of its own impulse, after this separation had been more and more firmly established during the course of centuries.

3. If now this priesthood, along with all its manifold duties

---

[1] P. 155.

[2] Ex. xxix. 37, xxx. 29, Num. i. 51, iii. 10, 38, xviii. 7.

[3] At any rate such narratives as those mentioned in the *History*, ii. 416 sqq., iii. 126, can refer ultimately only to the extraordinary dread with which the sacred ark and its custody was regarded. In the same way in Rome any one was at once to die who got under the sedan-chair of the Vestal virgins, Plutarch's *Numa*, x. Other similar ideas which were handed down in Israel from primitive times have already been explained on p. 155.

[4] As e.g. among the Romans the Vestals were honoured, as well as punished, just like goddesses, in the most superstitious manner. And even in regard to the ordinary *Flamen* what a profusion of superstitious usages there were, according to Gellius' *Noctes Atticæ*, x. 15!

and occupations, maintained its position as one tribe among the rest, it will of course follow that for its internal and external relations, it essentially retained an organisation such as all the tribes possessed.[1] This organisation, however, must have taken a different shape in accordance with the peculiar vocation of Levi and the various occupations included in its collective activity. Of these there are three in particular, different alike in dignity and power, and hence the sacerdotal office is itself divided into three grades: priest, inferior priest, high-priest. No doubt the character and sphere of many of the sacerdotal functions varied during the course of centuries to so extraordinary a degree that in the later periods it is difficult to recognise the institutions of the age of Moses and Joshua in regard to the inferior priests, and frequently too in respect to the high-priest. The whole nation gradually changed to an incredible extent in culture and manner of life, and a similar transformation must have largely affected just that tribe in which the most spiritual powers of Israel were concentrated soon after the founding of the community. Nevertheless the tribe always continued to be divided into these three hereditary grades of rank.

A. THE REGULAR PRIESTS.

1. The higher the outward position of the priests, the less can their laudable aims and occupations be brought under fixed rules, and legally prescribed for in mode and measure. Thus the historical passages of the Old Testament represent Aaron and his sons performing as priests many actions of the highest importance and fraught with richest blessings, whenever the needs of the moment instigated them to sacerdotal activity on behalf of the community, without there being any special regulations to impel them thereto. If, however, we regard that which the law defined as their official business, we see that the regular priest had to protect, as well as to uphold in perpetual vitality and purity, both the visible Sanctuary and also whatever was yet truly sacred in Israel, though invisible. Everywhere, accordingly, their primary duties consist in effective public action; and among these occupations the offering of sacrifice, and the whole care of the inner Sanctuary occupy so important a position that in one main section these two duties alone are named.[2] But this constant active supervision of everything sacred embraces many points which are here omitted for the sake of brevity, such as the

[1] P. 241 sqq. [2] Num. xviii. 1-7.

supervision and treatment of lepers,[1] and similar occupations, which in modern times are left rather to the police. In particular, certain priests must regulate the calendar on account of the sacred festivals,[2] and all weights and measures, on account of the sacrifices and the manifold offerings to the Sanctuary.[3] And as the guardians of what was holy in the community, they had also the duty of making, from time to time, the estimate (the *census*) of the people with the purifications connected therewith;[4] hence too, of compiling the genealogical registers.[5] To such action, however, must be added, as equally important and indispensable, the giving of instruction about all the numerous objects of sacerdotal duty,[6] as well in the assembled community as to individuals, this being done both on solemn or official occasions, and in reply to inquiries about doubtful cases. They must have had, therefore, an accurate acquaintance with their laws and customs as well as some intimate knowledge of natural objects; the latter being all the more needful the less these things were specially investigated by others. That in particular they had charge of the original documents of the laws was so thoroughly understood, that the Deuteronomist, writing at a time when loud complaints had long been made over the neglect of the ancient laws, is the first who brings this into prominence as one of their duties, especially in relation to the king, who was to be bound to observe the law.[7]

---

[1] See p. 157 sqq.
[2] Comp. *Hist.* i. 205 sqq.
[3] These offerings will be spoken of below. Comp. for weights and measures according to the standards of the later times 1 Chron. xxiii. 29. Even the heathen were glad to deposit their standards in a temple, see Börkh. *Metrische Unters.* s. 189 sqq. 227, 290 *nt.*; Letronne's *Recherches sur Héron d'Alexandrie*, pp. 9, 267 sq. At first the regulation of weights and measures was probably entirely in the hands of the priests; still in traffic among the people they must early have escaped any higher guidance, so that to observe correct weight and measure seemed merely a requirement of religion, both in ancient utterances such as Lev. xix. 35 sq. and in later ones, Amos viii. 5, Mic. vi. 10 sq.—On this account there was a distinction in Israel from the time of the monarchy between *sacred* and royal weights, measures, and coins; the former as the more ancient being also the greater. In our own days the investigation into the weights and measures of ancient nations has been prosecuted with great zeal (comp. the *Jahrbb. der Bibl. Wiss.* xi. s. 262 sq., and Vasquez Queipo's *Essai sur les systèmes métriques et monétaires des anciens peuples*, *Gött. Gel. Anz.* 1861. s. 657 sqq.). As, however, ancient Israel had nothing characteristic in this respect, the subject hardly concerns us here. For the monetary system in the earliest times see *Gött. Gel. Anz.* 1855, s. 1390 sqq., 1856, s. 798 sq.
[4] See below.
[5] The יחש of somewhat later writings, i.e. properly the *counting*, as it corresponds to the Ethiopic ኈለቈ (see *Jahrbb. der Bibl. Wiss.* v. s. 143), and the latter signifies properly *counting*, comp. حَسَبَ and حَسَبٌ.
[6] Lev. x. 8–11, Deut. xxxiii. 9 sq. Ezek. xliv. 23 sq. An example of the mode of speech in the community is given in the phrase Num. xv. 15 ; for הַקְהָל is certainly to be understood here as an address.
[7] Deut. xvii. 18 sq., xxxi. 9, 25 sq. During the earlier days of the monarchy

But this duty of giving instruction and replies to questions easily leads men to regard the priest as also a prophet, and to seek oracles from him. Moses had in reality been both, and it seemed as if his example might be followed. Throughout the whole ancient world, prophetism for the most part clung to the priesthood as merely a special branch of the latter's functions. It is true that it appeared in Moses with so wonderful a force and effectiveness as to tower far above the priesthood, and manifest itself in Jahveism as a thoroughly independent power. But though at this pure elevation it could not be hereditary, yet the craving for oracles even in all ranks of ordinary life was imperative down to the time of David, so that Jahveism was obliged for a long time to suffer it to be, in actual life, an appendage to the priesthood, and had to tolerate what it could not yet prevent. Nevertheless the Book of Origins, the only one which regulates the relation, confines the right of the oracle solely to the high-priest; and here, as will be explained below, it could best be tolerated. In common life, however, it was regarded down to David's time as a faculty which every worthy, especially every youthful innocent, priest, might easily possess.[1] The external means of which he would make use in order to obtain an oracle will be spoken of below in connection with the high-priest.

2. As the immediate vocation of these regular priests was to guard and to explain what was sacred, they formed a narrower sacerdotal circle within the priesthood. A consequence of this was an extension of the hereditary system, so that only the house of Aaron, i.e. only the priests who were descended from Aaron and his brothers,[2] attained this higher dignity. Nay even among these, a further distinction was at any rate legally observed—that only the descendants of Aaron were to manage the work connected with the altar; while the other members of his house, e.g. the descendants of Moses, were to take care of the sacred vessels which belonged to the service of the altar, and attend to other subsidiary matters.[3] In the early days when the laws were less stringently observed, any priest without distinction may have been taken at will for a private household as a full priest and utterer of oracles, as a 'father of the

---

it would appear from 2 Kings xi. 12 (2 Chron. xxiii. 11), that when a king was anointed just the original Decalogue was laid on his head over the crown, as an adornment and as a symbol that he would have to submit to the fundamental laws of the realm. Comp. the phrase Job xxxi. 36.

[1] See *Hist.* ii. 317 sqq.
[2] P. 259.
[3] Num. xviii. 1-7. Ezekiel calls these priests 'the sons of Zadok,' after 1 Kings ii.

household.'¹ But this the law never sanctioned.—When the two Aaronitish households of Eleazar and Ithamar had greatly increased in the course of centuries, and the magnificent temple required a far more extensive service, the qualified priests of the altar were divided into twenty-four houses (or clans), each of which had to attend to the service a week at a time. This arrangement may have existed from the time of Solomon, and it lasted until the close of this history.² The descendants of Eleazar, as the first-born of Aaron, had always the advantage here. They supplied sixteen of these houses, the descendants of Ithamar eight.³—In so far as the sacred service in this established order came with its labours, on the one hand, as a duty, with its advantages, on the other hand, as a blessing, both to every individual and to the entire tribe, one might say that it fell to their share by an unalterable divine *lot*. Such images were very common elsewhere.⁴ And this view of the position and of the duties of the priesthood is so happy, that it has been spontaneously introduced into the language of the New Testament.⁵

Yet the mere hereditary succession, and the rights by birth of priests, were subject to numerous exceptions in the case of particular persons from the very nature of the priesthood; so manifest was its perpetual superiority to the chance external existence of individual men. That no man known to be immoral might become a priest was so completely taken for granted, that the law wholly ignores the matter. But since also the human body in its full purity and health was deemed a sacred thing,⁶ the law required that even the body of one who approached the altar should be completely pure and unmutilated.⁷ He might in no way disfigure the hair of his head or beard, or his skin. This prohibition is laid on all the members of the community in the earliest and strictest legislation;⁸ but since it gradually ceased to be observed in the growing community, it is repeated by the Book of Origins at any rate for the priests. In the next place, he might have no corporal blemish, either congenital or incurred later through some injury. He might

---

¹ Judges xvii. 7–13, xviii. 4–6, 14 sqq.
² 1 Chron. xxiv. 1–19, xxviii. 13, 21; 2 Chron. v. 11, viii. 14, xxiii. 8, xxxi. 2, 16 sq. Comp. *Hist.* i. 363 sq. and iii. 247 sq., as well as v. 113, and the comment on the Apoc. iv. 4, in the *Johanneischen Schriften*, ii. s. 158 sq.—The first of these was Jojarib, 1 Macc. ii. 1, the eighth Abia, Luke i. 5.
³ 1 Chron. xxiv. 4.
⁴ *Hist.* ii. 255.
⁵ It is indisputable that the phrase in Acts i. 17 has led to the spiritual *office*, and hence to the Christian ministry itself as the possessor of this lot, being briefly termed the κλῆρος, as is already done in the *Constit. Apost.*
⁶ P. 163 sqq.
⁷ Lev. xxi. 1–9, 16–24.
⁸ P. 164.

be neither blind nor lame, disfigured neither at the nose or ears,[1] neither in foot nor hand, neither hump-backed nor bleareyed, nor even with a white mark in the eye ;[2] he might not be afflicted with the itch, or ring-worm, or even have but one testicle. Contact with the dead he should avoid more scrupulously than an ordinary man.[3] Only on account of one of the nearest blood-relations, of his parents, children, brothers, or unmarried sisters, not on account of any one else, even though he were a more distant relative, might he give way to the more violent outbursts of bereavement.[4] He might not even marry any one defiled by harlotry or public unchastity,[5] nor 317 yet a wife who was separated from her husband.[6]

3. The attire of the priest on duty was simple, but in conformity with his solemn dignity. We are very fully acquainted with it, but not, in its entirety, from any sources prior to the Book of Origins.[7] As this book describes it, it had undoubtedly been in use for centuries, but even here traces are not wanting of a still greater simplicity which must have been in vogue during the very earliest days of the community. It is to be noticed in general that only linen material, nothing woollen, seemed suitable for priests.[8]

Clothing for the feet is not spoken of in the Book of Origins. The priest must certainly have always gone barefoot within

---

[1] As חָרֻם certainly refers to mutilation of the nose (even in Saadia, Lev. xxi. 18, אחרם is to be read for اخرم), the context of itself favours the rendering of שָׂרוּעַ by ὠτότμητος which the LXX give ; and in the other passage, Lev. xxii. 23, the conjunction with קָלוּט (which is most correctly rendered ' mutilated at the tail ') and the context of the entire passage, support the same meaning. This שָׂרוּעַ must therefore be compared with شرا. That so frequent a thing as mutilation of the ears should not be noticed here is of itself unlikely.

[2] Even in בַּק and תְּבַלֻּל the LXX and the Peschito bring us close to the correct meaning ; for the formation of the latter see Lehr. § 157 a ; the בַּק, however, is certainly to be compared with بَدَّ, which signifies an ocular disease.

[3] P. 151.

[4] בַּעַל, Lev. xxi. 4, must be equivalent to elsewhere (besides what is said in ver. 2 sq.) properly, behind that, in the next

place ; it is therefore connected with بَعْدُ, and, in respect to meaning, directly with the Ethiopic 'ቦዐ', 'another.' There is no other way of rendering the word intelligible.

[5] P. 228 sq.

[6] Similar and in part more definite prescriptions are given in Ezek. xliv. 20-22, 25-27.

[7] Ex. xxviii. 4, 39-43, xxix. 8 sq., xxxix. 27-29 ; and Lev. viii. 13.

[8] This is most clearly explained in Ezek. xliv. 17, 18, comp. ix. 2. Wool was undoubtedly the simplest and earliest material for clothing, but as something taken from an animal it was deemed unsuitable for priests and princes among all ancient nations, and even among the Arabs down to the time of Mohammed. Comp. also Herod. ii. 81, Philo. Opp. i. p. 653, ch. 37, and p. 161 alone ; Plutarch de Is. et Os. iv., Jamblich. Vita Pyth. xxi. xxviii. (c. cxlix.). Josephus, Antiq. iv. 8. 11, strangely thinks that a dress of wool and linen was forbidden (p. 161) only because it was permitted for priests.

the Sanctuary itself, from an ancient dread of treating the sacred spot like a common place.¹—Garments for the legs were just as little worn by the priests in the earliest days as by other people of those districts. This we see from the command not to build a lofty altar which must be approached by steps, lest the person might chance to be exposed thereby.² But, according to the Book of Origins, such garments were always to be worn simply for the sake of decency. They were, however, short, and may have reached no further than half-way down the thigh. The material employed was twisted byssus.

The principal garment, a robe hanging from the neck down to about the knees,³ was made of thick chequered byssus, in substance like what we term *piqué*.⁴ It was not, however, sewed together out of separate pieces, but woven in a single piece by an art with which the ancients were early acquainted.⁵ This integrity and simplicity of the principal garment was evidently not unintentional. It was in conformity with the rest of the system of the earliest Jahveism, which everywhere showed a preference for what was pure and simple, as has already been made plain in so many instances.⁶ Wool, however, in accordance with what we have just said, was inadmissible for this as for all other sacerdotal garments.—This robe was secured beneath the breast by a very broad girdle, with long ends which hung down in front. This was made of twisted byssus; but whilst the colour of this material was white in all the remaining articles of the sacerdotal dress, so that a dazzling whiteness was its characteristic appearance,⁷ the girdle had the three variegated colours which (as will be explained below) were in other respects appropriated by the Sanctuary. For it was usual to manufacture girdles of the most ornate description, and in like manner this broad band was regarded as the special symbol of the sacerdotal office.

Finally, there was a turban of the same white byssus. Its

---

¹ Ex. iii. 5.
² Ex. xx. 26, from the Book of Covenants (vers. 23–26 form a set of five laws, as ver. 24 consists of two commands).
³ Ordinarily בְּתֹנֶת, in Lev. vi. 3 [10], also termed מַד.
⁴ What תַּשְׁבֵּץ is, Ex. xxviii. 4, is clear from the description of the מִשְׁבְּצוֹת, Ex. xxxix. 15–18. According to this decisive passage, elevations with four or more corners were thus named, and we thus learn what sort of byssus we are to understand.

⁵ According to Ex. xxxix. 27, χιτών ἄρραφος, John xix. 23. At the present day the *Ihram* or pilgrim-dress of the Mohammedan should still be made out of two plain unsewed, and if possible white, pieces ; comp. Burckhardt's *Travels in Arabia*, i. p. 161, Maltzan's *Wallfahrt*, i. s. 182.
⁶ Especially p. 121.
⁷ Hence the appearance of the angels and all saints, to which allusion is repeatedly made in the Apocalypse ; comp. in particular xix. 8.

shape is not accurately known to us; probably it was of simple form, but tolerably high. It was made secure beneath with bands, and was never removed during duty.

Yet before the priests might perform their actual duties in this attire, they must be solemnly consecrated in order that they may receive full authority for their office; and it was in this consecration that Jahveism showed most clearly what were its special demands and expectations in regard to its permanent agents. The ceremony itself was no doubt performed later by the high-priest; according to the Book of Origins,[1] however, Moses performed it for Aaron and his sons together, thus for the first time rendering a high-priest possible. The novice was first bathed in front of the Sanctuary, then attired in his full dress, but, previous to his assuming the whole of his adornment, he was solemnly anointed by pouring the sacred oil, to be presently described, over his head.[2] In the next place a young bullock was sacrificed for him as an expiatory-offering, a ram as a whole-offering, and lastly, a second ram as the proper consecration-offering. The last sacrifice served as the strongest consecration which was possible in Jahveism. With the warmest sacrificial blood the novices were streaked on the tip of the right ear, the right thumb, and the right great-toe— a consecration which was also applied in other cases.[3] After this the novices were sprinkled with the blood flowing at the foot of the altar and with the sacred anointing oil,[4] as though these drops were to impart their sanctifying efficacy with the utmost force to the man on whom they alighted, and transform him into another being. This was a usage which in the earliest days occurs elsewhere only in connection with treaty-offerings.[5] In the second place this consecration-offering was employed from that moment for initiating into the sacerdotal functions the novices who had been purified with such mighty efforts. The altar-pieces of the ram, with the accompanying portions of bread, were placed in their hands, as though they could now prepare a like offering for the altar themselves, and

[1] Ex. xxix. 1–36; Lev. viii. sq.
[2] It is therefore incorrect to think that according to the Book of Origins only the high-priest was to be anointed. No doubt he was pre-eminently termed 'the anointed.' Lev. iv. 3, 16, vi. 15 [22]; but these passages are from an earlier author; and that the expression according to the Book of Origins is only an abbreviation of the fuller title of the high-priest, and does not imply the existence of other priests who were not anointed, is clear not only from the more definite construction of those words in Lev. xxi. 10, but also from distinct explanations elsewhere, Ex. xxviii. 41 (in accordance with which xxix. 8 sq. is to be supplemented), xl. 13–15; Num. iii. 3. On the other hand, it is manifest that all the priests of the house of Aaron were not anointed, but merely the sacrificial priests, those from whose ranks the high-priest came.
[3] P. 159.
[4] P. 108.
[5] P. 68.

then the person performing the consecration placed these portions, with the usual ceremonies, on the altar. In the same way the right ham was also placed in the hands of the novices, whilst the breast, as the better of these two parts which were the priest's share of the thank-offering,[1] fell to the person performing the consecration, and was therefore not placed in the hands of the novices, who then had an opportunity of getting fully acquainted with both of these ceremonies. The remainder of the sacrificial meal was not, however, consumed as a thank-offering, since a consecration-offering originally coincides rather with an expiatory-offering.[2] It was to be eaten by the newly-consecrated priest in a purely sacerdotal manner as an expiatory-offering, and with this was completed the full initiation of the new priest into his office. For no less than seven successive days was this consecration-sacrifice to be repeated, always in full view of the whole community. And the fresh feelings and high spirits, as well as the happy results, with which a priest thus consecrated could enter upon his arduous duties—nay, how even the effulgent glory of Jahveh descends upon the community in consequence of his operations—are beautifully described by the Book of Origins in the case of Aaron,[3] and the most inspiring type is thus given for all priests in a similar position.

As to the rest, we know that the priests had another dress of a commoner sort, which they wore when discharging their ordinary duties; and when we remember how many occupations they had which would prove destructive to clothes, we shall not be surprised that the law permitted them to wear garments of a commoner and cheaper sort besides their magnificent attire. We do not, indeed, know the particulars about it, the passage in the Book of Origins which treats of this being lost;[4] but, from the name which it bore, we can tell that it was sewn, and admitted patching—not, therefore, like the

---

[1] See below.
[2] P. 67.
[3] Lev. ix.
[4] Ex. xxxi. 10, xxxv. 19, xxxix. 1, 41, comp. xxviii. 2, Lev. vi. 3 [10] sq., Ezek. xliv. 19. Its description should have stood somewhere before Ex. xxviii. 1. The name בִּגְדֵי הַשְּׂרָד probably signifies 'dress of sewing,' i.e. sewed, from שָׂרַד, סָרַד, to pierce, sew; שֶׂרֶד, a *stylus*; see the contrast above, p. 247 sq.—According to Ex. xxxix. 1, these garments were of variegated colours, but the LXX show that the words here may have been greatly altered. If it were not for the threefold repetition of 'to serve in the Holy place,' which was a regular phrase for 'to be employed in the sacred occupations there,' the passage Ex. xxxix. 1 would refer to what is said in Num. iv. 6-13 about covering the sacred appliances on a journey, and would be parallel to the Chaldaic סְרָד. In this case the division into verses would have to be everywhere changed. The LXX and other ancient translators manifestly no longer understood the word.

garments described above,[1] woven in one piece. The plain white linen garments, which the high-priest wore for penance on the annual Feast of Atonement,[2] were probably of the same sort. Then we can also understand how the Book of Origins can command the magnificent attire of the high-priest to be left as an inheritance by its first possessor.[3] Its very magnificence caused it to be little used after the consecration was complete.

—Of other points which the officiating priest had to observe at the Sanctuary and elsewhere during the days when he was on duty, nothing is mentioned, except that he was not allowed to drink wine or anything else of an intoxicating nature before his work.[4] As for the first time great stress is laid upon this command in the Book of Origins, it is probable that the character of the Nazirite's life, spoken of above,[5] had its influence in the matter. Not that the prohibition would not have been in existence before that time, but so conspicuous an example as that of the Nazirites could not fail to increase its stringency.

B. THE INFERIOR PRIESTS OR LEVITES.

All Levites who were not included in the house of Aaron associated around it and the Sanctuary over which it presided, as servants about their master, and as members of a tribe about their chiefs.[6] They were, in fact, bound to discharge the inferior duties of the Sanctuary; the character, however, of these duties changed extraordinarily in the course of time.

1. Originally they were before all things bound to defend the Sanctuary externally, and associated like a powerful compact troop about the sacred tent.[7] They were then undoubtedly armed and ready for battle, like any man of the ordinary people, and certainly often displayed their military valour when it was needful to defend this moveable Sanctuary, with its

[1] P. 278.
[2] Lev. xvi. 4, 23.
[3] Ex. xxx. 29. How important this became in the Graeco-Roman period is further described in the *History*, v. vi. [German Edition].
[4] Lev. x. 8-11. It is best to connect the words of ver. 10 sq. so closely with ver. 9 that the infinitive with -לְ continues the בְּבֹאֲכֶם in ver. 9 according to *Lehrb.* § 351 c. This shows that the meaning of the prohibition was originally more stringent than it was at the time when, according to Josephus (see p. 85 *nt.* 4), it was made to refer only to the service of the altar.
[5] P. 86.
[6] According to Num. xviii. 2-4, the tribe of Levi took its name from the fact, as though the meaning was *sacred association* or *sacred guild*; for it cannot be doubted that the word נִלְוָה, which elsewhere does not occur in the Book of Origins, is employed here only for the sake of the play upon the word *Levi*. And the Book of Origins nowhere gives any other etymologies, though it makes allusions of this sort. See p. 241 sq., 257 sq.
[7] Num. i. 48-54, iii. 5 sqq., x. 21.

perpetual fire, either against the attacks of foreign nations or against internal insurrection; for the heart and life of the community seemed wedded to the Sanctuary.[1] When the latter had a fixed abode, they kept ceaseless watch about it, and no doubt rendered other assistance of various kinds both at the sacrifices and in purifying the sacred place and the like. On a journey there must have been an adequate number of them to carry on poles all the various sacred appliances (to be described hereafter); but so stringently were they, in this as in all other cases, kept at a distance from the immediate presence of the Sanctuary, that all these sacred appliances were previously covered over with cloths by the superior priests.[2] To facilitate all these occupations a regular organisation was introduced among them in connection with their three main clans, and with a part of these arrangements we are very fully acquainted from the Book of Origins. The heavier duties fell upon them from the twenty-fifth or thirtieth year[3] to the fiftieth of their age, and to discharge these they were to be divided into three military companies. After this period of life they had only to await the casual orders of the superior priests and execute easy commissions. When we remember that all ordinary men had to serve in the army from their twentieth year,[4] we shall understand that the Levites were exempted till they were from twenty-five to thirty years old, only because they were expected to show more dignity and caution in their occupations. Nor can we doubt that the average age at which priests entered upon their office was no earlier.

To discharge these duties the tribe of Levi was reorganised. Previously its three main branches or clans had followed one another in the order Gershon, Kohath, Merari.[5] But when the house of Aaron from the clan of Kohath was raised to the higher sacerdotal dignity, this clan secured the first place. In camp the house of Aaron occupied the place of honour to the east; on the south, close to it, came the camp of the Kohathites; towards the west the Gershonites; towards the north the Merarites.[6] Similarly on the march, the Kohathites had the care of the vessels of the inner Sanctuary; the Gershonites, and in gradation the Merarites, of the more and more external

---

[1] P. 114 sqq.
[2] Num. iii. 14-39, iv. 4-16, x. 17, 21.
[3] The 30th year is always stated in Num. iv. 2-49, the 25th in the supplement viii. 23-26. Both assertions are from the Book of Origins, but the second is manifestly the more accurate. In 1 Chron.
xxiii. 24, 2 Chron. xxxi. 17, we find the 20th, in 1 Chron. xxiii. 3 the 30th.
[4] Num. i. 3.
[5] See more on the point *Hist.* i. 364 sq. and p. 241 sqq., above.
[6] Num. iii. 14-39.

constituents of the Sanctuary.[1] The whole organisation turned upon the pre-eminence of the house of Aaron, but it was founded upon an earlier basis, which can still be clearly recognised.

Those who are ordinarily called Levites, or the inferior priests, are the ones who gradually usurped the place of the earlier house-priests. When Jahveism made its appearance, it had from the first its own priests, and these stood as much above the earlier house-priests as the new religion did above the old. But this new priesthood was at first confined to the prophet Moses himself and Aaron, or at most to these two along with their nearest relatives. The inferior duties were still discharged by the earlier house-priests; and in private houses these long continued to hold office, as has been already described.[2] The efforts of Jahveism, therefore, were everywhere directed in the first instance to transfer the prerogatives of the earlier priests to the Levites, since the less perfect religion would always have found support from the former. And as a fact these efforts must have succeeded tolerably soon. As the whole tribe of Levi learned to gather itself compactly about Jahveism, and the whole of the rest of the nation learned to assemble more and more closely around this new Sanctity, the earlier priests, in public and gradually too in private houses, continually lost ground till they entirely ceased to exist.

At the date of the Book of Origins this transformation had been long completed, nevertheless a manifest reminiscence of it had been clearly enough retained. And in as much as its author conceives and sets forth the whole relation transfigured by the light of the higher religion, he gives us the following account respecting the call of the Levites. Properly all firstborn male children were holy unto Jahveh and to be presented to him as a gift, but he had revealed to Moses his willingness to accept the Levites in their stead, and had surrendered these substitutes to the service of the sons of Aaron. Hence they were also briefly termed *surrendered* servants, i.e. *bondsmen*.[3] This account distinctly presupposes that during an earlier period the first-born males really had been given to Jahveh for some sort of service, and were so far sacred. Without a recollection

---

[1] Num. iv., x. 17, 21, comp. below. Since the Kohathites as the bearers of the most sacred vessels were most in danger of the ban (p. 272), the chief prayers for indulgence are offered on their behalf, Num. iv. 17-20.

[2] P. 263 sq. Comp. Ex. xxiv. 5 with ver. 1.

[3] נְתוּנִים, Num. iii. 1-13, 40-51, viii. 14-19, comp. Ex. xiii. 11-16, and the simpler representation, Num. xviii. 6.

of this having been the fact the narrative would never have originated. For it is impossible to assume that the first-born human males are here mentioned merely on account of an external resemblance, and lest the first-born of domestic animals and the first-fruits of crops should have lost their sacred character. This would be to misunderstand and repudiate the entire historical consciousness of the Book of Origins. The book relates at the same time that the first-born males of every tribe, reckoned from those of one month old upwards, amounted to 22,373, while the number of the Levites was only 22,000; and that the redemption of the balance of 373 first-born was effected at five full shekels of silver a head.[1] We shall see hereafter that we have every reason for believing these numbers not to be imaginary, and it therefore follows that the first-born must once have been accurately counted. If they ever were really considered to belong to the Sanctuary, it would in the next place be impossible to assume that they were originally destined for human sacrifice, for apart from the wholly incredible number, we have already seen that such a purpose could never have been ascribed to Jahveh.[2] Nothing remains, therefore, but the supposition that the first-born had been previously regarded as house-priests, and, according to the Book of Origins, might and ought to have been regarded as perpetually bound to the service of Jahveh, unless the substitution of the Levites—an advantageous change for both parties—had been preferred. If the ancient house-priests were not invariably the first-born,[3] the majority of them were undoubtedly so, and this is sufficient for the above representation. The same conclusion follows from some brief remarks contained in the ancient Book of Covenants.[4] Hence at the consecration of the Levites[5]—it was quite otherwise at the consecration of the priests—the representatives of the community take an active part, in order to transfer to them those prerogatives which they themselves possessed and therefore could transfer to the servants of the Sanctuary. The priests and the national representatives perform the consecration, the former taking the lead all through. Each candidate for consecration was first sprinkled with the effi-

---

[1] What was the average price of an able-bodied slave may be gathered from p. 201 nt. 1, comp. Gen. xxxvii. 28, Ex. xxi. 32, nk. Zach. xi. 12. Children were of much less value, and so an average estimate for all without distinction of age might be tolerably low.

[2] P. 69 sq.

[3] P. 263.

[4] Ex. xxii. 28b [29b], comp. xxiv. 5. The latter passage explains the former, and it is impossible in the former, in spite of its brevity, to think of anything so entirely out of all likelihood as human sacrifice.

[5] Described in the Book of Origins, Num. viii. 5-22.

cacious water of atonement, which should, as it were, remove from him all the impurities of his former life;[1] while a priest, as we have already seen,[2] was sprinkled still more strongly with the sacrificial blood itself. When further his whole body had been shaved[3] and cleaned after the prescribed fashion, the national representatives, standing in front of the Sanctuary, laid their hands on him as though they desired to present him as a sacred gift, which presentation the high-priest then completed by means of the dedication already described.[4] He next offered on his own behalf, one bullock as a whole-offering and another, as an expiatory-offering; he was then brought before the priests, and was once more sanctified by the above dedication, after which he entered upon his office. No doubt a large number were thus consecrated at the same time.

2. It is very remarkable that, according to sundry historical traces, even women must have had certain duties at the Sanctuary similar to those of the Levites. These traces are, it is true, as rare here as in many other cases, yet here, as often elsewhere, they may guide us to a sufficiently secure position. We know that women had to appear and do duty on the east side of the Sanctuary, organised just like the Levites, and therefore at fixed periods;[5] also that metallic mirrors were attached for them to the great washing-basin.[6] Proper sacerdotal functions, whether higher or lower, cannot be ascribed to them. It was characteristic of the whole of Jahveism to confine these to men. But we know from other sources that dances accompanied by singing were performed at the Sanctuary by women,[7] and these mirrors would indicate something of this sort. If numerous women from each of the tribes always took part in these dances on festivals, there must still have been some constantly at the

[1] The water of atonement (ver. 7) would certainly be the same as that which we have already seen twice applied under a slightly different name, p. 151 sqq.
[2] P. 279.
[3] Of course this shaving was only temporary, and had only this one end in view, and therefore had nothing in common with what is spoken of as forbidden on p. 164.
[4] P. 73 sq.
[5] Ex. xxxviii. 8, 1 Sam. ii. 22.
[6] See below. The word במראות, Ex. xxxviii. 8, cannot be understood otherwise than as 'with the mirrors.' These were accordingly of metal like the washing basin, and the latter too may have been polished so that it could serve as a mirror. But the Book of Origins in some now lost passage undoubtedly spoke fully about the women who are only casually mentioned here. Nothing else will explain the abruptness and excessive brevity of this notice. Conjectures like those in Heidenheim's *E. D. V. S.* i. s. 120 sq. are to no purpose.—The LXX it is true understand צבא of *fasts*, and Philo utters some edifying remarks on the passage after his own style, *Vita Mos.* iii. 15. On the other hand the *Protev. Jac.* vii. x. xv. perhaps still contains some better reminiscences; Maria, as a servant presented to the Sanctuary, dances there and prepares the decorations for the temple. Comp. also 2 Bar. x. in Ceriani's *Monum.* i. p. 75.

[7] Ex. xv. 20, Judges xxi. 21. Distinct from this was the male dance at the Sanctuary, Ps. xxx. 12 [11], lxxxvii. 7.

Sanctuary who should know how to lead the dances, and they may have been the same as those who daily performed the sacred music there. That women who sang and played lived there, we know as a certainty,[1] as well as that the culture of the Muses was chiefly left to the women down to the days of David.[2] The singing and playing Miriam,[3] therefore, clearly furnishes us with the original type of these women about the Sanctuary. If in the morning a great festival was celebrated with sacrifices, it always passed towards evening, unless it was an occasion of mourning or penitence, into playing and dancing;[4] and the deep earnestness of Jahveism took care that these performances should remain artistic and grave.

Probably with these women there were also many of the inferior Levites,[5] just as from the time of Solomon the latter seem to have had all the care of the sacred music. In the earliest period the inferior Levites were, it is true, only too much occupied with military service and labours. Nevertheless it is obvious that the duties which the Book of Origins assigns them, as stated above, were regarded as only the most indispensable of their obligations, so that they might be of service to the holy place in many other ways. Without an active sympathy with the great truths of Jahveism, and without an endeavour to serve these by means of all available arts, they never could have become and remained even good inferior priests. We know too that occasionally, in the earlier days, one of their number raised himself to the highest power and offered sacrifice with his own hand, as was the case with Samuel.

3. As soon as conquest and the firm possession of the country secured the external power of the nation, the Levites too acquired increased opportunities for giving themselves up undisturbed to voluntary spiritual occupations. When the forty-eight cities of the conquered land were handed over to the tribe,[6] and in each of them a colony of Levites was settled, probably under the leadership of a priest of the clan of Aaron, they received along with each city a common, where they could pasture their own cattle, and in certain cases sell them to those who were about to offer sacrifice.[7] They had further a share in the prisoners of war,[8] and these they could employ as slaves

---

[1] From the fragment of a Davidic poem, Ps. lxviii. 26 [25]. Women beating drums occur also elsewhere in those regions, Barhebraeus' *Chron. Syr.* p. 216.
[2] See *Hist.* ii. 354 sqq.
[3] *Hist.* ii. 225.
[4] Comp. the description of a similar case, Ex. xxxii. 6.
[5] This may be inferred especially from 1 Sam. ii. 22.
[6] *Hist.* ii. 308 sqq.
[7] Comp. below under the Finances.
[8] According to the Book of Origins, Num. xxxi. 25–47.

in the more menial occupations which in the absence of such assistants they would have had to perform themselves. Even whole cities may have been given them on the conquest of the country whose inhabitants had their lives spared upon condition of their becoming 'hewers of wood and drawers of water,' i.e. the bondsmen of the Levites. The Book of Origins illustrates this at length in the case of the Gibeonites, the dwellers in a town not far from Jerusalem, whose descendants experienced so peculiar a fate under the first two kings that at the date of the composition of the Book of Origins they seem to have been a good deal spoken about.[1] Under such kings as David and Solomon, gifts to the Levites like these were renewed and multiplied. In particular they received at Jerusalem itself a number of hereditary bondsmen who had to perform the lowest duties at the Sanctuary; so that the name *Netûnîm* or *Netînîm*, i.e. Bondsmen, by which the Levites had been previously known, was now appropriated to these, who were not Levites. The particular tasks which were transferred to the latter are no longer known to us. The duties which they had to render were evidently very definitely determined, for we know that one particular establishment of this kind, originating with Solomon and undoubtedly charged with a special form of service, always retained the name of 'the slaves of Solomon.'[2]

Hence from the time of David and Solomon, it was all the more easy for the inferior priests to receive not only a new organisation, but also a higher vocation. The progress of the entire people in power and civilisation elevated them too, and, from the warlike troop of defenders of the Sanctuary, they became peaceful guardians of the great temple at Jerusalem and its treasures—musicians, and artists in its service, instructors and judges scattered throughout the entire country.[3] The progress of their development naturally produced constant efforts on their part to place themselves more on a level

---

[1] BK. Josh. ix. 23, 27, xxi. 17, comp. above, pp. 236, 238.

[2] Ezra ii. 43–54, 55–58, Neh. xi. 3, comp. 1 Chron. ix. 2, Ezra ii. 70, vii. 7, viii. 20, Neh. iii. 26, 31, x. 29 [28], xi. 21. The 'slaves of Solomon' were not so numerous; David is expressly mentioned in Ezra viii. 20, but the passage Ps. lxviii. 19 [18] refers to the same thing; comp. *Jahrbb. der Bibl. Wiss.* iv. s. 54.— We have now a great number of Delphic inscriptions about the sale of slaves to the temple, see Curtius in the *Gött. Nach-* *richten*, 1864, s. 137 sqq.; comp. in the *Quellinschriften*, s. 16.—In like manner at the present time there are eunuchs who have been given by rich men to the Ka'aba at Mecca and to the holy tomb at Medina in order to perform the inferior duties there, and who may never again be employed elsewhere. See Burckhardt's *Travels in Arabia*, i. p. 288 sqq., ii. p. 166 sq., 174, 181, Maltzan's *Wallfahrt nach Mekka*, ii. s. 240 sq.

[3] See *Hist.* iii. 248 sq., iv. 54, *Die Dichter des A. Bs.* ia. s. 274 sq.

with the superior priests, if not in regard to occupation at least in respect to dignity; so that the Deuteronomist no longer gives prominence to the rigid separation between hereditary superior and inferior priests. Indeed, in the later days of the kingdom of Judah, an attempt seems to have been made to place the mere 'Levites' on a level even with the sacrificial priests. Otherwise Ezekiel would not have insisted so peremptorily on the maintenance of the ancient distinction between the two divisions of the sacerdotal tribe.[1]

But if the Levites from David's time formed out of their midst a close company of the most practised musicians, the regular priests nevertheless always retain the prerogative of blowing the trumpets, the ancient instrument with which they, at the head of the army, had formerly during the days of Moses and Joshua, aroused the nation to battle and led them to victory.[2] With it in later times they still invariably summoned the community to the Sanctuary,[3] and commenced the worship, so that the Book of Origins deems it worth while to explain it at length, and to describe its proper character.[4] The Chronicler, again, is everywhere emphatic in declaring that the trumpets appertain to them alone; and the belief in the miraculous efficacy of their blasts in front of an engaging army was revived entirely anew even during the wars of the Maccabees.[5]

C. The High-priest.

1. In the high-priest, or as he alone was originally called 'the priest,'[6] the entire sacerdotal tribe was firmly bound up as a whole; and precisely this rigid unity which the whole upper and lower priesthood attained in him, became ultimately a main characteristic of the priesthood generally in Israel. The existence of this single personal and hereditary unity at its head was of course due in the first instance to the primitive tribal constitution of the nation. Aaron, or after his death, his eldest son Eleazar, stood at first at the head of his tribe, only in virtue of the ancient custom which gave every other

---

[1] Ezek. xliv. 6–16. Tolerably early they liked to be called 'priests,' as Ezra viii. 24 comp. 18 sq.; and again, in the last days of the second temple, the Levitical singers contended for the privilege of wearing the sacerdotal robe. *Hist.* vi. s. 556 [German edition].

[2] Of which the narrative Josh. vi. 4 sqq. only desires to give the most illustrious instance.

[3] P. 130.

[4] Num. x. 1–10.

[5] As may be inferred from the vivid delineations of the first Book of the Maccabees. How highly the later priests esteemed these trumpets may be seen from the picture of them on the triumphal arch of Titus; comp. Josephus, *Antiq.* iii. 12. 6.

[6] P. 261.

tribe its prince.[1] But in so far as he was the head of the sacerdotal tribe, he comprehended in himself in the highest degree all its rights and its duties, and became in the second place emphatically the personal and perpetual representative to the other tribes of the requirements of Jahveism, so far as it had ever legally become the national religion. And as a fact it was principally the need of more pronounced representation, before the whole people, of Jahveism and the priesthood in its service which caused the permanent necessity for the priesthood to have at its head an hereditary prince. The same need which had called forth for Jahveism generally a sacerdotal tribe,[2] led further to strongly concentrating all sacerdotal authority in a single person. In the same way Christianity, so long as it penetrated many nations like a foreign force, without having yet taken complete possession of a single nation, was compelled to crystallise and stiffen in a Romish priesthood and ultimately in the omnipotence of a Pope. And it is an astonishing fact that the succession of the high priesthood of Israel remained through all the centuries in the same house, and that even in a token such as this we may see the tough thread of a most uniform development which was nowhere possible in Antiquity save in this religion.[3]

It is true that the hereditary power of the high-priest within his own house down to the time of Solomon was not much more assured or widely extended than that of any other head of a tribe. From Aaron there were immediately descended two families, Eleazar and Ithamar. This Ithamar appears in the Book of Origins as legally exercising power and superintendence next after Eleazar, or as the superintendent of the inferior two-thirds of the entire tribe[4] and their occupations,[5] and the history shows that the descendants of Ithamar, for about a whole century after, possessed the same eminent dignity.[6] Under David and Solomon we find, along with these two families, two high-priests simultaneously recognised,[7] of whom the one may have taken a somewhat higher rank than the other, and had charge of different business. But the dignity was always retained within these two branches of the house of Aaron, and after the later days of Solomon it reverted solely

---

[1] P. 244.
[2] P. 262.
[3] It is a second question, which did not previously arise, whether among other nations the entire priesthood developed in a similar manner, e.g. in Peru. See G. Müller's *Amerik. Urrelig.* s. 386 sq.

[4] P. 282.
[5] Num. iv. 28, 33, comp. ver. 16.
[6] See *Hist.* ii. 409 sqq.
[7] 2 Sam. viii. 17, xx. 25, 1 Kings iv. 4; for the third priest mentioned 2 Sam. xx. 26, see *Hist.* iii. 268 sq.

to the elder branch of Eleazar. The changes which took place during the last century before the destruction of the second temple hardly concern us here.

2. But just because the essence of the entire priesthood of the community of Jahveh was concentrated in the one high-priest, whatever lofty qualities were expected or required of the priesthood in general, would be most strongly and peremptorily expected and required in him.

His whole being and life, yet more than that of the remaining priests, ought accordingly to maintain inviolate the highest purity. Not even on account of the death of his parents might he pass into a different condition, and manifest tokens of disturbance and grief, or leave the sanctuary. The virgin whom he took in matrimony must be a relative belonging to his own tribe.[1]

Yet while he, at any rate, alone of the whole nation, retained as much as possible a life of uniform unruffled purity, he had perpetually to attempt to expel all disturbances of the original purity and sanctity of the whole community, and banish every cloud in the clear heaven of the grace of Jahveh, who dwelt, mysterious and invisible, within the community. This he must do whenever there was serious occasion for it; especially, however, at the annual feast of the atonement, which will be described hereafter. Perpetually pure and joyous himself, he had perpetually to represent, within the consecrated circle of the community, the divine purity and joy. Nor is it difficult to imagine that, so long as the usages which grew up about him had not yet lost their first vigorous life, but were rather being developed for the first time, an unusual degree of spiritual power would be required to discharge such functions.

In the next place, oracles were expected from him. If the law tolerated this in his case,[2] if the Book of Origins even represents them as given him by Jahveh himself, it must be remembered, in addition to what has been said above,[3] that after the death of Moses this prerogative of the high-priest formed an indispensable constituent in the earliest constitution of Jahveism. For this constitution provided the realm with no unbroken line of authority from which a final decision could be sought in difficulties otherwise insoluble, except that of the high-priest. The possibility of obtaining a final decision at some permanent locality is an indispensable requirement of every kingdom. Antiquity everywhere endeavoured to

---

[1] Lev. xxi. 10-15.   [2] P. 275.   [3] P. 258.

obtain this by means of oracles, and in regard to only too many things. The high-priest, before the human monarchy arose, was the sole durable authority competent to give such a decision; and his high position would suffice to secure him from any suspicion of misuse of the oracular power intrusted to him. The questions put to him could not relate to the fundamental principles of religion, since the community was already in existence, and had been as fully developed by Moses as was at that time possible, but only to matters of national need and uncertainty or to momentous controversies in the community. And we still see clearly, from certain narratives, how much this oracle of the 'sacred lot' was actually employed in the earliest times, what implicit confidence was felt in it alike by the individual national leaders and the entire community, what good effect it often had in allaying disputes between powerful nobles,[1] and how momentous its influence often was in determining the fate of the nation.[2] Such a feeling springing up from below could not fail to exercise for a long time an elevating influence on the sacerdotal princes themselves. They knew that they bore the whole nation, as it were, on their shoulders and on their breast, and a purer sacred feeling might readily seize and enlighten them in solemn moments. Still, however, the occasions when this kind of oracle was sought after prevented the answer from coming from the spontaneous instinct of the spirit, whence the pure prophetic oracle of a Moses and of his genuine followers issued. If this was impossible, it was needful at once to seek the aid of an external medium. No doubt, the greater part of the nation, from the time of Moses to that of David and Solomon, and to some extent still later,[3] was always ready to look upon a great priest as an inexhaustible source of oracles; and even down to the time of Christ a word of the high-priest was readily deemed prophetic.[4] But since this oracle, at the time when it became legalised, was compelled to attach itself to an external medium, and could accordingly only maintain itself in the character of a final remnant of heathenism, it fell into disuse in the times succeeding Solomon in proportion as the power of pure prophecy was developed.

---

[1] Prov. xviii. 18; comp. xvi. 33.
[2] Such narratives as 1 Sam. x. 19-22, xiv. 41 sq., 1K. Josh. vii. 14-18, do no more than show how frequent was the use of this oracle in the earliest times; even freer representations, like those in the Book of Origins, Josh. vii., only become possible in consequence of this. In the same way mention of the lot is made in many passages in Homer; and if anyone is of opinion that the Greeks occupied a higher level in this respect, let him compare what Plato says in his *Polit.* v. 8 *ad fin.* and 9 *ad fin.*
[3] Hos. iii. 4 at any rate belongs here.
[4] John xi. 50.

3. The high-priest's hereditary possession of the oracle, his official duties, and the princely authority which was inherent in him, were also the causes which determined his external adornment, as it is accurately described in the Book of Origins.[1] His under-garments were the same as those of his 'brothers,' the ordinary priests.[2] Over them, when on duty, he wore the following magnificent attire:

First there was an upper garment of dark-blue byssus, woven like the under-garment in a single piece, but without sleeves; it had at the opening for the neck a collar woven thicker than the rest, so that it might not be torn in being put on.[3] On the lower skirt it had little tassels like pomegranates, of the three brilliant colours of the Sanctuary,[4] each tassel alternating with a little bell of gold. The sound which the high-priest, therefore, made in walking would serve, when he entered the place to which his duty called him, and him alone, viz. the innermost Sanctuary, to inform the God who reigned there inviolate of the approach of a man who ventured to tread that ground, but might not enter unannounced. Some such meaning of this, in itself strange decoration, is indicated by the Book of Origins itself; and this is explained by what will be described below in connection with the estimation in which the Holy of Holies was held.[5] It also follows, from the position where these little bells must have been attached, that this upper garment, at any rate behind, hung down far below the simple priestly dress. It is the proper state or princely robe with flowing train, such as princes wore during peace on solemn occasions,[6] only furnished with these bells in accordance with the special functions of the high-priest. In front the robe might have been somewhat shorter than the under-garment, so as to display the girdle of the latter.

Over this long robe a short covering for the shoulders was

---

[1] In the *Testamentum Levi* viii., its amount is reduced to exactly seven articles.
[2] P. 277.
[3] The expression כְּפִי תַחְרָא Ex. xxviii. 31-35, xxxix. 22-26, is always translated subsequently to the Targum of Oukelos, 'like the upper opening of a coat of mail.' The word may then be softened from תחרך and correspond to θώραξ.
[4] See below.
[5] A somewhat different notion in regard to this tinkling of the bells occurs Sir. xlv. 9, viz. that the Lord was thereby reminded of the people. But this is less obvious. According to the *Protev. Jac.* viii. there were just twelve bells. The bells of the Brahmins are similar.
[6] Where מְעִיל occurs in historical narratives it never denotes anything but the princely robe in time of peace, worn also in judging, Is. vi. 1. In itself it must have had originally a more general meaning, like בֶּגֶד, and therefore the derivative verb מָעַל, like בָּגַד, means 'to play under the *covering*,' to cheat, act unfairly. But wherever it now occurs it always signifies a robe of the kind we have described.

worn, and this was the first thing which was distinctively sacerdotal. It was a sort of short mantle, termed an *Ephod*, a name which originally signified the same as mantle or covering cloth,[1] but which now occurs only in a sacerdotal sense. It simply consisted of two shoulder-flaps, i.e. of cloth without sleeves, which covered little more than the two shoulders, and did not hang down much below them either before or behind. It simply surmounted, like an ornament, the long robe, from which it seemed almost inseparable.[2] The two pieces of which it consisted, however, were not separated somewhere under the shoulders,[3] but on the breast and back. At the top, the ends were only slightly connected together. Below, however, they were held together by a girdle, which was certainly very broad and a main feature of the attire, and without which the state covering would not be assumed.[4] It was different in kind from the girdle of the plain costume,[5] and bore quite another name; it certainly had not the hanging ends and resembled rather a mere broad band.—A covering for the shoulders such as this might also be worn by other priests; not indeed, according to the Book of Origins, which, with its constant preference for regularity in all arrangements of a national character, assigns such a distinguishing mark to the high-priest alone; but we know from other sources that any priest, or even any man invested with sacerdotal dignity, might wear on his shoulders such a garment made of plain linen.[6] For

---

[1] אֵפוֹד seems now to stand in Hebrew without any root, but it is indisputable that it is only an extremely ancient dialectic form of ببز, in which even the verbal formation is parallel, and thus corresponds to *pallium*; and in so far as it should be thought of as a short tight mantle, the LXX translate it very suitably by ἐπωμίς in the Pentateuch, and ὠμοφόριον 1 Sam. ii. 18. The Arabic word is wanting in Dozy's *Dictionnaire des Noms de Vêtements*.

[2] Hence the standing phrase מְעִיל הָאֵפֹד, 'the mantel-robe,' Ex. xxviii. 31, comp. ver. 6 sq., xxxix. 22, comp. ver. 2-4; otherwise Lev. viii. 7.

[3] Which is the opinion expressed by Joh. Braun in the huge learned work *De Vestitu Sacerdotum Hebræorum*, p. 466 sqq. He thinks that the covering for the shoulders consisted merely of small lappets on the front of the dress, the space between which was occupied by the oracle-bag. But according to Ex. xxviii. 28, xxxix. 21,

the latter was fixed not in, but on, the ephod; nor was it indispensable that an ephod should have such a bag at all. That the covering for the shoulders rather hung down below it appears also from Ex. xxviii. 27, xxxix. 20.

[4] This is plain from the clear description of this girdle, Ex. xxviii. 8, xxix. 5, xxxix. 5, Lev. viii. 7; it was only this which, as it were, made the ephod an ephod, hence the new verb אָפַד. It is plain also from 1 Sam. ii. 18, 2 Sam. vi. 14, that the girding was a main feature with the ephod. The name of this girdle, חֵשֶׁב, should be compared with حزم, the word חָבַשׁ is equivalent to חָשַׁב, to bind.

[5] P. 278.

[6] 1 Sam. xxii. 18, 2 Sam. vi. 14. The levitical Nazirite Samuel when a boy wore a little sacerdotal robe merely as a present, but received the ephod as a matter of course, 1 Sam. ii. 18 sq.

this very reason the one worn by the high-priest was distinguished in a twofold manner. In the first place it, as well as the girdle, was artificially worked with gold thread and with twisted threads of the three colours as well as white. In the second place, on each shoulder an onyx was fixed in a golden setting, on each of which six of the twelve names of the tribes of Israel were cut. These were to be memorial stones of the twelve tribes whom the high-priest represented, whose wellbeing he bore on his shoulders as it were in affectionate care, and in whose united interest he acted at the Sanctuary.

Somewhere about the middle, on the front side of this covering for the shoulders, was attached the bag which in later times has become the least comprehensible article of the high-priest's adornment. We must before all things remark that the article was essentially a bag, as on the one hand its name *Chóshen* declares,[1] and on the other its description proves. For it was a span in length and in breadth, had four corners, and, as we distinctly know, was double. If, however, this last expression still seems ambiguous, it is fully explained by an inner side, i.e. the side of the article turned towards the breast, being spoken of.[2] What distance apart from one another the two sides of the bag were, we do not know; but it was plainly no more than was necessary to grasp with the hand and to draw out what was preserved within. For we know further that there was something placed inside the article.[3] It was the receptacle of the *Urim* and *Thummim*. Now these objects, which as something placed inside must have been quite capable of being grasped in the hand, are not described either elsewhere in the Old Testament, or yet in the Book of Origins at this very passage—an omission which is very surprising, since in the case of all the other separate articles which belonged to the attire of the high-priests, the Book of Origins describes them at length. It is also manifest from many clear tokens that the words *Urim* and *Thummim* of themselves denote nothing save the oracle, and declare nothing about its kind or the instruments by which it was to be obtained. Alike the formation of the words

---

[1] חֹשֶׁן (in Josephus pronounced 'Εσσενέ), is really only a dialectic form for כִּיס, i.e. pocket, bag, a receptacle in which something may be preserved. No doubt the early translators no longer conceive of it so simply, and are manifestly embarrassed how to translate the word correctly; but we must go back to the original meaning. The word 'bosom,' Prov. xvi. 33, gives the best explanation. The translation λόγιον, *oracle*, in the LXX and Josephus, *Antiq.* iii. 7. 5, is a mere paraphrase.

[2] Ex. xxviii. 26, comp. 16; xxxix. 19, comp. 9.

[3] For the meaning of נָתַן אֶל־ Ex. xxviii. 30, Lev. viii. 8, see *Lehrb.* § 217 c.

and their meaning carry us back to an earlier epoch,[1] and they were undoubtedly employed long anterior to Moses in denoting a kind of oracle. Of themselves they mean only 'clearness (i.e. revelation) and correctness,' denoting therefore a clear correct utterance, a correct and trustworthy revelation. The same thing, accordingly, is also more briefly explained by Urîm,[2] less frequently by Thummîm.[3] But we know, from the early days when the oracle of the high-priest was in great repute, not only that the lot was used to finally decide disputes, but that it was regarded as something dependent on heavenly influence.[4] This all agrees with the 'judgment' of the high-priest too well for us to doubt by what means the decision was obtained. That the oracle of the high-priest could not from its very nature be entirely unfettered—that it needed an external medium—has already been remarked;[5] and of all external mediums by which a disclosure may be drawn forth, the one nearest at hand and least objectionable is the lot.[6] If, moreover, we compare the cases where the history speaks of the use of the sacerdotal oracle, it appears in the first place that it gave answers only to questions which were put in a definite shape, or else gave no answer at all; and in the second place that its answers were generally very brief, either affirming or denying, sometimes mentioning names, more rarely giving fuller indications.[7] This is most readily explained if two pebbles of different colours were shaken as lots in the 'bosom' or bag, and one of them drawn out; while any un-

---

[1] The words Urîm and Thummîm appear in the existing language only as proper names; תם occurs nowhere else in connection with oracles; even the use of the plural refers us back to an earlier linguistic period. Hence the Book of Origins explains these ancient names by a word from ordinary speech, כמשׁפט 'judgment,' Ex. xxviii. 15, 30, comp. Prov. xvi. 33. Nevertheless the Arabic تمائم, plural تمائم, Imrialquais M. ver. 16, with meaning of amulet, as well as فال, with the meaning of fortune, Journ. As. 1856. ii. p. 454, are possibly a relic of the use of these words for sacred things.

[2] Num. xxvii. 21, 1 Sam. xxviii. 6. From the latter passage it appears also that in contradistinction to this 'clear oracle' there was the dream-oracle, p. 259, which itself needed an interpretation.

[3] In the passage 1 Sam. xiv. 41; comp. Hist. iii. 35 sq.

[4] Prov. xvi. 33, xviii. 18.

[5] P. 291.

[6] Thus it also plays an important part in the religion of Confucius, which in other respects is so rational. Comp. too for the ψῆφοι μαντικαί at Delphi, Eudokia's Violarium, p. 349; Sûr. v. 4; and Journ. As. 1838, i. p. 226 sqq. On the other hand, the gleaming image of truth which the Egyptian superior judge wore as an ornament to the neck (Diodorus Sic. i. 48, 75) is almost too remote to be compared. We should have to suppose that the soothsayer sought for oracles in certain appearances in the jewels fixed above, as the Syrian priests did in the perspiration on their idols (Lucian De dea Syra, x. xxxvi. sq.). The Chron. Samarit. xviii. xxxviii. certainly thinks of a sudden growing brighter or dimmer of the individual jewels; but these jewels had a far more direct significance, and the seat of the oracle lay elsewhere.

[7] The particular cases besides those already mentioned are the following:— Judges i. 1, xx. 18, 27 sq.; 1 Sam. x. 19-22, xiv. 36 sqq., xxviii. 6, xxx. 7 sq.; 2 Sam. ii. 1, v. 17-25.

favourable premonitory symptom or disposition of the priest may have altogether prevented the trying of the lot and seeking an answer.[1] On such an occasion there may have been sundry preparations and arrangements of which we can no longer frame an idea. Personal acuteness and watchfulness on the side of the priest must undoubtedly have played as important a part as faith on the side of the questioners, and of the person to whom they applied for the decision. The main portion of the charm undoubtedly rested on the knowledge that this was the way in which, during the lofty period of the founding of the community, the most momentous decisions had been given through Aaron or Eleazar. If, however, the contents of the bag consisted, as we have supposed, of two small pebbles, in themselves of insignificant value, and possessing their worth only through the power of the oracle, a closer acquaintance with which was preserved only in narrow sacerdotal circles, then we can understand why they were not further described in the Book of Origins.

Such a medium for giving oracles—a pouch containing lots fastened in front of the covering for the shoulders—was indeed possessed by every priest who deemed himself competent to utter oracles; and, as at the moment when he was about to utter one, he must necessarily assume the covering for the shoulders, it became customary to speak of this garment in place of the sacerdotal oracle.[2] But that of the high-priest, who, according to the Book of Origins, alone should wear it, was decorated with extraordinary splendour to befit his dignity. The bag itself was to be made of the same material as the covering for the shoulders, but on its front side there gleamed from a golden setting twelve different jewels, arranged after the series of the twelve tribes in four rows, each being engraved with the name of a tribe. The twelve jewels are here named separately,[3] and although some of the names are now obscure to us, it certainly appears from the entire enumeration that such stones as the *topaz*, *smaragd* (emerald), *sapphire*, and *jasper* were widely distributed during the earliest times under the same Semitic names.—The bag was secured to the front of the covering for the shoulders both above and below. Above, at the

---

[1] Or if there were three pebbles they may have been distinguished by different ways of writing the sacred name יהוה, as was done by the Gnostics, Bellermann's *Abraxasgemmen*, i. s. 35. Many possibilities may be imagined here.—But the later writers were in the dark about the whole thing; according to Josephus, who describes the way of using it very confusedly, *Antiq.* iii. 8. 9, it had disappeared 200 years before his time, but rather was it wanting all through the period of the second temple, *Hist.* v. 171 sq.

[2] 1 Sam. xxiii. 9, xxx. 7 sq.

[3] Ex. xxviii. 17–21, xxxix. 10–14; comp. *Gött. Gel. Anz.* 1862, s. 1816 sq.

extremities of the bag, there were two golden rings, from which two chains elaborately woven out of gold were carried up to two golden buckles attached with hooks on either shoulder to the covering. Below, were two other golden rings on the inner corners of the bag, from which a dark-blue string passed through two gold rings, which were attached at the place where the two sides of the covering for the shoulder met upon the broad band.[1] The ornamentation of the entire fastenings of the bag was accordingly greater above than below.

This decoration of the oracle the high-priest was always to wear when in office, not merely when he was applied to for a decision. He had therefore to bear the twelve tribes alike on his shoulders and on his breast (his heart), to comprehend them equally in his love and his care. Finally, his head was adorned with a turban, which seems to have been distinguished from that of the ordinary priest by more artistic winding of the byssus;[2] and also by a gold plate bearing the inscription 'holy unto Jahveh,' and fastened to the front of the forehead with a dark-blue band. This was the most distinctive token of princely rank, so far as it appertained to a priest of Jahveh. It is itself termed the sacred consecration,[3] and indeed, this is the consecration, without which no true dominion of any sort can be conceived, and which must exist in all the more abundance, the higher and the more spiritual the rule of an individual man ought to be. The high-priest, however, ought perpetually to be the holy man of Jahveh, in a way in which no other man in the community was. It has already been noticed that an anointing of the head was connected therewith,[4] but in the case of the high-priest this was only the foundation already given by his dignity as a sacrificial priest.

As the prince of a tribe the high-priest had the same right

---

[1] Here again the representation of Joh. Braun is too far removed from the meaning of the words Ex. xxviii. 26-28, xxxix. 19-21.

[2] מִצְנֶפֶת, in opposition to מִגְבָּעָה, further described by Josephus, *Antiq.* iii. 7. 6.

[3] נֵזֶר הַקֹּדֶשׁ, Ex. xxix. 6; comp. xxviii. 36-38, xxxix. 30 sq.; the correct explanation of it is found Lev. viii. 9, xxi. 12. How the later writers regarded this πέταλον may be seen from the Apocal. and the *Protev. Jac.* v.—Totally distinct from נֵזֶר, which signifies merely consecration, and may have been nothing but a gold plate fixed in front of the forehead, is the עֲטֶרֶת, i.e. the proper *crown*. The latter is essentially a *circlet* like an encircling wall, hence is an image of a town, and so becomes the symbol also of the lord of the town. of the king. It was accordingly most suitable for a king like the ruler of Ammon whose kingdom extended outward from a town, 2 Sam. xii. 30, not for a king of Israel; and if Saul, according to the narrative 2 Sam. i. 10, already wore some ornament on his head, it was only the ancient נֵזֶר of the high-priest, which was simply connected with anointing, which equally belonged to the ancient high-priests. This supplements what is said *Hist.* iii. 272.

[4] P. 279.

to bear a sceptre as any other tribal prince; and that this originally was done, and that the old sceptre of Aaron was preserved for a long time afterwards, at any rate in the Sanctuary, must be inferred as certain from a variety of indications.[1] But the Book of Origins no longer regards this sceptre as a proper constituent of the high-priest's adornment. In fact, it only denotes the power of compulsion, and is therefore more appropriate to a prince with whom spiritual power is not the one closest at hand and most employed. On the other hand, the decorative symbol of holy consecration on the head became so characteristic a mark of the high-priest that he was thereby sufficiently distinguished from the other tribal princes, and for a long period no one else in the nation seemed worthy of a decoration even distantly resembling this.

The full dignity which invested him as representative of the community at the Sanctuary required finally that he should daily offer with his own hand a sacrifice on his own behalf, just as elsewhere daily sacrifice is offered for the king. We have already seen that this particular sacrifice maintained itself for a long period without its primitive simplicity being altered.[2]

It will further be easily understood that for occasions when the high-priest although living did not discharge his functions, he had a representative, who comes into greater prominence later on as the *second (high) priest*.[3] It was also the custom to call the heads of the twenty-four sacerdotal houses,[4] even if they were no longer on active duty, particularly if they were of peculiar dignity, 'arch-priests,' or sacerdotal princes.[5]

3. MAINTENANCE OF THE PRIESTS AND OF THE SANCTUARY.

THE FIRST-FRUITS AND THE TITHES.

It is not unimportant to consider, in the last instance, what were the means of subsistence possessed by this sacerdotal tribe. That the nation would have to provide for its maintenance in some way or other is, it is true, presupposed as a matter of course, but is also expressed clearly enough in the declaration 'Levi shall have no inheritance,' i.e. no such earthly property 'as the remaining tribes,' a declaration with which is most closely

---

[1] See *Hist.* ii. 19, 180.
[2] P. 117.
[3] כֹּהֵן הַמִּשְׁנֶה, 2 Kings xxv. 18 (Jer. lii. 24).
[4] P. 276.
[5] For the first case see Ezra viii. 24; x. 5, Neh. xii. 7, ἀρχιερεῖς, Josephus, *Antiq.* xx. 8. 8, and often in the New Testament; for the second case see *die drei ersten Evang.* s. 289.

connected the second, 'Jahveh shall be his inheritance.'[1] The priests therefore were not to have assigned to them, like the rest of the nation, the cultivation of the soil, nor in general to devote themselves to external acquisition. It was theirs to protect the true God alone in having perpetually to maintain and perpetually to advance his truths in this community. This is the invisible estate which is allotted to them for cultivation, not for their own immediate advantage, but for that of the community. But on this very account the community is bound to support them in such a way that they can live free for their vocation, without being anxious to acquire external goods. At any rate, so soon as the thing needed is not to lay the first foundation of a new constitution and religion, but to maintain what has been laid, an arrangement will be made to meet this particular case.

The priests would also have to receive and dispose of a great deal which did not directly serve to satisfy their own needs. The daily sacrificial service already described,[2] which was celebrated for the whole nation, required no slight expenditure. The maintenance, and even the first establishment, of the Sanctuary and of all the appliances which belonged to it, which the priests had to guard, required levies which it was the duty of the people alone to contribute.[3] If a correct estimation is to be made of the revenues of the priesthood of Israel, the needful expenditure on behalf of the Sanctuary itself must be taken into account; for, apart from extraordinary contributions from the nation, such as were made, e.g. at the first erection of the holy place, they had to defray this from their own income.[4] We shall then find that proper but not extravagant provision for the priesthood was made by the law.—We will now pass in review the particular sources of this revenue, having regard to their historical origin.

1. We must consider the first and earliest contributions to be those which were originally due to the spontaneous affection and thankfulness of the nation, but which gradually became fixed by custom and law and assumed the nature of taxes. This we can at once see to have been the case in regard to one of the most important of this contribution, viz. the *tithes*. To conse-

---

[1] The two declarations are closely connected, nevertheless the Deuteronomist is the first to bring forward the latter everywhere into prominence; Num. xviii. 20, 21-24, xxvi. 62;—Deut. x. 9, xii. 12, xiv. 27, 29, xviii. 1 sq.; Josh. xiii. 14, 33, xviii. 7; comp. Ezek. xliv. 28. Even according to the earliest legislation Israel 'was not to appear before Jahveh with empty hands' on festivals, Ex. xxiii. 15 b, xxxiv. 20; Deut. xvi. 16 sq.
[2] P. 114 sqq.
[3] Just as must be the case with religions of a more or less heathen character, Ex. xxxii. 2 sq.
[4] Hence disputes might arise on the point, comp. 2 Kings xii. 5 [4] sqq., and *Hist.* iv. 139 sqq.

crate to the Sanctuary in pure thankfulness towards God the tenth of all annual profit, was a primitive tradition among the Canaanites, Phœnicians, and Carthaginians.[1] The custom, accordingly, very early passed over to Israel; and when it is now related of Abraham and Jacob that they promised and paid tithes,[2] this is no doubt to present a model for their descendants and therefore for the people of the community of Jahveh; but it can as little be denied that tithes as a Canaanitish custom made their appearance in the primitive times, and might readily therefore be ascribed to all the tribal patriarchs. The Mosaic constitution introduced nothing new in this respect beyond the decree that they should be for the benefit of the Levites; nevertheless, so far as we know, it was the Book of Origins which made the first attempt to establish them on a legal basis. It declared that the tenth part of all the annual useful products of the soil, as corn, wine, fruit, as well as one-tenth of all new-born domestic animals, and therefore for the first time reckoned under the herdsman's staff, were due to the Sanctuary. The owner might redeem, i.e. replace by money to his own advantage, the vegetable tithes, if he were willing to pay an additional fifth of their value; but those of the cattle (since the priests could not well do without them on account of the public sacrifices) were regarded as irredeemable, and also (to obviate deceit) as unexchangeable, so that if any case of deceit were discovered, the owner forfeited at the same time the animal which he sought to give in exchange.[3] It was the duty of the inferior Levites, who were scattered throughout the whole country, to collect the tithes, and they had to apply them in the first instance for their own benefit, giving, however, the tenth part of these tithes to the superior priests, and bringing this to the place where the latter lived. It was this alone which fully consecrated the sacred employment of all property collected by the Levites and applied in the first instance for their use.[4]—Nevertheless, this institution, though established in the earliest days, seems

---

[1] Also among the Lydians (comp. *Hist.* i. 278 sq.) according to Nikolaus of Damascus in C. Müller's *Fragm. Hist. Gr.*, iii. p. 371; and among the Arabs before Mohammed, according to the Scholia to Hârit's *M.* ver. 69; among the Greeks it depended more on free-will, according to Xen. *Anab.* v. 3. 5, 10, 12.

[2] In the primitive narrative Gen. xiv. 20, where, however, the whole remark refers only to the tenth part of the military plunder then taken; also in the Fourth Narrator, Gen. xxviii. 22.

[3] Num. xviii. 21–24; Lev. xxvii. 29–33; the one passage must be supplemented from the other. Deuteronomy, quite in the spirit of the earlier legislation, adds the tithes of oil in the passages quoted below, comp. Num. xviii. 12.—Allusion is made to idolatrous dedication of tithes and first-fruits in Hos. ix. 1.

[4] Num. xviii. 23–32; this explains the passage 1 Sam. i. 21, in accordance with the more perfect reading of the LXX; comp. *Hist.* ii. 421 *ut* 2.

to have fallen again into disuse in the times succeeding Solomon. The Deuteronomist, at least, regards the tithes as a gift which man ought to make rather from spontaneous thankfulness towards God than from compulsion. The people were, if possible, to bring them like any other thank-offering, direct to the (great) sacred place, either in kind or in the shape of a pecuniary equivalent; and should a man fail to bring them for two years in succession, then he was at any rate not to delay bringing the whole sum in the third year.[1] The new imposts of the regal dominion had probably caused these more ancient taxes to be neglected, so that they reverted to their original condition of being free gifts. Nor is there any mention in Deuteronomy of animal tithes, and it is needful for Malachi to exhort his contemporaries against practising deception in bringing even the vegetable tithes. But in general, during the period of the second temple, when under the dominion of foreigners, it must have been more needful to seek to accomplish all aims by the spontaneous good-will of the laity.[2]

Still more natural than the paying of tithes seemed the bringing of the *first-fruits*. That man can safely and happily enjoy all the bounties which the soil produces only when he has gratefully consecrated its first shoots and fruits to the Deity as though they were too holy for himself,[3] was a view which prevailed in other parts of the ancient world besides Canaan. In like manner the products of the spring were deemed among many early races to be peculiarly holy; and how powerful such feelings of awe must have been in Israel during its primitive days will be explained below under the Easter festival. Yet a *ver sacrum*, as it was superstitiously vowed and offered by heathen kingdoms, though only in particular years,[4] could never be sanctioned by Jahveism; just as in general it established from the first a vital distinction between itself and heathenism in permitting individuals to make and fulfil onerous

---

[1] Deut. xiv. 22-29, comp. xii. 6, 11, 17 (also ver. 26), xxvi. 12-15; the last passage is most clearly expressed; it however permits, according to ver. 12, the tithes also to be paid at will at the local towns.

[2] Mal. iii. 8-10, comp. Neh. x. 36-40 [35-39]. xii. 44-47, xiii. 12. The Pharisaical extension of the tithes to all possible vegetables, as well as their doubling or even trebling, originated in an interpretation of the legal passages not warranted by history; although this penetrated even into the *Chron. Samarit.* xxxviii.;

comp. *Hist.* v. 166 sq. 196 sq. If, however, the tithes flowed in so plentifully during the final period, there is less reason for wondering at an avaricious strife having broken out over them among the priests themselves, a quarrel which Josephus indicates only too indistinctly, *Antiq.* xx. 8. 8; 9. 2.

[3] Comp. the beautiful image Jer. ii. 3; they existed also among the Arabs, Sûr. vi. 142.

[4] Livy *Hist.* xxii. 9 sq., xxxiv. 44; comp. Herod. vii. 197.

vows, but never allowing the kingdom, i.e. the priests in the name of the whole people, to enter into such engagements. All the more reason had it for making arrangements for a regular delivery of the first-fruits. These were to be brought to the Sanctuary from all the products of the soil, including oil and must. This is already commanded in the Book of Covenants;[1] but even the Book of Origins determines no fixed measure for them,[2] so that it was in the main left to the free-will of individuals. A portion of the corn just threshed on the barn-floor, and a cake from its first dough, must be presented as an offering by every household :[3] a practice which manifestly survived from the original Passover (see below), and like everything of the kind can only have referred to the barley-harvest, as the earliest in the year. The first-born males of sacrificial domestic animals are demanded on the eighth day after birth by the same Book of Covenants ;[4] the Book of Origins adds the pecuniary value of the unclean ass, with the provision that if its owners were unwilling to redeem it, it must be at once strangled as something forfeited to the Sanctuary.[5] If the Book of Covenants demands for the Sanctuary in corresponding manner the human male first-born,[6] this will be sufficiently well understood from the explanations already given;[7] still the Book of Origins expressly represents the inferior Levites as having taken their place as servants of the Sanctuary, so that five pieces of silver were all that was legally required for their redemption.[8] In the next place all first-fruits were so far deemed more holy than the tithes that they came directly to the sacrificial priests, not to the ordinary Levites ;[9] and in the houses of the former, they might be eaten only by persons

---

[1] Ex. xxii. 28 [29], where in the first part רֵאשִׁית is to be inserted with the LXX, and further on מְלֵאָה is to be understood of ripening corn and דִּמְעַ of wine. The expression Ex. xxiii. 19 a is shown by the context to refer rather to the Whitsuntide festival.—A fine reminiscence of how they used to be brought in procession with bulls, flutes, and pigeons, occurs *M. בִּכּוּרִים*, iii. 1–7.

[2] Num. xviii. 12–14 ; nevertheless the amount is to be determined from the passage explained on p. 166 as well as from Deut. xxvi. 2.

[3] Num. xv. 17–21. The LXX translate עֲרִיסֹת by φύραμα; and Paul is fond of allusions to it, 1 Cor. v. 7, Rom. xi. 16.

[4] Ex. xxii. 28 [29] sq.

[5] Num. xviii. 15–19 ; Ex. xiii. 11–16.

[6] In the brief expression Ex. xxii. 28

[29] b. But to avoid understanding this short phrase as though the first-born human males of Israel were required for the sacrificial fire, comp. what is said on p. 283 sqq. No doubt when the first productions of all other things were required for sacrifice it was only a short step to the bloody sacrifice of first-born sons, and the offering to Moloch was an evil piece of consistency, to which Ezek. xx. 25 refers. But this logical step was just one which Jahveism would not take.

[7] P. 263.

[8] Ex. xiii. 2, 15 ; Num. iii. 11–13, 40–51, viii. 16 sq. For the rest comp. below under the Passover.

[9] This follows from the complexion of the speech Num. xviii. 6–20, and the opposite case in ver. 21; and the same fact is still seen in the latest times, Josephus, *Bell. Jud.* v. 1. 4, comp. 2

who were clean.¹—By the time of the Deuteronomist, however, the offering of the first-fruits (with the exception of the Easter-offering to be explained below) had experienced a similar fate to that of the tithes, so that he speaks of them in quite the same fashion.² The only peculiarity is that he adds the fleece of the first-shorn sheep.³

Other perquisites accrued to the priests from various consecrated gifts as well as from the ban-gifts;⁴ and also from *military plunder*. All such plunder was to be equally shared between the active warriors and the rest of the nation in accordance with that spirit of equity which penetrated the entire community. This is required by the Book of Origins,⁵ and according to the main source for the life of David it was on occasion of an event in his earlier history that something similar first became a custom.⁶ The law made two claims on the booty for sacerdotal purposes, viz. one part in five hundred of the warriors' share for 'Jahveh,' i.e. for the purposes of the Sanctuary, to be handed over to the superior priests; and one part in fifty of the share of the rest of the nation for the ordinary Levites. This division only applied to every kind of living booty; all the noble and ignoble metals came entirely to Jahveh alone for the purposes of the Sanctuary,⁷ so easily contented was this nation in its earlier and better days! Nor can there be any doubt that these metals were invariably applied to the endowment of the Sanctuary, never for the support of the priests. And the former share of the priests in the spoil was sufficiently modest to prevent its inciting them to stir up wars. How entirely different in this respect was the fundamental constitution of Islâm!

When extraordinary needs occurred all these contributions became inadequate. The Book of Origins therefore makes the first erection of the Sanctuary with all its appliances an occasion for describing what should be done in such exceptional cases.⁸ On the one hand, appeal was made to the pure spontaneity of all ranks and both sexes, who were summoned to

¹ P. 149 sqq. Num. xviii. 11, 13.
² Deut. xii. 6, xiv. 23, xv. 19-23, xviii. 4, xxvi. 1-11.
³ Deut. xv. 19, xviii. 4.
⁴ According to p. 75 sqq.; comp. also Ezek. xliv. 29-31.
⁵ Num. xxxi. 25 sqq.; comp. 1 Chron. xxvi. 27 sq.
⁶ 1 Sam. xxx. 23-25; comp. *Hist.* iii. 105. This conjunction is of course very remarkable from an historical point of view; nor is it to be denied that the difference between the precepts depicted in the two passages is more apparent than real.
⁷ Num. xxxi.; comp. above p. 79 sq. and 77.
⁸ Ex. xxv. 1 sqq., xxxv. 4 sqq., 20 sqq., xxxviii. 21-31. But before Ex. xxxviii. 21 (comp. xxx. 11-16) the second way in which the means were to be furnished, viz. the taxation of all the adherents to Jahveh's Sanctuary, must have been explained, or at any rate their number given; and if Num. i. did not once stand here, the same thing must evidently have been here

contribute according to their will and their means, in short to dedicate to Jahveh an exceptional thank-offering.[1] On the other hand, a poll-tax was demanded from every man; and this, according to all tokens, is a solitary instance of a demand being made for such pecuniary subsidies during the times before the kings, unless a victorious foe extorted a tribute to be levied on all the inhabitants. The financial register evidently followed the military roll. Every man, from the twentieth year upwards, had to pay; nor can there be any doubt that during the time of Moses and Joshua the people of the 'community of Jahveh' were accurately counted and enrolled in military and financial registers,[2] although we no longer know how often such a sacerdotal enumeration and review of the nation was instituted. During the disorders of the period of the Judges such a universal census would no doubt share in the general disorganisation, so that it may have appeared a dangerous innovation when it was first revived on a totally different side under the regal supremacy.[3] The earliest registration, although serving military purposes as well, was essentially sacerdotal in its kind. Those who were registered were termed the enrolled of the Sanctuary, of Jahveh,[4] and were accordingly regarded as its vassals or clients, as citizens whose names were recorded in its sacred books.[5] Since, however, a census and registration of the entire people in remote Antiquity was always dreaded as a possible occasion of all manner of national misfortunes—on which account the heathen accompanied it with expiations—it was possible to demand from every man who was to be enrolled some small uniform contribution to the Sanctuary as expiation and protection money, such as the vassal pays his liege lord. In this way the Book of Origins explains the origin and meaning of this sacred contribution;[6] every one, whether poor or rich, had to pay half a shekel of silver. What, however, took

briefly mentioned; comp. Ex. xxxviii. 25 sq. Moreover we should expect that the levy and application of the silver, which according to Ex. xxv. 3, xxxv. 5, 24, was to be freely contributed, would have been mentioned previous to Ex. xxxviii. 31. Gaps like these in the extant remains of the old Book of Origins are not to be mistaken!

[1] P. 72 sq.

[2] See *Hist.* ii. 195 sq., 274 sq. Without such registers the division of the land which is spoken of on p. 176 sqq. would have been wholly impossible.—That these registers were in the first instance military rolls, is also shown by 2 Chron. xxvi. 12 sq.

[3] *Hist.* iii. 161 sqq.

[4] Ex. xxxviii. 21. Prominence is given in 1 Chron. xxiv. 6 to the fact that priests undertook the registration.

[5] According to the image Ps. lxxxvii. 4-7, and in corresponding passages.

[6] Ex. xxx. 11-16, xxxviii. 25-28; comp. Num. i. 45 sq. The *sacred* shekel which is required here had, as the ancient coin, far more value than the royal shekel; and we can see also from this term that the Book of Origins cannot have been written before the period assigned in *Hist.* i.

place at that time, might, according to the spirit of this typical narrative, recur again under similar circumstances; nor does it contradict the spirit of the narrative when at a later time an annual contribution to the temple was founded on this, the amount of which might be determined from time to time.[1]— This tax then produced 100 talents and 1,775 shekels; and, reckoning the talent at 3,000 shekels, this comes exactly to 603,550 half-shekels, which was the number of the men at that period.[2]

2. Another source of income was derived from certain shares in the sacrifices that were offered; unquestionably a usage existing long prior to Moses, which only took more rigid shape subsequently. The origin of all such perquisites caused them to be assigned to the superior priests alone, not to the ordinary Levites, nor could the law make any alteration here. But for reasons already given the share would vary greatly according to the different kinds of sacrifice.—From every animal burnt-offering the sacrificing priest received nothing but the skin;[3] this probably came to him from all other animal-offerings.[4]— From all animal guilt-offerings, as well as from all expiatory-offerings which did not belong to either of the highest two grades, the priests in common received the whole of the flesh over and above the small altar-pieces. Nevertheless this might be consumed only by the male priests, and by them only in the fore-court of the holy-place.[5] The same limitation applied to the corn-portions of the burnt-offering,[6] as well as to the twelve weekly loaves described above;[7] although a priest during David's time was rational enough to give some of it to men in distress who, though not priests, were free from corporal impurity.[8] All the rich corn and flesh portions, on the other hand, which fell to the priests from the thank-offerings, might be taken, like the first-fruits, to their own homes, whose members or slaves it might serve to support; but neither strangers nor even lodgers, nor yet the priests themselves if

---

[1] Comp. Neh. x. 33 [34] sq.: and the explanation of *Die drei ersten Evv.* s. 277 sq.

[2] From the later period of King Menahem we know, 2 Kings xv. 19 sq., that an Assyrian tribute of 1,000 silver talents was so levied on all the more wealthy and independent men in the Ten Tribes that each had to pay 50 (*royal*, i.e. smaller) shekels. These men, therefore, only amounted to 60,000. But at that time only the richer classes were called upon to pay this tax; and the gulf between rich and poor had been growing wider all through the centuries up to that date.

[3] Lev. vii. 8.

[4] Irrespective of the regulations of the *Mischna Zebachim*. xii. 3 sq., in contradiction to *M. Sh'qâlîm*, vi. 6.

[5] See above p. 65: comp. p. 62 sq.; 2 Kings xii. 17 [16].

[6] Lev. vi. 9 [16] sq.: comp. ii. 3, 10; comp. 2 Kings xxiii. 9.

[7] P. 115 sq.

[8] Lev. xxiv. 9: comp. 1 Sam. xxi. 4-7 [3-6].

their bodies were unclean, might partake of it.[1] According to the Book of Origins the breast and the right hind-leg were the two pieces which belonged to the priests from every thank-offering;[2] thus the matter, at the time when the Book was written, was arranged in accordance with ancient traditions. But we see from another tolerably ancient work,[3] that during the time of the later judges, there was often great arbitrariness displayed by covetous priests; and later on the Deuteronomist[4] assigns somewhat differently the (right) shoulder, the cheeks, and the stomach as the priests' portion.

3. A uniform and inalienable means of support was to have been afforded to the sacerdotal tribe after the conquest of Canaan, by the possession of the forty-eight small towns with their open spaces or common lands, of which we have already spoken.[5] Here too all the inferior Levites had their dwellings; and although they were not allowed to practise agriculture, they may easily have kept on the commons more cattle than were needed for their own use. We must at any rate infer from certain indications that they sold their cattle to others for the sacrifice, and that such cattle were held in high estimation.[6] Besides this, the Levites would let lodgings in such a town to strangers and take rent from them.[7] But it must be confessed that this possession was soon disturbed, and must have been completely broken up when the whole body of the Levites were crowded together in the little kingdom of Judah.[8] Here also, estates seem to have been assigned them, or those which they had long possessed to have been secured for them.[9] But their

---

[1] Lev. xxii. 2-16.
[2] See above p. 52; Lev. vii. 28-34; Ex. xxix. 22-28; Lev. viii. 25-29, ix. 21, x. 14 sq.; Num. vi. 20; comp. above, p. 279.
[3] 1 Sam. ii. 13-16.—Another danger for the priests lay in the requirement of expiatory-offerings; bad priests may have promoted transgression in order to receive the more expiatory-offerings, Hos. iv. 8.
[4] Deut. xviii. 3.
[5] P. 286 sq. Even at the present day there are villages in those regions inhabited solely by saints or their descendants, see Lepsius' *Briefe*, s. 193. 221; Richardson in *Ausland*, 1854, s. 113.
[6] When, namely, Num. iii. 41, 43, the cattle of the Levites are to take the place of all the first-born cattle of Israel, this evidently means more than that the latter are redeemable according to p. 79 sqq. The same fact explains how the priest could estimate a sacrificial animal which had to be offered, Lev. v. 15, 18, 25 [vi. 6]; comp. xxvii. 2 sqq.—The common extended a distance of 2,000 ells round the town, according to the correct reading of the LXX, Num. xxxv. 4 sq. We might indeed conjecture that the 100 ells of ver. 4 according to the Masoretic text denote the free ground allotted for small huts close to the wall, which according to Burckhardt's *Travels in Arabia*, vol. i. p. 16 sq. (octavo edition), are to be found in almost every Arabian town. Then the description of the tract for grazing would commence with ver. 5. But the context of the whole passage verr. 2-5 does not favour such an assumption.
[7] According to Lev. xxii. 10.
[8] *Hist* iv. 27 sq., 224 sq.
[9] According to Jer. xxxii. 6 sqq., xxxvii. 12; comp. 1 Kings ii. 26; here, however, the fields are being spoken of.

number was so excessive for this kingdom that they sunk into continually increasing poverty, and the Deuteronomist bespeaks for them almost public commiseration. For these later times, when many especially of the poorer Levites had no regular abode, the Deuteronomist made among others the following regulation : that a Levite who came from a provincial town to the metropolis, and was there employed in the temple-service, should share in the rich temple-offerings, and not merely be the guest of one of the twenty-four sacerdotal households in its turn.[1]

III. THE KINGDOM; ITS UNITY AND ITS AGENCIES.

In the way and with the freedom we have described the various powers and arts in the nation were developed. Hence it is a question of all the more importance how the unity of the kingdom was to be preserved amid such internal freedom and variety in the most diverse aims and occupations of life, and in particular what permanent institutions were established to protect it. There are, in addition to the government itself, pre-eminently two institutions whose business it is to uphold and confirm their unity as far as in them lies: the courts and administration of justice, which though distinct from the government promote the strength and unity of the kingdom, and the eternal constant activity of the true religion assuming a material shape for the whole realm in the single great Sanctuary. We shall have to keep in view, however, only that form of the kingdom which was founded by Moses and those of his time in the shape of the first strict Theocracy.

1. THE GOVERNMENT.

When the priesthood, as we have described above, during the creative early centuries of the existence of Jahveism developed so great and distinct a power, and the tribe of Levi

---

[1] P. 276. This is the most probable meaning of the words in Deut. xviii. 6-8; but then מִמְּבְרָיו is to be punctuated from מִכְרָה, 'entertainment,' 2 Kings vi. 23; besides, the use of לְבַד without מִן (comp Deut. iii. 5) would be very surprising, especially in this author. The phrase 'according to the fathers,' is an abbreviation for 'according to the father-houses, i.e. the families.' Comp. the Jahrbb. der Bibl. Wiss. vi. s. 97.—It is hardly worth while here to notice further the manifold erroneous views concerning the priesthood of the Old Testament which are always being put forth alike from the side of the over-free (comp. e.g. the Jahrbb. der Bibl. Wiss. x. s. 259), and from the side of the un-free. Of the latter kind is the superficial book of the Prussian Consistorialrath Lic. Küper Das Priesterthum des Alten Bundes, (Berlin, 1865).

almost became an Israel in miniature, it might well appear as though a true unity of human government was from the beginning more hindered thereby, than created and firmly established. Nevertheless, the real state of the case is somewhat different.

The ancient popular power now had the sacerdotal power for a companion. The two must mutually tolerate and endeavour to supplement each other. But it is a fundamental condition of all good government that the state should include two powers, each sufficiently strong and well-ordered to be able to examine into the other and preserve it as far as possible from errors. Of these one should consist as far as possible of eminent permanent individuals and should act as a guide, while the other should embrace the entire nation and should act as an examiner. Now both of these were here given, and at the same time the true God was regarded as standing above them both and really uniting them. But while Israel had long possessed a consultative assembly,[1] the sacerdotal power was at that time not only the younger power, something pressing to the front with new force, it had also, in virtue of being founded on the compact exclusiveness of a single tribe with a High-priest as its hereditary head, an internal solidity and unity which was wanting in the other tribes. It seemed therefore as though it must now far outstrip the popular power and become the paramount authority. And as a fact the High-priest after the death of Moses was not merely the possessor of the perpetual oracle and leader of all sacerdotal functions; he was also the president of the national assembly when it met,[2] and the permanent representative of the entire nation whenever it acted as a whole. If a military leader such as Joshua was required, the two were to cooperate in the best way they could; and that such a cooperation might lead to happy issues is shown in the example of Eleazar and Joshua.[3] 'The High-priest and the Elders (or princes)' or 'the High-priest, the General, and the Elders,' are phrases which denote the ultimate authority. If a solemn embassy was to be despatched, it was composed in corresponding fashion of one of the most eminent priests and twelve (or ten) of the heads of tribes.[4]

Yet if this would lead us to think that the sacerdotal power as the predominant one would tend in due course to become

---

[1] P. 246 sq.
[2] As is depicted vividly enough in Judges xix.–xxi.; comp. xx. 28. Similarly Josh. xxii. 30–34.
[3] Josh. xiv. 1, xvii. 4, xix. 51, xxi. 1.
[4] Josh. xxii. 13 sq. speaks of ten, elsewhere the number is twelve; comp. above, p. 256.

despotic and would suppress the popular freedom, what the history shows is the exact opposite. There may have at times been degeneracy in the house of the High-priest after the days of Eleazar and Phinehas, and the sons of Eli may not have been the only ones who covered the name of Priest with shame; but in the main the spirit of Jahveism, especially during the first centuries, was too strongly opposed to all arbitrary rule, and the limits of the sacerdotal activity in particular had been too clearly defined by Moses, for the popular liberties to have suffered much and long at the hands of the priests. It is plain that what really happened was that the power of the High-priest, as representing the unity and strength of the government, declined only too soon. The nation had not been long settled in Canaan before a popular government (democracy) was formed which was often only too free. This grew as far as was possible for it, especially within Jahveism, and during all the centuries down to the establishment of the monarchy it remained the normal condition.[1] We find the law declaring:

> *Thou shalt not follow the crowd—to an evil thing,*
> *Nor enter into strife—in order to flatter the crowd;*
> *To wrest the right of the noble, thou may'st not endeavour,*
> *Nor to exalt on high the lowly in his strife.*[2]

When this was written democracy was unquestionably as flourishing in Israel as it was, many centuries later, in certain Grecian free states. The moral strictness of the community which has been already noticed, since its exercise and its maintenance inviolate was entrusted to, and imposed upon, the whole nation, was by no means antagonistic to the development of a wide popular freedom; while the latter was so extensive, that so soon as discipline and power began to decay internally, it was itself dissolved and compelled to give place to arbitrary dominion (despotism). This whole subject is, however, more fully discussed in the third section of the second volume of the *History*.

---

[1] The dangers of a democracy cannot be more briefly nor more correctly sketched than in the laws of the very ancient passages Lev. xix. 15 and Ex. xxiii. 2 sq. Such commands as 'not to speak to please the crowd or even the lowly in the court of justice,' occur nowhere else in the Old Testament. Besides, the text of Ex. xxiii. 2 sq. is both corrupt and imperfect; the words in ver. 2 are probably too many, those in ver. 3 too few; לְהַטֹּת in ver. 2 seems to belong to ver. 3 as the commencement of a now imperfect member.

[2] Ex. xxxii. 2 sq. A similar state of things is described (where we should not have expected to find it) in the Book of Job, xxxi. 33 sq.; comp. xxix. 7.

2. THE ADMINISTRATION OF JUSTICE.

The way in which justice is administered is everywhere dependent on the mode of government and the fundamental principles which guide the latter. Its sphere of operations was, however, all the wider in those times, in proportion as the separation between the judicial and the administrative provinces was less distinct. In general the administration of justice was undoubtedly provided for in the first instance by the institutions which existed prior to Moses,[1] and which, revived by him, entered on a new lease of life. But on all points which were more closely connected with sacred things, which concerned what was pure and what was impure as explained above, the Sabbath, sacrifice, and the like, it was only the priests who were competent to decide; and as their power generally was then in its first bloom, their judgments were for a long period willingly sought after. The High-priest besides could give a final legal decision on all matters which were brought before him.[2] A court of justice can nowhere have a beneficent influence unless the people are first convinced of its freedom from prejudice (its impartiality); but we may imagine what the respect must have been for the highest sacerdotal court in Israel so long as the earliest Jahveism remained firmly implanted in the faith of the nation, and with its genuine, trustworthy oracle seemed also to furnish the best perpetual court of justice. In those first and fairest days of the pure Theocracy, it was possible to term this highest court and its administrator 'God' himself. That it became customary to do so, at any rate in the common speech of the time, may be clearly seen from the laws of the Book of Covenants, and certain other phrases which have survived from that period.[3] Moses, then Aaron and Hur,[4] after them Eleazar and others, were regarded in their days as the living depository both of the oracle, and of the best administration of justice. And even later, when the pure Theocracy was gradually melting

---

[1] P. 253 sqq.
[2] P. 290 sq.
[3] We may refer to the five-fold repetition of הָאֱלֹהִים, or more briefly אֱלֹהִים, as equivalent to 'sacred authority,' Ex. xxi. 6 (where, moreover, הִגִּישׁ must relate to it), xxii. 7 [8] sq., and xxii. 27 [28] (for the last passage see p. 256, *ut* 6). Besides these there are the phrases in Judges v. 8; 1 Sam. ii. 25; comp. *Hist.* ii. 412.
[4] Ex. xxiv. 14; for Hur comp. *Hist.* ii. 25, 29, *ut* 1. He seems to have been a sort of forerunner of Joshua, i.e. not to have been one of the tribe of Levi, and so to have represented the lay element.— What the Book of Origins may have taught concerning the courts and method of justice we no longer know, with the exception of what it says about the oracle of the high-priest, see p. 290 sq.

away, the Levites always retained a considerable share in the administration of justice. According to the Deuteronomist, the priests were responsible for the discharge of all judicial duties, and along with the king they formed the highest court of justice.[1] The union of the two standing powers also in this respect was a logical consequence which the course of time was sure to bring about. Even the inferior Levites, as they gradually acquired increased culture, became more and more qualified for judging the nation wherever it was dwelling.[2] The nation, however, certainly never permitted the right of sitting in judgment as assessors to be taken out of its own hands.[3]

Nevertheless the good administration of justice was always deservedly regarded in the community of Jahveh as something so hard to obtain, yet so desirable, in cases which were difficult to decide, or when judgments were difficult to execute, that during the earlier centuries new tribunals of justice readily sprang up; especially when the court of the High-priest gradually lost the power of executing the sentence. In this way the tribunals of most of the so-called Judges arose, a subject which is discussed elsewhere.[4] But even during the later highly civilised times, the number of judges in the narrow sense of the word, especially of men who were 'earnest, God-fearing, trustworthy, and not greedy of gain,' as the earliest law already requires,[5] was so far from being superabundant, that the Deuteronomist gave an express exhortation for their establishment.[6] The damages which a defendant had committed were assessed by arbitrators.[7]

In other respects we have very little definite information regarding the number, position, and legal training of the component elements of the ordinary tribunals. If the Levites, some of whom were undoubtedly always present even at the smallest courts when a question of any importance was at stake, were, so to speak, the members learned in the law, and if they, from their position, needed no special pay for their judicial services, then the rest of the assessors, chosen from the leading citizens, would still less be paid. The taking of 'gifts' however, from the seekers for justice, was on this very account all the more liable to be practised; and already the earliest law

---

[1] Deut. xvii. 8-13, xix. 17, with which xxi. 5 is to be compared; comp. also Ezra x. 14.
[2] Comp. 1 Chron. xxvi. 29.
[3] Comp. 1 Kings xxi. 8-10.
[4] *Hist.* ii. 357 sqq.
[5] Ex. xviii. 21.
[6] Deut. xvi., 18-20, comp. i. 16 sq.
[7] Ex. xxi. 22.

is urgent in its warnings against the danger to which judges were thereby exposed.[1]

The most important point nevertheless, is that the administration of justice was always public, and this all the more so the more important was the dispute to be settled. Publicity in legal procedure is rendered indispensable by the very nature of the case, and the constitution and the religion under which the ancient nation had to live promoted the impulse to this with the utmost effect. The community itself was thus regarded as having the final judicial decision.[2] Before its assembly were brought all the more important controversies, and without, at any rate, its acquiescence nothing of moment could be determined. And though this ancient sanctified custom of conducting judicial proceedings in public might be exposed to the influence of many both favourable and unfavourable events and endeavours, though the oracle might be regarded in dubious cases as a court of final appeal,[3] though the Judges, and then more definitely and constantly the Kings, might pronounce judgment for all who sought their decisions, still the public administration of justice before the assembled community was always reverted to as the permanent deep foundation of all judicial procedure;[4] and even the Judges and Kings sat to judge in public.[5]

Moreover, the judicial procedure always remained very simple. The plaintiff, of course, had to bring all the grounds of his accusation before the court in a well-considered and properly arranged form.[6] It was not compulsory on either plaintiff or defendant to be represented by advocates. All the more do the Prophets exhort those who have it in their power to undertake voluntarily the defence of the right, especially of those who would otherwise be defenceless and impotent, e.g. widows and orphans; and all the greater merit could a highly respected member of a community earn by indefatigable exertion on behalf of those who needed help.[7] The defendant,

---

[1] Ex. xxiii. 6-8, repeated Deut. xvi. 19, xxvii. 25. The same note is often heard in the Prophets.—According to Josephus, *Antiq.* iv. 8. 14, 38, every town was to have seven judges (and rulers) along with two levitical assistants; comp. what is said above on p. 249, *nt.* 2. According to Josephus this was then founded on Deut. xvi. 18.

[2] Num. xxxv. 12, 24 sqq.

[3] P. 290 sq.

[4] Prov. xxvi. 26; Deut. xxi. 18-21.

[5] As did even the last king, Jer. xxxviii. 7; comp. *Hist.* iii. 175 sq.

[6] This is עָרַךְ מִשְׁפָּט, *instruere causam*. Job xiii. 18, xxiii. 4. In general the poet gives us in Job's speeches some very clear glimpses into the whole administration of justice as it was developed among the ancient nation. Even many of the most beautiful and most sublime of the passages in the Prophets will not be understood unless we remember that the imagery is entirely borrowed from the judicial system of the nation.

[7] The fair type of whom is depicted Job xxix.

generally attired in mourning squalid garments, appeared, or rather was brought in by the plaintiff, and had to stand on the left of the latter.[1] If anyone was called upon by the tribunal to confess the truth, the judge first referred him to God with the words already spoken of, 'Give God honour and praise, and confess.'[2] If there was no documental proof, not less than two witnesses were required, at any rate in the more important cases.[3] The witnesses, as we have already remarked,[4] must place their hands on a criminal condemned to death, and must cast the first stones at him. The judgment was passed as soon as possible, and immediately executed; if it could not be at once passed, the accused was taken into custody and closely confined in fetters,[5] generally in a very simple fashion, his feet being secured in the stocks.[6]—Moreover, the judgment, at any rate from the time of David, was always set down in writing.[7] The court, unless it were that of the highest authorities, was held publicly in the market-place (at the gate), in the presence of the assembled community.[8] The penalty of death, however, was always inflicted outside of the town. Sabbaths, and festivals of equal importance, of course involved a suspension of all judicial business.[9]

That penal transgressions generally were prosecuted in this community with the utmost zeal, follows from the whole spirit which prevailed in it.[10] Hence also the means taken to detect a criminal were in the earliest days extraordinarily severe. If, e.g. a thief, or even a receiver of stolen goods were hard to discover, aid was sought from the public adjuration;[11] and even anyone privy to the theft who paid no regard to this was punished with death for contemning it if subsequently discovered and captured.[12]

---

[1] Zach. iii. 1 sqq., Ps. cix. 6 sq.; comp. Math. xxv. 33.
[2] P. 20, 220 sqq.—So in the earlier days Josh. vii. 19, and later John ix. 24.
[3] Num. xxxv. 30, according to the Book of Origins; Deut. xvii. 4–6; the case in Ex. xxii. 12, where one witness is enough, has been shown on p. 187 to have been of trifling importance.
[4] P. 42 sq.
[5] According to the image 2 Sam. iii. 34. comp. *Die Dichter des A. Bs.* 1 a, s. 141.
[6] See my comment on Job, s. 153 of the second edition.
[7] Is. x. 1 sq.
[8] Comp. Num. xxxv. 12, 24 sqq.
[9] That festivals in particular, e.g. the first day of unleavened bread, caused a suspension of the *justitium*, may indeed be understood of itself, but it is also expressly taught in the *Mischna, Jôm tôb,* v. 2.
[10] P. 135 sqq.
[11] P. 19 sq.
[12] This follows from the word in Prov. xxix. 24; but comp. what is said above, p. 62.

The Legal Modes of Punishment.

The amount of punishment inflicted for transgressions proved before a judge, and the mode of executing it, are, as a matter of history, subject to great variation according to the period and the nation. We can correctly estimate the condition of morality and discipline in any community and age by the kinds of penalties and modes of inflicting them which are there permitted or prescribed by law. In many respects we may find such penalties for the ancient community of Jahveh in the manifold onerous expiatory- and guilt-offerings, the remarkable stringency of which we have already observed.[1] Alongside of them, however, and on an independent basis, were particular punishments needful on civil grounds. We have already shown[2] that no expiatory-offering could ever remove or diminish the penalty for intentional wrong-doing, and that even for unintentional injury compensation must still be made. The purpose of the expiatory-offering was therefore, to put it briefly, to restore the disturbed peace of conscience. Nor was it possible to escape the civil penalties of a distinctly compulsory character where such had been decreed: and thus in this case even the ancient Theocracy must confess that there are two disconnected provinces of everything human, the civil and the religious.—We must now consider the various kinds of punishment more closely.

The law does not inflict imprisonment as a punishment. Only in the regal times do we find a command not to leave the precincts of a town as something intermediate between prompt punishment and complete acquittal.[3] Closer confinement, particularly in a foul and galling prison, was first introduced under the later monarchy.[4] In Egypt imprisonment was very early employed as a punishment, and is therefore frequently mentioned in the history of Joseph.

In like manner the ancient law did not inflict as a penalty banishment, i.e. the casting out from, and forbidding any return to, one's mother country. In the feeling of the ancient world, when the mother country was far more limited in extent homelike and known, it would have been regarded as equivalent to a capital sentence; therefore the early stringent legislation of the Theocracy at once preferred the latter in the

---

[1] P. 55 sqq.
[2] P. 56 sqq.
[3] 1 Kings ii. 36 sq., comp. ver. 26 sq.
[4] Jer. xxxvii.-xxxix.; comp. 1 Kings xxii. 27, BK. Is. xlii. 7.

case of sufficiently heinous offences. Only in the regal times does it occur as a slight mitigation of capital punishment, but even then chiefly as the mere result of royal displeasure.¹

Pecuniary penalties were inflicted by the law; but little use was made of them. In the regal times, on the other hand, there are many traces that they became far more frequent, so that complaints arose on that score.² And when the ancient law does require or permit pecuniary fines, they still appear more as mere payment for damages, so that the idea seems to be mainly that of compensation. Such payments, however, were always strictly insisted on, and one of the main purposes of all punishment was to ensure their being made.

Corporal chastisement by beating with sticks, the favourite punishment of the earliest Egyptians (as can be seen from their paintings), was, remarkable to say, totally unrecognised by the ancient law of Israel.³ It was evidently deemed too degrading or too Egyptian, and was consequently limited to the domestic relation between masters and slaves or parents and children. The Deuteronomist does indeed permit it, manifestly because by his time it had long become customary in consequence of the monarchical rule; but he adds that more than forty strokes shall never be inflicted, 'so that the wounds may not become too severe, and a brother (a fellow citizen) become too contemptible in the eyes of the rest.'⁴

Hence capital punishment was the more frequent; and nothing affords so clear a proof of the strictness of the discipline in the original Theocracy. It is true that when we take a general survey we see it was confined to two principal classes of offences: 1) Intentional desecration of the majesty and of the sanctities of Jahveh, without which the community felt itself unable even to exist, and as a fact really could not have existed among the existing nations of the earth; 2) Equally intentional desecration of what is sacred in individual human beings, i.e. the blood, the life,⁵ or of what has ultimately the same significance.⁶ But these two principal classes embrace, when taken strictly, a very large number of actual cases; and Jahveism accepted them all with the most logical and unbending

---

¹ According to the phrase 1 Sam. xxvi. 19; comp. *Hist.* iii. 97. Hence a revival of it under Herod the Great was unfavourably regarded by the teachers of the law, *Hist.* v. 437. Comp. above for the membership of the community, p. 237 sq.
² Amos ii. 8, Prov. xvii. 26.
³ That the passage Lev. xix. 20 does not concern us here has been explained on p. 214.
⁴ Deut. xxv. 1-3. From further scrupulosity the Rabbis forbade more than thirty-nine to be given, 2 Cor. xi. 24, Josephus *Antiq.* iv. 8. 21, 23.
⁵ P. 37.
⁶ Such as are spoken of on p. 190.

stringency, especially the particular cases in which that which was most holy in the community and seemed like its life and soul, was desecrated.

This capital punishment is always designated in the Book of Origins by the manifestly ancient legal phrase, 'that soul shall be rooted out from its nations.'[1] The meaning of this phrase cannot be doubtful;[2] but we only fully comprehend it when we remember two things. In the first place, the expression 'his nations' may be equivalent in the earliest language to 'his fellow-countrymen,' or even 'his fellow-tribesmen and relatives.'[3] In the second place we must remember that according to the earliest domestic custom,[4] every household and every tribe would make the utmost efforts to protect its own members and rescue them from their accusers. The phrase accordingly held its ground in the sense given by this primitive tenacious domestic custom : the guilty shall be put to death in spite of the efforts of his tribesmen and relatives to save his life. Hence it also appears that this phrase defines nothing concerning the particular mode of capital punishment.

In fact, the mode of capital punishment varied according to the particular cases, as has been noticed wherever we have already had occasion to speak of it. When the offence readily roused the wrath of the whole community, simple stoning in their midst was still very common.[5] An aggravation of this was found in burning;[6] in other cases where they wished to avert the wrath of Jahveh when it was threatening the whole nation, they hanged the criminal, though not till he was dead, publicly in the sun on a post, as an offering 'cursed by God.'[7] This spectacle the Deuteronomist seeks at a later date to mitigate by ordering the corpse to be taken down and buried before

---

[1] Thus in Gen. xvii. 14, and very often subsequently.

[2] It is convertible in the Book of Origins with 'shall be slain,' Ex. xxxi. 14 sq., which elsewhere in the Book of Covenants is the usual expression.

[3] עַמֶּיךָ interchanges with בְּנֵי עַמּוֹ in the very early passage Lev. xix. 16, 18. Fellow-tribesmen and relatives are denoted by the expression even in Lev. xxi. 1, 4, 14 sq. As an explanation of it we find in the Book of Origins itself, Num. xix. 20, the expression 'out of the community,' nay, even the phrase 'out of the midst *of its nation*,' which sometimes interchanges with the former (Lev. xvii. 4 and elsewhere) is certainly meant as an explanation. The Deuteronomist, however (xiii. 6 [5] and elsewhere), has in its stead the expression 'thou shalt root out the evil from thy midst,' so that its growth may not adhere any longer to the community.

[4] P. 168 sq.

[5] Num. xv. 35 sq., Josh. vii. 25.—Deut. xiii. 10 [9] sq., xvii. 6 sq., xxii. 24.

[6] Lev. xx. 14, xxi. 9; Gen. xxxviii. 24. According to Josh. vii. 15, 25, it would not be a burning alive, nor is this meant in 1 Kings xiii. 2, 2 Kings xxiii. 20.

[7] According to the phrase, Deut. xxi. 23; comp. Gal. iii. 13; therefore as a חֵרֶם, according to p. 75 sqq.

the evening of the same day.[1]—Throwing stones on to the grave of a universally execrated offender must early have become a national custom.[2]

If the case lay entirely between two persons, the one against the other (a so-called private revenge), then in the earlier times the person condemned by the tribunal was simply handed over to his pursuer and accuser for the latter to execute the penal sentence, unless the matter was settled by pecuniary compensation.[3]

So simple, but yet so strict, were the kinds of punishment and modes of inflicting them in the ancient community. More artificial, and therefore for the most part more cruel processes of capital punishment do not occur until comparatively late periods; and clear tokens show them to have been introduced from abroad, especially from the Egyptian, Assyrian, Persian, and other great military powers. Many of them have already been enumerated.[4]

3. The Sacred Text.

An outward image of all these highest means of perpetually uniting and strengthening nation and kingdom was obtained by the establishment of the high Sanctuary, which most naturally occupied the centre of the entire visible territory of this kingdom. But the influence of the peculiar history, and then the special form of life of the Theocracy as we have described it,[5] determined the peculiar construction of the external Sanctuary, which from the very first was to be the sacred centre and fairest place of assembly for the whole nation. And since it originated during the first creative epoch of the community, it did as a fact always retain in this respect an importance almost without a parallel; and during the calm quiet of the ordinary course of time it was even reverenced as the sublime and most worthy model for a sacred home of Jahveh, and its type was one from which the nation could never properly get free down to the final close of its history.

This Sanctuary had not at first, it is true, quite the same

---

[1] Num. xxv. 4 sq. (where the explanation is tolerably complete); 2 Sam. xxi. 6 sqq.—Deut. xxi. 22 sq.; Josh. viii. 29; x. 26.

[2] Josh. vii. 26; viii. 29; 2 Sam. xviii. 17; comp. *Itiner.* of Marcus Antoninus, xxxi.; Guérin's *Voyage Ar-* *chéol.* i. p. 81; Maltzan's *Wallfahrt nach Mecca*, ii. s. 286, 345 sqq.

[3] This will explain figures of speech such as occur in Isaiah i. 24, as I have there explained.

[4] P. 165 sq.

[5] P. 127 sq.

purpose to which it was subsequently put during the long series of centuries, and which it never again relinquished. Everything goes to show that at first, whilst the nation was dwelling in the desert under the leadership of Moses, it was the easily-moved tent-like abode of the great leader himself, which so far was always the principal centre of the wandering nation, and at the same time the place where Moses uttered oracles, since the person of national leader was then absolutely identical with that of the great Prophet. Whether at that time an altar was already connected with the tent, we do not know; the ark of the covenant undoubtedly from the very first occupied the most interior chamber of this tent. Not before the nation had for the first time become untrue to the higher religion to which they had pledged themselves, and a rent had been made in the first innocence of the community, did Moses set up this tent at some distance from the general camp—like a castle near a town—manifestly to protect it better in future from the first rage of a popular rising. From this time it began to be termed the 'tent of revelation,' because it had now become something different from the mere dwelling-place of the national leader, and was visited by Moses himself only when he was called upon to speak and to act as Prophet and supreme Judge. Nevertheless Joshua also entered the tent itself at that time in his capacity of constant companion and military officer of Moses. This enables us to see back clearly into the period before the tribe of Levi became the sacerdotal tribe,[1] and the house of Aaron acquired the exclusive right of entering the sacred tent. All this we know from the third author of the Primitive History;[2] and although he, as an inhabitant of the Kingdom of the Ten Tribes, found in the very position of the kingdom special occasion for emphasising this earlier state of affairs before the development of Levi to a sacerdotal caste, yet the account is completely in harmony with whatever else we know respecting the time of Moses.

If, accordingly, this tent even during the life of Moses was separated from the other tents, including his own, and became the sacred seat of the oracle, it is a matter of course that the reverence for it should have continually risen higher and higher, when various distinguished powerful men of the house of Aaron, an Eleazar, a Phinehas, and others, trod in Moses' steps,

---

[1] P. 260 sqq.
[2] Ex. xxxiii. 7–11. It is inconceivable that this tent should not be the same as the one whose arrangements, according to the Book of Origins, are described later, Ex. xxxvi. Comp. Num. xi. 26 sqq.

and the prerogatives of the tribe of Levi were fully developed. All divine worship as it was to be held in the midst of the nation, concentrated itself in strictly arranged procedure at this tent alone. After it had in this way become possessed during many centuries of the greatest possible sanctity which Jahveism could permit it to acquire, it is more closely described in the Book of Origins down almost to the minutest detail. For by the date of this book it had acquired in the course of centuries so extraordinary a sanctity, that, though it had been constructed by human artificers such as Bezaleel from Judah and Aholiab from Dan (whose names were still preserved),[1] yet it seemed at the same time to have been copied from a divine model exhibited on Sinai to Moses by Jahveh himself.[2] The most beautiful and perfect earthly Sanctuary conceivable seemed therefore at that time to have been here realised. Yet Jahveism always retained sufficient sense never to compare anything earthly and made by human hands immediately with the Divine, so that the whole Sanctuary only seemed to have been constructed after a heavenly model; just as man must as a fact always aim at and honour in every visible and earthly sacred object something which is yet higher and better. The two tables of the law were the only things which at that time seemed to have been derived still more immediately from God.[3] The Sanctuary is ultimately a single sacred thing which readily seems to comprehend in itself all the infinite Holiness and Truth imparted to man at a given period, nor can man place anything above it but God himself. And yet men existed in the Old Testament who regarded neither a magnificent sacred house nor yet even an ark of the covenant as absolutely indispensable.[4] This contradiction is not unintelligible; in the deepest spirit of the religion of the Old Testament itself it is only apparent, not real.—We must now, however, consider more closely the sacred tabernacle which acquired such importance in the course of history.[5]

1. The tabernacle itself had always its entrance towards the east, of old the sacred quarter of the heavens.[6] It was divided

---

[1] Ex. xxxi. 1-11; xxxv. 30-35; xxxvi. 1; xxxvii. 1; xxxviii. 22 sq.

[2] According to Ex. xxv. 9, 40, this model is to be shown to Moses at that spot, and although verr. xxvi. 30, xxvii. 8 (where הָרְאֵה is to be read for הָרְהֵ), substitute the *perfect* for the *participle*, nevertheless the discourse from xxv. to xxxi. is too coherent to allow room for the insertion of a narrative stating that the model was shown to Moses before the end of xxxi.; it must have fallen out from the following passage.

[3] P. 122 sqq.

[4] See above 120 sq., and Jer. iii. 16.

[5] Some parts of the following description have been already expounded in 1858 in the *Jahrbb. der Bibl. Wiss.* ix. s. 152-154; comp. also viii. s. 155.

[6] [See the plan at the end of the volume.]

into a principal chamber, and a smaller back-chamber, the former being briefly termed the *Holy Place*, the latter the *Holy of Holies*. In the first place[1] its four sides were built of strong planks of the acacia wood which grows in the desert, sometimes to a great height. These planks were each ten ells high and one and a half broad. At the bottom they were morticed into one another beneath the ground by two accurately-fitting tenons, each of which had previously passed through a hollow socket. These sockets were made entirely of silver, and projected above ground at any rate high enough to be easily seen. On the north and south sides twenty of these planks were erected in line, close to one another, forming a wall which internally was thirty ells in length. The western end was formed by six similar planks, supplemented by two corner-planks where the end joined the two sides. These corner-planks had their broad side in line with the western end of the tabernacle, and were divided (as though each had been made up of two planks) from the ground upwards, but only to the highest of the five rings, which will be described presently. Above this point they were undivided like the other planks.[2] As this partial division of the two corner-planks, which in other respects were just like the rest, is without reason as far as their immediate function is concerned, it must be explained from the fact of its enabling them to be at once recognised also from the outside. Now as the six planks at the middle of the western side would occupy a space of nine ells, and as an interior breadth of ten ells would be most suitable for a length of thirty ells, and as also the great temple of Solomon was constructed according to this very numerical proportion,[3] it follows that each of the two corner-planks lengthened the inner wall by only half an ell; from which it further follows that the planks were one ell in thickness. We know that the back-chamber, i.e. the Holy of Holies, occupied exactly one-third of the length of the tabernacle,[4] and was therefore ten ells long; it was also ten ells high; and if, as we have assumed, it was also ten ells broad, it would have the form of a perfect cube. Dimensions like this, equal in all directions, may have been

---

[1] If Ex. xxvi. 15-29, stood before ver. 1, the whole description in this chapter of the tabernacle would evidently be much clearer, but the same arrangement occurs Ex. xxxvi. 14 sqq. That in early times important transpositions of the text may have taken place herei s still shown by the LXX, in Ex. xxxvi.-xxxix.

[2] Thus Ex. xxvi. 24, is to be understood; comp. ver. 29, יִהְיוּ is 'so that they may be,' according to *Lehrb.* § 347a; comp. even the narrative Ex. xxxvi. 29.

[3] See *Hist.* iii. 235 sqq.

[4] It is true that we know this only from the indication in Ex. xxvi. 33; comp. verr. 2-6.

purposely chosen for this particular space which was to receive what was most sacred, and should furnish an image of the dwelling of the Most Perfect. Even the curtain-ceiling, as will be immediately explained, indicated in a sufficiently marked manner where the space which was sacred above all else commenced. In this respect, too, the temple of Solomon faithfully followed the pattern of the tabernacle. But as only the priests were allowed to enter any part of the interior of the dwelling, and yet the people were to see as much of the architectural proportions as was permitted by the overhanging curtains, and as these hung down so low (as we shall explain) that only the above silver sockets were visible from the outside, the number of the latter was brought up, evidently on purpose, to exactly one hundred, as though this large round number were to give a conception of the Perfection whose image this dwelling was to be.—Finally, in order to secure the whole wooden framework more firmly, on the inner side[1] five rods of sound acacia-wood were passed through rings which were fastened at regular intervals in each plank; these are the 'bars.' The middle one of these rods went all round the three sides without break, and was morticed at the corners so that the separate pieces of wood fitted accurately into one another. These rings, five times forty-eight in number (though only one of the rings on each corner-plank was of any real service), were all made of gold; moreover, the planks (though, as will easily be understood, only on the inner side) were all covered over with gold-leaf.

This splendid wooden framework was now covered over with curtains of corresponding magnificence. These were made of byssus, displaying the four colours which, when placed side by side, furnish an image of the rainbow, and were therefore most appropriate for the Sanctuary of the God of Israel, and re-appear wherever gay colouring seemed requisite in it, even in the attire of the High-priest.[2] These colours were dark blue, dark red (purple), bright red (scarlet), and light grey. There were also images of cherubs woven in the cloth. Each of these costly curtains, symbolical of heaven and of God descending thence, was four ells in width and twenty-eight in length, and was placed over the wooden framework so as to hang down on the outside of the latter, without reaching, however, to the ground. It was the

---

[1] This is self-evident, because otherwise the entire decoration would have been concealed on the outside by the curtains.

[2] P. 292. Just as the rainbow is mentioned in connection with the appearance of the cherubs in Ezek. i. 21.—When a single colour was enough, the dark blue (sky-blue) was always preferred.

less needful for them to do this, since these heaven-curtains were properly only to be the covering of the framework of planks, and hence of the two chambers. These curtains were loosely stitched together so as to form two breadths, each containing five curtains, the total width being forty ells; and the whole was so placed over the woodwork that the last ten ells hung down over the western end, and the junction of the two breadths came exactly over the division between the Holy Place and the Holy of Holies. This dividing line was marked on the covering by an elaborate union, which was visible from beneath. The edges of the two breadths terminated in fifty loops of dark-blue (sky-coloured) byssus, placed exactly opposite to one another, and each corresponding pair of loops was connected by a golden clasp.

This completed the tent-dwelling proper,[1] i.e. all that was seen of the tabernacle from the inside, and was erected and adorned for a dwelling. Now begins the further external clothing of this dwelling so as to make it a complete tent. For this purpose the first thing employed was a plain covering of goats' hair, such as was always a favourite for ordinary tents in those regions.[2] This was to cover the whole edifice externally, and therefore consisted of curtains each four ells in breadth like the former curtains which were visible only as a ceiling from the inside, but thirty ells in length, so that on either side it hung down one ell lower than the curtains of byssus. The front breadth of it, moreover, consisted of six curtains instead of five, so that it had a total breadth of forty-four ells. The foremost of these six curtains was to be laid on double, two ells of it being turned back, manifestly in order to give the whole a firmer hold at the front. The remaining two ells were to hang down at the hinder end beyond the curtains of byssus, so that at the end it hung down further than at the two sides. Where the two breadths met they were held together in like manner by fifty simple loops and fifty brass clasps, the latter, as will be readily understood, being fastened on the outer side. A second covering was thrown over this made of ram skins dyed a flesh colour, and a third of dolphin skins. We must suppose that each of the coverings would be shorter than the one below it, and also of course that they would be fastened, as in the case of other tents, with pegs (here of brass) and ropes.[3] Thus the tabernacle was better protected above than any other tent would be likely to be.

[1] הַמִּשְׁכָּן, which is everywhere carefully distinguished from the tabernacle, as a special and most precious part of the whole.

[2] See my comment on Canticles i. 5.

[3] These are casually mentioned,

Inside, the Holy of Holies was separated off only by a drop-curtain. This was naturally made of the same byssus as the one we have described, and was fastened by golden hooks to four pillars of acacia-wood, which like the planks were covered with gold-leaf and carefully secured in the ground with silver sockets. The drop-curtain itself was undoubtedly fixed behind them, so that the pillars would stand outside the ten ells, while a trifle further to the front hung the ornamental junction of the curtains of byssus.—In front of the whole tabernacle an outer drop-curtain of greater strength, probably twofold,[1] was hung on to five pillars of acacia-wood which were set up across the entire breadth of the tabernacle. It displayed the same colours as the internal curtain, but no embroidered cherubs; the pillars were in other respects adorned like the four internal ones, but had only brazen sockets.

In the next place, this tent-dwelling was surrounded by a large court open to the sky, and enclosed with less substantial materials.[2] The court had a length on the north and south sides of one hundred ells, and a breadth at either end of fifty ells. In what part of it the tabernacle itself stood is not stated exactly, but it would certainly have been well back towards the west. On each long side there were twenty pillars five ells high, i.e. round wooden posts[3] fastened into the ground with brass sockets. Each pillar had a capital overlaid with silver, beneath which was a thick silver ring; at the top on the inner side there was a silver hook, to which, as well as to a brass tent-peg fixed in the ground, a linen cloth, which went all round, was constantly kept stretched like a sail. This cloth was made of fine white byssus. On the west side there were ten similar pillars. How the corners were constructed is not

---

Ex. xxvii. 18; xxxv. 18; xxxviii. 20, 31. We see, however, from Num. iii. 26, 37; iv. 26, 32, that the pegs and lowest ropes of the tent were secured to the woodwork of it, while the remaining ropes belonged merely to the various curtains of the tent and of the court.

[1] מָסָךְ: on the other hand, the drop-curtain of the Holy of Holies is called פָּרֹכֶת הַמָּסָךְ, properly the curtain partition (the dividing curtain), Ex. xxxv. 12; xxxix. 34; xl. 21; Num. iv. 5, but more frequently merely הַפָּרֹכֶת, elsewhere also 'the sacred partition,' Lev. iv. 6, or 'the partition of the Revelation' (p. 125, note 1), xxiv. 3. It is surprising, and due to a manifest error, to find הַמָּסָךְ alone put for the inner drop-curtain,

Num. iii. 31, like διάφραγμα, Protev. Jac. xxiii.: comp. xxiv.

[2] Ex. xxvii. 9-19; xxxviii. 9-20; the latter description is in some particulars more perfect than the former. How the tent actually was erected may be briefly seen from Ex. xl. 18 sq.

[3] That the pillars were round (as is everywhere the most natural) follows from their הָשֻׁקִים; for these can be nothing but the thick rings which formed the cincture of the capital, just as the word slightly altered denotes the nave of a wheel, 1 Kings vii. 33 (according to the correct rendering of this passage).— Moreover, according to Ex. xxxvi. 38, the five pillars before the Holy Place were adorned in the same way, only with gold instead of silver.

explained here. They were therefore, no doubt simply formed in such a way that on the south side (to begin with that) there would be a row of twenty pillars, then a row at right angles on the west side of ten, then on the north side another row of twenty parallel to the first, and then again a row of ten at right angles to it at the east end. All the pillars were five ells apart. In front, i.e. at the east end, there were first three pillars [1] on either side, adjacent to those forming the two sides and supporting the same linen cloth as the latter; but on the five pillars in the middle twenty ells of the more costly linen cloth in four colours were hung as a drop-curtain, so that at the third pillar from the northern extremity, as well as at the third from the southern extremity, the two kinds of linen cloth were contiguous.[2]

2. From this description, which the Book of Origins gives with its admirable minuteness of detail and with thorough clearness in all the main points, we may easily infer how perfectly all the individual constituents of this triple edifice combined to express the thought that all these parts constituted only a single sacred whole, the sanctity of which, however, increased from the outside to the centre in three stages, so that it attained its maximum in the innermost Sanctuary.

The great Sanctuary in the community accordingly seemed to be itself divided in this manner. It is not only one Sanctuary, but three, and even if all are united in their higher aspects, they are stringently separated in their lower. And as a fact it could not well be otherwise. For when once an external appliance or vessel was recognised, not indeed as an image of God himself, but yet as the outward realisation of the fact of his dwelling and working in the community, which we have already seen to have been the case in regard to the ark of the covenant,[3] it was but a logical consequence that a most holy place and, as it were, a private dwelling, should be assigned within the Sanctuary itself to this pre-eminently sacred object. If, in the next place,[4] the Levitical priests alone were deemed fully qualified administrators, as well as guardians and defenders, of all sacred things, it would follow that the place of the visible Sanctuary, along with its appliances, should belong peculiarly to them. If, again, the priesthood was divided into three grades sharply separated from one another, the Sacred Objects which might be touched, and the Sacred Places which might be trodden,

---

[1] These are the 'doors and posts' which are spoken of in Ex. xxi. 6.
[2] The last fact appears now somewhat out of place, Ex. xxvi. 36 sq., and is
[3] P. 122 sqq.
[4] P. 263 sq.

must be divided into three corresponding sections separated by similar sharp lines.¹ The crowd of ordinary Levites could come no further than the forecourt; but as the sacerdotal standing and consecration of these Levites formed the point of transition to the laity,² the latter were also allowed to enter this court when about to offer sacrifice. It was not till the time of the Temple of Solomon that the nation was altogether excluded from this space and relegated to an outer forecourt.³ The Holy Place might be entered by priests of the house of Aaron alone, and even by them only when they had certain solemn duties to perform. The Holy of Holies might be entered by the High-priest alone, and by him only to discharge his most solemn function.

In one point the tabernacle was wholly unlike a heathen sanctuary, viz., in the law forbidding that it should contain any image of a god. But in other respects its construction was quite similar. A heathen sanctuary properly aimed at being nothing but a habitation for a god or gods, and was therefore itself of moderate size, and generally contained an interior space divided off for the reception of an image of the god. In the same way, the tabernacle was not intended for the community, and part of the moderate space which it embraced was divided off as a most sacred place for its most profoundly sacred object. A heathen sanctuary loved dark mysterious chambers; in the same way the two rooms of the tabernacle would naturally be very dark. Thus the very architectural construction of this greatest Sanctuary of the ancient Theocracy proved that although the intrinsic life of the latter was widely separated from that of heathenism, yet in its outward historical manifestation it still for a time fell back thither in many ways.⁴

¹ P. 273 sqq.
² P. 284 sq.
³ Comp. *Hist.* iii. 232 sq., 210 sq.
⁴ This is not the place to speak of the typical and symbolical meanings of the tabernacle, or the sacrifices, and the rest of the Old Testament. It rather belongs to the last days of the Old and the origin of the New Testament, and I reserve what I have to say on this point till I come to that period. The latest attempts to discover such significance in the tabernacle, with all its appliances, which have been made in Germany by Bähr (*Symbolik des Mosaischen Cultus*, bd. i. 1837) and Ferd. Friederich (*Symbolik der Mosaischen Stiftshütte. Eine Vertheidigung D. Luther's gegen D. Bähr*, 1841)

have the merit of expressing their views with great fulness of detail, and equally great seriousness. The former finds in the tabernacle an image of the world; the latter an image of the human body. Both are equally right, and equally wrong. No one will ever succeed in proving that even Moses himself ever thought of either the one idea or the other; how much less the nation!—So far as the mode in which the sacred appliances and localities were determined was felt by Antiquity to be significant, it has been explained here as we went along.—The most recent treatises *Über die Mosaische Stiftshütte*, by Wilh. Neumann (Gotha, 1861) and Riggenbach (Basel, 1862) are unfortunately thoroughly retrograde alike in their purely

3. The places where the sacerdotal functions were respectively performed, and the arrangements of the sacred appliances in regard to them, may now be easily recognised.

The *forecourt* had essentially a threefold purpose. First and foremost all sacrifices of the coarser kind were offered here —all animal- and corn-offerings. These were the offerings in which the sacrificing laity might take a more immediate share, and which for the most part they themselves presented. In it, therefore, as its most important appliance, stood a great altar,[1] usually termed the brazen altar, or from the most important sacrifice, the altar of the burnt-offering. This was probably placed right in front of the tabernacle, midway between it and the entrance to the forecourt. In every altar the chief thing is the hearth, but this one was far more elaborate than those which satisfied the community in its primitive days,[2] constructed merely of earth or stone, and readily erected even in later times beyond the precincts of the great sacred house. The one in the forecourt of the tabernacle, like all the other appliances, was made to be carried, and had, therefore, a framework of acacia-wood, which was only covered over with brass; in this a hearth of earth or stone could be easily laid wherever it might happen to be. Its length and breadth were each five ells, its height was three ells, its shape rectangular; but at the four corners were horns, i.e. crooked points, which projected far above the rest,[3] and might also serve to retain the larger sacrificial portions which were laid upon the altar. They were, however, to be made all in one piece with the altar, just as in general importance was attached to the sacred appliances consisting of a single piece; the nature of a sacred thing requiring it to be perfect and entire in itself.[4] Beneath these horns round the upper edge there ran a tolerably broad and thick belt,[5] which served to hold the whole framework better together. Beneath this, extending to the middle of the altar, was secured its sole adornment, a sort of network cast in brass, the particular form of which we no longer know.—Belonging to it were many fire-pans, shovels

---

historical and in their symbolical interpretation, though the latter is rather more sensible than the former.

[1] P. 117 sq.
[2] P. 121.
[3] According to Amos iii. 14, and other passages, these 'horns' can by no means have been so small as they are usually represented. Joseph. *Antiq.* iii. 6. 8, calls them στέφανοι, *crowns*; comp.

too 'Innumeris structam de cornibus aram,' Ovid *Her.* xxi. 99.

[4] The same was required in the case of the golden altar and the sacred lamp-stand; comp. also the instances on pp. 278, 292. It is still so 1 Macc. iv. 47.

[5] This is certainly the meaning of כַּרְכֹּב, according to the delineation, Ex. xxvii. 1-8.

and prongs, and ash-pans, as well as bowls for sprinkling blood,[1] all of which were made of brass. Our description, however, gives us no information respecting the raised platform on which the altar stood. That it did stand on some such elevation is proved beyond doubt both by other indications in the Book of Origins,[2] as well as by the example of Solomon's Temple, which in more important matters always followed the model of the sacred objects described in the Book of Origins. In the temple the hearth, and therefore the altar proper, was only four ells high, but its length and breadth were each twelve ells, or, including the brazen belt which surrounded it, fourteen ells. Beneath this belt was a second, which extended downwards a distance of four ells, and projected outwards so as to form a second terrace of the width of one ell, and lastly a third terrace extending downwards two ells to the ground, and again projecting one ell.[3] The latter two terraces must have been approached by steps, and however much the size of Solomon's altar exceeded that of the earlier one, the latter must have had similar steps, and in this respect, too, have furnished a model for Solomon's. At Solomon's altar these steps would undoubtedly be erected on the eastern side; also towards the east, probably the south-east, was the place where the ashes and other refuse were provisionally discharged.[4]

In the second place the forecourt served the regular priests as a place of preparation for their solemn duties in the Sanctuary itself. If one of them desired to enter the Holy Place, or if he had only to attend to the sacrifice on the great altar just described, he must first wash his hands and his feet. For this purpose a brazen washing-basin was placed on a brazen pedestal between this altar and the tabernacle, not far therefore from the entrance to the latter.[5] The pedestal is always carefully distinguished from the basin, and there was no doubt

---

[1] See p. 44 sq.
[2] See above, p. 74. The Book of Covenants, Ex. xx. 26; comp. Ezek. xliii. 17. does, it is true, prohibit the use of such steps, but only for the reason we have noticed on p. 278, which disappeared when the more brilliant and better arranged sacerdotal service described in the Book of Origins had become firmly established.
[3] We may supplement the brief words in 2 Chron. iv. 1, from the description in Ezek. xliii. 13–17, as he had no occasion here for departing from Solomon's example. The altar was accordingly ten ells high, with an entire length and breadth of twenty ells, the horizontal dimensions being no less, because the lowest, as well as the third terrace, projected one ell. I have explained Ezekiel's obscure description more fully here than I did in 1840 in my *Prophets*.
[4] According to Lev. i. 16; comp. vi. 3 [10] sq.—If, moreover, all great altars among the heathen as well generally had steps (comp. *Corp. Inscriptt. Gr.* iii. pp. 25, 27), they nevertheless varied much according to each particular religion; comp. *Hist.* iv. 171, as well as Is. xvii. 8, and elsewhere.
[5] Ex. xxx. 17–21; xxxviii. 8; xl. 7, 11, 30.

something special in its construction, but we know no more about either than has already been said.¹

In the third place, the numerous custodians of the tabernacle, for the most part Levites, had to keep watch within the forecourt. We have already explained that certain duties would be discharged here even by women.²

The *Holy Place* was used for the more delicate sacrifices which the priests alone offered, and the rest of the people, including the Levites, never saw with their own eyes. Here stood, in the first place, the sacred table, which was certainly one of the very earliest appliances of the Sanctuary,³ with the twelve loaves which were changed every Sabbath. It was made of acacia-wood covered over with thin gold-leaf, two ells long, one broad, and one and a half high. How far its four feet projected we cannot tell; it was, however, surrounded by a golden hoop, from which it would appear that the wood which composed it was of considerable thickness. The top was enclosed by a sort of fence, four inches high, which was itself surrounded by a golden hoop.⁴—Near this sacred table were preserved the smaller implements which belonged to the offering of the bloodless sacrifice; the large plates to bring and take away the twelve loaves, the small bowls out of which the incense was scattered, the larger and smaller cups for libations of wine.⁵ All these were made of gold.

But the Holy Place was a dark chamber, and if therefore the numerous duties which the priests had to discharge in it were enough to make it necessary to employ artificial light, this was another reason, in addition to those already mentioned,⁶ why a light should be kept perpetually burning there. A lamp-stand was accordingly so constructed as to fulfil this higher function. It had to carry seven lamps, of which one was to stand higher than the others,—a manifest reference to the week and the Sabbath, and thus become a most genuine symbol of Jahveism, and a materialisation of what was most sacred in it (the highest Sacrament). It was, moreover, to be wrought as artistically as possible, as one of the most sacred appliances. In the centre was one strong shaft (or rod) which terminated in a broad foot, and in which there were three knots or expansions. From each of the latter there sprang two arms,

---

¹ P. 285.
² P. 285 sq.
³ P. 27 sq.
⁴ Ex. xxv. 23–29; xxxvii. 10–16.
⁵ This is the most probable purpose for the small vessels spoken of Ex. xxv. 29; xxxvii. 16; comp. Num. iv. 7; vii. 13 sq. קְשׂוֹת was the smaller cup holding as much wine as could be poured out at once. We may notice everywhere how many words there are which are used only of such sacred appliances.
⁶ P. 114 sq.

PURPOSE OF THE HOLY PLACE.

one to the left and one to the right, the whole six winding aloft in a serpentine fashion. Each of these arms expanded in three places in the form of the calyx of an almond-blossom.[1] Each of the three double arms sprang from such another calyx on the central shaft; and above these six branches with their three knots the main trunk was continued with four similar calyxes, so that the main trunk with its seven calyxes projected a considerable distance above the six arms, and thereby gave a clear image of the exaltation of the Sabbath over the other six days.[2] In the last place, the seven lamps were secured in their respective places. The entire sevenfold lamp-stand was made of refined gold, of chased workmanship, but all carefully cast in a single piece.[3] Everything which belonged to it, the lamp-tongs, fire-cups, and oil-cans,[4] were likewise made of refined gold.

While the sacred table was unmistakeably derived from a primitive era long prior to Moses, and the sacred lamp originated in the Mosaic period proper, a third appliance probably did not originate till the time when the whole Sanctuary assumed its perfect form as described in the Book of Origins, viz. immediately after the conquest of Canaan. This is the golden altar, also termed the altar of incense.[5] It was made of acacia-wood, but covered over with gold-leaf, and was one ell in length and breadth, and two in height. It was encircled by a golden hoop, and in other respects, including the horns, resembled the great brazen altar. It became an altar for the priests alone, at which nothing but the most delicate substance might be offered, viz. incense; this, however, was to be offered without ceasing.[6] Even the pouring of libations of wine upon it is expressly forbidden by the Book of Origins,[7] although, as we have just said, the vessels for the purpose were kept in the Holy Place. Even as this altar properly represented the sacrifices of the priests in contradistinction to the ordinary ones, so

---

[1] If in the description, Ex. xxv. 31–40, xxxvii. 17–24, the word גְבִיעַ is always followed by the explanation 'knot (belly) and blossom,' this is entirely due to the fact that, besides its first meaning of 'calyx,' the word had already acquired a second and commoner meaning of 'cup.'

[2] In the sacred lamp-stand, which figures on the triumphal arch of Titus at Rome, the central shaft does not, it is true, appear to be higher than the rest, but then the image is not quite complete just at the top, and in other respects this lamp-stand does not quite agree with the pattern described in the Pentateuch. The meaning of the words in the Book of Origins is, however, clear.

[3] P. 326.

[4] According to Ex. xxv. 38; xxxvii. 21; comp. Num. iv. 9, 16. The tongs were used to remove the lamp from the lamp-stand in order to trim it afresh; with the fire-cup a light was then brought from the altar.

[5] Ex. xxx. 1–10; xxxvii. 25–29; xl. 5, 26 sq.

[6] P. 115.

[7] Ex. xxx. 9; but the first member of this verse must terminate with זָרָה.

it manifestly originated in connection with the fully developed sacerdotal powers of the house of Aaron, and was so far the most modern of this whole series of appliances. It was probably placed exactly in the middle of the Holy Place, while the sacred table would stand in the north-west, the sacred candlestick in the south-west corner.[1]

Either from the perpetually burning lamps or, as is more probable, from the fire which, though only a small one, was always kept up on this inner altar, the sacrificial priest was always to bring the fire for the great outer altar whenever it was required, especially therefore for the very first sacrifice which was offered upon it, and on other mornings and evenings if the fire which had been previously kindled there had died out.[2] All other fire with which a sacrificial priest approached the external altar was deemed *strange*, inappropriate, and unblessed, desecrating the whole Sanctuary, and fatal to the sacrificial priest himself, as though the despised gentle flame of the inner Sanctuary suddenly and spontaneously poured itself forth in a violent flood, annihilating the false fire and priest.[3] In like manner all perfumery was deemed strange and unholy in this sense, unless it had been prepared in a particular fashion, and in definite proportion from pure frankincense, mixed with three other sweet-smelling materials.[4] The balsam, too, with which both the tabernacle, with all its appliances, and also the High-priest, were to be consecrated, was to be prepared in a similar technical fashion.[5] Both the balsam and the incense were to be kept in the inner Sanctuary, and any imitation of them or application to other purposes would have been already regarded by the time of the Book of Origins as impious.

We have clear tokens that during the earliest centuries certain other sacred objects were deposited in this Holy Place which were never received into Solomon's Temple. A small vessel filled with manna was preserved here, and at first may have been annually renewed.[6] Here, too, was kept Aaron's sceptre,

---

[1] P. 44. Ex. xxx. 6; xl. 4 sq., 22-26. It will also follow from the name 'table of the countenance,' that the sacred table stood as near as possible to the Holy of Holies.—The erection of a smaller along with a greater altar occurred also in heathen temples, Herod. i. 183; Tac. *Hist.* ii. 3.

[2] P. 116.

[3] The law about what was foreign and what native fire is now wanting from the Book of Origins. We can, however, draw correct conclusions about the whole matter from the indication in Lev. ix. 24; x. 1; Num. iii. 4; xxvi. 61, as well as from the similarity of the foreign incense of which we are just about to speak.

[4] According to Ex. xxx. 34-38; comp. ver. 8.

[5] Ex. xxx. 22-33.

[6] *Hist.* ii. 222 *note* 2.

PURPOSE OF THE HOLY OF HOLIES.

of whose former real existence it is impossible to doubt.¹ Where the consecrated presents² were kept we cannot tell. Whether the two sacerdotal silver trumpets,³ which, according to the representation on the triumphal arch of Titus, were contained in the Holy Place of Herod's Temple, were then deposited in the ancient Mosaic tabernacle, cannot be determined from the Book of Origins.⁴ It is improbable, in so far as only objects of greater sanctity were preserved in the Holy Place; they seem to have been admitted later into Herod's Temple merely because mention was made of them in the Pentateuch.

The *Holy of Holies* contained nothing but the ark of the covenant, that one object of absolute sanctity with which nothing else seemed comparable. Here it ever stood in awful darkness, scarcely illumined on those rarest occasions when the High-priest entered with a censer.

Round about the whole Sanctuary there was still another environment to ensure its solemn quiet and security, and guard against the inroad of any disturbing element.⁵ We have even traces of a partiality for planting high trees in its neighbourhood, and the primitive custom we have already mentioned of distinguishing a sacred spot by such trees was retained in this way,⁶ though nothing of the sort was required by the law.

—This is the tabernacle with all its essential constituents as described in the Book of Origins. That it originated with almost all its appliances during the time of Moses, and that even its latest developments were not subsequent to the period

---

¹ P. 298. The expression 'before the ark of the covenant,' Ex. xvi. 34; Num. xvii. 25 sq., may refer to the Holy Place, since the ark of the covenant was only separated by the drop-curtain; and that this is the actual meaning follows more distinctly from Ex. xxx. 6; xl. 5. When the author of the Epistle to the Hebrews (ix. 4) places the golden altar in the Holy of Holies, the manna, and the sceptre, as well as the tables of the law, *inside* the ark of the covenant, his view arises from a literal interpretation of the words in Ex. xl. 4; xvi. 34; Num. xvii. 25.
² P. 71 sqq.
³ P. 288.
⁴ Num. x. 1–10; xxxi. 6.
⁵ This is to be inferred from Ex. xix. 12 sq., 21–23; xxxiv. 3.—How simple were all these ancient limitations in comparison with the artificial *seven purifications*, ἑπτὰ ἁγνεῖαι, with which those of a later date, according to Joseph. *Bell.*

Jud. § 10, *ad init.*, endeavoured to protect their Holy Place! What Josephus means there may be inferred from v. 5, 6. The whole of Jerusalem as a sacred city was to be forbidden ground: (1) To those who were suffering from *gonorrhœa*, p. 157; (2) To lepers, p. 157; the Sanctuary, in the widest sense, was to be forbidden: (3) To unclean women, p. 156; (4) To all women, with the exception of the women's forecourt, *Hist.* vi. s. 717 [Ger. ed.]; (5) The great forecourt to unclean men; (6) The priest's forecourt to unclean priests; (7) The Holy of Holies to all priests save the High-priest. Similar regulations occur in the Talmud.
⁶ P. 120. The fact appears from Josh. xxiv. 26; and that such trees were not wanting in even the later temple follows from the delineation in Zach. i. 8; Ps. lii. 10; xcii. 13 sq. But it is denied by Hecateus in Joseph. *Contr. Ap.* i. 22, p. 457.

immediately following him, is unmistakeably indicated by every token. All its constituent parts and appliances, wherever this was required by a roving life, were provided with rings through which poles for carrying, which were always kept in readiness, might easily be passed. This the Book of Origins everywhere describes as something essential. When it had to be removed, the High-priest first caused the drop-curtain of the Holy of Holies to be taken down by his most immediate associates, and laid as the most worthy covering over the ark of the covenant; over this was thrown a covering of dolphin-skins, and lastly one entirely made of dark blue byssus. The same hands laid a similar covering over the sacred table, then wrapped it, and all its vessels, and the sacred bread, in bright red byssus, and threw dolphin-skins over this. The sacred candlestick and the golden altar, with all that belonged to it, were covered in the same way with dark blue byssus and dolphin-skins. The brazen altar and the washing-basin were wrapped up in dark red byssus, and covered, with all that belonged to them, with dolphin-skins. Not till all this was done did the first division of the Levites commence carrying these things away; on the High-priest himself devolved the special care of the sacred oil, incense, and daily sacrifice. The second division of the Levites removed the various curtains and coverings of the tabernacle and the forecourt, with their appurtenances and other appliances of less importance. The third division took charge of the wood-work, with its appurtenances; the two latter divisions acting under the direction of the second High-priest,[1] and employing an adequate number of waggons.[2] It will be plain, from what we have said, how ingenious and appropriate were all these allotments and arrangements.

When the army (or the entire nation) was on the march, the tabernacle, surrounded by the Levites[3], was appropriately carried in the centre; in camp it was set up in the centre. This the Book of Origins describes as what was customary during the time of Moses;[4] and even if at a later time the tent

---

[1] According to Num. iii. 25 sq., 31, 36 sq.; iv. 4-37, with some genuine additions in the version of the LXX.

[2] According to Num. vii. 1-10. The question may be asked whether two waggons for the Gershonites, and four for the Merarites, would suffice to remove so many heavy articles. It is possible that the proportions of the tabernacle given by the author of the Book of Origins, manifestly from personal inspection, may not have been those of the light tabernacle of the time of Moses, but of a more expensive and heavier one, such as Israel's dignity required after the conquest of the land. The difference would not alter anything essential; what may be said on behalf of this view has already been noticed above.

[3] P. 281.

[4] Num. ii.-iv.; x. 11-28 (comp. Hist. ii. 275); also Ezekiel's imagery, xlv., xlviii. The meaning of the words in Num. x. 17, 21, is this—the inferior class

was carried by the side of the army, the Sanctuary always seems to have had a central position in the camp. Nevertheless, the different description of the Third Narrator of the Primitive history[1] shows that the tabernacle was also sometimes set up outside the camp. It invariably faced the east, an ancient custom, which maintained itself with great tenacity among the heathen.[2]

of the Levites, after they are ready to depart, are to wait till the superior *Kohath* comes up from the south side, and take its place at the head; comp. p. 282.

[1] P. 281 sqq.

[2] See Plutarch's *Numa* xiv.

HOW BOTH SIDES WERE SUPPLEMENTED IN THE COURSE OF TIME.

THE GREAT SABBATH-CYCLE.

When the sacred tabernacle we have been describing had been happily erected in the community which assembled round about Jahveh, and within it[1] the eternal sacrificial fire was joyously blazing, it seemed as though the existence of the established community of Jahveh in this state of development should be as eternal as that of the sacrificial fire. The words, 'They my people, I their God,'[2] along with the true religion, would seemed to have been realised in fact and secured in undisturbed existence. Jahveh had now, as it were, acquired a permanent peaceful dwelling among this single nation of the earth; and the rising column of fire and smoke, which hung without intermission over the visible Sanctuary, even if it were really only the result of the daily sacrificial fire, was deemed by the people, just because without it they would still have believed in the guardian presence of Jahveh, to be the visible image and realisation of this dwelling of the glory of the Most High in its midst.[3]

But no one can have understood better than the great founder of the community that in all this there was involved a joyous belief in the realisation of the true religion and community, as well as a sure confidence in the same, rather than the actual realisation itself. How little the divine demands for sanctity and righteousness of life, as they have been described above, were fully satisfied by the community, and how little all the national institutions which were built thereon would remain

---

[1] P. 115 sqq.
[2] P. 4.
[3] The description in Ex. xl. 43-16; Lev. ix. 23 sq., must be compared with the other in Num. ix. 15 sqq., in order to understand how the Book of Origins still reproduces an historical, very clear-sighted view of these matters dating from the primitive days of the community; comp. *Hist.* ii. p. 217 sqq. The later Rabbi-nical term שְׁכִינָה for this *dwelling* of God *in the midst* of his people, or the visible manifestation of this eternal glory, is taken from Ex. xxix. 45 sq, xl. 35.— There is a similarity in spite of differences in the belief that guardian angels conduct cooling winds over the Ka'aba and the Mohammedans assembled round it, Burckhardt's *Travels in Arabia*, i. p. 256 sq., 292 sq.

undisturbed, would have been made sufficiently plain to Moses by the incidents of his own long leadership, even if he would not have expected it for other reasons. No doubt there had been a time when by the establishment of the community of Jahveh all previous impurity had been, as it were, washed away, and the foundation was laid in the life of the nation for an entirely new, pure, holy commencement. So, too, there had been a time when these demands were not only plainly promulgated, but were also acknowledged by the nation as binding on itself. This was the commencement of an inner perfection and glory, corresponding to the above outward manifestation. Nevertheless, troubles began to arise again soon enough; and it became sufficiently obvious that even all the expiatory- and guilt-offerings, nay, that all temporal punishments, could not suffice to root them out. Indeed, it became evident that the gradual progress of time imperceptibly brought with it a variety of new evils, which in the end were mighty and perceptible enough, and which threatened to destroy the most intrinsic life of the entire realm.

Insidious evils like these, which are little amenable to law, and gradually work their way in with more and more disastrous consequences, are enemies from which, it is true, even our modern Christian kingdoms suffer; and many such have sprung into being, owing to the contingencies of recent centuries. Nor will it ever be possible, in the course of human history, to provide against all possibilities of evil which the future may bring forth. Make the best and purest start possible, and yet before long new evils will find entrance, partly from remnants of the former state of things, partly from the fresh impulses of the new condition, so long as humanity continues to develope, and stirrings of evil exist to remind man how far he still is from the goal of his history. Yet, in our case, the insidious evils need not inevitably become very dangerous. We have only to give fair play to the working, on the one hand, of the now perfected, extant, revelation of true religion; and, on the other hand, of the rich experience, capabilities, and knowledge, that have already been acquired. In the ancient world, on the contrary, especially in remote antiquity, even among the people of Israel, the inner work of true religion was not nearly so far completed that every man everywhere could easily tell what he ought to do, and what to leave undone; and there was far from being any superfluity, either of historical experience or of higher capabilities and knowledge, such as would suffice to establish, e.g. the civil law of debt upon unassailable principles.[1] Moreover, the insidious

[1] P. 181 sqq.

evils grow all the more dangerous in every realm, in proportion to the closeness with which it seeks to shut itself up in itself. And the kingdom of Jahveh rested on a very narrow self-contained nationality, and on a conscious sharp opposition towards all the other kingdoms of the existing world.

We can thus imagine how earnest would be the endeavours made by Moses and the other great souls of his time to encounter the inevitable deficiencies in the right way, and everywhere to restore the original purity and health of the body corp rate when it had been imperceptibly undermined. Nevertheless, the means which they adopted for achieving this end, and which then seemed the most effective and best, could not well have been obtained anywhere, save from the whole life and tissue of the ancient religion; so that what was already in force reappears once again here, only in a new and stronger form. It was essentially necessary to appoint certain longer or shorter periods, when all that had been overthrown or become exhausted might be restored to its original pure and healthy life; just as our modern representative assemblies meet at regular intervals to effect a grand purification of the whole condition of the nation. But what was specially characteristic of these ancient periods was, that, in order to satisfy more effectively the divine demands for holiness and uprightness, and supplement all that was defective, the human efforts and strivings towards God, as Antiquity understood them,[1] were at such times stimulated to the highest pitch. The endeavour to supplement all human action or endurance, wherever men felt this to be requisite in order to satisfy the divine demands for holiness and uprightness, took accordingly the form of sacrifice, as Antiquity understood it; and here we meet with the highest application of sacrifice which could possibly proceed from the ancient ideas in regard to it.

Similar institutions are to be found in the laws of many ancient realms, and still exist in Islâm, that belated shoot from the mighty stem of true religion, aiming at surpassing its two fellow-shoots which had already sprouted and grown great, but in reality remaining behind both. For a similar irrepressible feeling of an inner want, and hence a similar craving to supplement ordinary laws by more drastic measures, which are held in reserve, must have pervaded every religion and legislation which, although striving after the highest, yet fell short of its aim in something essential. But nowhere do

[1] Pp. 12-133.

we see this supplemental process carried through all possible details with so firm a hand, and bearing so palpably the mark of being due to one great thought, as we do in Jahveism. On a close investigation, it appears as certain as anything can be that these final offshoots of the ancient legislation sprang altogether, as the expression of a single idea, from the mind of the the arch-legislator.

So if the Sabbath was at once the highest and the most characteristic sacrifice of Jahveism,[1] the one in which the latter's whole meaning was most perfectly expressed, and which on that account strove with its whole power to penetrate all things, it became a matter of course that the great attempt to supplement all earlier laws should be connected with the Sabbath, and make this the sole point of departure. And, as a fact, no other foundation was so admirably adapted for the erection of a new high-towering stronghold, which should be a fortress capable of upholding and protecting all else. In regard to the determination of the above-mentioned longer or shorter intervals for a purification and restoration of the great Whole, the sabbatical number, Seven, was easily capable of a varied and extended application. And in regard to the general significance of such intervals, this too could be included in the higher significance of the Sabbath. For, as on ordinary sabbaths there was to be rest from the care and occupations of ordinary life, so on these greater sabbaths there was to be a universal cessation of ordinary national life; only their rest should embrace a wider sphere, and have in view remoter purposes. Yet, as the weekly sabbath rest, regularly recurring at the shortest intervals, only aimed at a fresh gathering up and strengthening of the spirit, and hence at a new vigorous commencement of work, so the greater and greatest sabbaths, recurring at longer and longer intervals, should bring greater and greatest rest with the sole view of restoring all the earthly constituents of the kingdom of Jahveh once again to their original and necessary purity, health, and uprightness. Only with this meaning and for this purpose was there a multiplication and wider extension of the simple sabbath as the firm foundation and centre of the organism of Jahveism. The fundamental thought is the same, only working in wider spheres in order to subdue unto itself a continually greater and farther-stretching province. From this follows the further important consequence, that what holds good in the smaller circle will repeat itself in the larger, only

[1] P. 97 sq.

on a more extended scale, so that nothing can be wanting from the larger which has been given in the smaller, until in the largest circle all that the fundamental thought is capable of producing is realised in fact.

The individual, as well as each particular community, ought to withdraw on every weekly sabbath from the toil and moil of common life, and seek strength in God for fresh activity. Starting from this fact, we observe three provinces, each one more important than its predecessor, which, in the progress of time, lose their original virtue and strength far more imperceptibly and gradually than the individual, but nevertheless to an extent which is at least evident and prejudicial enough, so that they, too, each require their several sabbaths at the proper periods. These three provinces are the following: the national character, as something still of vital importance to religion; the soil possessed by the nation, as the great instrument for its physical maintenance; and, finally, the whole kingdom itself, so far as it is a permanent institution of a human, and therefore perishable, nature. In this triple series of great provinces is contained everything outside the individual man and particular sections of the realm, which was liable to a gradual decay and destruction, merely under the influence of time, and which was all the more exposed thereto the longer the elements of decay remained concealed. But while the national religion and morals needed to be again refreshed and strengthened after a period reckoned in months, hence when possible once a year, the nourishing soil of mother-earth only required the same in the course of years; and the kingdom, although human and perishable, ought nevertheless to rest fairly upon such good laws and institutions, that only after the lapse of decades and centuries should it need a purification and revival extending to its fundamental basis.

In this way the simple weekly sabbath was supplemented by a *sabbath-month*, which was the seventh in the year, and as such determined the date of all the other annual festivals, i.e., of the greater sabbaths—just as the days of the week are governed by the higher and more sacred day,—and embraced all the simple weekly sabbaths in itself, as it was itself embraced within the circle of the year. This sabbath-month was again supplemented by the *sabbath-year*, which recurred every seventh year from the one which was chosen as the commencement, and furnished a starting point from which the whole series could be reckoned. This, in the last place, was supplemented by a *sabbath-sabbath-year*, which was the seventh sabbath-year (reckoned rather as the fiftieth year), and closed the entire circle in its wide embrace, so that each half-century was succeeded by another like itself. This is a brief sketch of the magnificent way in which all the other laws of Jahveism were supplemented and brought to perfection. We have now to examine the details more closely.[1]

This grand, constant progression of the sacred number Seven displays the progression of the three stages which are here reared upon the firm basis of the simple sabbath, or of the three circles which surround the latter as the vital heart of the whole. On every convenient occasion, however, in numerous ways within the various circles, the arrangements are regulated by this all-dominant number seven, or rather governed by the powerful conception of the Sabbath; so vigorous are the efforts of the latter to penetrate the entire sphere. And this fact at once appears in the first circle, because the nature of this circle cannot be absolutely simple, but involves many complications.

The Division of Time in the Ancient Nation.

Before we consider more closely the earliest form of the series of periods sanctified by Israel's religion, we must see what was the division of time in general which prevailed in the ordinary life of the ancient nation, since every subsequent calculation and division rests finally on this broad basis. We must, at any rate, acquaint ourselves more accurately with those facts which are somewhat difficult to understand, or peculiar. An established method of dividing the time through which men have to live is rendered indispensable by so numerous and inevitable requirements of common life, that most complicated divisions come into existence long before a higher religion tries to guide the life of a whole nation, and these maintain their place alongside and independent of the religion.

1. To commence with the sections of the day, it cannot be proved that a division into twelve, or, with the night, twenty-four hours, was introduced among the people of Israel in its

---

[1] The whole subject I had already treated in 1835 in an essay which was subsequently printed in the *Commentationes Soc. Reg. scient. Götting. rec.* t. viii., as well as in the *Morgenländischen Zeitschrift*, vol. iii. s. 410 sqq. With this the further remarks in the *Gött. G. Anz.* 1835, s. 2025 sqq., and 1836, s. 678 sqq., may be compared. Much that was said there is not repeated here.—A more remote consequence of the former essay may be found in the treatises of Kranold and Wolde *De anno jubilæo*, which obtained prizes at the Göttingen Jubilee in 1837. The theme of these essays was proposed by the late D. J. Pott, in conjunction with myself (although at that time I was a member of the philosophical faculty), and this gave me further occasion to write upon the subject in the *Morgenländischen Zeitschrift*, i. s. 410 sqq.—In regard to the most perverse treatises, written after 1852, by H. Hupfeld; comp. the *Jahrbb. d. Bibl. Wiss.* iv. s. 131 sqq.; ix. ss. 257–260; also viii. 223.

earliest epoch. On the contrary, such an assumption is controverted by all the tokens which we can now discover. According to these tokens, only the three main dividing points in the day which are given of themselves were used to designate, in quite general terms, the sections which preceded and followed them; so that the day was divided into three parts, or, if a distinction is made between the two halves of each of the sections thus given, into six parts. The *upright*, i.e. central, *point of the day* (from which it declines on either side towards night) i.e. noon,[1] when the sun stands, as it were, motionless right over men, was enclosed by the *double-noon*, or the time immediately preceding and subsequent. The *evening*, in the strictest sense, i.e. the moment of sunset,[2] was enclosed by the *double-evening*; the morning, i.e. sunrise, by the *double-morning*.[3] Any further accurate and permanent distinction between these three periods of the day cannot be shown to have existed. It is true that the limit of these three periods might be drawn nearer to their centres, and a narrower definition given, by the expressions *about the heat of the day*,[4] and *towards the wind of the day*, i.e., towards morning or evening.[5] It was also possible to distinguish the beginning and the end of each of the three main divisions of the day.[6] Besides these, the whole nation gradually learned to distinguish the exact moment when daily sacrifice was offered morning or evening.[7] In this way was made a beginning of dividing the day into a number of still shorter periods; but the three main divisions of the day were so far from being superseded, that the entire night was divided into *three* corresponding *night-watches*.[8] Each of the latter may, however, have been somewhat shorter than the former divisions, supposing the night to have been reckoned from the commencement of total darkness to the first, or rather the second, gleam of dawn. An arrangement, and corresponding reckoning, of *four* night-

---

[1] נְכוֹן הַיּוֹם, Prov. iv. 18.

[2] For עֶרֶב itself denotes the sunset.

[3] There is now extant in the Old Testament no dual of בְּקֶר, but that one is possible, and that at any rate the similar form שָׁחֳרַיִם occurs, is shown in my *Lehrb.* § 180a. The latter term must denote the time of the rosy dawn (the *primum* et *alterum diluculum*), the same as is still expressed in Syriac by the word ܨܦܪܝܐ, a dual corresponding to the διάφαυμα. *Protev. Jac.* xxiii., according to the Syriac translation edited by W. Wright.

[4] According to Gen. xviii. 1.

[5] The phrase itself, it is true, usually refers to the evening alone, Gen. iii. 8; comp. Cant. ii. 17; iv. 6; but the ancient word רוּחַ, which of itself likewise denotes a blowing, indicates the morning, as well as the evening, twilight; and distinctly means the former in Job iii. 9; vii. 4; Lam. xxx. 17.

[6] As in respect to the night watches, Lam. ii. 19; Jud. vii. 19.

[7] P. 116. Still the same, *M.* פסח iv. 5.

[8] According to Jud. vii. 19, and Ex. xiv. 24; 1 Sam. xi. 11.

watches,[1] only became possible in Palestine through the Romans, or more definitely through the introduction of Roman military dominion. It cannot, at any rate, be shown to have been in existence there earlier.

This division of the day into six sections may, by a gradual bisecting of each sixth, and by a strict limitation of the day to one-half of an entire day-and-night,[2] have developed into an accurate division with twelve hours in the day and twelve hours in the night. This at least is the easiest explanation of the choice of the number twelve for the hours. But this would only become possible by means of more artificial instruments for measuring time, such as sun-dials, sand-clocks, and the like. The invention of this division of time was ascribed by the ancients to the Babylonians,[3] although we now know from the hieroglyphics that the early Egyptian dynasties were acquainted with it. It came at last into use among the people of Israel;[4] and, as we know that King Ahaz was the first who introduced a sundial,[5] it may have suppressed the ancient division of the day more and more from his date in the eighth century onwards.

The influence of religion on either of these modes of dividing the day can only have been very trifling. The strict precision which was necessary in the sacerdotal arrangements of the entire daily divine service, as well as of the needful night-watches,[6] and other reasons which caused importance to be attached to this precision, did indeed prevent religion from remaining wholly without influence on other national customs and occupations in this respect. But there was one case in which this influence was very important. To connect the annual festivals with the full-moon, and to commence them in the evening, as though greeting her with a glad shout, was certainly a primitive custom, both among other races, and in the circle of nations from which in the earliest times Israel sprang. When Moses instituted the Sabbath, which, as described above,[7] is ultimately based on the lunar period, this custom was transferred to it as though it were to stand on an equal footing with the great festivals, in regard to time-honoured sanctity. Since, however, the Sabbath, as indicated above,

---

[1] Mark vi. 48 ; Matt. xiv. 43 ; Luke xii. 38.—All four are mentioned together, Mark xiii. 35.
[2] The νυχθήμερον.
[3] According to Herod. ii. 109. As a fact the Semitic word for *hour* is originally the pure Aramaic ܐܫܳܥܳܐ and is quite unknown in ancient Hebrew, though it travelled into Arabia and Ethiopia as well as into late Hebrew from the Aramaic.
[4] Distinct mention of it occurs first in the Aramaic speeches in the Book of Daniel.
[5] *Hist.* iv. 169.
[6] Pp. 114, 287 ; comp. Ps. cxxxiv. 1, 2.
[7] P. 97 sqq.

became the permanently preeminent day, to which every series of days was to return after a brief interval, it cannot surprise us that the remaining days should follow its precedent in so far that for sacerdotal matters each day commenced with sunset, at which moment the watches appointed for the day commenced their duty; and thus one day passed into the next, not during the hours of sleep, but while the occupations of life were in full activity.[1] But it must be allowed that this commencement of the ordinary day with the evening cannot possibly be adapted to all sides and needs of human life; and we even have a proof of how natural it is, in spite of all this, to reckon from morning to morning, in the sublime narrative of the creation, Gen. i. 1–ii. 4. Even the twelve hours, after they had been introduced, were reckoned from morning to evening.[2]

2. In this matter we only find further consequences of the strong influence exerted by the regard for the moon, an influence which must have maintained itself in this nation down from remote Antiquity, and which will be found predominant in other matters. The reckoning by months, in its primitive significance, and hence by lunar years, continued to prevail, and was closely connected with the celebration of the above annual festivals.

But the mode of reckoning by the solar year had likewise been long familiar to the highly civilised nations with which Israel early came into such close contact, the Egyptians, and the Arameans or Babylonians. Even the mode of adjusting the solar and lunar years in the course of time had already been calculated by their learned men with great accuracy; indeed, in essentials they had made the solar year the basis of all reckoning of time, and had introduced it into the actual life of the nation. The fact is, it is indispensable, on the most numerous and unavoidable grounds, for every more highly civilised nation to reckon time according to the solar year. The people of Israel made no discoveries in all these matters. They had long been firmly established among nations of far greater antiquity and early civilisation when Israel came into their midst, and could become a sharer of their knowledge and institutions. Not only, however, was Israel acquainted with the solar year generally, but also with the peculiar arrangement of it which had become customary among these nations, as we learn plainly enough from the way in which the history of the Flood was adopted and recast by the Book of Origins, a phe-

---

[1] To which allusion is already made in Ps. xc. 4, according to the correct rendering.

[2] This does not touch the question how the hours were reckoned by John in his Gospel.

nomenon which in this connection is extraordinarily instructive in many respects.[1] If the influence of a purely lunar reckoning finally got the upper hand in this nation, there must have been a very special cause for this; and on a closer inspection we cannot doubt that what turned the scale here was nothing but the mighty age of Moses and its spirit, transforming all the religious customs of those nations which, up to that point, had been exerting such influence. As Jahveism under Moses reverted in so many other respects to the greater simplicity and the sacred reminiscences of the ancient people, so now, in direct opposition to the custom of the Egyptians and other similar nations, the observation of the lunar period and lunar year, which must have been customary of old among the ancestors of Israel, again became predominant, and was made the basis on which the whole series of the sacred times of the nation should be established. So far as this new mode of reckoning proceeded from the impulse and power of the new religion, it must, before long, as we have already noticed,[2] have been intrusted for the most part to the care, the insight, and the learning, of the priests. And, as a fact, it intertwined itself the more inseparably with Jahveism, the more securely it established, and the longer it developed, itself. The traces, however, of the other mode of reckoning, by the solar year, never totally disappeared; rather was a constant endeavour made to reconcile the two modes one with the other.

Still another point of importance has to be considered. For the agriculturist, the solar year has its main and best marked division, and hence its new commencement, after the great harvest, and in a country such as Palestine after the vine-harvest, since this was there of great importance. Consequently to commence the year in autumn became the primitive custom in the countries about the Euphrates and the Tigris.[3] The same custom probably prevailed from the earliest times among the nations of Palestine before the people of Israel acquired a fixed settlement there; and even in Israel itself it was the traditional practice, as will be further explained below. If, never-

[1] See on this subject the *Jahrbb. d. Bibl. Wiss.* vii. s. 8 sqq. The principal points here are the 365 days, and the months of 30 days each. That this was the primitive custom in Asia outside Persian boundaries, I already noticed in reference to Israel in the essay in the *Zeitsch. für die Kunde des Morgenlandes*, iii. s. 417 sqq.; but the Egyptian mode of reckoning was the same, comp. Lepsius, *Chronologie der Aegypter*, i. s. 133 sqq.— But even in Israel the custom was retained of limiting a period of time to thirty days, e.g. in regard to mourning, p. 153; it was the same among the ancient Germans, *Berl. Akad. Monatsber.* 1862, s. 537–542.

[2] P. 273 sq.

[3] Comp. also Chowlson's *Ssâbier*, ii. s. 175 sqq.

theless, the commencement of the year in Israel (at any rate in regard to the annual series of great festivals which attached themselves to Jahveism), fell in the spring, as will be shown below to be the case, this phenomenon, too, leads us to the certainty that under Moses and in his whole legislation a new mode of reckoning time was adopted, which was alone deemed valid at least in regard to Sacred matters. No doubt, however, it would be long before the entire nation became accustomed to this innovation. It is true Moses could not have borrowed this way of commencing the year from the Egyptians, although they, too, originally began their year in the spring. The whole arrangement of times and festivals instituted by Moses is completely different from that of the Egyptians, and, where the ancient customs of Israel were not in accord with those of the Egyptians, Moses never abandoned the former, if he could avoid doing so. It is more likely that it was the spring-time when Israel took its departure from Egypt, so that the month of departure became the commencement of its whole national freedom, and Moses was fully justified in placing in the spring the festival of the deliverance of Israel, and the commencement of a new era. We shall, however, see below how long it was before the people could forget the earlier beginning of the year, which was so well adapted to their agricultural pursuits. The priests, from the time of Moses, might always commence the year in the spring to suit the series of festivals; but in ordinary narrative the Book of Origins is the first to reckon the months of each year in the same way.[1] And, when the nation was at last violently transferred by the Assyrians and Chaldæans to those countries about the Euphrates and Tigris where the custom still remained of beginning the year in autumn, this custom was all the more readily again exclusively adopted in regard to civil life. Under the Persians an attempt was made to restore the genuine Mosaic custom also in reference to civil matters;[2] but from the dominion of the Seleucidæ the nation became so accustomed to the Syrian mode of reckoning alone, that this henceforth seemed to have acquired in it an ineradicable and permanent position; and, as a fact, the opposition to the Roman Calendar becoming an additional motive, it maintained itself there down to the Middle Ages.

But even the nomenclature and enumeration of the months leads us to a similar conclusion. If we inquire how the names of the months first originated, what is their simplest

---

[1] See more on the subject below.
[2] See more detailed information, *Hist.* v. 183 sq.

explanation among every ancient people, we are led at once to the seasons of the year. It may almost be understood of itself that the distinction and naming of these seasons would form the earliest foundation of every mode of dividing the year. Now everything goes to show that in these countries of Asia and Africa the year was divided, in the first instance, into three equal periods. These existed in the primitive Egyptian calendar; and in the Hieroglyphic documents four months are reckoned to each of these periods in a very simple fashion.[1] A further step was to divide each third of the year into halves, and count six divisions; this became the legal practice among the ancient Hindoos,[2] and it must once have prevailed also in Syria and Arabia. The proof of this lies in the fact that in the calendars of the Syrians and Arabians two consecutive months are often distinguished merely as the first and second of a given period, and this period from which they are named is evidently a division of the year.[3] To distinguish a first and second month in such divisions would be unmeaning, unless the months were reckoned, at any rate in theory, according to the solar year; but this mode, as has already been remarked, was introduced sufficiently early. Finally, various causes would lead to giving the individual months separate simple names, founded either on the phenomena of the year, or upon the special sanctity and vocation of the month, or lastly (the most remote and latest ground) upon human celebrities.[4] But this would take place in different ways, according to the history of the particular nations; and thus in the Syrian, and again differently in the ancient Arabian calendar, numerous simple names of months sprang up along side of the double names referred to above. To distinguish the individual months by individual names was also the custom in Israel—judging from all our present knowledge—and these names were the same which the Phœnicians also employed, and which from the earliest days were peculiar to the land of Canaan.[5] The last step in this

---

[1] See Lepsius, *Chronologie der Aegypter*, i. s. 134.
[2] Comp. Kálidása's *Ritusanhára*.
[3] Among the Arabs *the first* and *the second* ربيع, i.e. *spring*; *the first* and *the second* جمادى, i.e. *winter*. Among the Syrians the year began at once with two pairs of months, *the first* and *the second Tishrin*, *the first* and *the second Kânûn*.
[4] As is shown by the Roman calendar, and still more by the newly-discovered, paltry, cringing, *Cyprio-Roman Calendar*.

[5] The names which occur are as follows:—(1) The *Abib*, i.e. the *Ear-month*, when the ears of corn show signs of ripening, comes first according to the spring reckoning. Ex. xiii. 4, xxiii. 15; Deut. xvi. 1 (the name is a good Hebrew formation according to *Lehrb*. § 149 a, and is wholly distinct from the Egyptian Ἐπιφί, which, moreover, belongs to a different season); (2) *Ziv*, the *flower-month*, comes second, 1 Kings vi. 1. 37; (3) The *Aetanim*, probably meaning the month of the *streams of water*, when only those rivers which never dried up were in existence

whole development is evidently to denote the twelve months by mere numbers—a practice which can be explained most easily by assuming that the ancient mode of dividing the year was entirely and suddenly changed by an abrupt transformation, and that one particular month had to be placed in a position of great preeminence, wholly unlike the former arrangement. If, accordingly, we find the Book of Origins beginning to designate the months in this way, merely by numbers starting with the spring,[1] this is a sacerdotal innovation which is in perfect accord with all the above tokens of some such transformation of the earliest Hebrew year. When at length the mode of dividing the year observed by the Seleucidæ came to prevail,[2] it brought with it the custom of using the Syrian names of the months,[3] and the earliest genuine Hebrew names were thus still more completely lost to memory. In just the same way the Hellenists in Egypt at that time employed the Egyptian names of the months.[4]

All these indications are finally in harmony with the fact, that the earlier and more general name for *month*, which was employed by the Hebrews as well as by the majority of Semitic

---

(a fact which must have been specially remarked on the festivals of this month), was the seventh month, 1 Kings viii. 2; (4) The *Bûl*, probably meaning the *rain-month* (comp. بال and بول), when the rain first begins (in November) was the eighth, 1 Kings vi. 38. If we now remember that the passage Deut. xvi. 1 merely repeats an antiquated phrase, it will appear that all the passages where these names of months occur are in the earliest works, viz. the Book of Covenants and the Book of Origins, the latter of which prefers elsewhere to reckon the months according to the sacerdotal method, but makes exceptions at suitable places in favour of using the ancient manner. Even these names of months are evidently Canaanitish, because they are neither Aramaic nor Arabic; but the meaning of them in general is far from being clearly recognisable from the ordinary language of Israel, so that of themselves they refer us to Phœnician. For the name *Bûl* has now been actually discovered in this last language (comp. the *Erklärung des grossen Phönikischen Inschrift von Sidon*, s. 20), as well as on a newly-discovered Cyprian inscription (comp. the essay on it in the *Gött. Nachrichten*, 1862, s. 460). There has also been found in the same language (5) the ירח כרפא, contained in the second Mal-

tese, the eleventh Carthaginian (Ges. *Monum.* p. 451), and several Kittaic inscriptions (comp. the *Gött. Nachrichten*, 1862, s. 546 sq.); and (6) the ירח מפל, in a lately-discovered Sidonian inscription (s. the treatise *Ueber die grosse Karthagische und andere neuentdeckte Inschriften*, s. 46); and (7) **עם, on a Phœnician inscription given in the *Journ. As.* 1867, p. 88. We are, accordingly, at present acquainted with four primitive and very different series of Semitic names for months. (1) the *Canaanitish*; (2) the *Aramaic*; (3) the *Arabic*; (4) the *Ethiopic*; quite distinct from the latter and very unintelligible. The question further arises how a fifth series, that of the Ssabians (Chowlson, ii. s. 34, 36), was related to them. The Mosaic series must be considered a sixth series, content to reckon the months by numbers.

[1] This brings us close to the question whether the custom of only numbering days of the week has the same origin. See, however, what is said on p. 101.

[2] P. 344.

[3] How closely this introduction of the Aramaic names of the months can be traced has been indicated, *Hist.* v. 183 *nt*.

[4] The Παχών and the 'Επιφί just mentioned occur 3 Macc. vi. 38, and are correctly reckoned after the Egyptian fashion at thirty days.

nations,[1] began about the same date to be replaced by another term, which of itself only signifies the *new-moon*.[2] We have already seen that the ancient sanctity of the new-moon, and of the lunar year experienced a revival under Moses; it cannot, then, surprise us that many of the technical expressions in this department should have been changed under the priests.

So powerful, on all sides, was the transformation which Jahveism effected from the time of Moses in restoring the ancient sanctity of the lunar changes, and endeavouring to connect therewith the whole reckoning of time. But one step further, and Moses would have done what Mohammed at last did, viz., established the sanctity of the simple month alone, and given up the solar year altogether; but the superior common sense of Moses preserved him from this step, by taking which Mohammed sufficiently proved himself to be the unwisest and most perverse of legislators. The solar year was not, and could not be, given up, if only because Moses retained so many and such important traces of ancient festivals which depended on it. But if it was to stand by the side of the lunar year, there was no other course but to continually make the two correspond as closely as possible; and the way to do this lay close at hand. For if the year was to commence with the great spring-festival, when the vegetable first-fruits appropriate to it were to be brought for sacrifice (as will be described below), it would not do to commence too early with the lunar year; but so often as by keeping to it they were so much behind-hand with the crops, that their was a danger of not being able to bring these first-fruits, they were compelled to insert an extra month before the regular twelve, in order to get right with the solar year. They were, therefore, always cognizant and observant of the solar year as well, and as a matter of course they were quite well acquainted with the intercalary days of the Egyptians and Syrians, though they could not employ them in the same way, when the lunar year was to remain the basis of the whole calendar, and all that was wanted was to ensure correspondence between it and the solar year. And we have in the above-mentioned history of the Flood[3] a clear proof of how

[1] This name יֶרַח is Hebrew and Canaanitish (Phœnician), Aramaic, Ethiopic, and Himjaric, and that it was once also Arabic is proved by its derivation ورخ. It is, therefore, undoubtedly the earliest, and hence the most widely extended Semitic word; but in Hebrew it is very rarely used in plain narration, and is rather a poetical expression, although even the poets just as frequently use the other term.

[2] חֹדֶשׁ. The interchange of these two names keeps pace almost evenly with that explained above of the designation of the particular months.

[3] P. 342.

perfectly the mutual relations of the two calendars were understood, at any rate, in thought, and could be represented in narration.

This insertion of an extra month[1] whenever it seemed needful to revert to the solar year is an extremely simple process; and, in contradistinction to the far more complicated Egyptian calendar, its very simplicity might recommend it to a mind like that of Moses. But how the insertion of a new month was arranged and proclaimed throughout the whole population, whether it commenced when the first light of the new-moon was again visible in the heavens,[2] or whether a more artificial process was adopted—these are questions which happen not to be alluded to in the Old Testament.

3. Early civilised nations like the Egyptians and Babylonians, calculated, in addition to the simple year, longer series of years in various ways, the latter differently from the former.[3] But it will be shown below that those which Moses established were of a distinct kind; and the only point of importance here is that if those other nations had their longer periods, he could the more easily establish similar ones in his own way.

I. THE SABBATH-MONTH AND THE SEVEN ANNUAL FESTIVALS.

1. THE TRACES OF PRE-MOSAIC FESTIVALS.

It may be assumed from the general considerations already adduced that Israel celebrated certain festivals long prior to those instituted by Moses; and according to all tokens, the constituent elements of the latter were essentially based upon such earlier festivals. But it is equally certain that these pre-Mosaic festivals were pure nature-festivals. In the changes of the seasons, and of the phenomena of heaven, nature always displays a gracious adaptation to the needs of man, giving him

---

[1] Which in the language of the later Aramaic times was only a new *Adâr*, i.e. last month.

[2] As was the case according to the description in the *M.* ראש השנה, ii. 1 sqq. during the final period before the second destruction of Jerusalem, and certainly this would have been the simplest for all the sacerdotal occupations. Comp. the *Jahrbb. der Bibl. Wiss.* xi. s. 253 sqq., and also what is said in the second edition of the *Prophets of the Old Testament* on Jer. xxxi. 6. The seventh day of the month spoken of in Ezek. xlv. 20 is not the sabbath; but it follows from Dan. x. 2–4 that the festival at the commencement of the first month might extend over two days, which is important on account of what is said below, p. 356.

[3] For the Babylonian cycles of years see Berossos in G. Synkellos *Chronogr.* i. p. 38 Goar; for the Egyptian, see Lepsius *Chronologie*, i. s. 160 sqq.

special opportunities and intervals, when he may rest for a considerable while from his ordinary toil and devote himself unreservedly to higher thoughts. Hence, among the most ancient nations, these festivals of the earliest type bore a great resemblance to one another; and the people of Israel had, in this respect, no preeminence over other nations, especially those nearly related to itself.

1. We may be sure that the celebration of the *new-moon* and of the *full-moon* was as customary in primitive times among the people of Israel as it is to this day among certain heathen races, especially the Hindoos, and in religions derived from Hindoostan.[1] Of the primitive celebration of the new-moon very important traces were preserved in the Mosaic arrangements, as will be explained below. That the full-moon, too, was originally celebrated in Israel, is proved by Jahveism placing the great spring- and autumn-festivals on the day of the full-moon, the 14th or 15th of their respective months.[2] The celebration of these two great annual festivals was so inseparably connected, down to the latest times, with the middle of the month, that all members of the community, who, either on account of bodily impurity,[3] or of being at a distance, had been unable to celebrate the Passover at the great gathering of the nation, were to keep it on the corresponding day a month later.[4] Again, the first king of the Kingdom of the Ten Tribes, when he wished the great autumn-festival to be connected with a new order of affairs for his subjects, had still to place it on the corresponding day of the following month.[5]

Where two externally distinct festivals are contained within a perpetually recurring circle, they readily seek to be distinguished from one another by internal marks also, as will be shown to have been the case in regard to the spring- and autumn-festivals. Whether a similar internal difference was traditionally observed between the celebration of the new-moon and of the full-moon, may at first sight appear doubtful. For

[1] Comp. Manu. vi. 9 sq. Max Müller's *History of Sanskrit Lit.* p. 490; Wilson's *Vishnu-Purána*, pp. 145, 275 *nt*, 538 *nt*; De la Loubère's *Description du royaume de Siam*, i. pp. 347, 351. Among the Buddhists in Arrachan and elsewhere even all the *four* quarters of the moon (the origin of the week of seven days, p. 98) are still solemnised, see *American Oriental Journal*, i. p. 238 sq.; Spence-Hardy's *Eastern Monachism*, p. 236 sqq. For the Chinese customs see above, p. 98.

[2] In the later Ps. lxxxi. 4 [3] the full- and the new-moons are still spoken of in general terms as sacred, although the thought of the full- and new-moons of the seventh month may predominate in the mind of the poet.

[3] P. 149 sqq.

[4] According to the Book of Origins, Num. ix. 9-13. Even the whole community when it was prevented from celebrating the passover in its proper month, postponed it to the corresponding date in the next month, 2 Chron. xxx. 2 sq.

[5] 1 Kings xii. 32, comp. *Hist.* iv. 27.

it is impossible to apply the distinction lying close to hand, which would make the celebration of the new-moon preeminently a penance with expiatory-offerings as its predominant feature, while the celebration of the full-moon would be mainly expressive of joy; since all our present knowledge goes to show that the new-moon, as the appearance of new light, was celebrated as a purely joyous festival.[1] Another distinction between them was, however, possible, and everything goes to show that this was permanently kept up. The full-moon was most suitable for great national festivals in those countries where the whole nation from far and near collected around its principal Sanctuary; in countries, therefore, where they might make their pilgrimage thither during the preceding nights, and commence the festival itself under the cool moon-shine.[2] The festival of the new-moon, on the other hand, bore more appropriately in every respect a domestic character; and all recognisable traces indicate that even in Israel this always continued to be its prevailing character.

No doubt lunar celebrations would as good as lose all meaning if a nation substituted artificial for natural months. But the ancient people of Israel, as we have shown above,[3] in addition to reckoning by the solar year, always continued to reckon also by the lunar year, and to bring the two into harmony by inserting an extra month every third year. It is true, we do not possess any direct testimony to this, but everything indicates it to have been the case. In particular, the two annual principal festivals were so largely dependent upon the arrangements of husbandry, and hence of the solar year, that this of itself would ensure a sufficiently speedy return to the solar calendar.

We have also already seen[4] that the week of seven days, as the approximate quarter of a month, had been long established in pre-Mosaic days, both in Israel, and among many other nations.[5] But the very rigidity with which Moses connected this weekly period with the number seven, caused it to pursue

---

[1] Comp. the passages quoted below in respect to the new-moon.
[2] Just as in those regions such festivals even now commence with dances at night, see Layard's *Nineveh*, i. p. 120.
[3] P. 313 sq.
[4] P. 98 sqq.
[5] Among the Hindoos the seventh or the eighth and the fourteenth day of every month (termed *parvan*, i.e. knots, divisions) have from the earliest times possessed a certain sanctity; comp. Mahâbh. Sâvitri, cl. 25; Wilson's *Vishnu-Purâna*, p. 275 nt; *Journal of the Royal Asiatic Society*, ix. p. 84-86. The same, however, was also the case with the days from the tenth to the twelfth, p. 87 sq. which is explained by what is said on p. 98. In the lunar month of certain Negro races it is still the Tuesday, not the Saturday, which is deemed holy, see *Ausland*, 1839, s. 1390.

an independent course by the side of the lunar period, without accommodating itself to the latter.

2. Of *Annual festivals* there were at any rate two recognised in Israel prior to Moses, one in spring, and one in autumn. These are the two—almost given of themselves in the great order of the phenomena of the heavens and the soil—which appear again among all the races consanguineous with Israel, as well as other primitive nations, as the most original of all annual festivals, and which, in particular, were to be found among the ancient Arabs.[1] Now the intimate way in which they were associated with the arrangements of agriculture and the entire life of nature, from the earliest times, gave rise to a contrast between them, through which the spring-festival received an entirely different significance and external character from the autumn-festival.

In autumn, after the gathering of all the crops of the year, including the latest, such as fruit and grapes, is complete, it is to this day in those warm regions a very prevalent and extremely ancient custom among the settled population, to spend certain special days of leisure and rejoicing out in the open air, living in arbours or tents, and there celebrating a great festival of thanksgiving and gladness. To keep, about this time, such a festival of arbours (as it was briefly termed), was always customary also in Israel;[2] and if the people gradually learned later to abandon the habit of marching in great crowds out into the open fields, and there building arbours for the autumn, such erections were at any rate set up on a small scale at the traditional period for the festival, on the roofs of the houses, in courts, or in market-places.[3] Hence this festival always retained in Israel a strong relish of the country. While the arbours were still built in the open fields, it was usual to form solemn processions, in which the people bore ripe lemons, and other such fruits, as well as tufts of palms and branches of cypresses and willows.[4] In later times the

---

[1] It has not been sufficiently noticed how closely, in the ancient Arabian calendar, the Muharram (the first month reckoning from the autumn) and the Régeb (the seventh) correspond with one another as festival months; comp. *Jahbb. der Bibl. Wiss.* x. s. 169 sq., and what is said below.

[2] The Book of Origins, Lev. xxiii. 42; comp. Hos. xii. 10 [9], where tents are once mentioned.

[3] Neh. viii. 16.

[4] This is the meaning of the words in Lev. xxiii. 40; the expressions 'tree of splendour' and 'tree rich in foliage' are plainly half poetical; the former is probably the citron, the latter the cypress. It need hardly be said that וְעַרְבֵי is still dependent upon עֵץ. The Samaritans and Karaites adhered more closely to the letter of this passage, disallowing all further decorations; comp. F. P. Bayer *De numis Hebr. Sam.* pp. 128–138.— Among the Babylonians the great Sakæan festival was a corresponding celebration. But even among the Nestorians, Jakobites, and others, as well as among the Mohammedans of those regions, a sheep-offering

more elaborate arbours within the city would be constructed of olive-branches, palm-tufts, myrtle, and cypress-boughs.[1] Even the magnificent libations of wine and water, which are mentioned from the time of the second temple,[2] may have had some ancient prototype, although it is not alluded to in the ancient law. With usages like these, as well as with costly sacrifices, the celebration of the autumn-festival would be kept up for a much longer time than the spring-festival. The great relaxation of the year was then sought and celebrated.

Totally different from this was the nature of the spring-festival. It was not so simple as the other, but, in the people of Israel, as well as other ancient nations, always possessed something of a double character. On the one hand, there was the presentation of the first-fruits of the new-year, accompanied by pious vows and prayers on behalf of the hoped-for blessings of the entire coming year. In Canaan, however, corn ripens so early in the year that the first-fruits of barley might be brought very soon after the spring equinox, at any rate from certain very favourably situated districts, e.g. the fields about the southern end of the Jordan, and the harvest of every kind of corn was over a good while before the expiration of our spring.[3] Now just as the earliest forms of every kind of sacrifice always include a human participation, so was it particularly to be with this primitive sacrifice. The first ears of barley just acquired were on the same day in part rapidly ground to flour and baked to unleavened bread, in part merely roasted at the fire or pounded in a mortar. The roasted, or pounded portion, was especially used for offering up on the altar, the unleavened bread as sacrificial bread for the human beings.[4] A natural addition to this was devoting an entire sheaf of the fresh ears to the altar. In these rites it was a stringent law that, until such a sacrifice was completely accomplished, none might dare to eat of the new bread.[5]

But, at the same time, the spring, coinciding with the commencement of the new year, is always a period of serious reflec-

in autumn has held its ground. See Badger's *Nestorians*, i. p. 229 sqq.
[1] Neh. viii. 15 sq.
[2] See *Mishnah Sukka*, iv. 9 sq. Allusion to it is made in John vii. 37 sq.— It is intelligible that many superficial heathens regarded this as a festival celebrated in honour of Bacchus, see *Hist.* v. 470 *nt* 1, and Plutarch's *Quæst. Conviv.* iv. 6. 1, 2. Comp. also the passage in Curtius' *Quellinschriften*, s. 16.
[3] Eight days after Easter Theodoricus still found ripe barley in the neighbourhood of Jerusalem, *De Locis Sanctis*, p. 69 (Tobler).
[4] According to the very ancient passage from the Book of Covenants, Josh. v. 11 sq., comp. Lev. ii. 14-16, and the representation of the Book of Origins, Num. xv. 17-21. That it was the first-fruits of barley follows both from the nature of the case and from 2 Kings iv. 42.
[5] Lev. xxiii. 14.

tion and anxious care for the future, of obscure transition over to a mysterious unknown, and of upward-gazing anxiety about the blessing or the bane which may be expected from heaven. At this period, therefore, man felt himself most strongly impelled every year to offer, wherever practicable, sacrifices of purification and reconciliation, not alone on account of particular transgressions of which he knew himself to be guilty, but also to secure the divine exemption and grace generally on the occasion of this uncertain transition, so that, as it were, if during the new year, his God were to visit him and call him to account, He might not slay him, as he perhaps deserved, but might graciously pass him over. Thus in the people of Israel, from the earliest times, an atonement-offering was an indispensable constituent of every spring-festival. It is called by a name of unmistakeable antiquity, not occurring in any other connection, *Pascha*, i.e. passover, exemption,[1] and even its usages as they were preserved in Jahveism betray a pre-Mosaic period. Even in the later times it ever continued to be a proper domestic sacrifice, which every household offered for its own exemption. Hence it was always to consist of a male animal, either of the sheep or goat kind, since such a one might generally be consumed at one meal by the members of a single household. If, however, there was a household of too few members, as many neighbours were to be brought in as would ensure its being wholly consumed.[2] This offering, itself

---

[1] This is the explanation of the name intentionally given Ex. xii. 13, 23, 27, comp. Is. xxxi. 5 (see also the *Jahbb. der Bibl. Wiss.* vii. s. 165 sq.). Closely corresponding is, therefore, the name τὰ διαβατήρια in Philo, *Vita Mos.* iii. 29, comp. Aristotle in Euseb. *Eccles. Hist.* vii. 32. This also gives the explanation of the custom of keeping the doors of the temple open during the night of the passover, which may have survived from a very early date, Josephus, *Antiq.* xviii. 2. 2. The Arabians term this sacrifice very correctly الحلّ i.e. *the redemption*, and they are therefore in the habit of adding the cognomen Abulfidâ to the name Ismaîl.—We have elsewhere alluded (*Hist.* iii. 136 sq.) to the fact that already in early days (as well as at the time of Christ) public executions used to be connected with this as the great purificatory festival; comp. *Mishnah Sanhedrin*, xi. 4 (where it is asserted of all festivals); a similar instance occurs in Porphyry, *De Abstin.* ii. 54, and still in Africa, *Ausland*, 1849, s. 466. 518.

[2] Ex. xii. 4, 43–46. We have a parallel usage in Islâm in the sheep and goats which annually on the tenth day of the Muharram are to be slain in the valley Mina (Munâ) on the slope of the mountain Arafat, not far from Mecca. This usage is described by Burckhardt, *Travels in Arabia*, ii. p. 56 sqq.; it has survived from primitive times, and is one in which it is most easy to recognise the traces of primitive pre-Mosaic religion among the nations connected with Israel. Still more parallel, however, was the sacrificial lamb slain previous to the time of Mohammed in the spring month Regeb (for the Muharram was originally in the autumn), Hârits *Moall.* ver. 69 Schol. For similar instances among the Jezids and Hindoos see Badger's *Nestorians*, i. p. 119 sq., 125.—It would appear from Deut. xvi. 1 sq. as though it were also allowed to sacrifice cattle; but according to 2 Chron. xxxv. 7–9, these ought to be regarded as a subsidiary offering, or rather as a thank-offering for the first day of the principal festival.

simply termed *pascha*, was unmistakeably an expiatory-offering, but the way of sacrificing it, even in the later times, was very different from the procedure with the regular expiatory-offerings. The head of the family, down to the latest times, himself slew the animal,[1] and streaked with its blood the lintel and door-posts of the house, as though to make atonement for the whole house and all who were contained therein celebrating the festival.[2] The bloodless animal, next to be made ready for the table, was not cut up into joints, but slowly roasted before the sacrificial fire with its limbs intact, to give, as it were, the clearest indication that a creature, which had but just ceased to live, had fallen, intact as it was, for men.[3] The only accompaniment permitted to the dish were certain bitter herbs.[4]

The accomplishment of a closer union between these two solemnities of the spring offered no great difficulties. The entire twofold celebration could not become such a joyous festival as that of autumn; in contrast to the latter, it became one of a very stern character. It was commenced with the expiatory-offering which was to be made in every house; not till man was thus purified could he venture to offer the first-fruits in public, and eat thereof himself. But even the unleavened bread, which was then eaten as a sacrifice,—composed of a pure unmixed substance, and made with the greatest simplicity and absence of all seasoning—might represent both the sternness and anxious care of that day, so that it might also be termed 'bread of tribulation.'[5]

2. The Festal Institutions established by Moses.

In some such way as this, sacred times were observed in Israel before Moses; and if, in addition to those we have mentioned, there were others, which was very probably the case, they were assuredly of less importance, and their celebration not so universal.

The superior mind of Moses was preeminently successful in bringing, out of the idea of the Sabbath, into this whole

---

[1] According to Ex. xii. 6; at a later date the Levites were also employed in this, Ezra vi. 20, comp. 2 Chron. xxix. 24 sqq.

[2] Ex. xii. 7, 22 sq., comp. Ezek. ix. 4; Apocal. vii. 1-8, and similar cases above, p. 159 and 279; for a parallel Roman custom see Böttiger's *Kl. archäol. Schriften*, i. s. 153; see too G. Müller's *Amerik. Urrel.*, s, 391 sq. At a later time this went out of usage.

[3] Ex. xii. 7, sq., 46; Num ix. 12; comp. Justin *contr. Tryph.* xl. The custom does not occur in connection with any other sacrifices in the Old Testament.

[4] Ex. xii. 8, Num. ix. 11—For the passover among the modern Samaritans see also Petermann in the *D. Zeitschr. f. chr. Wissensch.*, 1853, s. 201 sq.

[5] Deut xvi. 3.

series of possible sacred times, a single thought, and hence one firm connecting medium, and equally clear and beautiful bond of union. Just this fact may be most completely recognised from the still extant remains of the Book of Origins.[1] The new constitution would of course remodel many details entirely afresh, and many others it would establish more permanently; but, in the main, all that was done was to breathe upon things a spirit which transformed into harmony with Jahveism the meaning and purpose of all festive celebrations generally, and of individual festivals in particular. Thus very many of the earlier practices were still retained, and may be easily recognised under a transparent veil. It was characteristic of the whole of Jahveism [2] that the worship of Jahveh by the priests should run parallel with that by the community; and especially at the celebration of these festivals must this duality everywhere find expression. Parallel with all that the people were directed to do on the festivals, indeed independent of all this, arrangements were made for a sacerdotal celebration of every festival, with appropriate sacrifices and other rites. In particular, on festivals the sacerdotal sacrifices were increased. They accompanied the daily offering spoken of above,[3] but themselves assumed different forms in accordance with the various significance of the special festal days; and here we can observe an arrangement no less elaborate, though probably not equally ancient. The particulars are the following :

1. The commencement of the year, or at any rate of the first year, was fixed for the first month whose full-moon follows the spring equinox. This month the Book of Origins always terms simply the *first*, and counts the others in succession from it. In the Book of Covenants, on the other hand, it is called the Ear-month, as in it the ears of corn ripened.[4] Starting with this point, the annual autumn-festival was fixed for the seventh month. For the autumn-festival, occurring at a time when all

---

[1] Lev. xxiii.; comp. Num. xxviii. sq., and Ex. xii. sq.
[2] P. 113 sqq.
[3] P. 116.
[4] Ex. xxiii. 15; whence the expression in the passages Ex. xiii. 4, Deut. xvi. 1, may be derived; comp. on the other hand Ex. xii. 2, Lev. xxiii 5, Num. xxviii. 16.—With this is unmistakenly connected another deviation of the Book of Covenants: the autumn-month, the seventh according to the Book of Origins, is here the last in the year, Ex. xxiii. 16, comp. xxxiv. 22. This presupposes a wholly different commencement for the year, similar to that which was customary in Syria, and which from the time of the Seleucidæ prevailed even among the Jews in their civic life. As a fact, commencing the year in autumn, or still better after the great autumn festival, was best adapted to agricultural economy; and it is possible that in ancient Israel it was for the most part only the priests who always observed the spring commencement required by the Book of Origins, and certainly also by Moses. See p. 342.

business can easily be suspended, was traditionally the greater of the two annual festivals, and was celebrated, not only with the greatest joy, but with the most universal participation of the people, and was readily extended to the longest period. It was from the first a true national holiday; it was often termed simply 'the festival,'[1] and even within Jahveism it could never lose this, its natural feature. This was already reason enough why the *autumn-month* should tend to become, more than all the rest, the proper sabbath-month; and as the seventh in the series to form the exalted summit of the year, for which all the preceding festivals prepared the way, and after which everything quietly came down to the ordinary course of life, until the commencement of a new festal circle.

Hence this month was to be distinguished from all the rest, and receive a sacred consecration, by its *new-moon* being saluted more solemnly than that of any other, and even being exalted to the dignity of a special annual festival. With the remaining new-moons the law concerned itself but little. It was the ancient traditional custom for all the members of a family to celebrate them at home;[2] in ordinary life they were on a par with the weekly sabbaths;[3] on the part of the priests they were, it is true, honoured as proper festivals, with rich sacrifices, viz. seven lambs, two head of cattle, a ram, and an expiatory-he-goat.[4] But the law never insisted on their celebration by the whole people, or placed them on a level with the sabbaths. On the seventh new-moon, however, there was to be a public celebration of a great festival by all the people, during which work was suspended, and the importance of the occasion was to be loudly proclaimed by the priests from the Sanctuary.[5] It is therefore manifest that, at least according to the original intention of the legislator, this one new-moon, in the series of sacred days, was alone to be of real moment to the whole nation; and the law would hardly have remonstrated if all the rest had gradually ceased to be observed by the people.

2. While the great autumn-festival remained fixed for the full-moon of the seventh month, the corresponding spring-festival was appointed for the same day of the first month, so

---

[1] Hos. xii. 10 [9], Is. xxx. 29, comp. Zach. xiv. 18 sq. Deut. xxxi, 10 sq. 1 Kings xii. 32, Ps. cxviii.

[2] 1 Sam. xx. 5, 24, 27. From ver. 27 we see that the new-moon was celebrated by a feast on the day *after* its first appearance, and not till then; hence the πρ νουμηνια and νουμηνια, Judith viii. 6, corresponding to the προσάββατα and σάββατα *loc. cit.* Comp. also the lately recovered passage in Clemens Rom. *Hom.* xix. 22, where the new-moon is still placed by the side of the Sabbath, and bears too the worst significance.

[3] Amos viii. 5, Judith viii. 6.

[4] Num. xxviii. 11–15.

[5] Lev. xxiii. 23–25, Num. xxix. 1–6, comp. x. 10.

that their dates marked the commencement of two nearly equal halves of the year. Each of them had essentially the same dignity, and hence properly entirely similar arrangements. Nevertheless, their different place in the year produced a distinction between them. In the first place, the whole character of the spring-festival was far more serious than that of the autumn-festival; and, secondly, the whole series of celebrations during the first half of the year was related to those of the second half, as the weaker to the stronger, as a mighty upheaval to its necessarily still more weighty subsidence.

Just as every great sacrifice may be initiated by an expiatory-offering,[1] and just as a suitable preparation and purification should form the commencement of every sacred action,[2] so each of these two great annual festivals was preceded by a special festival of expiation, which was celebrated with great solemnity, in accordance with the serious nature of Jahveism. The principal festival itself, both in the autumn and in the spring, commenced immediately after the full-moon, and therefore on the fifteenth day of the month, and lasted an entire week; even here the number seven succeeded in keeping its ground. Nevertheless, this sanctification of a whole week was not meant to prevent the people from doing any work whatever for the entire space of seven days. It was only on the first, or also on the last as well, that ordinary occupations were to be suspended as on the sabbath,[3] and great congregational meetings held. In other respects all these days were only distinguished sacerdotally by richer sacrifices. On the other hand, the preparatory expiatory-festival was limited to a single day for both festivals, and originally at any rate it was fixed for the tenth of the month, both in spring and autumn, this being a day not too distant from the fifteenth, and, moreover, possessing, on its own account, a certain primitive sanctity.[4]

And as each principal festival had its preparatory expiation,

---

[1] Pp. 67 sq. 131.
[2] Pp. 42 sq. 106.
[3] In this sense the first day of unleavened bread is expressly called a 'Sabbath,' viz. in brief phrases where the meaning cannot be mistaken, Lev. xxiii. 11, 15; the meaning of this is always made clear by descriptions such as verr. 7, 8, 21, 25, 28, 35, 36; Ex. xii. 16. The more definite name for a day thus resembling the sabbath was, however, שַׁבָּתוֹן, derived from שָׁבַת.
[4] P. 98. It is really remarkable that Islâm still retains some traces of the same sacred numbers manifestly derived from pre-Mosaic times. The tenth of *Muharram* and of *Dulh'igg'eh* are both days of great importance in the arrangement of the festivals, see above p. 353 nt 2, Shahrastâni's *Elmilal*, p. 442 sq., and Burckhardt's *Travels in Arabia*, i. p. 255, 323, ii. p. 56, 75; Bartlett's *Forty Days in the Desert*, p. 159. The same is the case with the tenth of the lunar month of August among the Jezîds, see Ainsworth's *Travels*, ii. p. 185.

so too each was not brought to a conclusion without a joyous holiday, which equally with the former, lasted but one day. Each of these annual festal seasons accordingly was divided into three particular celebrations: the preparatory, the principal, and the concluding, festivals.

The preparatory festival of the spring celebration was the *Pascha*, to whose fame so many causes had contributed,[1] and which even in Jahveism never lost its character of a purely domestic expiatory-offering. That the law originally intended it to be observed on the tenth day of the month is unmistakeable. The corresponding expiatory-festival in the autumn is fixed for that date; and even the Book of Origins orders the paschal sacrificial animal to be selected and held in readiness on the tenth.[2] But just as it was this sacrifice generally at which the domestic and national customs held their ground most tenaciously, so here too the custom was retained of connecting it as closely as possible with the Feast of Unleavened Bread. Not till the fourteenth, during the last three hours before, and the first three after, sunset,[3] was the sacrificial animal slain and eaten. Thus, in contradistinction to the ordinary sacrifices, it remained a real night-offering, with which man entered upon a new period. But in this sense it was always appointed for the fourteenth, and in the earliest times at least, the view was strictly upheld that the Feast of Unleavened Bread did not begin till the following morning.[4] On the side of the priests this fourteenth day was not further celebrated.[5] But for the primitive religion this festival of purification with the succeeding principal celebration was always deemed an absolutely indispensable sacred rite for every single household, and indeed for every adult male—a rite which might not be omitted in any year whatever, and was on a par with circumcision, or rather was something even still more sacred.[6] Just because this remained the sole purificatory

---

[1] P. 353 sq.

[2] Ex. xii, 3-6, comp. too what is remarked in *Hist.* ii. p. 245 sq.

[3] This is at any rate the most probable meaning of the phrase בֵּין הָעַרְבָּיִם Ex. xii. 6, Lev. xxiii. 5. *Lehrb.* § 180 *a*, about the meaning of which there has been much controversy among later writers. The Pharisees and the Rabbis wanted to limit this period to the earlier hours before sunset, the Samaritans and Karaites to those after sunset. It is worthy of notice how the *Lib. Jubilorum*, xlix.

(p. 161 sqq. of the Ethiopic text), determines that the passover shall be observed from the last third of the day to the third third of the night, but that the slaying shall take place in this last third of the day.

[4] Josh. v. 11, comp. Lev. xxiii. 5 sq., Num. xxviii. 16 sq.

[5] This follows plainly from Num. xxviii. 16 sq.

[6] According to p. 110, with the consequences already treated more fully on p. 349 sq.

sacrifice which the individual had personally to offer, it was regarded, in the light of the extreme reverence in which the bloody sacrifice was held, as an annual debt which he was bound to pay unless he would make himself unworthy of membership in the communion. Hence comes its significance as a Sacrament. Only men were to partake of it, as circumcision applied only to them; and no portion of the sacrificial flesh might remain over even to the following morning.[1] But when in later days,[2] they became the more scrupulously anxious about purification, the closer the contact into which they were perpetually coming with the heathen, a law was even passed that no one might eat the passover who had on the same day entered a heathen house.[3]

The principal festival, lasting a whole week, but only observed as a solemn day of rest on the first and last day, was properly the Feast of Unleavened Bread, which was to be eaten during the entire week. That this unleavened bread was originally made of the very first ears of the barley-harvest (barley being the corn which ripens earliest), is quite indisputable.[4] But the Book of Origins already ceases to require definitely that it shall be made from the first harvest of the year, and as an historical fact circumstances soon arose which made this at times impossible. For if this festival in the second and third lunar year kept falling earlier and earlier, the commencement of the harvest would take place too late for it to be possible for the whole nation to eat unleavened bread made from it; the usage in this respect must become less stringent. Nevertheless, the original meaning of this festival was restored in another way, viz., by the rise of the custom for the priests, at any rate, to offer on the second day of the feast a fresh sheaf of barley in the name of the whole people. This might be deemed symbolic of the commencement of the whole corn-harvest, and it was expressly ordained that, previous to

---

[1] Ex. xii. 10, comp. ver. 46; even in the very ancient utterance Ex. xxiii. 18, the words 'offering' and 'festival-offering' denote especially the passover, as is expressly explained in the repetition of the Fourth Narrator. Ex. xxxiv. 25. At the passover, therefore, as a sacrifice largely left to individuals but stringently observed, everything holds good which was said about thank-offerings on p. 52; and in the case of the strictest thank-offerings the same stringency prevailed, Lev. xxii. 29 sq.—The *Liber Jubilorum*, xlix. (p. 163 of the Ethiopic) distinctly enjoins for the time of the temple in Jerusalem that the blood must be sprinkled upon the base of the altar and the fat cast into the fire.

[2] P. 155 *nt.* 5.

[3] According to John xviii. 28. The regulation of the schools then in force was by no means deduced merely from the words Deut. xvi. 4; it followed from the entire system of the later days, and is only accidentally wanting from the present Talmud.

[4] P. 352.

its presentation none might eat of the new corn in any form whatever. The day was to be marked, at any rate by the priests, like a simple sabbath of the second rank, i.e., with one sacrificial lamb in addition to the daily allowance of two.[1] In proportion, however, as the unleavened bread lost its natural significance, the more available did it become for receiving a higher, more spiritual, meaning which would not be unappropriate to the rank of this festival. The very close connection of the passover as a strict expiatory-festival with this principal celebration (for the two were only separated by a night),[2] caused the idea of a serious cleansing and purification to be continually passing over from the former to the latter. Thus unleavened bread soon came to be regarded not only as suitable for a serious time, but also as a symbol of that purity of the whole house, which was to be sought after afresh in the new-year; and the custom grew up of scrupulously removing, previous to this feast, every remnant of leavened bread.[3]

The joyous concluding holiday in the spring was postponed till somewhat later, in order that an interval might elapse during which the whole corn-harvest could be brought to a close, even if the principal festival was celebrated quite early in the year. This interval was to extend from the first day *after* the fifteenth,—from that day, therefore, which was deemed the day of consecration for the corn-harvest,[4]—for exactly seven weeks, as though this period, defined by the sacred number, were the consecrated spring-time during which the sickle was busy throughout the whole land until the blessing had been fully reaped in the harvest of every kind of corn. The day immediately following—the fiftieth day (Whitsuntide)—became accordingly the day of jubilee for the completed corn-harvest. It was named 'the festival of the corn-harvest,'[5] or more definitely 'the day of the first-fruits,'[6] and also 'the festival of

---

[1] P. 116. Lev. xxiii. 9–14.

[2] The Book of Origins, in passages like Lev. xxiii. 5 sq., Num. xxviii. 16 sq., xxxiii. 3, distinguishes both festivals accurately enough, but in other passages when it describes everything at greater length (Ex. xii. 14–20, xiii. 3–10) it clearly shows how much the two ran into one another by its time. The earlier Book of Covenants distinguishes the Feast of Unleavened Bread most sharply, Ex. xxiii. 15: at a later date the distinction altogether ceased, and the name Passover became the prevalent one, Deut. xvi. 1–6, so that the festival of seven days is even reckoned from the fourteenth day, Ezek. xlv. 21–24, comp. ver. 25. The same variation extends to the New Testament, Mark xiv. 12 (Matt. xxvi. 17) Luke xxii. 7.

[3] Ex. xii. 15–20, xiii. 7. This throwing away of all leaven corresponds with the custom of throwing away all old clothes and food during the Hindoo penance in the autumn-month, Manu, vi. 15.

[4] P. 359.

[5] In the Book of Covenants, Ex. xxiii. 16

[6] Book of Origins, Num. xxviii. 26.

THE DAY OF ATONEMENT.

the (seven) weeks.'[1] For then, in addition to the other appointed sacrifices, two loaves of wheat, made, moreover, of leavened bread as at a joyous festival and in contrast to that of Easter, were offered as the sacred first-fruits of the new wheat now gathered into the threshing-floors.[2] Throughout the entire nation too it was deemed one of the higher duties that every household should itself bring such a gift of first-fruits to the holy place, consisting of grains either roasted or pounded in the raw state.[3] Thus the presentation of the first-fruits which assumed such importance in Jahveism[4] was principally connected with this joyous annual holiday.—

The preparatory celebration in the autumn which took place on the tenth day of the seventh month was essentially distinguished from that of the spring in not being a terror-stricken celebration at the commencement of the year, which sought to avert the perils of the dim future and, as it were, the wrath of a new coming God, but in being rather a pure feast of penance which endeavoured to expiate all the human and national transgressions and impurities which had occurred during the year. For although the searching stringency of Jahveism, already described, required that every, even the smallest, impurity and defilement which had been contracted should be immediately expiated, yet the higher religion was well aware how little all the secret and slowly advancing desecrations were actually removed from the entire community. Hence this universal festival of penance and expiation was established in order that even all these might be expiated as far as human labour could avail, and that the community, as free as possible from all guilt, might celebrate with joyous feelings the great happy festival of the year which immediately followed. Both this origin and purpose and also its name, *feast of expiation*,[5] show its genuine Mosaic character. Here, more than in any other, the entire purpose and the absolute stringency of the higher religion found expression, and it was certainly this religion which first founded the festival. Only in one of its rites which, strictly speaking, is hardly essential, do we find a remnant of pre-Mosaic belief and life. The festi-

---

[1] Deut. xvi. 9-11, after Lev. xxiii. 15 sq.; comp. also Num. xxviii. 26.;
[2] Lev. xxiii. 17. 20.
[3] According to an earlier author, Lev. ii. 14-16, and in different language according to the Book of Origins, Num. xv. 17-21; in the latter passage only a cake of pounded corn is spoken of. That both passages may be quoted here and have the above meaning is indubitable. The Book of Covenants speaks very briefly on the point, Ex. xxiii. 19. Comp. above p. 352, *nt* 4.
[4] P. 301 sqq.
[5] יוֹם הַכִּפֻּרִים.

val, then, was by no means to be principally of a domestic character like the Passover, rather in contradistinction to the latter was it to become a thoroughly public festival. Accordingly, the people were not to offer any of the regular sacrifices, but a new one, which should go deeper and reach a more sensitive point in taming man's sensuous nature than the regular offerings. This was to be a rigid fast from the evening of the ninth to that of the tenth;[1] the solitary fast which Jahveism annually required.[2] The whole structure of Jahveism did indeed require that a sacrifice of the ordinary kind should be offered on this day, as its peculiar importance demanded; but this continued to be purely sacerdotal. It was a great expiatory-offering, to be made by the high-priest or his representative[3] on behalf of the entire community, and to be sacrificed with an amount of solemnity which was rarely observed on other occasions.[4] Not only the human members of the community, including the priests, were now deemed impure and in need of expiation, but even the visible Sanctuary as well, as though, like a wall between the nation and its God, it received all the stains of impiety which were incurred in the realm.[5] Hence the high-priest employed expiatory-offerings of two kinds: one, purely sacerdotal and serving especially for the atonement of the sanctuary; and another, which had special reference to the share of the community and must therefore also proceed from it. The latter bore quite a national stamp, and evidently forms that portion of the usages which was derived from a pre-Mosaic time and still retained subsequently. This particular custom was to present two he-goats before the sanctuary as a sacrifice, of which the one was selected by the high-priest for Jahveh, the other for Azazel, the lot being used to determine the selection. The latter name, in other respects unknown to us, is shown by its opposition to Jahveh to designate an evil spirit; and as the goat devoted to him was finally to be sent away laden with the whole guilt of the community into the desert where man dwelt not, he was evi-

---

[1] Lev. xxiii. 26, 32, xvi. 29-31, comp. Num xxix. 11, Acts xxvii. 9.
[2] P. 83 sq.
[3] Prominence is intentionally given to this fact in the words Lev. xvi. 32; comp. what is further said on p. 279, nt 2.
[4] That a great expiatory-offering like this was offered only on occasion of this festival, and that in consequence the Holy of Holies was never entered at any other time, although it is so assumed in Philo ii. p. 591, is not quite a correct conclusion from Lev. xvi. After the opening words in verr. 1 sq., and since the description does not distinctly refer to this festival till ver. 29, we should expect something different. And since the grievous defilement of the Sanctuary through the guilt and death of two priests in it, Lev. x. to which xvi. 1 alludes, had not yet been expiated, it is probable that provision for such a case was made after Lev. xvi. 34.
[5] P. 271 sq.

dently the evil spirit of the desert whom man drove from himself in horror, and to whom he was glad to send all the evil which he could not tolerate about himself.[1]—When in this way all things had been made ready for the sacred rite, then the highpriest, cleansed by a bath, assumed the simple white garments appropriate to him as chief penitent.[2] He next sacrificed as a sacerdotal offering a bullock for an atonement for himself and his house, and having filled the whole censer with glowing coals off the inner altar and with a profusion of incense, he then entered that so rarely trodden innermost sanctuary—where according to the ancient belief the sacred footstool[3] must immediately conceal itself in sacred smoke if the person entering were to remain alive and safe,[4]—and sprinkled the sacrificial blood seven times on and before the sacred footstool. Next, he sacrificed the he-goat which had been selected by the lot for Jahveh, sprinkled the sacred footstool with its blood in the same manner, pronounced the atonement for the external sanctuary and all human beings, and in conclusion similarly sprinkled the inner altar with the blood of both animals. All this he did in mysterious solitude, attended by no human creature. When the inherent guilt had been thus, as it were, liquified, he took outside the consecrated he-goat which had been devoted to Azazel, placed his hands upon its head in order to impart to it with audible confession all this liquified guilt of the nation, and sent it by the hand of a man appointed in readiness 'to Azazel in the desert.' Finally, after washing himself within the sanctuary from the impurity which had come to adhere even to him, he once more donned his magnificent attire, and sacrificed two rams, one on his own behalf and the other on behalf of the community, as a whole-offering, and presented along with it

[1] עֲזָאזֵל. Lev. xvi. 8, 10, comp. ver. 21 sq. is by its origin (from אָזַל to go away) just the same as ἀποπομπαῖος (the translation of the LXX.) averruncus, a fiend, a demon, whom man banished to a distance. The symbolical dispatching of the evil at the sacrifice is undoubtedly a genuine Mosaic rite, explained by p. 158, just as is the imagery generally, so peculiar to the ancient legislation and corresponding to the purpose of the law when it began to be put in practice; comp. the custom described in Hardeland's Daj. Gr. s. 372. But the fact that a demon is definitely placed in contrast to Jahveh, is opposed at any rate to the stricter Jahveism, and is manifestly a relic of preMosaic religion. Still it is an error to identify Azazel with the later Satan; historically at any rate they cannot be brought into connection. A similar representation of a prophetic character occurs later in Zach. v. 5–15; comp. too the ἐπικατάρατος in the Epistol. Barnab. vii.

[2] P. 280 sq.

[3] P. 123 sq.

[4] This is the meaning which evidently is contained in ver. 2, comp. ver. 13 (כִּי ver. 2 means but). We must, therefore, compare the bells on p. 292. It was an ancient belief that anyone who entered the Most Holy Place without due preparation and proper equipment might be struck down. Hence preparations of all kinds were made, and in particular for the purpose of evoking the sacred cloud in which Jahveh might become invisibly-visible, and appear innocuously. Comp. Jahrbb. der Bibl. Wiss. iv. s. 136 sq.

the portions for the altar of the two expiatory-offerings. This concluded the high celebration at the Sanctuary. In the mean time throughout the whole land the people were rigidly fasting and praying.[1]

The principal festival, termed the *Feast of Arbours*, then continued from the fifteenth of the month for a whole week, being celebrated with great rejoicing and the most universal participation of the whole people.—If, however, only the first day of it had to be celebrated in full national assembly, not the last as well, as was the case with the principal spring-festival, this may be accounted for by the fact that there was here no reason, as there was in the spring, for postponing the concluding festival to a later date. On the contrary, it was at once concluded on the eighth day, when the people mustering all the more strongly from the country and the arbours, once again marched in full procession up to the Sanctuary; and many would only join in this concluding festival. The general participation in the celebration of this annual festival is referred to even in its names.[2] And the whole autumnal festival is probably the one to whose evening celebration the people went up out of the whole land in pilgrimage to the temple, amid the sound of flutes and singing.[3]

—The connection of the four festivals of the seventh month, their mutual rank, and their common distinction from all the remaining annual festivals, are, however, most distinctly denoted by the number of the sacerdotal sacrifices. We have

---

[1] How much the later writers have to say about this sacred rite in particular and what various hues its usages assumed under their hands, may be excellently seen from Heb. ix. 13; Barnabas *Epistol.* vii. sq., repeated in Tert. *Contr. Marc.*, iii. 7, *Contr. Jud.*, xiv. It is instructive that the epistle of Barnabas appeals here to the younger Thorah, which at that time must have been much used and in high repute.—In a similar way 2 Chron. xxxv. 1-18 describes the particular form in which the passover was observed in later times, for just these two festivals had from the first in Israel so much that was peculiar and mysterious that their usages survived with very great vitality.

[2] עֲצֶרֶת, a word which properly means *assembly*, πανήγυρις, as the LXX translate it in Amos v. 21; it has this meaning also in Lev. xxiii. 26, Num. xxix. 35, Neh. viii. 18. Nevertheless the word also occurs with a wider significance,

and the Deuteronomist, who in xvi. 13-15 (like Ezek. xlv. 25) omits this concluding festival, gives this name to the seventh day of the Easter festival, in xvi. 8. Since, however, it became usual to give this name to any particularly sacred day, it was also given at a later time to Whitsuntide, Joseph. *Antiq.* iii. 10, 6. *Mishnah Rôsh hashana*, i. 2; Maqrizi in de Sacy's *Chrest.* i. p. 93, 98; while the Samaritans equally arbitrarily named the latter מִקְרָא, *Chron. Samarit.* xxviii. At any rate we cannot well suppose that עֲצֶרֶת properly means *conclusion*, ἐξόδιον LXX, Lev. xxiii. 36, and hence the concluding day of every festival.—Another name is *the great day of the festival*, John vii. 37, *Prot. ev. Jacob.*, i. ii.; any other festival was only called this when it fell on the same day as a sabbath. John xix. 31.

[3] Is. xxx. 29, comp. too, *Mishnah Sukka*, v. 1.

already seen [1] that these sacerdotal festival-offerings characterised all festivals without distinction, being an addition, not only to the daily sacrifice, but also to the special ones, which were peculiar to the particular festivals; the regulations about their number and kind have been already given.[2] Instead, however, of the two bullocks, which were the usual thing here, thirteen must be offered at the principal festal day of the seventh month, viz. on the seventh day there must be the sacred number of seven, while on each previous day, in gradation, one more must be sacrificed. And, in order to distinguish more clearly the three other festivals of the seventh month from the principal festival, and concentrate attention on the latter, only a single bullock was to be slain on them.[3]

3. The law accordingly made provision, in a way fraught with the deepest significance, for exactly seven annual festivals, three in the spring, and four in the autumn; even in this respect retaining the sacred number. It is true that the passover was early almost completely merged in the first day of Easter; but, as the people grew accustomed to observe also the last day of Easter week as a festival, the number seven preserved this most important significance for them, that, irrespective of those celebrated merely with sacerdotal offerings, there were seven days kept as holidays and festivals, or, in other words, there were seven annual sabbaths. Taken in this way, the number of the annual festivals was not excessive for a labouring population.[4]

The series of ordinary sabbaths, it is hardly needful to remark, was maintained independently of this entire succession of festivals, so that e.g. a festival might be immediately followed by a sabbath.[5] Any of the seven annual festivals which did not fall on a sabbath was observed, like the latter, with a total cessation of work, but it was permitted to prepare food on

---

[1] P. 355.
[2] P. 356 sq.
[3] Num. xxix. comp. xxviii., and Lev. xxiii. 18, sq.; in the last passage the reading is to be altered to harmonise.— The above remark was not made in the treatise of 1835, but it entirely confirms the first result arrived at then.—Since the first edition of this work I have also discovered that even the present Samaritans still reckon seven annual festivals, see Juynboll on the *Chron, Sam.* p. 110, Petermann's *Reisen* i. s. 287, sqq., and now the ancient Samaritan songs themselves in Heidenheim's DEVS. s. 422 sq., comp. s. 125 sq.
[4] For the three annual festivals which may have been first established during the time of the new Jerusalem, and which may be indicated in Judith viii 6 by the name χαρμοσύναι, see *Hist.* v. 166, (comp. *M.* תענית iv. 5) 230 sqq., 312, 358. It is noteworthy that the first two always fall on the fourteenth of a month, plainly after the model of the passover. In the case of the last, on the other hand, the arrangements in regard to the day were very peculiar. But it is undeniable that these later festivals clashed with the Mosaic series, and they were never celebrated sacerdotally.
[5] As at Whitsuntide in the year described by Joseph. *Antiq.* xiii. 8, 4.

it,[1] a thing forbidden on a regular sabbath.[2] This relaxation of stringency might appear needful, if only on account of the possibility of a festival and a regular sabbath following one another.

3. THE THREE PILGRIMAGES.

A festival, however, which is observed by the priests alone, is of less account than one which is also a holiday for the whole nation. The law, therefore, wished to distinguish three out of the seven festivals, and assign to them a greater importance, by making them days of pilgrimage, on which the men of the entire nation were to assemble around their great Sanctuary, as a body around its soul.[3] These three were the principal festival, and the fifty-day festival (Whitsuntide) in the spring, and the principal festival in the autumn; and it seems as though the choice between attending the first or the eighth day of the autumn-festival were purposely left to each individual man. It was this which not only first gave a national importance to these festivals, but also met their peculiar purpose of supplementing, as mentioned above, the institutions of Jahveism.

The national character would be deeply affected by all the men assembling together on certain great days in the year. They would thus not only strengthen one another in their common religion, but could also easily take counsel together on many other subjects. But it must be observed here that Jahveism imposed its yearly pilgrimages to a distant Sanctuary upon all men as a duty, and that it is the earliest law which displays the greatest stringency in this requirement.[4] This religion, therefore, could not dispense with so external a thing as a pilgrimage, and an appearance at a definite sacred spot at a particular time. When first she began to unfold her powers, they were not developed and strong enough to dispense with the support of nationality and locality. Even the smaller sacred spots, where each community assembled on sabbaths and festivals of a similar rank, would not suffice. She still felt an imperative need for strengthening herself anew from time to time from that support without whose aid she could have secured no foothold, viz. the nationality and the locality inseparable therefrom. Three times

---

[1] An inference from Ex. xii. 16.
[2] P. 105.
[3] A pilgrimage festival is חַג, one of the seven annual days is מִקְרָא קֹדֶשׁ according to p. 356, a festival which recurs at an appointed period is מוֹעֵד, and when work is suspended on such an occasion it is שַׁבָּת, p. 357 nt. 3.
[4] Book of Covenants, Ex. xxiii. 14–16, and especially ver. 17; a later redaction xxxiv. 18–24, and a repetition Deut. xvi. 16.

a year ought all the men of Israel to renew their strength for the service of Jahveh, by gazing directly upon the highest external Sanctuary, and witnessing together its splendid sacrificial cultus; and being once more brought together, they ought to feel themselves one great united nation, so that they may again become all the more the 'people of Jahveh.' So, too, did Islâm, from the time of the last years of its founder, believe itself unable to exist unless its confessors by annual pilgrimages bound themselves to the spot where it had first sprung into being; and, so long as a nation is nothing but a great camp, the arrangement has everything in its favour.

Of the details respecting these pilgrimages we have no particulars. In the early days after the conquest of Canaan, while the compact feeling of nationality prevailed, this law was certainly observed very strictly, although many might gradually reduce the three annual pilgrimages to a single visit.[1] Whether the Book of Origins required such pilgrimages at all, we do not know; at least we do not find, in its extant portions, the smallest definite allusion thereto. Nevertheless, the pilgrimage at the autumn-festival at any rate continued to be tolerably universal. No doubt, in proportion as the nation gradually spread itself out, and dwelt at greater distances apart, the complete execution of the law became more difficult. Moreover, in troubled times, experience taught that the national enemies availed themselves for purposes of invasion of the stripping of the more exposed districts of their fighting men.[2] And in any case, even under the Hagiocracy, no one incurred any penalty by the neglect of a single visit.[3]

But there was no way in which these festivals of Jahveh could acquire a more national character than by their connection with pilgrimages; and we can clearly see from the Book of Origins how close this connection between the Mosaic festivals and the entire national feeling, and hence the historical consciousness, of Israel, had already grown in the first centuries. Moreover, the natural religion could not fail to be continually more and more penetrated by a higher spiritual experience and therefore to become more historical and (at any rate temporarily) more national. It was involved in the regular order of development that within Jahveism the festivals should be continu-

---

[1] 1 Sam. i. 3, comp. verr. 7, 20, ii. 19; comp. with this also 1 Kings xii. 32, and p. 356 above, as well as *Hist.* iv. 239 nt. 1.

[2] A point taken into consideration in the repetition of the ancient law by the

Fourth Narrator, Ex. xxxiv. 25; just as Mohammed in his last Sura, ix. 28, takes a similar objection into consideration.

[3] As even the evangelical histories show, particularly that according to John.

ally losing more and more of their merely natural significance, and assuming a spirit peculiarly Israelitish and in harmony with the higher religion. Permanent festivals commemorating historical events cannot originate in a nation till it has won for itself permanent fame upon earth by actual great deeds and experiences. In Israel these festivals could only arise subsequently to the days of Moses and Joshua; but it is the mark of a judicious mind that no attempt was made to insert them as special festivals, which would only have disturbed the fair edifice already existing, but that they were united with the former kind. It is ultimately the same true God who is revealed to man both in history and in nature, and in some of the original Nature-festivals at any rate such a union was not far to seek. When the Book of Origins was written the Passover along with the closely succeding Feast of Unleavened Bread was already become a festival in historical commemoration of the great epoch when the community was founded, and even its ancient usages were already being more and more apprehended in this historical sense. As in every spring, man entered upon a new-year with fear and trembling, and should prepare himself for this step with serious reflection, so had Israel once stepped out of the fearful Egyptian oppression into its new life of freedom; and as it had been then rescued in an astonishing and glorious manner from most terrible danger, so should it with every new-year hope to be again redeemed by its true God from every actual or threatened disaster. The ancient trembling and quaking at the celebration of the Passover became, accordingly, a commemoration of the trembling haste in which the nation had once left Egypt; the use of unleavened bread seemed due to the fact that in the former hasty departure from Egypt there had been no time to leaven the dough; the custom of offering the first-fruits seemed to have originated at a time when the Egyptians were chastised by every punishment, even by the loss of the first-born and first-fruits, while those of Israel were preserved by Divine providence; and even the whole departure from Egypt seemed to have taken place in the same mysteriously consecrated night between the fourteenth and the fifteenth of the spring-month—the night when at a later date the two-fold festival always commenced. So thoroughly by the time of the Book of Origins was the original natural significance of the festival of the renewal and redemption of the new-year amalgamated with the historical remembrance of the great national redemption which had once taken place.[1] It is far

[1] Ex. xi. 4-8, xii. 1-xiii. 16; comp. also above pp. 352-354.

from improbable that Israel really did depart out of Egypt in this month,[1] (if not on that particular night), and that it was Moses himself who consecrated this ancient festival to the commemoration of the great historical national event, and that in accordance with this the whole conception was gradually framed which characterises the Book of Origins.—Far looser is the connection which the Book of Origins would establish between the Festival of Arbours and the time when Israel dwelt in the desert.[2]

It will also now be readily understood how it was possible that the annual festivals, when spoken of briefly, might be given as three in number. There is no contradiction here to the original number of seven as explained above ; but the word 'festival' must be understood in its narrowest sense, according to which it comprehended only those occasions when the pilgrimage was made and which of course had the greatest external prominence. It is in this sense that three festivals are spoken of in the Book of Covenants,[3] whose example is followed by the Deuteronomist.[4]

II. THE SABBATH-YEAR.

When in this way the year had repeated for six times its numerous ordinary and its seven superior sabbaths, its two kinds of sabbatical weeks and its sabbatical month, then the seventh year as the sabbatical year would be further elevated to a new, loftier stage of celebration.[5] The blessing of rest was then to be given to the soil of the entire country, the year was so far to be a fallow-year. The conception of the Sabbath, as it prevailed generally in Jahveism, recurs here only in a new application. For that the soil (especially if, as was the case then, it is not manured) should for its own sake lie fallow from time to time, that man had certain duties even towards it and might not perpetually exact, as it were, work from it,[6] was a feeling which was undoubtedly firmly established long before

[1] Another reason for supposing this, is the prominence already given it in the Book of Covenants, Ex. xxiii. 15 (xxxiv. 18). Even the ancient paschal song Ex. xv. alludes solely to this historical significance, so, too, its later imitation, Ps. cxiii. sq.
[2] Lev xxiii. 43. It was not before the time of the Rabbis that an historical significance was given to Whitsuntide, viz., making it a commemoration of the legislation on Sinai, because (Ex. xix. 1) this took place in the *third* month.—But even for the ordinary sabbath the Book of Origins tries to find an historical origin and type, pp. 103-105.
[3] Ex. xxiii. 14-17 (xxxiv. 18-24).
[4] Deut. xvi. Even Ezek. xlv. 18-25 adopts this enumeration, adding, however, in its scheme some new regulations quite foreign to Antiquity.
[5] Important solemnities, lustrations, and the like, which did not recur every year, existed among many ancient nations, e.g. the Greeks had a cycle of four or five years, and this bears a certain resemblance to the present case.
[6] The crops of the soil or the tree were

any conceptions about the Sabbath. But when the idea of the Sabbath was added, not only was a permanent period defined when the soil should rest, but this period was itself sanctified and its observance placed among the higher duties of man. Here, accordingly, the whole natural view in regard to the soil which prevailed in Antiquity found expression in the style peculiar to Jahveism. Even the soil has its divine right to the necessary, and therefore divine, amount of rest and consideration; even towards it man is not to be ceaselessly directing his lust for work and gain; even to it is he to allow a proper time for rest, in order that he may in turn reap the greater blessing. The soil annually produces its fruits as a debt which it owes to man, and on which man may reckon as the reward of the toil which he expends upon it; but just as there are times when the debt may not be demanded even from the human debtor, so is man at the proper time to let the soil alone without exacting payment from it.[1] And as the ancient law everywhere manifests a splendid consistency,[2] it desires that the harvest of every kind, even of orchards and vineyards, shall be renounced, nay that no purpose shall be entertained of gathering even the spontaneous crops of the year in field and garden.[3]

It is undeniable that the observance of such a sabbatical year would not be wholly impracticable. If it was known beforehand that in the seventh year no fields were to be cultivated and no harvest to be reaped, sufficient preparation could still be made for this time in the course of the six ordinary years; at any rate there would be no insuperable difficulty in doing so in a country where in most years the fertility of the soil exceeded the requirements of the population. Such inhabitants however as were really in need during the seventh year, or who may have been unable to lay by anything for the occasion, were at liberty to gather the fruits of every kind which would grow freely and abundantly on the fallows. This is especially permitted even by the law.[4] No doubt the influence of a higher faith would be re-

regarded in early days as the work which the soil or tree exerted itself to ripen of its own efforts.

[1] Hence the name שְׁנַת הַשְּׁמִטָּה, *the year of remission*, when payment of the debt due in other years would not be demanded, Deut. xv. 9, xxxi. 10; it is borrowed from the ancient legal passage about the sabbatical year in the Book of Covenants, Ex. xxiii. 10 sq., comp. Deut. xv. 2. Comp. the cognate ideas explained above, p. 182 nt 1.

[2] P. 7 sq.

[3] Special prominence is given to this direction in the account of the Book of Origins, Lev. xxv. 1–7. The strange use, arising apparently from a popular joke, of the word Nazirite to denote the vines and trees whose foliage (hair) is not clipped, Lev. xxv. 5, 11, is explained by what is said on p. 84 sqq.; it also proves both that by the time of the Book of Origins the Nazirites already formed a very ancient institution, and that the free growth of the vine was not unfrequent so that the sabbatical year must actually have been observed.

[4] Ex. xxiii. 11; Lev. xxv. 6 sq.

quired for an entire nation to make up its mind to provide for such a fallow-year; but that such a faith was not wanting is proved by the Book of Origins hoping that Jahveh would cause such abundant crops to grow in the sixth year as would, perhaps, suffice for the next three years.[1]

Anything different from or more than this was not involved in the original sabbath-year. The Deuteronomist, it is true, does not even mention this purpose in regard to the year, as though by his time it had become more and more difficult to put in practice; and no doubt it could not fail to be attended with increasing difficulties in proportion as the nation devoted its energies to production and trade, so that while one half was keeping holiday on account of the suspension of agricultural pursuits, the other half would have to work as usual. The remission of debts, however, which the Deuteronomist desires should characterise this year instead of the agricultural remission,[2] was evidently no original part of its observance, for in the oldest sources, as well as in the nature of the thing itself, 414 the former remission belongs to quite another category and properly appertained to the Year of Jubilee; as will be further shown below. The emancipation of a Hebrew[3] slave in the seventh year of his service is prescribed by the Deuteronomist in the same series of laws on account of the similarity of the ideas,[4] but he has no intention of abridging or lengthening the seven years in accordance with the fixed series of the years of remission or sabbath-years. This would be altogether impossible, because the six years of toil of such a slave was to represent the price of his redemption, and could not therefore be casually diminished or increased. These two regulations were brought under the ruling thought solely for the sake of preserving a certain similarity, and so far as this went of putting them in the place of the decaying sabbatical year.

But in a nation chiefly agricultural, such as Israel was during the first centuries, the cessation of agriculture involved a general cessation of all ordinary labours throughout the entire

---

[1] Lev. xxv. 18–22. The mention of three years is explained, if in the country the year was reckoned from autumn to autumn (p. 355, *nt.* 4), while in sacerdotal language such as we have here the year was commenced at the previous Easter. The year of rest would then extend to the second half of the eighth year, the deficiency signified here to the second half of the ninth year. Comp. below under the Year of Jubilee.—In complete correspondence with this childlike hope is the narrative in the Book of Origins about the ordinary sabbath as it existed in the typical days of Moses. Ex. xvi. 16–27.—For the rest the entire passage Lev. xxv. 18–22 is evidently misplaced, and should properly stand after ver. 7.

[2] Deut. xv. 1–11. Nevertheless the name sabbath-year is wanting here, though one can see, especially from ver. 9, that such a year is intended.

[3] P. 213 sqq.

[4] Deut. xv. 12–18.

year, so that as a necessary consequence the sabbatical year required rest not only for the soil but also for men throughout the entire nation, and the contents of the shorter sabbatical terms essentially recurred again in this greater cycle. But what did the legislator intend the people to do during this year? Were they to remain ceaselessly idle? No one can ascribe such nonsense to the great legislator. On the contrary, all other occupations besides ploughing, sowing, and reaping the fields were undoubtedly permitted; and as the ordinary Sabbath only caused toil to cease in order the more to set free and elevate the mind, so too in this year the giving instruction in schools and elsewhere, which at other times had far too little continuity and system, might then be taken up with all the more regularity and zeal both for children and adults. According to the Deuteronomist, at the Feast of Arbours in this year the law in its entire comprehensive range was to be expounded to the assembled people,[1] particularly to the younger members of it; here a relic of the ancient practice may have been retained.

III. The Year of Jubilee.[2]

1. When the cycle of seven such sabbatical years was expired, the immediately following fiftieth year was to be a sabbatical Sabbath-year, the so-called Year of Jubilee. This is the final and extreme kind of suspension which is possible in material things and in the midst of an established realm—a supension of the realm itself so far as this contains human elements which therefore stand in need of purification and rectification. The entire arrangement and the progress of the previous development of human toils and efforts in the kingdom were to be suspended so that everything which had gone wrong during the course of the just concluded half-century, and in which the evil though imperceptible at first was at length manifest enough, might revert to its pure condition, and the kingdom might arise with renewed and purified powers.

In a kingdom whose foundation is the true religion, the only things which can go wrong in the course of time and be set right again by human agency at particular periods, are the mutual relations in regard to the possession of the external goods of life. For the fundamental truths on which the whole

---

[1] Deut. xxxi. 10–13. Sundry indications imply that the Mohammedan month of fasting, *Ramadhân*, was originally utilised in the same way; see the passage in Nöldeke's *Geschichte des Qorâns*, s. 41.
[2] According to Luther, *Halljahr*.

existence of a nation and a kingdom rests,—its spiritual possessions—are given it in an inalienable and irrevertible form; or should any one of them grow obscure or completely fade from view, it cannot possibly be restored or revived at a predetermined date or by a mere edict of the government. But the relations and conditions of a nation's external possessions may go wrong to such an extent that gradually a few citizens become excessively rich while the majority become excessively poor, so that inequalities arise which lead to the weakness, or even the overthrow of the realm as a human institution. Human authority in ordinary times is tolerably competent to meet such threatening dangers, when the proper means for the purpose have a legal existence; and a legislator cannot easily have a more worthy task than to devise the proper means by which such inequalities, which imperceptibly arise in the kingdom and which are such strong incitements to seeking redress by violence and revolution, may be legally counteracted, and an outbreak of brutal rebellion be avoided.

Ancient kingdoms like that of Jahveh's, which had their human basis in an original conquest and division [1] of a fertile country, could moreover look back upon an original equality of possessions and privileges; and this equality would always hover before their eyes as a model, something to which they might hope perfectly to return, at any rate at particular periods. Experience, no doubt, soon enough taught that the division of landed property did not long remain unaltered as it was at first, and that many a Hebrew by birth, in spite of the prohibition against taking interest, soon lost, either through misfortune or idleness, his hereditary estate, or even his liberty. But all the relations of the state were in part so new and plastic, in part so simple, that it seemed possible to accomplish a return to the original purity and equality in the possession of what was indispensable by the appointment of a periodical year, if only the arrangement had the full authority of the law to start with and was faithfully submitted to by the whole nation.[2]

The immediate purpose of the Year of Jubilee was, accordingly, nothing more than to restore the hereditary estates described above [3] to the family of their original possessors, so that every one who was a full citizen by birth but who had lost his ancestral heritage, and hence also his place in his clan and tribe, might once again be offered the chance of a laborious but

[1] P. 177 sqq.
[2] Hence also in other ancient legislative systems, especially that of Lycurgus, similar legal provisions are to be found.
[3] P. 177 sqq.

independent and honourable life. Then would the discipline and honour of the families and tribes be upheld, and the proper constitution of the whole body be reestablished. No other property of any kind was touched here; but in the earliest times these hereditary estates constituted by far the most important property and penetrated deepest into all the relations of civil life. We must remember that the final claim on an hereditary estate was not extinguished with the death of its immediate owner, but passed to his descendants and relatives in accordance with the laws of inheritance valid in other cases. When accordingly the date for the restoration of the original possessions drew near, there would be sure to be many a decayed head of a family, or his children, eagerly awaiting the moment when the law proclaimed universal suspension of business. On behalf of the realm as such, moreover, the priests proclaimed on their trumpets with blasts of the loudest joy the arrival of the universal liberation. Thus the year, which rarely or never on other occasions was inaugurated by the priests and responded to by the people with such universal loud rejoicing throughout the entire land, received from its noisy commencement the name of the *Year of Jubilee*.[1]

If, in this way, the sole proper function of the Year of Jubilee was to restore the hereditary estates, it is hardly necessary to explain that this commencement must have dated from the preparatory day of the autumn-festival.[2] Not till the year's harvest of every kind was complete, would it be easy to accomplish a change in the ownership of the soil, and the autumn-

---

[1] The word יוֹבֵל in the Book of Origins, Lev. xxv. 10–12, has evidently already become a proper name for the *Year of Jubilee*, and there, as elsewhere, the abbreviation הַיּוֹבֵל is employed of the Year of Jubilee in the meaning already given. The LXX, therefore, could not see what to do except to translate it by ἀφέσεως σημασία, 'proclamation of the remission,' or even by ἄφεσις alone. But we see from the ancient passage in the Book of Covenants, Ex. xix. 13, as well as from the description in Josh. vi. 4–13, that by itself or when closely connected with קֶרֶן (horn) or שׁוֹפָר (trumpet), it originally denoted an ancient kind of trumpet. Now as the root יבל, cognate with the Ethiopic and the Aramaic בבב, may indisputably mean a sounding and shouting aloud, it appears that יוֹבֵל is a primitive word for *music* (formed according to *Lehrb.* § 156 *e*; comp. Gen. iv. 24), and that the name *music-horn* is only antiquated redundancy; the word would then finally be limited to the loud joyous shouts of the year of freedom, just as the Latin *ovatio* is ordinarily employed with a narrower denotation. The plural שֹׁפְרוֹת הַיֹּבְלִים is then to be explained by *Lehrb.* § 270 *c*. The derivation would no doubt be simpler if it could be shown that יֹבֵל meant a ram, so that the compound would correspond to the Latin *buccina*, comp. the treatise on *Die neuentdeckte Phönikische Inschrift zu Marseille* (Göttingen 1849), s. 16. But one must be on one's guard against supposing that the יֹבֵל, Ex. xix. 13, was originally identical with the שֹׁפָר, ver. 16, 19; it is derived, on the contrary, from the primitive narrative.

[2] I'p. 361 sqq. Lev. xxv. 8 sq. comp. p. 371, *nt.* 1.

festival, in itself of so joyous a nature, would in this year become a celebration of even far greater joy. But the establishment of the rights of ownership, the production of the necessary witnesses, and the decision of complicated claims, were processes not to be brought to a speedy conclusion, even though they were entered into with all zeal immediately after the autumn-festival; and in the mean time, when all rights of possession of the soil were insecure, and might be called in question, no one would be willing to cultivate the fields. This of itself would be enough to cause a universal suspension of industrial occupations generally, and particularly those of agriculture, so that this year, like the sabbatical year already described, became a fallow-year, and so far this greater cycle would include in itself the whole contents of the previous series. Hence the Year of Jubilee, in virtue of this all-embracing character, also became the most sacred year possible.[1]

Since, however, the Year of Jubilee, on account of its connection with agriculture, commenced in the autumn, we are justified in assuming, on the same grounds, that it would also expire in the autumn of the following year. Its terminal points would then include, not that year which would be the fiftieth according to the strict sacerdotal commencement of the calender in the spring,[2] but the last half of the forty-ninth and the first half of the fiftieth; although in ordinary speech it was always customary to call it the fiftieth year.[3]

---

[1] Lev. xxv. 10–12; in v. 12 יובל־קדש are to be connected, 'sacred jubilee,' according to *Lehrb*. § 287 *h*, in spite of the intervening היא.

[2] P. 355.

[3] That the Year of Jubilee cannot be simply the forty-ninth is certain from the descriptions of the Book of Origins. We might assume that it should have been the year *after* the seventh sabbatical year, in which case we should have to assume further that the latter began in the autumn of the forty-eighth year, since the sabbatical year ought certainly to commence in the autumn. Two sabbatical years in succession would not be inconceivable, as the prophetic image in Is. xxxvii. 30 shows. Still they would be unnecessary here, as the conception of the Sabbath would rather require that the seventh sabbath-year should be greater than its six predecessors, and thus be the Year of Jubilee. Hence it is best to assume that of the fifty years the first half of the first and the last half of the fiftieth would not be counted in reckoning the series of sabbatical years and jubilees, since the sabbatical year was considered to begin with the autumn, comp. above, p. 355, *nt*. 3.—With the later Jews themselves it was matter of controversy whether the jubilee was the fiftieth or the forty-ninth year. The most learned, as Philo, *De Decalog.* xxx; *Quæst. in Gen.* xvi. 1 (*Auch.* ii. p. 209); and Josephus, *Antiq.* iii. 12. 3 (comp. also the *Constit. Apost.* vii. 36), were always in favour of the fiftieth; if many, notwithstanding, preferred the forty-ninth, this was certainly due primarily to the fact that in the later times the sabbatical year was still observed and used in reckoning, while this was not the case with the Year of Jubilee. This is further proved in *Hist.* V. The first attempt on a grand scale to carry through the view that the forty-ninth and not the fiftieth was the Year of Jubilee is made in the *Liber Jubil.* (on which see *Hist.* I. 201, and comp. the *Jahrbb. der Bibl. Wiss.* iv. s. 79); but this is done by a purely arbitrary division of the primitive history. But comp. what is said below on the point.

2. The actual execution of the laws of the Year of Jubilee would modify in a peculiar manner many of the relations of ordinary life. The principal result would be that the price of an hereditary estate would not be equal to its freehold value, but would be estimated by the number of years during which the estate might be utilised before the next jubilee, and the buyer paid not for the land itself but only for its usufruct for a term of years, so that its value would diminish as the Year of Jubilee approached.[1] And since hereditary estates could not be bought or sold for all perpetuity,[2] i.e. not as freehold property, it was only consistent to allow the owner or his heir and representative,[3] to redeem the pledged estate at any period previous to the expiration of the full term, as soon in fact as he had money enough to pay for the usufruct during the time which was still to elapse.[4] Since all this tended very strongly to reduce the value of land, especially in troublous times or when wages for hired labourers were high, and a man who was compelled to try and raise money on his estate would often have a difficulty in finding a purchaser, the law exhorts all parties to mutual equity and kindness.[5] Houses in the open country and in villages were regarded as belonging to the hereditary estate; those which were protected within the walls of a town, and had accordingly a value in excess of the ground on which they stood, could only be redeemed by the original owner in the Year of Jubilee if he paid this excess in value; in case this was not done, the buyer acquired a perpetual right to them.[6] A further consequence of this was that aliens, if they wished to acquire real property in Israel which could be inherited, were limited to the acquisition of houses within walled towns.

These relations would also affect the priesthood in a peculiar manner. Since consecrated gifts generally were considered capable of redemption,[7] every hereditary estate which had been devoted to the Sanctuary without being placed under the ban, might be redeemed by paying the redeemable value together with the one-fifth of the same which was customary in the case of consecrated inanimate property. But should the owner have already sold his estate to a third party before presenting it to the Sanctuary, or if he were without either the means or the will to

---

[1] Lev. xxv. 13–17, 23, comp. 27 sq., 50–52, xxvii. 17 sq.

[2] This is involved in the expression לִצְמִיתֻת, Lev. xxv. 23, 30, whose root should be compared with صَمَدَ and اَلَدّ *eternal*, as well as with תָּמִיד. It was certainly a technical term employed only in trade.

[3] The *Gôel*, p. 168.

[4] Lev. xxv. 24–28; Jer. xxxii. 6 sqq.

[5] Lev. xxv. 14, 17.

[6] Lev. xxv. 29–31.

[7] Pp. 79 sqq.

redeem it on his own account, or at least to pay in the Year of Jubilee one-fifth of the value which it had at the time of the presentation, then, at the jubilee, it became the perpetual property of the Sanctuary. If on the contrary, any one presented a field which he had merely purchased from the original owner, the Sanctuary gave it up to the latter before or at the Year of Jubilee in case he discharged the liabilities due on its account.[1] On the other hand, houses in the Levitical cities, as well as the open spaces round about them,[2] were regarded as necessarily reverting to the Levites in the Year of Jubilee, since they formed their permanent and indispensable dwelling-places.[3] The immediate consequence of this was that these town-houses and commons could never obtain a high commercial value.

A further important consequence of all the changes here described was the impossibility of perfectly restoring in the Year of Jubilee the original ownership of property. To these causes others might be added, e.g. the complete extinction of a family. In every Year of Jubilee, then, what would be essentially a new register (Doomsday-book) of landed estates and houses would have to be compiled and set down in writing, in order to serve as a document throughout the following fifty years.[4] With this, the financial register already spoken of would evidently stand in connection.[5]

Whoever had lost his hereditary estate thereby sank, together with his whole family, into a servile condition. Such a man ought, according to the oldest law,[6] to have regained his freedom in the seventh year of his service; and when free, the way was open to him to earn by industry and skill sufficient money to redeem his hereditary estate even before the Year of Jubilee. If the jubilee occurred before he had served six full years, the liberation of his estate furnished him all the sooner with the means of emancipating himself. But after this most ancient regulation had gradually become obsolete, the Book of Origins desired that every serving-man of Hebrew blood (apart from the question whether he had an hereditary estate to hope for or not) should at any rate be emancipated and restored to his clan in the Year of Jubilee;[7] truly but a paltry remnant of the right which had secured him against having to serve more than six years! And

---

[1] This is the meaning of Lev. xxvii. 16-24.
[2] Pp. 286 sq., 306 sq.
[3] Lev. xxv. 32-34; in ver. 33 לא is therefore wanting before יגאל.
[4] This is even once casually indicated, Num. xxxvi. 4.
[5] P. 304.
[6] Pp. 213 sqq.
[7] Lev. xxv. 39-43; comp. ver. 10 *ad fin.*

since at that time many a Hebrew by birth would be in the service of an Israelitish half-citizen or his descendants,[1] the Book of Origins desires the privileges of the jubilee to be no less extended to such a serving-man, commands him to be set free at the Year of Jubilee, and allows his redemption at any time when relatives were willing to redeem him (as duty would require them to do) or when he himself found an opportunity for it; so that his redemption could be effected on easier terms the nearer the Year of Jubilee.[2] It seems that in such a case the average value of the yearly work of a day-labourer was made the basis of the estimate, just as in the case of the redemption of an estate the estimate was made on the average produce of the annual harvest.

3. These are the most essential features of the form which the Year of Jubilee had assumed at the time when the Book of Origins was written, and this of itself is enough to prove the entire groundlessness of the doubts raised by modern writers as to whether its celebration ever was actually observed. To invent laws, particularly such as are of extraordinary importance, is wholly foreign to the character of the Book of Origins. The law of the Year of Jubilee had moreover by its time developed its minutest details under a varied execution and experience, and had even passed through a varied history. That no mention is made of it in the miserably scanty historical narratives of the earlier centuries, is purely accidental, and can furnish no support for such doubts,[3] which are clearly refuted on other grounds. On a close inspection nothing is more certain than that the idea of the jubilee is the last ring of a chain which only attains in it the necessary conclusion, and that the history of the jubilee, in spite of its at first seemingly strange aspect, was once for centuries a reality in the national life of Israel.

But the observance of this law required not only the influence of a strong authority during the great year of the restoration of all original ownership of the soil, but also a permanent willingness on the part of the people to adapt all their commercial dealings to it. The same Book of Origins which on the one side bases this law on the truth that all members of the community are the direct servants of Jahveh, not the servants of men, and that they must therefore have an unfet-

---

[1] P. 236 sq.
[2] Lev. xxv. 47–54.
[3] No more than can the fact that the jubilee is not mentioned in the laws of the Book of Covenants, Ex. xxi–xxiii, for this account of the laws has come down to us in a shape very far from complete.

tered body and unencumbered estate in order to live worthy of their vocation,[1] is content to let it rest on the other side on the requirements of a genuine fear (religion) before Jahveh, which must impel the more powerful citizen to assist the less powerful to attain freedom for his property and person.[2] But the very sacred dread which the law here had to require would be likely to exercise in the course of centuries less and less influence in this respect in proportion as the national relations ceased to retain the simplicity which the law postulated. All interruptions of this kind would be the more keenly felt and the more pernicious in their effects in proportion to the development of the internal peace and well-being of a nation. Besides this, when a nation, from being engaged principally in agriculture, devotes itself readily to commerce and manufacture,—as did the whole of Israel from the time of Solomon—then the possession and cultivation of the soil itself will inevitably become an article of commerce and manufacture, and all manual labour will be based on relations which are totally left out of account in the above law. We have just seen that the original laws of Jahveism concerning the freedom of the person, and hence, too, those about property, no longer retained their original and proper shape by the time of the Book of Origins. The Year of Jubilee, whose benefits primarily applied only to property, is still insisted on here and is further extended to the personal freedom which could no longer be legally secured in any other way. But even the observance of the jubilee as regulated by the Book of Origins, evidently declined to such an extent from the days of Solomon, that the Deuteronomist is quite silent on the subject, and only endeavours to save the remission of debts in the seventh year, as well as, in like manner, the freedom of the person, by reverting to an antiquated regulation.[3] When the great Prophets of the ninth and eight centuries B.C. complain of the accumulation of too many acres in the hands of a few owners,[4] the law of the jubilee could hardly have been in force in the actual national life. Nevertheless the recollection of it never entirely faded away in the better class of minds, and its image is again most vividly present to the minds of the later Prophets and authors.[5] Its essentially

424

[1] Lev. xxv. 42, 55, comp. ver. 38.
[2] Lev. xxv. 17, comp. ver. 36, 43. Still more is the Deuteronomist xv. 9, in his regulations constituting the ordinary sabbatical year the time for a general remission of debts, obliged to rely on religion as the sole ground for the regulations.

[3] P. 370 sq.
[4] P. 185.
[5] Such allusions to the fallow-years and the jubilees occur Is. xxxvii. 30, Lev. xxvi. 34 sq. (comp. below); to the jubilee Ezek. vii. 12 sq., xlvi. 16–18 ; particularly as the time of the great investigation, restoration, and liberation, Jer. xi. 23,

pure and divine purpose was gradually esteemed all the more highly as the want of it was felt in ordinary life and nothing better was found to take its place.

The ancient law also recognised other great epochs in the life of the nation and realm,—epochs which seemed to it to possess a sacred character, and which brought with them a final decision as to the guilt or innocence of many citizens which man had previously been incompetent to give. The accused persons who had fled to a legal place of refuge were sure of their lives there, only as long as the high-priest lived under whose supremacy and, as it were, with whose consent they had fled thither.[1] With the accession of the new high-priest there seemed to commence a period of general new investigation and decision about all sins committed against life as something most sacred in Israel; so that the fugitive was either once more publicly recognised as innocent, and left at liberty to move about freely among the whole people, or else if in the mean time substantial grounds against him had been discovered, he finally expiated his transgression as the law prescribed. And when it was a king who wielded the supreme power in Israel, the same usage prevailed on occasion of the death of the reigning monarch and a new accession, only being more stringently executed in conformity with the regal dignity.[2] But all such extraordinary epochs, suspensions, and important new commencements, invariably involve violent disturbances of public and private relations which are most undesirable, and which only appear inevitable as long as the palpable deficiencies cannot be removed in any less violent manner. This we see most clearly in the great instance of the Year of Jubilee gradually sinking beneath its own weight.

---

xxiii. 12, xlviii. 44; BK. Is. lxi. 1 sq.— Moreover the BK. Ruth contains an allusion to the custom: Elimelek's hereditary estate was only purchased for a term of years, not in perpetuity, so long as the childless widow or the next-of-kin would not allow anything else. And since Jer. xxxii. 6 sqq. presupposes something of the kind, the execution of the law of the jubilee appears to have been once again recognised, at any rate as possible, by the national reformation under Josiah; but from that time to the overthrow of the kingdom fifty years did not elapse.

[1] P. 172.
[2] See *Hist.* III. 213 sq.

CONCLUSION.

THE HUMAN KINGDOM.

Even the final and most powerful of the means supplied by external institutions were, accordingly, insufficient to uphold the earliest form which was assumed by true religion in Jahveism. They could not permanently supply the deficiencies inherent in this form. Precisely the boldest system which could be erected on the given foundation of the earliest Jahveism and which ought to have served to protect all the other external institutions, was the first to fall. The Year of Jubilee did not permanently secure a restoration of the original independence and equality of the citizens. The sabbatical year did not avert the evil consequences of the growing desolation and loss of fertility of the soil which proceeded parallel with the internal decay of the nation. The obligation to perform annual pilgrimages did not prevent a lethargy gradually overcoming the original vitality of the national religion. And while these extensions of the sacred rest (of the Sabbath) which moderated human energy, and which in their youth were full of vitality, gradually became obsolete one after another, there was imperceptibly growing up within the community of Jahveh a wholly new form of energy, which after many temporal vicissitudes finally took such vehement possession of the entire nation that no more rest seemed possible until the earth itself, utterly desolate and disorganised, should begin the long-deferred celebration of all the ancient sabbaths.[1]

This new energy arose from the increasing needs of the Human Kingdom. It expended itself for a considerable period in actually introducing and developing in the realm this new power, which at the time of its first origin was only one power

---

[1] This is the meaning of the prophetic discourse, equally true and elevated, and dating from the eighth or seventh century, Lev. xxvi. 34 sq. 43; a discourse which, according to 2 Chr. xxxvi. 21, Jeremiah quoted in a passage which is now lost from his works.—In connection with such thoughts the *Liber Jubilæorum* (l. s. 164 sq. of the Ethiopic) subjoins its Messianic hopes, after referring to the sabbatical laws in Ex. xvi. and Lev. xxv. 'But its year (when the Year of Jubilee should commence) we have not indicated, until it shall come into the land (Canaan), and this on its part shall solemnize its sabbaths when they will remain in it: then shall they know the Year of Jubilee!' and again, 'The Years of Jubilee will vanish (i.e. will not be kept) until Israel, free from all unrighteousness and impiety, shall dwell for ever in the land securely and peaceably.' Here, accordingly, the Messianic era is put on a par with the Year of Jubilee and the Eternal Sabbath, to the exclusion of the idea that the jubilee had formerly actually been observed.

among others, like prophetism or the superior priesthood,[1] but which like these latter powers, intertwined itself more and more closely with the entire national life and furnished this for centuries with new life and vigour. It finally became a devastating storm, when, in spite of the centuries of its highest development, it yet failed to attain the summit to which consistency led it in the community of Jahveh, viz., the perfect king of the community of the true God—the Messiah. But all this has been already explained at greater length in the second era of the History of Israel.

[1] P. 257 sqq.

INDEX.

N.B. Where a number is distinguished by an asterisk, the principal section on the subject will be found on that page.

AAR

Aaron, 66. 232; family of, 275, 289; see High-Priest
Achor, or Achan, 77, 234 *nt.*
Adoption of children, 180, 210
Adjuration, 19, 313
Altar, 30, 54, 117 sqq.*, 128 sq.; the brazen, 326 sq.; the golden, 329
Amen, 20; threefold repetition of, 133
Animal-offerings, ground of their predominance, 36 sq.
Animals available for sacrifice, 31 sq.; unclean, 146 sqq.
Antiquity, characteristics of, 7, 24, 28
ANTIQUITIES OF ISRAEL, plan of the present work, 4 sq.
Ark of the Covenant, 122 sqq. see Holy of Holies
Assembly, the national, 246
Atonement, water of, 60 sqq., 152; day of, 124, 281, 361* sqq.
Avenger of blood, 168
Azazel, 362 sq.
Azkâra, 46

Baal, 229
Ban, the, 15, 75–79*, 84, 154 sq. 236 sq.
Banishment, 314
Beating as a punishment, 315
Birds, how offered for sacrifice, 32, 45; excluded from thank-offerings, 51; unclean, 147
Blasphemy, 220
Blessing, the, 15, 132
Blood, ideas about, 35–41*, 54, 147 sqq.; sprinkling of the, 44 sq., 62 sq.; shedding of, 104, 138
Blood-money, 169 sqq.
Book of Origins, aim of, 2; foundation of present work, 3
Bread of the countenance, the, 27
Bull, worship of a, 225
Burial, rites of, 153
Burnt-offerings, the, 46–50, 116

EXP

Census, 274, 304
Charity, 183, 186, 217, 219
Cherub, its symbolical meaning, 123, 321
Circumcision, 89–97; where in use, 90; origin and significance, 91 sq., 231; a sacrament, 95, 110; exceptional, 163
Cities of refuge, 172
Colours, the sacred, 278, 292, 321*; of sin, 60
Combinations, prohibited, 160 sq.
Compensation for damages, 175, 186 sq., 311
Concubines, 199 sq., 214
Confession, 65, 313
Consecration, 67 sq., 107 sq.; of priests, 279
Corban, 41, 81
Corn-offerings, 33, 45 sq., 49, 51, 62, 66, 117
Corporate associations, 257
Court of the tabernacle, 323 sq., 326 sqq.
Curse, the, 15
Curtains of the tabernacle, 321 sq.

Day, commencement of each, 341
Dead, contact with the, 149 sqq.
Debt, laws of, 181 sqq.
Divine service, 130 sqq.
Divorce, laws of, 203 sqq.
Drink-offerings, wine, water, broth, 34 sq. 50, see Libations

Egyptian customs, 30, 82. 90 sq., 146, 164, 198, 315, 342 sqq., 347 sq.
Elders, the, 215; committee of the, 248 sqq.
Entrails, objects of sacrificial art, 41
Epochs, the four great, 40, 103 sq., 138 sq.
Ephod, 224, 293 sqq.
Equality, spiritual, 230 sq.
Eunuchs, 164, 238
Expiation, purpose and means of, 55–59 limitations of, 57; feast of, 361

INDEX.

EXP

Expiatory-offerings, 55–66; distinguished from guilt-offerings, 57; three grades of, 61; disposal of the carcases, 63, 65 sq.

Fasting, 83 sq.; on day of atonement, 362
Fat, devoted to the altar, 41, 51
Feast of Arbours, 351*, 355, 364*, 369, 372
Feast of unleavened bread, the, 352 sq., 357 sqq.*, 368
Festivals, pre-Mosaic, 348 sqq.; annual, 351 sqq.; Mosaic, 354; the autumn-, 355, 364; the spring-, 356 sq., 360, 368
Fines, 315
Fire from heaven, 29
Fire, strange, 330
First-fruits, 301 sq.; presentation in spring, 75, 352, 360
Flood, the, 40; important in connection with the calendar, 342, 347
Footstool, sacred, 123 sqq., 363
Free-will offerings, 73, 303

Garments, sacerdotal, 277 sq.; of the high-priest, 292
Gifts, sacred, 71–81; temple-slaves, 75; ban-gift, 75 sqq.
Gleaning, 217
God, early dread of his wrath, 12, 55, 136; fear of losing, 113 sq., 133, 155
Government, 140, 232 sq.*; ancient form of, 307 sqq.
Guilt-offerings, 55–66; distinguished from expiatory-offerings, 57; grades of, 61; disposal of the carcases, 63, 65 sq.

Hair, 164, see Nazirites
Hands, meaning of laying them on the head, 42 sq.
Hereditary estates, 177 sqq., 207, 373 sqq.
High places, bamâh, 120 sq., 227 sq.
High-priest, the, 58, 288 sq.; had to give oracles, 290; attire of, 292 sqq.; sceptre, 298, 330; a president, 308; to enter the Holy of Holies, 325, 363; death of, 79, 172, 380
Hindoo customs and beliefs, 15 sq., 30, 36, 40, 44, 82, 174, 198, 209 nt., 345
Hired service, 185, 217 sq.
Holy of Holies, the, 320, 322 sq., 325, 331, 363
Holy place, the, 320, 322 sq., 325, 328
Human sacrifice, 27, 69 sq., 228
Hyssop, use of, 44, 151

Idolatry, 222 sqq., see Worship
Images of the Deity, 119 sq.; idols, 223 sq., 325
Imprisonment, 313 sq.

MUR

Incense, 35, 45, 62, 66, 205, 330, 363
Infanticide, 174, 189
Inheritance, laws of, 179 sq.
Interest, when forbidden, 182

Jealousy, ordeal for, 205
Jephthah, 70, 80 sq.
Jubilee, Year of, 372 sqq.; ceased to be observed, 379 sqq.
Judges, the so-called, 233, 249; the subordinate, 253, 310 sqq.
Justice, administration of, 310 sqq.; held in public, 312

Lampstand, the sacred, 115, 328*
Land, special laws in regard to, 177 sqq.; value of, 376; registration of, 377
Leaven, laws about, 34
Leprosy, 157 sqq.
Levites, 265 sq., 281 sqq.; their three clans, 282; substituted for the first-born, 283 sq.; their cities, 286, 306; their bondsmen, 287; seek to be priests, 287 sq.; collect tithes, 300; act as judges, 311
Levitical cities, 286, 306, 377
Libations, 27, 28, 34, 46, 329, 352
Local sanctuaries, 128 sq.
Lot, use of the, 224, 259, 276, 291 sqq., 295, 362

Magic, 16, 119, 260
Marriage, 190 sqq., 200; of priests, 191, 206, 277*; with the heathen, 193; forbidden degrees of, 196 sq.; ceremonies, 201 sq.; with a brother's widow, 207 sqq.
Meals, sacrificial character of all, 54, 68
Mercy-seat, see Footstool, sacred
Mincha, 36, 40, 46
Miriam, 159, 232, 286
Mohammedanism, 16, 83, 91, 147 nt., 175, 206 sq., 235, 303, 336, 347, 357 nt., 367, 372 nt.
Moloch, 70, 228
Months, 342, 345; names of, 345 sqq.; extra, 347 sq.
Moon, 99; the full- and new-, 341, 347; celebration of, 349, 356
Moses, special allusions to, 6, 28, 30 sq., 42 sq., 66, 70, 77, 85, 88, 92 sqq., 98, 100 sqq., 104, 107, 113, 115 sq., 121, 125 sq., 132, 135, 139*, 154, 158 sq., 175, 177, 180, 193, 195, 198, 209, 226, 232, 235, 238, 243, 248 sq., 251* sqq., 256, 261 sqq., 271, 275, 279, 283, 291, 300, 304 sq., 308 sqq., 318, 329, 331 sq., 336, 341, 343 sq., 347, 354, 361, 363 nt., 368, 372
Murder, 168 sq.; different cases of, 171 sq.

INDEX.

MUT

Mutilation of the body, 81 sqq., 89, 163 sqq.

Names given children at circumcision, 96
Nation, lofty feeling of the, 229 sqq., 234; admission into, 238; organisation of, 241 sqq.
Nature, respect for, 7 sq., 142 sq., 166
Nazirites, 51. 80, 84–88*, 152, 281
Nethûim, the, 287
North, supposed abode of the Deity, 44

Oath, the, ready use of, 16; language and application of, 17–21, 220, 313
Offering of thanksgiving, 52 sq.
Oil, sacrificial, 33, 35, 62, 205; of consecration, 108, 330
Oracles, 50, 126, 139, 224, 259, 275, 290*, 294

Parents and children, 188 sqq.
Passover, the, 33, 353*, 358 sq., 368
Patrons and clients, 179, 216*
Perpetual light and sacrifice, 49, 114 sqq.*, 330, see Lampstand
Pilgrimages, the three, 366
Pledges, 183 sq., 190
Plunder, how divided, 303
Polygamy, 195 sq., 199
Prayer, at first no fixed form of, 14; posture at, 15; public, 46, 132
Priesthood, the, 260–306; the earlier form of, 263 sq., 283; the Levitical, 265 sqq.; general function of, 269 sqq.; its three grades, 273; duties of the regular priests, 273 sqq.; their qualifications, 276; their garments, 277; consecration, 279; inferior priests, 44, see Levites; see also High-priest, Marriage, First-fruits, and Tithes
Prince, of a clan, 245; of the nation, 254 sqq.
Prophecy, 258; not hereditary, 266
Property, private, 141, 176 sqq.; sale of, 180; loan of, 181; stolen, 185 sq.
Punishment, right of inflicting, 134 sq., 137 sqq.; by parents, 189; different kinds of, 165, 198, 314*; capital, 104, 110, 138, 163, 165, 189, 191, 198, 220 sq., 223, 313, 315 sqq.*
Purification, 67, 107, 150 sqq.*, 159, 357

Rainbow, the, 104, 321
Rechabites, the, 88
Redemption of sacred gifts, 79 sq.; of tithes, 300; of hereditary estates, 180, 373 sqq.
Registration, financial and military, 304; of land, 377

TAB

Release from slavery, 213, 371, 377
Revelation, ark of, 125
Rulers, human, 137 sqq., 231 sqq., 241 sqq., 254 sqq.
Ruth, 209

Sabbath, the, 25, 97 sqq.*; day of rest, 102 sq., 313; recreation and instruction allowed on, 106, 372; a sacrament, 110; extension of its idea, 337 sqq., 365; the sabbath-month, 338, 348 sqq.; the sabbath-year, 338, 369 sqq., 372
Sacraments, 39 sq., 95, 108 sqq.; the three special ones, 110; contact with, 155, 221; the Passover included, 359
Sacred externals, the, 111 sqq.
Sacred places, 120 sq., see Tabernacle
Sacred times, 113, 116; based on the lunar calendar, 343, see Sabbath and Festivals
Sacrifice, 23 sqq.; origin and development of, 25; different kinds of, 27–106; two main divisions, 47; a sacrament, 39, 110; priests' share in, 52, 305 sqq., see Human
Sacrificial ritual, 42–46, 130 sq.
Salt, employed at every sacrifice, 34
Sanctity, inherent, 140 sqq.; human, 112, 167; national, 230
Sanctuary, the, 127 sq., 317 sqq.*
Saturn, connection with the week, 100 sqq.
Saul, 54
Scape-goat, see Azazel
Seventy, the, 247 sqq.
Sexes, opposition between them in sacrificial ritual, 33, 48, 53, 60 sq.; general relations between the, 190 sqq., 198 sqq.
Signs, early use of, 9 sq., 180
Sinew, the sacred, 148
Singing at the temple, 44, 46, 53, 108, 131, 285 sq.
Sin-offering, see Expiatory-offering
Slain-offerings, same as thank-offerings, 51, 53
Slavery, 75, 185 sq., 190, 200, 210* sqq.; privileges in, 212; release from, 213, 371, 377; attempt to abolish, 215; fugitive slaves, 217
Sprinkling of the blood, 44 sqq., 62 sq., 363
Stones, monumental, 21, 118 sq., 122, 226; magic, 119
Strangers, feeling towards, 216, 234 sqq.
Suicide, 174
Sun-dials, 341

Tabernacle, the, 317 sqq.; its heavenly model, 319; construction of, 319 sqq.; removal of, 332

INDEX.

TAB

Table-offering, the, 27, 115, 305; the sacred table, 328
Tamar, 209
Tassel, the, ordered to be worn, 231
Taxation, direct, 304
Ten Commandments, 126 sq., 185, 188, 190
Teraphim, 223 sqq.
Thank-offerings, the, 50–54; three varieties of, 52
Theft, laws regarding, 185 sqq., 313
Time, early divisions of, 339 sqq.; lunar months, 342 sqq.
Tithes, the, 299
Treaty-sacrifice, the, 21, 68
Trees, sacred, 120, 260
Trumpets, the sacerdotal, 130, 288*, 331, 374
Truth, regard for, 221 sq.

Unchastity, 72, 191*, 198, 201, 214
Unclean, what is, 144 sqq., 150; unclean animals, 146 sqq.
Uncleanness, personal, 156 sq.
Urim and Thummim, 294 sq.

YEA

Vassal-tribes, 235 sq.
Vow, the, 21; aim of, 22; laws about, 23*, 81, 83; of thanksgiving, 52, 72; influence on the ban, 77

War, laws of, 237; spoils of, 303
Washing-basin at the sanctuary, 285, 327
Wave and heave, 74 sq.
Wedding customs, 202
Week, origin of the, 98
Whitsuntide, 360
Whole-offerings, the, 46–50*, 116
Witnesses, 21, 176, 180, 313*
Women, general position of, 207; serving at the Sanctuary, 285 sq., *see* Singing
Worship, public, 46, 130 sqq.; idolatrous, 222 sqq.; of a bull, 225; of stones, 226; of Moloch, 70, 228; of Baal, 229; of stars, 100 sq., 229
Writing, use of, 21, 126, 181*, 313, 377

Year, lunar and solar, 342 sqq., 347; commencement of the, 343 sq., 355; of Jubilee, 79, 180, 338, 372*

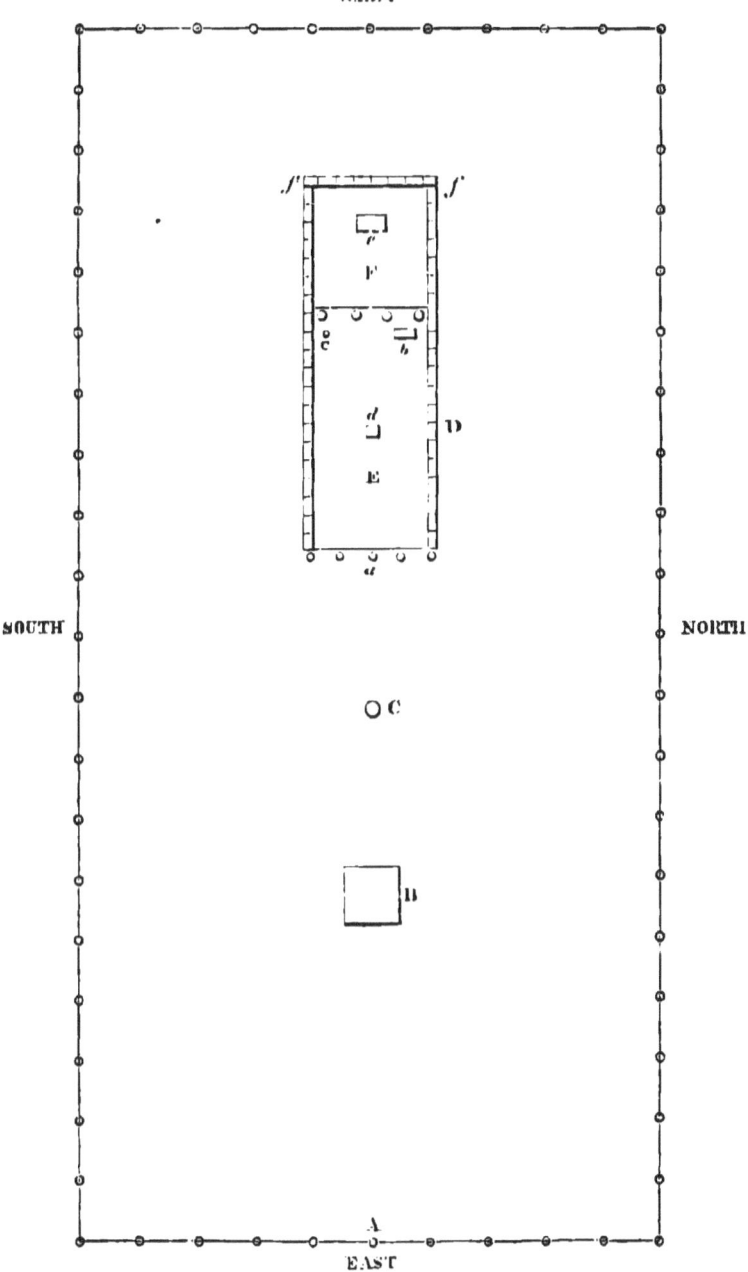

A Entrance to the Fore-court.
B The Brazen Altar.
C Site of the Washing-basin.
D The Tabernacle.
E The Holy Place.
F The Holy of Holies.

a Entrance to the Tabernacle.
b The Sacred Table.
c The Sacred Lampstand.
d The Golden Altar.
e The Ark of the Covenant.
f The Corner-planks.

www.ingramcontent.com/pod-product-compliance
Lightning Source LLC
Chambersburg PA
CBHW030428300426
44112CB00009B/909